THE STORY OF THE WORLD

THE STORY OF THE
WORLD

W. B. BARTLETT

AMBERLEY

This book has taken a number of years to research and write. I would like to gratefully acknowledge those who have supported me in this enterprise, both family and friends and professional colleagues at Amberley, especially Jonathan Reeve and Alex Bennett for their unstinting hard work and support.

First published 2014

Amberley Publishing
The Hill, Stroud
Gloucestershire, GL5 4EP

www.amberley-books.com

British Library Cataloguing in Publication Data.
A catalogue record for this book is available from the British Library.

ISBN 978 1 84868 104 0 (hardback)
ISBN 978 1 4456 3725 9 (ebook)

Typesetting and Origination by Amberley Publishing.
Printed in the UK.

CONTENTS

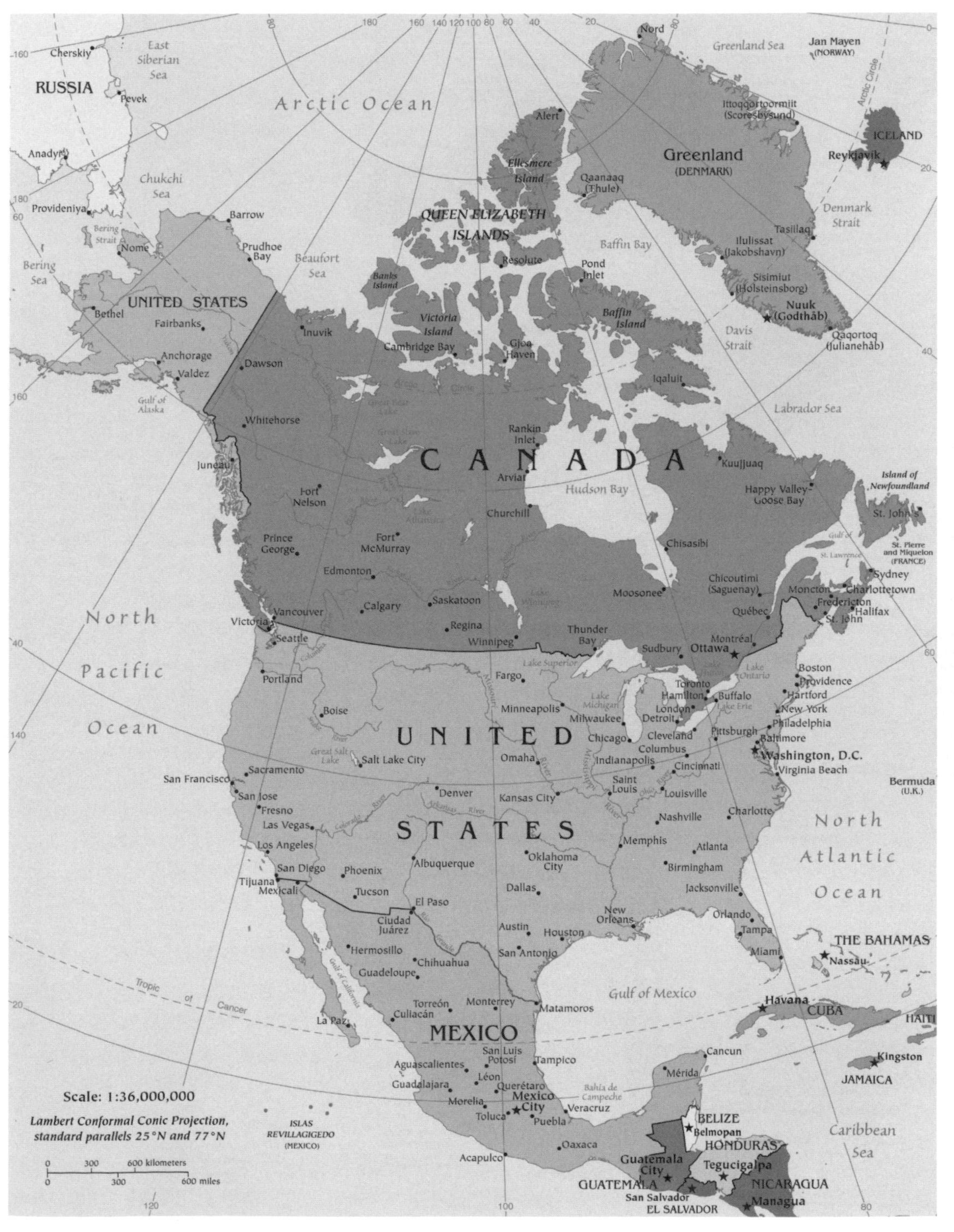

(Central Intelligence Agency)

(Central Intelligence Agency)

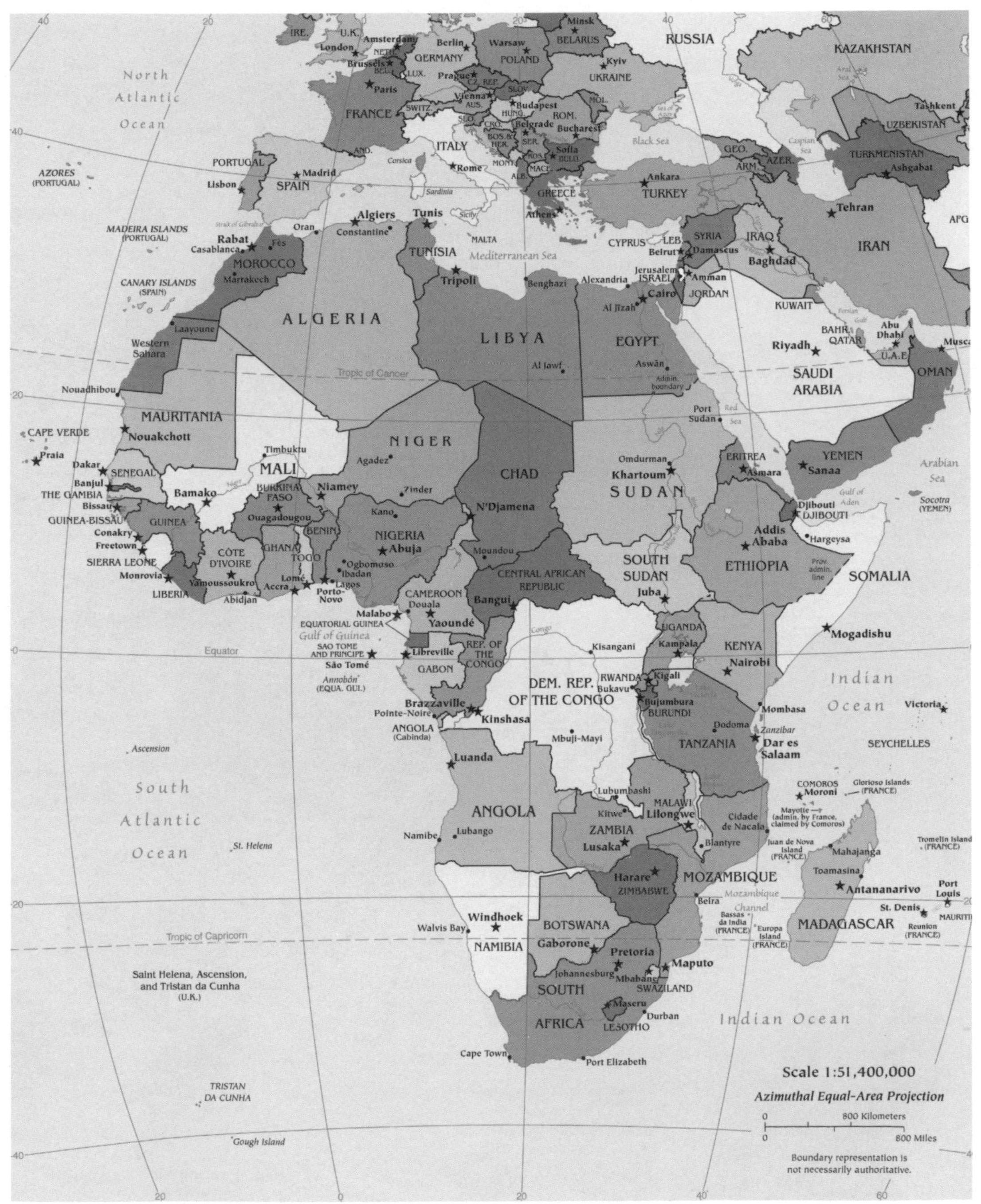

(Central Intelligence Agency)

(Central Intelligence Agency)

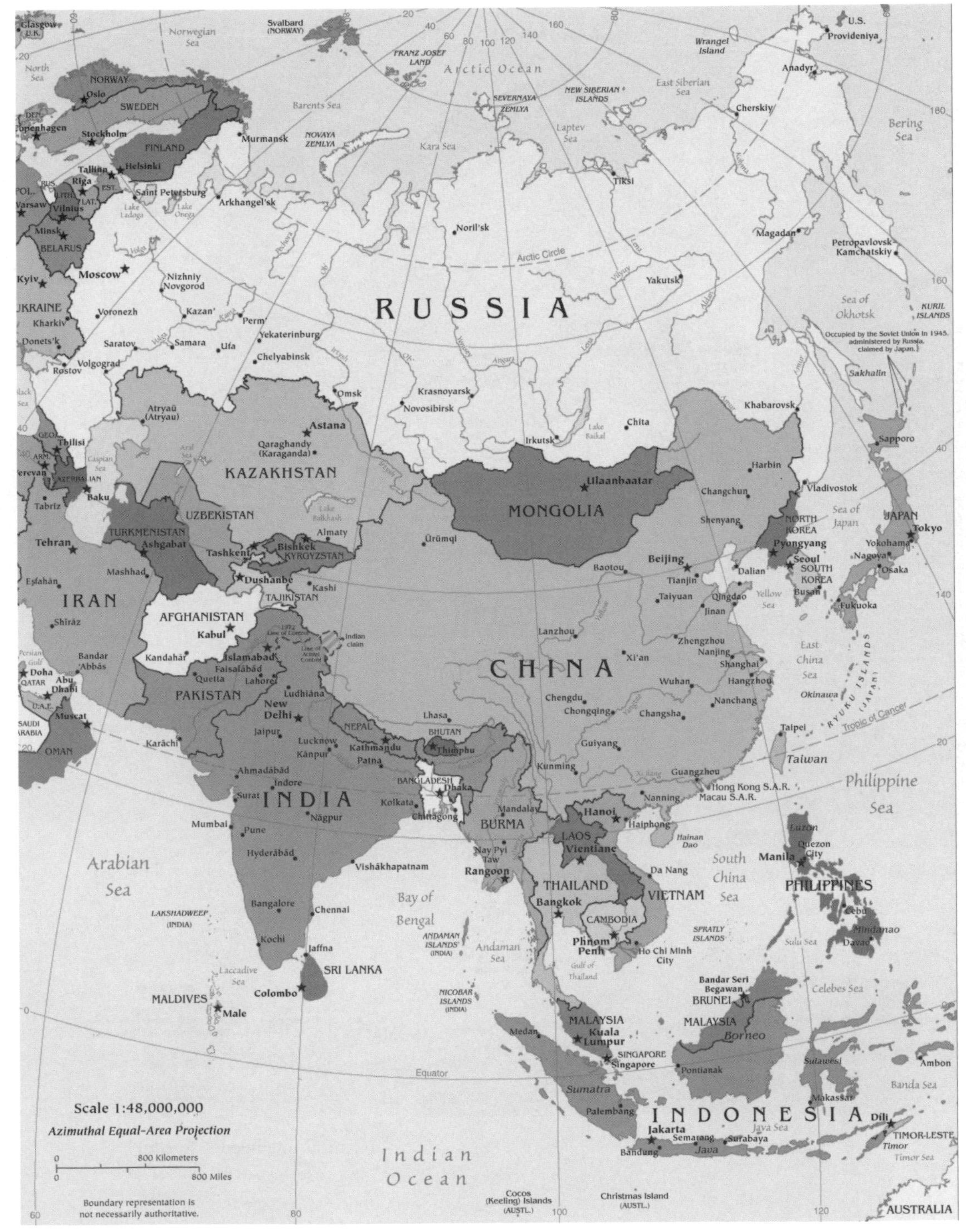

(Central Intelligence Agency)

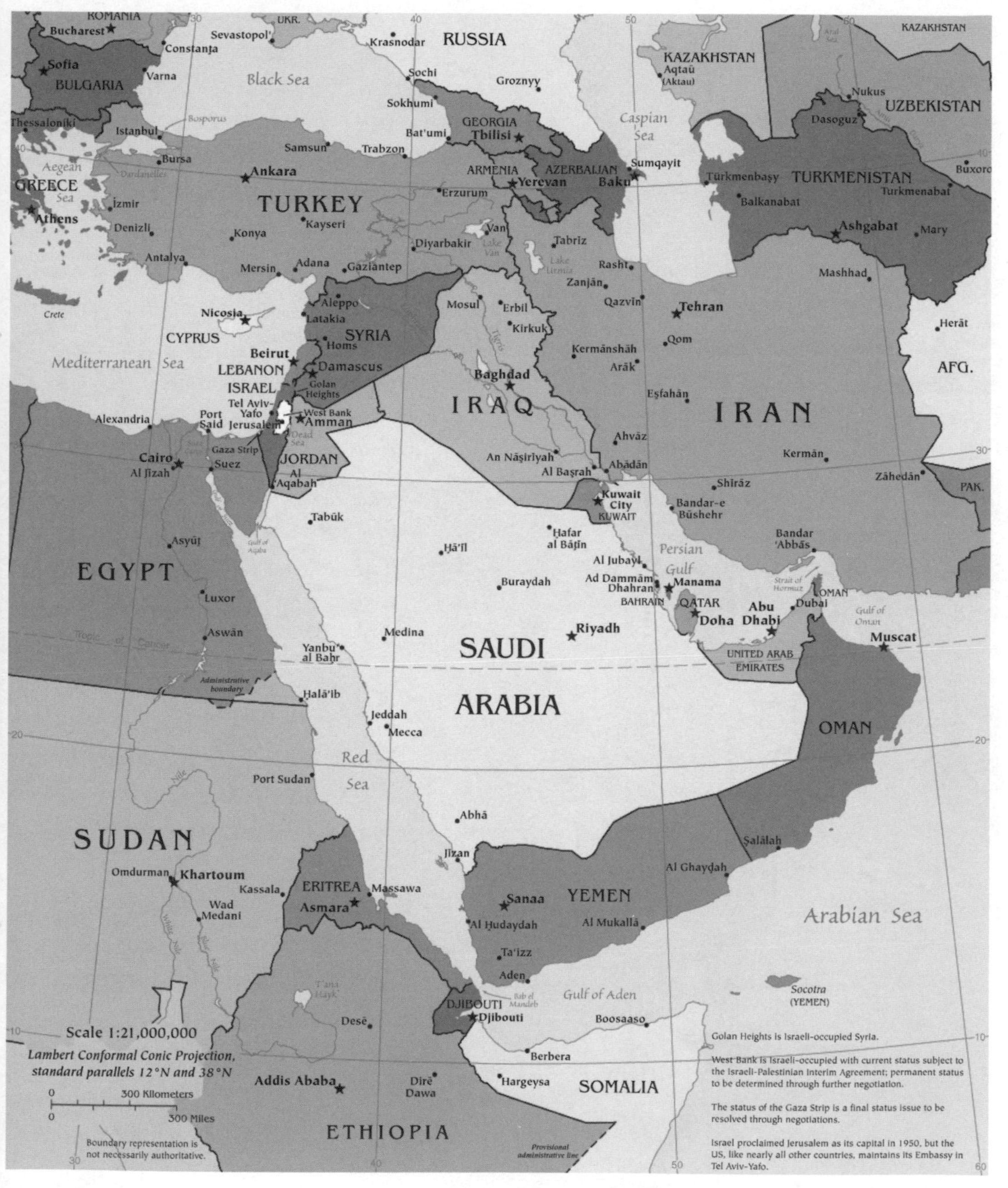

(Central Intelligence Agency)

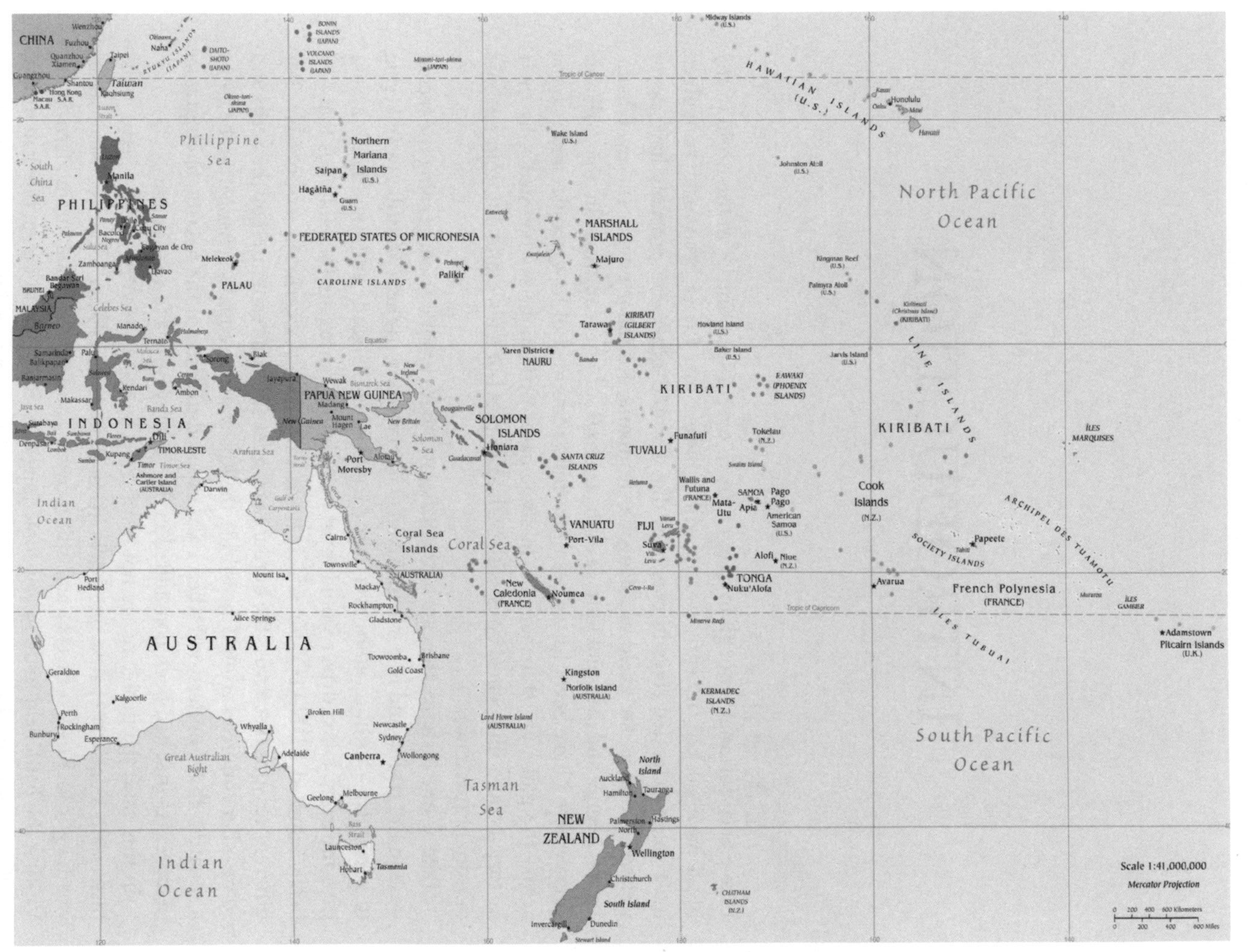

(Central Intelligence Agency)

INTRODUCTION

I have been fortunate enough to spend time in over fifty countries in the world in my life. I have worked in nearly twenty, which means that I have been lucky enough to have some extended stays in countries that I would otherwise probably have never visited, places as far afield as Mongolia, Romania, Rwanda, Egypt, Turkey, Ghana, Sierra Leone and Mozambique as well as most of the countries in the Balkans. Everywhere I have been, I have been forcefully reminded of how peoples and nations across the globe are still shaped – in some cases one might say haunted – by their history. I could fill a whole book with such examples but a few stand out from my own personal experiences.

Take as one instance the case of the Balkans, where emotions concerning the recent wars in the region and in particular NATO intervention in them are still raw in Serbia in particular – until recently, every time I arrived in Belgrade and my English accent gave me away, a taxi driver would insist on pointing out to me the buildings that had been 'bombed by NATO', for which I was presumably vicariously responsible. For different reasons just across the border (a frontier still not recognised by the Serbs and some other countries around the world), the Kosovars are equally sensitive on the issue, a situation that I understood when I was exposed to some of the horrific photographs of atrocities that had been committed in the country only a few years ago.

In this case, the problems are not just fuelled by recent history, for the Serbs' most historically significant battle, one that holds an almost sacred place in Serb consciousness, was fought in Kosovo in 1389 and still forms a point of reference for modern Serbs. Visiting the battlefield in 2009 was something of a shock for, to do so, one had to first of all pass through armed checkpoints, manned by foreign soldiers who were there to protect the monument from deliberate damage from those with whom the Serbs were recently at war (the same is the case for some of the magnificent Serb churches within Kosovar borders). The monument is a reminder of something sacred to the Serbs and therefore is a focus of resentment from their opponents in the recent conflicts.

Other places I have visited show the scars of history even more powerfully. In Rwanda, for example, the genocide of 1994 is very openly remembered and a visit to one of the ruined churches where thousands of non-combatants were brutally massacred is a harrowing experience. Even worse than the piles of human skeletons, many of them with tell-tale fractures in their skulls, were the piles of clothes, once worn by those who were slaughtered there not that long ago – somehow a discarded children's shoe can be the most distressing object of all.

I could go on – constant reminders of Soviet occupation in Tbilisi, Georgia; the still-surviving paintings on the walls of terraced houses in Republican or Loyalist Belfast; the comments of my Ghanaian guide at Cape Coast castle (the point of exit for many slaves taken away to horrendous lives thousands of miles away) about what 'my ancestors' did to 'his ancestors'; or the quasi-deification of Genghis Khan in Mongolia – all served to remind me how powerful history is, even if it is almost always a mythologised rather than a factual version of it that people refer to. Readers could add their own points of reference for reminders of history: the death camps of Auschwitz, Ground Zero in New York or the battlefields of the Somme and Verdun, for example.

What does all this mean? It means that history matters. It tells us where we have come from and who we are (and also gives us some clues about where we are going if we are not careful). It helps to explain why we think the way we do. It enlightens us as to our prejudices and misconceptions – if we are prepared to look at history with an open mind, which is much harder to do than one might think (even for a historian). We are all shaped to some extent by our upbringing and our environment and this makes objectivity difficult.

Yet the world is an incredible place, as much as anything for its cultural variety. We have so much to learn from each other, so much to respect in our own cultures and those of others, and yet history also teaches us that those who are different from us are somehow menacing; the 'Other' challenges our own perceptions of how the world should be, that is the way in which we see it and the way we believe it should be. Many of us welcome diversity in theory but struggle to completely assimilate the concept in practice, especially when other cultural paradigms are far removed from our own.

In attempting to assemble a history of the world there is inevitably some personal selection of what to put in and what to leave out. Foremost in my mind when writing the following pages has been to give some idea of how historical events have led to the world in which we live, in terms of both its positives and its negatives. An understanding of our world, and especially its history, is crucial, and misunderstandings can be disastrous – to take a topical example, the political and military analyses which led to the conflicts in Iraq and Afghanistan were hopelessly oversimplified (and this is not just hindsight; it has been obvious from the very beginning).

But I have allowed myself the luxury of another criterion. I have also tried to include references to individuals or events who, though often forgotten now, in their time played a significant role in history, sometimes regionally, sometimes globally. Hopefully in the process something interesting and new may come out for the reader.

Through it all I find a sense of both wonder and bewilderment. Wonder at the ingenuity of man, his ability to innovate, to survive and to thrive. Bewilderment at how the baser instincts of human nature are still never far beneath the surface. Time spent in Rwanda and the Balkans has reminded me forcibly of this, witnessing close-up reminders of very recent history that were shocking and disturbing – though they also spoke to me in powerful terms of just how resilient the human spirit can be.

It has been a remarkable history for our species, especially in the past few thousand years. There have been amazing breakthroughs in science, in medicine, in all kinds of technology. Yet it is as if a Pandora's box has been opened; the new technology could as easily destroy us as save us. This brings with it a solemn responsibility. Let us hope that the leaders of our world, all parts of it, use it wisely. And let us hope that, where we have any element of choice in the process, we all choose them wisely.

In the course of the journey I have travelled in writing this book I have learned a lot. There have been interesting facts that have emerged, taking me into areas that I had not been familiar with. But these are incidental to the main lessons learned on this voyage of discovery. It might seem odd to state them at the beginning of this book but they impact on much that I have written subsequently.

Two things in particular stand out – one practical, the other philosophical. Firstly I have been reminded that those who would understand history must also understand geography. Just where a nation happens to be on the world map has a remarkable impact on its journey. Looking at my own country, Britain, the narrow strip of water that separates it from Continental Europe has helped preserve it from invasion for a millennium. The same is true for Japan.

Sometimes these barriers may eventually be crossed – often with catastrophic results. For thousands of years the vast expanse of water that separated the Americas from Eurasia protected the cultures there from virtual annihilation. Within decades of the wide Atlantic moat being crossed, many of those cultures were on the edge of extinction. The vastness of the Sahara did the same for much of Africa for a while and indeed was only really counteracted when European invaders bypassed it via the ocean. China too was out of sight of the West for millennia; its existence was suspected from the trade routes that existed but Xanadu was unseen by the West to all practical intents and purposes until Marco Polo's epic writings.

On the other hand, nations can be unlucky with their position. Georgia, a narrow strip of land between the Caspian and Black Seas, has been criss-crossed innumerable times by powerful Turks, Russians and Persians, not to mention Mongols. Romania has similarly spent much of its history (as has Bulgaria) trapped between, for example, Ottoman Turks, Russians and Austro-Hungarians. Perhaps the best example is that prime trouble spot in the Levant around Israel, Lebanon and Syria, where religious tension currently adds to historical rivalry.

This in fact links to my second lesson learned. It is perhaps a statement of the blindingly obvious but one of the greatest evils ever to blight our world is colonialism. However much colonists try to excuse their behaviour, the process is doomed to lead to tragedy because it starts from the premise that the colonist and their culture is somehow superior to that of the colonised. At its worst this can lead to the deliberate destruction of the colonised culture, whose people are seen as inferior and even subhuman.

Lest this become the guilt-ridden thoughts of a Westerner, who indeed has been humbled by some of the sins that the West has committed, let me also say that colonialism is almost as old as time. Neither is it a solely Western phenomenon; witness, for example, the attempted colonisation of the Pacific by the military Japanese regime in the Second World War. Yet one might have hoped that after 2 million years of existence we might have learned to respect others who are different to us (provided that they too allow us to act out our differences). Sadly, we appear to be another 2 million years at least from learning this lesson.

There are many challenges in the way of the achievement of such a utopian aspiration. Nationalism is one: a source of fine and uplifting empathies in one respect, the origin of bitter division in others. The latter sentiment is sadly far too often exploited by self-serving politicians in furtherance of their own ambitions, often to the detriment of their fellow countrymen and women. Religion is another; tragic, abused, exploited religion – potentially the source of so much that is good and uplifting, often a vehicle for bigotry, distortion, mistrust. How many innocent millions have been slaughtered in the name of religion?

Yet religion too can be a power for good; it is the way that ideologues abuse it that is the problem. There are of course other sources for good; we find it in the arts, in music, literature, painting, sculpture and architecture, for example. We find it too in the selfless people who give of their talents, sometimes great, sometimes humble, to further the well-being of wider humanity. Let us hope that it is the latter group that shapes the spirit of the future. And let us hope that we learn from history, treasuring all that is best from it and doing our utmost to avoid a repetition of all that is worst.

A NOTE ON DATES

The further back we go, the more imprecise we are in our ability to supply accurate dates. Scientific analysis is needed to allow us to date with any accuracy, with techniques such as radiocarbon and potassium-argon dating. These are subject to margins of error that get bigger the further back we go.

Also, there is only so much of the world and its history that we have discovered. New archaeological discoveries are being made all the time – some were made as this book was being written. In some cases they moved back the timeline of man some hundreds of thousands of years.

I say all this as my introduction to a plea for understanding. I have tried to be careful in my use of dates but often there is no agreed consensus for ancient history and, even when there is, new discoveries and scientific advances can change anything and everything. In other words, for ancient history in particular a date in this book for a particular event may be in need of an update a day after publication. Therefore the reader should be aware that, even allowing for my attempts to be careful in my chronology, they may come across some expert with a dissenting view, especially for events in the 'BC' period. I hope the reader will show suitable forbearance and reserve their irritation for any mistakes that may be present as regards more modern, and therefore more dateable, times.

I make no apology however for using the well-known dating conventions of 'BC' and 'AD'. Whatever one's religious affiliations, they have been the common currency of dating in the Julian and Gregorian calendars for hundreds of years. Recently, however, political correctness has started to introduce the acronym BCE (Before the Christian Era) instead of BC, a symptom of creeping intolerance that I have no intention of repeating here.

1

GENESIS

The Beginnings of the World (The World Before 3000 BC)

Just how our world began is a matter of debate, enveloped in uncertainties that obscure the truth in a darkness as deep as the remotest recesses of the universe. It is the greatest of ironies that generations and civilisations long past were much more confident that they knew the answers to questions of our origins than we are. Archbishop James Ussher of Armagh, a seventeenth-century Christian prelate, even knew the time that it all began – the night preceding 23 October 4004 BC apparently (given changes in calendars, that would be 21 September 4004 BC in modern currency). Pre-Darwinian bibles often quote these dates in the margins as if they were statements of incontrovertible fact.

Ussher was far from alone in his confidence; various civilisations in many different epochs had their own equally strongly held beliefs that they knew the secrets of creation, including the date (though they would not of course have expressed these in Christian timescales). The Maya calendar was divided into periods of 144,000 days, known as *baktuns*, and they based their dating system on the number of these periods that had passed since the world began. Within the framework of their mythology, this gave a creation date of 3114 BC in the Western Christian calendar (famously, some 'experts' believed that they also showed that the world would end in AD 2012).

The method of creation varied too. Maori lore told how the world was formed when the female earth split apart from the male sky. In Chinese variants, a giant gave up his life to form the world. In Egyptian mythology, all was first a watery chaos before the first land was formed and all, it was feared, would return there if the gods were ever to be defeated by their enemies. Of course, in Old Testament versions of the creation tale the earth also came out of the water, on the third day of God's week-long construction project.

Modern scientific views of the beginning of the world are somewhat different from these now widely disregarded beliefs. Scientists now reckon the world to be some 4.6 billion years old (with the universe itself believed to be about 13 billion years old), giving a date of origin somewhat before those suggested by the seventeenth-century archbishop or Mayan priests. The earth did indeed come out of chaos, if that is what the universe may be called, but in a process known as 'The Big Bang'. This was the result of cosmic chemistry, not God, it would seem; there is little room for theology in the scientific mindset, as some great minds like Albert Einstein have lucidly explained. Einstein's view was that 'I do not believe in a personal God and I have never denied this but have expressed it clearly. If something is in me which can be called religious then it is the unbounded admiration for the structure of the world so far as our science can reveal it.'

Science, in other words, rules supreme. And scientists, among other things, love labels. This affection extends to world history, where a series of dry and dusty categorisations have been applied to a plethora of subjects. Take for instance the geological history of our planet. We have the Palaeozoic era, which extended from 570 to 230 million years ago, the Mesozoic (from 230 to 65 million years ago) and the Cenozoic (from 65 million years ago to the present time) which includes the Quaternary, in which we live now. Each of these have various subdivisions – our present age is set in the Holocene subdivision of the Quaternary.

The observant reader will have noticed that the closer we get to modern times the more labels we have. The 2 billion years before the Palaeozoic era are grouped together as one amorphous lump, the Proterozoic. The history of the world mirrors that of humanity: the further back we go, the less detail we have and the more sweeping the generalisations we make.

There have been times of dramatic change, of continental drifts of unimaginable scale and volcanic eruptions of such intensity that they changed the climate of the world. At one stage just one giant continent existed, named Pangaea. The continent was shaped like a boomerang and in the middle was an indented sea, giving the whole a form that looks eerily similar to a foetus. All this was one concentrated landmass, around it a vast ocean.

Pangaea eventually split into two. To the south was Gondwanaland, and at one time South America, Australia, India, Arabia, New Zealand and Antarctica formed part of this one huge mass while in the north the equally vast territory of Laurasia was separated from Gondwanaland by the Tethys Sea. They are now long gone, these old lands and ancient oceans, not even memories except in the odd geological anomalies that hint at their presence from time to time.

And then came life. Exactly when and how is doomed, it seems, to remain forever a matter of speculation. But new evidence is being unearthed, literally, all the time. Tiny bacteria probably came into being about 3.5 billion years ago. At the beginning of the Cambrian subdivision of the Palaeozoic, over 500 million years ago, it is believed that a jellyfish-like organism called *ellipsocephalus* swam in the seas. Early life continued to evolve in the water.

But then, through a miraculous process of evolution, life forms began to swap fins for feet. Eventually came the era of the dinosaurs. They had their own impact on man but only on his imagination for they were long gone by the time that anything remotely resembling *Homo sapiens* walked the earth. Yet their remains made a huge impact on humanity and fuelled his dreams of a 'Lost World' where dinosaurs still survived.

As men started to dig in the bowels of the earth they unearthed fossils, like photographic negatives of the giants that had once ruled the world. 'Dinosaur' means 'terrible lizard', which encapsulates well enough the profound impact that these creatures had on the imagination when men became aware of their existence, an existence that ended millions of years ago. The term was first coined by Sir Richard Owen in 1841. During the previous two decades new species of fossilised reptile had been identified and there was no convenient label for them, so one needed to be created; Owen's term fitted the bill and has stuck.

Later, scientists felt that the term was too all-embracing and further subdivisions were suggested; they may have fitted the bill too, but they stuck less well. So when the English palaeontologist H. G. Seeley suggested in 1887 that dinosaurs should be categorised between lizard-hipped 'saurischians' and bird-hipped 'ornithischians' he was scientifically accurate but failed to grip the imagination and his names were lost to all but specialists.

The dinosaurs were small-brained and we can safely assume that they did not philosophise about their place in the world. But if they had done so, they would no doubt have thought themselves masters of the world forever. However, their reign was finite. The most common consensus among scientists is that a cosmic catastrophe occurred some 65 million years ago, when a large body struck the earth and changed the climate disastrously. The huge ring of underwater *cenotes* that pockmark the Yucatan Peninsula in Mexico is believed to provide evidence of this event.

There is of course no guarantee that such a disaster will never strike the earth again, and it is quite likely that one day it will; a large meteorite that is believed to have struck the remote Tunguska region of Russia at the beginning of the twentieth century left behind it a trail of destruction but fortunately no widespread loss of life. It was on a far smaller scale than the hit that destroyed the dinosaurs, but was nonetheless a salutary reminder of how fragile the rule of man is. Certainly, the age of the dinosaurs ended with terrifying finality. Such, it seems, is the fate of all species; of all those that have ever existed on our planet only 1 per cent are still extant. Ultimate demise will, on the balance of probabilities, be our fate too.

How man came to be on the scene has also been a subject of intense debate. As the earth was created by God (or the gods), so was man placed on it by Him or them. That man was descended from the apes appeared to many, when it was first mooted as an idea, as an outrageous piece of blasphemy. Indeed, so radical was such a concept that it took Charles Darwin some twenty years to pluck up the courage to publish it; not surprising perhaps, as, in his adolescence, he seriously considered becoming a country parson. However, when he eventually committed his thoughts publicly to print, his book became possibly the most influential ever written outside a religious text – and in its own way it did of course have a profound effect on religion. It appeared to call into question man's understanding of the world and of his special (so it had previously been believed) place in it. Man's view of himself and his history was turned on its head.

Darwin is one of the most famous and influential of all scientists, certainly in terms of his impact on man's thinking, and it is worth briefly noting the four main tenets of his work. These are that the world and its species evolve, so that as new species develop old ones die; that the process is gradual and does not involve sudden leaps forward; that all creatures have a common descent (the most controversial statement of belief to those with strongly held religious convictions); and, lastly, that natural selection ensures the survival of the fittest; the latter belief has been used in an attempt to justify some terrible abuses over the years, especially in the colonial era between 1875 and 1945, when the advocates of Social Darwinism appeared to be in the ascendancy.

The primate family, of which *Homo sapiens* is a branch, neatly interlinks in time terms with the dinosaurs. The founding parents were shrew-like creatures, nocturnal animals, living about 70 million years ago when dinosaurs still roamed. Around 40 million years ago the first monkeys arrived, with the first apes found 10 million years later. Sometime between 4 and 14 million years ago (note the huge uncertainty in the date range, indicative of how little is known of our origins) came the hominids. Primates also evolved; chimpanzees, gorillas, orang-utans, all cousins of man. There would be two branches to this tree: 'pongids' and 'hominids', the former containing apes and the latter species of humanity. There is in fact still a very close biological similarity, with humans having a DNA structure that is 99 per cent similar to chimpanzees.

At some point, the branch which eventually spawned humanity began to emerge within the family tree – a process that took millions of years before humans evolved to their current design. Various characteristics marked man's development. There was the fact that he walked upright rather than on all fours. There was his use of tools (something that he noticeably shares with chimpanzees). Then there was the development of his brain, and it is indeed his skull shape that has been one of the prime definers of the different types of hominid that have been identified.

The theory of evolution should not be taken too far. Man has not come down in a neat line where one branch of the human family can directly be traced back to a predecessor. Various branches of our ancestors' family co-existed. About 2 million years ago, for example, several variants known as *Australopithecus* and *Homo habilis* walked the earth at the same time.

Within these branches, several subspecies can be noted. The so-called robust australopithecines were believed to be vegetarians, living on grasses, roots and berries. The gracile *Australopithecus africanus* in contrast were believed to have added lizards, eggs and small mammals to their diet.

Differences in the shapes and sizes of jawbones and skulls set these various subspecies apart. But in the end Darwinism won – *Australopithecus* failed to survive and the *Homo* branch of the family emerged (for the time being) triumphant – a steady increase in the size of the brain being a characteristic of his development. The shape of *Homo*'s brain too was different from that of his chimpanzee cousins in important respects. The temporal lobe, which is responsible for memory, and the parietal lobe, which integrates information received from the senses, became increasingly prominent.

Africa is considered to be the birthplace of early man, with strong clues to his origins found particularly in the Olduvai Gorge in Tanzania. Here, evidence of basic tool making has emerged, going back some 2 million years. However, inevitably not everyone accepts that Olduvai provides the only early evidence of such industries, with sites elsewhere in Morocco and Algeria also found. Other ancient sites have been identified in Jordan and Hungary.

But it is Africa that is widely believed to be the birthplace of mankind, the epicentre from which humanity rippled outwards across the globe. And it is always best to keep an open mind on these matters, because the story of our origins is far from complete and new developments add to knowledge all the time. At the time of writing discoveries just made in the Afar region of northern Ethiopia show evidence of stone tools being used to cut into animal bones that have been dated to 3.4 million years ago, 1 million years before the previously accepted earliest date for a creature something like modern man.

The *Homo* family had its own subdivisions. As well as *Homo habilis*, there was *Homo erectus*, evidence of whom has been found in China (known as Peking Man) and Java; *Homo neanderthalensis* (the renowned Neanderthal Man); and of course *Homo sapiens sapiens*, modern man. Early man left few physical remains other than his bones and his tools as a mark on the tapestry of world history; the latter have traditionally been used as a way of distinguishing different cultures of early man, allowing ancient cultures such as the Acheulian, the Clactonian and the Levalloisian (the first two identifiable by their hand-axes, the latter distinguished by flint flakes) to be identified.

There are clues in the naming of these early cultures that should act as a warning. All of them are based on European sites. This gives an insight into the fact that those who discovered them were European archaeologists, which runs the risk of focussing excessively on matters European to the exclusion of all other parts of the world, and this of course should be avoided. At this early stage it is important to recognise without equivocation that the part played by early man in Africa in human development was absolutely crucial and it is to these non-European parts of the world that we owe much of our subsequent development.

Every now and again, a hint of something we might call art emerges from the gloom of those distant days of early *Homo sapiens sapiens*. From a culture known as the Magdalenian, a carving of an animal that looks very much like a horse has been found. From Moravia (in the modern Czech Republic), a female figure with exaggerated buttocks and pendulous bosoms suggests a link with a fertility cult. A figure in ivory of such a 'Venus' found at Lespugue in France strongly suggests similar fertility undertones; its abstract qualities are such that it would not look out of place in a Salvador Dalí exhibition.

Man has had an interest in art for a very long time. An ox rib decorated with a series of double arc-shapes found in France has been estimated to be 300,000 years old. An amazing discovery of carved statuettes at Vogelherd in Germany included a well-crafted abstract mammoth and a human figurine. The mammoth has crosses carved in it, an expression of some abstract idea whose origin is now lost, which suggests that man has been a philosophical as well as a utilitarian creature for many thousands of years. And there are thousands of cave-art sites across other regions, particularly in Africa.

The crosses at Vogelherd suggest something else too: the ability to communicate ideas. A crucial part of communication, of course, is language. Here we move inevitably into the realms of hypothesis. Some have suggested that rudimentary forms of verbal communication existed up to 2 million years ago. The suggestion of the existence of abstract ideas among *Homo erectus* evidenced by some of their surviving artefacts adds substance to this theory.

Communication is vital to successful existence for many animals, of course. Dogs, wolves, monkeys, lions and many others hunt in packs, and for a relatively weak specimen such as *Homo sapiens* such tactics are vital to survival. But what more advanced language does allow is the expression of ideas, of philosophies, of mythologies, and this is what most sets man apart (as far as we can tell) from other species.

Cave paintings provide glimpses into the mindsets of early man, such as those at Lascaux in France, dated to around 15,000 BC (but now, since recent discovery, sadly deteriorating rapidly). Wall paintings on the caves at Pech-Merle show speckled horses; anthropologists have suggested that these images were used as part of ritual ceremonies. It has been noted that the attention paid to the depiction of animals in these subterranean art galleries is astonishing, whereas human shapes rarely appear and are drawn crudely when they do, almost in sketch form. Animals clearly played a key role in the rituals of the artists who painted these images, an understandable situation when they relied on them for food, clothing and myriad other uses (bones could be used as tools, sinews for strong twine, for example).

There is also evidence from very early on of a human attribute we would all recognise; compassion. Remains as old as 1.8 million years ago show evidence of hominids being inhumed with dignity. Others half a million years old show humans with physical handicaps who lived for many years with severely debilitating deformities; they could not have survived for so long without the help of others.

The first (and by far the lengthiest) periods of man's existence on earth were inevitably assigned a label too: the Stone Age. This was further divided into the Palaeolithic, Mesolithic and Neolithic periods (Old, Middle and New Stone Ages respectively). Traditionally, a Danish antiquarian, C. J. Thomsen, is credited with inventing the classification sometime around 1819, though not everyone agrees as others were working on similar labelling systems at around the same time. No matter; the divisions serve as a useful point of reference.

The vast majority of the 2 million years or so that a creature recognisable as a hominid has existed on earth belongs to the Palaeolithic. It was during those years, centuries and millennia that the subspecies to which we belong, *Homo sapiens sapiens*, evolved. The process and progress of that evolution is little known, understanding it being more down to some esoteric black art or estimation and speculation than undeniable fact. The evidence that remains is so incomplete that reconstructing the story of our early history is equivalent to reconstructing a Roman mosaic when we only have a fraction of 1 per cent of the tiles in our hands.

This means that studies of our early history are destined to remain areas of fierce debate, however much scientific knowledge may advance in the future. Take, for example, the story of Neanderthal man. The earliest evidence of him was uncovered in 1856 in Germany, three years before Darwin's *Origin of Species* made its controversial appearance in the world. The remains found at this time initially suggested to many scientists that the hominid owner of these fragmentary remains had been a brutish oaf, a lumbering and unintelligent specimen. That owner could therefore be no close relation of *Homo sapiens sapiens*.

Extraordinary theories were devised to account for this aberration. Bones that looked Neanderthal were often of bandy-legged individuals; one scientist explained this away by stating that they were the relics of a Cossack cavalryman in the Russian army that chased Bonaparte across Europe; that 'oafishness' must somehow be non-European gives a strong clue about the racial stereotyping of the time. Yet as more bones were uncovered across the world the widespread existence of Neanderthal man became harder to explain away.

Neanderthal is a name applied to remains found in Europe, yet discoveries of this subspecies have been made across the globe; it is simply that in different continents he has different names, and branches of the family tree can be found in remains uncovered in Africa, Central Asia and as far away as Java. Of course, many more remains, in all probability, lie undiscovered and others have simply been destroyed and lost forever, so his distribution may have been even wider than we currently know.

Eventually it was recognised that here was at least a cousin of *Homo sapiens sapiens*, hence the technical nomenclature of this hominid, *Homo sapiens neanderthalensis*. Strong links were recognised between him and *Homo erectus*, the hominids' chief representative on earth for most of his 2 million years here. Physically he was about 5 feet, 8 inches tall on average, with a large musculature, a longer and lower cranium than ours and a slightly larger brain capacity – the latter suggesting that rumours of his lack of intelligence have been greatly exaggerated.

He was also associated with some important developments in the evolution of man. He worked stone tools well; he is linked with cultures already mentioned in passing such as the Levalloisian. But he left us hints of other aspects of his life, far removed from his technology, for excavation has uncovered evidence of ritual burial practices. A grave in France housed the body of a teenage boy, lying on his side as if asleep (interestingly, Bronze Age burials in England tens of thousands of years later showed a similar positioning). Near him was a well-worked stone axe, perhaps intended to be of some use in the hereafter.

Other human remains in Central Asia had animal bones interred with them. Evidence of scratches on skeletons in some graves suggests that the flesh had been cut off the child buried there, perhaps as part of the ritual process of burying the remains or, more darkly, of some form of ritual cannibalism. The headless body of a young child in a shallow pit in France hints at other dark ceremonials.

Most intriguingly of all, a body found in the Zagros Mountains of Iraq suggests that it was interred with carefully arranged flowers; pollen traces identified these as including ragwort, hollyhock and cornflowers. These were not accidental deposits for they were carefully arranged, suggesting to some that the remains may have been of a medicine man, though it might equally have been a normal part of the burial arrangements of a prominent member of society. It is nevertheless intriguing to think that the role of flowers at funerals has a history stretching back at least 50,000 years.

The last unearthed remains of *Homo sapiens neanderthalensis* have been dated to about 40,000 years ago, during the same period in which *Homo sapiens sapiens* appeared. This has inevitably led to some debate as to whether he is a missing link in our evolution or just a cousin from a now-withered branch of the family tree. In fact, the answer is now known; remains from *Homo sapiens neanderthalensis* and *Homo sapiens sapiens* have both been found from the same period, therefore the two subspecies existed side by side. This poses the question of why Neanderthals disappeared: were they wiped out by the ancestors of modern man?

I am inclined to agree with Dr Richard Leakey, one of the leading anthropologists of the late twentieth century, that in fact the branches probably merged through a process of inbreeding (recent research findings in 2010 seem to support this). A number of scientists think that remains found in Portugal and Romania at the close of the twentieth century exhibit clear signs of both Neanderthals and their modern ancestors, that is to say these bones are from a hybrid. As is often the case, though, there are a number of modern scientists who hold beliefs to the contrary.

'Neanderthal Man' did not look that much different from us. Scientists have argued the case that it would be hard to spot a Neanderthal in a modern crowd and to prove the point a BBC presenter adopted the facial characteristics and supposed hairline of one of the subspecies and, dressed in modern clothes (animal skins would perhaps have given the game away), walked boldly down a crowded English high street. Only one of the passers-by walking the other way gave him a second look.

For most of his existence, man has been a hunter-gatherer, at the mercy of his world and with limited ability to influence it on anything except a local scale. All that has changed, in historical terms, quite recently, and with the increased influence has come increased responsibility, though man sometimes seems unwilling to recognise the fact. At Niaux in France, paintings of ibex and bison, elegantly and accurately drawn, still adorn the walls of a cave. Some of these animals have spears and arrows in their sides, showing that they were a source of food to the men who once lived here. Men developed spears and arrows, and also learned to work together in packs to drive prey, even large animals such as mammoths, over cliff-edges. Cave paintings of mammoths have been dated to be 35,000 years old.

Another old object, dated back some 13,000 years, is a carving on ivory of two reindeer swimming across a river. This find from France perhaps refers to a seasonal migration important locally as a means of obtaining extra meat and providing something of a feast for people who must more often than not have been used to famine.

Man must have been conscious from the very beginning of how much powerful forces were at play around him and this too led to the creation of mythologies to explain man's position in the world. Climate change, a currently topical subject, has been an issue for man ever since he walked the earth. Periods of intense glaciation have frequently made large portions of the earth's surface no-go areas for men, though these Ice Ages were broken up by warmer interglacial periods. These impacted greatly on the shape of the land and on the types of flora and fauna that lived in different regions of the world.

The (to date) last Ice Age ended some 14,000 years ago and the melting of the ice that followed had a profound effect on the shape of the world, as indeed did the Ice Ages themselves when great glaciers gouged out huge tears on the surface of the earth, moving enormous boulders along in their icy grip, ripping up great chasms that are now deep valleys surrounded on either side by towering mountains whose geological features, cols and corries, still testify to the immense power of nature.

The rising of the waters changed the geography of the earth considerably. Britain and Ireland, for example, became islands, and land links between Papua New Guinea and Australia disappeared beneath the waves. The bridge between India and Sri Lanka also went. Less well known is the effect that the removal of the weight of the ice had on the shape of the land; in Britain, parts of Scotland are still rising while the fringe of the South Coast is disappearing imperceptibly underwater. The warming of the earth was not all bad news for mankind, for areas that had previously been out of bounds as they had been gripped by the chilling embrace of the ice now became accessible.

Another area where the rising waters may have had a profound effect is in the Americas. It has been suggested that links between Asia and America go back at least 20,000 years, when the then land bridge between the two allowed nomads to cross from one to the other. I have met people who have suggested links between the music of Mongolia and that of the Native Americans, for example, connections that cannot belong to modern times but only to long-lost links thousands of years ago. Although I cannot advance this as a scientifically proven theory it is nevertheless an intriguing hypothesis and one deserving of further research.

We now know that human beings had an interest in music at least 42,000 years ago. In 2012, flutes made from bird bones and mammoth ivory were discovered in a cave in southern Germany, alongside evidence that the site had once been occupied by *Homo sapiens*. It has even been speculated that the development of music helps to explain the demise of the more conservative Neanderthals.

It took some time for the world to look as it does now. North-western Europe in 10,000 BC would have initially been mainly treeless, with Arctic flora the predominant vegetation. As the earth warmed, some pine and birch forests would have appeared. A continuation of the global warming of the time would have seen trees such as oak, hazel, lime and elm evolving (by perhaps 6,000 BC). Between 5,000 BC and 500 BC temperatures would actually have dropped a little to those we see today.

As the earth itself evolved, so did mankind. One area now becomes increasingly important in evolution: south-west Asia. Late Palaeolithic cultures were still composed of hunter-gatherers. However, the most vital of all of mankind's inventions was about to take place: the development of farming.

Farming meant that peoples could stay put, that the need to be nomadic had gone. This enabled permanent settlements to be established which in turn led to the possibility of specialisation of labour. This then fed the need for different skills and occupations to support a changed mode of existence, from humble bureaucrats, such as accountants and lawyers, to artists, architects, philosophers, scientists, storytellers and historians, in short to all the things that together make civilisation. We are jumping the gun, for it took a few thousand years to get there, but without the stable existence that farming made possible the journey would never have started. It was the start of a chain reaction that culminated in the world in which we now live.

The last years of the Palaeolithic were marked by developments in hunting technology, such as sharp, barbed harpoons (made of bone or antlers) used by the Magdalenian culture (who lived in what is now France). Little is known of the Mesolithic era that followed but, as it led into the epochal events of the Neolithic, these are critical years. There were of course no 'full stops' between Palaeolithic, Mesolithic and Neolithic, but the process was one of gradual and constant evolution, some developments being perhaps almost imperceptible on a day-to-day basis but over time having an enormous impact in terms of their accumulated effect.

The Mesolithic is one of the worst-defined epochs of all human history. Its name, the 'middle' Stone Age, suggests its character as a bridge between hunter-gathering and fully fledged farming in the Neolithic period. It is mainly characterised by the use of 'microliths', finely worked flint flakes used in particular for arrows and spear-points. Flint scrapers also become common.

It is difficult to ascribe precise points in time to this, or indeed the other Stone Ages, in any detail on anything other than a local basis. Of course, such ages did not have a defined beginning and end anyway (an unavoidable weakness of 'labelling') but rather experienced an indefinable merging of one into the next. In addition, transitional phases between these occurred at different times in different parts of the world. In some remote parts of the Amazon jungle or Papua New Guinea it could be argued that until very recent times some peoples still lived as essentially Neolithic communities. As a form of rather crude benchmark however, the Mesolithic community at Star Carr in England has been dated to 7500 BC. In contrast, the Mesolithic ended in the Middle East several thousand years before that.

So far the history of our subspecies has been discussed with only passing references to specific cultures. This is mainly because we have limited concrete evidence to state that such-and-such a culture was epoch-making in terms of its impact on our world. This is about to change with the emergence of the Natufians of the Middle East and their 'city' of Jericho. They were initially a Mesolithic culture, with many examples of the flint tools characteristic of such a definition. But among the flint relics that have been unearthed was one of enormous significance – a sickle.

We first know of the Natufians during the tenth millennium BC, when they were cave dwellers on the Mediterranean coast of the Levant. The sickles suggest harvesting, as do pestles and mortars with which to crush crops and presumably create the raw ingredients for bread. At the outset this does not necessarily mean settlement, for wild crops can be gleaned as well as deliberately planted ones.

But there are other early hints that this was more than a transient hunter-gatherer band. They built elaborate tombs in cemeteries, big enough to give evidence of collaboration between fairly large groups of people. And then there is Jericho, perhaps the earliest settlement in the world (certainly yet found), scarcely a village in terms of size but also dating back to the tenth millennium BC. This was surrounded by a stone-built wall with towers 30 feet high.

Elsewhere evidence of animal domestication can be noted. One such site has been uncovered in the Crimea and another near the Caspian Sea. Traces of herding have been found at Shanidar in Northern Iraq and have been dated to 9000 BC (possibly before crop-growing began). Man was settling down and along with evidence of farming there are also marked developments in social organisation. During the Neolithic period animal husbandry and the growing of crops marks a new way of life, one that foreshadows modern existence and is indeed its lifeblood.

However, it is quite easy to believe that, before domesticating animals, tribes followed meat herds in search of food – reindeer was a prime source of meat during the Ice Age as far south as France and northern Spain due to the colder conditions then prevailing and the much lower sea levels (up to 400 feet lower than now). Cave paintings and *objets d'art* maybe 15,000 years old show something rather like a bridle on horses. Horses' teeth dated back as far as 30,000 years show evidence of something called crib-biting, which is only found in modern times on tethered animals.

Some argue convincingly that the so-called Agricultural Revolution was not quite the dramatic and unexpected innovation that it has long been thought to be. Studies of other cultures that have survived into modern times, such as Lapps in the far north of Europe, have led anthropologists to suggest that this was not an overnight transition but one which happened over thousands of years when hunters would kill prey for immediate food needs but keep some for milk production or other forms of husbandry.

What is undeniable, though, whatever the speed of transition and its starting point, is that the Agricultural Revolution had an enormous impact on world population. It has been estimated that 10,000 years ago this stood at no more than 10 million. By 2,000 years ago that had gone up to 300 million. Our population now is well over 6 billion and rising. The Industrial Revolution of the 1800s has driven the latter part of this stunning rate of increase but none of it would have been possible without farming and the sedentary lifestyle that it allowed.

Interestingly the developments in agriculture seem to have occurred in several different parts of the world independently of each other (though of course the absence of evidence does not necessarily mean that there were no links between them, merely that none have yet been discovered). Significant agriculture began in the Middle East some 10,000 years ago in an area known from its shape as the Fertile Crescent. It appears in China about 7,000 years ago and in Mesoamerica (i.e. Central America) about 5,000 years ago. Most historians independently suggest that it also appeared in other parts of the world such as Papua New Guinea and Africa.

Africa looked very different until quite recently. The area we now know as the Sahara Desert was green and fertile until perhaps as late as 3000 BC. Archaeology has unearthed extensive evidence of hunting and fishing in particular in what was then a green and well-watered area. When the climate changed, and the sands began to creep, those who had lived there previously were forced to seek new lands to the east, west, south and north in order to survive, helping no doubt to provide impetus to the formation of new societies in the regions to which they relocated.

China has always been to some extent cut off from the rest of the world. A significant reason for this is straightforward geography. Surrounded by harsh steppes, precipitous mountains and arid deserts, and therefore isolated from the other great early centres of civilisation, the Middle East and the Indus Valley, its development occurred without a great amount of outside pressure until later times. The lands in between China and the rest of the world to the west were, if they were suited to anything, more useful for pastoral nomads than settled crop-growers. There was commercial traffic from fairly early on, but this was often through middlemen, and East and West initially had little detailed awareness of each other.

However, it is reasonable to assume that even in early times there was trading to some extent between quite dispersed areas on a more local scale. One excellent example concerns the Greek island of Milos. On the island a particularly distinctive kind of obsidian is found. Neolithic tools and blades made from it have been found around the Aegean but also in Malta, Italy and Egypt, leading to the assumption that somehow small vessels were ferrying it around the Mediterranean more than 7,000 years ago.

In the Fertile Crescent, settlements appeared such as the aforementioned Jericho as well as Uruk and Ur in Mesopotamia (the latter the original home of the biblical Abraham, though much later in time than the events being discussed here). Excavations show the people there to have enjoyed quite a varied diet. Sickles suggest harvesting (probably wheat, rye and barley in the main) but bone remains hint that they also ate rabbits, gazelles, goats and onagers (wild donkeys). Mussel shells and fish vertebrae show that rivers were a source of food too. Alongside cereal seeds they consumed berries, nuts and lentils.

It is also important to note that farming and the domestication of animals had a dramatic impact not just on man but on nature. In some parts of the world, such as the British Isles and much of Western Europe, it is impossible to find a landscape that has not somehow been touched by man, however wild it may look. It is a trend that continues and accelerates into modern times, with rainforests and other precious habitats from South America, across Africa and into Asia increasingly under terminal threat. Animals, too, evolved as a result of domestication. The ancestors of modern domestic sheep were called mouflons, animals with hair rather than wool, more like goats than anything else. This animal's modern successors appear much neater, tidier, groomed in comparison.

In Mesoamerica (in the main Mexico) on the other hand the major crop was maize. It is interesting that, despite the evolution of crops in Central America, tribes in North America lived the lives of hunter-gatherers until very recently, well into the nineteenth century AD, so the spread of agriculture was far from universal even in fairly adjacent areas. In Mexico, however, it took root in spectacular fashion. It is little surprise that chilli was one of the early crops of which evidence has been found here, as well as beans, squash and corn.

Agriculture, though, as already noted, did not arrive everywhere at once. In the coastal areas of Peru, for example, at the same time that Mexico was developing crops, sustenance came from the sea in the form of fish (anchovies especially). At one site, Salinas de Chao, the community consisted of 2,000 people, a sizeable settlement. Elsewhere, in the far south of Patagonia, the inhabitants were hunter-gatherers until just 200 years ago, as were the Aborigines of Australia until European settlers arrived.

Other more subtle developments distinguish Neolithic peoples from their predecessors. These include the development of pottery (easier in a fixed settlement than in a nomadic environment) and the shaping of stone axes by polishing rather than chipping or grinding. It seems from archaeological finds that farming precedes pottery making and therefore the term 'Pre-Pottery Neolithic' has been developed to describe such a period.

At Jericho, mud-brick buildings were developed inside the stone town walls. These began to appear in the eighth millennium BC but pottery traces on the site do not appear for another 3,000 years. The same sequence of events (though not the exact same timing) has also been found in Iraq, Anatolia and Cyprus. Another site in mainland Greece confirms that similar developments were also beginning to appear in Europe.

Along with the practical implications of farming and pottery making there are also remains that allow a glimpse into the soul of Neolithic society. Foremost among these is the site of Çatal Hüyük in Anatolia. The site has been dated to the sixth or seventh millennium BC. A collection of shrines has been excavated there, with rooms festooned with wall-paintings, as well as the horns and plaster-modelled shapes of bulls. Bulls are also widely seen in the wall-paintings; so too are leopards, and vultures soaring above decapitated human corpses.

Though research has been less extensive or successful in other parts of the world, it is safe to assume that similar developments were taking place elsewhere. The emergence of civilisation in the Indus Valley around 3000 BC for example cannot have come out of the blue and must represent the culmination of an extended period of evolution.

The Neolithic did not reach many parts of Europe until later, though, and this hints at a theme that will be referred to regularly in this account. The pace of development varied in different parts of the globe and therefore we will find ourselves for example talking about aspects of the Neolithic in Britain at the same time that we are considering much more advanced civilisations in Egypt, Mesopotamia or the Indus.

This might be inconvenient for the reader but reflects reality in any chronological account of world history. Even in our own age of globalisation there is still a vast difference between life say in parts of sub-Saharan Africa and that in North America. Technology and communication have narrowed the gaps but they are still there. How much more so must have been the case in times long past?

As the year 3000 BC approached, the world was on the brink of history. The first major civilisations were about to appear. These would leave behind them tangible evidence of their way of life. They would erect massive pyramids or other funerary monuments which would enable us to construct much more solid theories about their way of life (or death).

They would also develop something else which is crucial to historical understanding; they would write. This would give later historians the chance to understand their laws and their history. It also gives us a window into individual lives, which provides the colour that tints the monochrome landscapes of history. Without writing, there would be no Alexander, no Plato, no Ramses the Great, human stories that light up the darknes for good or ill. We could at best imply their existence. It is significant that we ha covered the 2 million years of human prehistory in one chapter and will cover the r 5,000 years in forty. That, as much as anything, shows how critical the emergen written language was.

2

PYRAMIDS AND MEGALITHS

The Dawn of Civilisations (3000–2501 BC)

What is civilisation? Is it, in the standard definitions offered by dictionaries, a contrast with barbarism or an advanced stage of social development? To me, it seems that it is easier to recognise civilisation when you see it than it is to define it. To gaze on monuments such as Westminster Abbey or, at the other end of the historical epoch, the Great Pyramid, is to see something that can only have been created and built by what we would regard as a civilisation.

Civilisation is characterised by a number of features, a written language that gives the ability to transfer information and record it for posterity being one of them. Evidence of a love of art and learning for learning's sake are other characteristics; interestingly, so-called 'civilised behaviour' is not – some of the greatest outrages in history have been committed by nations regarded in other ways as 'civilised'. At some time around 3000 BC, what I think of as civilisations began to emerge from the darkness of prehistory.

At last we have arrived at a moment where we can find an individual with a name, the birth of history itself. Admittedly Narmer (or Menes, his other title) has a firmer place in tradition than he does in history but his supposed achievements were significant, for he was the man who is said to have created the kingdom of Egypt and founded the first dynasty, the first of thirty-four such (although the last three were usurper dynasties from abroad and therefore do not merit a place in the official numbering system, i.e. there are thirty-one Egyptian dynasties and three foreign or foreign-related ones following on from this).

In around 3100 Menes succeeded in uniting Upper and Lower (Southern and Northern) Egypt (its Greek name; the country was known as 'Kemet' to the Ancient Egyptians), ongoing unification being the aim of most pharaohs who came after him, in the process creating the first nation state. An ancient mace-head is inscribed with an image of a man who wears just the crown of Upper Egypt and may therefore predate Menes; the presence of a scorpion on it has led to him being called 'King Scorpion'. By the king's side stands the falcon-shaped Horus, the sky god and one of the foremost deities in Egypt's pantheon. Apart from the fact that he supposedly united Egypt, little is known of this King Menes, but the achievement in itself is sufficient claim to fame.

The famous 'Narmer Palette' in Cairo Museum tells us much about early Egyptian history. As is often the case with this fascinating civilisation, we can tell much from pictorial representations, even if there are few words. There are two sides to the Palette. On one, Narmer is seen about to brain a man with a mace; the pharaoh is dressed in the crown of southern ('Upper') Egypt, while his victim appears to be a delta-dweller. This is therefore a symbolic representation of Narmer uniting Egypt by conquering the north.

The pharaoh figure, mace raised and about to beat the brains out of a victim, was a representation of power that would last for another 3,000 years in Egyptian art. But the Palette also carries other representations of violence; on one side there are ten decapitated corpses. All of them are bound so these were opponents cold-bloodedly executed and not killed in the heat of battle. On another part of the Palette, Narmer tramples his enemies. The message is clear and not at all subliminal; you resist this man at your peril.

From then on, each pharaoh strove to wear the crowns of both Upper and Lower Egypt, the 'White' and the 'Red' respectively. It was this unifying claim that was always perceived to be the foremost mark of a pharaoh's legitimacy and greatness. The pharaoh ruled over a unique land. Egypt was the Nile, a thin, watery ribbon its lifeblood around which a fertile strip, in places just a few hundred yards wide, supported life. The land by the river was known as the Black after the silt that lay on it, and its life-giving soil was deposited annually by the Nile inundation; black was also the colour of life and resurrection. Beyond it lay the Red, parched and largely lifeless, known as Deshret. Even now the divisions between the two are so marked that it is possible for one to stand, legs astride, with one foot in the 'black' and the other in the 'red'.

There are signs of fairly advanced societies in Egypt for some time before this, though. With some irony, mummified bodies estimated to date from 4000 BC have been found in the desert; the irony is that these were not deliberately preserved but desiccated accidentally by the sand, which provided better standards of preservation than later deliberate mummification attempts did. There are also more mundane signs of domestic life stretching thousands of years into prehistory. There is even evidence of toothpaste in Egypt dating back to 5000 BC, an unattractive-sounding substance made up of ground ox hooves, myrrh, powdered and burnt eggshells and pumice.

Where did the Egyptians come from? Did they come from the Middle East or, to the south, from Africa? The evidence suggests the latter. A grave in Nubia to the south is believed to predate the first pharaonic dynasty and includes statuesque references to a flail, a symbol that we frequently find later on many royal images in Egypt, and also the White Crown, later adopted by the pharaohs, so it seems clear that it was from here that the momentum for Egyptian culture came, though we would be foolish to also discount the later cross-fertilisation of ideas with the Middle East in its ongoing development.

Menes' son, Hor-Aha, would found the city of Memphis, one of the most important cities of the ancient world. Its main attraction was its central site, symbol of a newly unified kingdom. Nearby another important city, Heliopolis (its Greek name; in Egyptian it was 'On'), would develop as the spiritual centre, with Memphis as its political equivalent – two settlements which more or less flank modern Cairo, where the narrow ribbon of the Nile starts to split into its complex delta. At Heliopolis it was said the glorious phoenix bird would return every 500 years to burn itself to a pile of ashes and then rise reborn from the flames.

Hor-Aha met his death in unusual fashion, being killed during a hippopotamus hunt, a rare detail in a period that is still generally dimly illuminated with any flashes of personality. Little is known of the first dynasties, and individuals are largely anonymous. There is, though, a decent amount of statuary surviving to give us an insight into the religious beliefs of the times. There are also intriguing pictorial references to something that seems to represent human sacrifice.

Collectively the pharaohs of the first two dynasties (fourteen in number, spanning about 400 years) provide a foundation for the amazing events that were about to follow. Historians are disappointed at the lack of concrete history giving an insight into these early years, although there is widespread agreement that they must have been important in the light of what followed.

One thing is known, though, and that is that this period saw the development of the extraordinary pictorial writing known as hieroglyphs. And there are occasional glimpses of other aspects of the Egyptian story that do survive. In the unusual shape of a label for a pair of sandals there is an image from the reign of King Den (*c.* 2950), a picture inscribed, 'first time of striking the easterners'; the pharaoh can be seen, about to dash the brains out of a prostrate enemy. This is one of the earliest surviving war pictures, giving a graphic insight into conflict, a terrible state of affairs that was to characterise man's subsequent time on earth.

Following the ascension of Sanakhte (sometimes believed to be also called Nebka, though this is unclear) in around 2686 BC (he was the first pharaoh of the third dynasty), there were some particularly significant developments. One of the most outstanding features of the subsequent centuries is how over time the role of the pharaoh became increasingly linked to the gods. During the next 500 years of what was known as 'The Old Kingdom' pharaohs would come to be considered as the incarnation of Horus and then the son of Re, the sun god.

This was not all, though. There would also be an increase in the centralised nature of the state accompanied by major advances in construction skills. Centralisation allowed the state to take more advantage of the resources represented by Egypt's population. The enhanced building possibilities allowed ever more impressive state structures to be erected. The two would combine to allow the erection of one of the most amazing sequences of public buildings ever constructed – the Pyramids.

Calling them public buildings is perhaps stretching the truth. No member of the public could ever hope to enter them once they had been sanctified. However, building them must have entailed a huge public effort: they could not have been made by slaves alone. The sheer scale of the construction effort epitomises the fact that the pharaoh was the unashamed centre of power, and around his royal mausoleum lesser monuments, known as *mastabas*, were erected to house his leading officials as if they were to serve him in the next life as well as this one.

Two men were responsible for initiating the Age of the Pyramid. One of them, the sponsor, was the pharaoh Djoser, who united with a master architect called Imhotep to create the blueprint for a building project as yet unique in the world. The latter seems an amazing all-rounder, known as a scribe, a counsellor, a doctor, a priest and an astronomer in addition to his skills as a builder. His deification attests to his impact, for over 2,000 years later in the time of the Ptolemies he would be equated with Asklepios, the god of healing. Together these men masterminded the construction of the first pyramid.

It was not just its shape and scale that made this edifice so special, for it is the first known building to be constructed entirely of stone (though the material had been used in *mastabas* previously in the construction of inner burial chambers). This first pyramid was a step pyramid, with a succession of rectangular *mastabas* built on top of each other. There were many tunnels penetrating the monument, some constructed later on by grave robbers. Other members of the royal family were entombed in this vast structure, 358 by 411 feet at its base. But of Djoser himself nothing now remains, except (perhaps) a mummified foot.

The ruins of the step pyramid are still one of the most impressive sights in the world. This is because the massive funerary complex around it can still be seen in enough detail to imagine what it might have looked like in its pomp. For a pyramid was just the centre of a much larger site, with covered causeways to the Nile several miles away (along which the pharaoh's body would be carried out of sight of the masses), mortuary temples at the entrance to the complex, dozens of *mastabas* where his courtiers would be buried and a number of other buildings. The pyramid itself was just the epicentre of a vast spiritual complex.

Staring up at the still substantial remains, it is hard to ignore resemblances between this prototype pyramid and the ziggurats of Mesopotamia, suggesting a flow of ideas from west to east or vice versa. Inspiration also came from Egypt; the second-dynasty ruler Peribsen had a pyramid-shaped tomb. Other impressive remains from Saqqara include a carved frieze with four threatening cobras, hoods splayed wide, threatening any who dare disturb the pharaoh's repose.

The face of Djoser too can be seen in a life-size statue of him, the oldest we have of an Egyptian pharaoh. It was formerly hidden away in a chamber at the funerary complex that contained his pyramid. The eyes, once probably semi-precious jewels, are now gone, empty holes staring blankly into space. Djoser wears the dress of the *heb-sed*, the festival of rejuvenation held notionally once every thirty years though some pharaohs celebrated it much more frequently. It was an important ritual in which the ruler was born anew and given fresh life, in turn doing the same for his kingdom.

Djoser's successors also built pyramids though Sekhemket, who came immediately after him, did not get to use the finished product as his was incomplete when he died in 2643. The earliest construction projects were in the region of Saqqara near Memphis. For the pharaoh Snefru (reigned from 2613–2589) one pyramid was not enough

– he had two constructed. The first of these was unusually shaped and was called consequently the Bent Pyramid. Presumably the innovative techniques involved did not quite work out and the Bent Pyramid, rhomboid in shape, was abandoned though it remains an astonishing monument right on the fringes of the Egyptian desert.

Snefru was buried in the second pyramid he had ordered to be built, but remarkably he also completed a third for his predecessor, Huni. His north pyramid, the Red, was the first true pyramid (in the sense that the steps were filled in to give the edifice smooth sides) to be built. The exhibitionism and egotism these grandiose projects hint at seems entirely in accord with the few other glimpses we have of Snefru. One story that survives of him tells how, in a fit of boredom, he commanded his harem to row him around his palace lake dressed in nothing but fishnets.

But the burial chamber of Snefru, deep inside his North Pyramid, is perhaps one of the most evocative sites from ancient history remaining. For those brave enough to walk down the ramps stoop-backed, fighting off feelings of claustrophobia as they descend, the sensation when arriving at its heart in a huge though undecorated central chamber is quite overwhelming, even more so than in the chamber in Cheops' Great Pyramid, now normally overrun with tourists.

Construction of pyramids of this size tied up resources on a grand scale. Snefru's son Cheops (his Greek name; in Egyptian he is Khufu) was the backer of the Great Pyramid-building scheme though the actual architect, most unfairly widely forgotten given the brilliance of his creation, was a man named Hemiunu. Originally 481 feet high, it was the tallest building in the world until the nineteenth century AD. Herodotus, regarded by some as the first historian, wrote of the Great Pyramid 2,000 years later. He said that it took thirty years to build. It is one of the original Seven Wonders of the World and the only one that can still be seen.

This was an enormous engineering undertaking. Perhaps 25,000 men worked on it at any one time, organised into groups of stone-cutters and those deputed to drag the stones back-breakingly from the quarries to the evolving structure. They used massive stone ramps topped with timber rollers to help the workers haul the blocks up onto the pyramid. The men were organised in groups of ten, given daily targets and awarded bonuses of extra beer if they outperformed rival teams. But although the workers do not appear to have been slaves, the work itself was terribly demanding. The bones of some of the workers have been unearthed, showing broken limbs, stress fractures, bent backs. At a time when an Egyptian noble would on average live for fifty-five years, a worker could only expect to live for thirty-two.

The Grand Gallery led into the King's Chamber at the heart of the monument, an echoing void with a stone sarcophagus at its heart that is bigger than the entrance into the room, showing that it was placed there before the pyramid itself was completed. Around this pyramid were constructed smaller copies for Khufu's queens. Legends inevitably attach themselves to the building like bees to a honeypot. It was said that Khufu placed one of his own daughters in a brothel to raise money for its construction. She insisted that each client left behind a stone to be used in the building as well as money.

Khufu's son Khafre also built an impressive pyramid. Great slabs of granite were sailed up the Nile highway from Aswan, some 600 miles away. It looks taller than his father's 'Great' pyramid but it is in fact shorter; its position on slightly higher ground creates the illusion. But it is not his most famous monument, for nearby stands an enigmatic object carved out of local limestone, a strange creature with a human face and a lion's body: the mysterious Sphinx. This was part of Khafre's funerary complex and it has been suggested that the face is his; if so, this is one of the oldest large-scale royal portraits known to man. The sphinx had a special significance for the Egyptians, as the lion's body symbolised strength and the man's head wit and intelligence – something close to the perfect being.

Most of what we know about these years is gleaned from the monuments left behind. There is little other detail to go on. We can, though, surmise a fair amount from the pyramids. Egypt must have been a rich land, with good natural resources based around the thin ribbon of the Nile (the Greek historian Herodotus called Egypt 'the gift of the Nile'), perhaps enriched by trade, less likely by conquest (for wars would probably have left more marks than are now apparent). However, not all was pacific. Expeditions were led (possibly in person) by Snefru against Libyans and Nubians.

Some seafaring skills may also be surmised; Khufu's pyramid includes a wooden boat over 100 feet long, though navigation would most likely have been up and down the Nile (this particular boat is very slender), with some coastal navigation in the Mediterranean. It is known that cedars were acquired from Lebanon (Egypt is almost treeless), where the port of Byblos in particular became prominent, with ivory and gold also flowing from Nubia to the south.

Yet in the long term the pyramids were unaffordable. The strain on the economy was too great and although pyramids would be built for many centuries yet, pyramid building had peaked when Khufu died, quite early on in their life story. Five generations later, Shepseskaf had no pyramid and had to make do with a much humbler tomb. Later pharaohs would still build pyramids but they would be on a more modest scale. Equally the tomb of Menkaure, Shepseskaf's predecessor, had a pyramid which was much smaller than those of Khufu, Khafre and even Snefru (though it is still very impressive) – though recent excavations suggest that this may be because he died prematurely before the building of his monument had been completed.

What the pyramids do point at is the Egyptians' fixation with the afterlife (or at least the continuing of this earthly life in another world) although it is unlikely that it was just the thought of eternity that motivated their construction. These vast edifices are also status symbols that told of the king's greatness and wealth while he was alive as well as considering his needs when he was dead. But the entombment of everyday objects hints at the belief that those buried here were expecting to maintain an extravagant and regal lifestyle in the life beyond. Unfortunately for lovers of 'Mummy movies' there were no human sacrifices; these, which once numbered in the hundreds, had ended with the demise of the first dynasty, before the period of pyramid building began.

Many grave goods were stolen in later years but one chamber found close to the pyramid of Khufu in the tomb of his mother (also the wife of Snefru), Hetep-heres, painted a revealing picture. This tomb seems to have escaped the attentions of unwelcome guests for it appeared to have been untouched when uncovered in 1925. In it were two armchairs, a bed with a rather uncomfortable-looking pillow, a gold manicure set and twenty bracelets with dragonfly motifs. Although the sarcophagus was empty when found, the Canopic jars nearby were not – these contained her viscera, the earliest known use of evisceration in the mummification process.

The Egyptians had many gods, perhaps a result of the unification process when local areas each had their own deities, some of whom survived to become part of the new national pantheon. Each nome, or administrative district, would proudly lay claim to its own specific deity. Horus was possibly a god from Lower Egypt: he was the son of Osiris and Isis. Osiris' brother Seth was an evil being who resented him, invited him to a banquet, tricked him into getting inside a chest and then threw it in the Nile.

In the timeless myth, Osiris' body was retrieved by his wife Isis but then stolen and cut into pieces by Seth. These were then scattered across Egypt. Isis succeeded in regaining them and put him back together again using magic. She brought up Horus in secret and, when he grew to adulthood, he fought a bitter and eventually successful battle against Seth.

This is the Egyptian version of the war between good and evil, a standard motif of many religions. There is also an interesting link with later religious beliefs – in their own way Osiris, Isis and Horus form their own trinity. Other aspects hint at Christianity, for Osiris is effectively resurrected after his cruel death. For each pharaoh, this element of the tale had personal resonance for when an Egyptian died they became the equivalent of Osiris, the god of the Underworld, while when they lived they were Horus, god of life.

The greatness of Egypt is now best remembered through its art and its monuments. Although some art is colossal and speaks of power, other surviving pieces are surprisingly moving. A personal favourite is a painted limestone statuette of an important official named Seneb and his family. Crafted around 2550, the most incredible thing about it is that Seneb is a dwarf while his wife Nefert, a princess, puts one arm around his right shoulder and her left hand on his left arm. It looks like a caress of affection, not pity, and if so it would be in keeping for dwarves were respected and not scorned in Egyptian society and often held important positions.

Egypt might be the best-known civilisation to emerge at this time but others too developed that may be even older. Take Uruk in Mesopotamia for example (the region of Mesopotamia approximately equates to modern Iraq). By around 3200 BC the city could demonstrate a number of facets providing evidence that the age of so-called barbarism had been left behind. Other large settlements in Mesopotamia soon followed suit.

Writing was not the least of the inventions of these Mesopotamians, a pictogram-based communication system named by an eighteenth-century scholar, Thomas Hyde, as cuneiform. Mesopotamian script predated Egyptian hieroglyphs (though the Egyptians could claim a first of their own by developing writing on papyrus rather than clay, a great practical benefit as it was much lighter and made transportation of the information contained much easier; on the other hand, it does not survive the passage of time as well).

Other manifestations of Mesopotamian civilisation included specialised craftsmen, communal irrigation works and ceremonial centres. They built in mud brick, with vast walls protecting the citizens of the city states that developed. They erected temples and *ziggurats*, pyramidal towers with sacred shrines at their summits; the biblical Tower of Babel was one such edifice. The cities were large settlements; by 2800 BC it has been estimated that Uruk had 50,000 inhabitants.

Ancient Mesopotamians took delight in ambling through their gardens – Eden is reputed to have been here – and their boats sailed along the canals that had been erected, allowing an arterial network of transportation to develop and feed the growth of civilisation. By 2800 BC they were showing advanced skills in metallurgy (they had already been working in copper for 1,500 years), their artists painstakingly wove fine wire into ornamental filigree work and they worked in glass as well.

They also traded widely. Having little metal of their own, tin was brought in from Iran, Syria and Asia Minor. Gold came from Cappadocia, silver and lead from the Taurus Mountains and Elam in south-west Iran (this region had its own unique pictorial language, which appears in inscriptions before 3000 BC). Copper came from Oman, far to the south, and possibly also from the Caucasus region. Lapis lazuli, the dazzling blue stone much loved in antiquity, came from Iran and Afghanistan. Pine came from Lebanon and there were even shells imported from India.

This all provides evidence of a developed mercantile economy which must have required regular trading missions far afield to re-stock. This first Mesopotamian civilisation, which was given the name Sumerian, made a crucial technological breakthrough by developing the wheel (though they may not in fact have invented it), and they were also the first known glass-blowers. They practised astronomy, had a calendar and developed mathematics.

With their cuneiform writing, they developed bureaucracy (though the Egyptians also had a strongly centralised and bureaucratic state and may have done so earlier) – many of the written records surviving are mundane items beloved of administrators, receipts for cattle, milk, corn and sheep for example. Some of their vocabulary even survives in modern English, in words such as 'cane', 'alcohol', 'myrrh', 'saffron'. Their contribution to the development of civilisation has been rather overlooked though on occasion modern citizens of the world might curse their encouragement of the bureaucrat if they knew of it.

The Sumerians were polytheistic with a large pantheon of gods and goddesses, each city apparently adopting their own as a protecting deity special to itself. The *ziggurats* dominated the centres of their cities. Each year a young priest and priestess would ascend to the summit of these artificial mountains where they would copulate. Both participants would then be killed and buried, the aim being to symbolically propitiate the gods and ensure a fertile year characterised by an abundant harvest. The Sumerians had a rich array of legends and myths and it is now widely believed that the biblical account of the creation in the Book of Genesis actually emanated from their mythology through the story in which the god Enlil brought the world into being.

Politically, Sumer was composed of a number of city states, maybe as many as twenty of them, each autonomous but reliant on each other to an extent economically. There was predictably some inter-city rivalry and even conflict, but at this early stage it seems to have lacked the bitterness that epitomised, say, fifteenth-century AD Italy or the Greek city states in the latter part of the first millennium BC. The relative autonomy of these city states provides a marked contrast to the political geography of Egypt, with its one ruler.

The land between the rivers, which is what 'Mesopotamia' means (the rivers being the Tigris and Euphrates), was very fertile and this played a large part in helping civilisation develop there. Barley was the primary crop but there was also sesame, wheat, emmer and millet as well as dates, fruits and vegetables. Cattle and sheep were also domesticated. This land was a generous provider and the surplus that was not consumed by the Sumerians could be used for export to finance the purchase of all those imported commodities that Sumer relied on for its continuing development and prosperity.

We even know what the Sumerians looked like from the statues they left. They were short with large, curved noses. The men wore beards but no moustaches (unlike the Egyptians, statues of whom from the early periods show men with pencil-thin moustaches but no beards). They were clothed in sheepskins or garments of woven wool. They enjoyed a good feast and drank beer (the first civilisation known to do so) through long tubes of metal like prototype straws. Wrestling and boxing were popular with them and they were probably also the first people to enjoy watching a chariot-race.

It was once thought that civilisation arrived further east slightly later. Signs of an advanced Indian civilisation were believed to post-date Sumer and Egypt by probably half a millennium. In China it was almost certainly even later. Some argued in the past that this spread of civilisation may have been a result of some degree of colonisation, but the evidence does not seem to support this hypothesis. However, given the fact that we know that Mesopotamians were obtaining goods from India there can be little objection to the argument that ideas may have spread along the trading routes as well as provisions and in the process inspired the spread of civilisation – a cross-fertilisation of ideas rather than a process of conquest.

The theories may now need to be revised. A dig at Harappa in Pakistan in the 1920s uncovered a brick fortress associated with a large settlement apparently on a similar scale to those in Mesopotamia. Digging is ongoing and there are now suggestions that Harappa might date back to 3000 BC, making it contemporary with early Mesopotamian and Egyptian civilisation rather than later. Such is the carousel of historical knowledge that new findings next week might necessitate yet another reassessment of cause and effect as far as the sequencing of ancient civilisations is concerned.

In Western Europe, the move towards civilisation was a much slower process and would not arrive without the aid of outside impetus. While the Egyptians were building massive pyramids and impressive mortuary temples, the architecture of the megalithic builders was much more modest. However, what they did was still notable and must have posed a great challenge to cultures where only the most basic of building tools were available.

There are many megalithic monuments spread across Europe. A megalith may be a single standing stone or it may be part of a series of such stones used to assemble a basic structure which is held together by gravity rather than the use of cement. Megalithic structures are found not only in Britain but also across many parts of Europe including the Iberian Peninsula, France and Malta. The dispersal of such sites across a wide area, although stylistically different in many regions, had led to speculation that they are all in some way connected. Some argue that technology spread west from Egypt, enabling monuments to be erected in places thousands of miles away from the Nile. Advocates of this theory are known as 'diffusionists'.

There are some attractions in this theory. Many megalithic sites are found in coastal regions, which would encourage sea-borne movement of ideas. There is not a lot of evidence to support the existence of regularised trading or shipping links but a lack of such does not mean that such a situation never existed, merely that proof of it has never been found in sufficient quantity. Similarities in some building techniques between impressive temple sites in Malta and Stonehenge have also been used to support diffusionist theories.

Others, however, postulate that megalithic architecture appeared at different times in various European cultures purely by chance. There is not enough solid and irrefutable evidence to opt for one theory over another. There is enough corroboration to believe, though, that at some level there was interchange of ideas over a fairly wide area; for instance, pottery of this period from the Orkneys was very similar to that in southern England, and megalithic techniques in Brittany do appear similar to that in island Britain. However, this is very different to postulating links between Egypt and what was then the far West.

The temples in Malta are much more substantial than megalithic monuments in places like Britain, and if some of the construction techniques have similarities, the end products – the structures themselves – are very different. Maybe there was some movement of ideas from east to west, but only over an extended period and even then different regions adopted their own application of the technology. To argue that there was a widespread dissemination of such ideas is pushing the argument much further than the evidence will allow.

Such speculation highlights two particular problems that face the historian. Firstly, while areas like Egypt had now entered a historical period (that is, when written records, pictorial representations and chronicles add solid information to the time-worn remnants of architecture surviving from the period), further west we are still anchored in prehistory. A subtle illustration of this is that in Egypt we have now started to talk about individuals as well as cultures: such an approach is impossible without written records of some description.

The other problem is that of dating. To make sense of archaeology we need to determine a sequence of events. A huge step forward was made in 1949 when an academic from Chicago, Professor Willard Libby, established that all living organisms (animal or vegetable) contain a radioactive carbon element that deteriorates at a known rate when the host dies. By measuring how much carbon is left in the remains of such an organism when it is later discovered by archaeologists, scientists can establish when it died and, therefore, roughly how old it is.

This breakthrough was crucial to the dating of objects but is subject to margins of error. In addition, ongoing discoveries of new evidence as more archaeological remains are unearthed leads to a constant reassessment of dates. Therefore, dating of these remains is in an almost perpetual state of flux and as a result so is our view of the cultures that existed thousands of years ago.

What cannot be denied is the impressive nature of some of the megalithic monuments that remain. Of these, the most stunning of the earlier monuments was perhaps the site of Avebury (Stonehenge as we shall see reached its peak some time later than this site). This consisted of an outer circle some 365 metres in diameter surrounded by a ditch, originally 9 meters deep, 24 meters wide and 1.2 kilometres in length. Bearing in mind that this ditch was dug out with the use of tools like picks made of antlers and shovels made of the shoulder bones of deer, this is impressive.

This also shows that, just as was the case in Egypt, a significant amount of communal effort was required. It has been estimated that it would take 200 men over two years' solid effort to dig out the ditch and use the chalk to erect the soil circles around the monument. When we also consider the fact that the highest man-made hill in Europe at Silbury was erected just a couple of miles away, the construction effort was immense. It suggests that certain individuals, or institutions, had a significant degree of power to coordinate such activities and cajole, or persuade, communities to work together to erect such vast complexes.

We should return to the Middle East to conclude our review of this crucial period. At what was then the centre of the developing world, civilisation had now arrived and its rays were shooting out like a sunburst, illuminating areas further afield as they did so. The area these sunrays covered would spread and these early civilisations would themselves grow and, occasionally, thrive. But history does not stand still and it is the fate of all empires, and all civilisations, to grow old and stale and then die while vibrant newcomers take their place. Now that the process of civilisation had started it could not be stopped, but it could morph, like an amoeba, changing shape but never losing its essential vitality. The age of man had truly arrived.

3

FROM THE INDUS TO THE NILE

Civilisation Finds Its Feet (2500–2001 BC)

Civilisation was also establishing itself in the Indus region. Ships from here sailed to Mesopotamia, the inhabitants of which knew the lands further east as Meluhha. It has been speculated that the inhabitants of Meluhha shared a common root with the Elamites of Iran, demonstrating that it would be wrong to think of civilisations even back then as being a disconnected group of individual entities. Of the history of the Indus civilisations we know little, as their language has never been deciphered, but there are a number of substantial remains that bear testament to the sizeable cities that once stood in the region.

One of the greatest surviving ruins from this period is the Indian city of Mohenjo-daro, along with Harappa providing evidence of an early civilisation based around the River Indus (like the latter site, Mohenjo-daro is now situated in Pakistan). Laid out with well-ordered streets and a sophisticated drainage system, this appears to have been a society that would have enjoyed many of the benefits of technological advancement that citizens of Egypt or Sumer knew.

Substantial remains have survived until today and they give us indisputable evidence of well-planned housing; admittedly with few windows and packed closely together, but otherwise comfortable. In some streets in Harappa nearly every house has a bathroom. Another surviving clue to life in this period is a large bath at Mohenjo-daro, 40 feet by 20 feet, though it is not clear whether this was used for ritual or practical purposes. However, later Indian temples had ritual baths and it is tempting to assume that this was what the one at Mohenjo-daro was used for.

Many terracotta statuettes have also been found. These give us more insight into what mattered to the Indus civilisation; a large number of depictions of bulls show that these had a special significance to the people (a possible precursor of more recent Hindu practices and a link with traditions further west; the bull was sacred in Egypt and also in later Minoan civilisation).

One of the most amazing survivals is a small statue of a dancing girl, naked except for an array of bangles. With her genitalia accentuated, this figure oozes sensuality. Larger statues are less commonly found but one of them may be a god or a priest-king and has a steely, dominant look on his face though his eyes are blank, as if he can see into the soul of the onlooker without the need for them. Torsos from Harappa, now housed in a museum in Delhi, would not look out of place in later Greek architecture, so finely sculpted are their lines.

Other objects include small models of bullock-carts with wheels – they reached the Indus at an early stage, hinting at possible inspiration from Sumer. Possibly Sumerian merchants were dealing directly with people from the region – traders from the Indus may even have travelled to Sumer and seen such vehicles first hand. Or perhaps trade was through middlemen and the peoples of the Indus had only heard of wheels rather than seen them. In any event, it would be a fairly easy idea to assimilate, though copying it may have been less straightforward.

Camels and horses were used by the Indus peoples. They also had well-developed agriculture, harvesting peas and melons, as well as cotton – the first known instance of the latter being exploited domestically. They too had their own pictogram writing, unique to their civilisation.

Mohenjo-daro, which means 'mound of the dead', was on a ridge above a flood-plain and during the monsoon season it stood proudly above the enveloping arms of the waters as an island. There were even flood defences constructed a few miles away from the settlement to divert the Indus away when it was swollen by the annual deluge. Given the proximity of Mohenjo-daro to the Indus and the fact that the surrounding region could be flooded for four months a year it is not surprising that a good deal of communication was done by riverboat.

At its peak, the Indus civilisation covered a wider area than that of either Egypt or Sumer. There were some similarities between these civilisations but important differences too. There are few signs of warfare that have yet been found in the Indus region (though one should not think of this as a peaceful *utopia* either; cities sometimes had two layers of walls – why so, unless they were needed?). Neither have tombs been found of the scale of those discovered further west.

The Indus cities were neat and tidy but their major settlements were smaller than those of Sumer, with perhaps 30,000 citizens. Standard weights and measures were used over a wide area, suggesting a degree of centralisation. There was also a significant port at Lothal from which goods were probably shipped across the Persian Gulf; seafaring skills were clearly developing too. It is likely this was the preferred form of transport; it was easier to carry bulkier goods, for one thing. Another reason is that the land-route west posed horrendous challenges. Mountains and deserts acted as barriers across many routes, as Alexander the Great found out when he moved into the region from the west many years later.

But this early Subcontinent civilisation came to an end for reasons as yet unknown; the skeleton of a man found in Mohenjo-daro may have been of someone killed in the streets, suggesting that a violent denouement had brought it crashing down. This is a little-understood civilisation of which not a lot is known except for the cities themselves. No individuals are known to light up their history – the Harrapan civilisation, it has rightly been said, is one that lacks personality. Its end left a pall of tragic dimensions, hanging like a black cloud in a stormy sky, one that can still be vaguely sensed even now.

It is important to note that the Indus civilisation did not cover anything like the whole of what we now call the Subcontinent. The epicentre of its power was to be found in the area where Pakistan now exists. From here, influence rippled slowly down the west coast of modern India. However, it was far slower to affect the peoples of the Ganges Valley on the other side of India. It appears that influences there may have come from the opposite direction, from south-east Asia and China. In the latter, rice cultivation can be traced back to around 3000 BC and from here this crop spread to become the staple of other peoples in the region.

The land of Sumer was positioned as a potential bridge between the developing lands of east and west. Its wealth continued to grow and for the next 2,000 years cultures from this part of the world would vie with Egypt for the unofficial title of most powerful nation on earth. Like all civilisations, many of Sumer's aspects continued to evolve with time. By the time of the second half of the second millennium BC, the pantheon of Sumerian gods had more or less reached its final representation.

There was Ishtar; she was goddess of both love and war, something of an irony perhaps to members of modern hippy culture or discontented spouses in all eras. Three gods held prominence in the Sumerian pantheon: Anu, father of the gods; Enlil, lord of the air; and Enki, god of wisdom and of the life-giving waters which were the foundation of the agriculture that in turn gave Sumer life and nurtured it.

Attitudes to death were dark. In Sumerian lore we find Sheol, the origins of Hell, a place of darkness where man lived out eternity deprived of light and joy. Kings and queens of Sumer were interred along with their still-breathing servants, there to serve them in the life to come. For monarchs, eternity may have been less unattractive than to their subjects.

War too played an important part in Sumerian culture. The Sumerians recorded their history on carved stones, *steles*, with pictures, sometimes like antiquity's version of cartoons, telling their tales. One such carving, the Stele of the Vultures, can be seen in the Louvre. It shows those great birds of death flying through the air, carrying the heads of slain warriors. The victors' soldiers stand over the corpses of the slain in well-ordered ranks, protected by helmets and shields, armed with spears, battle-axes and swords. This is not merely a disorganised array of hastily assembled peasants; this is an army.

There is also evidence of another destructive force at work, one which is well known to the modern world: corruption. Inscriptions tell of cities run by corrupt priests, of workmen going unpaid, of apprentices having to pick through the rubbish to find scraps to eat. Exorbitant fees were charged by the priests for the burial of the dead, playing on timeless fears that the proper rituals of death must be complied with lest a terrible fate visit itself on those responsible for failing in their duties as the shade of the departed returned to haunt them. Taxes reached unaffordable levels, and the poor were forced to sell their children into slavery to survive.

In the city of Lagash, one of Sumer's foremost settlements, a king named Urukagina brought this exploitation to an end. He lowered the taxes and slashed the stifling bureaucracy that was smothering the life out of his realm. The power of the priests was broken and a relaxation in the legal code brought an element of freedom to classes who had previously suffered terrible repression. His reward was the loss of his throne, removed by King Lugalzaggesi of Umma, a neighbouring city. There was, it seems, barely an effort to rebuff the invasion: Urukagina had made enemies of too many powerful people, however laudable his motives might have been. Another painful lesson had been learned; how difficult it is for a man to be both principled and successful.

What has been called Sumer's archaic period (another convenient label) was about to come to an end, which it did in around 2400 BC. The emergence of an early giant of history was responsible for a new era. His name was Sargon, initially a cup-bearer, who launched a revolt and conquered Mesopotamia. The cup-bearing background suggests anything but a humble position, as the role had a major ceremonial importance and was second only to that of the king himself. Sargon's life story was, to say the least, interesting; it is said that his mother cast him into the river (his father was not known) in a basket of rushes – an uncanny resemblance to the biblical story of Moses.

The king whom Sargon served, the ruler of the Sumerian city of Kish, grew suspicious of him and sent him on an errand to King Lugalzaggesi, but just as in Shakespeare's *Hamlet*, the message he took asked the recipient to kill the bearer. Instead Lugalzaggesi marched on Kish. The city fell and the king fled into ignominious exile. Sargon, however, disappeared until he suddenly launched an attack out of the blue on Uruk. In a stunning victory for him, the city fell.

Lugalzaggesi marched on Sargon in turn but his army was destroyed in the battle that followed. Sargon led him back in triumph as a captive to the sacred city of Nuppur, leading him through the gates with a yoke round his neck. Sargon's powers of military organisation were impressive. Some believe that he recruited troops for his armies from as far away as Ethiopia and Egypt. Here was a militarist of the first rank; when he ate in his palace it was said he was accompanied by 5,400 soldiers. They used in particular a new weapon, the composite bow made of strips of wood and horn, far more powerful and longer-ranging than older types of bow. With such weapons, the Mongols would conquer much of the known world thousands of years later.

Sargon's men were Semites from the north of Mesopotamia. His capital was at Akkad (possibly near Baghdad, though no one knows for sure) and the Sumerians now found themselves increasingly an underclass. The Akkadian supremacy did not last long. Just 200 years later, a little-known group, the Gutians, who came from the mountains, emerged from obscurity and threatened to overturn the status quo. But the Akkadians in a way lived on as their language formed the basis of the later tongues of both Babylonia and Assyria. Many civilisations do not in truth die, at least not completely; in reality elements of them are reincarnated in a different, sometimes unrecognisable, form in those that replace them.

But the Gutians were, if Akkadian accounts are to be believed (as the losers in this war, they are unlikely to be unbiased), a destructive, wild people only interested in destroying the civilisation they found and not in any way adopting or enhancing it. They were described as having 'the minds of men, but the feelings of dogs, with the features of monkeys', 'snakes' and 'scorpions'. No conqueror had excited such opprobrium before; they were clearly detested by those they overran. And judging by the remains they left behind them when they eventually fell, they contributed precisely nothing to the progress of civilisation.

The last phase of Sumer was based on Ur, one of the oldest of cities. Surviving art suggests a civilisation focussed on extolling the powers of its princes. Whether this denotes strong centralised control, or the desire for such on the part of Sumer's rulers, is not entirely clear. Temples were built larger and larger, *ziggurats* taller and taller, the latter artificial mountains to substitute for the real ones which simply did not exist on the flatlands of Mesopotamia.

To the west of Mesopotamia, a warlike and nomadic Semitic tribe based in modern-day Palestine and Syria, the Amorites, was about to make its move. Sumer was already weakened by natural disaster; a succession of crop failures, probably caused by excessive salination from the salty waters of the great rivers, had already weakened society. Now incursions from the Amorites became so worrying that a great wall was built to keep them out. Like most great walls in history, this one failed to stop the deluge.

Sumer's time was passing. Like most civilisations, it never died, it was just subsumed by powers and influences so all-consuming that nearly all traces of Sumerian influence were ostensibly lost. Who now ponders on the fact that every time we use a wheel it is the Sumerians we have to thank or when we use a piece of glassware or admire an ornament made of the delicate substance we owe them a debt of gratitude? Just because we no longer recognise their importance, it does not in any way diminish their achievement. So many day-to-day objects in our world have traces of the technological DNA of Sumer concealed within them.

Another people, the Elamites, attacked the Sumerians in around 2000 BC. It was said that the Elamites were descended from the Hebrews, tracing their ancestry back to Shem, son of Noah. Several times in ancient history they would overrun powers in the region that appeared superficially to be far stronger than them. Now was one such time. The city of Ur fell, never to rise from the rubble. An old enemy of the Sumerians, the Elamites, dealt the final blow to this proud civilisation.

Sumer had played a crucial part in the development of world civilisation. As well as its technological legacy, it also bequeathed an example for later civilisations in Mesopotamia to emulate. It left behind great monuments, the *ziggurats* in particular; magnificent, religiously inspired edifices that seemed to touch the very skies, so high did they reach. One could do worse than refer back to one of the great pioneers of history in the early twentieth century, V. Gordon Childe, who said of one Sumerian town, 'One is no longer standing in a village green but in the square of a cathedral city.'

But now the Sumerian epoch was coming to its close as all great civilisations inevitably do. By the time that it did so, trading links between the various parts of the Middle East were strengthening. While we do not have enough evidence to assert confidently that expeditions from east to west and vice versa were day-to-day occurrences, surviving artefacts and writings do show that links were certainly there.

Even the Bible, in the early chapters of Genesis, describes how Abram (later Abraham), from Ur of the Chaldees, travelled west, first to Egypt and then to Canaan, where he became one of the great patriarchs of three world religions: Judaism, Christianity and Islam. The latter traces its genealogical roots back to Ishmael, son of Abraham and Hagar, for it was said that from him came the Arab races.

These stories of a common Middle Eastern heritage may well have been based on fact, a salutary reminder when we see the state of that divided and war-torn region of the world now. If we look at this biblical account at a level higher than that of the personal, the story of Abraham can be seen as a metaphor for the cross-fertilisation of ideas from Mesopotamia to Egypt and across the Middle East, now a melting pot of ideologies, technologies and other constructive impulses that were driving civilisation forward.

In Egypt, for example, pictorial evidence of trading links with Lebanon provides evidence of ongoing business between the two areas. Trading was still expanding and making Egypt rich. Pyramids continued to be built, such as that of Unas (died 2345). When this was excavated in 1881 by the archaeologist Gaston Maspero it was found that the interior was painted, the oldest example of such techniques found and a forerunner of the magnificent and hugely informative pictorial narratives that were to adorn the monuments of later Egyptian rulers.

Other remains from the period give us an insight into more humble lives. Cairo Museum contains a number of statues representing servants at work; one is stuffing a goose, another is a woman on her knees grinding grain, another is a man sifting it and a number show servants involved in brewing. They are artistically sublime but they represent lives of humdrum, labour-intensive toil beneath a beating sun. Another wooden statuette shows a porter, still in amazingly vibrant colour, carrying a wicker basket and a bag over his shoulder.

There are also exquisite limestone statues of more important figures, such as one of the family of a fifth-dynasty noble called Fifi. Beside him stands his wife, dressed in a skin-tight white dress (the statues are also painted) that would do justice to a twenty-first-century Hollywood actress. Their two children, a boy and a girl, sit either side of them. The males are tanned brown, symbolising a life in the sun, while the females are of pale white complexion, showing that noblewomen were expected to live their lives indoors.

Other magnificent statues represent various scribes of the era. These were important people and the statues are produced in such a way that this importance is obvious, being designed as if the scribal class was almost in possession of some magical and little-understood art. That they were bureaucrats is true but that they also were thinkers and creative talents is shown by the way they sit meditatively, almost yogic in their cross-legged stance. There were many different types of scribe to hint at their various functions, such as the *sab sesh* – 'the juridical scribe' – or the *sprw sesh*, 'the scribe of complaints'.

The scribes were crucial to the governance of Egypt, being the enforcers of the pharaoh, the bureaucrats who helped him govern. So too were the priests, the image of one of whom, Ka-aper, can still be seen in a wooden statue. His pot belly hints at a comfortable, well-fed life but Ka-aper looks serious, almost worried. His left leg is advanced in front of his right, a typical pose of Egyptian art, perhaps representing might, for the Egyptian army marched off on its left foot much as many modern armies do.

Pictures in Unas's mausoleum though suggest the presence of something disturbing which must have been a frequent occurrence in a country that was so reliant on the Nile flooding to exactly the right level: famine. Until recent times, when the Aswan Dam was constructed in the twentieth century, the level of the Nile flood was critical to the well-being of Egypt and was measured by Nilometers. Too high a flood and the land would be saturated and useless for cultivation; too low and the land could not be irrigated. Man was at the mercy of nature, and nature could be a harsh mistress indeed. Carvings from the time show people looking like walking skeletons, suggesting that malnutrition was rife at such times. So crucial was the river that in Ancient Egypt seasons were defined by their own peculiar calendar: *akhet* (inundation), *peret* (the planting season) and *shemmu* (harvest).

Little detail remains to describe the events of these years but there are occasional suggestions that all was not well. Pharaoh Teti (ruled 2345–2333) was given the moniker 'He who pacifies the Two Lands', suggesting that Teti was required to put down unrest and rebellion against his rule. This suspicion is confirmed by the suggestion that his reign ended when he was murdered by his own bodyguard. Three reigns followed, lasting nearly 150 years in total, and although these may superficially suggest a degree of stability, the more likely scenario was that they were representative of stagnation.

The reality was that Egypt was about to collapse. Egyptian history is typified by an amazing ability for the civilisation to reinvent itself. From time to time the system appeared to collapse, as the so-called Old Kingdom was about to do. There would then be an Intermediate Period, when the kingdom became a chrysalis from out of which a remarkable butterfly would emerge, hence the subsequent sequencing of a Middle Kingdom, another Intermediate Period and then a New Kingdom.

For a pharaoh, the ultimate test of success was how well he managed to keep Upper and Lower Egypt united. The rise of the different kingdoms, Old, Middle and New, coincides with the unification of the Two Lands and the intermediate periods that separate these kingdoms demonstrate a corresponding disunity.

In about 2181 the Old Kingdom ended in chaos. The last pharaoh of this period was Pepi II, who reigned for the remarkable period of ninety-four years (though it has been suggested that the extraordinary length of the reign is perhaps overstated as a result of a scribal transcription error). His reign is characterised by decentralisation, the breakdown of central power often being a precursor to meltdown in many ages and regions. The pharaoh tried to buy support, which had two unfortunate side-effects: his nobles grew more powerful while his control weakened, and his treasury was exhausted. Foreign adventures helped create an economic collapse.

Contemporary chroniclers were at a loss as to how to show their readers how great the chaos that followed was. They came up with the idea that the seventh dynasty that followed on from the reign of Pepi II had seventy kings who reigned for seventy days; unbelievable in itself but a simple literary device to illustrate the disintegration of Egypt at the time. The power of nobles, called nomarchs, became ascendant in direct contradistinction to that of the pharaoh.

There were invasions by 'Asiatics' (wandering Semitic tribes from whose stock the Amorites came) from the east, and local dynasties emerged in the vacuum caused by the evaporation of centralised control. At one stage, Egypt was so divided that the kings of the ninth to eleventh dynasties, the neat ordering of which gives the misleading suggestion of continuity, were in fact ruling in different parts of the country at the same time.

Not until 2060 did order start to emerge once more. Pharaoh Mentuhotep I, who inherited the crown then, reunited the two lands of Upper and Lower Egypt, effectively initiating the period of Egyptian history known as the Middle Kingdom. His reign started with intense conflict; his capital was Thebes and the Theban god of war was Montu, hence the pharaoh's name. A mass grave of the time excavated in the 1920s contained sixty soldiers, all slain in battle. Mentuhotep's position was secured when in the fourteenth year of his reign he crushed a revolt that started in the city of Abydos.

Externally, Mentuhotep protected Egypt's position by strengthening the kingdom's defences against invasion from the north while to the south he sought to increase trade contacts below the First Cataract, where modern Aswan stands. Egypt's imperial ambitions were generally more modest than those of the civilisations that later emerged, such as Assyria and Greece, let alone Rome, and prudence was often regarded as the most appropriate policy.

But despite the revival, the peak of pyramid building had long passed: Mentuhotep I built a fine mortuary temple (but not a pyramid) on the west bank of the Nile near to the rift in the landscape that would later be known as the Valley of the Kings. It is an impressive construction although the location of the tomb belonging to Mentuhotep II, who followed him, is unknown; it is believed to be in a cleft in the cliffs near to his father. However, the pyramids had not yet disappeared for good.

During the Middle Kingdom Egyptian art continued to evolve, though some features stayed constant throughout dynastic history, such as the traditional pose of a man standing with his left leg advanced in front of the right, which had also been seen in the Old Kingdom. Royal representations continued to show rulers holding the crook and the flail crossed over their chest, the symbols of Osiris.

But now faces started to wear inscrutable smiles, sometimes barely discernible but there nevertheless. Art started to become more abstract, though subtly so, with a slight lack of proportion between legs and bodies. These changes represented something in Egyptian society; slow change, subtle change, but still with strong links to the past, something that can be said to match well with most of Ancient Egyptian history.

To the far west, very different edifices to the pyramids and great tombs of Egypt were being erected. In the second half of the third millennium BC, megalith building was to reach its peak with the assembly of Stonehenge in its final form. The monument was erected in three stages spanning a thousand years. The famous horseshoe belongs to the later stages and the trilithons (where one horizontal stone rests atop two vertical ones) were held in place by carefully constructed pinions carved into the stones, showing significant masonry skills. Some of the stones came from west Wales, representing a long sea journey that must have tested the seafaring skills of the time to the limit.

Hugely impressive megalithic monuments existed in other parts of Europe such as the amazing stone rows at Carnac, Brittany. From them we have to work out what we can about the people that lived in these regions at the time, for we have precious little else to go on. What is clear is that here were people able to organise themselves, to run complex projects with limited technology and with underestimated engineering skills. One influential twentieth-century historian, Professor Thom, argued that there was evidence of consistent measurements being used, what he called 'the megalithic yard' (0.829 metres).

Just why these monuments were built is a matter of speculation. That there was a ritual purpose seems clear – ditches in henge monuments are inside rather than outside of the earth circles; in other words, useless from a defensive perspective – but whether or not they had further uses has excited the imaginations of many people over the years. Alignments between stones at key parts of the solar cycle (e.g. Midsummer's Day and especially Midwinter's Day) suggest links with worship of the gods of the day and the night, the sun and the moon. The most famous of these traces the rising of the sun on Midsummer's Day at Stonehenge over the Heel Stone.

Links with the sun hint at some universal beliefs. We will see later that the sun shines directly into the temple of Abu Simbel (constructed perhaps 1,000 years after the final phase of Stonehenge) on the morning of the spring and autumn equinoxes. On the other hand, the burial chamber of New Grange in Ireland predates Stonehenge by 1,000 years. It is a large, man-made mound with an impressive megalithic chamber at its core. There is a hole in the roof, through which sunlight shines and illuminates the whole passage through the chamber. This happens just once a year – just after dawn on Midwinter's Day.

Around 2,000 years later the heart of King Solomon's Temple was lit up at the equinoctial sunrises by the sun shining through a metal disc on its eastern gate. Christians even unwittingly acknowledge the sun today. The festival of the Roman sun god Solis was celebrated on 25 December, a date later borrowed by the early Church as that of Christmas. The power of the sun was acknowledged over a very long period of time, a natural focus of reverence for peoples of many generations and regions who were in awe of its life-giving power.

We must also consider what was happening in the wider world at this time. There is less to say because there is less surviving evidence, as many regions were still in what we would term a pre-historic phase, in the absence of written materials to flesh out the details provided by archaeology. We do know that by 2000 BC maize production had advanced sufficiently to result in a plant that is similar to that we know today.

Central America was the centre of this development. Further south, at around this time we see the first ancestor of what we know today as the potato. The sweet potato was well known to the peoples of Central America and it has been suggested that from here it spread slowly across the Pacific. If true, this may require a major reassessment for it suggests some kind of interchange between the Americas and the vastly dispersed and remote lands to the west (unless an accident of the ocean currents was somehow coincidentally responsible).

Such an interchange need not imply ongoing and regular links between distant lands at either extreme of the Pacific and is much more likely to have resulted from much shorter hops across the vast ocean. But this is the biggest ocean on earth, where few lands are truly close to each other. These clues suggest that we should be at least cautious before assuming that the Americas were a hermetically sealed vacuum and that the only movement ever was that one lost way back in time when immigrants from Asia first set foot on American soil. The east–west movement of the sweet potato, apparently on its own a trivial event, hints at other interchanges of far greater significance.

As the third millennium BC ended and the second began, the world was ripe for change. The Middle East would still be the driving force of civilisation, but Sumer, the first civilisation, was gone and other powerful forces would take its place. In India, events of enormous importance were about to take place that would help to shape the cultures that we know today from that part of the world. And civilisation would emerge in a new part of the globe, in the Mediterranean. The world, in short, was continuing to evolve at an accelerating pace.

4

ERUPTIONS AND UPHEAVALS

Civilisation Changes Direction (2000–1501 BC)

The story of the next 500 years is one of upheavals, both political and literal. Some of the world's oldest civilisations mutated and went into terminal decline, while other new civilisations stepped up to take their place on the world stage. It was as if the impetus of the first wave of ideas and technological innovations had been exhausted and a fresh explosion of energy was needed to keep the momentum going. Inspiration was about to arrive from a number of directions.

To sail into the harbour at Thira (Santorini) today is an awe-inspiring experience. Dazzling white buildings, houses and churches adorn the summit of its towering cliff-line, the icing on a rocky cake. It is the perfect picture-postcard setting, one that thousands of sight-seekers come to experience every year, in particular to witness spectacular Santorini sunsets as the golden disc slips down into the depths of the sea and heralds in the twilight. It is very hard to associate this place with an apocalypse.

Yet look closer and there are clues. There are several islands in the archipelago, with what looks like a giant, water-filled crater between them. A short boat ride to one of them just off the main island will take the tourist into another world. Step off the boat and the smell of sulphur will soon become unbearable. It is hot, not the humid heat of the Mediterranean summer but the sweltering suffocation of nature at its fiercest, for this is a volcano, still live, still potentially dangerous.

Sometime around 1500 BC (perhaps slightly afterwards) the volcano erupted with spectacular effect. It blew a great hole in the middle of what was originally one island, with a blast so enormous that the harbour at Thira, near what was once the centre of a composite landmass, now drops almost vertically 600 feet to the sea floor. Based on a similar eruption in Krakatoa in the nineteenth century AD, it seems probable that the tsunamis generated would have been huge. Right in the path of these vast walls of water was one of the first Mediterranean civilisations: Crete.

There had been a thriving Neolithic community on Crete since around 2500 BC and since then frequent trading links with mainland Greece. From that time progress on the island was rapid. A semi-mythical figure, King Minos, built a magnificent palace at Knossos, erected in around 1800 BC. It was said he was married to the daughter of the sun god. As is often the case when man and immortals mix, the result was disaster. The offspring of this hexed match was a mutant monster, known in mythology as the Minotaur. He was housed in a labyrinth and required an annual sacrifice until a Greek hero, Theseus, killed the beast.

Yet although Crete is now a Greek island and there were undoubtedly close links with mainland Greece when the Minoan civilisation was at its peak, this appears to have been a cosmopolitan culture. Goods were traded with Egypt and there are some connections between Egyptian and Minoan art. Based at the centre of the Mediterranean web, the Cretans' trading influence spread across the great sea even into Libya. Crete was at a commercial crossroads and her people took full advantage of their good geographical fortune. Indeed, Herodotus mentioned a labyrinth-like structure in Egypt near the city of Crocodilopolis which was a tomb. Nearby were references to the pharaoh Amenemhat III, who lived in the nineteenth century BC, synonymous with the Minoan civilisation, so it is as likely a speculation that the Egyptians inspired the Minoans as vice versa.

Crete was a fertile land – there is in the centre of the island a plateau high up in the mountains, the Lasithi, a veritable lost world where olives, fruit and vegetables grow in abundance, and it still feels a sacred place. Within the shelter of the mountains there is a cave, which nowadays is romantically lit by the flickering glow of candlelight. By tradition, it was here that Zeus, greatest of the Greek gods, was born.

Crete also has an excellent strategic position, midway between Greece to the north, Egypt to the south, Asia Minor to the east and the lands of the western Mediterranean in the direction of the setting sun. Vines also grew well on the island, and as a result wine production blossomed. Civilisation on Crete – known as the Minoan after Minos – grew powerful and rich, built on a heady mix of its well-developed agriculture and the seafaring skills of its sailors. That they were merchant adventurers seems clear enough, as historians have identified links to Sicily in the west and Syria in the east.

Despite the naming of the civilisation after King Minos – who may not even have existed – Crete appears to have been a fairly decentralised civilisation. In the absence of written records, the major evidence we have of its ways are again archaeological remains, especially the palaces for which the island is renowned. It appears there were a number of fairly autonomous small states in existence, recognising only the nominal hegemony of one supreme ruler.

Minoan art shows that the men in this society were beardless and the women liked to dress with their breasts exposed. Beautiful frescoes once adorned the walls of the palaces but many of them are now much decayed, which is a pity, for what remains is exquisite.

The Minoans liked sport and dancing but there was a darker side to them too. The story of the Minotaur hints at the significance of human sacrifice and archaeologists have found evidence to support the suggestion that the Minoans indulged in the practice, some indicating that children were among the victims and that the bodies of these unfortunates may have been eaten in some macabre ritual.

Little is known of the specifics of Minoan history. Its civilisation peaked for about 600 years. Then, in around 1500 BC, it collapsed. There are no historical accounts to explain its demise. Inevitably, the volcanic eruption on Santorini, just 70 miles away, is a prime suspect. Certainly the tsunami generated would have been of enormous ferocity and would have struck a blow of atomic proportions against coastal areas of Crete. Some have even suggested that evidence in Asia Minor points to a tidal wave an incredible 800 feet high.

It is not as widely accepted as it once was that the catastrophic events that overwhelmed Thira were responsible for the decline of Minoan civilisation, though the impact must have been horrendous given the short distance between Crete and the volcano. From archaeological evidence, it seems that there was an attempt by the Cretans to pick up the pieces and rebuild. But it is clear that the damage on the northern shores of Crete must have been substantial and the efforts required to recover must correspondingly have been great and potentially exhausting.

It is significant that archaeology has uncovered the remains of children in Crete from about this period, their bones scratched in the same way as those of animals butchered in Crete at the time. Their discovery with what appears to be a cooking pot is suggestive of cannibalism; whether for ritual purposes (the fall-back of many archaeologists for any unexplained artefacts, it seems) or just through starvation is unclear.

It is revealing also that a number of sites have been uncovered where substantial buildings have clearly been burned deliberately to the ground – on one site which stored olive oil the top of a container has been deliberately sliced off as if to literally add fuel to the fire. This is evidence of a cataclysmic downturn in Minoan fortunes. This may suggest foreign invasions though some historians think a more likely explanation is a civil war, perhaps predicated around support for rival gods in the pantheon of Crete. In any event this is clear evidence of something dramatic happening to bring about a decline in fortunes.

Yet for all that, perhaps the cataclysmic epic of the Thiran apocalypse lives on in myth, in one of the most famous tales of all. Nearly a thousand years later, Plato wrote of a mystical land, a rival of both Athens and Egypt, which was wiped out by a deluge of epic proportions. Of course, the whole concept of Atlantis is highly suspect and, reading Plato, much of the so-called evidence he presents suggests a land much larger than Crete, which had been powerful long before it and was located in the Atlantic. He describes events that suggest a volcanic holocaust, of a land where 'there occurred violent earthquakes and floods; and in a single day and night of misfortune all your warlike men in a body sank into the earth, and the island of Atlantis in like manner disappeared in the depths of the sea'.

Probably no one will ever know whether Atlantis was real or a figment of a quite brilliant imagination. But the flimsy evidence we have, based on Plato's vivid prose, might just contain a folk memory explained by the cataclysm at Thira and the subsequent disaster that struck Crete.

While the Minoan civilisation came and went, eventually falling to the power of colonists from Greece, in the distant lands of Mesopotamia the balance of power was also shifting. In the north of the region, Amorite tribes were rising to prominence.

One of them grew dominant and laid the early foundations of what would become the Assyrian Empire. To the south, another empire was formed, based around the city of Babylon.

This was a time of great uncertainty in the region, when minor kings entered into alliances as a matter of almost everyday politics, and political rivalry was rife. Through it all, though, Babylon became the major power, effectively picking up the baton dropped by Sumer. The Babylonians replaced the god Enlil with their own Marduk in the story of creation; the ultimate symbol of one regime's victory over another is the triumph of the victor's gods, greater even than the replacement of a conquered state's laws, as such substitutions fundamentally affect the core beliefs of the vanquished.

This was the time of one of the first known law-givers, Hammurabi (reigned 1792–1750 BC). Babylonian law made for rough justice (reminding one of the old maxim, often the first lesson for legal students, that one should never confuse law with justice). One of its elements was the so-called river ordeal, where the accused in a criminal case was required to swim a long way underwater. Following a process eerily reminiscent of medieval trial by water for alleged witches, if the accused survived, then they were deemed innocent.

Another of the laws of Hammurabi has a familiar ring about it:

> If a man destroys the eye of another man, they will destroy his eye. If he breaks the bones of another man, they will break his bones.

This is better known to us from the Old Testament phrase 'an eye for an eye, a tooth for a tooth'. Alongside creation myths and stories of the Great Flood, the maxim provides convincing evidence of the cross-fertilisation of ideas across the Middle Eastern region, which has been perpetuated within the religious teachings of some of the great religions – in the Torah, the Quran, the Bible – now universal articles of faith.

The laws give us an insight into many facets of Babylonian life. Included in them were details of the price fixing to be used in the trading of goods, evidence of a highly regulated economy. Hammurabi prided himself on his justice, claiming that his rules were handed down direct from Shamash, the sun god, who was responsible for justice. There were nearly 300 rules listed. This was not a new set of regulations, a bold new framework within which Babylonians would live their lives, but rather a codification of pre-existing rules.

Many of them covered the day-to-day details of Babylonian life, for example rules concerning marriage and divorce. An important aspect of what they tell us was that law had become secularised whereas earlier it had been the preserve of the priests. Non-priestly law courts adjudicated on issues, something that marks a diminution in the powers of the priestly caste.

Hammurabi was no bleeding-heart liberal, far from it. His laws were tough, and the death penalty was freely applied for a variety of offences. He was also an autocrat, as he needed to be to survive. Babylon was still a relatively new city, just over a century old, and it was surrounded by potential enemies. By a combination of diplomacy, treachery and effective military tactics he managed to become the ruler of the most prominent power in Mesopotamia.

Hammurabi was gifted with great energy, ruthless determination and a range of talents. He built impressive cities, strong fortifications, imposing temples. During his reign some of the earliest mathematical texts were produced as well as treatises on geometry. For the early part of his reign he was in the shadow of Shamshi-Adad I, King of Assyria, and Rim-Sin of Larsa. However, he managed to build up enough power to dominate the southern cities in Mesopotamia and then take Assyria.

The story of Hammurabi attests to the earlier influences that had shaped the region in which he ruled. He was himself of Amorite stock but the code that he had assembled was written in the Akkadian language. The peoples of the region were a fusion of earlier cultures. He seemed to have ushered in a golden age that brought together some of the strongest elements of previous civilisations in Mesopotamia.

But the danger of a strong tyrant such as Hammurabi is that, when they die, the state they have constructed can quickly fall apart in the vacuum left, and such was the case with early Babylonia. Towards the end of this period, another power became involved in the politics of the Middle East. The Hittites developed in Central Anatolia with their capital at Hattusha. Although their roots are obscure, by 1650 BC they dominated Anatolia and in the reign of Mursuli I (1620–1590 BC) became much more ambitious, taking Aleppo and then sacking Babylon itself. By the time they got there, the city was already a pathetic shadow of its former self, the glories of Hammurabi nothing but a dim and distant memory.

However, this initial period of Hittite history itself ended in chaos, with dynastic disputes ripping their society apart. Following the assassination of Mursuli, bitter infighting broke out and the power of the Hittites declined for a time. A succession of rulers all saw their reigns end in the same way, by the assassin's knife or other violent means. Great walls have been found, massively thick, their scale giving strong clues as to the warfare that had become endemic in Hittite society.

This was a troubled period in history and life across the Levant in particular must have been terrifying for ordinary people. In Egypt, there was also ongoing evidence of turbulence. Pharaoh Amenhemet I (reigned 1991–1962 BC) was forced to put down rebellions at the start of his rule. He also launched expeditions against the 'Asiatics' who lurked on his kingdom's borders in Palestine (immigration and the problems that it supposedly causes is by no means an issue solely of the modern era). He himself would be murdered.

Amenhemet has Hamlet-like qualities, for an Egyptian tale relates how his ghost returned to his son in a dream. He told him how he was attacked and killed by his guard while sleeping after supper. He gave him kingly advice, particularly warning him not to get too close to his people; a pharaoh should always encourage a degree of respect, even fear, in his subjects.

During the reigns of Amenhemet's successors there is increasing evidence of wider trading relationships involving Egypt. Relics found there include cups from the Aegean and the Levant, cylinders from Babylonia and amulets made of lapis lazuli from

Mesopotamia. Egyptian finds from the Minoan palaces of Crete speak eloquently of cross-Mediterranean traffic (the Egyptians called the sea 'the Great Green'). This was a long way from full-blown globalisation but trade was taking place over a wide area.

To the south there were trading expeditions from Egypt to the semi-mythical land of Punt, 'God's Land' (now widely believed to have been in the region of modern Somalia). From here all kinds of precious goods arrived including incense, gold, sandalwood, ebony and ivory. Giraffes and baboons were also imported from here, intriguing novelties and hints of lands to the south imperfectly understood by those in Egypt. The Red Sea was the watery highway that gave access to these strange and stimulating worlds with a great cross-desert highway linking the ports on the Egyptian coast to that other aqueous lifeline, the Nile.

But Egypt was a land with problems. The power of the nomarchs was still a great threat to that of the pharaoh. Foreign adventurism was not unknown either. Senusret III (reigned 1878–1839 BC) launched a number of heavy raids into Nubia, prized for its rich mineral resources. To assist in this, he ordered a canal to be built around the First Cataract to link up again to the Nile further south. Senusret was proud of his military prowess; an inscription celebrating his Nubian expeditions said, 'I carried off their women, I carried off their subjects, went forth to their wells, smote their bulls: I reaped their grain, and set fire thereto.'

He left a state boundary further south than any yet seen in Egypt but he also launched expeditions into Syria; if trade was spreading, war was too. In Nubia, Senusret left behind huge mud-brick fortifications, some of which were still impressive until modern times when sadly they were lost beneath the waters of Lake Nasser, formed when the Aswan Dam was constructed.

Then in 1806 BC something remarkable happened; a woman became pharaoh. Although little is known of her, or of her reign, Queen Sobeknefru broke a long line of male pharaohs. Although she only reigned for three years, this was a significant development. By the time she reigned, it appeared that Egypt was developing nicely, trade was good and all was well with the world. But her reign marked the end of the Middle Kingdom.

Horrific evidence survives that difficult times were approaching. Pharaoh Seqenenre died in around 1574 BC. His skull has been found and bears witness to the terrible death he suffered for in it are the marks of a dagger, a spear, an axe and possibly a mace. He was attacked by at least two people. Unlike most pharaohs, his corpse was not properly embalmed. He was clearly done to death in battle. He suffers the further indignity of now being on perpetual display for the benefit of gawping tourists as a star exhibit in the Egyptian Museum in Cairo.

These were violent times and the nature of the pharaoh's death evidences the disruption then extant in Egypt. In 1663 BC, a new regime had taken control in the north. The people behind this coup were known as the Hyksos, 'Desert Princes'. These people were foreigners and as a result the period of their rule came to be regarded as a national disgrace. Initially, they had entered Egypt as peaceful immigrants. However, when they saw the clear decline of pharaonic power they were quick to take the opportunity they identified (a situation that later Roman emperors would also understand very clearly).

The Hyksos were of Semitic origin and their most secure bases were in the Delta, but in 1720 BC they launched a devastating raid on Memphis. They came originally from Phoenicia (in the region of modern Lebanon) and they brought with them their gods such as Astarte, the mother-goddess. Few of their monuments remain, for they would eventually be overthrown and, suffering the fate of many foreign invaders, history would be rewritten and all traces of their rule would be eliminated by the Egyptians who overthrew them.

The Hyksos were military innovators and give us the first definite example of the use of the chariot in warfare. They were also great archers and their military technology gave them a significant advantage over their Egyptian foes. They never conquered all of Egypt, though, and a rump state ruled by a pharaoh continued in the middle of the country. Eventually a fightback was launched. The son of the butchered pharaoh Seqenenre, Ahmose, led the charge against the Hyksos. Serving under him was a warrior also named Ahmose. The latter's exploits were recorded on the walls of his tomb. The inscription tells how he received the order of the Golden Fly (described once as 'the Egyptian equivalent of the British Victoria Cross').

The Hyksos were chased back into Palestine and another period, 'the New Kingdom', began in the Egypt they left behind. By a quirk of fate we know more of these pharaohs than most others because we can still look at them. A large number of their mummies have been found in caches in or near the Valley of the Kings. This accident of fate came about because of the concern of priests who, in around 1000 BC, were so unnerved by the predations of grave robbers that they hid the mummies of about forty pharaohs in one cache and sixteen in another.

Amid all these historical events we get occasional clues that the Egyptians still had an imperfect understanding of the world. Their calendar had 365 days in every annual cycle and there was no allowance for leap years (the concept of these was initially developed by the Romans). This meant that from time to time dates would get out of synch.

In the reign of Amenemhet III (1842–1797 BC) an expedition was sent to Sinai to collect turquoise ore. According to the calendar, this should have been winter and the harshness of the desert should have been tempered. But the calendar was seven months out and it was the middle of summer. The expedition got roasted; as a later Egyptian chronicler put it, 'Winter is come in summer, the months are reversed, the hours in confusion.' The calendar would only in fact collide with reality once every 1,460 years – a so-called Sothic period (a year being in reality 365 days, 5 hours, 48 minutes and 45.51 seconds long).

Although the Middle East still appeared to be the crucible in which the developments of civilisation was forged, great events with massive import for the future of the world were taking place elsewhere. Harappan civilisation seems to have ended in India around 1750 BC for reasons which are not yet clearly understood. Heavy floods might have played their part, for the Indus region was prone to disastrous instances of these.

However, recent research has cast doubt on this theory and instead argues that precisely the opposite was true. It suggests that there was once a great river, now long dried up, in the region upon which many towns and villages were situated. The river may even have found a place in ancient Indian folklore in the shape of a goddess with the magical name of Saraswati, 'River of Lakes'. Digs have unearthed terrifying clues as to what happens when a world slowly begins to fall apart.

In fact, it appears that it may have been a combination of events that caused the demise. In an early, and salutary, example of the impact of climate change, there does indeed appear to be evidence of flooding hitting Mohenjo-daro and other cities. Great buildings were subdivided into much smaller living units and public buildings were taken over for private use, both suggesting that the area of available habitable land was shrinking.

There is disturbing evidence of a loss of standards and worse. Rubbish appears to have lain freely in the streets but so too did bodies, lying unburied where they were struck down. In a classic symptom of a threatened civilisation, people buried personal treasure, presumably because they were leaving; having planned to return to disinter it one day, they never did. At the port of Lothal, where stood the world's earliest known dock, it appears that a fire destroyed much of the city, along with a massive flood. Long-distance trading seems to have ended and it appears that the use of writing declined and perhaps disappeared altogether.

What happened after these early Indus civilisations declined is a debate that is still bitterly fought out today. The world over, peoples have sought to interpret history, subconsciously or otherwise, in a way that suits them in terms of supporting a particular political or ideological viewpoint. In recent times, communist regimes provide the most obvious example but they are far from the only case as we shall see. Owning the narrative of history is one of the most important targets for ruling elites to aim for.

Such debates affect India as much as anywhere, a proud and ancient land which has recently (in historical terms) found its feet again and is now rising with the aspiration and potential of becoming a world superpower. Where India comes from in terms of its historical roots is more than a trifling point of academic interest to Indians.

In 1786, Sir William Jones, a British judge based in Calcutta, noticed connections between ancient Indian ('Sanskrit') languages and Greek and Latin. He was convinced that they were too marked to be coincidental. Others had noticed it too, even before him. To them, it appeared that the common roots suggested a common ancestry. In other words, inhabitants of ancient India and parts of ancient Europe were, in anthropological terms, cousins. From these linguistic connections, the concept of 'Indo-European' language emerged.

Names of countries and settlements are often more suggestive of origins than many realise. The names Eire and Iran both have the same root, for example, one which links them directly to a people known as the 'Aryans'. And it is these people who are also widely believed to have moved into the Indus Valley and formed a new and vibrant civilisation there. But some Indian scholars are unhappy with the claimed connection, as are politicians who see a not very subtle attempt to justify past European rule in India in the theories. Of course, the Nazis infamously adopted the theory of Aryan supremacy as a way of justifying the unjustifiable.

But that there was a connection seems unarguable, though the sequence of events can be disputed (perhaps the Aryans were in India first and then their influence spread outwards from there: a more acceptable interpretation to some politicians). As one piece of corroborating evidence some texts were found in the former kingdom of the Mitanni in northern Syria. Dated to 1380 BC, they read perfectly as Sanskrit even though they are a long way from India.

One of the gems of the Indian world of the time is the great hymn collection, the Rigveda. These tell tales of gods but also give hints as to the origins of the writers, somewhere in the region of the Caspian and the Aral Sea. They appear to have been unaware of great cities such as Mohenjo-daro and Harappa, suggesting that they did not conquer the old Indus civilisations but rather moved in like squatters into a metaphorically empty house. The Aryans were warriors and by nature pastoralists: it cannot be said that their presence was an immediate step forward for Indian civilisation, which rather declined (or probably had already declined before they got there) but they did have a significant impact on the future of India.

China too was about to take a quantum leap forward in terms of its civilisation. The first known Chinese dynasty was the Xia, dating back to 2100 BC, about whom little is known. A project organised in China in AD 1996 dated the dynasty to between 2070 and 1600 BC. Before they emerged, the rule of the land passed to the strongest but the founding king of the Xi, Yu, passed the kingdom on to his son and so a dynastic system was introduced. Much later Chinese histories, dating to around 300 BC, suggest that the Xi emerged from a period of great upheaval ushered in by massive volcanic activity and consequent chaos.

Their successors, the Shang, assumed power in around 1700 BC (though alternative sources suggest dates up to two centuries later), though their history is also obscure and their territory was a relatively small region based on the Yellow River rather than the giant we think of as China today. As always in the absence of written records, we have to base our understanding of the civilisation on artefacts that have survived the destructive passage of time, an incomplete set of data on which to do so. Unless care is used in the process of interpretation then we may end up with a prejudiced and unbalanced view of how they lived.

Chinese tradition asserts that the Shang won power from the Xi when their leader, Tang of Shang, defeated the last Xi king at the Battle of Mingtiao. Although they left limited references to their rule behind, a major discovery took place near the modern city of Anyang in the AD 1920s. An array of relics unearthed gave fascinating insights into the ways of the Shang. They gave credence to a long-held belief that the Shang had practised divination based on the shoulder-bones of animals, a shamanistic belief that would be still used by peoples such as the Mongols 3,000 years later.

There is also irrefutable evidence of human sacrifice, which, however uncomfortable it may make modern human beings feel, has played a core part in belief systems the world over from the beginnings of known history. A royal tomb at Anyang contained forty-five complete skeletons as well as those of birds and animals. Other buildings also contain the remains of animals and young children, in what appears to be a clear example of a propitiatory offering to some divine being. Warriors were buried to guard the entrances and others to perform a similar function inside.

Sometimes several hundred people were interred as a grim gift to the gods to provide the users of the building with their protection. War chariots were also buried, giving us an accidental insight into military tactics of the time (the development of chariots by the Hyksos shortly before may suggest long-distance links through which ideas could pass). From these, we know that each chariot would have had a driver, an archer and a warrior wielding a dagger-axe; the heavy tanks of their day. There would be five of these vehicles at the centre of each Shang fighting unit, in front of them twenty-five infantrymen and to their right 125 others.

They were also expert craftsmen, arguably the most talented workers in bronze ever. Bells, axes and mirrors have survived but also magnificent food and wine vessels, with bewildering swirls of geometrically intricate circles requiring remarkable expertise in casting. Remains uncovered also provide the earliest evidence of that archetypal tool of Chinese cuisine, the chopstick.

The Shang legacy was crucial to the development of China. They developed their cities as well-proportioned squares, a form of town planning that has survived in China to this day and on which later settlements such as Beijing would be based. Unusually, they saw the world as a giant square, with their small square at the centre surrounded by a larger one composed of the countries they knew about and the outer, largest square made up of the unexplored *terra incognita*.

In common with the rest of the world, the Shang had much to learn about the planet on which they lived, but important strides had been made towards the spread of civilisation in the east. The first sentences of one of the world's most remarkable stories, of that great power that would be China, had been penned. Nearly four thousand years later, fascinating new pages continue to be written.

5

NEW BEGINNINGS

Assyria and Greece (1500–1001 BC)

The end of Minoan Crete, whether caused by a natural disaster of massive proportions or other more mundane reasons, presaged the rise of another power in the Mediterranean. Into the vacuum Crete's demise left behind stepped regimes from mainland Greece. The next 500 years saw the rise of a new power on the peninsula followed by its subsequent decline. Their demise was marked by so-called barbarian invasions, leading to what became known as the Dark Age of Greece. Mesopotamia too was to experience its own Dark Age. Everywhere there seemed to be a loss of vibrancy and vitality, and, although it suffered less than others, even Egypt was affected.

The great culture that rose and then declined in Greece was based around the city of Mycenae, on the Peloponnesian Peninsula. By 1600 BC, the civilisation here was already burying its kings in elaborate tombs that evidenced well-developed skills and the ability to organise labour in a sophisticated and organised fashion. Significant amounts of precious goods accompanied these kings on their journeys into Hades, suggesting that there was plenty of wealth around for the rich, too.

From its very beginnings, the Greek political landscape was composed of a number of city states jockeying with each other for regional supremacy. However, by about 1500 BC Mycenae had reached a more powerful position than any other state on the peninsula. From very early on, there was a close link between Minoan Crete and Mycenae. Mycenaean tombs housed liberal amounts of Minoan art. Other remnants of knowledge give hints of links too; the legend of the Minotaur preserves a folk memory that the Mycenaeans killed the son of King Minos and, in return, were forced to send a number of youths across the sea to Crete as sacrifices to the ferocious beast.

Ignoring the more outlandish elements of this myth, perhaps the story contains a significant germ of truth. Leaving aside stories of monsters half-bull and half-man, perhaps the story tells us that Mycenae for a time paid tribute to Crete, with the island kingdom holding the upper hand. But things changed; just as Theseus conquered the Cretan Minotaur, so too does Mycenae seem to have turned the tables on the island kingdom. By about 1400, we find that Mycenaean art dominates in Crete, rather than vice versa, and the great palace of Knossos appears to be in the hands of a Mycenaean ruler.

But it must not be assumed that Mycenae was overlord of all Greece. The city states there all took pride in their independence (there seem to have been six or seven of such states at the time, each larger typically than the states that existed in Greece's later golden 'classical' age). This was a confederacy but one where, at some stage, Mycenae for a time appeared to be first among equals. Later, archaeologists uncovered the remains of a great stone-built city at Mycenae, with a gate over which lions looked threateningly on those who entered. This Lion Gate gives us one of the oldest coats of arms known.

This was architecture on a massive scale, the stones used so large that the style is known as Cyclopean after the giants of Greek mythology. This was a Bronze Age civilisation in its prime, whose kings were buried in large chambers filled with treasure, with gold a particularly prized commodity. There were slaves too, organised in groups of twenty to thirty, some from Asia Minor famed for working with the plant known as flax or, in Mycenaean, *linon.* The Aegean cultures at this time were closely connected though, sharing a common script known unimaginatively as Linear B. But it was during the age of Mycenaean pre-eminence that one of the most evocative of all dramas was perhaps acted out.

It has been said that myth is the smoke of history, that is that we should be careful dismissing what we might regard as legend as it might be a useful pointer to a hard core of what is fact. The story of Theseus is one case in point. There are enough signs of bull worship from Cretan remains to suggest that a sacred bull was indeed worshipped, even if it was not half-man. Here, the myth preserves a trace of original history. We should remember this wise caveat particularly when considering one of the most dramatic of all ancient stories, that of the siege of Troy.

Did such an event happen? Belief that it did was strengthened when the German archaeologist Heinrich Schliemann (who also dug at Mycenae) uncovered in the nineteenth century the remains of a town that appeared to be in roughly the right place (though his cavalier archaeological techniques and moulding of evidence to suit his own pre-conceived ideas succeeded in destroying much of what he hoped to uncover. There were nine successive settlements at Troy and he picked the wrong one to excavate.).

If Troy was indeed sacked by the Greeks then it seems to have happened in around 1250 BC (the archaeology on the site suggests a disastrous fire at this time). This is five centuries before Homer wrote his epics, the *Iliad* and the *Odyssey*, but like all great storytellers of ancient times, he would probably have been committing to print stories that had been transmitted orally from time immemorial.

This is indeed epic writing. The first words of the *Iliad* set the tone. 'The Wrath of Achilles is my theme, that fatal wrath which, in fulfilment of the will of Zeus, brought the Achaeans [Greeks] so much suffering and sent the gallant souls of many noblemen to Hades, leaving their bodies as carrion for the dogs and passing birds.'

What follows is one of the greatest stories ever written. Those not fully familiar with it may think of it as a tale of glory but it is anything but. There are no real winners; the Greeks only triumph after a decade, their losses are immense and Achilles, the anti-hero of the tale, pays for his brutal defilement of the corpse of the Trojan hero Hector with his own death. The tale is a warning, much loved by the Greeks, of the dangers of hubris. Achilles has been blessed by the gods but their gift is flawed, for he is almost immortal but not quite. He can only be killed by a wound in his heel and, knowing this, we know that his death is inevitable. One cannot be 'almost immortal'.

The story also points out some old lessons. The dangers of an attractive woman on the judgement of a besotted man are there. This is most obvious in the story of Helen of Troy of course but is also there when the Greeks are struck by a plague when their leader, Agamemnon, refuses to hand over the daughter of a priest of Apollo, named Chryseis, back to her father. Agamemnon then falls out with Achilles over another beautiful woman, Briseis.

All of this was a good story well told and also an anachronism; the Greeks did not exist in the form that Homer knew them when Troy was attacked. However, it is known that there were Mycenaean colonies in Asia Minor and there is every reason to think that there would be rivalry between them and a city that enjoyed a prime position for trade close to the entry to the Black Sea. Even the far-fetched tale of the Trojan horse makes sense if thought of as a metaphor for a traitorous betrayal by something, or more likely someone, invited into the city by the unsuspecting citizens.

The story of Troy was part of a harsh trend. Mycenae suffered in these years too, at the same time that Egypt, the Hittite Empire and the kingdoms of Babylon and Assyria were experiencing serious problems of their own. This was a turbulent, violent epoch. In about 1200 BC, the Mycenaean city of Sparta was burned to the ground. Mycenae itself was also set ablaze, though its citadel managed to hold out. The problems were caused by invaders from the north named Dorians, a people without writing skills or the ability to work in bronze, which the Mycenaeans were so adept at.

But this was not a sudden demise but a long, lingering death. The fires in the Mycenaean cities occurred over a period of a century. Perhaps the story of Troy explains the demise to an extent; the tale that the Greek invaders were hit by an outbreak of plague, the foreign adventurism, the extended wars. Perhaps all of this is a cryptogram for the fall of Mycenae.

This period also saw significant changes in Egypt. In 1498 there had been a coup, one not involving any violence but rather the subtle brushing aside of a child pharaoh, Tuthmosis III. He was elbowed out by his co-regent Hatshepsut, the wife of the deceased Tuthmosis II. She claimed she was empowered to do so because she was operating on the orders of her 'father', the god Amun. She also invented two fictitious coronation ceremonies: an earthly one, and an otherworldly one in the presence of the gods when she was a child.

The power behind the throne was Hatshepsut's royal steward, Senenmut. It was rumoured that relations between pharaoh and steward were rather more intimate than would be normal between an official and his ruler. During Hatshepsut's reign a major trading expedition was launched to the land of Punt. The event was celebrated in some memorable wall carvings that survive to this day. Despite any romantic images that Hatshepsut might conjure up, her mummy suggests an overweight woman with very poor teeth. Indeed, in some ways it would be wrong to think of Hatshepsut as a female ruler. She went out of her way to masculinise herself. She insisted on being called 'king', not 'queen' and 'he', not 'she'.

It was not as if women had no power in Egyptian society; far from it. Women had legal rights and at some stages in Egyptian history the line of descent was matrilineal.

Women were therefore important – there were, after all, many female deities, of whom Isis was only the most famous. But in Hatshepsut's masculine portrayal we see that a pharaoh was expected to possess the attributes of the male.

Hatshepsut died in around 1483. Her lasting monument is the quite magnificent temple she built at Deir el-Bahari, near the Valley of the Kings, though this was not her tomb, which was alongside those of her fellow pharaohs in that dusty vale of death on the west bank of the Nile. With her death, Tuthmosis III at last achieved power and was quick to do all he could to erase the memory of the woman who had kept him from his inheritance for so many years. In a quasi-Stalinist revision of history, her name was omitted from the king lists of Egypt that followed, the shame of her usurping to power being too great to acknowledge even posthumously. The narrative of history was quickly rewritten.

Tuthmosis has been called the Napoleon of ancient Egypt. He led his army into Palestine, into a region where Egyptian influence had declined during the reign of Hatshepsut. One particular target was the city of Megiddo, halfway between Egypt and Mesopotamia: this was the first of many battles over the centuries at a place better known by its Greek name, Armageddon. Brave in battle to the point of recklessness, here was a general who led from the front. For eighteen years in succession he led his army against Syria, its moves being coordinated with those of an Egyptian fleet that kept it supplied from the sea.

One extraordinary relic surviving from the time is a small gold cup presented to a general, Djehuty. The general was supposed to have captured the town of Jaffa by hiding his men inside earthenware jars. This may well be the origin of the well-known tale of Ali Baba and the Forty Thieves. We know that Djehuty was a real person for his tomb was found at Saqqara in AD 1824. Sadly, the find was poorly recorded and the artefacts found inside sold to a number of different museums, leaving behind little trace of their provenance.

When Tuthmosis died, he left a border further north than any other Egyptian pharaoh. But in so doing, he brought his country into direct confrontation with other emergent powers in the Middle East. One group in particular was increasingly significant in the region. This was the Mitanni, descended from the same racial stock as the Aryans who had impacted so vigorously on India.

A clash between the two was inevitable and war broke out. A third force was present here; the Hittites. They had something of a death wish; their internal disputes weakened them perilously. Despite the fact that they made great play of their formal succession rites, with rigid rules that the royal bloodline must at all costs be protected, the death of each king was normally followed by a violent series of upheavals.

For the time being, the Hittites were unable to intervene too vigorously and a status quo of sorts was agreed. The Egyptians and the Mitanni agreed a border that tracked the Orontes River in Lebanon, which meant that the land of Canaan, soon to be much desired by a group of Semitic nomads from the west, remained at least theoretically in the Egyptian sphere of influence.

Egyptian society had evolved significantly since the early days, but religion still played a crucial role. There were many gods, from the Egyptian version of the Holy Trinity – Osiris, Isis and Horus – to the jackal-headed deity of the dead, Anubis, the crocodilian

Sobek or the feline Bast. Every god had their own speciality, sometimes several. The dwarf Bes protected against snakes but also helped women in childbirth. Ibis-headed Thoth was the scribe of the gods and the inventor of writing. It was as if the universe was too big, its complexities too immense, for one being alone to be in control of it all.

This multi-stranded view of religion was at the heart of the ancient Egyptian beliefs. The thought that any other view might be acceptable was anathema. Therefore, the acts of Amenhotep IV, who ascended to the throne in 1350 BC, appeared to be heretical, to threaten the very survival of an ancient way of life. He is better known by the name he later adopted; Akhenaton, the servant of the Aten.

To subsequent generations of Egyptians, Akhenaton would appear to be little short of a regal anarchist. Perhaps perturbed by the growing power of the priests of Amun (ancient priests had no compunction about mixing religion with politics – it would have been unthinkable to them not to do so) he attempted to refocus all worship on the Aten, the disk of the sun. Aten was not a new entity – the disk had been worshipped during the Old Kingdom. But now its status was elevated to a level where all other deities were left in the shade of its dazzling solar presence.

Akhenaton declared himself the intermediary between man and Aten, at a stroke making the priesthood irrelevant and destroying their power. Behind him, manoeuvring him through the choppy waters that were inevitably whipped up by his radical theology, was his beloved wife Nefertiti. A new city was built, Amarna, constructed as a place to concentrate worship focused on the Aten and his earthly representative, the pharaoh.

To look on the art of Akhenaton's reign is to gaze at something unique in Egyptian history. Statues of him are extraordinary; the face is elongated as are the ears, the hips curvaceous as if he were a woman, the lips pursed, pouting and almost sensual. This has led some historians to suggest he was somehow deformed. This appears a quite extraordinary viewpoint; it is unbelievable that a pharaoh would let any sculptor who carved him as a figure of mockery live (though what we regard as deformity would not necessarily be so regarded in Egypt, hence the positive treatment and regard for those who were dwarves).

Instead the statues should be read symbolically. The childbearing hips appear to be an allusion to fertility and the pharaoh was responsible, as the representative of the gods (or, in Akhenaton's case, the god), for the fecundity of his kingdom. Thus he is both male and female not in a literal sense but in terms of his divine responsibilities. The other extraordinary physical characteristics allude to the fact that he is no mere mortal but himself a deity whose physical characteristics defy normality.

Although Akhenaton is understandably best known for his dramatic impact on Egyptian religion, and what simplistically appears to be a very early example of monotheism (though it was not, for he did not argue that other gods did not exist, he merely effectively ignored them), he also played his part in destroying the Mitanni civilisation. Amenhotep III had arranged an alliance with the Hittites against the Mitanni. Akhenaton reversed this for a time but later turned lukewarm against his erstwhile Mitanni allies. Although he did not go to war with them, he left the field clear for the Hittites to move on their western frontiers. The Mitanni soon found themselves in a pincer movement for, from the east, Assyrian forces also moved in. The Mitanni were vanquished, their civilisation consigned to a footnote to history.

The new religion in Egypt did not long survive Akhenaton's death. Many of his subjects must have hated the innovations that he forced on them, denying the legacy of the past 1,500 years and threatening the very foundations on which they believed Egyptian greatness was built. The new city he had built at Amarna, at what must have been enormous cost and effort, was quickly abandoned. His successor was a young boy when he inherited Akhenaton's troubled legacy and he would only reign for nine years. Not a great deal is known of the events that occurred while he was pharaoh, yet he was the most famous Egyptian of all. His name was Tutankhamen.

It is, of course, the discovery of his tomb that has led to his fame. It is by no means the most impressive in the Valley of the Kings. To journey warily down the steps of the nearby tomb of Horemheb, for example, is to embark on an expedition that leads so deeply into the bowels of the earth that it truly feels like an entrance into the Underworld. Tutankhamen's resting place in contrast is much smaller, almost humble in comparison.

But it was the amazing collection of grave goods that were found, unknown to the robbers who would otherwise have gorged themselves on them, that left its mark. When the English archaeologist Howard Carter opened the tomb in November 1922 he not only unleashed a highly dubious curse but also generated a huge amount of newsprint on which an incredulous and stunned readership feasted greedily.

Tutankhamen's inner coffin was made of solid gold and weighed 110 kg, his gold death mask – one of the most incredible and recognisable artefacts of Egyptian art – over 10 kg. Like a larger-than-life Babushka doll, there were three coffins, one inside the other, all held within a stone sarcophagus. Ironically, the corpse had been badly mummified and was in a terrible state. Two stillborn foetuses interred in the tomb hint at a personal tragedy. One is tempted to speculate, given the amazing artefacts that survive in what is supposedly the tomb of a relatively minor pharaoh, on what we have lost with the pillaging of the grave goods of some of the greats.

Yet although Tutankhamen died young, and even though he is best known for his tomb in the Valley of the Kings, he did play his part in history. His name gives the clue for the reference to Amun, the old Egyptian god, symbolising his rejection of the Aten. All references to the disc of the sun were removed. The world was not yet ready for monotheism, or something close to it.

Tutankhamen might be the most famous Egyptian but the only pharaoh to be called Great was Ramses II, whose long reign spanned the years from 1279 to 1212 BC. Here was a man who did everything on a Cecil B. DeMille scale. Even the monuments of former pharaohs were claimed by him, their names removed and replaced by his own (yet more narrative reclamation). Greatest of all, though, was a monument he built for himself, the incredible temples chiselled in the rock to the far south of Egypt at Abu Simbel. They were painstakingly moved when Lake Nasser was formed, an amazing feat of engineering in its own right.

Now, it is protected by a hidden concrete dome built into the hills behind it. Tourists can enter both the ancient temples and their camouflaged dome, the latter like something out of a James Bond film. With its four huge statues, each 60 feet high, standing guard next to its small entrance door, this is one of the great monuments of antiquity. When the sun rises on the morning of the spring and autumn equinoxes, its rays shine directly into the Great Temple and light up three of the four smaller statues of the gods, situated 200 feet inside the rock. In a placement of supreme symbolic significance, the only one that is not lit up is that of Ptah, god of the underworld.

This most magical of days, when there are twelve hours of daylight and twelve hours of darkness, marks a turning point in the year when days in the Northern Hemisphere get longer and those in the Southern shorter, or vice versa. Associating archaeology with key dates is not restricted to Africa or Europe either; the great pyramid at Chichen-Itza in Mexico, a Maya creation postdating the Egyptian monuments by several thousand years, has a snake's head at the bottom of a long column which is illuminated by the sun to create a long, coiling snake's body just twice a year – at the equinoxes.

It was possibly during the reign of Ramses that an act of great significance to future history was played out. The Hebrews had lived in the Delta for some 400 years. For most of that time they lived apparently in concord with their Egyptian neighbours. However, as their numbers increased, their hosts became more hostile; concerns over immigration are nothing new (and the Hyksos were Semitic immigrants into the country too, so the nervousness was understandable). Eventually, the Hebrews were enslaved and forced to participate in Egypt's ambitious construction projects. But at last they famously left and made their way, after a forty-year journey, to Palestine.

The Exodus is a minor event in Egyptian records and most of the information we have about it comes from the Old Testament. To his people, Ramses' greatest claim to fame was his alleged victory (usually thought of as a draw by neutral observers) at Kadesh in Lebanon against the Hittites. Despite proclaiming a great triumph, Kadesh remained in Hittite hands. A peace treaty was agreed at the end of the battle, original versions of which still survive. They are the oldest examples of such documents surviving and a copy now adorns the foyer of the United Nations building in New York.

Yet Ramses milked his supposed triumph for all it was worth and inscriptions extolling his heroism and military genius were put up with wild abandon. Regardless of his bluster, his death at the age of ninety-two must have felt like the end of an age to many Egyptians, equivalent in its own way to how many British subjects would have felt when Queen Victoria died in AD 1901. Among his many claims to fame, he had fathered over 100 offspring.

Amazingly, the face of Ramses can still be seen. His mummy, hidden away from grave robbers in a cliff-side cave, was found in the twentieth century and can now be viewed in the Cairo Museum, his face exposed to the glare of voyeuristic sightseers. Despite the excited claims of tourist guides, it is in many ways a sad sight. We look down upon a wizened old man, his arms abnormally shrunk due to the drying up of the body following mummification so that they appear little more than emaciated twigs on a shrunken branch. His appearance is freakish and slightly macabre. It is hard to look on this old man and see in him the face of greatness.

In many ways Ramses' reign marks the swansong of Egypt. His building projects were on a truly Herculean scale. Abu Simbel is the greatest of them but immense too were the temples at Luxor (which he added to, though the bulk of the building was done in the reign of Amenhotep III) and Karnak (Seti I and others also undertook substantial chunks of the work here), with its sacred lake and superb position by the Nile. Then there was the Ramasseum, a gigantic mortuary temple. Dying in 1212 BC, his most significant successor was Ramses III. This later Ramses's most significant act was to fight off a confederation of invaders known as the Sea Peoples (some Philistines, others possibly from Sicily).

Fierce attacks from other invaders were driven off and the pharaoh had to survive a plot against him led by one of his minor queens in what was evocatively known as the Harem Conspiracy. Among the charges against the defendants was that they had indulged in an ancient form of voodoo by constructing images of Ramses to perform evil magic on. In a bizarre twist, several of the judges in the case were also charged of being seduced by some of the defendants. They were sentenced to have their noses and ears amputated. Ramses III died before any verdict was delivered, an unsatisfactory end to an energetic reign (a medcal report released in AD 2012 following a scan on his mummy said that his throat had quite possibly been cut, hinting that a successful assassination attempt had been made on his life). Following his demise in 1151, his kingdom slowly slipped into a lethargic old age, facing a long, lingering death over the next thousand years.

Now the Middle Eastern world, the centre of evolving civilisation, went through a period of crisis. The Hittites suffered more than anyone. The demise of the Mitanni removed a buffer zone between them and the Assyrians. The Assyrians also nibbled away at the edges of Babylonia. The ruler of Assyria awarded himself the honorific title of 'king of the world' (which was something of an exaggeration for someone who did not even rule all of Mesopotamia). King Shalmaneser I invaded Hittite lands, taking allegedly 14,400 prisoners and blinding them all (a traditional Assyrian punishment that had the obvious if cruel benefit of rendering the victims useless as soldiers in the future).

The Hittites suffered greatly from famine, leading to poverty and general decline. The Assyrian king Tukulti-Ninurta invaded their empire, proclaiming proudly, 'I filled the caves and ravines of the mountains with their corpses.' He also sacked Babylon and took away the images of the gods that he found there. There were many on his own side who said that no good would come of this sacrilegious act. Babylon was less important as a trading city than it was as a place of great spiritual significance. In this part of the world at least, it was more important to respect the gods of an opponent than to humiliate them, for it was said that the gods would take their revenge for the shame visited on them.

Tukulti-Ninurta was a man obsessed with his own publicity. He built monumental edifices in his capital city Assur, an attempt at self-proclaimed greatness that many, including Adolf Hitler, would try to emulate in the future. But the wise sages who said that pride went before a fall were finally proved right, for, after thirty-seven years, Tukulti-Ninurta was deposed and killed by his own son. The new ruler of Assyria attempted to redress any damage by returning the Babylonian gods to their former home, but it appeared to do little good as Babylon was sacked by the Elamites soon afterwards.

The period around 1200 BC was one when many in the centre of the world, as the Middle East then was, must have thought that their way of life was about to plummet into an abyss. Much of the decline experienced by all the major civilisations in the region appears to have been caused by a common set of problems, namely famine and disease leading to a generalised economic downturn. Egyptian decline has already been noted; the borders of the country contracted, first Sinai, then Nubia, being lost. Law and order deteriorated and the economic decline meant that foreign trade virtually dried up, with Byblos in Lebanon refusing to do business with Egypt anymore.

The Hittites were effectively wiped out during these traumatic years. They were attacked from all angles, being invaded from Cyprus and the Aegean and exposed to raids from fierce tribesmen, the Phrygians, from Thrace (modern Bulgaria). Their capital, Hattusha, was destroyed and only isolated bastions of the Hittite Empire, such as Carchemish on the Euphrates, remained. Surviving cuneiform texts from Hattusha speak of almost annual raids against tribes known as the Kashka to the north and east; the Kashka merely retreated out of range. The Hittites died of exhaustion.

Even today, Hattusha remains a place full of atmosphere. The ruins of the city, now in the main just foundations, climb up a steep, rocky slope. The stumpy bases of the walls blend with the rocks so perfectly that it is hard to differentiate what is man-made from what is natural and indeed natural features were utilised by the Hittites for a number of their buildings. It is as if someone has placed an ancient city scattered around the hillsides of a steep-sloped Scottish glen.

The city, which covers a large area, is split into upper and lower elements. The upper was the site of the sacred buildings, with many temples; Hattusha was known as 'the city of a thousand gods' as Hittite foreign policy seems to have involved an assimilation of the deities of conquered peoples. Links with other civilisations can also be discerned, in particular the 'Sphinx Gate' demonstrates the close ties with Egypt and the Hittite cuneiform language shows links with Assyria. Intriguingly, there is a long underground passage, corbelled in an almost identical fashion to the great tomb at Newgrange in Ireland – what links, one wonders, might there have been between these disparate groups way back in history?

The Hittites are representative of some of those peoples who, in their time, were a great regional power but who were overwhelmed by stronger forces that they were unable to resist. There was military defeat, but they were culturally overpowered too. Indeed, even during their peak they were under cultural influences from elsewhere. The clues are in their cuneiform language as well as their gods and their symbolism, such as the double-headed eagle that was so resonant of Mesopotamia.

We know the kings of the Hittites but only by name; of their biographies we are sadly deficient in knowledge. Just occasionally we get a glimpse of them and their status. They were not gods when alive, though they became so after death; rather they were high priests. There is a tantalising clue to one individual in a hidden-away cleft in the rocks, just a few miles from Hattusha. At the sanctuary called Yazılıkaya, there is a series of carvings on the rocks. They are almost exclusively of gods; some of the great ones, such as the weather god Teshub and the sun goddess Hebat. Others are only minor deities, unknown and forgotten by now.

There is only one human being represented here, and that is a great Hittite king named Tudhaliya IV. Presumably the sanctuary was created for him, probably by his son. One of the best-preserved of the largely eroded carvings is of the king himself, in the embrace of the god Sharruma. Sharruma has his arms around his shoulder and is noticeably bigger than the king, a symbolic confirmation of his divine rather than human status. The god appears to be leading the king somewhere, presumably to the afterlife. It is an appropriate representation too for the fate and demise of the Hittite Empire.

Soon after Hattusha went up in smoke, a man with imperialist ambitions took over in Assyria. Tiglath-Pileser beat off the Phrygians, who had pushed through the detritus of the Hittite Empire and now threatened his own, but defensive action was not enough. His great war chariots, and his equally important road-building engineers, pushed westwards, adding more lands to his expanding empire. Carchemish, virtually the last remnant of the Hittite Empire, was taken. Tiglath-Pileser even went dolphin hunting in the Mediterranean; a symbolic act that confirmed conquest by the dipping of toes in the great sea which others would later emulate.

At the same time, Nebuchadnezzar I became King of Babylonia, reigning between 1125 and 1076. He led a fightback against the Elamites, including an audacious smash-and-grab raid on their capital city, Susa. He showed all the hallmarks of superb generalship, launching the assault during high summer; such acts were thought to be impossible in this arid region at such a time of year. In the meantime, Babylon and Assyria picked fights with each other, indulging in hit-and-run raids across the porous borders.

But these bursts of activity disguised the underlying problems. Crop failures and sickness hit home here too. At the same time, sensing the weaknesses of such failures in these sedentary societies, nomadic Aramean Semitic tribes moved in for the kill. They launched heavy raids on both Assyria and Babylonia, further weakening the already struggling societies there.

It was at around this time that a society previously little known to the world emerged. Some cultures have long since disappeared but, while they lived, they played a crucial role in the development of the world. One such group was the Phoenicians, who lived along the Mediterranean coast mainly in what is now Lebanon. Much of what we know of them is derived from archaeology and the historians of other societies, particularly Egyptian and Assyrian, but also from that invaluable source of historical information, the Old Testament.

Their major cities were not new; places like Byblos, Sidon and Tyre had been in existence for many years. The Phoenicians had probably been in the area for a considerable time (their language was Semitic like other groups in the region) but the release of external pressure due to decline elsewhere in the Middle East allowed them to emerge into the light of day from the pre-dawn shadows they had previously lived in. The terrifying attacks of the raiders known as the Sea Peoples left a vacuum into which the Phoenicians stepped. Sidon appeared initially to be their main base. By around 1100 BC, there were clear signs that Egyptian interference, which had previously been symbolised by the flow of supplies of cedar wood to the land of the Nile, was over.

The Assyrians still paid the occasional visit in search of tribute to the region – hence Tiglath-Pileser's dolphin hunting off the coast – but this was more of a symbolic statement of dominance over the peoples there than something representing an actual and permanent state of affairs. As time went on, the Phoenicians would become stronger and more influential in the Mediterranean sphere. By 1100 BC, they had undertaken some extraordinary journeys, sailing to the other end of the Mediterranean and establishing a colony in what is now Cadiz, Spain, as well as other sites along the Iberian coast.

It is important to realise what Phoenicia was. It was not a unified state but a kind of dispersed Levantine version of the Greek city state political structure. Throughout its history, there were a number of states, each under their own ruler. Often they would co-operate, but not invariably so. On occasion, invaders of the Lebanese littoral would find themselves aided by one city state against another. What did unify the Phoenicians was a culture, their gods (though there would be a good deal of independence here too) and a propensity for seafaring, adventure and trade (often allied to opportunistic acts of piracy).

The world of the Middle East was to an extent an interconnected one where life in Egypt, Greece, Crete, Phoenicia, Asia Minor and Mesopotamia impacted to some degree on lives elsewhere in the region. The affairs of India and China were less impacted by those of the Middle East but they too saw significant changes in this period. In about 1200 BC, the great hymn cycle, the Rigveda, was written. Little survives that we can call history but the Rigveda does at least tell us much about the religion of the peoples of the Subcontinent at this time.

There are ten cycles in all, called *mandalas*. These are hymns in praise of the gods and guidelines for ritual services and sacrifices; effectively a 'Book of Common Prayer' for worshippers. These deities are in the main nature gods, representative of the ways of the Aryan peoples. They include Indra, the ruler of the pantheon of gods, and Mitra, the sun god, both of whom are referred to in documents of the Mitanni civilisation, demonstrating a common ancestral link.

This amazing collection of poetry, preserved now for over 3,000 years, tells also of the writers' views of history. They spoke of strange ruins that they did not fully understand, thinking that the residents of places like Mohenjo-daro were forced out by Agni, the god of fire. They themselves spread out from Turkmenistan, over parts of Afghanistan, west into Kurdistan, where the Mitanni found their short-lived home, and south-east into what is now Pakistan and India. Their language suggests, though, that they have largely concealed links with the histories of many other nations, for traces of it can be found in English, Welsh, Gaelic, Latin, Greek, Persian and several of the major Indian dialects.

The reasons for their mass migrations are not clear but climatic reasons have been mooted as a major factor; the Aryans were, in effect, chasing water. They forced their way into India by a mixture of violence and carefully chosen alliances with local magnates. The Aryans, like many migrant groups in history, were not one homogeneous whole but a collection of about thirty different clans. Their weapons were made of iron, giving them a vast superiority over their opponents. Their society was made up of three main estates – priests, warriors and farmers, a virtual mirror image, incidentally, of the three castes of Western European medieval society. It also provides the loose basis of the caste structure that lives on in India to this day.

Also in around 1200 BC, one of the greatest of Shang emperors, Wu Ting, was ruling in China. The Shang had become spectacular workers in bronze, and they also developed their own unique form of writing. This was a system of ideograms, which combined pictures, leading to a large and complex alphabet, the ancestor of modern

Chinese. The evidence of this writing has been found on bones used in rituals. Priests carved their answers to questions posed by those concerned with a variety of issues on these bones. The contrast between this region and the cultures of the Middle East was further emphasised by Shang burials, huge pits dug into the ground.

Wu Ting, who reigned for sixty-three years, went on campaign in the north-west of China. The Shang had often found it difficult to govern in their part of the world. Their capital city had changed location five times in 300 years, a most unusual phenomenon that suggests that they were either extraordinarily poor at making up their minds or found it difficult to assert their authority. Eventually their empire started to fall apart, riven by internal division. The exact date of this regime change is a subject of much debate, and a variety of dates have been suggested, ranging from 1137 to 991 BC.

One Shang emperor, Wu-yi, mocked the gods of his opponents and was struck down by lightning, a just punishment so many thought. Under his great-grandson, Chou, the Shang declined still further. Not without his talents, Chou allegedly misused them. He loved wine and women, and taxes increased to finance his excesses; his popularity dipped still further due to his domineering concubine Ta Chi. He was also viciously cruel.

Wen, a wronged noble, plotted his revenge against his errant master. Heading an army of 50,000 against one 700,000 strong led by Chou, he appeared to have little chance of success (though the extreme numbers are suspicious, such alleged disparities being used often throughout history to play up the significance of a stunning victory). However, his men, the Zhou, were equipped with war chariots. Further, they were united whereas the Shang army was full of discontented soldiers. At the crucial point in the battle that followed (the Battle of Muye), many of the Shang soldiers turned on their own generals and the battle was lost. Chou was killed as his city was burned around him, and the Shang regime was overthrown to be replaced by the Zhou.

The Zhou were good empire builders, setting up a network of city states over an expanding area, each with its own lord but all recognising the supremacy of the Zhou ruler, an experimental form of feudalism. To add to the impression, peasants were required to work the land and pay over a proportion of their produce to their lord. Each lord was required to present himself and some of his men to serve the king in a military capacity. At one stage, the monarch retained fourteen standing armies with which to protect his power, though these were much needed because there were many raiders from the west to guard against – a recurrent theme in later Chinese history.

This had been a very disrupted and disruptive period. Much had changed during this half-millennium and some groups – the Mitanni, Minoans and Hittites for example – had disappeared altogether. The Mycenaeans were absorbed into the new Greek cultures that started to form. The Assyrians and Babylonians still survived but were under great pressure. The Egyptians were also faced with an uncertain future but they seemed to be able to reinvent themselves forever. The Shang had been dethroned by the Zhou and the Aryans were creating a new way of life in India. Everything had been turned on its head. This had been a bewildering and unsettling time of uncertainty, but the period of change was still far from over.

6

THE SECOND AGE OF CIVILISATION

The Emergence of Greece and the Rebirth of Assyria (1000–750 BC)

In about 800 BC, a poet from the coastal plain of Anatolia, at the point where it abuts the Aegean (Izmir, ancient Smyrna, is one of the prime candidates), or maybe from one of the islands in the area, produced two great works. But when Homer wrote his epics, the *Iliad* and the *Odyssey*, he was writing of an age long lost in the mists of ancient memory, not of well-remembered history. The Greek civilisation in which he lived was one that was just emerging, like a many-coloured and beautiful butterfly from a chrysalis, into a bright new dawn.

It had, however, gone through its own Dark Age in between the fall of Troy and the birth of Homer. The Dorian invasions from the north had not wiped out Greek culture, for otherwise it could not have re-emerged as it did as the centrepiece of one of the most glorious of all civilisations. But the Dorians left no records and the stories of those distant centuries are lost, barring a miracle as yet uncovered, forever.

The Greece that came out of the other side of this dark tunnel was composed of several societies who came to share a common Greek language. They would not have called themselves Greeks but would have used a name similar to Hellenes, which we now very occasionally call them. Their language only appears in about 750 BC, but that does not mean it did not exist before then, merely that we have not yet found any evidence to predate this time.

These people shared not only a language but a pantheon of gods. For these, epic poems like the *Iliad* provide invaluable background information. The chief of all the gods was Zeus, whose qualities are displayed in the lofty nicknames allocated to him by Homer, monikers such as the Marshaller of the Clouds, the Darkener of the Skies, in other words the supreme being who controls all the elemental forces of nature and can direct them at those who displease him with spectacular and fatal effect (similar to the Norse god Thor).

The Greek gods are a large family but the lives they lead are not those of domestic tranquillity, rather of a fractured clan who are constantly seeking to outdo each other. The other gods are overshadowed by Zeus; they recognise his superior power but this does not stop them trying to win by guile what they cannot gain by force. Throughout

Greek mythology we find stories of other deities, such as Zeus's wife Hera, or his daughter Pallas Athene, trying to beguile him, though he almost invariably comes out on top.

All of this is something of an allegory of Greece itself. Throughout its ancient history, the peninsula was dotted with city states, all seeking to increase their power by the use of calculated alliances or, if the opportunity offered itself, by force of arms. This comes through in the *Iliad* too, for Agamemnon of Mycenae, who leads the armies at Troy, is merely the head of a confederation of other Greek states. If this was ancient history disguised as myth to Homer, it was also to a significant extent the story of his own time too.

Several different peoples came together in a culture that bound them together, however loosely. The Dorians, Mycenaeans and Ionians (who inhabited the western coast of Anatolia, modern Turkey) may have had their own political priorities and there was no doubt a good deal of one-upmanship whereby one city state and its government tried to gain the upper hand over another, but their shared language, myths and pantheon acted as a kind of mortar to give them a shared view of what the world as a whole should look like. However, their world was about to become more fragmented, with smaller city states emerging, polities that would be based more on cities (Athens, Sparta and Corinth for example) than wider regions.

Religion played a large part in their lives and frequent festivals to the gods were held. The most important of these took place at Olympia, in the shadow of the mountain on top of which the gods themselves perched and watched (very, very closely if the myths are to be believed) the affairs of humankind. In about 776 the king of a small city called Elis journeyed to the famous oracle at Delphi. The oracles would become renowned for their ability to tell the future. However, great care had to be taken in the interpretation for, like an ancient Greek version of Nostradamus, the oracle tended to talk in riddles. The danger was always that the recipient of an oracle's advice tended to hear what they wished to hear, with occasional spectacular adverse results.

The King of Elis wished to discover how battles between the Greeks could be brought to an end, which gives an insight into the martial values that the city states held and implies that this was a rough, tough world to live in. The oracles came up with one of their better ideas, suggesting that the games held in honour of the gods at Olympia should be declared a time of truce.

As in modern times, the Olympic Games never brought peace (on the very day that the Beijing Games began in AD 2008, Russian tanks trundled into Georgia) but they did offer at least the hope of it. From then on, the Games were held every four years, for a period that eventually ran into months. It was a splendid concept – like so many other splendid concepts it was flawed in the execution, but a reminder to all and sundry that war was not part of man's inevitable lot on this earth.

However, a problem for the various peoples who inhabited the Greek peninsula was that the stock of workable land was limited by sea and mountain. There was simply not enough viable territory to go around. As a consequence, Greek outposts appeared wider afield. Whether or not these were colonies is a matter of debate; some of them certainly seem to have held a nominal allegiance to states back in the 'mother country' but they must have developed considerable latitude in their politics given the distances involved and the difficulties in communication that these indicated.

Some of these outposts were in Ionia, where Homer himself came from, but these Hellenic adventurers also looked westwards for outlets for their energies too. Their ships journeyed the watery roads to Sicily, founding what would become great cities such as Syracuse. From here, an expansion to the mainland Italian Peninsula was a logical next step. Greek trading posts began to sprout up around, for example, the Bay of Naples. Greek culture began to take root across an ever-growing expanse.

There were other peoples already living on the Italian Peninsula, who did not yet have the organisation or the technological capabilities of the Hellenes but shared some cultural similarities, particularly from the use of a closely connected group of languages based on what would become known as Latin. One such group was centred around the banks of the River Tiber.

There were two towns close to each other here, called Lavinium and Alba Longa. The latter was an offshoot of the first, set up when the population of Lavinium became too large. As often happens, the two towns, once joined by an umbilical cord, became rivals, though both shared a king. In around 776, this ruler's name was Numitor. He was dethroned by his brother, Amulius, who then murdered his nephews so that they could not displace him and commanded that his niece, Rhea Silvia, should forever remain a virgin so that she could not produce an heir to threaten him.

As in many such tales, the gods were not happy with this scandalous behaviour and one of them, Mars, the god of war, seduced Rhea Silvia and she then fell pregnant and produced twins. News of this soon leaked out and Amulius, in a fit of temper, ordered that they should be thrown in the Tiber and drowned. However, the best-laid plans of such villains often end in frustration due to the intervention of fate. The twins were found in the rushes by a she-wolf who brought them up as two of her own brood.

They were soon found by a herdsman who named them Romulus and Remus. In the best tradition of such tales, the two boys grew into fine young men, overthrew the traitorous Amulius and restored Numitor to his rightful position. The twins then built a settlement on the site of the place where they had been saved from what seemed a certain death. However, this did not conclude with the fairy-tale ending desired. The two brothers grew envious of each other, each wanting to outdo his sibling. It was not long before the two came to blows, as a result of which Remus was slain and Romulus became sole ruler. The settlement they had built, Rome, was named after him.

This appalling finale was played out, according to tradition, in 753 BC. Archaeologists confirm that a settlement stood here sometime between 1000 and 800 BC but the remainder of the story has fantastical elements that are impossible to take literally. However, as in the story of Troy, maybe there are elements of truth in all this, of two factions in the early settlement of Rome of which one eventually emerged triumphant. Although it would be centuries before Rome emerged as a superpower, even at its zenith the Eternal City would often be at the mercy of mobs and factions.

The glory of Rome lay far in the future; that of Assyria had seemed to be in the past when the first millennium BC began. The nomadic Aramean tribes had appeared to undermine the very foundations of Assyrian greatness. But, like a dying star, there would be one last flare-up of this giant of Mesopotamia before it was subsumed by a new superpower in its own part of the world.

The instigator of this revival was a king named Ashur-dan II. He launched a ferocious fightback against the Arameans, who had usurped large chunks of land which had traditionally been part of the Assyrian patrimony, though he did not recover all the territory that had been lost. Instead he strengthened the core heartland of Assyria and helped make it secure. Villagers who had been driven out were encouraged to make their way back to their traditional homelands, refugee returnees who helped to put steel back into Assyria having for so long been tossed about by Aramean incursions.

This was merely the beginning of a newly expansive Assyrian Empire, built on a foundation of terror and ruled with a grip of iron. Babylon had always been a forbidden fruit for kings of Assyria, even when the old city had been so weak as to provide easy pickings for a much more powerful neighbour. This was the sacred city of Marduk, the great Babylonian god, and no good would come of desecrating its sanctity. For a while Babylon was safe, but it must have looked on in awed horror as its northern neighbour appeared to be sharpening its claws again.

In the reign of Ashurnasirpal II (911–859 BC) the Assyrians felt confident enough to move northwards. A new city was built up at Nineveh, protected by massive gates guarded by gargantuan statues half-bull and half-human, looking on in terrifying disdain at those who walked through the entrances they flanked. These monumental statements of power can still be seen in some of the great museums of the world, among the most potent symbols of any ancient culture that have survived the passage of time. Anyone looking on them for the first time cannot misinterpret the message of absolute power that they were meant to portray as they guarded the great wooden gates of wealthy, mighty cities.

In a statement of intent, Ashurnasirpal also crossed the Euphrates, one of the great boundaries of the ancient world. He then pushed on to the sea, washing his weapons in the Mediterranean. He followed this with a march down to the border with Babylonia, sacking a city right on the frontier as a warning to his southern neighbour to respect him, but he did not attempt to take the city of Babylon itself.

His son Shalmaneser III took up the gauntlet when he died. He also crossed the Euphrates, but unlike his father he did not leave the smaller nations he found in Palestine alone. For several centuries now, a Hebrew nation had been in existence, worshipping Yahweh, Jehovah, the one true god in a pure and monotheistic fashion. There were twelve tribes in Israel, but not at first a kingdom. The first king of this emerging nation was named Saul but it was his successor, David, who really created a coherent state.

David is one of the great heroes of Judaism and recent discoveries in AD 2005 of what some claim to be his palace in the Old City of Jerusalem have provoked fierce debate. Some say that the archaeologists who support the claim are inspired more by a desire to assert that this particular area of the city is part of the Jewish heritage, rather than any search for archaeological knowledge. Others naturally say that this is not true and that the site is really linked to David. This ongoing debate is a reminder that many people are very happy to claim that history is on their side in a particular argument without necessarily letting facts get in the way. Objectivity is not always a key feature of historical analysis.

The story of David introduces an important ingredient for those who wish to understand history. First of all, our historical record of him, contained in the Bible, was probably written 300 years after his life, which would in normal circumstances cause its accuracy to be regarded with some scepticism. But these are not normal circumstances, for the Bible as we know it is more a book of religious instruction that a historical record. Therefore, many Jews or Christians would not take kindly to having its reliability questioned any more than a Muslim would be happy for the details of Mohamed's acts outlined in the Quran to be queried or a Buddhist would feel comfortable with alleged inconsistencies in the life of the Buddha.

The historian therefore sails into choppy waters when they enter into a debate on the historical accuracy of a religious figure or text and sometimes objectivity is difficult. Archaeology can add or subtract credence from the historical record, but the task is not always easy. However, excavations at Khirbet Qeiyafa in Israel in 2008 did uncover a complex gate to the fortified small city there, which has been dated to the time of David, suggesting that the state there was at that moment a reasonably powerful if small kingdom. An excavation at the site of Tel Dan, also in Israel, in 1993 unearthed a black basalt *stela* inscribed with the words 'House of David', so we do have some supporting evidence for the existence of David other than the Bible.

David's son and successor, Solomon, who is believed to have reigned just after 1000 BC, had managed to take advantage of the relative weakness of far bigger neighbours to carve out a localised dominance for himself (again, whether or not archaeological evidence to support the existence of a king called Solomon has been found remains a matter of bitter debate). To the north and dotted along the coast had been powerful local enemies, the Philistines, but they had been subdued. The Egyptian kingdom was heading towards another of its regular periods of decline and was currently too self-absorbed to involve itself in the affairs of Palestine. To the east, the Assyrian revival had not yet gathered momentum.

According to the Bible, Solomon achieved local dominance and became a wealthy king renowned for his wisdom. In honour of his god he had built a magnificent temple, which would become one of the most sacred sites in the world. He also built up strong trading networks, reaching down as far south as the tip of Arabia, from whence the fabled Queen of Sheba may have come. But Israel had declined after Solomon's death. The kingdom split into two, the rump of Israel in the north and Judah in the south.

Phoenicia lay adjacent to these territories. During the time of King David, some Phoenician lands had come under the control of the Israelites, though Tyre always remained independent. King Hiram of Tyre was on good terms with King Solomon and provided building materials for his great temple. Trade cemented their alliance. The Phoenicians naturally supplied cedar wood, their prime export, to Solomon and he in return traded grain and oil. The Phoenicians had also started their colonising activity by this time, with a settlement being set up under their dominion in Cyprus.

By this time, the Phoenicians were already setting out on the adventurous naval expeditions for which they would become famous. One such, in conjunction with Solomon, was down the Red Sea to the land of Ophir (either in Somalia or Yemen); the fleet came back laden with gold. (Could this be the source of the mysterious tale of King Solomon's Mines? An interesting speculation but nothing more, sadly.)

One thing the Israelites and Phoenicians did not generally agree on was religion. The Hebrew people were generally monotheistic, though it should be noted that there are frequent references in the Bible to experimentation with the gods of other nations. One such incident was that of the Golden Calf, where Yahweh was believed by some of the Children of Israel to have deserted his people, and they turned to other gods instead. At other times, so the Old Testament tells us, they worshipped the god Baal, who was a Phoenician deity.

The Phoenicians were polytheistic. The main goddess was Astarte (the Biblical Ashtoret or Ashtoreth), who later became regarded as synonymous with the Greek Aphrodite, while Baal, the principal god, may be regarded as a similar being to Kronos, or perhaps Zeus. Phoenician cities would adopt their own chief god, so we might find Baal described as 'the god of Mount Sephanon' or 'lord of the promontory', for example. There were many other lesser gods too, now little understood, like Dagon, probably the god of wheat. There was also a young god, killed and resurrected, whose original name in Phoenician is unknown but who became the Greek Adonis.

To the south of this region, the Egyptians had, since about 1070 BC, been involved in internal infighting that had weakened them significantly. However, around 950 a Libyan general, Sheshonq, had managed to unite the kingdom. He inveigled himself into a position to declare himself pharaoh. As a way of securing his dubious claim, he resorted to the oldest tactic of all; he would enhance his legitimacy by restoring Egypt's lost glories through foreign conquests.

The Hebrew territories in Palestine had by then lurched into a period of decline following the death of Solomon. Divided as they were, they seemed to be ripe for conquest. Sheshonq I led his armies towards Jerusalem. Despite the fact that he did not conquer the city, he returned home laden with booty. This included the finest riches of the temple treasury. The only way the King of Judah, Reheboam, could keep his throne was to buy off the attackers with the most precious treasures in his kingdom. Sheshonq returned to Egypt well satisfied. He did not really need to possess these lands when he could help himself to Judah's riches.

However, this resurgence of Egyptian power was a temporary phenomenon. The country soon plunged back into a state of perpetual chaos, dividing into a number of parts all at each other's throats. A sure sign of the confusion that shaped the political landscape in Egypt was the coexistence of twenty-second, twenty-third and twenty-fourth dynasties all ruling simultaneously in different parts of the country. In such a situation, further adventures into Palestine were unlikely.

Therefore the weak Hebrew kingdoms were left alone until the reign of the Assyrian king Shalmaneser III (858–824 BC), who now decided to lead his army against that of

Israel. Despite the perception that the Assyrian army must have been stronger than that of their opponents, it appears that the battle that followed was bitterly fought, with heavy losses on both sides. In the end the Assyrians decided to withdraw, with the Hebrews, for the time being, still free.

This does not appear to have been the end of the matter, however. On a monument known as the Black Obelisk there are carvings that show a number of kings paying tribute to Shalmaneser. One of them is Jehu, the King of Israel. The reality appears to be that Israel could only survive by the use of careful alliances with neighbours such as the Aramean tribes, whose main base was at Damascus, or the Phoenicians on the coast of Lebanon. These old alliances had now evaporated, perhaps mismanaged, and Israel could not stand alone. Not yet a conquered nation, Israel nevertheless was forced to pay tribute to the Assyrians to survive.

Phoenicia was also forced to regularly pay tribute to the Assyrians during this period. An advance into the region is mentioned in 852 BC, although a battle fought appeared to be indecisive. Between 848 and 846 BC, there are nevertheless Assyrian records claiming that Tyre and Sidon paid tribute to Assyria. By the time of the death of Shalmaneser in 824 though, Phoenicia appeared to have been largely left to its own devices. The Phoenicians were soon back on their naval adventures. An internal squabble in around 813 BC led to the sister of the Phoenician king (a man named Pygmalion) fleeing across the Mediterranean and establishing a base at a place called Carthage.

These west Syrian adventures did not offer the most desirable conquests for Shalmaneser, for whom a far greater prize was about to become available. The King of Babylon died, a situation which led to a vicious succession dispute between two of his sons. Shalmaneser stepped in, initially putting one of the claimants on the throne. He strengthened his position by marrying a son to a Babylonian princess. This was, for the moment, enough.

He then turned north-west, towards the region known as Que, a tiny remnant of what had once been the Hittite Empire. Renowned most of all for its silver mines, Shalmaneser helped himself to its riches. He then swung in the opposite direction, towards the Elamites in Iran. These were raids, calculated to extract tribute and a policy of non-interference. Two minor tribes were among those in the region who complied. Known as the Mada and the Parsua, they would within a few centuries become better known as the Medes and the Persians.

Shalmaneser could not ensure the loyalty of Assyria, let alone the rest of the region, and when he died he was in the process of putting down a revolt. He appointed his son Shamshi-Adad as king instead of his previously nominated heir, who was at the head of the revolt. This was a major conflict and at one stage Shamshi-Adad fled to Babylon to seek sanctuary. He retook Assyria with Babylonian help but was obliged to accept a subsidiary relationship to the King of Babylon as his price. He had no option but to concur, but he never forgave the insulting manner of the Babylonians.

Safely installed, he then resolved to get his own back on Babylon. He led a great army down towards the city. When a Babylonian force came out to meet him, it was systematically destroyed. A puppet king was installed on the throne of Babylon but when he rebelled soon after, Shamshi-Adad decided to drop all pretence and claimed the throne for himself. When he died in 811, he was the first man to be king of both Assyria and Babylon.

During this period (the dating is a matter of ongoing and vigorous dispute, though followers of the Baha'i faith date the following events to around 1,000 years before Christ), an important new religion developed which was to be the dominant creed in Persia until the advent of Islam nearly 2,000 years later. It was preached by a man named Zarathustra (Zoroaster in the Greek variant of his name), who espoused the doctrine that there was a supreme deity among the gods whose name was Ahura Mazda. This god was the creator of all that is good and led the forces of righteousness in the ongoing battle against evil.

The faith still survives today, with its sacred flame guarded zealously by Zoroastrian priests. The flame burned on Mount Asnavant, where the prophet himself meditated for years on the secrets and meaning of life. There was much that later religions found attractive in his doctrines: the concept of free will, of final judgement, of heaven and hell, of one god. Judaism, Christianity and Islam were all influenced by these teachings: Islam regarded Zoroaster respectfully as one in a sacred line of prophets and his followers were accorded positive treatment as 'Peoples of the Book', along with Jews and Christians.

On the far side of Asia, the ruling Zhou dynasty found itself under pressure. Those nominally in command of the region of China that they ruled found themselves constantly threatened by petty princelings always looking for an opportunity to further their own vested interests. In an attempt to counteract this, a complex bureaucracy was created, with kings attempting to govern through administrative conventions and regulations. The difficulty was compounded by raids from barbarians striking at the heart of China's developing civilisation, a recurring theme for thousands of years.

There were also occasional revolts and coups, and it was not unknown for Zhou emperors' reigns to be ended by an assassin. There were also periods of famine and drought and, at a time when such events were linked superstitiously to divine approbation or otherwise for an emperor, such situations inevitably undermined a ruler's credibility. Earthquakes sometimes struck with similar results; they undermined not only the foundations of buildings but also of the state itself.

Barbarian assaults increased in intensity, sometimes aided by dissatisfied elements within the kingdom. The most serious of these was launched by a group of invaders known as the Quan Rong. The Zhou king, Yu, called on his nobles to help, but his plea fell on deaf ears. Yu was killed fighting for his kingdom and his palace was then razed to the ground. His concubine, with whom he was besotted and whom he had made his queen, was taken back with the Quan Rong as part of their booty.

This dramatic denouement had a drastic effect on the kingdom, for the capital, Hao, in the west of the country, seemed to Yu's successor P'ing to be too exposed in its situation. So in 771 he moved his capital to Loyang in the east of the region. It would remain the centre of the Zhou dynasty for the rest of its life, which was to last 500 years.

We are moving ever closer to a period where our knowledge of history is clearer, where written records are more voluminous and archaeological evidence more easily deciphered. The Middle East in particular had become a centre of civilisation, as had India and China as well as Greece. Elsewhere events are less easy to interpret, largely because written records do not exist. The only reason for giving these areas less attention is that we know less of them, and there is therefore less to say.

However, from these regions, still in what we would term a pre-historic period, there are occasional signs that hint at important future outcomes. Take for example the Olmecs in what is now Mexico. By the beginning of the first millennium BC they had become established in the region. What we know of them is largely limited to archaeological evidence, but from this we know that they built great earth pyramids. These they festooned with magnificent carvings and impressively shaped artefacts of jade.

The civilisation spread from its base in eastern Mexico down into regions such as El Salvador. Where they originate from we do not know and most other things about them are speculative. It has, for example, been suggested that the hieroglyphic systems which would eventually evolve in the Americas would originate with them, but this is unproven. However, what is more certain is that the Aztec pantheon of deities originated with the Olmecs, and there is therefore a strong suggestion of continuity with this early civilisation and its own great pyramids, which the Aztecs later developed into the great monuments we can see today.

Inevitably we will return to one thing time and again: that history works at a different pace in different parts of the world. Most of Africa, parts of Europe and all of the Americas and Australasia at this time developed in splendid isolation on all but a local basis. In certain regions there were interconnections though, the east Mediterranean and Greece for example. India was to an extent also connected via trade mechanisms. We are by now on the verge of an era where in some parts of the world the political geography was about to become more interconnected, and the affairs of cultures and regimes previously separate were about to become more intertwined, with sometimes drastic results.

7

MELTDOWN IN MESOPOTAMIA

The Final Glory of Assyria and the Brief Revival of Babylon (750–600 BC)

Assyria had been a powerful player in the politics of Mesopotamia for a millennium. However, it appeared that its best days were now behind it. The incursions of the nomadic Arameans showed its apparent weakness to its neighbours and they, like wolves scenting an injured prey, nibbled away at what they believed to be the remains of Assyria.

These were changed days. Shalmaneser IV, who came to the throne of this decaying kingdom in 783, was forced to enter into alliance with Jeroboam II, the King of Israel, to fight off further Aramean attacks. To seek the help of what was a relatively weak state in the times of Assyrian greatness would have been unthinkable, but, by now, the unthinkable had to be thought.

To the north of Mesopotamia, a group of people known as Hurrians, descendants of the now submerged Mitanni, chiselled out mountain kingdoms for themselves. Assyrian bullying in previous centuries had forced them to unite in coalitions, bound together by a common enemy that appeared to threaten their very existence. They had been an easy source of slaves in the now disappearing days of Assyrian glory and they longed for revenge against those who had previously exploited them cruelly.

Strangely, they envied parts of the Assyrian way of life – though this was perhaps not so strange, as many later so-called 'barbarian tribes' would adopt some aspects of the Roman way of life when Rome went into decline. They adopted Assyrian writing and royal customs but this did not lessen their resentment or their determination to turn the tables on their traditional oppressors. The Assyrians called them the Urartu, from which title the traditional resting place of Noah's Ark, Ararat, takes its name. Assyrian attacks attempting to dislodge them from their mountain fastnesses failed to budge them.

As if being eaten up by a vigorous tumour, Assyria was also decaying from within. Increasingly its nobles ruled with a huge amount of local discretion, ignoring royal authority with impunity. Perhaps worst of all, Babylon, the ultimate symbolic prize in Mesopotamia, declared its freedom from Assyrian rule. The Urartu, buoyed by all these signs of terminal decline, took over much of the lands once held by the Hittites in the west and entered into alliance with two rising powers, the Medes and the Persians, in the east.

The very walls of Assur began to decline, there being neither the money nor apparently the will to keep them in a good state of repair. Caleh, the administrative centre of Assyria, even attempted to break free. Assyria was in free fall. Then Pul, once governor of Caleh, seized the throne, a tarnished prize, almost in the gutter. He then changed his name, adopting that used by former and far more successful Assyrian kings and, as Tiglath-Pileser III, he proceeded to rebuild the realm he had usurped to a position of previously unmatched greatness.

There was no warning of this resurgence, which made it all the more astonishing, but the violence that accompanied it was severe. For centuries, Assyria had had to stand by almost helplessly, watching while its power crumbled. Now, in its efforts to re-climb the greasy pole to achieve dominance in the region, it appeared that there would be no lengths to which its ruler or his successors would not go. Decades of brutality probably never witnessed anywhere before were about to be unleashed.

Tiglath-Pileser's initial problem was that Babylon too had a strong ruler, Nabonassar, who was a Chaldean (from the southern part of Mesopotamia bordering the northern shores of the Persian Gulf). He was too strong to dislodge so Tiglath-Pileser entered into an alliance with him. Despite his origins, Nabonassar was at war with both Chaldeans, men of a shared origin within himself, and with Arameans. Tiglath-Pileser offered to help him but instead stuffed Babylonian cities full of his men. When Babylon finally fought off its external enemies, it was only to find that Tiglath-Pileser had annexed it by stealth.

Nabonassar was too weak to resist and instead remained as a client king. Tiglath-Pileser then moved north, against the Urartu. In a harsh campaign, much of this difficult terrain was conquered though the Urartu king fled north to rule over an emaciated rump of the territories he had once held. In 743 BC the Assyrians moved into Phoenicia, establishing provinces there, though some cities, including Byblos and Tyre, managed to retain a degree of autonomy while being forced to pay tribute to Tiglath-Pileser.

In the eastern part of Asia Minor, a people called the Phrygians had established themselves. The region was overwhelmed by the Assyrian advance but the west held on. The Phrygians here sought a new king and asked their oracle who it should be. He replied that it should be the first man who subsequently arrived in a wagon. He was a farmer, and his name was Midas, another man who is more strongly established in myth than he is in history. He married a Greek woman, and traded with Greek cities on the eastern shores of the Aegean, making him immensely rich, hence all those stories of his touch that turned everything to gold.

Tiglath-Pileser let him be, with too many targets elsewhere to worry about. A civil war in Babylon needed his attention following the death of Nabonassar. Putting it down, he decided to drop all pretence and entered the city to claim it for himself. The Chaldeans too were cowed into submission. When Tiglath-Pileser died in 727 BC, Assyria was much more secure than it had been for centuries.

Tiglath-Pileser's successor, Shalmaneser V, was an obdurate man who was determined to build on the successes of his father. He spent five years besieging the Phoenician port of Tyre and then devastated Israel (still a separate state from Judah, with the city of Jerusalem, in the south). Israel had sought help from an unlikely source in Egypt, traditionally so often an enemy; however, now both were threatened by this resurgent and acquisitive empire based in Assyria.

Not that it was clear who ruled in Egypt, which had declined spectacularly. To the south of Egypt, Nubia had often been under the thumb of the exploitative kingdoms downstream (downstream, given the flow of the Nile, in this case meant the north). It had by now managed to break free and form its own kingdom, a mixture of Egyptians and other Africans from further south. Its capital was on a bend in the Nile at Jebel Barkal. It modelled itself on Egypt, worshipping Egyptian gods and indulging in royal marriages between close relatives such as brothers and sisters as the pharaohs did.

In fact, in many ways Egypt and Nubia were extensions of each other. The Nubians had a strong culture of their own though one that was heavily linked to Egypt. Traditionally Nubia had been composed of two entities, Kush and Meroe, but by 1000 BC the former was in the ascendancy in Nubia (which may be roughly equated with the northern part of modern Sudan). The Nubians were famed for their skills as archers, and a remarkable survival in Cairo Museum sees forty models of them marching in organised ranks carrying their bows and striding out barefoot towards their enemies.

To protect themselves from the Egyptians, the Nubians built themselves a new capital at Napata. As Egypt grew weaker and Nubia stronger, the divided states in the chaotic northern lands decided to put aside their differences and unite in a campaign against the Nubians. However, they were overwhelmed and as a result a Nubian king, Piankhi, found himself ruler of Egypt; the servant had become the master and the Nubians, who had so often provided their highly regarded troops for Egyptian armies, now found themselves in charge. For a while, Egypt would at least remain undisturbed by Assyria. Shalmaneser had other targets to distract him and anyway he died soon after.

Any thoughts that this might somehow remove the intense pressure on the as yet unconquered parts of the Middle East were ruthlessly dispatched soon after. Shalmaneser's successor, his brother Sargon II (who came to the throne in 721 BC), was one of the mightiest and most feared of all Assyrian kings. There are strong suspicions that his was the hand behind his brother's sudden death and, if his reign did indeed begin in blood, this was a completely appropriate portent for the years of pain that were to follow.

Israel was one early target, with its capital Samaria not subdued during Shalmaneser's campaigning. Sargon brought the siege there, which had been dragging on for ages, to a successful conclusion. He then introduced one of the most disturbing of all his policies to those he captured, that of mass deportation, ostentatiously claiming that 27,290 of the captured Israelites were strewn like chaff blown by the wind across a wide sweep of land from Asia Minor in the west to the lands of the Medes in the east.

The Arameans were also brutally subdued. Assyria even developed its sea power so that its navy, too, became formidable. Sargon's ships swept across the narrow divide between the Asian mainland and the island of Cyprus, forcing it to pay tribute. He then turned on the Urartu. The mountain kingdom, or at least the rump of it that limped on, had managed to maintain a precarious existence in the north. Defended by a series of warning beacons which had been erected on the highest points of the mountains, creating an early alarm system should the country be invaded, even this remote land was not safe from Sargon's ruthless determination.

In a well-planned, methodical campaign, Sargon led his army into what remained of the Urartu. In the tough fighting that followed, the Urartu king was forced to flee for his life and his emaciated kingdom shrank even more, though it still survived with a tenacity that was admirable. Sargon then returned to crush an attempted usurpation of power in Babylon. So great was his reputation that ambassadors came from as far afield as Egypt and Ethiopia seeking to protect themselves from the Assyrian juggernaut. When Sargon died in 704, Assyria was feared across the Middle East.

Sargon was succeeded on his death by his son Sennacherib. The accession of the new king was quickly followed by a revolt in Babylon. An initial attempt to restore Assyrian rule in the city was rebuffed. As was often the case in such situations throughout history, it was a big mistake to defeat a superpower for it made a crushing response an inevitability. Winning a battle was one thing, winning a war quite another.

The Babylonians attempted to reaffirm their loyalty to Sennacherib when he arrived outside their gates with a huge army soon after by opening them wide. This merely made it easier to sack the city, taking, it was said, a quarter of a million people off into a life of slavery and teaching Babylon a lesson Sennacherib hoped she would not forget in a hurry. The king then turned his attention to the west, where storm clouds were brewing.

As he turned in this direction, he learned that an Egyptian army was moving up to confront him. The King of Judah, Hezekiah, fearing the Assyrian threat, had entered into an alliance with the Egyptians, and so too had the Chaldeans. Judah's ruler had demonstrated his loyalty to the alliance by holding as a captive a local king who had been a supporter of Sennacherib. This no doubt seemed a bold and worthy move when the Assyrians were hundreds of miles away but it appeared merely foolhardy when a large body of their soldiers turned up outside of Jerusalem.

In the face of the massive threat to his holy city, Hezekiah quickly capitulated and let his high-ranking captive go. This was enough for Sennacherib for the moment though he made a mental note to hand out more appropriate retribution at a later stage. Having put down more opposition locally, he soon after returned to Jerusalem, this time to punish it thoroughly.

A great army tied a suffocating noose round the city. The end, it seemed, was a foregone conclusion. However, just when Jerusalem appeared to be on the point of capitulation, the Assyrians were forced to move off by an outbreak of what sounds like plague. Pious Jews in the city attributed this naturally enough to the intervention of Yahweh, though Mesopotamian invaders had, as it turned out, certainly not finished with Judah yet.

Domestically, Sennacherib's reign is notable for his establishment of the city of Nineveh as his capital; it would remain so for the remainder of Assyria's independent existence. He also led an army into Elam to punish its people for their constant aggression and troublemaking against the Assyrians. To do so, he employed a mercenary navy of Phoenician sailors from Tyre, Sidon and Cyprus. They sailed down the Tigris and were then transferred across land to the Euphrates, where they completed their journey to the Persian Gulf. His army were victorious wherever they went and a crushing triumph was won.

The Elamites, though, were a dangerous and determined foe. They burned for revenge and plotted carefully to get it. Six years after Sennacherib's triumph the time had come. One of the darkest moments of Assyria's entire history was at hand. A lightning raid across the border succeeded in capturing the heir apparent and taking him back to Elam. This must have infuriated Sennacherib, but worse was to follow.

Babylon had been a constant thorn in the side for recent Assyrian kings. Now the Elamites overthrew Sennacherib's representative in the city and installed their own. The Assyrian king came down from the north in a terrible rage. In graphic detail, the chronicles tell how he cut out the entrails of his enemies, struck off their testicles and 'tore out their privates like the seeds of cucumbers in June'. Alongside narratives that tell how his horses were swimming in rivers of blood, it is clear that Sennacherib was not a happy man.

Like an angry lion with a thorn in his paw, Sennacherib now moved down on Babylon itself. To understand the significance of what followed, it is important to recognise the place that Babylon held in the ancient world. This was a sacred city, not just to Babylonians but to Assyrians too. The god Marduk, whose earthly home was Babylon, was respected, even feared, by the Assyrians. There were many in Nineveh as well as Babylon who would have been worried at any mark of disdain towards him.

Unconcerned at all this, Sennacherib came storming through the gates of the city. When he had last taken Babylon, although he had treated its people harshly, he had taken care to protect its fabric. Not this time. He commanded his soldiers to torch the city, razing everything, temples and statues of the gods included. Then he dug trenches to flood what was left. It was a brutal attack, perhaps one of the harshest and most complete sacks of all antiquity. Even Assyrians muttered that nothing good could come of such sacrilege.

All Sennacherib's immediate enemies seemed to be bested. Given his violent life, his end was apt. There is no further mention of his heir apparent, which must surely mean that he was put to death while an Elamite hostage. Then, seven years after his devastation of Babylon, Sennacherib was assassinated by his own sons while making offerings to the gods in Nineveh.

This act of patricide led to a veritable explosion within Assyria. From the mess that ensued, one of Sennacherib's sons, Esarhaddon, emerged as king. Despite the apparent strength of Assyria, it was soon under immense pressure. A new force of nomadic barbarians had emerged, Cimmerians, who were even now pushing into Phrygia. Among those who perished in the violence they unleashed was the renowned poor man made good, Midas. He was buried in a mausoleum at Gordian; constructed of wood, it is currently the oldest known edifice made of timber still surviving (though it should be noted that not all archaeologists think that the tomb attributed to him is in fact his).

Esarhaddon moved up to face up to the Cimmerians and destroyed them in a bitter fight. He now turned his attention further afield towards the oldest remaining civilisation in the world, Egypt. The Middle East was now set for a clash of the superpowers, though one was seemingly in the ascendant, the other struggling desperately to reignite past glories. However, since the installation of a pharaonic dynasty from Nubia, an element of stability had been reintroduced and Egypt was more united than it had been for some time.

The Assyrian attack on Egypt was vigorously resisted with aggressive tactics. The pharaoh Tirhakah moved his army up to Ashkelon on the coast of Palestine. Esarhaddon was forced back and Tirhakah returned to Egypt as a conquering hero. But shortly after, in 671, Esarhaddon was back. The Assyrian king led his men in a devastating attack that punched through the Egyptian borders as if they were made of paper. The Egyptian army was swept aside with almost complete impunity. The Assyrians marched on Memphis, thrashing Tirhakah's army in a decisive clash there and forcing him back to Nubia.

Esarhaddon's tactics now were simple. The former pharaoh's family, who had been captured more or less en masse, was taken back to Nineveh as hostages for Egypt's future good behaviour. Governors supposedly friendly to Assyrian interests were installed in the country. However, as soon as Esarhaddon's back was turned Egypt broke away from its new overlord. Esarhaddon, no doubt infuriated at this unwelcome change of allegiance, led his army back towards the Nile but never made it as he died on the way.

His successor Ashurbanipal determined to complete what his father had started in Egypt. This time his army marched as far south as Thebes (modern Luxor) and took some of Esarhaddon's hostages back from Nineveh, where they were put in charge of affairs in the re-conquered country; they had presumably been suitably trained as to what was expected of them. However, Egypt refused to lie down and a revolt, led by Tantamani, son of Tirhakah, was initially successful.

An Assyrian king could not afford such a reversal on his curriculum vitae and Ashurbanipal resolved to lead another army to Egypt and crush the country for good. He returned to Thebes and sacked the city in a ruthless act of destruction that became a byword for terror. Religious monuments such as the Temple of Amun were razed and the city looted of all its many treasures. Now, with the job done, Ashurbanipal installed a man he knew he could trust, a local warlord named Psammetichus who had been in alliance with him, as sole ruler of Egypt.

Except that Psammetichus had no intention of being a puppet to an Assyrian puppeteer. He quickly took advantage of the distance between Assyria and Egypt by increasingly asserting his autonomy. Eventually entering into an agreement with Gyges, King of Lydia (in Asia Minor, now Turkey) to co-operate against the Assyrians, he turned on Assyrian soldiers stationed in Egypt in a night of the long knives and ejected them from the country. Psammetichus had managed to make himself a genuine pharaoh, free to operate without foreign control.

Phoenicia, too, was kept under the Assyrian thumb. The parts of this narrow strip of land that lay between the Mediterranean on the one side and the Lebanese mountains on the other had come under increasing domination from the resurgent power to the east. Tyre had always tried to hang on to as much independence as possible and kept its own king. When it rebelled, the uprising was quickly crushed. Although the king hung on to his throne, he was less successful in retaining his daughter, who was taken back to the regal harem as a concubine.

Further revolts were to break out, though. When others aspired to succeed where Tyre had failed the response was brutal:

> The people of Ushu, who had not cowered before their governors, and had not paid their tribute, their yearly gifts, I slew. Among those insubmissive people I applied the rod. Their gods, their people, I carried off to Assyria. The insubmissive people of Akka [Acre] I slaughtered. Their corpses I hung on stakes, surrounding the city with them.

Assyria undoubtedly appeared to be the dominant power in the Middle East; the images of these wretches on blood-stained poles are appropriate pictures to sum up these terrible years. The secret of Assyria's success was its well-organised army, with well-drilled and armed men, specialising in the various elements of warfare – infantrymen, archers and cavalry – with tactics that pulled these together in a coordinated fashion. With their weapons of iron and ruthless discipline it seemed that none could resist the Assyrian juggernaut. Yet in all these triumphs lay the seeds of Assyria's ultimate demise.

The Greeks had a word for it – hubris, what modern vernacular might term 'believing your own publicity'. The Assyrians believed that they were destined to rule the world. One Assyrian king indeed, not content with the moniker of 'ruler of the world', named himself 'ruler of the universe'. All great empires, however omnipotent they appear to be at the time, are doomed to fade away – one of the greatest lessons of history, and one that always has to be learned anew. And often, convinced of their own supremacy, these empires parade across the world stage oblivious to the dangers that eventually overwhelm them.

To the east of Assyria lay Madua, home of the Medes. In the past disunited, a kingdom had now been formed there, centred on their city of Ecbatana. This was one of the most amazing settlements of the ancient world. It had a series of seven walls. The city was designed in such a way that each succeeding wall was at a higher level than the one outside of it. In medieval military architecture such a style became very fashionable. Known as 'concentric castles', these later fortresses gave defenders a huge advantage as archers could fire on attackers from several lines of walls at once. What is less well known is that Ecbatana was designed in such a fashion 2,000 years before.

To add to the visual effect, each level of the walls had bastions painted in different colours. Working from the outside in, these were white, black, red, blue, orange, silver and gold respectively. Inside the inner layer was the royal palace itself. The city, built at an altitude of 6,000 feet above sea level, must have made a stunning impression on any who saw it.

In the year 675 BC, the king of the Medes, Phraortes, attacked and conquered the Parsua. Sensing weaknesses inside Assyria itself, he then audaciously attacked Nineveh, the empire's heart. His attack was beaten off but, in another sign of imminent demise, the Assyrians – overstretched by their extended conquests in recent times – were forced to ask for help from barbarians to protect their frontiers. Their allies were Scythians from what are now known as the Russian steppes. Initially the tactic appeared to be successful.

The Medes and Persians were repulsed so vigorously that Phraortes was slain and his throne taken by Madius, chief of the Scythians.

All this happened in the reign of the Assyrian king Ashurbanipal, but his apparent triumph bought only temporary respite, for his brother was jealous of his position and started a vicious civil war against him, based on the recently rebuilt city of Babylon. Almost inevitably, the rebels were helped by that other old Assyrian enemy, the Elamites. Ashurbanipal pushed down to Babylon itself, initiating a horrific three-year siege. During the course of the siege, it was said that the Babylonians were so desperate for food that parents ate their children to survive.

When the city at last fell, a bloodbath of colossal proportions was unleashed. Ashurbanipal gloated that 'their carved up bodies I fed to dogs, to pigs, to wolves, to eagles, to birds of the heavens, to fishes of the deep'. His bloodlust was not yet sated and he moved into Elam, sacking Susa itself. Thousands of Elamites were deported to the region of Samaria in Israel. But he failed to push home his advantage and instead left Elam to its own devices. It is true that its power was broken, but this merely left a vacuum for opportunistic neighbours to step into.

It was the Parsua tribesmen who moved into the breach. They advanced into a broken Elamite kingdom with no resistance. The Assyrians left them undisturbed and the Parsua established a more permanent home for themselves, to which the name of Persia eventually became attached. When Cyrus I became king of the Persians he still accepted the overlordship of Madius but it was only a matter of time before this changed.

Records for the latter part of Ashurbanipal's reign are sketchy but from what we can glean from them it appears that the king faced increasing internal pressures, perhaps explaining his failure to stop the Parsua advance. Towards the end of his life, effective rule passed to his son Ashur-etil-ilani for reasons which are unclear but are likely to have been associated with violence. The Scythians were attacking Urartu, in the Assyrian sphere of influence, with impunity. Josiah, King of Judah, was also attacking Assyrian territory in the west in Israel itself.

Ashurbanipal died in 627 BC, and what followed was the complete meltdown of Assyria. A vicious civil war followed, with three different factions fighting for various rights in the kingdom. The chaotic scene was further convulsed by events in Madua. The Medes had been biding their time to overthrow their Scythian rulers and that moment had arrived. Taxed to the point of poverty by the Scythians, the Medes rose up against them and overturned the ruling regime. Their king, Cyarxes, organised his men into an efficient fighting machine, ready for action at a moment's notice.

In the meantime, Assyrian affairs deteriorated still further. In the south of the country, Nabopolassar, a Chaldean, pushed up towards Babylon. The cities in the region were powerless to resist his advance and the great city soon fell to him. He pushed on further into Assyria proper. At his side were new-found allies, the Medes and the Persians led by Cyarxes.

The Medes and Persians then took Assur. The allies then moved on Nineveh itself. A huge counter-attack by Scythian troops was rebuffed and at last the city fell. The inevitable orgy of death and rapine followed. The ejected Assyrians asked the Egyptians for help. A decisive battle against the Assyrian–Egyptian alliance was fought in 605 BC. Nabopolassar was old now and his army was led by his son and heir, Nebuchadnezzar. The conflict, which took place near the ancient city of Carchemish, appears to have been bloody and brutal. At the end of it, it appears the Assyrian army had been wiped out. The power of Assyria was broken, never again to be seen. A new power was about to announce itself to the world to take its place.

Another was forming in the western Mediterranean. Early references to Carthage immediately after its foundation are rare, but by about 650 BC the Carthaginians had established a colony on Ibiza. Rather like a child who has decided to leave the nest, Carthage had copied some of the habits of the eastern Phoenicians whose adventurism had given birth to the city but had now, other than that, largely gone its own way. Although other evidence of expansion at this time is scant, the modern holiday destination of Mahon on Minorca seems to derive its name from the Phoenician *Magon*. It is important to note, though, that these new colonies did not really become a Carthaginian Empire, as most of them developed a significant degree of autonomy in classic Phoenician tradition.

Our recent focus has been exclusively on the Middle East and the Mediterranean, where events would have a decisive effect on the shape of future world history. The demise of Assyria and the rise of the Medes and Persians was one crucial outcome. Although it was not yet clear, the power of Egypt was about to disappear too. Elsewhere, the future direction of Greece and even Rome had started to become more apparent; to these changes we will soon return.

However, there were also significant developments in China at this time. The west of the region ruled by the Zhou (bearing in mind that we are to an extent playing fast and loose with the term 'China', which was still a region centred on the Yellow River, much smaller than the country we know in modern times) had been virtually abandoned by the dynasty. King P'ing also stood by, powerless, while key members of his nobility jostled for position against each other.

This merely presaged greater problems in the future. Matters came to a head in the reign of Hsi, who came to the throne in 682 BC. The impetus behind a catastrophic series of events was once again a series of barbarian incursions. These came from two directions: the Ti from the north and the Yi from the south. One of the nobles supposedly accountable to the king was the Duke of Qi, in the east of the country. He looked on askance as the young king seemed to be incapable of providing leadership to resist the barbarian threat.

He therefore decided to claim military leadership of the Zhou lands for himself, declaring himself hegemon. This was certainly for selfish reasons but it did introduce an element of organisation into the forces facing the barbarians. In practical terms the Duke of Qi was in control of Zhou China, but he was content to let the king remain on the throne, a mere pawn albeit one living in some luxury. Even when Hsi died early, the duke made no attempt to seize his title for himself.

This established a precedent. However, there were other developments too that foreshadowed the future as far as China was concerned. During the reign of Hsi's grandson Hsiang, there was a vicious internal battle led by the king's brother, who wished to seize the crown for himself. In order to do so, he invited two barbarian tribes, the Ti and the Jung (also to the north), for assistance. Although initially these plans did not come to fruition, and a truce of sorts was hammered out between the two brothers, this was only a postponement of the problem.

Following the death of the hegemon of the day (who had been acting as a mediator between the hostile siblings), Hsiang decided to attempt to seize back power for himself. He approached the Ti for help, offering to marry a princess of their tribe if they would assist him. This was, as any ruler with a modicum of common sense would have realised, tantamount to inviting a cuckoo into the nest.

Ti help did Hsiang no practical good, for their invasion came to nothing. Seeing that they had brought him no benefit, he decided unilaterally to cancel their agreement and annul his marriage. This was a terrible miscalculation. The Ti, incensed at the arbitrary injustice of this cynical move, invaded Hsiang's lands. The king was forced to flee his capital. Into the breach stepped his warring brother, Shu Tai. He offered to marry the barbarian princess himself. His offer was accepted and he established a new capital at Wen, just 30 miles away from his brother's old seat of power.

Hsiang was not finished, though. He approached Duke Wen of the Chin, one of those noblemen who nominally recognised his authority as part of the Zhou kingdom, for help in removing the new regime. It was duly done, Shu Tai being slain in the process. Duke Wen was declared hegemon and proceeded to grab even more power and status than any of his predecessors had. To the south of the Zhou territories, which had established a strong degree of autonomy, a different tack was tried: a vast wall to keep the barbarians out. It was not what we call the Great Wall of China, but one of its early ancestors (in fact, what we think of as the Great Wall is a series of constructions added to and joined together over time). Elsewhere other parts of the Zhou lands also became more independent, until the king merely became a figurehead with little real influence and even less real power.

Four features may be identified here, which, taken as a whole, provide a neat summary of much of Chinese history for the next 2,000 years. Firstly, internal disputes had weakened the Zhou from within, leaving it an easy prey to external influences. Secondly, barbarian tribes did their utmost to take advantage of the chaos that ensued, often, it must be said, helped by elements of the Zhou elite themselves. Thirdly, the ruler had become a man with no real power, at the mercy of the fickle support of his nobles. Lastly, great walls had been built in an attempt to keep out the barbarian threat; against a determined enemy, they would prove to be surprisingly ineffective.

The events we have considered here were important in setting the scene for what was to come, for the world was on the verge of great changes. The century that now loomed, the years between 600 and 501 BC, was to be one of the most crucial in the story of mankind, as it did much to shape the direction of future history. Some dramatic developments were to ensue.

8

PHILOSOPHERS AND WARRIORS

The Lives of Confucius and Buddha and the Rise of the Persian Empire (600–501 BC)

The events of the sixth century BC were some of the most important in history. During this period a great Persian Empire was created, one which was to play a huge role in Middle Eastern affairs for a thousand years (and, in the way it then helped to shape the Islamic world, far beyond that, right through to the modern day). Equally as significant was the emergence of two very different philosophers in India and China, for the teachings they developed also continue to influence large portions of the world into our own times.

The East has a reputation for mystical religion that differs significantly from the West. The West, of course, has had its mystics, such as Thomas Aquinas or Saint Augustine, but in modern times even the Western world appears generally to look eastwards for its mystics if it looks for them at all. Two of the greatest figures of the East in both philosophical and historical terms are the Buddha and Confucius.

But sweeping generalisations must be avoided, however tempting they appear. The teachings of these men were very different. The philosophies espoused by the Buddha have little in common with those of Confucius. Neither would it be true to say that either man, great though they were, was universally representative of his culture. There were plenty of people within their own societies who held very different views than they did.

As always, it is impossible to understand the impact of deep thinkers such as these without appreciating something of the contemporary politics of the regions in which they lived. By this time, India was composed of a myriad of different groups, often at war with each other but also capable of negotiating a kind of precarious coexistence if the moment suited. A number of these kingdoms were named in Buddhist writings, with sixteen of them being specifically mentioned.

Many ancient societies were governed in a sensitive alliance between the secular, as epitomised by kings, and the religious, whose representatives were of course priests. Kings would seek the approval of the priesthood and there were occasions when some would suggest that the latter became too powerful – such happened from time to time in Egypt. But on the whole an equilibrium was struck. However, such was not the case in India.

Here, the *Brahmans* achieved dominance over the secular. They developed a complicated and constricting code, the precursor of the still-existing Indian caste system. Sacred Hindu writings described them as 'the highest on earth, the lord of all created beings'. This was a region run by ritual and convention and both of these were set and their observance monitored by the *Brahmans*.

There were those though who came to feel that this domination was plainly wrong. The Buddha was not the only reformer of his age in India. Before him came a man named Nataputta Vardhamana, born into a tribe called the Jnatrika, who did not live within the sixteen kingdoms that then represented the core of India but in the periphery to the north, where tribes entered into confederacies to protect themselves. As a man of about thirty years of age, he rejected wealth, no mean gesture when he himself was a prince; an almost Franciscan tale, in fact. After many years' contemplation, he rejected the role of the *Brahman* and argued that man should look after his own salvation and that the only way to spiritual fulfilment was to turn his back on the world and its material attractions, its money and its passions.

The prince became known as *Mahivira*, 'the great hero', and his creed as Jainism. In his teachings are a number of the tenets of subsequent mystical Indian creeds. Five main features were outlined. These were *ahisma*, non-violence against any living beings; *satya*, the requirement to tell the truth; *asteya*, a rejection of thievery; *brahmacharya*, the rejection of sexual passion; and *aparigraha*, a rejection of all that is material. Among the major figures of modern times to be influenced by Jainism was Mahatma Gandhi.

After *Mahivira* came the Buddha. Early twentieth-century historians dated the Buddha's life to the period between around 563 and 483 BC. The date, as ever when we go back this far, is a matter of ongoing debate – many scholars now tend towards a later date of around 400 BC for his death, but I see little reason to quibble too much about dates when new research is almost bound to suggest a further correction one way or the other in the near future.

Siddhartha Gautama was a prince too, also from the tribal periphery around India (believed to be in modern Nepal). He grew up in a palace, was a husband and father and wanted for nothing. One day, out on a drive around the vicinity of his palace with his charioteer, he saw an old man, his body broken and decaying, and saw for himself the horrors of extreme old age. Not long after, he saw a corpse rotting and a man stricken with the most terrible disease. Soon after, at a party, he saw women who were extremely beautiful when awake, but when asleep ground their teeth, snored and looked generally repulsive. All these signs convinced him that all material life was false.

It was a very human fear of decay and death therefore that set him on the road to meditating about the true meaning of life. He developed a belief that the only way to perfect peace was to become free of existence itself. This was a rejection of everything the *Brahmans* stood for. They argued that existence was one long and infinite series of deaths and rebirths. The former prince, however, opined that a perfect rejection of all material matter would in the end lead to *nirvana*, a state of nothingness.

He also argued that man must find his own salvation; he could not rely on a *Brahman* to do it for him. This was a total rejection of their power – to them, an extremely radical and dangerous idea. Siddhartha became known as a Buddha, an enlightened one. Many adherents flocked to his creed, which seemed to offer hope where before there had been little. Not that his religion ever subdued Hinduism, which would eventually claim its place as India's premier religion, which it remains. But Buddhism was the first religious creed to be exported outside of its region of origin on a large scale, and would become prominent in places like China and other parts of the Far East.

The teachings of the Chinese philosopher known to the West as Confucius were very different. Again, the environment in which he lived shaped his beliefs significantly. The Chinese hinterland was at this time, frankly, a mess (as it would remain to some extent into modern times – some of the most violent conflicts in human history took place in China right into the twentieth century). It was characterised by lords fighting for petty advantage, paying the nominal Zhou king little or no respect. Barbarian interlopers continued to pick away at Chinese territory.

In around 606 BC, the duke of the region of Chu, in the south of 'civilised' China, came to prominence. His region was strong whereas the centre of Chinese territory, the homeland of the king, was weak. He picked away at other dukedoms and then moved into the Zhou lands themselves. He used as his excuse the need to eject troublesome barbarians from the king's lands and he did not remove the king. Yet not long after, he began to call himself a king too.

The position of king had a revered status in China. It is notable that, despite the often parlous state of the institution, most kings managed to survive, admittedly often without any real power but able to retain a title at least. This move from the Duke of Chu was irrefutable evidence that the kingship was a damaged prize.

During the decades that followed, the downward slide of the Chinese monarchy continued. In the year 521 BC, the Zhou ruler King Ching died after a mainly uneventful reign of over two decades. On his death, a bitter succession dispute broke out between two of his sons. Several years of death and destruction followed. At the end of them, Confucius (actual Chinese name Kong Fuzi; the Latinised version was given to him by Jesuit missionaries two millennia later) emerged.

Confucius was the antithesis of Buddha. He believed that life should be run according to well-defined rules of society, that law and order could be guaranteed by each man knowing his place. He was a great believer in what he saw as necessary formalities – for him, there was a right way and a wrong way to do most things and man should pride himself on doing things properly. He was a man who, to put it plainly, was an advocate of 'the good old days', who believed that human beings should look back to what had once been for their code of life, a traditionalist with a rose-tinted view of the past.

Confucianism is not in everyone's eyes a religion. There is little discussion of spiritual matters in this philosophy but rather ethical and philosophical teachings about how to live one's life. Confucius outlined the merits of loyalty to one's family, the virtues of ancestor worship and the need for the young to respect their elders. It is a set of beliefs, a code, built on traditional values and conventions and it is this that seems to have made his teachings, recorded in a work known as *The Analects*, so attractive to large parts of ancient Chinese society, and indeed of many segments of Chinese society since.

He was famed especially for his *Golden Rule*, which in many ways predates one of the most profound teachings of Christianity: 'Do not do unto others what you do not want done to yourself.' It is easy to see how such a value had so much to commend it in a society riven by internal violence. These words were those of a man who was fed up with the descent into anarchy that he saw around him in the Zhou lands. The clue is in the use of the negative 'do not', rather than the later Christian, and positive, 'do'; this is a prescriptive code rather than one of freedom. An understanding of the difference is key to understanding Chinese views of the world.

The ongoing internal conflicts in China forced Confucius to move around and seek sanctuary from the violence. This made him more convinced than ever that men should know their place in the world and should show deference to those whose position merited it. Much more than a radical religious reformer, Confucius was the ultimate civil servant. His teaching of due deference to others was to set the tone for Chinese life until very recent times, and in its way still does – Confucius was one of the greatest of public enemies for the modern Chinese Communist Party, who wished to change the way that the people saw themselves as part of their political revolution.

A contemporary of Confucius was Sun Tzu, a general who wrote a well-known treatise on warfare. His *Art of War* still has its readers now on a worldwide basis. During his life its readership was restricted to a small group of people in China, which is a shame, as a few thousand miles to the west, in Mesopotamia and Iran, his words would have been greedily consumed by the generals of the armies of the region, who seemed to be permanently employed.

This was a turbulent century for Mesopotamia. At its outset, the great city of Babylon was seemingly resurgent. At its end, Babylonia had been eagerly devoured by an up-and-coming power to the east. The early years were ones of Babylonian conquest and expansionism, led by a dominant king, Nebuchadnezzar II. He is most famous for his conquest of Jerusalem and the deportation of most of its population to the famous 'rivers of Babylon' where, according to the Old Testament Book of Psalms, the Jews wept when they remembered Zion. Judah's king, Jehoiakim, had attempted to survive by recognising the nominal suzerainty of the Babylonian king as he conquered large chunks of Syria.

However, this was just an attempt to buy time. Jehoakim courted the Egyptians under pharaoh Necho II and, when the moment seemed right, entered into alliance with him. A battle between the armies of Egypt and Babylon ended in a draw, but the power of Egypt was still fragile. Necho had grand projects inside the borders of his country to keep him occupied, notably the construction of a canal between the Mediterranean and the Red Sea (predating Ferdinand de Lesseps' Suez Canal by 2,400 years).

Necho employed Greek and Phoenician sailors to crew his ships. One party, sent to explore the Red Sea, carried on and ended up sailing right around the coast of Africa and back through the Straits of Gibraltar, the first known circumnavigation of Africa.

This was an inspiring cocktail, a heady mix of engineering prowess, derring-do and adventure. Unfortunately, it did not help the abandoned Jews of Judah one bit for they were now left on their own to face up to the might of Babylon single-handed.

Fortunately for them, there were other distractions to keep Nebuchadnezzar occupied for a while. However, the death of King Jehoiakim in 597 BC acted as a catalyst for a Babylonian attack. When the Babylonian army moved on Jerusalem, the city surrendered without a fight. The royal family were taken back to Babylon, where they seem to have lived a comfortable existence. There was no widespread pillaging of the city and a Babylonian governor was appointed with no resistance. Life went on largely as before. That, however, was not the end of the matter.

It was the misjudgement of a Judean king that brought down the full wrath of Nebuchadnezzar on Jerusalem. Despite the lessons that might have been learned from Jehoakim's failed alliance with the Egyptians, a successor, Zedekiah, tried to resurrect it. He succeeded in encouraging the pharaoh Psammetichus II to send his army to face the Babylonians. One of Zedekiah's prophets, a man whose dire prognostications were so dark that all pessimists have been named honorary 'Jeremiahs' after him, warned the king to abandon this policy but was predictably ignored.

Unfortunately for the people of Jerusalem, he should have been listened to. The Egyptian army was routed and chased out of Syria. The peoples of the Nile would no longer intervene in Judean affairs and Zedekiah's country was again on its own. A systematic conquest of Judah then followed, slow and deliberate but all leading to an inevitable conclusion. Town after town fell, until at last only Jerusalem – the greatest prize – was left.

The siege of the city was tightly laid, without pity or compromise. Famine predictably broke out inside Jerusalem, as, equally unsurprisingly, did disease. This went on for two years, until Zedekiah shamefully abandoned his people and fled. The walls were breached and the Babylonians stormed in, their bloodlust up after their extended siege of the city. Zedekiah himself was chased, his army – many of whom managed to break out – were caught and annihilated, and the king himself was at last captured.

Although not a man particularly marked for savagery in those troubled times, Nebuchadnezzar's next actions were those of an angered and frustrated ruler. The punishment of Zedekiah was as cruel as it could be. His sons, who were still children, were killed in front of him, and then he was blinded so that the last thing he ever saw was the death of his own heirs. He was then taken back to Babylon, a pathetic symbol of Babylon's triumph.

He was at least spared watching the rape of Jerusalem. All his officials were slaughtered in cold blood, then the Babylonian army was told to torch the city. They did this with grim relish and the skies above Jerusalem were soon lit up with the haunting half-light of flickering flames. As the terror-stricken inhabitants were dragged off into lives of harsh slavery in strange lands, they looked on in despair at Solomon's great temple and its sacred Holy of Holies disappearing in a pall of smoke. The whole city, even this, its most famous and hallowed edifice, was left a total wreck. It was 587 BC and one of the saddest stories in the tragic history of the Jewish people had been written, one which powerfully haunts their psyche to this day.

The Jews went to Babylon, where Nebuchadnezzar had built his famed Hanging Gardens, a ziggurat whose various levels were festooned with flowers and trees, a statement of luxury that the impoverished Jewish slaves may have looked on with a mixture of awe and bitterness. But Nebuchadnezzar was to meet a mysterious end, allegedly going mad, no doubt according to some a punishment from Yahweh for his blasphemy. His demise in many ways marked the end of Babylon, for no man of greatness replaced him and within half a century the city would cease to exist as an independent entity.

Babylon's nemesis was Cyrus, who became king of the Persians in 559 BC. The Greek historian Herodotus tells a classic tale of mystery and intrigue to illustrate how he was born to greatness. A man named Astyages was king of the Medes, still the dominant power in Iran. He had a vivid dream that his soothsayers interpreted as giving warning that a child of his daughter Mandane would inherit his kingdom; not necessarily troubling in itself, as it might merely mean that the succession skipped a generation.

However, in a subsequent dream he was further warned that this succession would not be peaceful but that this child would seize the crown from him. By this time Mandane had given birth to a son, none other than Cyrus. She was lured to Astyages' capital at Ecbatana and orders were given that Cyrus should be killed. However, the herdsman to whom the job was given could not go through with the deed and instead took the boy home to his wife where, as if in a fairy-tale of antiquity, he grew up in anonymity.

It is a classic story, echoed in other mysterious tales, with details reminiscent of personalities as diverse as Moses, Romulus and Remus and King Arthur contained within it. Of course, at the end of it all Cyrus finds himself back at court, the dastardly plans of his grandfather having been averted. At this, Astyages took a terrible vengeance against the man to whom he had delegated Cyrus's murder, an official named Harpagus. He invited Harpagus to dinner and served him meat that was in fact the cooked body of the official's recently murdered son. When he then told Harpagus what he had just eaten, the official kept his composure, an amazing feat in the circumstances, but probably the only way of staying alive. Inwardly, he burned for revenge.

Like Cyrus, Harpagus bided his time. He plotted quietly with disaffected individuals who resented the increasingly repressive rule of Astyages. A trickle of support became a flood. This support gravitated to Cyrus, who, in contrast to his repressive grandfather, inspired confidence and loyalty. He raised an army and set off at its head towards Ecbatana. There was no resistance for no one had any time for the king. He was easily dethroned but, perhaps surprisingly, lived out a comfortable life in easy captivity and eventually died of natural causes.

With the Medes now safely united with the Persians under one king, Cyrus next moved on Lydia in Asia Minor and conquered it. However, he seemed to have inherited some of the viciousness of Astyages for he employed terror tactics as a way of subduing resistance. He ruled his lands with a rod of iron, though he supplemented his firmness with the judicious use of patronage to buy support. He delegated well, instructing Harpagus for example to take Ionian Greek cities on the Aegean coast. The result was a cosmopolitan empire unlike others seen before, with several different racial groups – Lydians, Greeks, Medes and Persians – recognising Cyrus's suzerainty.

Cyrus also moved his armies east and reached the banks of the Indus, though he did not cross it. However, the most enticing target was Babylon, the fabled city itself. Babylonia now had two kings. One ruled in the south, in Arabia: a man, Nabonidus, whose name has attracted little notice over subsequent centuries. The other was much more famous: Belshazzar, renowned for the biblical incident of the writing on the wall.

Babylon was his territory. In a famous incident in the Old Testament, Belshazzar was one day enjoying a splendid feast in his palace when a mysterious hand appeared and wrote on the wall the strange words 'Mene, Mene, Tekel, Parsin'. Daniel, a Jew in his entourage, interpreted the words as a sign that his worship of idols had led to Yahweh decreeing that he and his kingdom should come to an end or, as he more dramatically put it, the king had 'been weighed in the balance and found wanting'. That very night Cyrus's men stormed into Babylon, taking the city and killing Belshazzar.

The reason for Babylon's demise was a combination of exhaustion and its divided rule. When Babylon fell, it was a clever piece of tactics on Cyrus's part that was responsible for its death. The River Tigris flowed right through the city but it was so deep that no one had bothered to defend the city at the particular point where it entered. Cyrus, however, dug ditches to divert the river away and the water levels plummeted. The Persians merely walked through the gap and took over.

There was a fierce fight when they did so, even though the end was unavoidable once the walls had been breached. On 14 October 539 BC Babylon fell, this time for good. Once force had taken it, though, Cyrus was quick to use his wits to secure his triumph. The co-ruler Nabonidus had distanced himself from the Babylonian god Marduk and Cyrus now claimed to enter it as the defender of the deposed deity. It was a canny move, ingratiating the Persian conqueror with his new subjects.

This was another, subtler, side of his character. He followed it by implementing a well-thought-out plan. He let the Jewish exiles in Babylonia return to Jerusalem and gave them express permission to rebuild their temple there. The building they constructed was a poor shadow of its former great self, and some who remembered the glories of Solomon's magnificent tribute to Yahweh wept tears of shame rather than joy when they saw it, but later generations of the Jewish nation remembered the acts of Cyrus with gratitude.

Cyrus would die an inglorious death, struck down in a minor skirmish in a remote corner of Central Asia. He found himself involved in a battle where he had seriously underestimated his enemy, a warrior queen by the name of Tomyris. She cut off his head and put it in a pouch filled with blood. She had promised to sate his thirst for blood and this was her way of doing so. She did later relent, though; recognising the greatness of the man whose death she had brought about, she allowed his body to be taken back for an honourable burial in a magnificent mausoleum in Pasargadae in Persia.

Cyrus's eldest son, Cambyses II, took his place. He abandoned his father's capital at Pasargadae and moved it to Susa, once the capital of the Elamites. Perhaps inspired by Cyrus's example and wishing to outshine even him, he set his sights on the conquest of Egypt, still a fabulous prize even though its halcyon days were long in the past. Cambyses produced something even Cyrus could not – a fleet. He conscripted Ionian sailors from the shores of Asia Minor to man his ships, as well as skilled naval men from Phoenicia. Then he launched an ambitious amphibious assault on Egypt.

Faced by a new pharaoh, whose father had died and left him the throne even as the Persian army and navy was on its way, Cambyses won himself a great victory and now found himself lord of Egypt as well as most of the Middle East. The Persian Empire was expanding at an impressive rate of knots. This conquest was a significant achievement but it was the last of his reign for he died soon after.

Following Cambyses's death, there was a coup led by his spear-bearer, an ambitious and shrewd man named Darius. Having manoeuvred his way to the throne, he set in train a sequence of events that were to reverberate across time as some of the most momentous of the ancient world. A very capable general and administrator, Darius decided to sacrifice quantity for quality and, instead of relying on hordes of conscripts for his army, decided to assemble a small and select band of professional warriors. There would be 10,000 infantrymen and 10,000 cavalry, trained unceasingly in the skills of war.

His first task was to restore order in Persia. As a usurper, it was no surprise that Darius's right to rule was questioned, but any doubts were quickly dispelled by force of arms. Darius divided up his lands into large administrative provinces that he called *satrapies*, each under the control of a hand-picked and trusted *satrap* as governor. They were his eyes and ears, ruthless in putting down any signs of trouble while he was busy elsewhere.

This was just as well, for he had great plans to occupy him. He moved his men far to the east and crossed over the Indus. India was not unknown to the Persians. Iran, the area where the Persians lived, means 'the land of the Aryans', the Aryans having of course populated much of India as well. But there had never before been any Persian attempt to conquer lands in India. Now Darius pushed on into India, not the whole country but the northern segment we now know as the Punjab.

Then Darius turned west, to the campaign for which he was most famous. To the north of Asia Minor, where the country of Georgia now exists, was a bridge of land with the Caspian Sea on one side and the Black Sea on the other. To the north were warlike tribes known as the Scythians. Constantly on the lookout for easy pickings, the Scythians were skilled and violent raiders who made drinking cups from the skulls of their enemies. Darius decided to bring them to book.

His plan was to launch a huge pincer movement against them by crossing the narrow Bosporus Strait and heading onto the mainland of Europe. He would then sweep up northwards in a wide arc to attack them from the rear. It was an audacious plan that required extraordinary feats of engineering to make it a reality. Getting the army across the narrow strip of water, less than a mile wide, involved his engineers making a pontoon bridge by tying up boats side by side from one edge of the waters to the other and then laying planks across it to create a makeshift road.

They marched across a vast, permanent road that Darius had ordered to be built right across Asia Minor named, appropriately enough, the Royal Road. Thousands of soldiers crossed over the strait. For the first time in recorded history, Asia was invading Europe. Brilliantly executed though these arrangements were, the plan had a fatal flaw. The Scythians were nomads. They had no cities for Darius to attack and conquer. Instead, like the rapid horsemen that they were, they just rode away from him and disappeared into the hinterland of the steppes.

Darius had brought an army into Europe and its *raison d'être* had disappeared with the strategic withdrawal of the Scythians. This was no problem; he would find another. To the south lay Macedonia and, beyond this, the city states of Greece. The Macedonians capitulated at once. Darius demanded of them the traditional tribute of earth and water, symbolic surrendering of the lands and waters of the country, and they complied at once.

The Greeks to the south were panic-stricken. They were divided and at odds with each other. Prominent among the states were Athens and Sparta, two entities with very different views of the world. It was Sparta that took up the mantle of resistance, with one of its kings, Cleomenes (Sparta uniquely always had two co-kings at its head), marching on Athens, whose citizens were even now squabbling among themselves, to put some bite into resistance.

Unbelievably, the Athenians saw the Spartans as the enemy and sought to retain their independence by approaching the Persians, of all people, for help. It was only when their delegates arrived at the court of Darius that they truly realised what the price of that alliance would be. Nothing less than complete submission to Darius would do. Their delegates lied their way out of the Persian camp and back to Athens. The Athenians, realising they were on their own, fought off the Spartans without outside help.

Soon after, another Greek city asked for Persian aid. This was Miletus, an Ionian city in Asia Minor. A Greek adventurer here asked for Persian ships and men to help him conquer the Cyclades, which he would then hand over to Persia for a price. However, this plan backfired and instead the Persians found themselves having to put down a series of revolts. When Athens sent ships to help fight the Persians, it made war with the might of the Persian Empire inevitable. It was 500 BC and one of the great wars of pre-Roman times loomed.

These events shook the very foundations of the evolving civilised world around the fringes of the eastern Mediterranean. There was, further west, another event whose immediate impact was more local but whose longer-term consequences were profound. The city of Rome had initially been dominated by the neighbouring local superpower, the Etruscans. Various local tribal groups had competed for pre-eminence: Etruscans, Sabines and Latins. It was a volatile mix that often set off an explosive chain reaction. From the beginning, Roman life, indeed the city's very existence, was protected by violence.

Rome developed as a monarchy. However, it was protected by its people, who were expected to arm themselves and fight when the occasion demanded. This made the citizenry assertive, which in turn undermined the autocratic rule of the kings of Rome. This explosive situation erupted with Vesuvian ferocity when a proud and debauched man, Tarquin, usurped the throne. His coup succeeded but was followed by despotic and exploitative rule. Trying to govern through fear, his strong-arm tactics succeeded only in bringing about his own downfall.

His son raped a Roman noblewoman, Lucretia, whose shame was so great that she killed herself. Her husband displayed her body in public, a move that inspired an outpouring of anger on the part of Rome's citizens. Tarquin was out of the city when these feelings led to a full-blown uprising. Tarquin journeyed around Etruria, the home of the Etruscans, in an attempt to assemble an army with which to retake his city. However, Etruria was already in decline, its moment in the sun already passing. Although they did provide troops to help the deposed king, the Roman army fought them off vigorously. But the Etruscans tried again and moved on the city with a fresh and stronger force.

Rome had walls on only three sides, the fourth being protected by the fast-flowing Tiber. There was a bridge across this, the only means of egress from this direction. An army sent to stop the approaching Etruscans fled across it to the city. Only one man stayed to fight, a soldier named Horatius. While his colleagues struggled desperately to break down the bridge, Horatius held back the Etruscans on his own. When the bridge was eventually demolished, he fell into the water but managed to swim across to his own side (or so the story goes; even the Roman writer who recorded it, Livy, accepted that it might well have been apocryphal).

The end was an anti-climax. The Etruscans did not give up but a long-lasting siege was eventually ended by a truce, effectively an honourable draw. Nevertheless, this meant the end of the monarchy and the beginnings of the Roman Republic. A treaty shortly afterwards with a rising power in Africa, Carthage, was made in Rome's own name, a sign of its rising power and self-confidence.

Carthage had in fact been spreading its wings. It had previously entered into an alliance with the Etruscans. The Carthaginians needed allies in the region. The Greeks had begun colonising Sicily, a Carthaginian sphere of interest, and the two groups had come to blows. A battle against aggressive pirates in the western Mediterranean ended in a decisive victory for Carthage and the Etruscans prevented the Greeks from expanding further west in Sardinia and Corsica.

There was still a long way to go before Rome became a regional, let alone a global, power. A new group of people had made their way into the north of the Italian Peninsula. Known somewhat loosely as 'Celts', they had wandered across Europe somewhere between 600 and 500 BC, having originated as an Indo-European group in the tract of land between the Black and Caspian Seas that had spawned other Indo-European peoples. By about 630 BC, they had established a society in Austria, in a culture known as the Hallstatt after one of the sites there that was later excavated.

Their weapons were of iron and they seemed to have exulted in warfare. But they had other traits too. They were entrepreneurial traders, and they imported many goods through a busy, bustling town in the south of what is now France known as Massalia (now Marseilles). This included tin brought in from Cornwall, showing that even the British Isles were now starting to be drawn into affairs on the European continent. Eventually, the Celts would establish a vibrant presence across Europe and into Britain and Ireland. Their incursions into Italy were eventually to bring them into conflict with Rome in what became a battle for survival for the small Latin state.

Indeed there are some interesting examples of the cross-fertilisation of ideas between the Celts and other civilisations. There are similarities, for instance, between Greek Pythagorean philosophy and aspects of Celtic belief. Elements of Celtic folklore appear in Roman writings, such as the story of Valerius Corvus, who was saved in single combat with a Gaul by the helpful intervention of a crow.

The perception that the Celts were somehow 'barbarian' compared to the civilised Romans and Greeks is a vast oversimplification and indeed, in the context of the world 2,500 years ago, plain wrong. It depends how supposed superiority is measured. The famous Roman Pliny the Elder would admit a few centuries later that the Celtic plough was vastly better than its Roman equivalent. Judgement against the Celts probably arises from the fact that they made little use of a written language, preferring instead a reliance on memory, hence the famous bards, though they did have some writing, as evidenced by the inscriptions on stone in a basic line script known as ogham (though when this started to be used is disputed).

Considering all these events, it is difficult to avoid the conclusion that this century was one of the most important ever. At the end of it, a Persian superpower had been established that was to last a millennium. It would remain important even beyond that and even today Iran has a global significance out of proportion to its size. Oil may be the primary reason, but it would be foolish to ignore the contributions that Persian civilisation has made over the years.

The impact of Confucianism was also massive, helping to shape Chinese paradigms for millennia. These may have changed in recent times, as China has emerged as a more quasi-capitalist society. Nevertheless, as leopards do not change their spots, so peoples do not change their characteristics overnight and there is still a strong residual Confucian influence present there.

Buddhism, too, still has many adherents, mainly in eastern Asia, and remains one of the great religions. At the beginning of the twenty-first century AD there were estimated to be 376 million Buddhists in the world. In 2008, there were estimated to be 6.7 billion people living on Earth; therefore over one in twenty of the world's population is a Buddhist.

Space has precluded more than a passing reference to another crucial influence on world civilisation, but we are about to remedy that deficiency. The evolution of Greek city states has been referred to, but little has yet been said on their philosophies and systems of government. However, the century that was about to begin would bring Greece into the centre of the stage, though for a time it seemed that its very existence as a collection of independent city states was in grave doubt.

9

THE GREEK CENTURY

The Triumph and Self-Destruction of Greece (500–401 BC)

It might be romantically said that history truly begins with this century, for during it the man said to be its father, the Greek Herodotus, lived. He was a collector of tales of (to him) recent history and for the first time attempted to scrutinise them for accuracy and consistency. Having undertaken this preliminary forensic analysis, he then committed them to writing with a verve that brought them to life. Helpfully, as far as accuracy is concerned, his most famous work, the *Histories*, tracing the development and events of the Greek–Persian Wars, took place at a time not far removed from when he lived.

Born early on in the century in Halicarnassus (now Bodrum, in Turkey), he was an avid collector of information and an inveterate traveller, which suggests a man with a keen interest in understanding the world, an assumption borne out by his works. Exiled from Halicarnassus, he then went to the nearby island of Samos and later is thought to have lived in Sicily and Macedon. He eventually died in about 420 BC.

For a long time, historians believed much of his writing to be fanciful. But there are clues that there is a strong basis in fact for a good deal of what he recorded. One story tells of sailors who journeyed south and eventually found the sun on the right-hand side of the ship even though they were heading west – which is exactly what happens when crossing the Equator and heading into the Southern Hemisphere. His recording of events in India shows that, even then, the region was known as far west as Greece.

He also knew of regions further to the south of the Mediterranean. When he visited Egypt he travelled up the Nile to Elephantine (modern Aswan) but, although he did not go on, he was told of other cultures further down the great river. He spoke of the 'Ethiopians' in their big city of Meroe – at that time the Greeks called any African to the south an 'Ethiopian', while those in the north were 'Libyans' (Ethiopian in Greek means 'burned faces').

Others knew of distant lands too; for example, there is evidence that during this century an explorer from Carthage in North Africa sailed as far down the African coast as Sierra Leone. His name was Hanno and the brief record of his voyages would later appear in Greek in a later work known as the *Periplus* (a word which means 'a sailing-around'). A number of such documents were produced over the centuries, each one listing the ports and coastal landmarks that a sea captain could expect to find when sailing down a coast.

Pliny, the later Roman writer, says that Hanno was under orders to try and circumnavigate Africa. He leaves tantalising clues as to how far he got, including references to hippopotami. He also encountered a hairy beast that his interpreters called a 'gorilla' and from this we know that he got at least to Sierra Leone and possibly as far as Congo, for this giant of the natural world is found in both regions.

Almost contemporary with Herodotus was another Greek historian, Thucydides (*c.* 460–395 BC). He was born in Athens and wrote in a factual manner that contrasted with Herodotus's approach, which tended to adopt a more moralistic interpretation of events and their causes and effects. Thucydides was a political realist, an early exponent of the theory that it is might rather than right that matters.

It is in his subject matter that we see the greatest contrast, for while Herodotus wrote of a Greek triumph, Thucydides detailed the events of a Greek tragedy, an exercise in self-destruction where Greece tore itself apart, the loose alliances between its city states breaking down completely and generating a devastating sequence of events that left it exhausted. For as well as the glorious triumphs of Marathon and Salamis, this was also the age of the Peloponnesian War, when Sparta and Athens, along with their respective allies, fought themselves to a standstill.

The Persians lost their wars with Greece, so perhaps it is unsurprising that there is no record of them surviving in any Persian archive and our evidence therefore all comes from a Greek perspective, so of course a glossy varnish may have been put on this epic. But this is nevertheless a tale of monumental events, of victories against the odds, of heroic self-sacrifice and the most glorious defeat of all time, one that would rival the tales of the combatants' ancient ancestors on the fields outside Troy 1,000 years earlier.

The revolt of the Ionian Greek cities, on the eastern coast of the Mediterranean in Anatolia, against Persian overlordship at the end of the sixth century BC had received Athenian assistance. The uprisings continued and a serious outbreak in Ionia saw the Greeks there take the key city of Sardis in a surprise attack. In what seems to have been an unfortunate accident, a fire broke out and most of the city was destroyed. Darius, king of the Persians, was angered beyond measure at the loss of this wealthy city and gathered together an army to retake what was left and punish the rebels for their perceived crimes.

The Ionian army was shattered at a battle near Ephesus and the rebels that were left took to their ships (these were also Persian, having been seized earlier on in the rebellion). They moved on a small Persian city called Byzantium by the Bosporus Strait and then did all they could to stay out of the reach of Darius. However, the rebel fleet was destroyed when caught by a Persian armada with 600 ships – nearly twice the number available to the Greek rebels – near Miletus. The Persians then moved on Miletus, where the revolt had begun, and unleashed hell on it, killing the men and taking the rest of the population off into slavery.

With Ionia now subdued, it was time for Darius to punish the Athenians for their involvement in the revolt. His first attempt was a failure, ruined when a storm destroyed the Persian fleet, and he was not ready for another attempt until 490 BC. There was on this occasion no land force marching to Greece – everyone was on board 600 ships. Initial landings in Greece went well and resistance crumbled until it seemed that Athens, alone now that most of her allies had been subdued, must fall.

Athens sent for help to Sparta, famed for its warrior ethos, but the latter wanted to avoid any involvement in what might have seemed a lost cause (modern generalisations that the Spartans were a band of warriors spoiling for a fight for the sake of it are a ridiculous exaggeration). Using the excuse that the time was not right for their involvement because it was a religious holiday (they were certainly a very superstitious people so this much may have been true as well as convenient), they refused to come. Athens was on its own.

An Athenian army was sent out to do what it could to fight off the Persians. Battle was joined by the Bay of Marathon. The Athenians won a stunning victory, largely due to their disciplined tactics, with their foot soldiers (known as hoplites) working in a compact unit, forming a united front with their spears pointing in front of them so that the whole looked like a gigantic hedgehog. Forced back, the Persians panicked and many drowned in nearby marshes. A fair number made it back to the ships, though, and sailed off. The subsequent debriefing with Darius, who was a man of violent temper, must have been an interesting one.

There was a fascinating subplot to these events. The Athenians had sent a runner to Sparta before the battle asking for their help. His name was Pheidippides and he covered the distance of 150 miles in two days. After the Battle of Marathon, a runner took the news of the triumph back from the battlefield to Athens, a distance of 26 miles and 385 yards to be precise. Once he had gasped out his news, the runner (who may according to tradition also have been Pheidippides though there are several rival claimants to the honour) collapsed and died. The modern athletics marathon covers the same distance as this epic run, an ongoing tribute to a hero who would otherwise be long forgotten.

It is always dangerous for anyone to defeat a superpower in a battle (ask the Zulus who defeated the British Army at Isandlwana in 1879 or the Japanese at Pearl Harbour in 1941), for, inevitably, an aggrieved sense of damaged pride means that a much stronger response is certain. The victors were heroes, all except the Athenian general Miltiades, who later failed to take the Persian-controlled island of Paros and died making his way back to Athens to explain his failure (Athenians did not much like men who were too successful and, much as is the way with modern sports stars and a cynical media circling for blood, loved to cut them down to size).

In 486 BC, just after he had put the finishing touches to another invasion force financed by a vigorous tax-collecting campaign, Darius died. His son Xerxes took his place. His first task was to put down an uprising in Egypt but once this was done he turned his thoughts back to Greece again. More ships were needed, and these needed to be built. The logistics were complicated by the need to build another pontoon bridge across the Bosporus and it was not until 480 BC that he finally set out.

The Greeks, though, had not been idle. They had been building ships too; less of them than the Persians had, but sharp-prowed and built with a view to ramming and sinking any vessel foolish enough to get in their way. The Athenians built alliances as well as ships. In 481 BC, they put together the Hellenic League with thirty other Greek city states, great and small. The Spartans were also ready to fight the Persian threat. For now at least, most of Greece was wise enough to sense a common threat.

The Greeks realised that the strong army with Xerxes meant that they had to pick their ground carefully. The north would not hold for long and it was pointless putting up a defence there. In AD 1815, Wellington fought a decisive battle at Waterloo. He is said to have remarked to one of his generals that he had seen the ground some time before and put it in his pocket. The Greeks had also put a prime battleground in their pocket and were now ready to produce it. It was called Thermopylae.

At the time, Thermopylae was a narrow pass between the mountains on one side and the sea on the other (in modern times, the waters have retreated and the effectiveness of the pass as a defensive spot is therefore harder to realise). It could be held by a small force against a much larger one as the latter could not deploy all their superior numbers.

The Spartans had sent one of their two kings to lead their troops. His name was Leonidas. With a force of allied Greek troops he managed to hold the pass for three days. Herodotus gave a ridiculous number of 5,283,220 men in the Persian army, but most modern commentators would accept an estimate of 100,000 soldiers as being reasonable – still a massive army. Among them were the crack 'Immortals', 10,000 strong.

On the first day of battle, the Persian army hammered away at the Greek forces, who were protected by a wall. Leonidas cleverly used his men in relays; the narrowness of the front meant that he did not need them all at once. After a day of frenetic fighting and with nothing to show for it, Xerxes sent in the Immortals. In common with all the soldiers he had sent in before, they crashed against the Greek wall, made both of stone and flesh, with no success, though incurring a large number of casualties in the process.

On the second day, all was as it had been on the first. The Persians threw themselves on the Greeks and were beaten back. But then, a breakthrough from that most dangerous of weapons – a traitor's knowledge. There was a pass through the mountains which would enable Persian soldiers to cross above the Greeks and then come down and attack them from the rear.

During the night, Persian soldiers made their way through the mountains in the moonlight, in what was undoubtedly a heroic venture in its own right. When the Greeks woke on the next morning, they found that they were in danger of being surrounded. As the sun rose and lit up the skies, both armies prepared for battle. The Greeks brought out an animal to sacrifice, an essential part of a Spartan's preparation for battle. Just a few miles away, Xerxes made an offering to the sun.

The moment for battle was at hand. It would be decisive, for there was no escape for the Greeks now, and it would be brutal, for the Persian losses had been heavy and they would want the debt of blood owed them paid off in full. Leonidas, according to Herodotus, had his morning meal and then advised his men that 'this evening, we shall dine in Hades'.

Most of the troops with the Greeks had been sent away to safety by Leonidas. He, as is well known, stayed with just 300 of his men (there were also warriors with him from the cities of Thebes and Thespia; their sacrifice is, rather unfairly, usually forgotten). It was said that the fighting on this third day was as heavy as that on the previous two, even if a Persian success was now almost inevitable. Leonidas was, sadly for the storytellers, killed quite early on (not what is required of a hero at all; he must of course be the last man standing). So ferocious was the Greeks' defence that the Persians finally killed off the survivors with arrows fired safely from a distance.

Xerxes appears to have been incensed at the losses he incurred. Leonidas was decapitated, even though already dead, and his corpse was crucified. Xerxes had his victory but it was a Pyrrhic one. For this was the most successful defeat of all time, the Spartan (and allied) sacrifice an inspiration to that and future generations. The epitaph written for the brave 300 by the Greek poet Simonides remains one of the most moving ever penned, the epitome of sacrifice, with the immortal lines, 'Go tell the Spartans, passer-by, that here obedient to our laws we lie.' Even now, nearly two and a half millennia later, this gallant defeat is known as an example of heroic martyrdom in defence of a lost cause.

But the cause was not, after all, lost. The Athenians had a heroic warrior of their own but he fought on the sea rather than the land. His name was Themistocles and he prepared to defend Athens behind what the oracle at Delphi had termed her 'wooden walls'. But for the city itself there was nothing that could be done. It had to be abandoned to the far from tender mercies of an angry Xerxes. Its priests were left to pray to the gods from the sacred Acropolis, but the rest of the population were taken to sanctuary on the island of Salamis nearby. From here, they would have seen the columns of smoke pluming up as the Persians proceeded to destroy their precious city.

The Athenians placed their fleet of sleek, quick triremes provocatively in the bay, in full sight of the Persians. Xerxes, now feeling much better having ravished Athens, settled himself down on a stool to watch what he believed would be a foregone conclusion when he sent his fleet in. It was September 479 BC and the first truly decisive sea battle in history was about to be fought.

Themistocles had in fact sent a secret message to Xerxes saying that he wished to desert. He had no such intention but the trick worked. Xerxes was now supremely confident and sent his fleet into the narrows. In the straits, the Persians could not make their numerical superiority pay against the more manoeuvrable Athenian triremes; a kind of naval Thermopylae. The Persian fleet was shattered, and with it all hopes of conquering Greece.

Xerxes returned to Persia, leaving his general Mardonius in command of the troops that were left. The next year, a Greek army led by Pausanias, nephew of Leonidas of Sparta, defeated the Persians at Plataea. Another Greek victory at sea, at Mycale off the coast of Asia Minor, forced the Persians to pay attention to the war against Ionian Greek cities and to leave mainland Greece well alone. Greece, however, had not finished with Persia.

The victory paved the way for further Greek expansion. Greek colonies would appear across the Mediterranean. However, although the trireme was the platform on which the triumph of Salamis was based, in the long run it posed serious problems for longer journeys. The large numbers of men required to propel the vessels necessitated significant volumes of food and water to keep them alive and fit. This in itself would limit the duration and reach of voyages. The long-term answer lay in developing alternative forms of propulsion that would adequately deal with the problem, such as the evolution of effective sailing ships.

The Greeks expanded their world. For example they moved into Colchis, now part of modern Georgia. In the small city museum in modern Tbilisi known as the Archaeology Treasury, there is perhaps one of the most exquisite collections of ancient gold and silver jewellery still in existence. They evidence breathtaking craftsmanship, delicate links of precious metal interspersed with precious stones in a fusion of Greek and local traditions; evidence of a coming together of two great traditions. Colchis was the land of gold and it was said that grains of it ran freely in the rivers and the locals fished for it with the skins of sheep – the probable origin of the famous tale of Jason and the Golden Fleece.

While these events were going on in Greece and the surrounding region, there were movements taking place elsewhere that were to have a huge impact in the future. The normal caveats on ancient history apply; we cannot be certain as to exact dates and, with little detail on specific happenings to latch onto, only general periods may be talked about anyway. But it is generally thought that by about 480 BC monastic life had started to become established in India.

The ways of these monks were little different than those of Buddhist holy men and women alive today. Both men and women, monks and nuns, gave up their secular lives to put on the humble garments which were all they owned. They had no other worldly possessions, living off alms. They travelled around the parts of India where their faith had started to become established, preaching and teaching as they went. It is remarkable to think that two and a half millennia later there are still some Buddhists living in broadly the same fashion. There were significant developments in China, too. In about 471 BC, the great philosopher Confucius died. His followers endeavoured to preserve his thoughts by committing them to writing.

It is also believed to have been in around 480 BC that Celtic migrations across the Channel to the British Isles began in earnest. These movements, which were to change the racial profile and characteristics of the British Isles forever, emanated from the Low Countries and France, where the kingdom of Gaul would become the most powerful of all Celtic nations until smashed by the legions of Julius Caesar four centuries later.

In Britain the Celts gradually built small kingdoms of their own, often keeping themselves occupied by wars with each other. Over time (and this was a long-term process, not one of a few decades), great hill forts were built, usually on hilltops where keen eyes could observe what was going on in the distance. The banks of many of them still exist, in areas like Dorset and Wiltshire in the south of England, their palisades of timber long gone, the round huts of those who lived there having disappeared many centuries since, their ditches shallower and their ramparts more rounded. But many remain impressive and, to any with a sense of imagination, vivid. In the imagination they are still unconquerable and defiant.

There were important developments in science taking place at this time too. In 475 BC, a scientist called Parmenides who lived in Elea in Italy declared that the world was a sphere; so much for those who believe that everyone was a member of the Flat Earth Society until a few hundred years ago. But the world was still full of superstition as well. In 480 BC, a Greek army had failed to follow up the triumph of Salamis because it had been frightened to do so due to the evil omen of an eclipse.

In the meantime, when Xerxes returned to Persia it was as a failed commander. His losses in Greece caused him great angst. The Ionian Greek cities on the coast were exposed to the full wrath of Persia as a form of vicarious vengeance. The Spartans suggested that they should be abandoned as a lost cause. However, other Greek city states argued against this policy and it was decided that, for the time being, they should be defended.

This small difference of opinion was only the tip of a very large iceberg. Now that the Persian threat to mainland Greece had been apparently defeated for the foreseeable future, the Greeks soon began to fall out among themselves. Two rival parties formed, with Sparta heading one side and Athens the other.

When considering both these city states it is important to avoid simplifications. On the one hand, Sparta may be thought to be a military superpower whose men were motivated by thoughts of glory. This is indeed in many ways true, as from the age of seven all Spartan males were groomed for fighting, but it misses out an important part of the truth. Because the Spartan men were trained for war, and Spartan women were similarly expected to devote their lives to bringing up future Spartan supermen, others had to be found to do the everyday jobs that oiled the wheels that enabled life to go on.

The Spartan solution was simple. They have left us several words. One is 'laconic', from an alternative name for Sparta, Laconia. This word is derived from the Spartans' well-known propensity to keep their conversations short and sweet. Another less well-known word is 'helot', defined as someone who is ruthlessly exploited. This is derived from the name given to those serfs who kept Sparta going. Unlike other Greek cities, Sparta enslaved Greeks, not individuals but whole communities. Their reason for living was solely to provide the Spartans with all that they needed to keep their military economy afloat. They had no rights and no hope. Let us dispense with one simplification at once. There was no glory in this.

Athens may be thought a beacon of democracy in comparison, but actually it was not. For some citizens, it is true, the concept had meaning. The city was run (since the so-called Athenian Revolution) by its better-off inhabitants, who debated and took collective decisions on the key matters of the day. Those who were not well-heeled had no such rights. As one modern writer put it, this was 'more like a dictatorship of the proletariat'.

Athens' legacy to the future world would be most of all the idea of democracy. It would be much expanded in the centuries to come so that all the population would have democratic rights, but in other ways democracy as we now think of it is much more restricted than it was in Athens. Typically, modern democracies do not give the right to vote on every key issue to every citizen (those enfranchised in Athens could vote on a wide range of issues) but entrust politicians with the job of acting on their collective behalf. Regardless of the rights and wrongs of communism, there was some truth in Karl Marx's famous quote which may be paraphrased as 'democracy is one minute in a ballot booth every five years'.

As the century went on, tensions in Greece grew. The Athenians withdrew from the Hellenic League and set up their own version, the Delian League, composed of their allies, some of them reluctant partners. Sparta set up the Peloponnesian League, which became its major rival. Each side sought to dominate Greece. This was nothing to do with two rival philosophies trying to outdo each other. This was a plain, old-fashioned fight for power.

It was perhaps just as well that the Persians were too preoccupied to take advantage of this disunity. Xerxes proved to be a deeply flawed man and a fairly awful king. He never took responsibility for the setbacks in Greece. Instead he turned to a life of debauchery, famed for his sexual excesses and his love of a pretty woman. When he ordered his wife Vashti to display herself before the leading men of his kingdom, she refused to do so. Xerxes was so incensed that he immediately sent her away and sought a replacement. According to the book of Esther in the Bible, Xerxes (called there Ahasuerus) happily listened to his counsellors' advice when they said, 'Let there be fair young virgins sought for the king.' A strange and rather erotic series of auditions then followed before a suitable replacement was chosen. This biblical tale of Xerxes's lust is backed up by Herodotus, who tells other stories of the king's roving eye.

Few can have been distressed when Xerxes was murdered by one of his eunuchs in 465 BC. The throne was taken, after a struggle, by his youngest son, Artaxerxes. Rebellions broke out in the meantime across the Persian Empire. Distant Egypt was one of the areas involved. The Egyptians sought help from the Athenians, who were delighted to oblige. But they had overstretched themselves. The rebel leader, Inaros, was eventually defeated and crucified. A serious Athenian reverse in about 456 BC saw her fleet defeated and her army retreating hurriedly across the Sinai Desert.

This aggressive activity on the part of Athens was representative of her current philosophy in Greece where she was increasingly assertive, one might say bullying (though she may only have been doing this because she too had been bullied). Under her famed leader Pericles she sought out every opportunity to expand her interests. Aegina, virtually on her doorstep, was forced to join the Delian League about the same time that the Athenian fleet and army was being bested in Egypt. Having successfully rebuffed the unwelcome attentions of would-be Persian conquerors, Greece was about to go to war with itself.

After the Persians had been ejected, Athens had decided to rebuild its walls. Sparta objected, saying that any walls should be restricted to the Peloponnese, a ludicrous stipulation that Athens quite naturally ignored. During succeeding decades, tensions between the two great city states grew in intensity. Throughout this period, Athens had become increasingly aggressive. When in 460 BC the island of Naxos tried to withdraw from the Delian League it was forced to remain in it.

In the same year, Sparta marched its army into Boeotia, close to Attica. The Spartans said they had been invited in by the Boeotians, but it was also suggested that a party in Athens, opposed to Pericles' leadership and wishing to see the Athenian concept of democracy suspended, had also been in contact with them. In any event, the Athenians themselves sent a force into Boeotia, and a conflict ensued. The Spartans had the better of it but not decisively so. The first blows in the Peloponnesian Wars had been struck.

These early years of warfare in the conflict appear to have been desultory. The Thirty Years' Peace was agreed in 446 BC. In these years of peace, Pericles ordered the construction of one of the greatest and most iconic buildings ever built. The Parthenon replaced an older building on the Acropolis which had been destroyed by the Persians. It was built to honour the city's protector, the goddess Athena. Its subsequent history has been a sad one; an Ottoman ammunition dump stored in the structure was destroyed by a stray Venetian cannonball in AD 1687, causing considerable damage, and the Parthenon's precious marbles, the notorious Elgin Marbles, were taken away by the British Museum in AD 1816 – for a fee, it must be added. The Greeks would surely respond that it was quite an insufficient one, no doubt arguing too that their heritage should not be for sale at all. The marbles remain a subject of bitter contention between the governments of Greece and the United Kingdom today.

But at the time the Parthenon was a glorious achievement, undertaken under the supervision of the renowned architect Phidias. It was completed by 432 BC. As one modern writer noted, it 'enjoys the reputation of being the most perfect Doric temple ever built.' Doric architecture had first been developed in the sixth century BC. It was a simple style; architecture became more complex as it developed through the Ionic and Corinthian periods, which came later. The Greeks invented the entablature which topped the colonnade and enabled it to support a hipped roof. It has been said that ancient Greek architecture is their greatest legacy to the modern world, for all subsequent European architecture is indebted to it.

By the time that the Parthenon is known to have been completed, Athens and Sparta were at war again, this time with no holds barred. The dispute was ignited by the Corinthian colony of Corcyra, whose masters were in league with Sparta. The people of Corcyra enlisted Athens' help in breaking away from Corinth, and both Athens and Sparta quickly progressed down the road that led to all-out war. Most of the early battles were minor affairs, most notable for perhaps one of the most eloquent pieces of oratory ever written.

In a speech honouring the fallen, Pericles extolled his listeners to fight for the glory of Athens and what she represented. He told them, 'You must realise yourselves the power of Athens. Feed your eyes on her from day to day till love of her fills your hearts; and then, when all her greatness shall break upon you, you must reflect that it was by courage, sense of duty, and a keen feeling of honour in action that men were enabled to win all this.' This appeal to ideals still has the ability to touch the heart millennia after it was first uttered.

The war lasted for nearly thirty years, with a short and poorly kept period of truce in the middle. In 407 BC, in an extraordinary about-turn, the Persian king, Darius II, entered into an agreement with the Spartans. The Spartans themselves appointed a new commander, Lysander, to lead their navy. In the next two years, he won a series of victories against Athens. Then he besieged the city itself. By now, Athens had nothing left to give and surrendered. The Peloponnesian War was at an end and Sparta was the victor. The Long Walls were smashed and the Athenians began the energy-sapping process of rebuilding the shattered fabric of their city.

We have in the main considered the history of the well-known city states of Greece in this chapter. Perhaps it would be appropriate to end with a civilisation that has been largely forgotten. Far to the south of Egypt, between the sixth and fifth cataracts of the Nile, the kingdom of Kush built a new capital called Meroe. Kush was a Nubian state, at some times dominated by Egypt, at other (less frequent) times able to lord it over the kingdom to the north.

Meroe took the place of Napata, further north (perhaps at a safer remove from the troubles that had beset Egypt over the past few centuries). It became a terminus for caravan routes to the Red Sea. Round about, the region offered good grazing and agricultural land and was rich in iron ore and wood. It became rich but also found a role as a repository of Egyptian tradition. Here, great stone pyramids were built, commemorations of a time long past in Egypt. Although smaller and steeper than those immortal monuments of Khufu and Khafre, there is no doubting where their inspiration came from.

The language of those who lived in Meroe is not understood but they used a form of hieroglyphs for their ceremonial writing as well as an everyday script, simpler to write no doubt but still indecipherable. Over time, Meroe became an anachronism. While Egypt fell under Roman domination, Meroe managed to retain independence (though the Romans would triumph against the state, their victory was not decisive).

Meroe survived until around AD 350, when it faded away and died. The cause may have been defeat in battle, economic decline, failure of the crops or, as it often is, a combination of factors. This ancient civilisation has largely faded from consciousness as far as history is concerned, which is a pity as the archaeological sites that remain, such as the temple of Naqa, give a fascinating insight into a world now largely lost.

On the far side of the world, there were significant developments in Mexico. The people called the Olmecs reached the zenith of their power in the period 700–400 BC. The centre of their settlement was in the modern states of Tabasco and Veracruz. Their great city was La Venta but there were also important sites at Tres Zapotes and San Lorenzo. There was a highly organised political and religious super-class in control of their civilisation. There was also a surplus of agricultural production, which enabled specialists in various crafts to develop.

Several art forms developed. One of them involved the carving of large stone humanoid heads, some of which were nearly 9 feet high and weighed 40 tons. Jade was also worked and was very highly valued. Statues half-human, half-jaguar continued to be crafted; this remained so for centuries – in eighth-century AD Mayan civilisation, a were-jaguar appeared in folklore! But the Olmecs had by then long died out. In the absence of historical records no one knows why, though merely being overwhelmed by other emerging cultures appears to be the most likely reason.

By the time this century closed, a powerful new force was developing around the city of Teotihuacán, which would emerge as the most impressive settlement in Mexico though that process would take hundreds of years to reach its conclusion. Over time, vast stepped pyramids started to emerge, to the honour of the Moon and the Sun and the chief deity Quetzalcoátl. He was regarded as a benign god, the deity who had given mankind the gift of agriculture. This would not though prevent the development of a cult of human sacrifice developing, leading to rituals of blood that would colour the febrile imaginations of future generations whose worlds were as yet unknown to the inhabitants of Mesoamerica.

10

WEST *VERSUS* EAST

The Age of Alexander (400–301 BC)

This was a century of great men. Consider the cast list; it includes individuals such as Alexander the Great, Plato and Socrates. Profound philosophies were developed that would shape the world's thinking for centuries. Momentous battles would be fought and significant conquests made. There would be an important expansion of geographical understanding too. In 320 BC the Greek navigator Pytheas wrote of tin imported from Cornwall, of the icy land of Thule (Iceland) six days sail to the north of Britain and of amber mining on the Baltic. He wrote of Britain that much wheat was grown but it was all threshed in barns, 'because they have so little sunshine and so much rain' – some things, apparently, have changed little. But Europe was opening up and, if distant lands were still cloaked in mystery, their existence was now clearly known.

Epic events were about to be played out, in particular around Greece, developments so momentous that they would change the shape of the world. Through what began as the most ambitious attempt at global conquest yet, the worlds of west and east were about to meet and exchange ideas and assimilate some of each other's thoughts. This was the age of Alexander the Great, one of history's most famous and controversial characters. It was also, though, the age of Chandragupta, one of India's greatest early kings, who would build a mighty empire of his own. Their two worlds, largely unknown to each other at the start of the century, would end up living cheek by jowl at its end.

As the century began, the Greek hinterlands were exhausted by decades of war and infighting. Athens had been decimated by plagues as well as conflicts. She revived economically though, with banks being established and the port of Piraeus expanding. Sparta, however, began to self-destruct. An unsuccessful attempt to usurp power by Lysander was symptomatic of ongoing problems. But alongside these political uncertainties Greece continued to contribute in other ways to the world, for it was about this time that the Hippocratic code was laid down.

Hippocrates was born around 460 BC on the island of Kos. Known as 'the Father of Medicine', he rejected the traditions and superstitions that existed at the time concerning healthcare and instead sought to create a rational and scientific approach to his subject. He argued that health problems were not caused by the gods as a punishment to mortals for their disobedience or disrespect but were rather a result of issues such as poor diet or the environment in which people lived. Noted for the strict discipline and professionalism that his teachings encouraged, the oath that he included in the corpus of his works provides, in a modified form, the basis of many modern medical ethics systems.

Another famous Greek of the time was Socrates. Renowned for his philosophical insight, it is ironic that few of his writings survive. His claim to fame rests instead on the fact that other famous writers, including Plato and Aristotle, were inspired by him. He taught that human beings should live their lives with a focus on self-development rather than material wealth.

However, it was his constant questioning of everything accepted as the norm that made enemies of some powerful people. In 399 BC, he was brought to trial by his fellow Athenians on charges of sacrilege and corrupting the young. Found guilty, he was sentenced to death. He met his end when he took hemlock. He could have escaped but chose not to do so – after all, what self-respecting philosopher would show he was scared of dying?

It was one of his acolytes, Plato, and the latter's pupil Aristotle, who laid the foundations of western philosophy, the influence of which was to spread widely across the globe as a period of 'Greek' (actually Macedonian) conquest loomed. Plato went on to write in 385 BC his *Symposium*. He established an academy teaching mathematics, astronomy, other sciences and philosophy. In a blow against a traditionally male-dominated society, women were allowed to join it.

Not long after he completed his most famous work, the *Republic*. This lays out the rules for an ideal society, warns of the delusive power of poetry and suggests that kings should at least be taught by philosophers. The next year Aristotle arrived to become his pupil. Plato's writings continued to have an effect across the world for hundreds of years after his death. One of those he influenced was the astronomer Eudoxus of Cnidus, who taught the Greeks about the motion of the planets in a way that was not perfect but advanced the understanding of the heavens considerably.

Aristotle was equally as influential as Plato; in all probability, in medieval times he was even more so. He developed new theories of physical science that were the template for the teachings of scientists the world over until modern physics developed. Yet he was not invariably right. He subscribed to the geocentric theory of the universe, which argued that the earth was at the centre of the solar system (a belief that persisted until AD 1500). As teacher of Alexander the Great, he had a significant influence over the would-be world conqueror and strongly held that the Greeks were superior to the 'barbarians' of Persia and the eastern world. In later years his relationship with Alexander would deteriorate, not helped by the fact that Aristotle's nephew, Callisthenes (the king's expeditionary historian), was put to death on his orders.

Despite these spectacular personalities, political life in Greece was still based on shallow foundations. Persia may have been ejected from the Greek mainland but she still exercised a significant influence on Greek affairs. Internal debates continued to threaten Greece. Sparta launched a war against Athens in 395 BC. Athens responded by asking for Persian assistance. In 393 BC, the Athenian 'Long Walls' were rebuilt with Persian help.

This was realpolitik of course; Athens had been decimated by the Peloponnesian Wars. Nevertheless, it is strange that her citizens, whose emotions were still inflamed by the burning of its sacred buildings by Xerxes nearly a century before, looked east for help. Not long before, many Spartan soldiers, eager to earn a living now that their city was bankrupt after the extended and debilitating conflict, found employment as mercenaries in the Persian army. At times, it must have seemed unclear who had won the wars against Xerxes and who had lost.

Far across the globe, as yet mostly a closed book to the west, a new empire was emerging in India. It was known, after its founder, as the Nanda Empire. Short-lived (lasting just about a century), it stretched across much of northern India. Its rulers appear to have emerged from humble origins and their power was based on the huge resources devoted to building up their military strength. Contemporary accounts speak of an army of 200,000 infantry, with tens of thousands of cavalry, and thousands of chariots and war elephants. Their main significance is that they are often considered to have created the first truly Indian Empire but also that their massive forces emerged as a block to Alexander the Great's later moves east.

In the meantime, there was about to be a dramatic and decisive sea change in Greek affairs, a turn of events that would eventually send shock waves rippling out across the world. Philip of Macedon was born in 382 BC. Macedonia was heavily influenced by Greek culture but the Macedonians were something of a breed apart, rough, tough and regarded as little better than barbarians by their cousins further south (suspicion between Greeks and modern Macedonians living in what is called rather cumbersomely the 'Former Yugoslav Republic of Macedonia' remains an important, divisive part of south-east European politics to this day). By 359 BC Philip had become regent of Macedonia. He had three factors in particular in his favour: a good number of men to call on to fight for him, wealth (a large gold-mine had recently been discovered in his territories) and, most of all, extraordinary political acumen allied to an incisive military mind.

Shortly after becoming regent, Philip had already started to nibble away at smaller Greek cities close to his orbit. By 353 BC, he was ready to push further south. His advance was blocked, though, at that impenetrable barrier, the Pass of Thermopylae. It took ten more years but eventually Philip was challenging Athens itself. Acutely aware of the danger, the famous Athenian orator Demosthenes urged his fellow citizens to spare no effort in resisting the rising power of Macedon.

Then in 338 BC a decisive conflict was fought, the Battle of Chaeronea, at the end of which Athens and her Theban allies were defeated – Demosthenes was allegedly one of the first to flee the field. Soon after, Sparta too was forced to accept Macedonian supremacy. The battle was decisive for it marked the effective end of the power of the Greek city states.

Philip's reputation only suffers because his son was one of the greatest military geniuses of all time. But Alexander the Great, who would become King of Macedonia in

336 BC, inherited a formidable fighting machine from his father. Philip's army was well disciplined and well armed, built around powerful infantrymen armed with enormous spears. The secret of their success was that they fought as one, operating en masse in compact phalanxes, solid formations of infantry moving together in close coordination, advancing like a juggernaut, steamrollering over everything in its path with terrifying inevitability. Under Philip it had been as unbeatable as it would be under Alexander, although its operations were on a much more local scale.

Alexander paid tribute to his father's legacy if the words of his chroniclers are to be believed. According to them, he said to his troops when they eventually stopped their eastward advance in India that

> he made you a match in battle for the barbarians on your borders, so that you no longer trusted for your safety to the strength of your positions so much as to your natural courage … It was due to him that you became masters and not slaves or subjects of those very barbarians who used previously to plunder your possessions and carry off your persons.

But if the one-eyed Philip (the other eye had been lost in battle) was a formidable parent, so too was Alexander's mother, Olympias. It was said that she was a snake worshipper and she was certainly a lover of the mystic arts. She was also a dangerous person to make an enemy of. Philip put her aside for a younger woman who bore him a son. When Philip was murdered in 336 BC most believed that she was behind the plot, both to avenge herself and protect the position of herself and her son.

Alexander was proclaimed king. So too, in that same year, was Darius III, who was enthroned as the ruler of Persia. Just over a year before, Philip had already proclaimed at the Council of Corinth that he would lead an army to free the Greek cities in Ionia from Persian domination. Alexander had altogether bigger ideas. After putting down revolts close to home, in 334 BC he led his army across the Hellespont and into Asia. He would never see home again.

Shortly after crossing, Alexander played out a fantasy that he must have always dreamed of. He was a lover of the tales of Troy and seems to have modelled himself on Achilles, from whom he claimed descent (prominent Greeks often claimed to have divine or semi-divine ancestors). His friend and lover Hephaestion became Patroclus, the beloved confidante of Achilles who was tragically lost at Troy. Given this, it must have been a powerful and inspirational moment when the army stopped at Troy to pay homage to their legendary ancestors and heroes, and Alexander and Hephaestion ran naked around the supposed tomb of Achilles in celebration of their illustrious predecessor.

There were, soon after, more mundane matters to attend to. Darius, naturally, was not prepared to let the army get very far before driving it back across the sea. The first decisive confrontation of the war took place not far into the journey, on the River Granicus. In the battle that followed, the Macedonians had a numerical advantage though the Persian army was reinforced by a significant number of Greek mercenaries, demonstrating that this was not simply a war between Greece and Persia. Alexander was wounded but his army was triumphant and proceeded to advance further into the hinterland of Asia Minor.

To the solidity of the infantry phalanx, Alexander had added the speed of cavalry, his famous 'Companions'. It was an impressive combination. Darius brought up his main army to face the Macedonian threat. The two armies met at Issus, close to where the south-east corner of Asia Minor abutted the north-west corner of Syria. Nowadays, in the shadow of the clouds from nearby power plants, it is hard to realise that this spot saw one of the decisive battles of history.

The battle was won by the shattering charge of the Companions, who smashed through the forces facing them as if they were not there. Darius, in his war chariot in the Persian centre as was the custom, managed to escape. Great treasure fell into Macedonian hands, none greater perhaps than the wife, mother and children of Darius himself. They were all well treated.

Rather than moving on Persia itself, Alexander instead advanced down the Mediterranean coast. He tried to enter Tyre but was resisted by the citizens. This was a foolish decision, made perhaps because the Tyrians felt secure as their city was on an island. This did not matter to Alexander, who painstakingly built a causeway across the few hundred yards of sea that cut it off from the land. The city fell and most of the garrison paid a painful price for their intransigence, being crucified by the infuriated Alexander, who had been delayed for seven months.

Alexander then moved into Egypt. The power of the kingdom had declined greatly. Ironically to the south the kingdom of Meroë had reached greater heights than ever before, perhaps because it was relieved of pressures from the north. It was agriculturally self-sufficient and well supplied with iron. It had in many ways become more Egyptian than Egypt itself; for example, 223 pyramids are known in Nubia, about twice as many as have been evidenced in Egypt. The great temple of Musawwarat es-Sufra – 'The Great Enclosure' – was a significant site of pilgrimage for worshippers of Amen. They also traded with shadowy lands further to the west across the arid regions there and it is known that a trading centre existed at Jenne-Jeno in Mali from around 400 BC.

But Egypt itself was on the wane and had been under foreign control for some time. The Persians were unpopular there (they had been ejected at the beginning of the century but had subsequently returned) and the Egyptians welcomed Alexander, if not quite as conquering hero, at least as someone who was eminently preferable to the current alternative. Alexander responded positively to their friendly greetings, adopting their gods and then setting off across the desert to the remote oasis of Siwa.

Even now a place apart from the rest of Egypt, set as it is in the hidden centre of a sea of sand, here was the sanctuary of the god Ammon, who had become synonymous with the Greek Zeus. At Siwa Alexander had an oracular consultation, the contents of which were kept secret. However, the visit made a profound impact on Alexander that lasted for the rest of his short life. It was even said that when he died he left instructions that he should be buried at Siwa.

Despite the fact that there were Greeks fighting alongside the Persians, Alexander had sold the campaign to his army as a war of revenge for former outrages against Greece.

To achieve retribution, he had to crush Persia but that could wait for a short time. He established a new city on the Egyptian coast of the Mediterranean, which he named Alexandria. He was not, it seems, a modest man; over thirty Alexandrias appeared across the lands that he conquered.

Then finally he moved in 331 BC towards Persia. Just to the west of Persia itself, a decisive battle was fought at Gaugamela. There were wide plains in front of the Macedonian position but, despite the fact that the battlefield seemed to be tailor-made for the Persians and their scythed chariots, being flat and open, Darius's army – which was numerically vastly superior – was shattered. It was simply no match for Alexander's well-disciplined and increasingly experienced army, particularly as it had been further buoyed by an unbroken succession of victories.

Following this triumph, Alexander moved into Babylon where again he was treated as something of a liberator. Here, sights greeted the eyes of the former herdsmen from Macedon that they could barely comprehend. The great wealth of the city was staggering and offered Alexander the opportunity to finance further adventures. The magnificence of its architecture and the inescapable signs of its former greatness overwhelmed even Alexander, for whom the city seemed from then on to hold a special affection.

But the conquest was far from over. He then moved into the heartlands of Persia where he was less enthusiastically greeted. The great cities of the motherland fell to him, Susa and Persepolis in particular. It was in the latter that Alexander, a ruthless man and like most Macedonians of the time an inveterate drinker, burned the magnificent palace, one of the most opulent of the ancient world, while he was in an alcohol-induced stupor.

The fate of Persepolis, described by Alexander as 'the most hateful city in Asia', was a grim one. His troops had suffered enormously as a result of this long, gruelling and seemingly never-ending campaign. They were rewarded by being allowed to do with the city as they wished and an orgy of rapine and looting followed. The treasures of the palace, though, were reserved for Alexander (before he burned it down). The wealth it contained was staggering. It was valued as being worth nearly 130,000 talents of gold. To give that some perspective, it was equivalent to 300 years' worth of income for Athens. With this kind of funding, anything was possible.

However, Darius still had to be caught and Alexander resumed the chase. The Persian king fled towards the periphery of his empire but was eventually killed by his own shrinking entourage. One of them, his general Bessus, declared himself king in his stead. The chase resumed with increased intensity; Alexander needed to overcome a kingdom, not just one man. Bessus was pursued right across the seemingly impassable Hindu Kush, 14,000 feet high. He was eventually captured and died the most excruciating death, impaled after being cruelly mutilated. The last of the Persian kings had been definitively wiped out.

Alexander was now in little-known lands in Central Asia. He saw great cities which even then bestrode crucial trade routes from east to west, such as Balkh and Samarkand. In the latter, he slew one of his chief lieutenants, Cleitus, the same man who had saved his life at his earliest battle with the Persians, the fight on the Granicus. Cleitus had allegedly argued that Alexander was becoming a victim of his own publicity, that he had over-inflated views of himself; the king, who was again intoxicated, speared him in an uncontrollable rage. As soon as he had slaughtered the man who was one of his most trusted advisers, Alexander collapsed in a flood of tears.

In Central Asia, Alexander decided to marry. By now, some of his own men were querying his adoption of local customs. He dressed like a Persian and seemed to enjoy the virtual deification of his person by his Persian subjects; this was traditional in Persia but unknown in Greece. His choice of bride was a local princess, Roxana. She was renowned for her beauty, her nickname being 'little star'. The locals had a sense of pride in the match; they were still telling the story when Marco Polo passed through nearly 2,000 years later. However, Alexander's Macedonians grumbled at his choice of a foreign bride.

Alexander was an inveterate traveller, fascinated by the world that was opening up in front of him. He wished to reach the ends of the earth but had no idea where that was. Now, he moved his men towards India. They marched into the Punjab, by now a vast, lumbering army laden down with thousands of camp followers. They crossed the Indus, fighting off armies that included terrifying war elephants (though these could be as dangerous to their own men as to the enemy if hurt). But when they reached the River Beas, the army would go no further. They had been away from Macedon for eight years and, not unreasonably, wanted to go home.

Alexander was enraged but in the end even he could not lead an army this exhausted and frustrated. Arrangements were made to return west. On the way, Alexander was seriously injured in a reckless assault made at the city of Multan, possibly inspired by his pique that his men had refused to follow him further across the Beas. His constitution was badly affected and he would never truly recover his vigour again.

Leaving India at last, he marched along the coast while his general Nearchus went with some of the men by sea. Alexander led the army through a desert waste known as the Makran, allegedly the most awful event of the entire extended expedition. At last, decimated by hunger, thirst and disease, the army arrived back in Persia. In Susa, mass marriages of the Macedonian generals to local women took place. Provisions were made for the 10,000 children that had been born to native concubines while the army had been on the march.

Alexander never left the Middle East, nor did he want to. In places, his story remains so famous that he has still not left it – in Persia 'Iskander' is still remembered with revulsion. His life was now in Persia and Babylon. New expeditions were planned, with Arabia apparently next on the world tour. But increasingly he became an embittered and isolated man, old well beyond his years. The death of his beloved Hephaestion in 324 BC seems to have devastated him; the doctor who had failed to cure his lover was put to death. The year after, on 13 June, Alexander himself died, appropriately enough in Babylon. He was not yet thirty-three years old but had lived more fully than most men would do in a thousand lifetimes. The cause of death was unknown. Liver failure is a strong suspect but there were widespread rumours of poison, not administered by Persian enemies but by Macedonians who wished to wander no longer.

The Macedonian conquests provide one of the epic stories of history but they also played a crucial role in the spread and interplay of cultural interfaces. Greek culture, with its philosophies, political practices and artistic achievements, was disseminated across a huge empire but at the same time other influences were appended to the mix to add in their own way to Greek achievement. Within a few years of Alexander's campaigns, for example, we find statues of Buddha from the north-west corners of India but with unmistakable Greek artistic influences.

The Macedonian king is one of the great heroic figures of all time to many. But to some he was, and is, a tyrant, the two-horned one, the Accursed. In Iran he is still the target of bitter resentment. The last Shah of Persia could not bear to speak of him. Once Alexander had passed through, the smell of death and decay lay thickly over the proud Persian Empire that he had steamrollered. An ancient Persian oracular text had described how 'all Asia shall suffer a yoke of evil, and its soaked earth shall drink much blood'. That powerful prophecy had come true with a vengeance.

Alexander's empire was too large to rule without the unifying influence of his colossal personality and within months of his death it had started to disintegrate. There were soon after six different parts of the empire with different rulers: Ptolemy (Egypt), Seleucus (Babylon and Syria), Antipater and Cassander (Macedon and Greece), Antigonus (Phrygia), Lysimachus (Thrace) and Eumenes (Pontus). Ptolemy began a pharaonic dynasty, one that would last until the time of Cleopatra.

The succession dispute led to a deluge of bloodletting. Alexander's mother Olympias was murdered by Cassander; so too, soon after, were Alexander's young son and Roxana. It was not until 301 BC that the decisive battle in the war of succession was fought at Ipsus. There were huge armies involved, about 70,000–80,000 on each side. Lysimachus and Seleucus led one party against that of Antigonus on the other side. The former had more war chariots than the latter and was also armed with war elephants. In a brutal conflict, Antigonus was killed and his army destroyed. However, much energy and human capital had been expended in this fight and it left the empire exhausted.

The use of war elephants hints at close relationships between the Macedonians and an emerging Indian leader, Chandragupta. Seleucus had been consolidating his empire as far as India. Beginning negotiations in 305 BC, he had entered into an alliance with Chandragupta, who gave him a present of 500 war elephants (those that featured at Ipsus). In 303 BC Seleucus left behind his ambassador Megasthenes at the court of Chandragupta while he moved back west to his appointment with destiny. Megasthenes continued to send back informative reports to his master.

These events took place on the north-western periphery of India. Meanwhile, Chandragupta had managed to become the ruler of significant chunks of other parts of India too. He came from a small kingdom called Maurya. In 321 BC he had taken advantage of the unpopularity of the Nanda dynasty, which ran its territories ruthlessly, and overthrew it.

He then established his own Mauryan Empire, which incorporated the Ganges Valley. This was just the beginning of the expansion of his kingdom. By the time the empire reached its maximum extent it would control 80 per cent of the landmass of the Subcontinent. To put this in perspective, it was the greatest empire measured in the proportion of Subcontinent territory controlled until the Mughals came along in the seventeenth century AD (they were only subsequently outdone by the British at the height of the Raj).

The deal struck with Seleucus was a way of opening up roads to further expansion. It gave Chandragupta access to territories bordering the Indus Valley too. He moved into the vacuum that he had negotiated and moulded Taxila into a city that became famous for its scholars and their love of learning. It suited Seleucus's purpose too as it enabled him to concentrate on affairs further west while feeling confident that the agreement with Chandragupta protected his back. But it has also been suggested that Seleucus had no choice, having lost heavily in battle against the forces of Chandragupta, though there is little evidence to support this supposition.

Chandragupta's origins are obscure. Some said that he was the illegitimate offspring of a Nanda prince, others that he was the son of a peacock tamer. Wherever he came from, what he did is in far less doubt. His empire would stretch from the borders of Afghanistan in the west to Bengal and Assam in the east, while it reached as far north as Nepal and Kashmir and as far south as the Deccan Plateau in central India. With the aid of a hugely talented prime minister, Chanakya, Chandragupta managed to build the largest Indian state seen up to that time.

This was a remarkable king but the evidence suggests that he was an equally remarkable man. He embraced Jainism in later life (he did not live long past forty) and voluntarily gave up the throne so that he could concentrate solely on spiritual matters. It was said that he starved himself to death while engaged in a fast in a cave in a ritual detachment from all material distractions known as *aparigraha*. His grandson Ashoka would become perhaps the most famous of all ancient Indian kings.

To the north-east, immune from these events (though rumours must have surely filtered through the trade routes before long), there had been some violent upheavals in China too. The Chin region in the north had fallen apart in 403 BC, in the year, the chronicles said inscrutably, that the Nine Tripods shook. As a result some of the still fragmented Chinese states got bigger. The greatest gainer of all in terms of territory was in the west, where the Ch'in state grew considerably larger. But it was a traumatic time, as the label given to it suggests, for the decades that followed were known as the Warring States period.

At the start of this period (which ran from 403 to 361 BC) there were nine states but by its end there were four dominating. To the east of the Ch'in were the Wei and the Qi, while to the south the large state of the Chu ran both north and south of the Yangtze. The Ch'in lived in an area that was effectively a backwater, but that all changed with the arrival at the court in 361 BC of a nobleman called Shang Yang. He was the son of a concubine from the Wei territories and as such was debarred from real power. Perhaps this gave him his motivation and his energy to help build a Ch'in dynasty.

Given free rein, he first of all introduced a draconian legal code into the Ch'in homeland. Even the ruler's own son was sentenced to death when he broke a minor law, though it was eventually decided that this punishment was inappropriate and his tutor was executed instead. Then it was agreed that progression through Ch'in society should be on military merit, not accident of birth. Men were encouraged to till the land by being given their own private plots. But there was a sinister side to this new rule; all Confucius's works that could be found were burned.

All of this was building up to a period of Ch'in conquest. In 340 BC their army moved on Wei territory, which fell easily. However, the architect of this triumph, the brutal Shang Yang, was living on borrowed time. A new ruler took over in the Ch'in territories soon after. His name was Huiwen and he was the ruler's son whose teacher had been executed as a vicarious punishment for his misdemeanours some years before. He ordered that Shang Yang be arrested but he fled. However, he could find no hiding place, for the law decreed that no one could give shelter to a stranger unless he carried an official pass. He had none and was soon caught, an irony indeed as this harsh regulation was one he himself had introduced.

He was soon after tied up between four chariots that were then sent charging off in four different directions. But despite this vicious act of elimination, Huiwen continued to govern by the rules that Shang Yang had set up. They were harsh but they were certainly useful. They had helped establish the Ch'in as the rising power in China (a region which was named after them).

In Europe, a new region was on the verge by now of becoming far more influential. The Italian Peninsula had become a fault line where four major groups came into potentially explosive contact with each other: Greeks, Carthaginians, Celts and indigenous Italians. To the last category belong the Etruscans, whose peak was now in the past, but also the emerging power of Rome.

In the south, Sicily was a flashpoint, particularly between the Carthaginians and the Greeks, the latter especially strong in their main base of Syracuse. In 398 BC, there was a 'night of the long knives' directed by the Greeks against the Carthaginians and many were slaughtered as a result. The year after, the Carthaginian general Himilco led an army against Dionysius of Syracuse, hell-bent on revenge. He failed and returned to Carthage, where he publicly humiliated himself in every temple and then starved himself to death.

This was not the end of Carthaginian dreams of revenge, but Dionysius was sufficiently invigorated by his triumph to invade the south of Italy proper in 391 BC. He was not initially successful but was a resilient and determined campaigner. By the time he died in 367 BC, he had established a Greek foothold there and offered a foundation for further expansionist efforts.

Rome was still not securely established and as yet was far from a superpower. Gauls continued to pour over the Alps and attempted to carve out a kingdom for themselves in the north of Italy. In 391 BC, they advanced down the Italian Peninsula and defeated a Roman army at the Battle of Allia. Rome had been so exhausted by fighting local wars that her army was hugely outnumbered. The Gauls were at first so taken aback by the paucity of the force facing them that they were reluctant to attack, thinking the Roman tactics a ruse. Realising eventually that they were not, they stormed into battle and slaughtered the Roman army.

For six months, Rome itself was under siege until only the Capitol, atop a hill in the middle of the city, held out. But the Gauls were unable to push home their advantage. It has been prosaically suggested that the Romans bought them off. More romantically, another story tells how an attempt to take the Capitol was beaten off when the sacred geese of Juno, who were housed there, acted as surrogate guard dogs and their cackles alerted the garrison just in time as the attackers attempted to catch the defenders by surprise.

Rome then decided that more needed to be done to protect it. One way it sought to do this was by conquering adjacent territories to create a buffer zone to defend the city. The Servian wall was also constructed around Rome as a further line of defence. At least twice more (in 358 BC and 350 BC) the Gauls came back to try again, but once more without success. There were important non-military developments too. In 347 BC, Rome became a monetary economy when coins were introduced to it for the first time, though there was something of an economic crisis when it happened.

Later on in the century, the Romans were often up against local rivals, the Samnites. They proved a very difficult opponent and Rome was often on the wrong side of a defeat. The Roman army had adopted the phalanx system much loved by the Macedonian army. However, in 315 BC they decided that this was no longer an effective tactic. They took away the long spears that their men had previously been armed with and instead gave them short swords and javelins. This would become the basic armament of Roman infantry when the empire was in its prime. Out of the bitter lessons of defeat Rome had learned the secrets of military success. It was now on the verge of the campaigns that would eventually lead to the conquest of much of Europe, western Asia and northern Africa.

Yet, at the end of this remarkable century, we must return to the epic story of Alexander. Not only was this a tale of epic proportions, it was also an event that had a dramatic impact in opening up the world. The impact of Greek civilisation on India was profound. By the third century BC, Pythagoras' Theorem would be known in China. A century after that, we believe that the Chinese met Westerners, merchants on the Great Silk Road, for the first time. Many centuries later, Islamic culture would also be heavily influenced by Hellenistic philosophy, and Plato in particular would be honoured. The dramatic movement east by Alexander would play a major role in all this.

Alexander is a man who courts controversy. None of us can be assessed in terms of black and white. We are all complex, capable of acting emotionally and irrationally. But few men can ever have written their page in history with so much complexity in their mind and their soul. Tyrant or inspiration, a man of violence or a man of vision? It depends on an individual's point of view, but surely he was all of these and more.

The last word should go to a modern Pakistani scholar from Taxila, almost Alexander's furthest point east on his excursion into India, for few could say it better:

> Alexander belongs not only to Greece but to the Islamic world, and to Pakistan and India. For this is one of the greatest events in the history of the world.

11

THE CHINESE REWRITE HISTORY

The Ch'in Dynasty Is Founded (300–201 BC)

The fractured political landscape of China was about to become much more unified. The region was on the verge of seeing a reversal of the disintegration that had epitomised the recent past. In 259 BC, the armies of the western Ch'in state defeated their regional enemies in a battle on the Yellow River. There was a massive slaughter of captives in the aftermath. Three years later, the last Zhou emperor was forced to stand down.

In 246 BC, the Ch'in dynasty was formally established, led by its 'First August Emperor', Shih-huang-ti. Having repelled Hun raiders, the new emperor attempted to turn China from its feudal structure into a totalitarian police state by introducing communal landholdings and standard weights and measures. His unification of the disparate states he conquered ended with what might be regarded as the first approximation of what we now know as China.

The country was divided into administrative units and Shih-huang-ti ensured that no relatives of officials were posted to prominent positions, putting a brake on nepotism. He trusted no one. But his achievements were not all autocratically based. He built a large number of new palaces, one for each defeated enemy. He modelled his capital Hsien-yan on the Milky Way, reflecting an interest in astronomy. He also introduced a standard calendar to his kingdom. Roads and canals were built on a grand scale, improving the basic infrastructure of the region. These were all positive achievements on an impressive scale.

But he also began to raise armies bigger than any previously seen in China. All private weapons were collected and melted down, limiting opportunities for future private feuding. In 225 BC, he started work on a 'Great Wall'. Walls had been built here before, but this was on an altogether different scale, stretching 2,000 miles in total, taking twelve years to build. Shih-huang-ti was told by his soothsayer to bury 10,000 men under it to ensure its success. Even the emperor was shocked at this, so instead he buried one man with the name 'ten thousand'.

Nevertheless, many died as a result of the harsh construction conditions. The slaves and peasants who were conscripted to work on this enormous structure had few rights. Shih-huang-ti was a ruthless man, happy to eliminate any, great or small, who stood in his way. He was aided by an equally ruthless lieutenant, Li Ssu. In 223 BC, in an act known as the Burning of the Books, piles of old records and historical accounts were burned, although a copy of Confucius's teachings was retained. Attempting to control the narrative of history was a dictatorial way of controlling the people, a trick often emulated since.

It was a capital offence even to discuss the old teachings. The year after the burning, 460 Confucian scholars were killed, their knowledge and philosophy being a threat to this attempt to control the minds of the citizens of the region. There was another shadowy figure behind this policy, a draconian philosopher Han Feizi, who castigated scholars, merchants and artisans alike, classing them under the headings of the so-called Five Vermin. 'In the state of an enlightened ruler there are no books written on bamboo slips: law supplies the only instruction.' Books on medicine, divination and horticulture were excluded from the Burning but everything else went up in smoke.

The emperor died in 210 BC. He left a huge underground tomb, a vast pit in which the workmen responsible for constructing it were buried alive. It was protected by crossbow booby traps, a trick that would have done justice to an Indiana Jones film. But this was not all. Alongside him were 8,000 warriors, 130 chariots with 520 horses and 150 cavalry horses, all made in terracotta. Each individual soldier in this famous terracotta army, only discovered in AD 1974 and now one of the most famous of all archaeological finds, has a different face, so close was the attention to detail. As he dominated his people in life, Shih-huang-ti's continued legacy continues to grab the headlines in death.

Shih-huang-ti left a weak successor, Er Shih-huang-ti. He attempted to enforce his rule by brutality but only succeeded in causing a mutiny. In 206 BC he was deposed and committed suicide. This brought an end to the Ch'in dynasty, a generally harsh period in Chinese history.

Ch'in rule enforced a ruthless legal code where the laws were savage and brutally administered. There were a number of punishments imposed for wrongdoers. In ascending order of severity, they were branding of the forehead, cutting off of the nose, cutting off of the feet, of the genitals, flogging and then death. Li Si, the man who introduced these draconian measures, suffered them all when he was punished after his overthrow, finally being cut in half. All his family were killed too. However, from the wreckage of the state a new and longer-lasting dynasty, the Han, was about to emerge.

India too was to see the emergence of a mighty ruler. In 297 BC, Chandragupta abdicated and his son Bindusara succeeded him. He extended the Mauryan Empire south to Mysore. He was known to the Greeks as *Amitrochates*, 'slayer of enemies', the title of a conqueror, but little else is known of him. However, he is known to have had continued contacts with the Seleucid Macedonians.

In 272 BC, Bindusara was succeeded by Ashoka, one of ancient India's greatest kings. As a young man he was sent to Taxila to put down a rebellion. Here he learned the arts of war but also those of love, taking a mistress of great beauty, Devi, who was believed to be a Buddhist. Although she bore his children, he did not marry her. Nevertheless, it was suggested that her Buddhist teachings were eventually to have a profound effect on Ashoka.

Ashoka did not initially find the job of king an easy one. On his accession, he had to fight his brothers for the throne. Once securely established, he started to expand his kingdom but initially failed to subdue the lands of his neighbour in Kalinga (now Odisha). However, in 260 BC Ashoka tried again, completing the conquest of most of the Indian Subcontinent by defeating Kalinga in a bloody battle (only the land of the Pandyas in the south stayed independent). His treatment of Kalinga was harsh in the extreme, with tens of thousands of deaths in the slaughter that followed the battle, and mass deportations to boot.

Ashoka was a brutal ruler, with his early achievements including a grim torture chamber in Patna to punish his enemies and subdue his opponents. However, in 258 BC he underwent a profound conversion experience. He was now overcome with revulsion when he looked back on the bloody nature of his conquests and became a Buddhist. 'The slaughter, death and deportation of the people is extremely grievous and weighs on the mind,' he explained. He then encouraged missionary visits by Buddhist monks (one allegedly to Greece), even sending a cutting from the tree under which Gautama Buddha sat to Sri Lanka as he did what he could to export Buddhism to the wider world.

These diplomatic and religious missions are mentioned in rock inscriptions that survive, our main source of history for the period. They illustrate that Ashoka exchanged diplomatic missions with western rulers such as Antiochus II, Ptolemy III and Antigonus II. Ongoing contact would continue to be made with the West over the next 100 years. The basis for an infrastructure of a flow of information and ideas from east to west and vice versa had now been established.

Ashoka was clearly a changed man. In 256 BC, he founded hospitals and herb gardens and encouraged the education of women. He also engaged in ambitious road-building programmes. In addition, he went on a pilgrimage around the Buddhist sites of his kingdom. This was perhaps not just an exercise in personal religious expression but a way of cementing an expanding empire together. He appears to have grasped the eternal truth that an idea is a much surer way of building unity than the rule of force. But he also espoused tolerance of other religions – a concept in many ways well ahead of its time.

Ashoka, also known as Dhammashoka, 'the Just', is a much revered figure in Indian history. He reigned until 232 BC but there are hints that in the last years he lost control of his kingdom when he married a young wife, Tishyaraksha, with whom he was besotted; she was, it was said, an evil and manipulative influence. As in China, his empire soon began to decline following his death, disappearing in fifty years as the Greco-Indian kingdoms to the north-west and Bactria began to eat into it.

By the time Ashoka became ruler, Greece was already changing, with its perspective increasingly eastward-facing. In 300 BC, Athens and Corinth had been the most important Greek cities, but their economies were now in a state of decline. An important new city was founded in Syria at Antioch by Alexander's successor Seleucus. However, he maintained his capital at Seleucia, on the west bank of the Tigris opposite Ctesiphon, where he exercised an absolute monarchy with a kingdom structured along Persian satrapy lines.

To the south-west, Ptolemy, ruling in Egypt, had established his own kingdom with an effective bureaucracy, run in the main by Greeks. A vibrant Jewish community played a particularly strong role in financial matters and Greek science blossomed at the dynamic and hugely influential new port of Alexandria. Ptolemy devoted himself to science and set about creating a new Egypt.

But both men were growing old and needed to think about their successors. In 293 BC, Seleucus handed over the lands he held west of the Euphrates to his son Antiochus. In 285 BC, Ptolemy abdicated, handing over Egypt to his son, who became Ptolemy II. Great achievements followed on.

In 283 BC, construction of the Pharos of Alexandria, a towering lighthouse that was one of the Seven Wonders of the World, began, with Sostratus of Cnidus as its architect. Shortly after, the island of Rhodes became home to another Wonder, its great Colossus, a huge statue (105 feet high) of the Rhodian patron-god Helios. Chares was its architect and it is said that he committed suicide rather than deal with the fact that the costs of its construction exceeded the initial estimate. Many modern civil servants must be glad that such action is no longer expected when a cost overrun occurs, though the statue lasted for only half a century before collapsing during an earthquake.

In the years that followed, political unrest continued to disturb the tranquillity of the fragmented Macedonian Empire. Seleucus invaded Macedonia and killed its rival king in 281 BC but the year after he himself was assassinated. In 279 BC, a horde of Gauls poured down the Greek peninsula through Macedonia. They were halted just before Delphi but diverted to Asia Minor, where they established a small province of their own (Galatia, the home of the New Testament Galatians).

Internecine fights continued throughout the empire as the century progressed, ripping Alexander's political legacy apart, but in Europe new powers were slowly gaining recognition. In 273 BC, Ptolemy II sent an embassy to Rome (the city would send a return delegation). The power of Greece was, in a political sense, already in retreat in many places (though not yet fully in Syria, Egypt or the parts of India that were in Greek hands). However, their contribution to the world of ideas was unabated.

There was so much verve and drive exhibited during these years that a sample of developments will have to suffice to sum up the period. In 250 BC, Hero of Alexandria invented a steam engine, a device that automatically opened doors, and a water clock (though only the latter was turned to practical use). At around the same time, Ptolemy II encouraged the Jews in the city to have their holy book translated into Greek. Ptolemy was very careful to preserve the separate identities of the Greek, Jewish and Egyptian populations in the city, though later such differentiation would turn into distrust that would ultimately lead to out-and-out violence; such outbreaks based on ethnicity were nothing new and are still all too obvious in the modern world.

One of the great Greeks of this time was the mathematician Archimedes. He was born in Syracuse on Sicily in 287 BC. Founded by Greek settlers half a millennium previously, the city became one of the greatest of all antiquity, surrounded by walls that stretched for some 22 kilometres. Archimedes is most famous for developing the theory of displacement and his renowned 'Eureka' moment but in 230 BC he invented a huge pleasure boat with its own sports deck, garden deck and pleasure bath and a stadium 407 feet long. A great idea in theory, it was too expensive to run and was sent to Egypt with a cargo of corn to help with a famine. Therefore, the life of what might loosely be termed the world's first luxury cruise liner came to a distressingly practical early conclusion.

This was also the age of a generally obscure Greek kinglet whose name lives on in the English language, though of his own life little is known. His name was Pyrrhus, King of Epirus. In the year 299 BC he went to Egypt as a hostage but returned to his kingdom four years later with the help of Ptolemy I. In 287 BC he took advantage of ongoing weaknesses in Macedonia to declare himself king, only to be driven out the following year. An inveterate opportunist, it was only a matter of time before he found himself embroiled in upheavals further afield.

In 282 BC, Rome declared war on the city of Tarentum (now Taranto on the heel of Italy). Having failed in Greece, Pyrrhus opted to try his hand on the other side of the Adriatic and chose to ally himself with Rome's enemy. Two years later, he invaded Italy with an army of 20,000. Near Heraclea, a great battle was fought in which Pyrrhus's twenty elephants wreaked havoc and the Roman cavalry was swatted aside. Rome was defeated but the losses of Pyrrhus were almost as great as his opponents'. This was his first 'Pyrrhic victory'.

Next year, he advanced on Rome. Attempts to bribe Roman officials and frighten them with the surprise appearance of an elephant failed. Another Pyrrhic victory at Asculum soon afterwards encouraged Pyrrhus to engage in ever more frantic peace approaches to Rome. While this was happening in the north of the Italian Peninsula, on Sicily Carthaginian forces attacked Syracuse. The people of Syracuse appealed to Pyrrhus for help but his intervention did little practical good.

In 275 BC Pyrrhus suffered a heavy defeat in a battle with Rome and returned to Greece with just a third of his original army. Captured elephants appeared in a Roman triumph, the first known instance of a celebration that would one day mark a series of great Roman victories. Back in Greece, Pyrrhus invaded Macedonia and ejected its ruler Antigonus II. However, Antigonus fought his way back in. Pyrrhus then tried his luck attacking Sparta and Argos, and was killed in the latter when a woman threw a tile at him from a window, an ignominious end to a very ambitious but largely unfulfilled man's life.

In the meantime, Rome had been cementing its rise. In 299 BC, the Third Samnite War broke out when Samnites from the Italian Peninsula in alliance with Gauls and Etruscans attacked Rome. Three years later, they were prepared to advance on Rome but their combined forces were defeated at the Battle of Sentinum. By 291 BC, the Third Samnite War had come to end, with Samnite autonomy recognised by Rome but with the latter clearly triumphant. It was not until 283 BC though, when Rome defeated the Etruscans and Gauls at Lake Vadimo, that they became effective masters of north and central Italy.

Carthage, in the meantime, was pushing north across the Mediterranean from her African base. By 270 BC, she ruled both Sardinia and southern Spain and had effective control of the western Mediterranean. She possessed most of Sicily too, though Syracuse held out. She did not have huge military resources of her own and had to employ large numbers of mercenaries. With Rome pushing south down the Italian Peninsula, it was almost inevitable that the two powers would collide with each other.

In 265 BC, the spark for confrontation was lit in Messina, Sicily. An internal dispute there led to the city asking for help from both Carthage and Rome. Both responded favourably. The Carthaginians got there first but were ejected when the Romans arrived. Angered at this turn of events, Carthage sent a force to Sicily which was beaten off by a Roman army led by Appius Claudius.

In 263 BC, the Romans attacked Syracuse and forced its king Hieron to enter into an alliance with them. The following year, the Carthaginians were defeated by Rome at Agrigentum. The Carthaginians had elephants in their army but they caused more trouble for their own side than for their Roman enemies. Agrigentum was taken and its people enslaved by Rome.

If Carthage held an ace, it was to be found in her seafaring skills. In 261 BC, Rome started to build a navy by making 100 copies of a grounded Carthaginian ship. Just one year later, they scored a crushing victory over the Carthaginians at Mylae near the Straits of Messina. Their victory owed much to a 'crow's bill' (*corvus*), a hinged and hooked boarding plank; sea battles at the time were fought more like land battles rather than owing anything to naval strategy.

This First Punic War appeared to be going Rome's way. In 258 BC, the Romans took Corsica from Carthage, strengthening their position in the western Mediterranean. Another Roman sea victory at the Battle of Cape Ecnomus two years later gave them the confidence to consider crossing over to Africa. Soon after, an armada sailed across the Mediterranean with the hope of taking Carthage itself.

But then, just when a Roman victory in her first overseas venture seemed inevitable, the Carthaginians launched a fightback under a Spartan mercenary, Xanthippus. The Roman commander Regulus was captured and a Roman fleet sent to rescue the army was wrecked.

A stalemate then ensued for some time. The Romans captured the naval base of Panormus on Sicily in 254 BC but could not complete the conquest of the island because they did not have sufficient command of the sea. The year after, another Roman fleet was wrecked. In 250 BC, the siege of an important base at Lilibaeum on Sicily was begun by Rome but her fleet was defeated. In an attempt to break the deadlock, Regulus was returned to Rome under terms of parole. However, he advised Rome not to surrender. He then returned to Carthage, as agreed under the terms of his parole. His honourable actions did him little good as he was allegedly then tortured to death. His wife took out her anger on two Carthaginian prisoners, who met a similarly gruesome end.

Rome was by now a major city; a census of the time gave her a population of 297,797 (though this is not always considered a reliable figure). The Carthaginians though were divided and failed to unite against Rome. Her leaders were more interested in carving out new estates in Africa than the war. They sent a new general, Hamilcar Barca, to Sicily but the Carthaginian politicians did not adequately support him. This was very much a portent of the future.

In the parts of Africa further south, history was still shrouded in obscurity. Yet from time to time glimpses emerge from the mist to enable us at least to understand something of what was happening. For example, during this century it appears that a people emerged from among the tribes known as the Soninke and became a powerful trading bloc in the territories around the upper reaches of the Niger River. The kings of this nation were known from the local word 'Ghana' and the first stirrings of a significant African nation on the West African coast were in evidence.

These changes in West Africa were little felt further north, where war raged on. Between 246 and 242 BC, Hamilcar wore the Roman defenders of Sicily down. However, Rome would not accept defeat and she determined to build another fleet. This led to a decisive Roman naval victory off Lilybaeum in 241. It left the Carthaginians on the island isolated and Carthage was forced to accept harsh peace terms. Carthage abandoned all claims to Sicily and agreed not to sail in Italian waters and to pay an indemnity of 3,200 talents. Her army was, however, allowed to return home. The doors of the Temple of Janus in Rome were shut to symbolise peace, as was the custom. They would not stay closed for long.

Towards the end of the First Punic War, in the year 247 BC, one of the great warriors of ancient history, Hannibal, was born. Seven years after his birth, Rome had taken over full control of Sicily and stationed a legion there. Her rule was harsh, with taxes levied at a much higher level than in Italy. Her policy was to turn Sicily into the breadbasket of Rome, while Roman farmers turned more to olives and vines, the luxury end of the market, now that Sicilian grain was freely available. An important side effect was that the occupation of Sicily introduced Rome to a full-blown Greek culture for the first time.

Rome's victory appeared to be complete, while the defeat of Carthage seemed to have led to her inevitable demise. Between 240 and 237 BC, Carthaginian soldiers returning home were not paid their arrears and were badly treated. It is always dangerous to have groups of discontented soldiers with time on their hands around and this insensitive treatment merely served to ignite a powder keg. A terrible civil war broke out where the proletariat joined the mercenaries. Only after much effort was the revolt put down.

In the meantime, Sardinia had joined the revolt against Carthage, and Rome took the opportunity to annex the island. By 237 BC, the Carthaginian general Hamilcar, who had crushed the rebellion back in Carthage, was sent to strengthen Carthaginian bases in Spain. He saw it as a chance to re-establish a force that could fight back against Rome. According to legend, he made his young son Hannibal vow eternal enmity towards Rome. Still a boy, Hannibal moved to Spain, where he grew up in Gadir (Cadiz). He would not see Carthage again for many years.

It was a while before Carthage was in a position to intervene again in Roman affairs. Some time was spent by the Carthaginians in establishing themselves anew in Spain, where the death of Hamilcar by drowning in 230 BC cannot have helped. His son-in-law Hasdrubal took over, establishing the city of New Carthage (Cartagena) there. In the meantime, Rome had other distractions. Those persistent Gaulish raiders invaded Roman territory again in 226 BC, though they were defeated at the Battle of Telamon the year after. In 222 BC, the Romans took the Gauls' base at Milan from them.

In the meantime, Hannibal had been developing into a powerful young man with a brilliant military mind. When in 221 BC Hasdrubal was murdered, Hannibal took command in his stead. In 219 BC, in a statement of intent, he attacked the Celtic city of

Saguntum, which was an ally of Rome. This was tantamount to a declaration of war. The Romans sent Quintius Fabius to Carthage to negotiate but discussions soon broke down. The Second Punic War was about to begin.

Hannibal's plan was hugely ambitious. He would lead his army over the Rhone in the south of Gaul and across the Alps into Italy. This was no spur-of-the-moment decision, as spies had been looking for the best routes into Italy for years. His army was said to number 100,000 and was accompanied by fifty elephants. A Roman army was sent to intercept it but arrived too late.

The crossing of the Alps was a nightmare. Wild tribesmen attacked Hannibal's army as they passed through the mountains. Narrow paths were caked in ice, and men and beasts alike fell to a terrible death down sheer precipices. The crossing took fifteen days and Hannibal was said to have lost 36,000 men in all, as well as many of the elephants.

In December 218 BC, with Hannibal now safely across, the Roman consuls Publius Scipio and Sempronius marched out with what troops could be mustered to face the Carthaginians. Scipio was wounded in a skirmish and only saved by his young son, Scipio (later known as Africanus). Sempronius suffered worse though, being heavily defeated on the River Trebia, losing a third of his men. The elephants that remained played a key part in the battle but then began to suffer from the winter cold.

Worse was to come for Rome. In 217 BC, Hannibal won a great victory over her army at the Battle of Lake Trasimene. The fight took place in thick fog and there were heavy Roman losses. Morale in Rome plummeted and the spectre of defeat loomed heavily over the city. Quintius Fabius took over the Roman defence and introduced scorched earth defensive tactics.

The year after, one of the great battles of history was fought. Rome, with an army said to be twice the size of Hannibal's, suffered a devastating defeat at Cannae, east of Naples – it was said that there were 70,000 dead. Hannibal's tactics were to face the mass of the Roman soldiers, thickly bunched together, with a thin line and leave the bulk of his forces on either flank. He himself was in the front line to encourage his men.

When the Roman mass was sucked in by its attacks against the vastly outnumbered Carthaginian centre, Hannibal's flanks attacked and overwhelmed them (for students of later history, these tactics are surprisingly similar to those used by the Zulus in their rise to power in southern Africa). Quintius Fabius had previously been removed, having not pleased the Senate with his defensive tactics, but was now reinstated. The city of Capua sided with Carthage and his army wintered there.

Hannibal was winning major battles but he had not won the war. The problem once more was back in Carthage, where a niggardly government refused to send reinforcements. Stalemate ensued again, this time in Italy rather than Africa. In 215 BC, an attack by Carthage on its lost colony of Sardinia was beaten off. Hannibal captured the important city of Tarentum but hesitated to march on Rome. No reinforcements could be spared from Spain because Rome had launched a counter-attack there. However, Carthage did succeed in persuading Syracuse to rebel against Rome.

For years, Hannibal wandered around Italy with his army. By 212 BC, Rome had twenty-five legions and a quarter of all Italian men under arms. Hannibal's moment had passed, though his achievements were still impressive as he managed to keep an army in the field that was composed of many different races: Mauritanians, Moroccans, Greeks, Spanish and Gauls, as well as Carthaginians. Corn supplies were failing. Rome encouraged a rebellion by Numidians in Africa. Hasdrubal, Hannibal's brother, dashed across from Spain to put it down. In 211 BC, Hannibal marched on Rome but failed to take it. Capua fell to Rome and was severely punished for its alliance with Carthage. This was a bitter war of tit for tat, a boxing match with two heavyweight fighters standing in the ring slugging it out, with neither side managing to strike a knock-out blow.

The Roman fightback continued in Spain, when Scipio Africanus took over in 210 BC, one year after Syracuse had fallen to the Romans (the great Archimedes was killed in the sack that followed as out-of-control soldiers looted the city). By 207 BC, the Carthaginians were being driven out of Spain. Hasdrubal retreated over the Alps to join Hannibal. He sent a letter to tell Hannibal he was coming but it was intercepted. This enabled the Romans to lay an ambush in which Hasdrubal was killed; his head was subsequently thrown into Hannibal's camp.

By 206 BC, Scipio had returned to Rome in triumph but his success was resented by the Senate. They allotted him no legions but gave him command of Sicily. He accordingly recruited his own army including survivors from Cannae and a small cavalry arm. But Hannibal's power was now waning, unsupported and deserted by the government of Carthage as he was.

They needed him again in 203 BC, when Carthage itself was under threat from Scipio who had taken an army across to Africa to attack it. Close by the city at Zama, the two armies came face to face. Scipio and Hannibal met for the first time, the latter offering peace terms which did not interest Scipio at all. All-out victory was his only aim. Cannae must be thoroughly avenged.

The Roman legions were now battle-hardened; most of Hannibal's troops in Africa were mercenaries. The Romans devised ways of rendering useless the Carthaginian elephants; they instructed their musicians to play trumpets, the blare of which caused the elephants to stampede. Their soldiers were told to open up gaps in their ranks to let the pachyderms pass harmlessly through.

The battle was a rout, with Scipio the victor. Harsh peace terms were agreed. Carthage was to give up all but ten ships and to pay an indemnity of 10,000 talents. All overseas possessions were to be renounced and her foreign policy was to be linked with that of Rome. Hannibal was allowed to remain in Carthage and join its senate but was later forced to flee after a plot against him. He could have won the war with Rome if his own government had supported him but they did not.

Hannibal's ultimate tragedy was to be turned on by those who owed him so much. Their short-sightedness had made the demise of Carthage inevitable and the exponential rise of Rome more certain. From now on, the power of the Romans soared like the early-morning sun rising inexorably higher in the sky; Carthage, on the other hand, was now heading towards the twilight. A new power was rising, one that would create an empire that would dominate southern and western Europe, northern Africa and western Asia for hundreds of years.

12

DESTINATION CHINA

The Opening of the Great Silk Road (200–101 BC)

The world was on the verge of becoming much more interconnected. A trade route was about to open that would connect China to the Middle East and through it, indirectly, to the lands around the Mediterranean. The road that was opened would be a great arterial route for centuries, a highway along which goods would flow well into the Middle Ages. Though both east and west would stay, for most people, distant and little-known lands, the goods that would flow along the trade routes would help to increase awareness, at least among the educated class and those few rich enough to avail themselves of the luxury items that were now available.

Evidence of these connections reveals itself from time to time in archaeology, such as with the gold Roman coin found in China, decorated with an image of Bacchus and dated to the second century BC. Trade the other way may be intimated by the discovery of silk in 3,000-year-old Egyptian mummies, though this may have come through middlemen rather than direct from China.

Silk indeed played an underestimated part in the development of trading links. In the first century AD the Roman emperor Tiberius complained that so much silk was being bought that 'ladies and their baubles are transferring our money to foreigners' – this has a surprisingly contemporary ring to it in the globalised economy of the modern world but demonstrates that complaints about levels of imports are nothing new. So great would the problem become that Tiberius prohibited the wearing of silk to solve it.

All of this stemmed from the opening up of the Silk Road. However, there were other great changes taking place that would also alter the shape of the world during this century, particularly in the forms of a rising power in the West and another in the Middle East, both able to step into the breach created by declining powers elsewhere.

The rising power in the West was Rome, whose conquest of Carthage made her the superpower of the Mediterranean – *Mare Nostrum*, Our Sea, as the Romans would call it. Now she looked eastwards and in particular to Greece, which seemed to be weakening. Sensing decline, the Romans made plans to become a world power. Macedonia did not own the great empire it once did but was still a prominent player in the Greek peninsula. In 200 BC, the Second Macedonian War broke out between Macedonia and Rome.

By 197 BC, the Macedonians were forced to sue for peace. Placated, Rome turned to building her armies. Non-Roman Italian troops were recruited but these soldiers were denied the privileges of citizenship. In the meantime, the aristocracy and the Senate that governed Rome grew stronger and further apart from the masses of the ordinary people, the *plebs* as they were known.

In the meantime, other parts of the now fragmented empire that had once belonged to Alexander continued to squabble with each other. Between 200 and 198 BC, Antiochus, ruler of the Seleucid Empire (in the main Syria and Mesopotamia by now), waged war on the Ptolemies in Egypt and wrested Judea from them. He was about to receive encouragement to attack Rome from her greatest rival. In 195 BC Rome demanded the surrender of Hannibal by Carthage. Instead, Hannibal went into exile and approached Antiochus, urging him to take on Rome.

The city states of Greece were now organised under the umbrella of the Achaean League, which had been formed by a number of cities in the northern Peloponnese in the previous century. They had initially fought against Macedonian domination but with the defeat of the now declining power to the north by Rome they tried to strengthen their position further. They took up arms alongside Antiochus, who moved into Greece to beat the Romans back. However, Rome won a significant victory in 192 BC on the old battlefield of Thermopylae. Antiochus was forced to retreat but Scipio Africanus, the victor over Carthage in the Second Punic War, persuaded the Senate to send troops to follow him into Asia Minor. Rome was now starting to empire-build on three continents.

Antiochus was defeated in a further great battle at Magnesia in the south-east of Greece in 190 BC and fled back towards Syria. Hannibal went on the run, first of all to Crete, then to Bithynia in Asia Minor. The Romans eventually caught up with him there in 182 BC when a visiting consul demanded that the local ruler surrender him. Seeing that the Romans were closing in on him and that there was no escape, he took his own life, a tragic end to an ultimately unfulfilled career.

It was said that he had carried the poison which killed him around in a ring with him for a long time, expecting such an end. If the legends are to be believed, he was defiant even in death, leaving behind a letter in which he said, 'Let us relieve the Romans from the anxiety they have so long experienced, since they think it tries their patience too much to wait for an old man's death.' It was a suitably acerbic comment on the implacability of Rome's hatred for anyone determined enough to oppose the nascent superpower.

By this time, Antiochus was also dead and had been succeeded by a much less able ruler, Seleucus IV. To the east of his empire, in Persia, another great power was emerging. The Parthians, who were now dominant in the region, were nomad warriors of great skill and perseverance. They were particularly renowned for their abilities as both horsemen and archers. They were also ambitious and opportunistic. As the Seleucid Empire began to decline they started to push its borders back inexorably towards Syria.

In the meantime, Greece was descending into chaos and there was a growing feeling that only Roman conquest would restore order to the region. In 172 BC, a Third

Macedonian War with Rome was underway. This time its outcome would be definitive. The King of Macedonia, Perseus, overstretched himself, though it seemed at first that he had the upper hand. His armies were initially successful and by 169 BC had trapped a Roman force at Tempe. However, Perseus did not push home his advantage, an error that he would come to regret. The following year, the Roman general Aemilius Paulus won a decisive victory and took Perseus prisoner. He would die a captive in Rome.

The region of Epirus, in the north-west of Greece, had allied itself to the Macedonians and was about to pay a heavy price for its decision. Aemilius took his revenge, destroying seventy of their towns and taking 100,000 captives into slavery. Another 1,000 prominent Greeks from the Achaean League were taken to Rome as hostages for future good behaviour. Macedonia itself was split into four states. Regulations were so strict that intermarriage between citizens of each of them was prohibited.

The Middle East too was about to experience great tension. Judea was about to become the centre of a revolt against Seleucid rule. Problems had been simmering just beneath the surface since 175 BC, when the Seleucid emperor imposed worship of Zeus on the Jews. He even insisted that pigs, that most unclean of animals to Jews, should be sacrificed in the temple. This was, of course, the ultimate insult and blasphemy of the highest order. The Jews were powerless to strike back at once but had to wait their moment until the time was right.

Now, with Seleucid power seemingly on the wane, their time had come. The revolt was launched by a Jew named Mattathias. He died not long after the uprising started but his place was taken by one of the most famous of Jewish freedom fighters, Judas Maccabeus, who took over leadership of the rebel armies in 166 BC. He led a persistent and aggressive guerilla campaign of a type for which the Jews would later become famous, particularly against Rome over 200 years later. By 164 BC, he had retaken Jerusalem and cleansed the temple. During the Middle Ages, he was much better known to the wider world than he is now and even Handel dedicated an opera to him, from which the famous song 'See, the Conquering Hero Comes' is taken.

The Seleucids approached Judas after his victory and offered the Jews full religious freedom if they would lay down their arms. Matters had gone much too far for that and nothing less than full political freedom would be acceptable. In 161 BC, the unthinkable happened and Judas became an ally of Rome, hard to believe when later relationships between Jews and Romans were so hostile. Judas died in battle that same year but his reputation at that time was high indeed.

The power of Rome continued to rise but there were still Romans who fretted that Carthage might make a comeback. The attitude of the Romans towards the city since the end of the Second Punic War gave little sign that they wished to repair the damage to the relationship caused by the fighting. Carthage was given fifty years to raise the indemnities imposed upon it at the end of the war but managed to raise the money forty years early. Rome refused to accept it, instead preferring to have leverage over Carthage on an ongoing basis.

Rome continued to grow, establishing a colony near the Pillars of Hercules in Spain in 172 BC. By 159 BC, there were 338,314 Roman citizens. But as Rome grew bigger, tensions between her and Carthage rose once more to critical levels when in 153 BC the latter approached the former for help. Strict arms controls had been placed on Carthage. The king of her North African neighbour Numidia, a man named Masinissa, had taken advantage of her weakness to encroach on her territory.

Carthage now asked Rome for permission to fight back. The Romans responded by sending a delegation to Carthage to find out first-hand what was going on. One of its members was an old and respected statesman, Marcus Cato. He was shocked when he arrived in North Africa. He had expected to find Carthage a poor, ramshackle city. Instead what he found was a vigorous, powerful and wealthy metropolis. He returned to Rome convinced that, if Carthage were not destroyed, she would soon be a threat to Rome once more.

Carthage took matters into her own hands anyway by ejecting Numidian interlopers from her lands. Back in Rome, Cato argued passionately that nothing save the destruction of Carthage would suffice – she was simply too powerful to be allowed to live. Eventually, in 149 BC an impossible ultimatum was sent to the city – Carthage should be abandoned and rebuilt at least 10 miles away from the sea, unthinkable given Carthaginian reliance on sea power. When a Roman army turned up outside the walls to enforce this demand, the government of the city surrendered. However, the rest of its population was not so easily cowed. They turned on the leaders, killed them and prepared themselves for a fight.

The Romans laid siege to the city. Their commander, Scipio Aemilianus, built a gigantic mole to cut off the city from supplies. Eventually, the legions broke through the walls. A desperate series of hand-to-hand battles followed as Carthage was taken street by street. A last stand of the Carthaginians took place at the Temple of Eshmun. The wife of the Carthaginian commander Hasdrubal dressed herself in her finest clothes and then threw herself and her two children into the flames that greedily devoured the sanctuary rather than be captured or slaughtered on the spot.

The city was razed to the ground and the Carthaginian lands were sold or leased to Roman opportunists. The city itself was levelled and salt sown over the site so that nothing would grow there ever again. It was said that Scipio broke down when he saw the city burning, terrified at the sight of what he had done and that the same would be meted out to his own city one day; it would, but not until half a millennium later. A new Roman province of Africa was established soon afterwards. But Carthage had effectively been wiped from the face of the earth.

There were, though, still significant powers to the south in Africa, beyond the orbit of Rome. An inscription in a funerary chapel at Meroë speaks of a Queen Shanakete, who was clearly the predominant ruler at this time and is the earliest known example of a pre-eminent queen, for she enjoys a subtle difference from Hatshepsut who, although a woman, ruled as a king. The queens of Kush and Meroë would become the main rulers of the dynasty or were at least co-equal with their husbands.

Rome was now fighting on two fronts, being also embroiled in Greece. It was that ancient great power, Sparta, that acted as the catalyst for this renewed situation. The Achaean League was now taking joint decisions on many of the key issues that faced

Greece. In 149 BC, when Sparta was unhappy with one of these decisions, she opted to appeal directly to Rome. A Roman diplomat was sent to see if he could resolve the dispute. He made his decision in favour of Sparta. When he announced this in the city of Corinth he was badly beaten up. It was an insult that Rome could not afford to ignore.

Tensions spilled over into Macedonia, where a revolt broke out against Roman authority. It was crushed and Macedonia, which had managed to retain the trappings at least of a form of autonomy, was now made a province of Rome. When Corinth was also taken, its people were enslaved en masse and Greece effectively became a province too, watched over by the Roman governor of Macedonia.

Rome was being maintained by an influx of slaves from all parts of the Mediterranean. The sweat of their brows and the toil of their bodies provided the labour on which Rome's greatness was founded. In an age where most manufacturing and agriculture was of a labour-intensive nature, the presence of thousands of souls providing cheap labour to drive the economy was vital. In common with all slaves, these Roman vassals had no rights and were, as a rule, harshly treated.

With little to lose save their lives, which were not worth much anyway, it was inevitable that there would be slave uprisings and in 134 BC the most serious yet started in Sicily. Around 400 slaves turned on their master, renowned and hated for his cruelty, and slew him and his family. The intensity of the eruption that followed would have done Etna proud. Thousands of slaves joined the revolt, outnumbering the local Roman garrisons that tried in vain to put the genie that had been unleashed back in the bottle. It took three years for Rome to triumph in what was known as the First Servile War and the repercussions that followed were predictably brutal.

If Rome did not always manage its empire well or fairly, much the same could be said of the way it managed itself. Rome was governed by its Senate but there were other posts of importance too. Tribunes were appointed annually to represent the affairs of the common man. But the common man's voice was rarely heard. Rome was governed for the benefit of its aristocracy. There was a desperate need for land reform so that everyone could theoretically share to some extent in the riches of Rome, but the people were generally not allowed to do so. Soldiers retiring after long military careers were shamefully treated when it was their blood and often the lives of their fallen comrades that had carved out the empire.

Understandable resentment bubbled away. These feelings were expertly tapped into by the tribune Tiberius Sempronius Gracchus, elected to his post in 133 BC. He tried to institute land reform and grant more rights to the plebs. He attempted to bring in laws that would limit the amount of land that any man could hold. But in so doing he trod on the toes of many powerful Romans, who saw in this young upstart a direct challenge to the extravagant lifestyles they lived and the absolute power they enjoyed.

These were just the opening gambits in a political power game. Gracchus's rivals tried to put a stop to the reforms by using their veto in the votes that were taken on them. Gracchus responded by using his veto to stop everyday business decisions being taken. Rome ground to a halt. A tribune was only supposed to stand for one term but when his year was up Gracchus put himself up for re-election. His enemies let it be known that he planned to make himself king, the most heinous crime possible in the Republic of Rome. A riot broke out and Gracchus was beaten to death in the violence that followed. His body was thrown into the Tiber.

Scipio Aemilianus had been a mentor to Gracchus, who had taken part in the final battle for Carthage. Now he was called back to restore order to Rome. He was shocked by Gracchus's attempts at reform which he felt threatened the very fabric of the state. But he himself fell victim to the violence, murdered by Gracchus's supporters.

This was far from the end of the problems facing Rome. Tiberius Gracchus had a young brother, Gaius. He took up the mantle that had been brutally torn from the shoulders of his elder brother. In 123 BC Gaius himself was elected tribune. He courted popularity by doling out bread to the poor, speaking to their stomachs proving the most eloquent form of oratory. However, his attempts to democratise Rome by granting citizenship to all Italians made him widely unpopular.

Rome continued to expand. In 122 BC a territory was carved out in the south of France between the Alps and the Pyrenees around Narbonne. This province later became known as Provence. In the same year the Balearics were added to the empire. Gaius was now elected for the second time but he wished to join the empire-building himself, so he left Rome for a while to help establish a colony at Carthage.

It was a mistake, for while he was away his enemies plotted against him. Many said that his decision to go to Carthage was doomed as the land was cursed. When he stood for tribune for a third time in 121 BC, he failed. A riot broke out and, just like his older brother Tiberius, he was killed. His headless body was thrown into the Tiber along with the corpses of 3,000 of his supporters. But Rome would remain in ferment for a while yet.

While simmering civilian unrest threatened to bring down Rome, in China it had violently erupted to bring down the Ch'in and commence the years of Han rule. The Han had taken over power in 206 BC when a group of labourers were late in arriving to carry out some work that they had been ordered to undertake. Under the harsh rules of the Ch'in, this meant that some of them at least would be executed even though the weather had been appalling and there was nothing they could do to arrive any earlier than they did.

With nothing to lose, they turned on their persecutors and from this small beginning an unstoppable wave of anger grew, overwhelming the hated Ch'in as a result. It was an interesting object lesson that if you treat people so badly that they have nothing to lose by resisting, then eventually someone will resist. It is a lesson that dictatorial regimes throughout history have had to relearn. Modern dictatorships seem no more in touch with this reality than those that ruled millennia ago.

The first Han emperor, Gaozu, was from peasant stock. His major qualification to rule appeared to be that he had seventy-six moles on his left thigh; this was at the time considered to be a lucky omen. He was no great lover of scholars; the eminent Chinese historian Ssu-ma Ch'ien described how 'whenever a visitor wearing a Confucian hat comes to see him, he immediately snatches the hat from the visitor's head and pisses in it'. But he was an astute politician, who knew when to be brutal with dissidents and when to use a lighter touch. China was still threatened by powerful internal divisions and he had to tread carefully to keep his throne.

The great threat of nomadic raiders also continued as strongly as before. If anything, the danger had increased as the tribes had formed themselves into a confederation, known as the Hsiung-nu (which means 'slave with a corrupted soul'), who are first recorded as appearing in the third century BC. The name of one of their early leaders survives: Mao Tun. When Gaozu led a massive army against him, he adopted the well-worn methods of nomad armies throughout history. He merely retreated before the army sent against him until it began to lose its discipline. Then, when it had started to become uncoordinated, the nomads turned, forcing Gaozu to fight for his life.

Suitably chastened, Gaozu sought peace with Mao Tun by handing over one of his daughters to be his wife. It did the trick but Gaozu did not live long to enjoy peace, for he died in 195 BC after just a few years' rule. His death led to the effective usurpation of power by his dowager-empress Gaohou. Although she could not rule in her own right, she arranged that a line of several child emperors should rule whom she could dominate completely.

She had been one of many wives of Gaozu but she had made short work of a number of the others when he had died. The fate of the Lady Qi, who had been his favourite for a time, was appalling. She was deprived of her eyes, her hands and feet were cut off, her ears were burned, she was given poison to strike her dumb and then she was thrown into the stinking waste of a privy, where visitors could come and admire what Gaohou called 'the human pig'. But when Gaohou died in 180 BC, there was a massive outpouring of blood as all her relatives and supporters were slaughtered.

Hsiung-nu incursions grew progressively worse. For sixty years, since their first appearance, they had forced the Han emperors to buy them off with lavish tributes and the marrying-off of imperial princesses. This was not enough for them and in 170 BC they were invading Xinjiang. This was clearly a threat that would not go away.

The new Han emperor, Wen-ti, ruled with great tact, a welcome change from recent decades. His empire was again threatened by barbarians, a new grouping known as the Yüeh-chih. Ironically, the Hsiung-nu acted as a buffer state and the Yüeh-chih were effectively diverted away westwards and the Han state was saved from further threat. They moved west and eventually arrived in Bactria. Here, they came into contact with the remnants of the Greek state created by Alexander.

Their arrival caused many of the remaining Greeks to head south across the mountains and into India. Here, some of the Greeks that remained had become more Indian than European. The greatest of them was King Menander I, who came to power in the Indo-Greek Kingdom in around 150 BC. Despite the fact that the coins surviving from his reign show him in Greek armour and display Greek writing on them, he is remembered very favourably in Buddhist texts. During his reign, despite the pacifist qualities claimed for him in these writings, he extended the borders of his kingdom eastwards, conquering Hindu lands as he did so.

To the north-west of these lands, the Parthian Empire was expanding under its emperor Mithridates I. The Parthians moved closer to Babylon and established a base at the old Persian palace of Ctesiphon. They held a number of large and powerful cities. Their agriculturists grew crops for food and vines for pleasure. Their traders carried their surpluses far and wide and made Parthia rich.

This was the country in which, in around 130 BC, a Chinese adventurer named Chang Ch'ien arrived. He was in many ways a Chinese mirror image of Marco Polo and his journey had been a remarkable one. In 140 BC, a new Chinese emperor had been installed, Wu-ti. He had soon after sent Chang Ch'ien on a mission to see what lay to the west of China. His start was an inauspicious one; he had been taken prisoner by the Hsiung-nu and his imprisonment, though not a harsh one (he was given a wife by his captors), lasted for ten years before he escaped.

He journeyed first of all to Bactria and then on to Parthia, where he was warmly received. His visit laid the foundations for future closer ties. Under the next Parthian ruler, Mithridates II ('the Great'), closer trading links were initiated. Parthian envoys were sent to China, and in return Chinese delegations made their way west. From this diplomatic courtship, a long-term relationship blossomed. A great trade highway was set up, along which Chinese goods flowed to the Middle East and vice versa. This was not a straightforward task; fierce tribes had to be subdued en route. But at the end of it all, the Great Silk Road had been established. It would be the most important link between east and west until the epic journeys of Christopher Columbus spun the world around on its axis.

Wu-ti's reign would last for fifty years. During it, the Han Empire expanded consistently. When he came to power, the currency was in a mess; private mints had grown up across the land, leading to rampant inflation. Wu-ti eventually put a stop to this. He took over control of the economy by introducing widespread monopolisation. In 113 BC, he unilaterally declared all existing coinage void and set up his own mints whose currency would alone be valid in the future. This helped finance ongoing expansion; new lands were conquered in southern China and north Vietnam (then collectively known as the kingdom of Nan Yüeh). In 108 BC, he would also establish a colony known as Lak Lang in northern Korea.

This was the original command and control economy; prices and incomes were rigorously regulated. But the wealth Wu-ti controlled was put to good use. He engaged in a large number of construction projects, and developed bridges, canals and irrigation channels, all measures to improve the infrastructure and agriculture of China. Despite these laudable achievements, Wudi was a brutal autocrat who meted out harsh punishment to any who annoyed him. One was the historian Ssu-ma Ch'ien, perhaps the greatest of all Chinese court historians. In a massive volume of work, he painstakingly outlined all the key events he knew of in Chinese history, creating a blueprint for future court historians to emulate (in terms of quality, none of them succeeded).

However, Ssu-ma Ch'ien incurred the wrath of the emperor when he defended a general who had attracted his lord's ire. Wu-ti had ordered that Ssu-ma Ch'ien should be castrated. This was equivalent to a death sentence, for the Chinese sense of honour demanded that a man mutilated in such a fashion should take his own life. Ssu-ma Ch'ien however defied convention, determined to finish the work that he had started but not yet finished. Given the knowledge that he subsequently imparted to future generations, it was fortunate indeed that he acted in such a fashion.

Wu-ti also fought back hard against the threat from the Hsiung-nu. He entered alliances with other states and groups who were enemies of the raiders. He also developed a strategy of attacking the Hsiung-nu bases in the far west, conquering them and then installing garrisons to prevent them retaking the territories that had been lost and settlers to act as a buffer against them. He also extended the wall westwards, though it was not a continuous barrier and in some regions just isolated watchtowers were installed with handily placed beacons ready to be lit at a moment's notice. Topographical features were utilised as natural obstacles to the Hsiung-nu and much was left to the discretion of local commanders. A message to one of them still survives:

> The colonel, his subordinates and 2,000 soldiers will occupy a new land in order to install a defensive and agricultural garrison. The governor will have to set the scene, using natural obstacles; he will build a wall to oversee the land. May there be no negligence.

During these momentous years, there had been other important delegations visiting Parthia. The Romans in Asia Minor were alarmed at the ascendant Parthian power. They sent Lucius Cornelius Sulla to keep an eye on affairs along the Mesopotamian border and he met a delegation sent by Mithridates II on the Euphrates. The Parthians sent a message of peace and co-operation to the Romans and for the time being Rome and Parthia were on good terms. It was a situation that would not last.

Sulla returned to Rome, where he would play an important role in the development of the empire. This was, not unexpectedly, a result of playing a key part in the tangled power politics of the city. The Republic was characterised by a corrupt political landscape, where those who wished to rule would prostitute themselves to the highest bidder in order to advance their own ambitions. The tangled web of bribery and intrigue that characterised the situation came to a head in 118 BC.

This crisis in Roman politics was caused by a seedy attempt at usurpation by a North African ruler named Jugurtha. He had seized the throne of Numidia, near ancient Carthage, encouraged to do so by Roman officials who suggested that Rome would not intervene in his unlawful scheming provided that he paid the correct price for her non-intervention. Wise enough to heed this advice, Jugurtha sent generous quantities of gold and silver to Rome, which seemed to convince the city's politicians that they should not interfere.

In the meantime though, his rival and cousin, Adherbal, had arrived in Rome to present his own case. The Senate decreed that Jugurtha should share his kingdom with Adherbal. They might have felt that they had shown the wisdom of Solomon in exercising this decision but Jugurtha did not share this view for he soon arranged for Adherbal to be killed on his return to Africa.

The Romans were incensed at this insult and a consul, Bestia, was sent to Africa to bring Jugurtha back into line in 111 BC. He made little progress, another generous contribution from Jugurtha convincing Bestia that the king had been much maligned. Rome was becoming increasingly annoyed at Jugurtha's cunning and the next year an army was sent to bring him under control. Sadly for them, Jugurtha was as able a soldier as he was a politician and the army was trapped in the desert and forced to surrender.

Military defeat was the most unpalatable of all things to the Romans. They were already under threat in Italy, a group of Celtic tribes known as the Cimbri invading and creating havoc. Rome needed a hero. They found one when, in 108 BC, Gaius Marius was elected consul. The next year, he formed a new army and appointed Lucius Cornelius Sulla to his staff. Marius led his army into Africa, penetrating deep into the Sahara but, despite some key victories, he failed to trap Jugurtha, who found sanctuary with his father-in-law, King Bocchus of Mauretania (which approximately covers the area of modern Morocco and part of Algeria).

It was Sulla who broke the logjam, using that most potent of weapons, money, to buy the cooperation of Bocchus. Arrangements were made for Jugurtha to be kidnapped. The deed was done and this wearisome opportunist, who had for fifteen years made a fool of Rome, was brought back to the Eternal City. Here, he was the key attraction in the Triumph that entered Rome, marking the victory of Marius and Sulla. He died in 104 BC in the prison known as the Tullianum, where he starved to death.

There was still much to be done. The Celtic Cimbri had been winning battles against the Romans again and Marius was re-elected consul with a brief to defeat them. Marius implemented vital reforms to the Roman army. The heavy spear, the *hasta*, was replaced with the lighter *pilum*. Rome was to recruit its cavalry from other nations. Legions were given names and numbers. They were professionalised and for the first time each legion carried an emblem, the famous eagle, which would become the best-known of all military totems. Marius, relatively little remembered in modern times, was effectively the founder of the standing Roman army, the replacement for the much more unreliable and less trained citizen militia of previous times.

Marius's reforms were a resounding success. The Cimbri and their Teutonic allies were routed, firstly at the Battle of Aquae Sextiae in 102 BC and, the year after, at the Battle of Vercellae in the Po Valley, where it was said that 120,000 of Rome's enemies were slaughtered. At the same time, a Second Servile War was fought and won in Sicily against an army of oppressed slaves.

The triumph of Marius seemed complete. After the Battle of Aquae Sextiae, he had ceremonially burned a vast cache of captured arms to honour the gods. As the flames ascended skywards, news arrived that Marius had been elected consul once more. But in this very year, largely unmentioned in an as yet unknowing world, a child was born on 12 July who would far eclipse Marius. He was not from the highest ranks of the Roman aristocracy, but by the time he died some fifty-seven years later, Gaius Julius Caesar would have transformed the world in which he lived. His century was about to begin.

13

THE OLD AND THE NEW

The Death of Ancient Egypt and the Triumph of the Roman Empire (100–1 BC)

It is hard to underestimate the influence of Rome on world history (though Hellenists might argue that much of their cultural achievement was built on Greek foundations). The avenues of power in Washington DC give an insight into the cultural impact; the Capitol building is a relatively modern successor to the great architecture of classical Rome and the spirit of the ancient civilisation itself is reflected in the design of many great architectural edifices around the world (the Brandenburg Gate in Germany is another example of a modern statement of power that has undeniably Roman architectural roots). In the West, certainly, those who seek to be great emulate – in their architecture at least – Rome.

Rome lives on too in legal systems across much of the world as well as in everyday speech; many Western European languages – French, Spanish, Italian for example – have Roman roots. Such languages are called 'Romance' or 'Latin', terms that betray their origins in the tongue of Rome. Rome also helped to preserve the Hellenic legacy and protect it for future generations. In addition, Rome's role in adopting Christianity was crucial in laying the foundations for the spread of one of the world's great religions. All of this influence would not have been possible without the events of the first century BC, a world-changing period in every sense of the word.

Roman history during this period is one dominated by the relationships between key individuals. The great events played out by them would affect not only Europe but also Africa and Asia too; even in India the power of Rome would become known. Some of the great names from the time have survived: Julius Caesar, of course; Octavian and Mark Antony too. But others played key roles too and their parts need to be brought to the fore.

The century began with Marius and Sulla continuing to vie for power. Marius, after being re-elected consul a number of times, suffered a damaged reputation through scandal and was forced to disappear from public life for a time. Rome itself was a place of simmering threat. By 95 BC, many Italians had entered Rome and obtained citizenship. In an anti-immigrant response which in many ways echoes problems found even in our own times, those of 'pure' Roman blood rebelled against this process and as a result a number of non-Roman Italians were struck off the electoral roles. In response to this, a number of secret Italian societies were set up; something else we are still familiar with.

Although Roman power was on the increase, it was not universally unchallenged. Asia Minor was one area of friction. In parts of it, King Mithridates of Pontus acted with a great deal of autonomy. In 92 BC, the King of Cappadocia was ejected by him. Rome would not tolerate this resurgent power and Sulla, who was by now protecting Rome's interests in the region, had reversed the situation by force.

Mithridates posed a great threat; not for nothing was he known as 'Mithridates Magus', 'the Great'. His ancestry was impressive, as one of his forbears was Darius I, King of Persia, and his bloodline also included some of the foremost generals of Alexander the Great. He sought to build an empire that would dominate the Black Sea and Anatolia; he could not do so without entering into headlong confrontation with the might of Rome.

Further action might have followed Sulla's triumph but for trouble much closer to home. Rome was bitterly divided in its approach to dealing with the ongoing problem of the Italians of non-Roman extraction. In 91 BC, a prominent official called Livius Drusus attempted to enfranchise all Italians but was murdered for his pains. There were perhaps other reasons for his demise; he had debased the currency by issuing coins made of copper rather than silver and rampant inflation had resulted. Not long after, the Italians revolted and the so-called 'Social War' began.

The fight was a hard one. Although Rome won an inconclusive victory, the war ended with many Italians being granted Roman citizenship. Perhaps taking advantage of this distraction, by 88 BC Mithridates had conquered parts of Asia Minor and slaughtered a number of Roman and Italian officials in the process, gaining retribution for his earlier defeats. But rather than uniting in their response, Romans instead started to fight among themselves.

Petty personal gain was at the heart of the problem. It was perhaps inevitable that two such powerful figures as Sulla and Marius would fall out sooner or later. Sulla was given command of an army to face up to Mithridates but Marius, who had been trying to rebuild his fading career, attempted to take command off him. Fighting in the streets of Rome followed, as a result of which Marius fled and was declared an outlaw.

Rome had been guilty of underestimating both the threat facing it and the ambition of Mithridates. In 88 BC, the King of Pontus crossed the Hellespont and invaded Greece. There were those in Greece who were far from enamoured of Roman domination. Athens took advantage of the invasion to side with Mithridates and rise up against Rome. Asia Minor was no longer the problem; for Rome the issue to be faced was now much closer to home. Sulla sailed with five legions and landed in Epirus, determined to end the threat.

In 86 BC, he took Athens and pillaged it although, appreciating its heritage, he was careful not to destroy it completely. Then he moved on Mithridates's army, under its general Archelaus, which was resoundingly beaten at the Battle of Chaeronea. But it was to Rome's shame that, back in the capital, petty politicking was still undermining the defence of its fledgling empire. Cinna, the consul left in charge of Rome, stirred up trouble and was forced to leave after a riot. He joined up with Marius, who was desperately seeking a way of recovering his lost position. Cinna and Marius succeeded in re-entering Rome, where they launched a short reign of terror. However, Marius died of pleurisy soon after though not without first of all awarding the post of Priest of Jupiter to his nephew Julius Caesar. It was Julius's first public position and an early hint of an ambitious character developing.

In 85 BC, Sulla won another victory in Greece, as a result of which Mithridates was chased back across the Hellespont. Not long after, Sulla and Mithridates met near Troy and agreed the terms of a peace treaty. The terms offered to the defeated king were lenient and probably reflected the fact that Sulla wished to get back to Rome to protect his own position as quickly as possible. His job in the east done for now, Sulla hurried back towards the city to eject Cinna, who had declared him an outlaw in his absence. Cinna had overreached himself. His poor decision making had led to a financial crisis in Rome and there was little public support for him. He was forced to flee the city and was killed by his own troops soon after.

In the meantime, Sulla had landed at Brundisium and was advancing northwards in triumphal procession. By his side was an ambitious politician and general, 'Pompey' (more correctly known formally as Gnaeus Pompeius Magnus). But when Sulla entered Rome in 82 BC, he completely mishandled the situation when he instituted another reign of terror. He had drawn up a list of those he wished dead, cloaked under the bureaucratically innocuous title of 'the Proscription'.

Sulla had misjudged the situation and in 79 BC he was forced to retire. However, his own violent tendencies were to get the better of him. The year after, he ordered an enemy to be strangled in his presence. While he was watching, one of his blood vessels burst and he collapsed and died, a victim in the end of his own bloodlust. This appeared to leave Rome open to the rule of other ambitious predators, one of whom, Lepidus, soon advanced on the city. However, he was beaten off and chased away by Pompey.

By the year 77 BC, Pompey had rounded up the rebels but refused to disband his army. Rome (in which by now the young Caesar had obtained a reputation as an orator in the law courts) held its breath, fearing a grab for power. However, the year after, the threat of Pompey was brought off for a time when he was given command of the army in Spain.

Further east, Mithridates was not yet finished. He was now emboldened to take Bithynia, which had been bequeathed to Rome by its late ruler. Rome had had enough and in 73 BC drove Mithridates from his kingdom. He would return a few years later in a brief resumption of power, but would be finally defeated. He fled to the Crimea, where he eventually took his own life, unable to cope with the low ebb to which his fortunes had plummeted. He had been unable to best the power of Rome. He was far from the last to be in such a position.

Rome continued to have problems of its own closer to the heart of its empire. In 73 BC, one of the most famous revolts of all time broke out. A group of gladiators, unhappy with their lot, turned on their masters. They were led by a man called Spartacus. A small army sent to put out the flames of revolt was overwhelmed by the revolutionaries, who used their fighting skills to great effect. Larger armies arrived but these too were defeated. However, the ambitions of Spartacus were limited; he did not want to overturn the Roman political system, he just wanted to go home.

An army led by Crassus was given the task of putting down Spartacus's rebellion with six legions. Crassus was both extremely rich and very powerful in Rome, and under his sponsorship the career of Caesar had continued to rise. He now defeated the gladiator's army totally. When it was clear that the battle was lost, Spartacus charged straight for Crassus. He was killed in the attempt (a different ending than Hollywood aficionados might expect). Of his men, 6,000 were crucified in a long line along the Appian Way. But Crassus had many enemies in the political hotbed of Rome and even in victory the divisions within the city were exposed – when Pompey returned to Italy soon after, he tried to claim the credit for the victory from Crassus.

Glorying in their triumph over Spartacus, for which both men sought credit, in 70 BC both Pompey and Crassus were elected consul (this was the same year that the poet Virgil was born, most famous for his tale of Aeneas, the fugitive from Troy). One of Pompey's first tasks was to clear the Mediterranean of pirates. Piracy was a major problem; a few years before, Julius Caesar had for a time been the prisoner of pirates on Rhodes. He had been ransomed but later returned with a force, captured his former jailers and crucified them. Caesar was proving a dangerous man to cross.

In 66 BC, Pompey was given the authority to lead an army to the east, a move supported both by the eloquent orator Cicero and Caesar. It was Pompey that finally brought an end to the career of Mithridates. However, even the greatest empires have their limits, as Rome was about to find out. Rome received an approach from Parthia, which suggested that the Euphrates should be the natural boundary between the two empires. Pompey, ambitious for more than this, refused to strike the bargain. The ensuing tension was a sign of approaching conflict between the two powers; in the end, Rome would have decidedly the worst of it.

Back in Rome itself, law and order was a major issue. He who wished to rule in Rome also needed to rule the mob. Pompey, though, stayed in the east for the time being. In a move of immense significance, he imposed himself as arbiter in a dispute over the ownership of Antioch. He had earmarked the region for Rome, marking the end of Seleucid power once and for all. By 63 BC, he had cemented his position by making both Cilicia and Syria Roman provinces.

That same year he moved into Judea, where he took Jerusalem, showing little respect for Jewish religious sensibilities about the temple in the process. The often antagonistic relationship between Rome and Judaism (and its eventual offspring Christianity) was a strange one. Rome frequently absorbed the religions of conquered peoples; it did so with the Greek gods more or less en masse. Greek Zeus became Roman Jupiter, Athena became Minerva and Ares became Mars, for example. Even native religions were tolerated and sometimes celebrated. The waters at Roman Bath would be named Aquae Sulis after a Celtic water goddess who became linked to Minerva.

However, the monotheistic religion of Judaism seemed to posit too much power in one individual god, something that seemed to threaten the very fabric of Roman rule. In the biblical record, Jesus Christ said when asked whether the Jews should pay taxes to their Roman overlords that they should give unto Caesar what belonged to Caesar and unto God what belonged to God. This to modern ears seems a clever answer but the thought that God could have a claim on any earthly possession (other than the occasional symbolic sacrifice) was one that powerful Romans would have vehemently argued against.

By 62 BC, Pompey had returned to Italy. For a time he perhaps considered keeping his army intact, with a view to grabbing power in Rome. This would have been a direct challenge to the Senate. However, in the end he chose to disband his army. This did him few favours, for he was not well received by the Senate. He had been very successful in the East, in truth too successful for the Senate's liking. He was not well received by them as he posed a threat to their power. Caesar, who was made Praetor, an important public position, now made a note of their attitude to the returning victor for future reference.

Caesar was undoubtedly a rising power by this stage. In 60 BC, along with Pompey and Crassus, he formed what was known as the first triumvirate, effectively composed of the three most important men in Rome. But he had a surer political touch than any other man in the city. When he was made Consul in 59 BC, he introduced agrarian laws by which war veterans received lands at the expense of aristocrats. He also passed the *leges Juliae*, legislation which defended the common people against bribery. Cynics might think that this was his way of securing his power by winning over the army and the mob. Certainly the Senate did not take kindly to moves that undermined their own position.

However, events in Gaul were about to drag Caesar away, perhaps to the relief of some of the Roman senators. Migrations and raids into Gaul threatened Rome. A series of tribes were subdued by the armies that Caesar led to beat them back. Then in 55 BC he sent a prominent Gaulish captive, Commius, across to Britain as his ambassador. Upon landing there, he was immediately put in chains. This was an insult to Rome and in response Caesar led his armies across. In a short but sharp campaign, the armies of the southern Britons were conquered, their leaders sued for peace and Commius was returned. But for the time being Britain, though now a tributary power to Rome, retained its independence. A second expedition the year after also did not bring final, decisive victory and, on both occasions, the Roman fleet had been seriously threatened by the weather, not the last time that the relatively narrow Channel crossing proved a formidable obstacle.

The year after, Caesar was joined in Gaul by Mark Antony, who would become his closest confidante. He would need him. In 52 BC, the Gauls revolted, led by a fierce warrior, Vercingetorix, the chieftain of the Arverni tribe from the Auvergne region in what is now France. Initially he was triumphant. However, Caesar then won a massive victory when he turned the tables on a relief force that attacked him when he was laying siege to the fortress of Alesia. This secured Gaul and on a personal level gave Caesar a great triumph. His star was in the ascendancy, as were his levels of ambition.

At the time of Caesar's triumph in Gaul, Rome was reeling from a massive defeat far to the east. Crassus had rashly decided to invade Mesopotamia, leading an army said to contain 70,000 foot and 4,000 cavalry. Across the Euphrates, near the town of Carrhae, he came face to face with a large Parthian force. The Parthians had a huge advantage with their archery, which they used to fire from a distance, easily penetrating the Roman armour. Seeing that the battle was going badly, Crassus sent his son Publius in at the head of a charge but he was surrounded and killed himself rather than be taken alive. The Parthians cut off his head and stuck it on a pole.

Just two days later, Crassus himself was killed. His head was cut off too and taken back as a token of victory to King Orodes II of Parthia. It was said that the king ordered that a play should be produced to mark the victory, in which the head of Crassus performed a starring role. The defeat was total. Most of the Roman army was killed or captured, along with their precious eagles. It also secured the borders of a Parthian empire that stretched from the Euphrates in the west to the edge of China in the east.

Caesar, in the meantime, began to move back to Rome. Just as in Pompey's case, his triumphs had turned the Senate against him. Perceiving a threat, they refused to make Caesar consul. He moved towards Rome with his army. As he got closer, frantic messages came from the city, entreating him to disband his legions. He came to a small river called the Rubicon, physically so insignificant that no one now knows where it was. Symbolically, though, this was a massively important barrier, for if Caesar were to cross it then he would be at war with Rome.

Caesar, as is well known, crossed over the physically small but symbolically crucial barrier. Responsibility for the defence of Rome was given to Pompey, but he decided to abandon the city to Caesar and instead led his armies to Greece, accompanied by the politicians and famous orators Cicero and Cato. Caesar mopped up all resistance in Italy and then took Sicily and secured Spain, though his army was defeated in Numidia. However, one of his key lieutenants, General Labienus, defected to Pompey. Caesar's ambition was making a lot of enemies.

Caesar followed Pompey to Greece and defeated him decisively at Pharsalus. Pompey as a result fled to Egypt, where he was immediately assassinated. Nevertheless, Caesar sailed across the Mediterranean to ensure that the country was suitably inclined towards him. When he landed, he came face to face with Egypt's queen, Cleopatra. One of history's great love stories was about to be written.

There was no doubt now that the ancient Egyptian civilisation was in its death throes. It had only lived this long because of the injection of Greek blood in the last few hundred years, but the effects of that transfusion were wearing thin. The last years of the Ptolemaic dynasty were approaching. There had been signs of decline for decades.

Cleopatra had been born in 69 BC and had been a co-ruler with her brother, the last of the Ptolemies. He had been dethroned in 58 BC and had appealed to Rome for help in his reinstatement. Rome was never slow to intervene in the affairs of another state if it saw an opportunity in the situation. Now Caesar had arrived in Egypt and in the ongoing succession dispute that was threatening the country's stability, he was quick to side with Cleopatra. The queen has often been feted as being the fairest of all women and it seems that Caesar was genuinely smitten (though, interestingly, coins from her reign do not always suggest a woman of stunning beauty).

But tragedy attended this conquest. When Caesar took Alexandria its great library was destroyed by fire. Around 700,000 priceless documents went up in smoke, including the *History of Egypt*, written by the priest Manetho, which outlined the thirty dynasties of the country, a system that we still use. It was a tragic and irreplaceable loss which has only been partly compensated for by the efforts of archaeologists in recent times.

But the Romans were unable to take everything in their path. Further south they came up against a stubborn stumbling block in the shape of the armies of

Amanirenas, the Queen of Nubia, who was able to force an agreement from Caesar that he would leave her kingdom alone if she did not interfere in the affairs of Egypt to the north. Amanirenas acknowledged her Egyptian antecedents even in her name, Amani being the Nubian equivalent of 'Amen'. Her kingdom still had access to the Red Sea and through this access to markets as far away as India and as close to home as Arabia.

However totally Cleopatra may have captured Caesar's heart, there was still an empire to be won. Caesar now embarked on a grand tour of the Levant, marching through Syria and Asia Minor with his legions and defeating Pharnaces, son of the late Mithridates of Pontus, en route. He then journeyed back to Rome, but there was still more fighting to be done even now. He took ship back to Africa, where he crushed the remaining forces of Pompey's supporters at the Battle of Thapsus in Carthaginia.

The fighting was still not quite over but Caesar's thoughts now started to turn towards other matters. A Roman colony at Carthage began to develop and nearby Numidia became a Roman province. Caesar returned to Rome and was made Dictator and ten-year Consul. He was now close to being an absolute ruler in Rome. He then decided to celebrate his victory in the bitter civil war that had been fought.

Declaring an armistice with his Roman opponents, he arranged a great Triumph in which Vercingetorix was paraded. The Gaul had fought bravely but little good did it do him, for he was killed soon after, probably strangled in his prison, the Tullianum. There were other, more peaceful, matters to attend to for Caesar. He introduced a new calendar of twelve months. The year was to be made 365 days long, with an extra day every four years; in effect, this was exactly the same as current measurements of what constitutes a western year except for the fact that the Roman calendar did not allow for non-leap years at the end of every century.

In 45 BC, Caesar led his armies to Spain where he defeated Pompey's sons and his former lieutenant Labienus at the Battle of Munda. It was a terrible, hard-fought battle in which little quarter was asked or given; Caesar later said that he had fought many times for victory but never before for his life. This was the end of the civil wars, for the time being at least. Returning to Rome, Caesar increased the size of the Senate to 900 and began the rebuilding and repopulation of both Carthage and Corinth. He even began the cutting of a Corinth canal.

Caesar's position now seemed unassailable. However, perhaps hubris was now beginning to weave its tangled web, convincing the great dictator that anything he wished for was there for the taking. In February 44 BC, Mark Antony, Caesar's most loyal supporter, offered him the crown. There was a pathological hatred of all kings in Rome and Caesar was perhaps testing the water to see how the Roman public would react to his complete usurpation of power. If so, the reaction cannot have been positive for he refused the offer, which he would not have done if the crowd had been on his side.

But he did not heed the warning signs. On the morning of 15 March, he made his way to the Senate. According to legend, his wife begged him not to go as she had been warned of evil portents. Caesar, however, was unafraid and made his way into the Senate. The mood there soon turned ugly. The senators began to crowd Caesar. Then, to his horror, the flash of a knife, followed by that of a dozen others. His body was hacked to pieces and the great Caesar slumped to the floor in a pool of blood.

Ironically, this did not halt the rush towards monarchical rule, or at least towards something closely related to it. Caesar's adopted heir, Octavian, his grand-nephew, returned from Illyria and immediately claimed the succession. Even the gods were disturbed at these momentous events for, during funeral games held in Caesar's honour, a comet streaked across the sky.

The knives that cut the thread of life from Caesar ushered in a period of dreadful bloodletting. A second triumvirate was formed soon after Caesar's death, formed of Mark Antony, Lepidus, one of Caesar's closest confidantes, and Octavian. Cleopatra took advantage of the upheaval by killing her own brother Ptolemy and eliminating him as a rival. Cicero, the great orator, was assassinated in a purge in Rome.

This was not just a period of political intrigue but also one in which the civil war was reignited. Two of the leading conspirators against Caesar, Cassius and Caesar's close friend Brutus, were defeated by the forces of Antony and Octavian at the Battle of Philippi in 42 BC. Rather than be taken alive both men killed themselves.

This victory won, the triumvirate now divided the world between them, Africa to Lepidus, the East to Antony and the West to Octavian. It was now that Cleopatra was about to write the second chapter of her love story for, at Tarsus, Antony met her and quickly became besotted with her. There was a problem here, for Antony was already married to Octavian's sister, Octavia. In 37 BC he peremptorily returned her to her brother and took Cleopatra in her place.

Affaire de couer or no, this was also a political and a personal insult to Octavian. Antony was clearly an increasingly ambitious man, which made him even more disagreeable to Octavian. Antony attacked Parthia, though his efforts there did not meet with success. He then invaded Armenia. Octavian was biding his time, waiting for an opportune moment to strike back. Lepidus had been forced into an unsought retirement, meaning that the empire was now to be divided between two men rather than three. This was still one too many to be sustainable in the long run.

In 33 BC, Cleopatra claimed that her son Caesarion was fathered by Caesar himself and was therefore his heir. The year after, Octavian declared war on Antony. Antony and Cleopatra wintered in Greece, satisfied with the gains they had made. But Octavian's army moved down on them, defeating their fleet at Actium and forcing them to retire to Alexandria. Octavian took advantage of this situation to have himself declared Consul on a recurring annual basis.

Rome sent her armies to Egypt. Seeing that the game was up, Antony took his own life, as did Cleopatra, traditionally by the bite of a snake, an asp (these events taking place in 30 BC). Equally as likely as this all too convenient and romantic end for Cleopatra was the possibility that Octavian had a potential focus for opposition eliminated. Cleopatra was the last queen of the Egyptian line, the concluding full stop of a line of dynastic succession that stretched back 3,000 years.

Truth be told, it was debatable how much undiluted Egyptian blood coursed through her veins. Sea Peoples, Nubians, Assyrians, Persians, Greeks and others had worn the double crown over the centuries and millennia. But this was a conclusion, symbolic or not, to one of the greatest of all historical epochs. There would be no more dynasties. As if to ensure this, the would-be heir apparent, Caesarion, was executed.

In 29 BC, Octavian returned to Rome in triumph. The year after, the Senate was purged and reduced in numbers to 600. In 27 BC, Octavian took the name Augustus and became the first emperor of Rome. But he seems to have longed for peace to enjoy the privileges of rank. He reduced the army to twenty-eight legions and released 100,000 men. Great architecture appeared, for example the first Pantheon in Rome, built by Octavian's lieutenant Agrippa. In 25 BC, the doors of the Temple of Janus were closed in a symbolic assertion that peace had broken out across the empire, the first time this had happened for 220 years.

It was not quite so in reality. For example, Spain was in rebellion for seven years, with Cantabrian tribes fighting a heroic but ultimately doomed campaign against Rome. After the conquest tin mines opened up in Iberia, causing production from those in Cornwall to slow down (globalisation was something of a problem even then). This was an empire whose influence extended across the known world. Goods flowed to and fro from China along the Great Silk Road.

In the same year that the doors of the Temple of Janus were formally shut, a trade mission set out from faraway India. Stories of Rome had reached as far afield as this. Exotic gifts were sent west, including snakes, tortoises, pheasants, tigers, a monk and an armless boy who fired arrows with his toes. The delegation took four years to reach its destination; it would have been interesting to see the looks on the faces of Rome's citizens when it arrived.

As befitted a Roman emperor, martial matters were occasionally to the fore, showing that the doors of the temple had been closed prematurely. Octavian/Augustus threatened Parthia to such an extent that the standards taken at Carrhae thirty-five years previously were returned along with the few prisoners of war who still survived. There were also campaigns waged against tribes in the Balkans and along the Danube. The power of Rome was still increasing.

They even crossed the Rhine, into the tangled forests of Germany. There were a number of tribes in the area, strong-willed and unwilling to be subservient. Frontier incidents were frequent. To protect against raids across the Rhine into Gaul, the Roman legions made punitive expeditions against some of the tribes. Archaeological evidence reveals well-organised logistics, with the legionaries and their auxiliaries being fed on Mediterranean vegetables and even spices from India, showing that trade links between west and east were already strong. In 9 BC, the Romans reached as far east as the Elbe. Yet those who believed this presaged ultimate Roman conquest in Germany missed the fact that victories in the region were followed by intense difficulties in hanging on to the gains made.

In the latter years of the reign of Augustus, an event at the time unremarked upon took place in Bethlehem. There is no historical record to back up the supposed birth of the man who would become known as Jesus Christ, these matters being ones of faith rather than certainty. The date of his birth is, bizarrely, a matter of debate too, with the most popular date being 4 BC. What cannot be doubted, however, is that the birth of Christianity would change world history, as would the onset of other great religions such as Hinduism, Buddhism, Judaism and Islam. Belief systems are the province of theologians and philosophers but historians ignore their impact at their peril.

Shortly before, the man known as Herod the Great, client king of Israel, expired. King since 40 BC, he had become a friend of Rome, making a state visit to Rome itself in 18 BC. He was a ruthless man whose path to power was a murderous one (among his many victims was his wife, Mariamne, victim of a trumped-up charge of plotting to murder him). Once he had gained power, though, he embarked on ambitious building programmes. In 10 BC he had completed the rebuilding of the city of Caesarea. He completed a new fortress at a place called Masada which would achieve notoriety a hundred years later.

Herod's end marked a diminution in Jewish autonomy. There was trouble in Jerusalem when the religious group known as the Pharisees had tried to pull down the Roman eagles that had been put up in the temple. They were massacred as a result and a Roman legion was ordered in to keep control in Jerusalem. Herod's son, Herod Antipas, succeeded to the throne of Galilee shortly after his father was said to have ordered the Massacre of the Innocents mentioned in the Bible, an attempt to destroy the child whom, it was said, was supreme over all earthly kings. Antipas would play his own part in the life of Jesus, being king when Pontius Pilate was the Roman governor in Judea.

Close by these lands, the territories of the people known as the Nabateans reached their zenith. Semitic traders on the road between the Mediterranean and Arabia, their foremost city was Petra – the 'rose-red city half as old as time' as it was described by the nineteenth-century Swiss explorer Johann Burckhardt, who rediscovered it (for the West at least – local inhabitants had always known it was there).

Petra remains one of the most evocative and exotic sites on earth, an ancient city frozen in time, spectacular and seemingly eternal. Its people, beneficiaries of the trade arteries that stretched from the Roman world to the desert vastnesses of Arabia, have long been gone but their city remains one of the most iconic memorials to history on the planet. Its breathtaking architecture, a unique fusion of Mesopotamian, Greco-Roman and Arabian styles, speak of a vibrant trading community that picked up ideas as well as wealth from those with whom it did business.

This century had seen the formal creation of a new empire. Rome would dominate Europe (or the southern half of it anyway) for the next half-millennium. Its history would be one of the most splendid of all civilisations and its legacy is still profound. And yet Rome would, like all empires, eventually decline and fall. In the year 2 BC one of the seeds of its own destruction was sown by the formation of an elite bodyguard, the Praetorian Guard, which would become the maker and destroyer of many a future ruler of Rome. There are two great recurring lessons of history: the first that nothing lasts forever and the second that the agents of destruction often come from within. These were lessons that Rome, like all great empires, would find out for itself but only when it was too late to change the course of history.

14

THE WORLD GROWS SMALLER

The Growth of Trade (AD 1–100)

One of the most remarkable literary works remaining from ancient times, one long forgotten in most quarters, is the *Periplus of the Erythraean Sea*. It was produced sometime between AD 70 and AD 80 by an Alexandrian Greek trader, Hippolus, but parts of it seem to replicate a far older work by an early Carthaginian explorer, Hanno. Its importance lies in the definitive statement it provides of geographical knowledge at the time. Details are given of trade routes to places as diverse as Eritrea or Yemen but also to other places further afield. Some of these are not surprising, being, after all, fairly local trade routes. More interesting perhaps are the details of contacts with regions much further away.

These include accounts of twenty different ports in India, the most important of them at Muziris in the south of the country on the Malabar coast. Corroborating evidence of these links may be found in the shape of Greek and Roman temples erected by merchants visiting there. Coins of the emperors Tiberius and Nero have also been uncovered by archaeologists in Muziris alongside piles of Roman *amphorae*. The trade was two-way; it is intriguing that in the midst of the ash deposits that covered Pompeii in the catastrophic explosion of Vesuvius, there was a statue of the Indian goddess Lakshmi.

Among the items that made their way west were items such as pepper, coral, ivory, cotton, Chinese silk and pearls. Merchants would effectively co-finance expeditions to collect these, clubbing together to pay for the trip and in return taking a share of the profits. These goods would have made a significant impact on the lifestyles of the better-off sections of Roman society, although it is debatable how far down the benefits trickled. By the same token, trade must have helped finance the lives of wealthy Indian merchants, though it should be noted that India was far from one united country then – rather a number of different states, as it had always been – and not everyone would have shared in the benefits there either.

The other interesting aspect of the *Periplus* is that it clearly establishes the limits of such contacts too. The narrative describes how Tamil traders from the south of India journeyed up to a great port on the Ganges. 'Beyond this country there lies a great inland place called China, from which raw silk and silk yarn and Chinese cloth are brought overland,' it states, showing that knowledge of China was certainly in existence. However, no one from the

West travelled there, for 'this China is not easy to reach … People seldom come from it and not many go there.'

In other words, contacts between China and Europe were still in the main conducted through middlemen. 'The lands beyond these places, on account of excessive winters, hard frosts and inaccessible country are unexplored,' explains the *Periplus*. One-to-one contacts did not exist and China was a shadowy, mysterious region, cloaked beneath impenetrable, enveloping clouds. It was destined to stay that way to Europe for many centuries.

China did have some awareness of Europe, though its understanding was very constrained too. Not long after the *Periplus* was written, China found itself struggling against renewed attacks from nomad warriors, the Hsiung-nu, better known in the west as 'the Huns'. This threatened the Silk Road, which, in addition to providing the maritime routes between the Middle East and India, was an important conduit for goods east and west. In response, the ruling Han dynasty sent out a general, Pan Ch'ao, to beat off their attacks.

He did so with some success, inadvertently forcing the Huns westwards, towards Europe, on which they would ultimately descend with frightening ferocity several centuries into the future. Pan Ch'ao reached the Caspian Sea, where he heard of a mighty power further west. He sent reports on the greatness of Rome, for this was the power spoken of, back to China.

This was above all the century of mighty Roman emperors, many of them tyrannical, a few of them of dubious sanity and some remembered even now for their vices far more than their virtues. It was also the century when a new religion introduced itself to the world but when an older one, Buddhism, was exported to China with significant long-term effects. A new power would emerge in the north of India, while Parthia was strong enough to continue to hold its own in the Middle East against even Rome. In short, this was another crucial period for the future of the world.

The century began with Rome's first emperor, Augustus, ageing and seeking an heir. He had not been lucky in this respect, failing to father a son. He did, however, have a daughter, Julia, who had been married off several times in vain attempts to provide a son to solve the problem after a fashion. Her third husband, Tiberius, was a somewhat cold and calculating character but, in the absence of a better alternative, he it was who was finally designated as the heir of Augustus. Yet this only entitled him to Augustus's possessions, not his throne. In the new and still evolving constitutional position of Imperial Rome, there was as yet no clear succession policy in place as far as the emperor was concerned.

By the year AD 13, it was obvious that Augustus had not long left for this world and Tiberius was given equal powers with him. A year later, Augustus died. On his deathbed, so it was said, he summoned his close confidants to him and asked them to applaud the crafty game he had played throughout his long life (he was well into his seventies, a good age for the time). It was a stylish end to a life lived to the full.

In terms of its international position, the century had already seen some significant events for Rome, not all of them positive. In AD 2, the Euphrates was agreed as the border between Parthia and the Roman Empire. This was in effect only a holding position and there would be more clashes between the two powers as the century progressed. Four years later, Rome intervened in the affairs of Judea, making it a province. Perhaps she was worried about the powers and aspirations of Herod the Great, who had died in 4 BC. The temple he had built had been an impressive project, providing strong evidence of an emerging regional power. Rome had been unnerved by these developements and decided to break up Israel and Judea and thereby weaken it. This would have significant consequences a few decades later.

To the north of Rome, the forests of Germany provided cover for aggressive tribesmen, 'barbarians' as the Romans would have seen them. Rome's attitude to the Germans is well summed up in a near-contemporary poem which threatened that 'cold chains will bind the great kings of your race, by neck and hand, with fear on every face'.

But this was difficult to bring about in practice as gains made in summer expeditions were frequently lost straight away when the Romans were forced to retreat to winter quarters. In an attempt to bring the Germans under control several Roman legions had been sent to subdue them in AD 9. However, they were up against a formidable leader, Arminius, who led the legionaries deeper and deeper into the woods, a ploy helped no end by the fact that he had been brought up as a Roman and was playing a clever game of pretending to be Rome's ally while planning her downfall. He was merely luring the Roman army into a trap, wiping them out bit by bit until the legion came up against a strong, prepared position, effectively a wall that Arminius had ordered to be constructed at the heart of the forest.

Once the Romans stumbled across this, the German warriors turned on them. Inundated by attacks from the flanks too, the legions were overwhelmed and forced to retreat. Huge numbers of them died during the battle, known as that of the Teutoburger Wald, one of the greatest ever defeats suffered by Rome. Germany would, in the main, continue to remain out of bounds for the legions for the foreseeable future. Roman 'civilisation' had been outfought and out-thought by the 'barbarian' hordes.

A line had been drawn that marked the outer boundaries of Rome's territories and realistic ambitions. Rome was not, after all, invincible. The legend of Arminius would be used many centuries later and, like the stories of many otherwise long-lost heroes, his almost mythical deeds would be employed as a powerful symbol of rising nationalism. In Germany in the nineteenth century a great statue of him was erected, rising high above the forests around where the Teutoburger Wald was believed to be.

Tiberius was not a popular emperor and in later years developed a flair for cruelty and sexual excess. For the last few years of his reign he had effectively retired from the public eye, living in unbelievable luxury on his estate on the dream island of Capri. There had been events in his reign that were surprisingly resonant of issues that would recur again right down until modern times, particularly when all Jews were expelled from Italy in AD 19 when one of their number was accused of obtaining money under false pretences. Persecution of the Jewish community has remained a disturbing and terrifying nightmare since, as we know only too well.

The Jews would also be at the heart of another series of events whose repercussions resonate down the centuries. When Pontius Pilate was appointed procurator (effectively governor) of Judea in AD 26, it would not perhaps have appeared to be a plum position. The Jews whom he was to govern were renowned for their passionate religious affiliations and their proud protection of their heritage and traditions. These were not necessarily qualities that the Romans appreciated among those they saw as a subject people.

Soon after Pilate's arrival, a prophet appeared, a wild and passionate desert-dweller named John. He said that he was merely the advance guard for a man far greater than he. He made powerful enemies, particularly in the shape of Herod Antipas, nominal king of Galilee (a separate political entity from Judea but still under the thumb of Rome). It was said in the Bible that John attracted the enmity of Herod's stepdaughter Salome when he insulted her mother and she insisted that he must be eliminated after famously dancing before the king. In other quarters it was suggested that John was dangerously fomenting political dissent. Whatever the reason, he was seized, imprisoned and then executed.

But this did not remove the problem, for the prophet whose coming John had foretold, a man named Jesus of Nazareth, was about to embark on his short but hugely significant mission. Preaching radical ideas about man's place on earth, his relationships with his brothers and his need to prepare for another, far more important, life to come, the impact of his teachings in the long term would be huge.

Sometime around AD 30 (the year is not known for sure) Jesus embarked on what appeared to be his final mission in Jerusalem. It was on the fourteenth day of the Jewish month of Nisan (3 April in the western calendar) that Jesus and his disciples shared their Last Supper. That same evening, he was seized and taken before the Jewish High Priest Caiaphas. The next day he appeared before Pontius Pilate for judgement (this being a Roman province, life-and-death decisions were down to the procurator). Pilate famously washed his hands of the decision and handed Jesus over to be crucified. The rest of the story is well known.

Of course, the preceding few paragraphs take as their source the Bible, which was not written as a historically accurate account but as a statement of religious beliefs. That said, we rely on other 'single-source' accounts for our knowledge of ancient history so we should treat it as a source of no lesser or greater historical veracity than other books of the time. And what cannot be argued against in a historical sense is the impact that the Bible made and the way the actions of its professed believers shaped the course of history.

That was not the end of Jesus but it was not the end of Pilate either. In AD 36, he put down a Samaritan revolt so brutally that even the authorities back in Rome were unnerved by his violence; governors were expected to avoid escalating trouble whenever possible. He was summoned back to Rome, his career effectively at an end. He returned to a city where not only great events were being played out but much more mundane occurrences were having a positive effect on daily life. The well-developed glass-blowing industry in Rome was reaching its zenith; around this time the Romans came up with the idea of putting glass in their windows. By the end of the century, Roman citizens would also be reaping the benefits of false teeth – history is, after all, a mixture of the great and the seemingly trivial.

Tiberius, suffering from an imperial curse it seemed, also struggled to provide an heir. He had initially nominated his nephew Germanicus to succeed him (his own accession had established the principle of a hereditary handover of the powers of emperor). Germanicus, however, had been thoughtless enough to die before Tiberius did in AD 37, and so it was his son, Gaius Caesar, who took up the imperial mantle in his place.

The name Gaius Caesar might not be well known but he had a nickname, Caligula, 'Little Boots', by which he is most widely remembered, manly for the wrong reasons. He had been a popular general and this had helped ease his way to the Imperial throne. On becoming emperor, he had continued his martial exploits. In AD 39, he had led an army towards the Rhine but at the last minute veered off towards the English Channel. Britain, still unconquered despite Julius Caesar's efforts nearly a century earlier, was his target but Caligula was diverted before he crossed. Britain was safe – but only for a few short years.

If Britain was saved for now, the citizens of Rome were not. The supreme prize had turned Caligula's head. The emperor decided now to declare himself a god; not a first in human history of course, but providing convincing evidence of his growing megalomania. This also led to other excesses. The Roman treasury was soon exhausted by his extravagance. Increasingly cruel characteristics emerged too, such as when the son of Juba II, King of Mauretania, was brought to Rome in AD 40 and starved to death.

Accusations of madness followed on. It was even said that the emperor planned to make his horse a consul (though this, it must be pointed out, was not necessarily a sign of madness but could have been a satirical comment on how little Caligula valued the consulship as an institution now). At any rate, in AD 41 the Praetorian Guard, who increasingly began to see themselves as kingmakers, decided that enough was enough and assassinated the so-called madman. His place was taken by his uncle, Claudius.

This would be a century of much turbulence in Rome, at least as far as its emperors were concerned. It was a period that was to see similar problems emerge in China too. A succession of young kings in quick succession was brought to an end when a usurper, Wang Mang, seized the throne in AD 8. He would introduce extreme repressive measures, including the mass nationalisation of land. His usurpation brought a temporary end to the Han dynasty.

However, authoritarian leaders everywhere have always struggled to subdue the masses who, when their lot becomes too harsh, see little to lose in revolt. Within a decade of his succession, secret societies were evolving, plotting to remove Wang Mang. One of them was known as the Red Eyebrows, named after the colour that they painted their foreheads to distinguish them when they broke into open revolt. A series of peasant uprisings progressively brought the usurper to his knees.

Although the participants in these revolts were unable to establish an administration of their own to replace that of Wang Mang, by AD 23 they had succeeded in overthrowing him when he was killed in battle. China had suffered a series of disasters, economic and natural (drought and famine in particular being a problem). Attacks from Mongolia increasingly sapped the strength of the ruling regime and in the end it died of exhaustion. A new dynasty was established, or rather an old one – the Han – was reinstated. It moved its capital east, hence the name it is normally known by, the Eastern Han, to distinguish it from its predecessors.

Roman expansion continued as the century progressed. In AD 43, Mauretania, long a sphere of interest for Rome in Africa, was made a province, the same year that Britain was invaded again. This time, four legions made the short but dangerous crossing from Gaul, led by Aulus Plautius. Their landing was unopposed (a mutiny among the legions assembled to invade had lulled the Britons into a false sense of security) but when they advanced they were faced by a British leader, Caratacus, whom they swept aside. Emperor Claudius followed with reinforcements (possibly accompanied by elephants). The process of conquest continued until AD 47 when a border was established. Caratacus continued to raid across it but was eventually betrayed by another British queen, Cartimandua, queen of the Brigantes tribe.

Cartimandua's actions emphasised that Britain was far from united in its response to the Roman threat. The land was still divided into tribal territories and in fact the invasion had been partly organised in response to pleas from disaffected British tribal leaders for help in restoring their fortunes. A number of tribes in the south of Britain had been on good terms with the Romans since Caesar's time and had profited from trade with Rome. Resistance to the invasion came in the main from tribes further north and west who had not benefited from these trading links or had deliberately chosen to stay aloof from Rome. Tribes to the south were therefore much better disposed towards the Romans. Many an invasion in history has been helped by the self-interest of powerful figures in the lands targeted.

The initial process of conquest was not easy; during the excavation of Maiden Castle, the largest of all Celtic hill forts, which was attacked by the Romans on their way west, a skeleton was unearthed with a large ballista bolt still embedded in its spine, graphic evidence of the ferocity of the fighting. However, military garrisons were established to keep the native population under control, and towns grew up around these and trade began to prosper. This was facilitated by the building of roads which linked the garrisons but also the towns around them and Britain began to become a profitable part of the Roman Empire.

However, trouble was not far away. In AD 60, the king of the Iceni, one of the British tribes in the east of the country, died. He left his throne jointly to his wife Boudicca (known to later generations as Boadicea) and Rome. According to Tacitus, the Roman historian, she was harshly treated in the arguments that followed this division. She was flogged and her two daughters raped. She was incensed at these abuses and a vicious revolt broke out, with the situation quickly escalating out of control.

At the same time, the governor of Britain, Suetonius Paulinus, began a campaign into Wales, denuding the province of troops when it could be least afforded. While he was on the island of Anglesey in the west, destroying the last vestiges of Celtic Druidism, further east the country was ablaze. Supported increasingly by other tribes who resented Roman excesses, the towns of Colchester (Camulodunum), St Albans (Verulamium) and London (Londinium) were attacked and thousands massacred. Paulinus returned with his legions and eventually defeated Boudicca in a crushing victory. She took her own life rather than be captured. However, Rome again had not appreciated the mismanagement that led to these problems; Suetonius was recalled as a result and his successor told to be more conciliatory.

By this time, Rome was ruled by one of the most notorious of all emperors. In AD 54, Claudius had been poisoned by his wife, Agrippina. Her seventeen-year-old son, Nero, now became the ruler of Rome. Violent tendencies and an unstable temperament quickly became apparent. A year after becoming emperor, Nero had his stepbrother Brittanicus killed when Agrippina began to favour him. As well as seeing him as a political threat, it was also said that Nero was jealous of his superior singing voice.

In AD 59, Nero decided to kill his own mother, Agrippina. Appearances still mattered so he tried to bring about her death by subterfuge. He had a specially designed boat made which would be self-collapsing, hoping to drown her in the process. When she survived this attempt, all pretence was dropped and she was beaten to death. Despite these violent events, above all else here was a man who wished to be adored. At one stage he tried chariot racing but then turned to stage performance, being an accomplished performer on the lyre, a musical instrument with Greek antecedents.

Nero's private life became increasingly chaotic and violent. In AD 62 Nero got rid of Seneca, his mentor, and divorced Octavia, his wife (who was put to death soon after). Instead he married his mistress Poppaea, ignoring the fact that she already had a husband, Otho (whose impact on history was not yet over). This presaged the darkest and most sinister days of Nero's life. In AD 64, a great fire broke out in Rome and large parts of the city were destroyed. There is little evidence that Nero really did sing while Rome burned, and his response to the disaster was that of a very concerned emperor. He devised great plans for rebuilding Rome, but it was here that the problems started.

His schemes were so grandiose that they were completely unaffordable. Vicious purges were initiated in an attempt to eliminate people whose main crime was to be rich, for Nero wanted their wealth and would stop at nothing to get it. A reign of terror descended on the city from which none was safe. He kicked to death his own wife Poppaea, pregnant with his heir, over some minor offence to his pride. Terrible though this was, it was not the last or the greatest offence of Nero, who then became besotted with a young man, Sporus, who reminded him of Poppaea. He had him castrated and dressed as the wife he had murdered.

Nero also visited Greece, where he attended the Greek Games. In a farcical display, he was awarded 1,808 prizes in the competitions there. The audience was forbidden to leave the Games while he was performing, a prohibition which extended to pregnant women who went into labour in his presence. Given these disturbing manifestations of instability, the patience of Rome wore thin. In AD 68, a widespread revolt broke out, involving legions from Spain and Gaul as well as the Praetorian Guard. It quickly became apparent that Nero was so universally detested that virtually no one would protect him. He fled Rome but, being caught by those who wished to destroy him, he took his own life (aided by a servant) rather than be taken alive.

Now the new faith of Christianity was starting to develop from its humble beginnings. Yet for a while it seemed that the small church Christ left behind him would not last for long. When Rome had burned, Nero had needed scapegoats and he had chosen the small group of Christians in the city for the part. He alleged that the fire was a deliberate act of arson on their part. The persecution that followed was a hammer-blow against a faith that had plenty of other issues to concern it. The early decades of Christianity had been marked partly by evangelism and partly by internal dissent. There was debate particularly about whether the religion should retain its Jewish roots or whether it should also be open to non-Jews, 'Gentiles'.

These debates were argued out with passion and often bitterness. One of the most prominent supporters of the cause of the 'Gentiles' was an unlikely convert: Paul, a Roman citizen who had been an early persecutor of the new religion. He was beheaded in Rome during Nero's purge while another leading early Christian, Peter, Jesus's disciple, was crucified (he was not a Roman citizen so his punishment was harsher). Many of their co-religionists were also slaughtered in the outpouring of violence that marked these dark times.

Religiously inspired confrontation was a recurring theme. Another great faith, Judaism, was about to face its blackest day. Relations with Rome had often been difficult. When Herod Agrippa died in AD 44, they deteriorated badly and a revolt broke out when a Roman soldier tore up a religious scroll. This uprising was put down but a far more dangerous one was to follow. This broke out in AD 66 when the unpopular procurator Florus was on the receiving end of a ferocious outpouring of hatred which overwhelmed a Roman legion sent to put it down. The fortress of Masada, high up on sheer cliffs on top of an arid desert plateau by the Dead Sea, also fell, but violence was not just directed against Rome. There was fighting between Jews and Gentiles, and it was also not long before different Jewish factions were at each other's throats too.

However justified rebellion might have been, it could never be tolerated by Rome. Nero, still emperor when the revolt started, despatched the experienced Vespasian, a veteran of the conquest of Britain, to put it down. Vespasian had incurred the wrath of Nero when appearing bored during one of his performances and was perhaps lucky just to be exiled to Greece, where he spent his days indulging himself in his favourite hobby, beekeeping.

On arriving in Judea and taking up a rather more active assignment, Vespasian launched a systematic campaign to bring the Jewish rebels to heel. He captured the town of Jotopata, where an important commander, Josephus, was located. Faced with the prospect of certain death unless he helped the Romans, Josephus did his best to keep in their good graces. As well as trying to bring the war to a peaceful end which somehow managed to protect his own people from the wrath of Rome, he also wrote a history of the war, our main source of information on it.

The death of Nero brought chaos back to Rome. There was a succession of emperors claiming the throne during the following year. Galba, the first, was assassinated after rashly trying to diminish the power of the Praetorian Guard and stop bribery and corruption in Rome. Next came Otho, divorced husband of the unfortunate Poppaea. He did not last, but the final claimant did. This was none other than Vespasian himself, elected emperor by his troops in Alexandria. However, he could not hope to claim the title of emperor *in absentia* and so he returned to Rome, leaving the final acts of the war in Judea to his son Titus.

Titus moved on Jerusalem in AD 70. A siege of 139 days followed, during which the city was systematically reduced. Resistance was stoic but doomed, though the Jewish defence was fragmented as there were a number of groups that were at violent odds with each other (one, especially, called the *sicarii* were fanatical and gained a reputation for their zealotry and penchant for assassination). When the Romans at last broke into the city, their revenge was absolute. It was said that Titus wished to save the temple but if this was so then his objective was unfulfilled. There was fighting around the sacred building and a fire broke out in the melee. It took hold and the Jews looked on horrified as Herod the Great's magnificent homage to Yahweh was obliterated.

It was a terrible day in the tragic history of the Jewish people. That same year the last book of the Christian New Testament, the apocalyptic Revelations of St John the Divine, was written on the Aegean island of Patmos. This was of course coincidence, but it was a singularly appropriate time to write of the end of the world.

The year after, Titus returned to Rome where he shared a Triumph with Vespasian. Vespasian, the first commoner to become emperor of Rome, introduced a frugal reign and brought in fresh provincial blood to the government of Rome. However, he was harsh in his treatment of the conquered Jews, many of whom he sold into slavery. Jews were also forbidden to proselytise and their lot was generally a tough one.

This was not the end of the suffering of the Jews, far from it. In AD 73, the daunting citadel of Masada was taken from them after a three-year siege that involved the erection of a 375-foot-high ramp up the side of the mountain on which it stood (much of this remarkable piece of engineering is still visible 2,000 years later). At least that is the traditional account of the siege, though it now seems that the ramp took advantage of a completely natural incline already there and that the fighting covered a much shorter period than three years.

Rather than be taken alive, most of the Jews at Masada, men, women and children, took their own lives. Less remarked but in some ways even more important for posterity (though the legends created at Masada continue to exercise a significant influence over modern Jewish consciousness), an ascetic community at Qumran by the Dead Sea was overrun at around the same time. Those fleeing buried some scrolls in the caves round about. They would remain undiscovered until the twentieth century, when the re-emergence of the Dead Sea Scrolls had a dramatic effect on modern understanding of ancient history.

Vespasian reintroduced stability in a generally parsimonious decade of rule and on his death in AD 79 was succeeded by Titus. Titus's reign was short and unlucky; one wonders whether devout Jews saw this as a punishment for his actions in Jerusalem. Rome was further seriously damaged by several major fires and then plague broke out while he ruled. Despite these adverse events, the brief reign of Titus was also to see one of the most remarkable architectural achievements of history, the completion of the immense Coliseum in Rome, said to hold 50,000 spectators.

Titus was also emperor when one of the great natural disasters of history occurred, adding to the general impression that he was an unlucky ruler. The cities of Pompeii and Herculaneum were built in the shadow of Mount Vesuvius but the volcano had not caused any problems to the citizens in living memory. Then in August AD 79, the very year of Titus's accession, ominous rumblings were heard. On the 24th Vesuvius exploded with colossal intensity. Great plumes of searing ash were thrown into the air, descending in thick, asphyxiating clouds on the cities. Thousands died, unable to outrun the forces of nature, their bodies cloaked in shrouds of pumice that would freeze them in time until later generations dug them out of their igneous graves.

Titus did his best to alleviate the sufferings of the survivors but his reign was a troubled one and many superstitious souls were perhaps glad when it was over. His place was taken by his brother Domitian, a harsh and often cruel emperor. During his reign the empire continued to expand, as did the state of knowledge. There were probing raids across the Rhine, and a Roman fleet completed the circumnavigation of Britain. Then in AD 86, a tribe known as the Dacians crossed the Danube from a region in what we now call Romania. It was the first barbarian incursion into the empire for many years but it heralded future problems.

The Dacians, under their resourceful leader Decebalus ('the brave'), had been forced to move by mass migrations to their north-east, driven on by tribal movements of Sarmatians from Central Asia. Similar events, but on a completely different scale, would eventually bring down the empire itself, though this end was still a long way off. Rome responded by crossing the Danube and fighting a harsh war in the Dacians' own territory.

Eventually a province would be established there, though it would not last for long. Its influence did though. Romanians even now proudly claim their descent from Rome (hence the name) and prove the fact by pointing out that their language is based on Latin, in contrast to most other countries in the region who use Slavic languages and have a Cyrillic alphabet. A statue of Romulus and Remus with the she-wolf who played such a key role in the birth of Rome now stands in Central Bucharest to mark the link. The province in Romania marked the furthest extent of the Roman Empire in the region.

Domitian proved to have inherited the vices of some of his maligned predecessors. In AD 88 he too declared himself a god. Astrologers and philosophers, whom he mistrusted, were ejected from Rome (they were later kicked out of the rest of Italy too). In a comical side effect to a generally harsh rule, in AD 88 the emperor wrote a book called *On the Care of Hair*. This cannot have been especially well informed, for the writer Suetonius gleefully tells us that the emperor went bald.

Violent excess characterised later years of his reign. In AD 92, Domitian had Christians executed for refusing to worship his image. Four years later, he had his secretary executed. His crime? This was the same man who had helped Nero commit suicide three decades earlier. It is perhaps no surprise that Domitian himself was murdered in AD 96, killed by his own wife. There was widespread elation at this act. All statues of the late, unloved emperor were destroyed by order of the Senate, grateful for the intervention of his spouse. He was succeeded by Nerva, who ruled for only two years before dying and being replaced by Trajan.

We began this chapter of history by looking at the links that existed between east and west, so it is perhaps appropriate to return east to conclude it. Christianity had begun to spread east fairly early on and there is a tradition that the apostle Thomas journeyed to India to the court of Gandhara in AD 50 or thereabouts. He was martyred there according to the legendary accounts but his missionary movements were not the only significant ones at the time (he was not the only one – less well-known is the story that the apostle Bartholomew ended his days as a martyr in what is now Azerbaijan).

About fifteen years later, envoys were sent by the Chinese to India to study Buddhism. This encouraged the efforts of Indian missionaries to journey to China in return and

Buddhist holy men were soon making the long and arduous trek to the country. There they began to make a significant impact on Chinese culture (though, as was often the case in such movements, their initial impact was largely restricted to the higher echelons of society). The effect on Chinese art, too, was profound.

There is also evidence of links between China and a mysterious island to the east. In AD 57, the records tell us that there was a delegation sent from the islands of Japan to China. There had been little mention of the islands previously in history, though there is evidence of humankind there as far back as half a million years ago. Up until 15,000 years ago Japan was connected to the Asian mainland by a land bridge and this must have facilitated the free movement of hominids to and fro. Japan was not by any means a backwater; the oldest known pottery, some 13,000 years old, has been found there, but the rising of the seas did inevitably isolate Japan to an extent from developments elsewhere.

This isolation began at the start of what is known as the Jomon period. Farming came later, dated to around 4000 BC. Around 3,000 years after this, rice and maize appear to have arrived from the Asian mainland. At a similar time there were also invasions of the islands from across the sea (though the introduction of rice predates these invasions, suggesting that there were trading links before these conquests were launched).

This was the start of what became known as the Yayoi period. Japan was at this time a very fragmented region with a number of small, petty states fighting to survive by the use of warfare or judicious alliances. Increased levels of rice production, which were encouraged by the invaders, led to a corresponding upsurge in permanent settlement (many Japanese inhabitants appear to have been hunter-gatherers until a relatively late stage compared to developments further west) and also the growth of dominant social elites. Around the first century AD an upsurge in silk production on the islands might well have led to trade delegations such as the one to China noted above.

There were also other important developments in Asia. Sometime around AD 80 a new group exploded into parts of the Indian Subcontinent. Led by a warrior called Kujula Kadphises, the Kushans established an empire that would spread from Bactria in Central Asia in the west to Kashmir in the north of India in the east. The Kushans were formed of nomadic tribes, the Yüeh-chih, who had been expelled from the borders of China and forced west – yet another piece in the jigsaw that would lead to the dramatic descent of migrating hordes into the Roman Empire in the future.

Given their position, the Kushans exerted significant influence on the overland trade routes between east and west. As a sign of how cosmopolitan parts of the world were starting to become, they adopted much of the Greek language for their own. In the west, they rubbed up against the borders of Parthia, a state that had managed to survive the century despite several Roman attempts at intervention (particularly around control of Armenia, which was essentially a buffer state between Rome and Parthia). As the century ended, Parthia appeared to have more than held its own against Rome, but the Roman Empire still appeared to be the real superpower. That view, however, would appear increasingly illusory in the future. Rome had reached its limits and a long period of contraction was about to begin almost unnoticed.

15

WAR AND PEACE

Parthia and Rome at War and the Further Emergence of China (AD 101–200)

Far out of sight of Europe and Asia, across the as yet unexplored Atlantic Ocean, a new civilisation had begun to emerge in South America. There are no historical records by which to date it but archaeologists reckon that it was around AD 100 that a civilisation known as the Moche began to emerge in what is now northern Peru. It was probably not organised as a centralised state, so historians assert, but as a conglomerate of a number of individual, smaller entities that shared a culture and something of a world view.

The Moche were particularly distinguished for their pottery, which often featured human faces moulded on the front of their vessels. Their pottery is also often erotic, showing human beings in the act of coitus, possibly suggesting a strong link to cults of fertility or maybe, less esoterically, sexual voyeurism. They lived in the main in adobe buildings, most of which have long since been looted and destroyed, but the fragments that remain suggest that they used richly decorated murals to decorate their properties.

We find in the Moche many elements of darker practices that would emerge later among other cultures in the area, notably the Incas of Peru or, further to the north, the Aztecs and Maya of Central America. There is definite evidence of human sacrifice, and decapitation appears to have been a much used ritual. Scholars have identified a recurring figure in Moche iconography, the so-called 'Decapitator', a spider-like monster who appears holding a head in one hand and a knife in the other. There are also hints that victims were held for several weeks and tortured before being ritually despatched.

The Moche had links with civilisations further south, of which little is known. One was the Nazca culture, famous for carving hundreds of mysterious lines in the southern Peruvian desert, symbols that have been variously interpreted as ritual representations of the gods or, by some more adventurous commentators, landing zones for alien spacecraft. Rather more prosaically, there was certainly trade in *guano*, an important fertiliser. The Moche also used mummification for their dead.

In Europe, as the century began, Decebalus continued to cause trouble for Rome. Deciding that he must be controlled once and for all, Trajan invaded Dacia. At his side was a young, ambitious man named Hadrian, a lover of all things Greek to such an extent that he was known as 'the Greekling'. Although Decebalus was defeated, he led a revolt between AD 104 and AD 106 which was finally put down by the Romans. Decebalus and his leaders held a final feast as the outcome of the war became certain, at the conclusion of which they all committed suicide. Trajan held celebratory games in Rome at which captive Dacians were forced to fight as gladiators.

In AD 107, Trajan sent ambassadors to India (presumably to the Kushanṣ). The emperor went on to be a hard-working administrator, credited with the maxim 'it is better that the guilty should remain unpunished than the innocent should be condemned', a philosophy that has a very progressive ring about it. He also had a social conscience, encouraging the development of agriculture and introducing state mortgages. He commanded that a corn dole, a distribution of food, should be handed out to the poor.

Trajan's architectural achievements were impressive too. He ordered the construction of a magnificent bridge across the Danube in the Iron Gates region which was over 3,500 feet long and remained the longest arch bridge in the world for over 1,000 years. It was guarded at either end by a *castrum*, or fort, which all travellers had to pass through to cross the river.

Although still a minority sect, and destined to endure further persecution in the future, Christians continued to gain more of a foothold in the empire. Early on in the century, they started to bury their dead in the catacombs outside Rome. It was here that the earliest traces of surviving Christian art appeared. At times the catacombs would be refuges, hiding places in times of persecution, but they would also become time capsules, giving us an insight into the early Church that would otherwise be lost.

Far away on the other side of the world, in AD 105, a Chinese official, Ts'ai Lun, told his emperor that he had discovered a new form of writing material better than silk or bamboo. It was made of rags, fishnet, bark and hemp. It was in fact paper, and Ts'ai Lun had made a crucial discovery, that of a material that continues to be very important down to our own time. However, it did him little good; when he was implicated in an intrigue with the empress he was executed.

Whenever two superpowers are neighbours, confrontation is almost inevitable. Sometimes this is at a political level, at others military conflict ensues. A showdown was brewing between Rome and Parthia, one that had been inevitable since the two powers started to come into contact in the Middle East. In AD 112, the Parthians invaded Armenia, long a buffer between the two regional superpowers, and Trajan decided that the power of the Parthians must be broken.

That same year Trajan had erected his famous column in the forum of Rome commemorating his Dacian triumphs. Composed of eighteen blocks of marble, each weighing 50 tons, it was a massive construction. On it, carved in relief, were scenes of the Roman army in action and of the dramatic conclusion to the war. Not only does it provide permanent evidence of the glory of Trajan, it also gives historians lasting insight into the way the legions were armed and how they fought.

There is also evidence surviving of other, more mundane, matters from Trajan's reign. In AD 116 the physician Soranus of Ephesus (but living in Alexandria) wrote a treatise on contraception and abortion for mothers whose lives were in danger. This was not the first mention of contraception in history. Egyptian records dating back to 1850 BC mention a very unattractive intrauterine substance made of crocodile dung or honey and sodium bicarbonate. The Ebers Papyrus, dating back to 1550 BC, mentions another intrauterine substance made of dates, acacia and honey. While this might seem an unlikely mixture, in fact the chemical reaction produced results in the formation of lactic acid, which is still widely used in spermicides.

In the meantime, Rome continued to expand at the expense of Parthia. Between AD 114 and AD 116 Trajan systematically conquered large chunks of Parthia, including Ctesiphon, one of the oldest and most prestigious cities in the region. Mesopotamia, Armenia, Assyria and Parthia all became Roman provinces. Trajan also reached the shores of the Persian Gulf but regretted that he was too old to emulate Alexander and move on to India. However, he built a Red Sea fleet instead, through which he hoped to control trade with India. He had discovered that it can be more profitable to dominate trade routes than to conquer countries.

Trajan installed a puppet emperor in the conquered lands and returned west. However, the region was still far from subdued and revolts broke out in his wake. He had learned another home truth; it is one thing to conquer, another to subdue permanently (a lesson that we still have to relearn in our own time). Worn out perhaps by his intense campaigning, he suffered a stroke and died on the way to Rome.

In AD 117, Trajan was succeeded by the 'Greekling' Hadrian, who opted for a change of approach in international affairs. He believed that Rome was overextending itself dangerously and reinstated the Euphrates as a border with Parthia. A great lover of Greek art forms, he wore a beard in deference to their culture, the first Roman emperor to do so. He also showed some populist tendencies, attempting to win over the masses by putting on games and publicly burning tax records, effectively declaring an amnesty for all those who owed taxes to the state.

In AD 121, Hadrian set out on a tour of his empire. Frontier fortifications were improved and he confirmed that the empire's European borders should be based on the Rhine and Danube. In AD 122 he visited Britain and ordered that a wall should be built to divide Britannia from the barbarian lands to the north. Completed in AD 127, Hadrian's Wall is one of Rome's most famous monuments, though it is minuscule compared to the Great Wall of China, being less than 100 miles long.

It is important to remember Hadrian's approach to empire when considering the building of his wall in Britain. Its existence may superficially appear to offer evidence that the tribes from the north were causing so much trouble on a regular basis that great efforts were required to keep them out. But in the wider context Hadrian's strategic insight must be acknowledged. Faced with a number of rebellions at various times across the empire, ranging from Britannia to Mauretania and across to Egypt and Judea, he realised that the most sensible approach was to hold what he had and not seek further expansion.

However, there is circumstantial evidence that Hadrian's mission to Britain was required because of serious unrest there. The historian Fronto wrote in the middle of the century to the emperor Marcus Aurelius, reminding him of the troubles faced by his grandfather Hadrian when he remarked, 'What great numbers of soldiers were killed by the Jews – and what great numbers by the British.' Clearly some violent disturbances had been taking place, leading perhaps to the loss of large numbers of soldiers. Some historians suggest indeed that the disappearance from the historical record of the Ninth Legion, which simply vanishes without trace, can be put down to its annihilation in Scotland, though there is as yet a lack of conclusive evidence to prove this.

The wall was manned by troops from far afield, including those from Dacia on the other side of Europe. It was Rome's policy to integrate soldiers from conquered territories into her armies. The evidence that survives suggests that discipline in the army was tough, even brutal. Corporal punishment was frequent, often bringing the victims to the point of collapse and even death. No soldier below the rank of centurion was allowed to marry. Recruitment was for a twenty-five-year stint, much of an adult lifetime in those days.

The harshness of the regime explains both the effectiveness and the unthinking brutality that the army demonstrated in battle. The legions also became very cosmopolitan, with auxiliaries recruited from across the empire for their very specific skills. So Gauls would be recruited for their abilities as horsemen, and stone slingers from the Balearics were attached to the armies, where they would fight alongside Batavians (from the region of the modern Netherlands) who were famed for their ability to cross rivers in their armour and then fight when they reached the other side.

In AD 129, Hadrian visited the Middle East on what would turn out to be a fateful trip. He first journeyed to Palmyra, at the fringes of the Syrian desert, which had taken over from Petra as the dominant Roman city on the trade routes east. However, when visiting Alexandria, his favourite, his homosexual lover Antinous whom he worshipped, was drowned in the Nile. Hadrian was married but had no children and although he treated the empress with all due deference publicly he does not appear to have felt real affection for her. In contrast, he was devastated by the loss of Antinous, building a city in his memory.

That same year Hadrian visited Jerusalem, still largely ruinous after its sack by Titus, and ordered its rebuilding. However, in the process he was very insensitive to the Jews, ordering a ban on circumcision and commanding that they honour Roman gods in the rebuilt city of Aelia Capitolina, as Jerusalem had become. In response, between AD 132 and AD 135 there was a vicious revolt led by Simon Bar-Cochba, regarded by some of the Jews as a Messiah. The uprising was brutally crushed, the province was renamed Palestine and Jerusalem was declared a forbidden city as far as the Jews were concerned. This was the beginning of the period of long exile and the creation of the Jewish diaspora, from which the Jews would not begin to recover for many centuries.

The latter years of Hadrian's reign were characterised by repression and the brutal removal of opponents. Hadrian died in AD 138 and was replaced by Antoninus Pius.

Before his death, Hadrian had made a poignant last visit to see the sea, a very human touch for a man who seemed one step removed from a god. However, wanting to ensure that his legacy was recognised by future generations, Hadrian ordered the construction of a vast mausoleum in Rome.

His successor, Antoninus, inaugurated the most peaceful and perhaps most prosperous of all Roman reigns. Trade delegations were received from, and sent to, different parts of the world. There were also important developments in science that marked his reign. A geographer in Alexandria by the name of Claudius Ptolemaeus ('Ptolemy') coined the terms 'seconds', 'minutes', 'parallels' and 'meridians' for the first time, though he underestimated how far away India was in his geographical calculations.

Ptolemy's work had been preceded by the geographer Marinus of Tyre, who was active around the beginning of the century. He was the first to assign latitudes and longitudes. His maps were the first of the Roman Empire to show China (called Shera). He also believed that there should be an opposite to the Arctic in the south and coined the name 'Antarctic' for these unknown regions.

In his view the inhabited world stretched from Thule (Shetland) in the north to 'Agysymba' in the south (a now lost sub-Saharan country). In the west, inhabited lands began with the semi-mythical Isles of the Blessed (also called the Fortunate Islands) to Shera in the east. He calculated a circumference for the world of around 33,000 kilometres, an underestimate of about 17 per cent.

The relative shrinking of the world was having an impact on other areas further afield. One such was Axum in northern Ethiopia, which was mentioned in the *Periplus*, where it was noted that Axum was an important staging post for the ivory trade. It also acted as a link between the Mediterranean and India, in particular through two major ports, Massawa and Assab, on the Red Sea. By this time the trading links that these served had become much more important than they had been in the past. Axum became the most vital of all links between African trade and Rome, taking the place of the ancient kingdom of Kush, which had once been pre-eminent in this area.

These developments were to be the springboard for future expansion in Axum. Agriculturally, the region was much more fertile than it is now and there was a significant surplus to export. This helped the country's economy to grow; so too did the trade in other products for which Axum was a middleman. Ivory has already been mentioned, but exotic animals were highly prized as novelties and these were also traded. Axum grew rich enough to look at expanding through conquest and in particular gazed across the Red Sea to the ports of Southern Arabia, which it began increasingly to covet.

Great changes had been taking place in India during these years. Around AD 120–150 the Kushan Empire was ruled by its most powerful emperor, Kanishka the Great. His fame was widespread and he is remembered in the legends of China, Mongolia and Tibet and even referred to in Japan. Buddhists in Sri Lanka talk of him as one of the four pillars of the faith, though he is also known to have worshipped Persian fire gods – in other words, he was a man who was hedging his bets in a spiritual sense.

A great statue of Kanishka survived until very recently. It showed the emperor wearing a kaftan and riding boots. Tragically, it no longer survives, having being smashed to pieces by nihilistic Taliban members in 2001, though other images of him remain in India itself. Kanishka enthusiastically embraced many brands of religion and his multiculturalism bred a style of art, part-Greek, part-Buddhist and part-Persian, that was exotic and previously unheard of. There is an Arthurian quality to him, however, for he is a man who is much more marked in myth and legend than in irrefutable historical record – until recently even the date of his reign was subject to great uncertainty (another reminder that historical perspectives change all the time as our knowledge increases).

He also built one of the greatest edifices of ancient times near modern Peshawar, a massive *stupa* (shrine) 300 feet across and reputedly 600 feet high. There are those who argue that its height was greatly exaggerated, but if these reports were true then it made the *stupa* the highest building yet built. When a Chinese monk, Fa-hsien, came here 250 years later he called it the greatest of all Buddhist buildings; 'There was not one comparable to this in its solemn beauty and majestic grandeur,' he said, confirming that this was indeed a magnificent monument to the great Buddha.

The Kushan Empire benefited greatly from trade with both Rome and Han China. Economists have calculated that this empire held in its hands 30 per cent of world GDP at the time, more than either Rome or Han China. It also drove forward the spread of Buddhism. A Kushan monk, Lokaksema, translated Buddhist holy books into Chinese for the first time. Kanishka adopted a new brand of Buddhism, known as Mahayana. Before this, the figure of Buddha had been referred to in abstract form: a wheel, a footprint, an empty throne, for example. This new brand showed him in human form as the cross-legged, meditative figure we see so frequently today.

But the great Kanishka's end is shrouded in mystery. There is no confirmed account of his demise, but the legends make frequent references to assassination. If so it would have been a poignant conclusion to a great reign, but perhaps a fitting one as some of the great names in history (Alexander and Julius Caesar for example) and legend (Arthur and Robin Hood, to name but two) have also met their ends in suspicious and controversial circumstances. Such is the required end, it seems, for real heroes whose memory survives the passing of time.

In Rome, despite the tolerance of Antoninus, the empire still proved difficult to govern. Famine in Rome itself threatened to turn the mob on Antoninus, a situation only avoided when he made distributions of food from his own resources. There were rebellions in Egypt (AD 152), Britain (AD 154), Dacia (AD 157) and Africa (AD 160), demonstrating that even under a good ruler it was very difficult to hold the empire together, a worrying precedent for the future. This was despite the emperor's repeated injunctions to his officials to avoid excessive violence in their actions and even to masters to abstain from harsh treatment of their slaves.

Antoninus died in AD 161 and was replaced by co-rulers previously designated by Hadrian in Marcus Aurelius and Lucius Verus (though the first of these men would prove far more effective and durable than the latter). This division of powers was a foretaste of things to come and also an indicator that the empire in its current form was too big to govern. There were soon revolts against the new rulership, notably in Parthia. Eventually, in AD 167, Ctesiphon was taken by Rome again though Parthia was far from subdued. Uprisings also had to be put down in Britain as well as on the German border.

In AD 166 and AD 167 important events occurred that might perhaps be connected. In the first of these years Chinese accounts say a Roman trading mission reached Tongking. The year after there was plague in Rome as well as in other parts of the empire such as Asia Minor, Greece, Gaul and Egypt. It has often been suggested that the arrival of the Black Death in Europe 1,200 years later was related to contacts with the Mongols and trading links might have also been responsible in this earlier case. However, this time it appears that the plague spread from west to east rather than vice versa. It reached China by AD 173, where it lasted for eleven years.

Taking advantage of the weakness caused by the plague, 'barbarian' invaders adjacent to the Roman Empire attacked across the Danube, including a particularly tough tribe known as the Vandals. In the fighting that followed, 20,000 Roman soldiers were slaughtered. Marcus Aurelius assembled a ramshackle army in response to this dangerous threat. He hired mercenaries including Germans and Scythians to fight back the invaders, another predictor of things to come. In AD 169 there were other barbarian invasions, including raids into Spain and attacks by the Lombards on the Rhine.

These events show that the famed *Pax Romana* was a myth. With such an extended empire, governed in many cases with brutality and exploitation, and with seemingly incessant barbarian raids taking place that threatened the lands held by Rome, there could be no permanent peace. Later ages would sometimes see Ancient Rome as a time of stability and law and order. It was so only as far as Rome was able to crush all opposition underfoot. Once its grip weakened, as over time it did, it would begin to fall apart.

Marcus Aurelius prided himself as a philosopher but he was also a stern judge and essentially a conservative. He was not a friend of Christians, whom he regarded as obstinate, but during his reign the mystical rites of Mithraism became more established. In the city of Lyons in Gaul, forty-seven Christians were massacred after Marcus Aurelius had spoken out against strange sects – a criticism deemed to include Christians.

The barbarian raids were eventually fought off for the time being. In AD 176, Marcus Aurelius awarded himself a Triumph in Rome, having also defeated a challenge to his rule from another Roman general and established a peaceful frontier on the Rhine with the Germans. Captured barbarian soldiers were put to work on imperial estates within the empire, importing non-Roman cultural elements, a policy that would many years hence lead to dramatic repercussions. As Marcus Aurelius grew old, he made his son Commodus co-ruler. In AD 180 he died at Vindobona (Vienna) and was duly succeeded by Commodus.

The year after, Commodus returned to Rome, where he adopted a debauched lifestyle. He became a gladiator (his exploits made famous in modern times by the film of that name) and courted popularity by extravagant gifts to the people. He had, it was said, a harem of 300 women and a similar number of boys. There was further trouble in Britain when 'barbarians' from north of the Antonine Wall (a less substantial earthen barrier built to the north of Hadrian's Wall) crossed over and attacked Roman territory to the south. There were more revolts in Germany too but these were also put down. Despite the vices and maliciousness of its emperor, Rome remained strong. Commodus, however, suffered from the same megalomaniac madness of other flawed emperors and in AD 189 placed a bust of himself on top of a statue of Apollo in one example of an inflated ego.

During the reign of Commodus, events of great moment were taking place thousands of miles to the east. By the year AD 184, the Han dynasty in China was suffering from the long-term effects of the misrule of eunuch ministers who were both corrupt and self-serving. The palace eunuchs had first appeared about a century before, since when they had proved almost universally troublesome. Han China was effectively suffering a long, drawn-out death.

There were several popular risings against Han rule, the best-known called the rebellion of the Yellow Turbans. This was led by a magician who claimed to have supernatural powers by means of which anything was possible. It was not only political disintegration that caused the demise of the Han. As a result of a series of almost biblical natural disasters – floods, plagues and an invasion of locusts included – public confidence in the regime had evaporated. Chinese emperors were deemed to rule by what was known as the Mandate of Heaven. It seemed as if heaven had withdrawn its support.

One factor that is often overlooked when considering the demise of great civilisations is the effect of natural catastrophes. The most obvious example, mentioned earlier, is the possible destruction of Minoan Crete by the tsunami resulting from the volcanic eruption on Thira in the Mediterranean. However, sometimes it is the cumulative impact of successive disasters such as floods or earthquakes, often followed by famine and occasionally war, and such was sometimes the case in China (where, as already mentioned, there had recently been a plague too), which was exposed by geography and climate to fairly regular occurrences of such events (a situation also mirrored in modern Japan, which has seen more than its share of such traumatic events).

The Yellow Turban uprising in AD 184 was documented in a work known as the *Tzu-chih T'ung-chien*, which appeared nearly a thousand years later but appears to have been based on much older records. Government forces drove back the initial attacks but their momentum was too great to be so easily defeated. By AD 189, the rebels were approaching the Imperial capital, Luoyang. While this was going on, there was a dramatic outbreak of palace in-fighting when the emperor's generals and his eunuch advisers turned on each other, with the latter in the end losing out.

China descended into anarchy, with disaffected peasants again heavily implicated, strong enough to overturn the ruling regime but not to set up an alternative government of their own. In AD 189, Hsien-ti, the last ruler of the Han dynasty, became emperor. A young boy, he was no more than a puppet. This was entirely in keeping with what had happened in the preceding decades. A succession of children had been appointed emperor, only then to be dominated both by powerful courtiers and interfering relations. Their reigns had been short and tragic.

In AD 192, there was a further rebellion. The boy emperor was imprisoned and the long years of Han rule were effectively at an end. There was no real change for the vast majority of the Chinese people, merely a replacement of one set of absolute rulers with another. However, Chinese history was about to make a change of direction.

The Han had been crucial to the development of China. They were one of the longest-lasting of all dynasties and contributed greatly to the idea of a 'Chinese' culture and state. For all the flaws that were so evident during the centuries when they reigned supreme, their impact on the subsequent shape of China was profound. Future generations would look back to their time with respect if not affection.

Back in Rome, Commodus was becoming increasingly paranoid and unpredictable. In AD 192, members of the Praetorian Guard, nervous for their own safety, poisoned him. He lingered on obstinately but was finished off anyway when he stubbornly refused to die. Anarchy ensued and, in a shameful act, the Praetorian Guard offered the imperial crown to the highest bidder. Eventually, from the chaos, a new emperor, Septimius Severus, emerged. Between AD 197 and AD 199, he engaged in further fighting with the Parthians and there was more trouble in Britain when the barbarians reached as far south as York (Eboracum). Hadrian's Wall was clearly not doing its job and the fact that tribes from the north were able to cross over it may suggest problems with finding enough manpower to defend it, an early warning of the sense of stretch that was eventually to overwhelm the Roman Empire.

In summary, there were signs that Rome was already struggling to maintain its territorial and political integrity as the century ended. There had been rebellions to put down, barbarian raids to fight off. To do so, Rome had been forced to employ mercenaries who would in the long term damage the legions as a powerful fighting force. Even more worrying perhaps was the internal squabbling, the desire for petty gain, most strikingly evidenced in the actions of the Praetorian Guard. All of these factors were clear signals of a major disaster that was looming, one that would in the end bring down the might of Rome forever and change the face of Europe and the Middle East to a point where it was unrecognisable.

16

DECLINE AND DIVISION

Rome in Retreat (AD 201–300)

This was a turbulent century. Unmistakable signs of decline manifested themselves across the Roman Empire, with dramatic consequences for the future of that great power. In retrospect the symptoms of terminal and inevitable demise appear so obvious that it seems as if an observer needed to be blind to fail to see them. There were many of them. Some were internal; for example, as the century progressed it seemed as if a bewildering carousel was whirling around, and each time it stopped another emperor would be on the throne. The army had effectively become kingmakers.

Other internal symptoms included the onset of major economic problems, examples of urban decline and a suffocating bureaucracy which was itself a product of a keenly felt desire of the emperors to centralise control in an attempt to retain power. These internal weaknesses were linked to a marked increase in the levels of 'barbarian' incursions across the empire's borders. Although Rome was to be overwhelmed by a succession of such invasions in the fifth century, it is important to realise that these were just later events in a long-term process that began two centuries earlier and perhaps even before that.

The tone was set at the start of the century when, in AD 203, Plautianus, the head of the Praetorian Guard, was made consul for the year. He was a very influential figure and the position he held is significant as it highlighted the fact that the Guard was playing a crucial role in defining the political context of Rome. Nevertheless, just two years later he was murdered, with the emperor's son, Caracalla, implicated in the act. It is also significant that, early on in the century, banditry was prominent across the empire from Egypt to Gaul. One brigand, Bulla Felix, became very famous in Italy. This decline in law and order also symptomised a diminution in central power and did not presage well for the future.

The power of Rome had long been challenged by the emergence of Parthia as a force in the Middle East. However, when in AD 208 Ardashir became King of Persis, a vassal kingdom of Parthia, it was probably largely unremarked upon outside the region. Parthia was at war with itself, and its king, Artabanus V, was fighting to get half of his empire back. He had little time or inclination to worry about Ardashir.

Ardashir's capital was at Persepolis, a major city of the ancient and long-dead great Persian Empire. But that faded glory was about to be resurrected and Ardashir was the man who would give it its initial spark of life. There were legends that said he was descended from Darius the Great himself; if this were indeed so, he would prove the most worthy successor the family had seen for some time (though such illustrious ancestors were often claimed for many ambitious leaders over the centuries, so such claims may not necessarily be true).

On the far side of Asia, the Chinese Han dynasty was going through its last rites. A general, Ts'ao Ts'ao, had effectively become the power broker in the region. The last Yellow Turban rebels were crushed in AD 205, but after such a long period of violence and a comprehensive breakdown of law and order there was no fight left in the rulers of the country. Too many of them were driven only by self-interest for a fightback to be launched. A decisive battle was fought between Ts'ao Ts'ao and his enemies at the Red Cliffs, on the Yangtze River, in AD 208.

Ts'ao Ts'ao was to suffer a crushing defeat. His enemies launched a small fleet of ships against him, packed with oil and other flammable materials. Then, when the moment was opportune, they set them alight. The historian Ssu-ma Kuang tells how 'the fire was fierce, and the wind was strong, and the ships went like arrows'. The fire spread quickly, sowing havoc in its wake, and soon 'smoke and flame stretched across the sky and a multitude of men and horses were burned or drowned or died'.

The fireships had done their work and Ts'ao Ts'ao's beaten army tried to flee. Their escape was hampered by the state of the roads, which the inclement weather had made virtually impassable. So ended Ts'ao Ts'ao's hopes of reuniting China. When he died in AD 220, his son took up the reins of empire soon after and the last Han emperor resigned, formally marking the end of the dynasty.

So across the world mighty powers appeared to be in decline but, despite its many problems, Rome was still capable of operating in an expansionist fashion. Between AD 208 and AD 210 an invasion of Scotland was attempted in an effort to subdue a troublesome neighbour to the north of the empire's boundaries. The emperor Severus reached as far up as a point to the north of Aberdeen. Yet even now there was trouble brewing on the far side of Rome's empire. On the northern shores of the Black Sea and around the Danube Delta a tribe known as the Goths were becoming increasingly aggressive, perhaps pushed on by migrations of tribes from the east to their rear. A deadly domino effect began, one which would ultimately have critical results for Rome.

Severus was proving himself a supporter of the army, whose power he expanded at the expense of the Senate. Legionaries were allowed to marry when on active service, the first time this had happened and an attempt perhaps to buy the support of Rome's soldiers, which an emperor needed if he were to survive. The sons of legionaries automatically became Roman citizens regardless of their origins. Soldiers' salaries were increased by 50 per cent, putting pressure on the exchequer. This helped secure the emperor's power base but at the expense of increasing the influence of the army to a point where it was very difficult to control.

Urban life in the Roman Empire began to decline as economic pressures started to manifest themselves. *Colonii* of foreigners were located on Roman estates, a practice followed by private landowners due to a lack of slaves. The general economic decline of Rome had begun, exemplified by higher taxes, falling trade and a devaluation of the currency. It was estimated that by the middle of the century, up to 15 per cent of all agricultural land had fallen out of use though some areas, such as Egypt, were enjoying a boom as a result of decline elsewhere.

In AD 211, Septimius Severus died at York. His final advice to his sons was to 'enrich the army', an appropriate epitaph on a reign in which its power had increased significantly. With his death, campaigning in Britain ended for a while. His sons Caracalla and Geta become co-rulers. Severus would be the last emperor to die in his bed for eighty years, though it was also said that the ambitious Caracalla had hastened his end and murdered him.

Caracalla soon proved his cruelty and ruthlessness by murdering his brother Geta and then having his body burned. That was only the beginning of the bloodshed. It was also reported that 20,000 of Geta's party were killed in an attempt to protect Caracalla's position. In an attempt to quieten opposition, he also made huge donations to buy them off. The Praetorians were hostile to him at first, seemingly being much more inclined to side with the murdered Geta, and took some time to decide to support Caracalla. However, they too were bought off with bribes. Caracalla paid for these by selling Roman citizenship to all free adult males in the empire.

A reign of terror followed these events. In AD 215, Caracalla visited Alexandria, where reportedly he had thousands of the citizens put to death. Then he moved on Parthia. As well as being cruel, Caracalla also had unmistakable delusions of grandeur. Part of his army was given the grand title of 'Alexander's Phalanx'; he had them armed in ancient Macedonian style. He tricked the Parthian king Artabanus V into camp with an invitation to marry his daughter and then attempted to seize him. Artabanus escaped and then invaded Syria.

But this emperor was no Alexander and he was loathed even by his own men. Near the ancient battlefield of Carrhae, Caracalla was murdered by some of them. The story goes that he had been suffering from stomach cramps and his men took the chance to kill him when he had jumped off his horse and pulled his breeches down to defecate in a hurry, perhaps an appropriate commentary on his reign. Macrinus, head of the Praetorian Guard, then declared himself emperor. However, it was no easy thing to explain away the death of a Caesar and he declared Caracalla a god. But the war with Parthia was over for the time being, a peace following soon after, bought by Macrinus at exorbitant cost.

Many of his men resented him for it and he was soon after overthrown by a rival faction and executed. He was replaced by Elagabalus, perhaps one of Rome's worst emperors (which is no small claim). He proved to be decadent to an incredible degree; he was, the *Augustan History* graphically remarks, 'the recipient of lust in every orifice of his body'. He adopted strange religious rituals, in one of which he tried to circumcise himself but instead only succeeded in partly castrating himself.

It was during his reign that, thousands of miles to the east, the puppet Chinese emperor Hsien-ti was deposed, marking the formal end of the Han dynasty. This introduced a forty-five-year period of anarchy and terror known as the period of the Three Kingdoms to the East. China split into various warring territories. In the south was the Wu dynasty, based on its capital of Chien-yeh, now Nanjing. Liu Pei ruled in the south-west from Chengdu as head of the Shu Han dynasty. Ts'ao P'i, Ts'ao Ts'ao's son, reigned in the north. This was the preface to nearly three centuries of virtually uninterrupted war in China.

In Rome, Elagabalus was overthrown in AD 221. When he heard a lynch mob coming to get him, he hid in a public toilet but was found, killed, dragged through a sewer and then thrown into the Tiber with his body weighted down. His place was taken by Alexander Severus, who attempted to limit the power of the army and increase the might of the Senate and the aristocracy. Taxes were reduced and money lent at low rates of interest (4 per cent) in an attempt to boost growth, as modern economists would call it. He also encouraged the development of trade associations and attempted to curb excessive immorality. He engaged on a building programme of roads, bridges and aqueducts. In addition, he put a stop to the persecution of Christians.

In the meantime, Artabanus of Parthia had been involved in a bitter and drawn-out civil war which turned his attentions away from external affairs. He eventually defeated his rival and took back Ctesiphon, which had been lost to him for a time. But the final moments of Parthia were approaching, and in the year AD 224 the clock at last struck twelve. In that year, Artabanus V of Parthia was overthrown by Ardashir of Persis. There were three great battles, at the end of which Ardashir was triumphant, killing Artabanus on the Plains of Hormizdagan.

Ardashir declared himself 'King of Kings'. This was significant as it was the honorific title also assumed by the rulers of Persia in its prime hundreds of years before. It linked this would-be descendant of Darius with the old, great Achmaenid kings of Persia. He started a new Persian dynasty, named after his tribe the Sassanid. Here was a man who recognised the power of religion, which, by defining a set of ideals and ideas, provided a mortar by which his subjects could be bonded together. He strengthened his position by adopting Zoroastrian teachings and producing a new edition of its holy book, the Avesta.

His adoption of Zoroastrianism was an appeal to ancient roots, firmly engrained deep down in the Persian psyche, a link with a golden age which had gone long ago but which he now hoped to revive. In recognition of this, he also reintroduced the old satrapy system with his appointees at the head of the satraps as military governors – those from his own tribe were given the honorary title of shah. This contrasted with the system that had recently been the norm in the region, under which vassal kings were allowed to retain power but too often abused it by rebelling. By putting his own men in post, he was tightening his grip on Persia.

But he also had ambitions further afield. By AD 230, Rome had received news that Ardashir was advancing through Mesopotamia on the Roman province of Syria and in the process declaring a new Persian Empire. Alexander Severus sent a mild letter suggesting that Ardashir should be content with what he already owned, but predictably it had no effect. Realising that he would have to fight to protect his empire, for the next three years Severus fought a hard campaign against Ardashir, who eventually withdrew.

In the meantime, another of those symptoms of impending decline was about to appear. Perhaps aware that Rome was distracted in the east, German tribes attacked from across the Rhine and Danube. Severus moved on them but his troops were undisciplined and he was forced to buy the raiders off. This was taken as a sign of weakness. Severus's legions mutinied and killed him (yet another symptom of imminent decline and an over-powerful army). This introduced a period of total anarchy into Roman affairs, a time in which thirty-seven men would be declared emperor in thirty-five years.

The first of these, the Thracian Maximinus, was acclaimed emperor by the legions themselves. He was a huge man, said to be 8 feet tall and able to wear his wife's necklace on his arm. However impressive his physique may have been, he did not understand the secrets of survival in Rome and when he began to tax the aristocracy heavily it was inevitable that they would start to plot against him. In AD 238, a full-scale rebellion broke out led by an eighty-year-old called Gordian, who was defeated (his son, also named Gordian, was implicated too). However, Maximinus was then killed by his own men. As a result Gordian III also became emperor in AD 238 – the third imperial claimant in a year.

This lethal combination of internal disintegration and external pressures was about to result in a perfect storm descending on the empire that threatened to blow it apart. AD 240 saw perhaps the gravest threat to Rome since the time of Hannibal. She was attacked from several directions simultaneously, a coincidence of events that threatened to overwhelm her straining defences. There were rebellions in Africa and northern German tribes, known as the Franks, attacked the empire from across the Rhine.

In the same year, events in Persia were also to take a threatening turn. King Ardashir was assassinated and was succeeded by his son, Shapur I (who may have been a co-ruler with his father for a while if numismatic evidence has been interpreted correctly). He was a man of great ambition, impressive drive and no little talent. He would continue his father's expansionist policies but would also prove a strong ruler. At Shapur's coronation, a young mystic named Mani declared himself a messiah. He borrowed doctrine from many other faiths including Zoroastrianism and Judaism and formed a creed called Manichaeism, which divided the world into the realms of Light and Darkness.

Mani's writings tell us much of the times in which he lived and it is revealing that he wrote of four great empires in the world: Rome, Persia, China and Axum. The last has often been overlooked but it was a great power in its time and reached its zenith in around AD 220. From its great cities of Adulis and Axum, merchants and soldiers alike set out. Axum was already an old civilisation but it was now about to experience its greatest period. It managed to achieve significant regional influence, in part because of the decline of two other great powers. To the north, a weakened Meroë enabled expansion across the land while to the east the decline of Saba in Arabia opened up the sea routes to Axum (whose core territories were approximate with modern Ethiopia).

While all this was happening in Africa, a Roman emperor could not ignore the growing threat from Persia and in AD 242 Gordian III opened the doors of the Temple of Janus in a symbolic statement that the empire was at war, then started out for the east. The army was led by a general named Timesitheus who defeated the Persians in the following year and drove them over the Tigris. However, he then fell ill and died. Command of the army then passed to a man known as Philip the Arab. It was not long before Philip stirred the army up against Gordian, who was overthrown and killed. After negotiating an expensive peace with Persia, Philip returned to Rome to attempt to cement his claim to power.

However, as was now being proved on a regular basis, it was much easier to become an emperor than it was to remain one. By AD 249 there was widespread discontent at having an Arab as emperor, even though Philip appears to have tried his hardest to be a worthy ruler. During his reign he had declared an amnesty for those in exile, put down brigandage and built roads to help in the military effort to protect Rome against barbarian invasions.

In that year, there were several rebellions against Philip. He sent his general Decius out to pacify them. However, during the campaign Decius was declared emperor by his army. He then marched on Philip, who was defeated in battle and killed. The deterioration of law and order in the empire was now alarming. Some of the legions deserted to the Goths, who had crossed the Danube and ravaged Thrace.

The Goths probably came from Scandinavia; a later writer, Jordanes, told how they were a tough people, 'like no other race in their sufferings and blessings, because during the longer days they see the sun returning to the east along the rim of the horizon, but on the shorter days it is not thus seen'. Jordanes also categorised the Goths in two groups: the western half, the Visigoths; and the eastern, the Ostrogoths. The Gothic invasions seriously undermined morale within the empire, and Decius, whose claim to the throne was based on force alone, sought to unify the citizens by giving them a scapegoat on which to blame Rome's ills. The Christian sect was a convenient target, and in AD 250 the twentieth Pope (who was not yet a particularly important figure in the wider world) was martyred.

Little good did it do Decius, for the following year he was killed by the Goths while on campaign. His son died with him and another general, Gallus, was declared emperor. He was forced to buy off the Goths with a sizeable ransom. But the unrest within the empire had encouraged the Persians to invade Armenia. Matters went from bad to worse and in AD 253 plague hit Rome. Gallus was killed by his own men and he was replaced by Valerian, destined to be Rome's most tragic emperor (though he was certainly far from the worst).

The situation facing him was dreadful. Shapur had sacked the important city of Antioch on the Mediterranean coast. The Franks and other tribes were raiding from the north. Rome appeared to be under threat from many directions. Faced with these challenges Valerian responded with some very sensible measures. He split the empire in two, realising that it was too big for one man to rule, and gave the western half to his son Gallienus. The Roman cavalry was strengthened (it was always its weakest arm), imitating the Persian tactic of using heavily armoured cavalrymen as shock troops. Instruments of war like catapults and ballistae were also improved.

Still the attacks kept coming. In AD 256 the Franks attacked Spain by sea, the Goths invaded Macedonia and the Persians descended on Mesopotamia and Syria. The year after, the Goths crossed the Black Sea and landed on its southern shores, attacking Roman bases there. By AD 259 the barbarians had broken through to the heart of the empire, with Alemanni from the north crashing into Italy, though they were eventually defeated at Milan. The Alemanni were a hotchpotch grouping, as their name (*alle Männer* meaning 'all men') would suggest (it is also the source of the French name for modern Germany, Allemagne).

It is not surprising that there are clear signs of economic decline during these years. In Britain, Frankish and Saxon pirates were raiding the shores and archaeologists have found clear evidence of slum conditions in the once wealthy town of Silchester and the complete abandonment of an amphitheatre at Verulamium. In retrospect it seems that the sensible thing to do would have been to defend the empire's heartlands, in essence a continuation of the Hadrianic policy of a century earlier. However, Valerian decided instead to face up to the Persian threat and in doing so made a great tactical mistake.

Valerian led an army east to fight off the threat of Shapur once and for all. The Persians had moved up to Edessa and it was towards this city that Valerian led his legions. On approaching the Persians, however, Valerian changed tack (it was said that his army had been decimated by plague) and tried instead to negotiate a settlement (this may have been his idea all along, of course, and if this were so then his policy was more Hadrianic than might first appear). However, he was caught off guard, led into a trap and captured (though for the record it should be stated that this is one version of the tale – the other is that there was a battle that Valerian lost).

And so an emperor of Rome became a prisoner of the Persians, a humiliating state of affairs that struck to the heart of Roman honour and pride. Valerian was cruelly treated by his captors, being used, it was said, as a stool on which Shapur climbed every time he mounted his horse (a technique in humiliation that Timur allegedly copied a thousand years later).

Shapur also had a rock carving crafted, showing Valerian kneeling in submission before him. When Valerian eventually died, his skin was stripped from his body, dyed vermilion and placed in a temple. This was not just gratuitous cruelty; it was also an ongoing reminder to Rome of its place in the world. Every time a delegation came to the Persian court they could be reminded of the inferiority of Rome compared to the greatness of Persia.

Shapur, surprisingly, failed to press home his advantage. When he led his army westward, it was defeated by Odenathus, Rome's vassal king in Palmyra, at Ctesiphon. Odenathus declared himself king of the lands to the west of the Euphrates, effectively in the process also declaring himself independent of Rome. There was not much, to be frank, that Rome could do to argue.

There is little to say of Chinese affairs in this period. This is because there is only a small amount of information on which to draw. However, there are occasional rays of light breaking through the darkness. With China now divided in three, each state was looking after its own affairs. In around AD 250 the southern Chinese state of Wu sent envoys to Funan (now Cambodia) while the northern state of Wei sent a delegation to Japan some time in the previous decade, showing that each was concentrating understandably on its near neighbours as far as external affairs were concerned.

Some accounts of this time survive in the *Wei Chih* (*The History of Wei*) which tells us more of the visit to Japan. Japan was a very divided land but the strongest kingdom within it was that of Yamatai, ruled by a shaman-queen, Himiko. It was said that she 'occupied herself with magic and sorcery, bewitching the people'. She lived in a fortress, guarded by 100 men and served by 1,000 female servants (there was just one male attendant, who was her conduit with the outside world).

It appears that her kingdom had been a tributary of China for nearly 200 years and in return her kings received the Chinese stamp of approval. The delegation from China delivered Himiko cloth, jewels and mirrors as gifts. She responded with presents of cinnabar, cloth and slaves. Himiko died in AD 248 and was buried with 100 of her sacrificed servants in a large tomb some 100 paces across. She was eventually replaced by a thirteen-year-old girl, Iyo.

By AD 265 the northern Chinese kingdom of Wei had begun to exert some authority over other local kingdoms and founded the Chin dynasty. Its power was far from absolute but it was definitely in the ascendancy in the region. There were notable scientific achievements to report on during this period in the region too. Perhaps one of the most significant is found in the work of Pei Xiu, a geographer, who produced a large map of China in eighteen sections.

In the west, Gallienus was to face many of the same problems that Valerian had. The famous eighteenth-century historian Edward Gibbon, who wrote *The Decline and Fall of the Roman Empire*, perhaps the most famous secondary-source history book ever written, famously summed him up by describing him as 'the master of several curious but useless sciences, a ready orator, an elegant poet, a skilful gardener, an excellent cook, and most contemptible prince'.

Gallienus had to cope with ongoing barbarian raids. In AD 268 the Sarmatians poured through into Greece, destroying some of the great names of history: Athens, Sparta, Corinth and others. The year after, Gallienus won a Pyrrhic victory against the Goths in Thrace and was soon after killed and replaced by Claudius II.

The highlight of Claudius's short reign was a crushing victory against the Goths where, it was said, 50,000 of the enemy were killed. He had little time to enjoy the victory, though, for he died of the plague soon after (it must be said that his natural death was a remarkable exception from the general rule at the time). He was replaced by Aurelian. The Roman historian Eutropius called him cruel but admitted he was 'an emperor necessary for the times'.

After winning an initial battle against the Goths, Aurelian then made peace with them. Dacia was handed over by Rome as part of the settlement as the empire reverted to its traditional borders on the Rhine and the Danube. The Vandals were pushed back across the latter frontier and the Alemanni were ejected from Italy, a task in which Aurelian was helped by Vandal cavalry.

In the east, there was at the time a remarkable ruler in the city of Palmyra; a queen, Zenobia, who claimed descent from Cleopatra and Antony. She was certainly beautiful, famed for her long, luxuriant, ebony-black hair. Palmyra had once been part of the empire but had gone her own way. Zenobia had even attacked Egypt but had been unable to take Alexandria. Aurelian now sent his commander Probus to bring her back into the fold. Some in Rome underestimated the challenge, but Aurelian assured the doubters that she was a determined warrior with considerable military acumen. After a hard siege, Palmyra fell. Zenobia fled on a camel but was caught on the Euphrates and brought back.

As the Roman army returned west, stories came in that Palmyra had revolted. Aurelian led another army against it and this time taught it a harsh lesson. It would never recover. What had been a vibrant and wealthy city, a heady mix of Roman, Hellenic and Semitic culture, now turned to ruin. Those ruins still stand, a stunning memento in the Syrian desert to a golden age now faded from view. When Aurelian came back to Rome, a lavish Triumph was laid on, with Zenobia as its star attraction. During the procession she was led in chains but was afterwards allowed to live out her life comfortably in Hadrian's old but luxurious villa at Tivoli.

This victory could not conceal the danger that Rome was increasingly facing. Rome had existed for centuries without walls but this situation was no longer viable. The Eternal City was duly fortified, as were other key parts of the empire. In an attempt to restore Rome's economic fortunes regulation was increased, for example on trade corporations, and Aurelian took measures to stabilise the currency, which had been hit heavily by inflation. However, the wealth of Rome was being stifled under a suffocating blanket of heavy taxation.

In AD 275, Aurelian was murdered by a group of army officers. The army gave the Senate the task of appointing a replacement; they chose a seventy-five-year-old, Tacitus. He punished the murderers, whose actions had given him the chance of glory, by executing them and sent an army to fight the Goths. During his short reign, which lasted just a year, a Christian saint, Antony, retired to the desert in Egypt; this was the beginning of Christian monasticism, at first solitary in nature, later to be characterised by larger communities of like-minded recluses. At around the same time, St Denis began to convert people in Paris to the still relatively new faith.

Probus replaced Tacitus and continued to try to pacify the empire, ejecting bodies of Franks, Goths and Vandals and putting down unrest in Britain, Egypt and Illyria. In AD 281, Probus held a great Triumph in Rome where a huge variety of prisoners from different enemies was displayed for the populace to ogle at. However, Probus could not control the army and they turned on him too, killing him at his birthplace in Sirmium. A civil war broke out, at the end of which Diocletian was successful and became emperor. Here at last was a man with a claim to greatness.

Diocletian was not the first emperor to realise that the empire was too big for one man, but he did take greater steps to address the problem than anyone else had. He appointed a co-ruler in the west, Maximian, who would make Milan his capital, while he himself would rule the east from Nicomedia near Byzantium.

To cement his position, Diocletian encouraged the development of a cult around his imperial status; he did not receive a good press from later pro-Christian writers because he was not a friend of their faith. Virtually becoming a god in his lifetime, Diocletian asserted that he was the earthly embodiment of Jupiter and that Maximian was the same of Hercules. He evolved this image still further by wearing robes of silk and cloth of gold, along with shoes studded with jewels and a pearl diadem.

At first it seemed as if nothing had changed. The commander of the Roman fleet at Boulogne, Carausias, crossed over to Britain and declared himself ruler there after being outlawed by Maximian. He later defeated Maximian in a naval battle and was acknowledged as a co-ruler by the emperors of both west and east in AD 290. He performed a useful role in this capacity, keeping down the raids of Saxon pirates.

In the meantime, Rome's position had been strengthened by developments elsewhere. The Franks had sued for peace in Gaul, while Diocletian had signed a peace treaty with Persia and then put down a revolt in Egypt. With some signs of stability returning, Diocletian now instituted one of the most radical constitutional reforms in Roman history. He decided that there would be two emperors (*Augusti*) in east and west, as there were now. However, each would be helped by a nominated heir, a Caesar, who would automatically replace him after twenty years. They would have joint but absolute power. All laws would be issued in their joint names but there would be no need for Senatorial approval.

There were other major reforms too. A vast bureaucracy was formed (said by the writer Lactantius to be formed of half the population) and a system of 'state socialism' was established with a managed economy. The coinage, frequently devalued in the recent past, was tied to gold, and most production was nationalised. Taxes were increased, as a result of which tax evasion became rife. A sinister force of tax police was set up; they would often be accused of using torture in their attempts to collect the money that was due to them. In many respects, it almost appeared to be an early precursor of the worst of communism.

It was perhaps as well that Persia had been weak in recent years while Rome had so many problems to cope with. However, in AD 296 a strong king, Narses, emerged and attacked Rome's ally in Armenia. There had been one major consequence of Persian expansion in this century; the decline of the Kushan Empire in India (they were also attacked by Huns).

The historian Michael Wood describes the Kushans as 'harbingers of the modern world'. The links they formed with China produced a vibrant response in both regions, with the cross-fertilisation of ideas spread both by trade and the movement of Buddhist ideals. Buddhism, with its rejection of traditional caste ideals, facilitated travel and trade by removing barriers that had inhibited them in the past. India was about to change direction and new, vigorous cultures would soon become apparent as a result.

There were other civilisations emerging too, in areas of the world that had so far been dimly lit outside of their own immediate environment. In Central America a new culture was emerging, one which owed much to the Olmecs of old. The Maya in Mesoamerica had an advanced culture in several important respects. Their mathematical system allowed for the existence of a zero. They recorded their language in a form of hieroglyphs, though they left no written records. Our knowledge of them relies much on epigraphy, that is the study of writing on stones.

The Maya been developing for some time but the first dateable reference to them occurs on a *stela* that includes the name of a king, the evocatively named Leafy Jaguar. This can be dated to AD 292, though as Leafy Jaguar claims to be the eighth ruler of his dynasty we know that the Mayan civilisation was older than this. This was the start of what is labelled by historians (loving labels as much as ever) as the Early Classic Mayan period, which would last from AD 250 to AD 600.

Yet these dates are subject to constant revision and it may be that by the time this page is read it will already be out of date. For example, a room recently discovered at San Bartolo in Guatemala, decorated with astonishing murals and nicknamed 'the Sistine Chapel of the Maya', has been radiocarbon dated to about 100 BC (early traces of the Maya in the so-called Pre-Classic period have been dated to 1200 BC).

The major feature of this culture was its ability to support a number of expanding cities, many of them geographically close to each other but seemingly not usually part of a bigger empire. As elsewhere in the history of the world, the Mayan people shared a culture but not necessarily a ruler. There is strong evidence of trade. The centre of Mayan culture was to be found in what is now Central America around Guatemala and Belize. Other areas were useful providers of goods across the Mayan zone of influence. The Yucatan, on the coast of Mexico, provided honey, salt and marine products, while the highland areas in the region provided jade, obsidian and basalt.

Cities had been in existence locally for some time but now they started to grow. There was, for example, Tikal in Guatemala, the city of Leafy Jaguar. But the cities were often at war with each other. This was a violent and militaristic society, and it seems likely that one of the reasons driving this state of affairs was to obtain slaves for the dark practice of human sacrifice. So Tikal, for example, was often at odds with Calakmul, just over the border and now in Mexico. Ongoing fighting was to mark civilisation in this part of the world for many years to come.

The world was now on the cusp of significant change. As the century ended, in the Middle East Persia was re-emerging as a threat to Rome. In AD 297 Galerius, Diocletian's Caesar, was sent to defeat Narses but instead suffered a humiliating loss, though he did at least manage to escape. His humiliation was made worse when Diocletian forced him to walk behind his chariot as a mark of his shame. There were rebellions in both Egypt and Carthage that needed to be put down too. But the humiliation did the trick. In AD 298 Galerius, perhaps spurred on by his sense of dishonour, inflicted a heavy defeat over the Persians, who were forced to concede Mesopotamia and five provinces across the Tigris. Peace with Persia had been won – it would last for forty years. It was only by the skin of its teeth, but Rome was hanging on.

17

CHRISTIANITY COMES OF AGE

The Flowering of the New Religion (AD 301–400)

After nearly three centuries of slow and sometimes fragile evolution, Christianity was about to come of age. From its troubled first days, when it seemed more than once that persecution would stifle the faith at birth, it would grow into a potent force. After its stuttering years of adolescence, it would ripen into maturity with staggering speed. By the end of the century, it would feel self-confident enough to put an emperor of Rome in his place. It was a stunning turn of events, only surpassed perhaps by the dramatic emergence of Islam a few centuries later.

The Roman empire was faced with dark and harrowing dangers, against which military force alone was not enough to survive. To increase its chances of living on, Rome latched onto an idea in the hope it would prove sufficient to protect her and return her to past glories. Although the advancement of Christian fortunes had a huge impact on the future shape of the world, it was a hope that would not be fulfilled as far as the survival of the empire was concerned, at least in the west.

For the old days were passing. New powers were gathering in the north and in the east. Termed 'barbarians' by the Romans, they were rather peoples caught up in a deadly game of dominoes where migratory pressures pushed vast masses of humanity west against the borders of the empire and eventually over them.

The driving force behind most of these movements was nomadic warriors from Central Asia and beyond to the borders of China. The Huns appeared as harbingers of doom when they eventually clashed with the Roman Empire but they impacted on India and China too. They were the first powerful expression of those forays driven by land-hunger and naked aggression that were to culminate in the Mongol Terror a thousand years later.

But Rome began the century as a pagan power, still paying due deference to the gods of old, Jupiter and his pantheon. Diocletian, the emperor as the century began, was an affirmed opponent of the Christians. He encouraged a belief in Rome that the Christians used 'bad magic' when they crossed themselves. It touched a superstitious nerve in the Roman people and they happily turned on the Christians in response to their prejudices. The 'Other' has always found itself subject to outbreaks of persecution, whatever guise it takes.

In AD 303 intense persecution of the Christians began in earnest. Rome, nominally still governed by its four rulers (though Diocletian certainly appears to have been the strongest of them in terms of his influence), issued a decree that all churches should be destroyed, Christian books burned and the property of the faith's adherents confiscated. The Cathedral of Nicomedia was burned down in an act calculated to strike fear into Christians. However, they did not stand meekly by and take this abuse, and soon afterwards they retaliated by burning down Diocletian's palace. The concept of turning the other cheek had clearly not yet caught on.

Diocletian was no friend of the Christians but his time was running out. The end of his reign was remarkable, for it was not brought about by an act of war or assassination but by his own voluntary retirement. This should not have come as a shock, for Diocletian had always said that his period of rule was time-limited. The surprise was more that he had kept his word.

In AD 305, he did as he had always said he would do and abdicated. In a deeply symbolic gesture, he pulled off the imperial purple in front of his people and then put on the robes of a mere citizen of Rome. Then he made his way off to his farm, where he felt far more comfortable than he did in an emperor's palace, for he had been born a common man and did not seem to appreciate the trappings of luxury and power much. His co-emperor Maximian was more reluctant to let go of power but he grudgingly stood down too.

The succession was passed on in the way planned. Constantius and Galerius took up their positions as co-emperors. Galerius proved himself a stern opponent of the Christians, though less so than Diocletian. However, in his reign the first British Christian martyr, St Alban, was sacrificed. The most powerful figure in Britain was its governor, Constantius, who led a successful expedition in AD 306 against the troublesome Picts who had been raiding from north of Hadrian's Wall. At Constantius's side was his son, Constantine, a young man of great ambition and no small talent. When Constantius died at Eboracum (York) soon after, the soldiers of the legions in Britain proclaimed Constantine *Augustus*.

It was one thing to proclaim Constantine emperor, quite another for him to acquire real power. Maximian, who had returned to power, and Galerius both unsurprisingly resisted his attempt to muscle in on a share of the empire. But by AD 307 he had taken Gaul. In that same year he also married a young woman of remarkable force, Fausta, who would if anything urge him on to even greater things. When he then fought off invading forces of barbarians from the north, the Franks and the Alemanni, a share of power at least was assured.

His position was about to strengthen still further. Infighting between the three co-rulers of the empire continued, but in AD 310 Maximian was captured and committed suicide. It then emerged that Galerius was suffering from a terminal illness. He appears to have been haunted by his harsh acts against the Christians for he first of all stopped his persecution of them and then asked them to pray for him. It did him no good, for soon after he died.

This left the way almost clear for Constantine – almost, but not quite. The mantle of opposition was picked up by Maxentius, the son of Maximian. He raised an army and occupied Rome. Constantine moved on him, realising that he could not rule until Maxentius was defeated. He descended on Rome with his army, ready for a decisive battle. At this moment we appear to move from the realms of history into those of myth, yet the story we are about to consider became a core part of the events that led Rome from paganism to Christianity. As the two armies prepared for battle, a sign in the sky was seen. It was a cross, the symbol of the Christians.

Of course, in modern secular society such miracles appear hard to believe, and the answer may be in Roman approaches to historiography. Roman historians would frequently introduce literary devices called *topoi* into their writings. These introduced supernatural explanations to make sense of the course of history. The famous first-century historian Tacitus made use of such devices, telling his readers that otherwise inexplicable Roman defeats, such as those initially suffered by legionaries at the hands of Boudicca, had been preceded by instances of a statue of Victory turning its back on the city of Camulodunum, as if to disown Rome. The cross in the sky could be considered a similar *topos*.

Constantine ordered his men to paint the sign of the cross on their shields in response to this portent and they marched into battle armed with this Christian iconography. He then led them towards the Tiber, crossed at a certain point by the Milvian Bridge. The two forces fought toe to toe but Maxentius's army was inexorably forced back. As they crossed the bridge, it gave way under the weight of the soldiers on it, throwing a number of them into the water. Maxentius was among them and he was unable to escape from the fast-flowing stream and drowned. Constantine was now undisputed master of the city of Rome, which he marched in to take. One of his first acts was to disband the Praetorian Guard, which showed both wisdom and courage.

This still did not mean, though, that Constantine was now undisputed master of the whole empire. There was still a rival in the east, Licinius. They met in Milan and agreed to co-operate. Constantine was a strong supporter of Christianity, seeing in it an idea that could unite the empire, though he was not yet a Christian himself. The two co-emperors agreed to stop the persecution of the Christians (though Licinius was not an adherent of the faith either).

However, Helena, the mother of Constantine, did become a Christian and she would later have a dramatic impact on the young religion. Years later, she would go to Jerusalem where she ordered the building of the church of the Holy Sepulchre over the supposed site of the tomb of Christ. She would also claim to have found the True Cross, setting off a vigorous trade in Christian relics that would last for more than a millennium.

After the meeting, Constantine moved west and Licinius back east after marrying Constantine's sister. However, the amicable feelings expressed when the two men met were a sham and soon afterwards they went to war with each other. Constantine defeated Licinius in Pannonia (a territory that approximately covered the western half of modern Hungary and parts of other surrounding states such as Serbia, Croatia and others) and gained all of Roman Europe except for Thrace. Licinius retired to Nicomedia, where he had previously reinstated the persecution of the Christians. He required all his soldiers to worship pagan gods, the ancient deities whom he argued had led to Rome's triumphs in the past.

There were still many perils to face, both external and internal. In AD 319 Constantine faced the barbarian hordes on the Danube while his son Crispus did the same on the Rhine, winning a victory in the following year. Also, in AD 320, a Libyan priest, Arius, developed what became to orthodox Christians a terrible heresy, denying that Christ was co-equal with God. He was defrocked, but some took his side and there were increasing signs of an impending schism within a religion where theology was both complex and a source of argument.

The barbarian threat was still the major problem, though. Between AD 321 and AD 322, Constantine ejected the barbarians from Roman Dacia (the portion that had been retained south of the Danube) but then crossed over into northern Dacia, abandoned by Rome some time before. Peace was made between the two parties but it did not extend to the eastern empire. The year after, there were more invasions, this time into Thrace, but Licinius took no action so Constantine took it upon himself to eject them. Seeing this as unmerited interference, Licinius declared war on Constantine but was defeated.

This was the end of Licinius. Brother-in-law of the emperor or not, he was assassinated soon after, following accusations of renewed intrigue against Constantine. This left the latter free to concentrate on introducing more stability into the empire. Key to this was ending the schisms in Christianity, Constantine's Big Idea. It could not cement unity in Rome if it were not itself united, so the moves towards schism needed to be halted and reversed.

He therefore summoned the leaders of Christianity to Nicaea (now Iznik) in Asia Minor, determined to reunify the faith. He was now a confirmed supporter of Christianity (though still not himself a Christian) but the search for a solution to the schisms was not because of theology but because of politics. At the council, the Arian heresy was at the heart of the debate. The 318 bishops present vigorously argued about its merits, with Athanasius, secretary to the Bishop of Alexandria, leading the opposition to the heresy. The Nicaean Creed was developed during the synod. This stated that God and Christ were of one substance, reaffirming the co-equality of the two. The council decided against Arius, who was excommunicated and his teachings burnt.

In AD 325, Constantine took another step of major significance when he dedicated a new city on the site of Byzantium which he called Nova Roma. It would soon become far better known by the name it took from the emperor who had founded it: Constantinople. It would be a power on the world stage for the next thousand years and would then carry on as a great city, though under new rulers, and with a new name, into modern times. In that same year, Athanasius became Bishop of Alexandria, in which capacity he became a redoubtable supporter of monasticism and St Antony.

However, Constantine's reign was often stormy. Soon after these events, Crispus, the son of Constantine, and possibly Fausta, the emperor's wife, were executed along with the son of Licinius, presumably for plotting (though there has been no conclusive proof uncovered to confirm the validity of any accusations of this sort). These were brutal acts more in keeping with the reign of Nero than the first Christian Roman Emperor. Constantine's mind returned soon after to affairs of state. In AD 330, Constantine officially made Constantinople his capital. Rome had been in decline for a while, partly because of a decreasing population brought about by family limitation and infanticide over a period of 200 years.

This transfer may suggest a move of power from west to east, and a triumph of Greece over Rome in the long term. Yet though Hellenism certainly figured prominently in the new capital, it did not obliterate everything Roman. It is true that Greek became the universal language of the empire in the long run, but even then Latin remained the language of officialdom. Even the city itself was consciously modelled on Rome, with its seven hills and similar array of administrative districts. It was in essence Rome without the Roman Senate, and maybe this was the intention all along.

Yet it was also a city that, despite Constantine's personal caution on the subject of Christianity – he still refused to publicly acknowledge it as his own creed – was dedicated to the new God that his empire had been required to embrace. The emperor erected a great column in his new city, which stated emphatically, 'O Christ, ruler and master of the world, to You now I dedicate this subject city, and these sceptres and the might of Rome.' This was, then, officially a city of Christ and His religion.

As an interesting aside, a man called Nicholas was named Bishop of Myra a few hundred miles away along the southern coast of Asia Minor in that same year, AD 330. He would later become St Nicholas, associated in modern times with regions far colder than the balmy Mediterranean. He became known for his generosity and his secret gift giving, hence his transformation into his commercial alter ego, the modern Santa Claus. He was also allegedly responsible for saving the life of a sailor by miraculous means, and so he became the patron saint of sailors too.

All this was, as Dickens would put it, the Ghost of Christmas Yet to Come. Constantine had far graver matters to concern him. Barbarian invasions affected Rome not only directly but also in other, less immediate, ways. In AD 332, the Sarmatians of the steppes of what would later be Russia asked Rome for help against the Goths. The emperor's son, Constantine II, duly defeated them and took the chieftain's son as a hostage to Rome.

Soon after, Vandal refugees running away from the Goths were allowed to settle across the Danube. It seemed like a humanitarian move but future attempts to copy it would lead to a disastrous denouement. In any event, humanitarianism probably had nothing to do with it; the Vandals probably seemed like a useful buffer against the Goths. The Roman Empire rarely – if ever – did anything without its own interests being paramount.

Constantine died in May AD 337. He had only just been baptised, hedging his bets at the personal level almost to the end. In later years he had been an enthusiastic patron of the arts, benefiting from the wealth that he had won control of when he became sole emperor. But even he seems to have realised that the empire was simply too big for one man. On his death, the empire was split between three of his sons: Constantine, Constantius and Constans.

The eastern half of the empire went to Constantius. He decided to wage war against Shapur II, King of Persia, in Mesopotamia. Shapur had been king for three decades, winning the throne after a period of infighting. Persia appeared to have weakened and there had been a long period of peace between her and Rome which was now coming to an end. But Shapur was no weakling. He was a strong ruler who had treated

Christians particularly harshly, and he was no slouch as a warrior either. The war ended inconclusively.

Further west, it did not take long for the infighting to start. In AD 340 Constantine II was killed in battle against his brother Constans. The empire was now effectively divided in two. But it needed to be strong, for in AD 341 the Franks invaded Gaul. The year after, Constans forced them to sue for peace. That winter, the Picts and Scots (confusingly from Ireland) in Britain combined and threatened Wales and the west of England for the first time. The nibbling away at the edges of the empire was continuing. But even now there were significant developments outside of the military sphere. Christianity continued its advance; in AD 341 an imperial edict prohibited pagan sacrifice, undermining the old gods still further. At around the same time, the monastic system was being gradually introduced into Europe by Athanasius.

But Christianity could not yet assume that it was triumphant. Old pagan beliefs remained barely concealed beneath the surface. A sarcophagus in St Peter's in Rome dated to AD 359 has a representation of a young Christ portrayed above a figure of Zeus, an uneasy hedging of bets by the former occupant of the tomb, one assumes. By this time Constans had been overthrown; he was an unpopular and unwise ruler as it turned out. In the east, Constantius had waged several wars against Persia but without any definitive conclusion. The balance of power in the Middle East had oscillated several times, but it had not as yet found a new equilibrium.

In AD 360, a new emperor was proclaimed in Paris. His name was Julian and he was a lover of those old gods, as time would prove. However, his claim was naturally not undisputed. He had more barbarian incursions in Britain to distract him, and Constantius decided to fight his claim too. Julian moved east to confront him but before their armies met Constantius died, giving Julian a free run.

Julian now declared himself emperor, with his capital at Constantinople. He also declared himself a pagan, earning himself the uncomplimentary epithet of 'the Apostate'. Old temples were restored to honour the traditional gods once more. Christians were not persecuted, although they lost many of their privileges. But Julian was not a vicious persecutor of all faiths for the sake of it. During his reign, a start was even made on the rebuilding of the Jewish temple at Jerusalem.

Julian then moved on to his next challenge: Persia. In AD 362, he moved his army to Antioch and prepared to invade. Rather than face him, Shapur adopted a scorched earth policy in the face of his advance. The Romans moved on Ctesiphon but were then lured into the desert and attacked. Julian was mortally wounded in the fight. Jovian, the captain of the guard, took over and made peace, though at a heavy cost, ceding large chunks of land to the Persians.

By this time, the pressures around Rome's northern borders were growing exponentially. A vast nomadic migration composed of Central Asian tribesmen, the Huns, was spreading across the steppes, an unstoppable wave that overcame everything in its path. In an attempt to escape the chaos that they brought with them, whole tribes packed up all their possessions and fled as fast as they could.

The Huns were well known to the Chinese much further east. At the start of the century, in AD 304, a Chinese-educated emperor, Liu Yüan, formed a 'Hun Han' dynasty based on old principles. Tea drinking had by now started to appear in China, probably learnt from Tibet, but beneath this veneer of genteelism there were many threats facing the region. In AD 316 the Chin dynasty abandoned northern China to the Huns (the whole of China by now being very fragmented). As a result, the Han Hun dynasty became more fully established. A Hunnish invasion of China through the Great Wall (again a rather ineffective barrier) then continued and also extended into Siberia.

What was about to happen in China mirrored in some respects the imminent demise of the Western Roman Empire. Tribesmen from outside the Chinese borders had been invited to settle in China; it seemed easier to do this than to carry on fighting off their raids. However, once settled they started to worry away at the fabric of Chinese society from within. As a result the fourth century was a period of almost uninterrupted internecine warfare within China.

The chaos that ensued led to a corresponding breakdown in the social fabric. There was widespread famine as agriculture was badly affected, there was a marked increase in the number of fortifications built in the region and there was an upsurge in criminal activity, especially banditry. There was also a mass refugee migration as disaffected northern residents fled towards the promise of a more stable life in the south – all in all, a turbulent and frightening period in history.

The barbarian migrations continued to have an impact further afield. Nomadic tribesmen do not generally write comprehensive histories and we have to construct the movement of the Huns from a glimpse here, a hint there. We know that by around AD 355 the Huns had begun to advance westwards into Russia. They overwhelmed and absorbed the Alans but other tribes tried to move out of their clutches. Among them were the Goths, and their movements were to have dramatic repercussions for Rome itself.

External pressure on the empire's frontiers continued to grow until AD 375, when Rome was again ruled by two emperors, Gratian in the east and Valens in the west. It eventually became irresistible. The Visigoths north of the Danube were heavily defeated by the Huns. With nowhere else to go, the survivors were given permission to cross the river into Roman territory. However, once they arrived they were very shabbily treated. This was both an inhumane and a foolish policy. Although beaten by the Huns, they were still a dangerous enemy. With no other option, they revolted against the Romans who had treated them so badly.

Their first triumph was the conquest of Thrace (in the region of modern Bulgaria). Valens had no alternative but to gather an army to meet them. His army met them near the city of Adrianople. In what was a decisive and historic battle, the army of Rome was shattered on the field. In the rout, Valens himself was killed. Constantinople itself now appeared to be in danger but, fortunately for Rome, though the Visigoths were fine warriors in the field, they had no experience of siege warfare, so the major cities of the empire were safe for the time being.

Neither was this the only area in which Rome was under attack. Britain in particular was a target. Between AD 368 and AD 372 Britannia suffered from concerted attacks from Picts, Scots, Saxons and Franks. Major shore defences were built in an attempt to fight off pirates, some of which, particularly those of Porchester and Pevensey, remain as stunning examples of military architecture. Rome sent Count Theodosius over in a successful attempt to restore order. But there were other threats against the rule of Rome. Irish forces were regularly raiding Wales, led by their famous king Niall from his base at Tara, while the Franks had by now occupied most of north-west Gaul.

In AD 379, the same year that Shapur II of Persia died after a long and successful reign, Theodosius became emperor of the Eastern Roman Empire. He vigorously took on the Visigoths, forcing them to make peace. He introduced a policy of retaining their loyalty by employing them as mercenaries. These events were in sharp contrast to the state of the Western Roman Empire, which was beginning to implode. In AD 383 it was seized by Magnus Maximus, who defeated and killed the reigning emperor Gratian near Paris. He gained control of Spain and Gaul, but Hadrian's Wall was overrun and its useful life was now at an end.

Theodosius decided it was time to renew the peace with Persia and the two powers decided to divide Armenia, that old bone of contention, between them (the existence of gold mines in the region may have helped make it so attractive to both parties).

In the meantime, the Church was still sorting out its doctrines. In AD 386 Pope Siricius declared that all married priests should be defrocked, bringing to a decisive conclusion decades of debate about whether or not priests should have a wife. The early Church indulged in exhaustive debate about sexuality, with some extremists arguing that the whole act of sex (and by definition marriage itself) was wrong. They did not care that the logical extension of their arguments against procreation was the demise of the whole Church on earth through natural causes; it was only the life to come that mattered.

In AD 389, there was a trial of strength between the Church and the emperor. In that year Ambrose, the Bishop of Milan, refused to administer Mass to the emperor unless he entered the cathedral as a penitent. After hesitation, Theodosius did as he was told. It was an important, symbolic moment in the history of the battle for supremacy between Church and State that was to last for the next thousand years. But it was only the beginning of the conflict, which would last for millenium until the onset of Protestantism in some areas of Europe, which seemed to symbolise victory for the secular power.

There were however some unfortunate by-products to emerge from the increasing power of Christianity. In AD 391, Theodosius proclaimed that all pagan temples in his empire were to be closed. In Egypt, where the priests kept alive a knowledge of hieroglyphics, the closures meant that within half a century all understanding of them had disappeared, not to re-emerge for a millennium and a half. It was a loss made all the worse by the destruction of the temple of Serapis in Alexandria, along with many of the records that had survived the terrible fire that had consumed the city when Julius Caesar took it 450 years previously.

The challenge to Roman supremacy posed by the barbarians continued to grow. The emperor of the west, Valentinian II, was assassinated when advancing into Gaul against a Frankish chief named Arbogast. Arbogast now became a kingmaker and appointed a weakling, Eugenius, as a replacement emperor. Theodosius came over from Rome to restore order and killed both Arbogast and Eugenius at the Battle of the River Frigidus. Theodosius now became emperor of both east and west, reuniting the empire once more.

The reunification did not last long. In AD 395 Theodosius died after proclaiming his sons Honorius and Arcadius emperors of west and east respectively. The following year Stilicho, the son of a Vandal, gained control over Honorius. He decided to stop employing the Goths, an act with fateful consequences. In response their leader Alaric now sought to carve out a kingdom for his people. He descended through the Pass of Thermopylae and sacked the Temple of Eleusis, though he spared Athens. Stilicho advanced and made peace with the Goths, letting them set up a state in Epirus. But the Goths had not finished with Rome yet.

The era of the barbarian invasions was far from over. It would also threaten a new and glorious power in India. In around AD 320 in the Magadha area of India (around the Ganges) the first ruler of the Gupta dynasty, Chandragupta, established a kingdom. He built up his territories with a combination of approaches that would be replicated many times across the world over the centuries, partly by conquest, partly by a judicious marital alliance that brought him a great deal in terms of inheritances. He took a new title, *Maharajadhiraja*, which means Raja of rajas, which seems like a copycat version of the Persian King of kings. Such hyperbolic titles became the norm for the Indian kings; one later version would be *Rajarajadhiraja*, which literally means king of king-of-kings.

The Guptas were not part of the highest social order in India but they married into a family that was: the Licchavis. They had a venerable and prestigious heritage. Chandragupta's queen, Kumaradevi Licchavayah, was shown on coins alongside him, something that had previously been unheard of. The Licchavis had previously conquered land in Nepal and it is probable that they and the Guptas ruled adjacent territories.

Chandragupta was succeeded in AD 335 by Samudra Gupta, who was the man who really put the new dynasty on the regional map. Much of the information we have on him is on a single pillar in Allahabad, perhaps one of the most famous of all Sanskrit inscriptions. Another one was found by British archaeologists; it had been dug up in the eighteenth century and injudiciously used as a roadroller. Samudra would expand his kingdom over most of India, using much of the treasure paid to him by vassal states as funding for his love of the arts. Buddhist art flourished gloriously, reaching its apogee under his successor Chandragupta II in AD 375.

The Allahabad Pillar contains a wealth of historical information. It provides a long list of kings and regions who were conquered by Samudra. They refer to wide-ranging campaigns: movements against Madras, battles in Bengal and probes into the Punjab. Other kingdoms, while remaining notionally independent, made obeisance to Samudra; these included parts of Nepal, Sri Lanka and Assam. He was known sycophantically as 'conqueror of the four quarters of the earth' and was regarded as a living god. It was a perception that the king and his successors assiduously cultivated. Each of them played out a year-long ritual called the Horse Sacrifice, which was a symbolic affirmation of their power, commemorated by the issue of superb golden coins.

However, Samudra seems to have been wise enough not to gloat in victory. Conquered kings were allowed to keep their lands if they were suitably submissive to him. As one writer, John Keay, wisely said, 'A world-ruler did not actually have to rule the world; it was enough that the world should acknowledge him as such.' It was a mantra that later would-be conquerors would copy consciously or otherwise; Genghis Khan would be one good example.

Later sources, which cover the period patchily and not always convincingly, suggest that Samudra was succeeded on his death by Rama-Gupta. He attempted to remove the powerful satraps of Malwa in central India. When he failed to do so, they forced him to give up his queen as the price of failure. The lady, Dhruvadevi, was famed for her beauty and she was seized eagerly by the Satrap of the Shakas, the Scythian dynasty of kings.

But the shame was too much to bear for Rama-Gupta's brother, another Chandragupta. He dressed himself as Dhruvadevi (which may suggest a number of things, including a wonderful acting ability on his part or a possibility that the lady was not quite as beautiful as she was claimed to be), inveigled his way past the palace guards and slew the satrap. With Rama-Gupta now, to coin a colloquialism, 'damaged goods', Chandragupta claimed the throne as well as the supposedly delightful Dhruvadevi. His subsequent reign was commemorated by an iron pillar in Delhi that still remains, a 'rustless wonder' as it has been called, for it shows few signs of corrosion.

Chandragupta declared war on the Shakas and gained control of north-west India. It was a long haul and fighting may have gone on for as long as twenty years. In the end, it is the mundane that tells us what happened. The coins that the satraps had been issuing in central and western India later bear the image of Chandragupta, speaking eloquently of his ultimate victory. It was an important triumph, for it gave him access to the ports of the Gujarat on the western shores of India and this in turn made him the master of considerable wealth from international trade.

Chandra proclaimed himself Vikramaditya or 'Sun of Prowess'. He gained control of the north-western land approaches to India too, but in the process eliminated a potential buffer state between him and the Huns. Such a buffer was needed as the Huns were still ambitious and their threat all-embracing. In AD 387, southern China had been saved from invasion by them at the Battle of Fei Shui but northern China continued to suffer at their hands. From China to the borders of Rome, the impact of their incursions was felt. Few places in the known world were safe from them.

Some were saved from such pressures by their geographical isolation. Rather than being threatened by the upheavals, Japan decided to add to them. There are accounts that in AD 369 the Japanese invaded Korea and set up a small colony there. A source of these stories of Japanese colonialism in Korea is the *Nihon shoki*, the *Chronicles of Japan*, penned in AD 720. This, and a counterpart written at around the same time, the *Kojiki*, the *Record of Ancient Things*, was written at the behest of an emperor who wished to establish the legitimacy of his claim to the throne by restating his family's mythical antecedents.

As such, the books are not reliable sources of history. It is rather like relying on Mallory's *Morte d'Arthur* as a trustworthy evidential basis for the history of fifth-century Britain. Many historians discount these stories of colonisation in Korea at this time. However, the fact that there were links between Korea and Japan of some sort at this period is widely accepted. Korea was divided in three – Paekche and Silla in the south and Koguryo (after which 'Korea' is named) in the north. There was also a small confederation of tiny kingdoms in the middle of the country. From Korea, both writing and Buddhism made the short crossing to Japan, with great significance for the future of what would eventually become a superpower.

During this period we have the first evidence for an early civilisation in a part of the world whose history is as yet little understood, western Africa. Civilisations in Egypt and the surrounding regions are well documented and we know a fair amount about them. For example, it is believed that by around AD 315 the Jewish community in Ethiopia accounted for half of the population (and continued to play a prominent part there until recent times, though much of the community has now emigrated to Israel).

Further south and west, though, the evidence is obscure, as if seen only through frosted glass. However, archaeological evidence suggests that between AD 300 and AD 800 there was a flourishing community at Jenne-Jeno in modern Mali. The population here is estimated to have exceeded 25,000 and there is evidence of well-developed housing, built of mud brick, and reasonably sophisticated social organisation. There is no sign, however, of religious or large public buildings, so civilisation here appears to have gone down a different road than elsewhere. In particular there appear to have been no palaces, so on the surface at least there is no evidence of a strong leader dominating the rest of the community.

These regions were protected from the 'civilising' influences further north and east by the vastness of the Sahara desert. The word 'protected' is used advisedly for, although there is much to be admired in civilisations such as those of Egypt or Meroe, the history of colonisation demonstrates that for most colonised peoples 'civilisation' often only comes at an awful price in terms of exploitation and abuse. That there was trade from early on is probable; entrepreneurs are of course famed for their risk taking, and a camel ride across the desert was surely an acceptable price to pay for some of them. However, the difficulties of distance and terrain meant that it was far harder for a conquering army to cross it than it was for a group of merchants.

The world, or at least that part of it covering Europe and western Asia, was now at a tipping point. As the fifth century approached there were unmistakeable continuing signs of decay and decline in Rome. Yet the ultimate demise of the empire in the century that followed only appears inevitable with the gift of hindsight. The stability reintroduced by Theodosius appeared to offer some hope that the barbarians could be bested, but it was a false dawn, as would soon become apparent. The barbarians were on the move and would have a dramatic impact across most of the known world, certainly in Europe but also on an ongoing basis in China, and finally in India too.

18

THE WORLD RESHAPED

The Triumph of the 'Barbarians' (AD 401–500)

By AD 400, Hindu Brahmans were increasing their power in India at the expense of the Buddhists while Sanskrit was becoming a literary language and Hindu epics were being written down. India, in short, was starting to take shape into the region which we now know. Not that it was by any means a united entity or indeed shaped in a fashion that we would now easily recognise. There were still independent peoples in the south of the Subcontinent, Kadambas, Gangas and Pandyas for example, while in the north the Gupta territories spilled over into what is now Pakistan and parts of Nepal and possibly Afghanistan (though this is not unarguably proven).

The Guptas provided something of a golden age. It was not just their own propagandists that said so. In AD 405 Fa-hsien, a Chinese traveller, reached India and reported back to his masters on its wealth and its freedoms under the Guptas. It was a marked contrast to what was happening in China for, in the same year, the Chinese poet T'ao Ch'ien retired from the imperial court, saying that he was tired of 'crooking the hinges in his back.' Chinese society was run by ritualistic obedience to those who ruled, much as Confucius would have wanted it to be. Fa-hsien undoubtedly found much to admire in India in contrast to what he was used to. China had by now entered what historians have labelled 'the Period of Disunion', a time that spanned four centuries between the Han and the T'ang dynasties.

It is a confusing period. It is not that no records exist of this long interlude. We have names aplenty but China in these years was divided and had split down into smaller units. The cohesion applied, however imperfectly, by the dynastic rulers was absent and the period was confused and hard to make sense of. Perhaps this is why Fa-hsien noted with emphasis that he was able to move in a great deal of safety around the Gupta territories, not something that he would necessarily have been able to say of his time back in China.

The Period of Disunion was one that saw a rapid breakdown in centralised control and a resultant increase in the power of local warlords. This was not a time for social justice; the rich generally did all they could to protect and enhance their position at the expense of the poor, whom they exploited mercilessly. Slavery had always played a prominent part in China, as it did with most ancient civilisations. In common with slaves elsewhere, those in China had no rights; the women were used as concubines, the children of slaves were destined to a life in bondage themselves and their faces were marked with tattoos as a symbol of their servitude that could not be concealed.

With widespread poverty, few rights, chaos aplenty and great uncertainty about the future, it is no surprise that many people were ready to turn to religion. This goes a long way to explaining why Buddhism, exported from India, took such firm root in China, a process that continued throughout the fifth and sixth centuries. Ironically, its fortunes were on the up in China in direct contrast to how they were going in India. Its teachings that, to quote a definition, 'everything mundane is impermanent and ultimately dissatisfying' must have struck a chord with those who had little to cherish in this life.

Buddhism had already moved north-westwards from its point of origin around the Ganges and had found a strong base in what was then part of the Indian patrimony but now forms part of Pakistan and Afghanistan. This was important, for it was an area where there had been a fusion between Indian and Greek influences and, because it was from these Central Asian areas that Buddhism made its way to China, these joint influences also made their way there too.

It is important to note that to speak of Buddhism as a coherent, joined-up entity is a great simplification. There were different styles of Buddhism (over time these would include, for example, Mahayana, Theravada and Zen Buddhism) and, although there were holy men, the whole concept of the faith was one of man finding himself, which meant there were great opportunities for adherents to experiment with the teachings that suited them most.

Buddhism had a great impact on Chinese art. Before it arrived, there had been no tradition of painting images – or carving statues – of the gods and deities of China, but Buddhism changed this. However, it was not universally welcomed. Supporters of Confucianism unsurprisingly did not like its rejection of their philosophy or its approach, which effectively rejected many of the conventions of Confucian life. From time to time, Chinese rulers would turn on it too. But Buddhists were exempted from taxes by rulers who supported them, which would deprive their successors of significant revenues.

There was a religious rival to Buddhism too, Daoism, with its concentration on yin and yang concepts and its preaching of sexual self-control and balanced diet as a way of prolonging life. It was a belief system that had developed in particular since the time of the Yellow Turbans and it was again unsurprising that it did not take kindly to Buddhism. No religion likes a rival and the two faiths competed for the devotions of people both north and south. Buddhism as a rule came out on top but Daoism continued to have its advocates and to win new recruits too.

There was great tension then in China, which contrasted with Indian civilisation at the time. Law and order was one of the abiding impressions Fa-hsien's visit to Gupta lands left with him. He also noted that, although the caste system existed there, it was not as ingrained as he might have anticipated. Certainly those who disposed of the bodies of the dead, the Chandalas, were a definite subclass, firmly grounded at the very base of the social pyramid. But there were few others who seemed to be particularly disadvantaged by the caste system.

Trade was also flourishing once more, both by land and sea. When Fa-hsien eventually returned to China, it was by sea from Bengal. He stopped off at several locations en route including Indo-China and one of Java, Sumatra or Malaya (the exact location is unclear). In India, religion at this stage was more a question of individual conscience than would sometimes be the case in Indian history. Although Hinduism was definitely on the up, Buddhism still survived and had a number of adherents.

It was during the reign of a long-ruling Gupta king, Kumara-Gupta (AD 415–455) that worrying threats to this 'utopia' first emerged. One of them was a rebellion in Malwa, an unstable region of Central India that had a reputation for attempting to assert its independence. Another was the challenge posed to the Guptas by the race of people called the *Hunas*, better known in Europe as the Huns. Originating in China, a branch of this marauding people known as the White Huns (or the Ephthalites) had established themselves in Bactria by the mid-fourth century, wedging themselves between the Gupta lands to the east and the Sassanian territories to the west. In the fifth century, they began to directly challenge the Guptas.

They also advanced towards Lake Aral, from which direction they threatened the Persians. The Persian king Bahram V managed to keep them at bay for a while, but this was only a temporary respite. By AD 484 Balas, the King of Persia, was forced to pay tribute to the Ephthalites, who had by then formed a kingdom between the Caspian and the Indus. They were a serious headache to everyone who came into contact with them, being able to move quickly and overwhelm the more static defences of those who were challenged by them. Not averse to being employed as mercenaries if the occasion demanded (the Eastern Roman Empire, Byzantium, for one, took advantage of this), they certainly much preferred the part of raiders.

The threat to India was initially repulsed by a son of the king, Skanda-Gupta. Not only did he fight off the Huns, he also managed to engage in some major building works. But he was the last great product of the Guptas. He became king himself but after his death in AD 467 a succession of short-lived reigns was played out by a number of unsuccessful rulers. The last decades of this century were typified by an inexorable decline in Gupta greatness. This presaged a permanent decline in the face of renewed Hun threats in the following century.

Europe was about to be turned on its head much earlier. For a while now, barbarian incursions had been sucking like rapacious leeches at the lifeblood of Rome. Now that great empire was about to die. 'Mutate' might be a better word, though, for in the east Rome would be reborn in Constantinople, a distorted though not unattractive variation on what the traditional empire had been, increasingly a mix of Roman imperialism and Hellenistic culture, a distinctive and unique creation which took many old ideas but gave them new life.

In the west, the situation was rather different. The leaders of the 'barbarian' invasions would attempt not so much to overthrow Rome as to become it. The heritage of Rome was a considerable thing, capable of becoming an inspiration as well as a source of contempt. However, what came out of the other side of this process was unrecognisable from what went into it and there was no doubt that the Rome of old was, to all intents and purposes, dead, even if aspects of her would be reincarnated in a new life that reshaped Europe in particular.

The danger for Rome sprang from the fact that many of the barbarians had actually settled inside Rome's borders. With a vast frontier to patrol, manpower was always a challenge for the empire. There were 250,000 troops to defend Rome and its vast borders. Many were deployed on the frontiers, typically the better troops. There were also forces behind the lines, generally of lower quality, who were theoretically available as a reserve to back up any part of the frontier line that had been breached. However, with constant strains on manpower the Romans decided to plug the gap by employing barbarian troops, *foederati*. While this might have been pragmatic, it was also risky.

The century had begun appropriately enough when, in AD 400, Gainas, a Goth, led a rebellion in Asia Minor and became in effect the ruler of Constantinople – an event that set a trend for the following decades. However, his reign did not last long before he was expelled from 'Nova Roma' and chased over the Danube, where he was killed by the Huns. This too was an appropriate portent of things to come as the Huns were to play a huge role in the events of this century right across Asia and Europe.

However, it was the leader of another tribal grouping who was to set his mark on the first years of the century. In AD 401 Alaric invaded Italy. In response, the usurper Stilicho, who was to play an important role in forthcoming events, denuded Britain of troops. He would certainly have been unaware of the long-term impact of events taking place on the island that year, which would also have vital repercussions. In the west of England, the son of a Roman official possibly living near the Severn Estuary was captured by pirates and taken to Ireland as a slave. The following formative years of the boy, named Patrick, would help to shape the future of the Emerald Isle and also of other parts of Western Europe in terms of the spread of Christianity.

Links between mainland Britain and Ireland had existed throughout the Roman Empire. Although Rome was never to attempt to invade Hibernia, trading links had certainly been present. And it would be wrong to think that there was no link between the Celtic tribes before the Roman conquest of Britain. The presence of tribes such as the Brigantes in both the north of England and in Ireland cannot be coincidence and must denote a common origin. Now the process would become two-way. With the weakening Roman Empire, a tribe called the Scotti would send settlers over to south-west Scotland; they would eventually become a fundamental element in the formation of the kingdom that would ultimately be named after them.

In Europe, Stilicho advanced into Italy and the next year fought a drawn battle at Pollentia with Alaric. The official emperor, a weak and unimpressive man called Honorius, bribed Alaric to leave the peninsula. It was an action that lacked glory, an approach that was, frankly, fully in keeping with this emperor. Honorius then deserted Milan and established a new capital for himself at Ravenna, on the Adriatic, a place that was easier to protect from the barbarian hordes that increasingly endangered his empire – his only positive legacy, as Ravenna would become a great city.

Alaric was not the only threat to concern the Western Roman Empire though. In AD 405 a barbarian named Radagaisus assembled a composite army of Ostrogoths, Vandals and others and invaded Italy. Stilicho sprang into action again, saving Florence from Radagaisus and presenting him in chains to Honorius. But the effort required to fight off these repeated attacks was taking its toll. The following year, the Romano-British, in despair at being deserted, elected their own emperors: first Marcus, then Gratian. Neither of them survived long.

While Vandals and others were overrunning much of Gaul there was yet another usurper in Britain, one more Constantine, who crossed the English Channel to try and enforce his claims to the throne. While this was happening, in AD 407 the slave Patrick, after working as a swineherd, returned home to Britain an older and wiser man and soon travelled to the continent to train as a priest.

A showdown between Honorius and Stilicho was imminent. The emperor's pride would certainly have been offended at being so reliant on one of his generals. He was therefore easily persuaded when his chancellor Olympius, a weasel of a man, persuaded him to have Stilicho murdered along with many of his Vandal soldiers. This was a miscalculation of the greatest magnitude for it invited the Vandals to attack Italy in search of revenge, while removing the one Roman general capable of standing up to their leader, Alaric.

Alaric duly invaded Italy again, his Vandal warriors supplemented by large numbers of discontented mercenaries. With no effective force to eject his army, he was soon besieging Rome. It was only a matter of time before the Eternal City's population began to starve. Alaric did not necessarily want to bring Rome to its knees and was bought off twice but each time he later returned. Success breeds success and it was not long before many barbarian slaves joined Alaric. Even as Italy was under assault, Vandals and their allies poured into Spain and plundered a number of rich cities. The empire was beginning to disintegrate.

Then in AD 410 the unthinkable happened. Outraged by the duplicity and the vacillation of Honorius, Alaric returned to the gates of Rome, determined to exact retribution from the city. A slave opened the gates to the hordes outside, who poured through the unprotected portals of the city. The Visigoths streamed through the streets of the city, looting it thoroughly. Rome fell after only token resistance and was sacked, though the churches of St Peter and St Paul were spared. Buoyed on by his success, Alaric headed towards Sicily but died in the south of Italy.

He was buried in memorable fashion. The course of a stream was diverted and then a grave was dug in the dried-up riverbed. Alaric, 'king of all' as the name means, was reverently interred along with some of his booty. Then the stream was released back onto its original course and the grave was lost forever beneath the waters. The captives who had been forced to dig the tomb were then put to death so that the secrecy of the spot might be preserved (an act resonant of the burial rites of other great 'barbarian' leaders such as Genghis Khan nearly a millennium later). But Alaric's death did not save Rome. Alaric was not the cause of its decline, he was a symptom and a beneficiary of it. It was a long-term deterioration, which was further evidenced when, around AD 410, Roman legions sailed away from Britannia for the last time, leaving the island on its own.

All the Goths wanted was a land to call their own and perhaps a semblance of acceptance and legitimacy from Rome. Alaric's brother-in-law Ataulf married Honorius's half-sister Placidia soon after the chieftain's death and set up a state in Gaul, nominally as a vassal of Rome. These dramatic events turned the world on its head and Roman citizens struggled to make sense of it. Between AD 413 and AD 426 one of them, the renowned theologian Augustine, wrote his *City of God*, a work that examined the reasons for the fall of Rome and argued that it was not the fault of Christians.

Augustine's influence on his world, and on that which followed in the medieval period and beyond, was immense. He developed concepts of free will, predestination and sin that still shape Western thinking today, even in an increasingly secular society. He acted as a bridge between the Roman world and the medieval and post-medieval eras (many may now be secular and refute organised religion, which of course they are entirely free to do, but they would be greatly in error if they were to deny the impact of religious thinking over the centuries on the way that we all think). He later became Bishop of Hippo in North Africa.

In AD 415 Ataulf was assassinated and replaced by Wallia, who was amenable to helping Rome out if the price was satisfactory. Between AD 419 and AD 420, Wallia, bribed by Honorius, campaigned to retake Spain on behalf of the emperor, which he duly did. The Vandal tribes he defeated retired to the far south of the Iberian Peninsula, where they established a kingdom in Vandalusia (Andalusia).

In AD 423 Honorius died. He had been a weak and ineffective ruler, at the mercy of the stronger characters who surrounded and advised him, often poorly. He was a pale shadow of some of the great names who had preceded him in previous centuries and he was in most respects completely out of his depth in facing up to the challenges that faced him. Predictably enough, there was now a struggle to succeed him as emperor. The year after, a Roman soldier, Aëtius, who had been a hostage among the Goths and Huns, invaded Italy in support of a usurper, John, leading a barbarian army.

Between AD 426 and AD 428, Aëtius campaigned in Gaul against the Goths and the Franks but the barbarian threat still cast an ominous shadow over much of the declining empire. In AD 429 a bishop, Germanus, came to Britain to combat a heresy known after its founder as Pelagianism. While he was there, he took up the sword against Saxon invaders, winning a great victory, allegedly after the battle cries of 'Hallelujah' that went up from his troops had terrified the enemy.

Further south, the Vandals under Genseric made the short crossing to Africa from Spain, having been invited over by the Roman governor Boniface, who was jealous of the rise of Aëtius. They moved on Hippo, the home of Augustine, who died during the siege that followed. Although the great thinker was dead, his theology would live on. Among his most important writings were those on the concept of the 'Just War', which outlined the situations in which a Christian was allowed to fight. Such doctrines were widely examined as part of the justification for the Crusading movement over 500 years later. To a significant extent, they even shape moral attitudes to war today.

Alongside such deep thinkers as Augustine, this was also an age of other great Christian mystics. One of them, Simon Stylites, had climbed a tall column in Syria, intending to make it a place where he could meditate undisturbed on the mysteries of the universe. He would spend the last thirty-seven years of his life here. Always an ascetic – it was said that he never ate or drank during the time of Lent – he was frustrated by the repeated interruptions he had to deal with while living in a terrestrial home. Unfortunately for him, his very public wish to be left alone did not work. Fascinated by such extreme devotion, pilgrims came to see him from far and wide, consulting him by shouting up questions to the top of his column (the remains of which, a sad, stunted rock a few feet high, may still be seen).

In AD 431, peace was made with the Vandals and Boniface went to Ravenna where he defeated Aëtius but died soon after. That same year, an event of widespread significance was acted out. The fight for Christianity's heart and soul was fought long and hard in the early centuries of the faith's existence. In this environment, there were deeply felt and sometimes violent disputations, and many sects regarded as heretical by others sprung up. At the Council of Ephesus, one such group, known as Nestorians after their leader Nestorius, were excommunicated. Over time, the Nestorians migrated eastwards, being welcomed first in Persia and later in China. They would later find a home among the Mongols.

At around this time the ex-Irish slave, Patrick, was made a bishop at Auxerre, and soon after set out to convert the Irish. He met the king at Tara who, though he stubbornly stuck to his traditional beliefs, did allow Patrick to set out on an evangelising mission. The message that he preached caught the imagination, and a number of converts were won. Over time a particular Celtic type of monasticism would flourish in Ireland and would then be carried by missionaries to Scotland and into the north of England. The Irish missionaries would be the torchbearers who would help reignite the Christian faith, which the pagan barbarian conquerors threatened to extinguish. Isolated on the far fringes of Europe, Ireland escaped these incursions and provided a haven and a springboard from which a reconversion of Western Europe could be launched, an event whose importance to later civilisations should not be underestimated.

The best-known barbarian warlord of all was about to appear on the scene. In AD 433 a man named Attila became co-ruler of the Huns with his brother, who conveniently died soon after. Attila may have been illiterate but he was very intelligent. He was also ferocious; he would later be known by Christians as the Scourge of God. In the early years of his reign he consolidated his kingdom, whose capital was probably on the site of Buda in Hungary. Both emperors, at the time Theodosius II of the east and Valentinian III of the west, bribed him to behave himself. It was a tactic that worked – for a while at least.

Further incursions elsewhere kept the empire occupied. In AD 435 the Burgundians made peace with Aëtius but were then attacked by the Vandals. Three years later, parts of Iberia were overrun by the Suevi (or Suebi), a Germanic tribe. The Suevi had entered into a confederacy with the Alemanni and had attacked south from Germany (where their name lives on in the region of Swabia), attacking parts of Lorraine and Switzerland before a number of them founded a kingdom based on northern Portugal and Galicia in north-west Spain. Then Genseric, an opportunist sensing weaknesses to be exploited, broke the peace with Rome and attacked Carthage. He would utilise its superb strategic position to make it a base for piracy and coastal ravaging by seaborne cavalry. It was not long before he was leading an invasion of Italy.

Genseric was king of both the Vandals and the Alans. The barbarian invasions were a bewildering period of history; bewildering but not unknown. The story of the Alans provides an interesting example of what happened during these chaotic times. They originated from lands by the Caspian Sea and became known both to the West, through the writings of Strabo, and to China, through a work known as the *Shiji*, at around the same time in the first century BC.

They were known for their skills as horse archers and grew more powerful in the latter years of the Roman Empire. During the second and third centuries AD they frequently raided the Danubian and Caucasian provinces of Rome. The writer Ammianus Marcellinus noted of them that 'the Alani are men of great stature and beauty; their hair is somewhat yellow, their eyes are terribly fierce'. They were also mentioned by the Jewish historian Josephus.

But towards the end of the fourth century, they were overwhelmed by the Huns and a number of them fled west. Here they joined with the Vandals and the Suevi in their attack on Gaul. They also allied with the Burgundians and they even helped Rome in facing the threat of the Huns. Subsequently, a number moved to Spain where they allied with the Vandals against the might of the Visigoths, who eventually emerged triumphant in the Iberian Peninsula. Their story acts both as a summary of the domino effect created by Hun incursions and as evidence of the frequent tribal alliances that typified the times. They epitomise the fact that there was wave after wave of incursions, eventually overwhelming the defences of Western Europe.

It will be obvious by now that the death of Rome was a long and drawn-out one, a death of a thousand cuts. Further evidence of this came in AD 441 when the Huns crossed the Danube and attacked the Balkans, taking both Belgrade and Sofia in the process. As a consequence, the Eastern Roman Empire's protection money was trebled. As Viking raiders would find a few centuries later, where a wealthy nation was prepared to buy you off, it was always worth returning in the future and asking for more. The Huns' incursions had a dramatic negative impact on the region and on the Danube as a carrier of commerce in particular.

In AD 446, Britain sent to Aëtius in a vain appeal for help. By this stage the Angles, Saxons and Jutes were starting to attack in strength with the aim of settling as well as raiding. However, Rome had too many distractions elsewhere, for soon afterwards the Huns entered Thrace, Thessaly and Scythia, sacking towns with great cruelty as they went. Theodosius II bought them off once more and they turned to the Western Roman Empire. Britain was now alone.

The *Anglo-Saxon Chronicles* note that, in about AD 449, 'Vortigern invited the Angle race here and they then came to Britain in three ships at the place Ebba's Creek'. Vortigern is believed to have been a British king with authority over southern England as far as Kent, and he invited Angles under Hengist and Horsa to settle to help him against the Picts who were invading Britain from the north. Once invited in, the Angles would not be leaving again.

As far as the wider empire was concerned, the crisis point with the Huns had now been reached. The success of the barbarian horde was based on its mobility and speed; Hun warriors were cavalry, wedded to their horses, but also outstanding marksmen with the composite bow, which they could use with great accuracy and power even from horseback – much as their descendants the Mongols could. Unfortunately the Romans did not yet seem to realise their enemy's superiority. In AD 450 Theodosius II died and his successor Marcian refused to continue the tribute to Attila. Valentinian III followed suit in the west.

This in itself was enough to ignite a conflagration. The spark that set the powder keg off, though, came from an unlikely source. Honoria, Valentinian's sister, was banished for misconduct and sent a ring to Attila as a token offering, along with a plea for his help.

Attila pretended to take this as a proposal of marriage and as his dowry he demanded half the kingdom. Soon after, overrun from north, south and east, it seemed that the last rites of Rome were finally being administered. By this time Franks were spreading through the Netherlands, taking their Teutonic language and paganism with them. In the north, the Slavs of northern Russia were being pushed into German states by the Huns, creating an even more chaotic domino effect that threatened to demolish what was left of the empire.

When Attila's demands were refused, he launched a full-scale invasion of the west. Trier and Metz were burned and at the head of a huge army he approached Paris and then Troyes. A Roman army moved out to meet him. In a decisive confrontation, Attila was heavily defeated at the Battle of Châlons in June AD 451. The victorious Roman general was Aëtius, while at Attila's side were both Franks and the Visigoths led by the old warrior Wallia, who was killed in the fight. But with Aëtius were also many barbarian allies – Visigoths, Burgundians, Alans, Bretons and Saxons included – so this could no longer be called a triumphant Roman army, but one which was largely Germanic.

Despite the defeat, Attila was able to extricate much of his army and retreated to Italy in good order. Milan bought him off, but the emperor Valentinian III retreated from Ravenna to Rome and sent Pope Leo I to parley with him. There was a force on its way from Constantinople and plague in the Huns' army, so Attila now decided to return to his capital. He had not long to live. Soon after, he was found dead in bed with a burst blood vessel after over-celebrating at a wedding feast. His empire was divided among his sons, and the threat to the west was effectively over, from this direction at least.

The involvement of the Pope in this sequence of events shows how his role was becoming increasingly important. Roman emperors like Honorius and Valentinian did their utmost to abdicate the responsibilities of the empire while enjoying all its sybaritic benefits, which left a vacuum. While their self-serving emperors hid behind their walls in Ravenna, Roman citizens looked for a lead. Some found it in the service of local magnates, who started to build up their own private armies. Others, however, turned to the Church. During the fifth century the numbers of new recruits increased. No doubt many spiritual reasons were the main driver, but for some the prospect of an existence that was tax-free at a personal level may have helped.

Economic decline was one of the major reasons for Rome's demise. The tax burden had grown increasingly heavy, acting like a great millstone pressing Rome's citizens to death. Collection of taxes was overseen by a burgeoning bureaucracy, which of course in itself cost money to run. All this sounds strangely resonant of life in many parts of the western world in the early twenty-first century.

Furthermore, the burden fell disproportionately on the poor, particularly in rural areas where it often became uneconomic to carry on farming by the time that taxes and rents were paid. A famine, or even just a mediocre year, could drive workers of the land to the brink of starvation. To some it seemed better to be a slave, for the 'free man' at his lowest level was not really free; he had to stay put and work his land to pay his taxes, so he was forced to remain where he was. He had no mobility, just like the slave, but he was in addition forced to live an unrewarding life of struggle just to earn a pittance and, after he had paid his taxes, survive at basic levels of existence. In bad years indeed he might well not survive at all.

Attila's death did not make much difference to Rome, which continued to self-destruct. Valentinian III ordered the murder of Aëtius, a poor reward for his stunning victory at Châlons. He himself was then assassinated and a puppet emperor, Avitus, put on the throne. Genseric, still looking for easy pickings, saw an opportunity and looted Rome. He took away the empress Eudoxia and her two daughters as part of his prize, a shame that must have been felt greatly by this proud city with its magnificent history but increasingly tarnished present.

It was clear that Rome's best days were behind it. By now much of northern Italy was in a terrible state. Towns were walled, farms had been abandoned and the population had shrunk dramatically. Rome's population had dropped from 1.5 million two centuries before to 330,000. A time of chaos and frequent changes of ruler in Rome now followed, with the Visigoth Ricimer as the power behind the throne. He had a counterpart in the east, Aspar the Alan, who made Leo the Thracian the eastern emperor in AD 457.

The empire was becoming increasingly fragmented. Either in the light of their military triumphs or as reward for co-operating with Roman generals, more and more barbarian kingdoms were starting to emerge, with Gaul in particular increasingly strong and independent, and recognising at most the nominal authority of Rome. Even where this was so, it was meaningless, for the legions were no longer capable of enforcing any domination over these emerging powers.

The story went on with monotonous predictability. Whether it was the Vandals capturing Sardinia or Euric and his Visigoths conquering Spain and Marseilles, everywhere the eagle hung its head in shame. Even when the western and eastern empires united in AD 468 in an attempt to defeat Genseric the Vandal in Africa, they failed. Germanic tribes invaded Italy, and the empire, especially in the west, continued to head towards its yawning grave. In Gaul, Clovis became King of the Franks in AD 481, establishing the Merovingian dynasty that would be one of the most important of these so-called Dark Ages in Europe. A few years later he hammered a Roman army sent to keep him in check at Soissons. Clovis was married to a Christian and would later be baptised. This was important as it demonstrated that many pagan warlords were prepared to adopt Christianity in an attempt to court legitimacy.

Only towards the end of the century did Rome find any sort of stability and by then the western empire was dead. In AD 476 the Roman emperor Romulus Augustulus was deposed by a Germanic chieftain, Odoacer. Romulus was the last truly Roman emperor. But, as the historian Michel Rouche noted, 'the Roman Empire of the West had expired, but at the time nobody noticed its passing'. This is true; there had been so much upheaval that the removal of yet another emperor cannot have seemed at the time to have permanently changed the face of Europe. And, although it was a crucial event, it was only one in a long series that had led to this point.

But if Rome died at all, the process of death was a long, drawn-out one. As another historian, Michel Fossier, noted with great prescience, great cultures do not die, they just grow old and mutate. He was right to emphasise the point. Rome's legacy lived on – and for that matter still does – in language, in legal systems, in art, in road networks (a number of roads in Britain, for example, still follow ancient Roman routes) and in a thousand and one other ways. This was indeed mutation, a continuation of Roman ways in new packaging, rather than death, even though the Rome that had spawned these great ideas and overseen a thousand years of development had now gone.

There was no doubt that, even though its influence lived on, the empire as it once was in all its glory was no more. The long process of decline continued. In AD 488, Theoderic the Great, leader of the Ostrogoths, crossed the Alps to attack Odoacer. He defeated him and took Milan. Fighting went on for years longer until in AD 493 Theodoric invited Odoacer and his son to a feast to discuss peace. He promptly assassinated them.

Now secure as the leader of Rome, Theodoric extended his realm to the western Balkans and Sicily, and started to govern independently, though remaining nominally subservient to the emperor. He was respectful to the Senate in Rome, and gave two-thirds of the land to the Romans, one-third to the Goths. He built himself a small palace in Ravenna. Nominally, Rome still had an emperor, Zeno, based in Constantinople. But it was an illusion for he had no power to enforce any such claim and his interests were decidedly in the east. Although a 'barbarian', Theodoric proved to be one of the greatest leaders of Rome – in fact if not in name – for many a year.

On the far side of the world, in a part of the globe still far out of the sight of Europe and Asia, the Mayan culture was beginning to advance. During the century a series of figures made their mark. They usually have names that we might more readily associate with Native American tribes of the north; Sun Born of the Sky, Stormy Sky or the more prosaically named Corrugated Nose, for example. However, although their names have survived, stories of their deeds are harder to find. Because of archaeology we know something of how they lived their lives; objects such as drinking cups or jade ornaments carved in the shape of animals give us an insight into aspects of their everyday existence, but not of their important actions in life.

But once more we can discern here that the story, as in previous centuries, is of independent cities that might have shared a culture but did not share a ruler. One of these was Tikal, the city of Stormy Sky, which established control over satellite towns 50 kilometres away. Another city that was established in about AD 426 was that of Cópan. This site is particularly important as surviving evidence links it to a great city in Central Mexico known as Teotihuacan. This was a hugely important centre with towering pyramids and enormous influence over much of Central America.

The nature of that influence, however, is sadly obscure. Whether it was extended through conquest or solely through peaceful cultural links remains one of the great debates for American historians. A number of different groups, not just the Maya but other less known peoples, such as the Totonacan culture, were also linked with Teotihuacan. Although much of the city's history is lost, its great ruins are not. They were revered by the Aztecs who came later, and they then astonished the Conquistadores when they invaded Mexico.

But the main focus on the shaping of the modern world continued to take place in Europe and Asia. Here, profound changes were about to take place. Europe was about to enter what was labelled (somewhat lazily) the Dark Ages, while India was to suffer some significant upheavals too. China would not emerge into the relative stability of the T'ang dynasty for over a hundred years. Yet for all the dramatic and, undoubtedly to many at the time, disturbing events that were about to take place, these forthcoming years would have their part to play in shaping the world in which we now live.

19

THE AGE OF ARTHUR?

Europe Begins to Take Modern Shape (AD 501–600)

We are about to enter what is known in the West as the Dark Ages. That name is unfortunate, for a casual interpretation of what might have occurred in these years might lead one to assume that nothing very important happened. It is too easy to see these years as ones in which little of significance took place, a period of no achievement best skimmed over as quickly as possible.

Many would go further than this, believing that the decline of Roman civilisation marked a return to barbarian values. This much is implicit in the approach to art and architecture in the period a thousand years later known as the Renaissance, which modelled itself extensively on the glories of Rome, as if harking back to a golden age long gone.

Yet although it is true that much was lost, it is a serious error to assume that nothing took its place save chaos. Chaos there was, but from it modern Europe emerged. If there is darkness, it is only because we know little of the detail of what happened. However, of what occurred at a high level we may be sure, and this is of crucial importance.

It is ironic that the best-known personality of the century might not actually have lived at all. Historians are agreed that, if the man known as 'King' Arthur lived at all then it was at the beginning of this sixth century, when the invasions of Saxons were starting to bite into British territory. Arthur, who was not a king at all even if he was a real historical figure, may have been a *dux bellorum* or *leader of the battles*, a cavalry commander who led his men successfully against the armies of the would-be conquerors. A near-contemporary writer, Gildas, wrote of twelve major victories against the Saxons that might well have related to Arthur, or so we might think. The only problem is that he does not mention Arthur at all.

It is not until several hundred years later that Arthur begins to be named, starting in the Welsh Easter Annals, which record key events in the manner of an almanac. He also gets a mention in the writings of Nennius, another later Welsh monk. A British poem from the Strathclyde region, written in the seventh century, talks of a great warrior, though noting that 'he was no Arthur', suggesting that the legend of Arthur was already well established. From such unconvincing scraps of information are we forced to attempt the construction of a hypothesis. It is all a long way removed from the Arthur of fairy-tale castles with his Knights of the Round Table, the creation of later medieval writers like Chrétien de Troyes and Thomas Mallory.

Putting the semi-mythical Arthur to one side, there were decisive events taking place in Europe, both east and west, throughout the century. In particular there would be a remarkable resurgence in the fortunes of the Roman Empire, followed by an almost as dramatic subsequent decline. Constantinople had become the inheritor of Roman civilisation yet it was a divided city, with tensions often at melting point between the various factions that characterised it.

It is tempting to think of violence attaching itself to sporting events as an exclusively modern phenomenon but this is not so. In sixth-century Constantinople outbreaks of fighting, brawling and often murder attached themselves to the events played out at the hippodrome, the great arena where chariot races took place (now a relatively quiet open space in front of Hagia Sophia in modern Istanbul, with just two columns surviving from antiquity to hint at its more illustrious past; its tranquillity contrasts markedly with the bustling nature of the rest of this sprawling city or the noisiness that would have typified it in antiquity). Two competing factions emerged, the Greens and the Blues, named after the colours that they wore. An outbreak of violence at the beginning of the sixth century involving these two factions was said to have left 3,000 dead. This does put modern football hooliganism into some kind of context.

As a result of the actions of these groups in Constantinople, what has been called a 'code of violence' developed, characterised by vandalism such as the destruction of public statues. There were not only brawls at the hippodrome; members of the factions regularly carved curses on lead tablets directed against their opponents. Of course, it was not just about sport. The Blues represented the interests of the palace, the Greens the city, simplifying itself as an ongoing squabble between rulers and plebs. These problems did not come out of nowhere; in the previous century there had often been food riots. As modern sports hooliganism is in part a manifestation of social tensions, so too were the outbreaks of violence in Constantinople in these times.

There were great social pressures facing the Eastern Roman Empire, as we shall see. This gave the Church a bigger role in providing charity to the poor, especially in the larger cities like Constantinople, Jerusalem (not large in population terms but hugely important in the Christian world), Alexandria and Antioch. The emperor when the century began was Anastasius, who put a great deal of effort into fortifying the walls around the city of Constantinople. He also adopted less popular measures when he put a stop to the fighting between wild animals and human beings that had taken place in the arenas for many a year.

The adhesive that glued the empire together was a highly effective bureaucratic administration which would largely rely on taxing the rural population. Traditionally payments would be made in kind, with grain or clothing for the army, for example. Anastasius had in the late fifth century made gold coin payment obligatory, but this was often overlooked in practice. Landowners were also required to provide services such as road maintenance as a part of their taxation requirement.

Religion played a key part in the Byzantine world. Byzantium was obsessed with demons, with threats to the soul, and existed in a climate of dark and brooding introspection. This was a Christianity that even at this early stage was showing marked differences from Catholicism. The role of the Pope was one area of contention, a point of dispute that would eventually create a gap the size of a chasm. Here in the east the patriarchs of Rome and Constantinople were given equal importance with each other, while other patriarchs, such as those of Antioch, Alexandria or Jerusalem were also treated as important.

However, even here the eastern patriarchs were often at each other's throats over doctrinal issues. The Monophysite philosophy, another of those incredibly intense debates about the nature of Christ that marked this period in Christianity's development, created widespread antagonism; there were, for example, riots against it in Constantinople in AD 512.

In a secular modern society it is hard to understand what all the fuss was about but in sixth-century Byzantium these debates were keenly and fiercely fought, and feelings ran very high. The eastern provinces in particular were more Monophysite in character than others, which helped to increase their theological distance from Rome. The urban bishops too were important pillars of the community, a significant calming influence and key in other ways through their involvement in urban building projects.

While the eastern part of the empire was taking on a new shape, in the west, Europe was largely unrecognisable from what had existed there two centuries before. Gaul and the Low Countries were especially changed. Various tribes had moved in and now fought over the land vacated by Rome. The Visigoths and the Franks in particular came to blows. In a vicious campaign between AD 507 and AD 510 the Visigoth king Alaric II was killed by the Frankish ruler Clovis at the Battle of Vouglé near Poitiers.

Yet it is interesting to note that Clovis was made a consul and a patrician by Anastasius. Though the writ of Rome (or, to be more accurate, Constantinople) did not extend in reality to Gaul, in theory this was still Roman land. It is particularly suggestive that Clovis was happy to be associated with the rule of the old empire and go through the formalities of being a notional vassal king. In practice, if he had chosen to declare total independence then there was little that the emperor could do about it. Anastasius had distractions elsewhere to keep him occupied. Between AD 502 and AD 506 he had been forced to fight a war in Armenia with a resurgent Persia. The war had an inconclusive result and a seven-year truce was signed. He could not be confident that it would hold.

In AD 511 Clovis died and left his empire to be divided by his four sons. He had established a new capital city at Paris, where he died. His wife retired to the church of St Martin in Tours. Rules of Frankish inheritance would play a significant part in future history. The requirement to divide lands between all sons would lead to a diminution in the power and vitality of the Frankish nation. In addition, a Salic law of the Franks which stated that 'of Salic land no portion shall go to a woman' would crucially affect future generations; Shakespeare made great play of this in his justification of the English king Henry V's invasion of France in 1415.

However, Gaul was not France. The boundaries of Clovis's kingdom were very different from those of the country we know now. They extended over the Rhine into part of what is now Germany. Here they came up against the Alemanni. This kingdom also took in the Low Countries. Although it extended to the Pyrenees in the south-west, in one area another tribe, the Burgundians, had an independent land of their own (Burgundy).

Rome, it appeared, had gone from the west forever. However, it was about to enjoy an extraordinary renaissance. This seemed highly improbable when in AD 515 the Huns broke through the Caspian Gates into Cappadocia in Asia Minor, only a few hundred miles to the east of Constantinople. They were continuing to have an influence on world affairs and were still creating persistent problems for those they came into contact with. Given their geographic dispersion, they continued to exert pressure on both Byzantium and Persia by their domination of the overland trade routes from China.

Anastasius died in AD 518, to be succeeded by an elderly figure, Justin. Justin had no heir and he left the management of state affairs to his nephew Justinian. One of his most significant acts occurred in AD 523 when he deprived pagans of all public offices. Three years later, a great general made his debut when a man named Belisarius was given his first task, to fight off the Persians.

In AD 527, Justinian succeeded as emperor and so began one of the great reigns of history. He was not necessarily a striking figure to look at, and was described as being of 'short stature, wide shoulders, flat nose, curly hair, a bit bald-headed, with a rounded face, mirthful, grey-haired, and a noble-minded defender of the Christian faith'.

By his side sat a great empress, Theodora. She came from an inauspicious background, being the daughter of a bear-keeper in the hippodrome. It was also widely believed that at an earlier stage she had been a prostitute. Looking at the magnificent mosaics at the church of St Vitalis in Ravenna, which depict both emperor and empress in their pomp, such humble, even vulgar, origins are hard to believe, yet the stories are consistent and frequent.

Justinian was a man of great energy; it was said that he never slept. He was deeply inspired by tradition and conservatism and had a great feel for Roman history. Perhaps it is fitting that in the year of his accession to the throne, a monk, Dionysus Exiguus, developed a dating system using the measurement of 'Anno Domini' – 'AD' – for the first time.

One of Justinian's first acts was to codify the law. The code of Justinian was not in any way innovative; it collated existing legislation (in a similar way in which the renowned lawgiver Hammurabi had acted thousands of years before). Its importance was in its definitiveness. This code was a point of reference for all future jurists to access. In case there was any danger of ongoing contestation on the law, Justinian had all the source documentation on which it was based destroyed. Soon after, he ordered the closure of the Platonic Academy of Athens. There was no room for philosophising in the eyes of this essentially conservative man. However, the loss of some great thinkers as a result of this rather draconian action had a benefit elsewhere, as many of those made homeless by Justinian's decision moved to Persia.

This was also a time when significant social changes in Byzantium accelerated. A movement to the towns had been a noticeable trend for some time and after AD 530 it seemed to gather strength. This led to some social problems. A law from Constantinople in AD 539 referred explicitly to recent rises in crime rates as well as a worrying influx of young and exploited prostitutes of peasant origin into the city (another tragic social trend that can still be seen in modern times, as sex trafficking from poor nations continues to be a problem).

Foreign affairs continued to dominate the empire though. In AD 530, Belisarius defeated the Persians at Dara. The year after, Chosroes I, probably the greatest of the Sassanid kings, came to the throne. There had been a period of bitter civil war preceding his accession, in which the north-eastern part of his empire (the lands around Bactria in Central Asia) had been much affected. These territories, centred on Balkh, threw off adherence to Zoroastrianism, the traditional religion of Persia, and instead embraced Buddhism. Balkh would allegedly become home to 3,000 Buddhist monks.

The internal disintegration of Persia that these wars were symptomatic of in the long run spelt supreme danger (and ultimately cataclysmic decline) for the ruling class in the country. This decline was delayed by the actions of Chosroes, although matters were too far gone for him to reverse the trend completely. He would prove a worthy opponent and emulator of Justinian. He too codified his law, created a standing army and improved the road system. He tolerated Christianity and surrounded himself with scholars from India and Greece, determined to create a reputation for learning in his court.

By now Belisarius had been recalled to Constantinople, having won the first of many victories for Byzantium. His presence was needed there. The city was in ferment, with open rebellion in the air. Disorder had been fomented by ongoing disputes between the Blues and Greens. The rebellion was ruthlessly put down. Justinian then patched up a peace with Persia, for he had ambitions elsewhere to occupy him and did not want an ongoing threat from the east to distract him.

The dream that drove him was the recreation of a world that appeared to most people to have gone for good; nothing less than the rebuilding of the old Roman Empire dominated his thoughts and motivated his actions, a cause in which he would be magnificently assisted by his superb general, Belisarius. The first target would be North Africa, now a territory held by Vandal barbarians who had crossed over from Spain.

It is important to note that many of the barbarian tribes were now Christians. However, Christianity itself was a source of dispute and on occasion downright hostility. Christendom at this stage was a collection of theoretically theologically united peoples divided by a common religion. The Arian heresy (as some saw it) had caused much bitterness within the Christian ranks, with some seeing its assertion that Christ was not of the same nature as God as a statement of common sense while others saw it as an outrage. The Vandals were in the Arian camp and had vigorously persecuted dissenters from these beliefs.

Between AD 533 and AD 534 Belisarius took the great symbolic prize of Carthage easily but was then recalled too early; Justinian soon developed an unwarranted jealousy of his triumphant commander. Belisarius later had to return and save the city from counter-attack. Elsewhere, events were going in Justinian's favour. The death of Athalric, king of the Goths, helped and only confirmed what was already suspected, that the Gothic kingdom was now in decline. Justinian was now inspired to up the odds considerably. After forming an alliance with the Franks, he sent Belisarius over the Mediterranean with the aim of reconquering Italy.

Belisarius's next port of call was Sicily, which he successfully subdued. Between AD 536 and AD 540 he then waged an all-conquering campaign on the mainland. He took Naples and then finally entered Rome, a dream becoming reality (though the city itself had lost much of its former glory, its name would live on forever). Witigis, king of the Ostrogoths, besieged him there for a year but at last gave up the unequal fight. Belisarius then returned to Constantinople, his reputation soaring to mountaintop heights on the back of his great victories. Not everyone was pleased though. Justinian was increasingly jealous of his success, and the relationship between the two men would become even more strained from then on.

When Belisarius came back to Constantinople, a spectacular new sight met his eyes, one that continues to inspire until this day. Between AD 531 and AD 537 the magnificent church of Hagia Sophia ('the sacred wisdom' – it is not and never has been called Saint Sophia, which does not stop travel guides and even the occasional historian from calling it such) had been rebuilt after the previous building had been destroyed by fire following a riot by the mob, in the aftermath of which Justinian's crushing response left 30,000 citizens dead.

Hagia Sophia's most famous feature was and is its magnificent dome. It rises 55 metres high above the floor and has a span of 77 metres. Today, it remains an awe-inspiring sight of immense scale, its vast walls being large enough to comfortably contain most other major churches in Christendom (although the dome has had to be rebuilt several times after damage from earthquakes and general wear). By the time it was finished, Justinian claimed to have outdone even Solomon. More than anything, it was a statement of a direct association between the emperor and the Almighty. It was fully in line with his philosophy as emperor; in his famous code he asserted his right as ruler to have supremacy over even the Church.

Yet if Hagia Sophia is the period's lasting architectural legacy to the world, the building of massive walls around the city was even more important. The walls, with huge towers spread along them, enclosed the land perimeter of the city, impenetrable armour against any barbarian horde that might come up against them. Even by the sea, walls were erected which would prove to be awe-inspiring barriers to rebuff any invader. Not for nearly seven centuries would they be breached.

But just when the triumph of Justinian appeared to be inevitable, another threat appeared to challenge his ultimate victory. In AD 539, Chosroes of Persia declared war on Byzantium. With the empire's forces occupied in the west, Chosroes enjoyed a successful campaign. Reasserting a symbolism last employed by Assyrian kings over a thousand years before, he signified his triumph in Asia by bathing in the Mediterranean. So harsh was the punishment inflicted on the region that archaeological evidence suggests that neither Antioch nor Aleppo ever fully recovered from the raids they suffered during the campaign. The year after, Chosroes raided further north. Justinian bought him off with large amounts of gold and negotiated a five-year peace.

For the truth was that Justinian had other urgent problems to address on the domestic front. A plague had reached Constantinople from Ethiopia via Egypt. It lasted from AD 541 to AD 544 and shortly afterwards was followed by an epidemic that decimated livestock. The empire also faced serious economic challenges. Given the parlous state of imperial finances, Justinian was forced to raise taxes, assisted by a hated finance minister, John of Cappadocia. He also introduced wage and price regulations.

But he continued to encourage trade with India. This had been helped in AD 527 when the leader of the White Huns had been deposed. The Hunnish invasions of India began to run out of steam and a degree of stability returned to the trade routes. In an attempt to develop the economy still further to take advantage of this, Justinian had new harbours built on the Black Sea. However, he was not always helped by his consort. Between AD 542 and AD 548, Theodora became a defender of public morality, building a shelter for fallen women. This in itself was not a problem. What was a problem was her opposition to her husband's religious orthodoxy, supporting the anti-establishment Monophysites and becoming a friend of the eastern rather than the western Church.

It is also important to note that references to a 'Dark Age', often ascribed to this period in history, have a very Eurocentric tinge to them. In Axum, for example, a sixth-century visitor wrote of the marvels he saw in what was now a very Christian land. Everywhere the writer, Cosmas Indicopleustes, saw 'churches of Christians, bishops, martyrs, monks and recluses by whom the Gospel of Christ is proclaimed' (modern Ethiopia, the descendant of Axum, still boasts one of the oldest branches of Christianity in the world and its conservative practices, when observed, seem immediately to provide an unbroken link with antiquity). Trade and contacts with Arabia were still vibrant and to a great extent Axum was shielded from the violent upheavals so obvious in the Mediterranean world. In fact, Axum was so strong that the country was able to launch an invasion across the Red Sea and occupy Yemen for fifty years during the sixth century.

Within Europe, holding on to Italy proved a greater problem for Justinian than taking it. Between AD 543 and AD 546 the Gothic king Totila raided the peninsula, taking Rome but sparing it from a sack. When he moved to Ravenna, Belisarius retook Rome but the fact that it had been lost in the first place did not augur well for the future. The Byztantines proceeded to beautify Ravenna, confirming it as the major city of Italy at the time. Justinian, anxious to reunite the eastern and western Churches, wrote an important theological commentary, *The Three Chapters*, trying to get the Pope in Rome to support its conclusions. As much as anything, it was an attempt by the emperor to reassert the unity of an empire that, like a phoenix, had emerged from the ashes of the shattered Rome of old.

However, it appears that all was still far from well between the emperor and his foremost general. When Belisarius was recalled to Constantinople, Totila took advantage of the vacuum left and took back most of Italy. In AD 550, a eunuch, Narses, was sent in place of Belisarius to combat Totila. Over the next three years, Narses defeated and killed Totila, and the Goths were finally ejected from Italy. But it was significant that Belisarius needed Lombard mercenaries to do it. Italy was financially ruined when the Gothic Wars ended. This was not, after all, the Rome of old; the city had an estimated population of 40,000. The Senate petered out, a shadow, barely discernible anymore, of the dominant body it had once been. When Justinian called an ecumenical council in Constantinople soon after, few western churchmen attended.

The latter part of Justinian's reign was devoted to more mundane matters. For example, rather than importing silk from China he instead imported silkworms as a way of breaking the Chinese monopoly over the trade. A silk industry was started in Syria and also in the Peloponnese, where the region of Morea was named after the mulberry tree so important to the manufacture of the fragile material. But this was a harsh, uncertain world and when plague and famine hit Constantinople between AD 556 and AD 558, Justinian turned increasingly to theology. This world, he fully appreciated, was transient in its glories.

Justinian also had further barbarian incursions to contend with. In AD 558, a group that had played little part in earlier movements appeared on the scene, more warriors from the steppes of Central Asia known as the Avars. In that year, they sent a mission to Constantinople and some of their warriors ended up by serving in Byzantine armies. In the following year, more barbarian horsemen appeared, Bulgars who crossed the Danube and advanced on Constantinople. With little option, Justinian recalled the out-of-favour old warrior Belisarius who, with a small force, brilliantly saved the city.

The Byzantines and their emperor sought to reinforce their position and were not too choosy about how they did it. In AD 562, Chosroes of Persia and Justinian signed a fifty-year peace agreement. Under the terms of the deal struck, Chosroes would be paid 30,000 gold pieces a year, in return for which he would renounce his claims to territories around the Black Sea and Caucasus. It was not long before Belisarius was back in disfavour. The year after this deal was agreed, he was imprisoned for six months on a charge of conspiracy but then released. Two years later he was dead. In a final, vindictive act, Justinian confiscated half of his property. Justinian himself died in November, to be replaced by his nephew Justin II.

It was a magnificent reign in which large chunks of territory had been re-appended to the empire in a way that was unthinkable just a few years before. It had been a marvellous period of achievement, on the home as well as the international front. But much of the triumph was attributable to Belisarius, a man of genius whose contribution to the emperor's glory cannot be overstated (though Justinian does not appear to have particularly appreciated the fact). Justinian's reign had been magnificent, though his shabby treatment of Belisarius diminished the emperor somewhat. However this was no rebirth, no new Golden Age, but the last glorious moment of an empire that was in its death throes. Byzantium would live on, at times gloriously, at times not, for another 900 years, but Rome was dead.

By AD 567, the barbarians were back in Italy. Lombard tribes, pressed by the Avars, crossed the Alps into the plains by the River Po, reaching what would eventually be called Lombardy. There were simply no troops there to fight them off. Some of the residents of the peninsula fled, a group of them setting up home in a marshy lagoon by the Adriatic where they would, they hoped, be safe. These were the very first beginnings of what would become the great city of Venice. But by AD 573, most of Italy had been lost by the Byzantines once more. This time, there would be no revival.

Byzantium also had to contend with Persia once more. In AD 571, Chosroes, that long-lived and able king, ejected the Ethiopians from the parts of Arabia that they had been controlling for some time. They had first moved in from Axum in AD 525, making the short crossing of the Red Sea to destroy the local Himyarite monarchy that had previously ruled there. They had been encouraged to do so by the Byzantines, hoping to profit from having an ally in control of the potentially troublesome lands of the desert to the south, independent and warlike Arab tribes who did not take kindly to efforts to keep them on a leash.

At around the same time, a boy was born in Mecca, centre of pagan tradition in the peninsula, the home of the fierce Quryash tribe, proudly protective of their culture and traditions. Unremarked upon at the time, the birth of Mohammed would have enormous long-term consequences. However, this was still in the future. Faced with a resurgent threat from Chosroes, Justin II renewed the war with Persia. In the following few years, the ageing Chosroes achieved some success against the Byzantine armies. When Justin died in AD 574, he was replaced by Tiberius. His strategy was simple: face up to Persia and let the west takes its chances against the barbarians.

By AD 578, the Byzantines under their general Maurice had defeated Chosroes, who retired to Ctesiphon. When Chosroes died the year after, he left a sound administration in Persia that would be largely inherited by the Muslims when they burst onto the scene over half a century later. Sensing a weakness following the death of this vastly experienced ruler, Maurice continued his campaigns against Persia, winning many victories in the process.

Given Maurice's victories, it was no surprise when he took the place of Tiberius when the emperor died in AD 582. But Byzantium had deep-rooted problems to face. In AD 588, the army mutinied against Maurice because of problems over pay. Maurice also tried to impose religious orthodoxy, in particular in Armenia and Mesopotamia, by force if necessary; it was an effort to maintain unity, but in this it was also counter-productive.

Barbarian incursions continued to add to the pressure. Slavs in particular had flooded into the Balkans, an event that had a profound future effect on the region and its racial composition. During the reign of Justinian the great emperor had been forced to build sixty-eight fortresses in his native Dardania (now in the region of Kosovo) alone to keep them out. They had already reached Corinth by AD 578 though the Avars had been bought off with generous amounts of protection money.

Persia had started to disintegrate after the death of Chosroes I. Chosroes II, who succeeded in AD 590, was displaced for a short time by a Persian general, Bahram. Chosroes fled to

Syria, where he sought Byzantine protection. Maurice, glad to have a young ruler on the throne of an arch-rival, restored the crown to him, hoping to have an inexperienced puppet whom he could dominate as a neighbour. Maurice then returned to the Balkans, which the Avars had started to infiltrate, and drove the barbarian invaders back.

By the time the century drew to a close, Maurice was finding it difficult to raise enough men to face the Avars, who had been killing the hostages that they had been holding. Manpower would be a perennial problem for Byzantium, as also would the wide extent of the territories notionally under its control. By this time Byzantine-held territories in both Italy (which were now little more than a rump) and Africa had governors with a high degree of autonomy, unmistakable signs that the dispersed empire was proving difficult to hold.

Now largely isolated, a lonely ship in the middle of a barbarian sea, the diminished city of Rome was home to an institution that would slowly rise to a position as powerful as any in Europe. In AD 590, a man named Gregory became Pope, the first monk to do so. He rigorously enforced the celibacy of the clergy, confirming in practice what had existed in theory for a while. He also diverted Church money to charity rather than grandiose building schemes, which had been the focus of expenditure in the past.

In AD 596, moved by some young Angle slaves (he called them 'angels' in a quite appalling pun) for sale in the marketplace at Rome, he sent one of his clerics, Augustine, to reconvert the English, whose faith had been substantially lost due to the arrival of pagan Saxons and Angles. When he arrived in England the following year, Augustine failed to ally himself with the native Christians who were there (a small group already existed) but was nevertheless well-received by Ethelbert, King of Kent, and his Christian Frankish wife Bertha. Allowed to evangelise, Augustine became the first Archbishop of Canterbury.

However, the Church owed much to the tenacious and dedicated efforts of the Celtic Church in Ireland. While invasion after invasion swept over the virtually undefended borders of Europe, on its very edge Christianity found a foothold which would act as a protector of its young traditions. The monks on whom Christianity depended lived spartan, self-denying lives, often in out-of-the-way places, none more so perhaps than the remote Skellig Michael, an isolated rock off the south-west coast of Ireland and the last stopping point before the wide open spaces of the Atlantic and the as yet undiscovered lands of America.

In the same year that Gregory sent his mission to England (AD 597), far to the north an Irish Christian evangelist, Columba, died on the sacred isle of Iona off the coast of Scotland, where he had founded a highly influential establishment from which in the future many missionaries would go out and preach. He was the spearhead of a peaceful Christian invasion of Britain from the north. This onslaught had been launched from Ireland and involved a particular brand of monasticism based on some of the very first eremitical principles. This made its way southwards into the northern part of what we now call England. The new breed of Christianity, the non-Celtic version introduced by Augustine in the south, slowly spread north. Before long, the two would be in vigorous theological conflict.

The monastic movement was to play a crucial role in the protection and development of knowledge in Europe. From the early reclusive hermits who had gone to live in remote places in the deserts of Egypt and Syria (and were then emulated in places on the other side of Europe like Ireland), new monastic movements were to develop and formulate rules by which the monks who chose to live in communities should live – St Benedict and his Benedictines being a particular example. They became centres for knowledge as well as religion – for example, many orders insisted that monks who were illiterate when they joined should quickly be taught, to rectify the shortcoming.

Across what we now call Asia, some decisive events had taken place, or at least some decisive outcomes had been achieved. By the century's close, Japan had become one culture and nation, a huge step forward in the formation of what would eventually become a regional giant, though that eventual conclusion was a long way off.

However, although subsequent Japanese history would be typified by an inward-looking stance, outside factors had played a key part in uniting Japan. Not for the last time in history, the close proximity of Korea on the Asian mainland assumed significance. The dynasty that brought Japan together, the Soga, came from a Korean bloodline. They also brought over a number of priests to cement the creation of what was effectively a state religion.

In our modern world, in a post-religious phase in some parts of the globe at least, we have perhaps lost sight of the importance of religion as the mortar that can hold society together. Religion as a unifying factor was of course not a new tactic; Constantine had done the same in Europe a few centuries before, while many centuries earlier Akhenaten had alienated his people when he tried the same in Egypt. In AD 592, the Japanese emperor Shotoku had given his country a written constitution based on Buddhist teachings. His reign also encouraged the arts and sponsored the growth of learning by bringing in scholars from Korea and China.

The Soga undoubtedly saw Buddhism as a way of confirming their own political authority, and the imperial power became closely connected with the state religion in a way that associates of the Emperor Hirohito in the twentieth century would surely have recognised. In many ways, the Japanese practice of statecraft began to emulate that of China, almost in a way that suggested that the fledgling nation wanted to establish its credentials and legitimise itself by copying the example of a much longer-established power.

Yet ironically, as a form of stability was introduced into Japan, China continued on its roller-coaster ride through history. In AD 549, the Buddhist emperor of south China, Liang Wu-ti, saw his capital Nanking overrun by rebels. The cycle of disintegration followed by closer integration proceeded apace. Forty years later China was reunited under Wen-ti of the short-lived Sui dynasty.

Although still concentrated on its own internal affairs primarily, the influence of the outside world continued to shape China. A Sui cave shrine from the period has pronounced Hellenistic Buddhist influence; a Greek artistic influence allied to an Indian religious one being recognised in China is compelling evidence of a degree of wide cultural interchange.

It was not that the Sui were without their own ideas. They introduced the Equal-Field system, an attempt to reduce the gap between rich and poor with a surprisingly progressive ring about it. Buddhism spread here too. Most ambitious of all was an amazing engineering project. A Grand Canal across China had existed in part since the fifth century AD. The Sui now brought it together as one huge waterway. At over 1,100 miles long, it became the longest canal in the world.

However, in the event this scheme became symbolic of the reasons why the Sui were doomed to fail. In its own way, the Sui Grand Canal was rather like the pyramids of Egypt: a massive drain on resources that could not be afforded. The Sui years were typified by a ruthless centralised control, epitomised by the standardisation of coinage, which may have been a good idea in economic terms but also was a way of tightening state control.

The Sui overreached themselves, embarking on ambitious and ultimately catastrophically expensive wars. They quickly lost their vitality and it was not long after this ebbed away that they lost control of China too. Unpopular because of their exploitation, the people turned on the Sui and turfed them out after three short decades of power typified by amazing energy but ultimate self-destructiveness.

The major event of this period to affect India was the demise of the Gupta dynasty, which had been in power from around AD 300. Despite their longevity and eminence, they remain an enigma. They left no great architectural edifices to provide material evidence of their strength and little is known of their administration, their policies or their domestic or international adventures. Their greatest legacy, interestingly, is the world's foremost sexual encyclopaedia, the *Kama Sutra*.

Even the manner of their death left little mark on history. There was no final, dramatic denouement, no massive funeral pyre on which their culture was incinerated. It was a long, unremarkable demise, hastened no doubt by Hunnish incursions in the north but brought about ultimately by exhaustion and old age. Yet their legacy lives on in other, largely unrecognised ways. By AD 516, the Indian astronomer and mathematician Aryabhata was writing on eclipses, quadratic equations and the power of Pi. And at some time towards the end of the century, Indian mathematicians started using the number zero in their calculations.

Although much change had taken place in recent times, nothing had given warning of what was about to appear. Yet in the long run, the demise of Rome and the ongoing struggles to survive in Persia and Byzantium had started to create a vacuum. Into this vacant space a new power was about to emerge, creating a vital energy and force, the impact of which would resonate down to the core of international politics into our own era. No part of the world would be unaffected by it in the end. The youngest great religion was about to evolve and the world would never be the same as a consequence.

20

A NEW WORLD POWER

The Emergence of Islam (AD 601–700)

Recent decades had seen the growth of tensions between Byzantium and Persia, frequently leading to campaigns between them both which were both expensive and debilitating for each side. The pendulum would swing wildly from one side to the other, with Persians and Byzantines enjoying short-term ascendancy for a while before the balance swung back again. Although it was only obvious in retrospect, this was very dangerous and for one of the combatants indeed fatal, for their obsessive concentration on each other meant that both Persia and Byzantium failed to watch their backs just at the crucial moment when a new world power was emerging.

In the face of the Persian threat, Byzantium seemed to show every sign of wanting to commit political suicide. A revolt under Phocas in AD 602 saw the army turning on the current emperor, Maurice. Maurice tried to appease the all-powerful mob by the old technique of laying on lavish games for their entertainment – one leftover of old Roman politics, where he who controlled the mob could also hope to control power. But Maurice's attempts did not work and, after his failure, he fled across the Bosporus to seek help from Byzantium's arch-enemy, the young Persian king Chosroes II.

Phocas's supporters caught up with Maurice before he could make good his escape from Byzantine territory and promptly killed him. Given his attempts to consort with the enemy, this was completely understandable. But it gave Chosroes a good excuse to march on Phocas, as Maurice had become his ally. Chosroes took full advantage of the opportunity. Large tracts of territory in Asia Minor were seized by the Persians and the power of Byzantium tangibly continued to evaporate.

The Byzantines were quick to seek to change weak and unsuccessful emperors, something which makes the longevity of their world one of the more remarkable feats of history. Maurice's deposition did not seem to improve matters significantly, if at all. By AD 609, the Byzantines sought another change and the son of the governor of Roman Africa, a young man named Heraclius, moved on Constantinople, displaced Phocas and set himself up as emperor instead.

At first, it seemed that the disastrous demise of Byzantium would continue. Chosroes II in AD 614 took the Holy City of Jerusalem, unleashing shattering violence on its inhabitants in the process. The comprehensiveness of the sack that followed was horrific and mirrored that inflicted on it by the Romans centuries earlier and that which would be visited upon it by the Crusaders nearly half a millennium later. It was a triumph that humiliated the Christian faith as the Persians seized the relic of the True Cross, one of Christendom's most sacred symbols. Egypt and most of Asia Minor also fell to Chosroes in the next few years.

The usurper Heraclius seemed an unlikely saviour during his first decade in power. He appeared powerless to drive back the Persian surge but he also faced challenges from other directions. By AD 618 the Avars were at the very gates of Constantinople and the emperor himself barely escaped capture. Persia was clearly in the ascendancy in the fierce conflict that was being fought, and demanded a heavy price, including 1,000 horses and 1,000 virgins, for peace. Byzantium hung on grimly.

These terrible reverses for Byzantium gave absolutely no hint of what was to come. In one of the great campaigns of history, between AD 622 and AD 625 Heraclius launched an incredible fightback. Helped by the fact that an ageing Chosroes had effectively retired from campaigning, all the losses Byzantium had experienced were reversed. It was a change in fortunes that was so unexpected that it seemed little short of miraculous.

The battle that appeared to cement the ultimate triumph of the Byzantines took place against the Persians at Nineveh in AD 627. But perhaps the greatest victory for the religiously motivated emperor was the retaking of Jerusalem, when he restored the sacred city to Christian ownership. As he rode through the streets of the Holy City in triumph, Heraclius could barely imagine that he would lose it again for good a few years later to a power that few in the world were as yet even aware of.

Persia was dying as a result of these wars, emaciated and starved of resources. The end of Chosroes II was tragic and brutal in its cruelty. He was overthrown by his own son, Kavad, and forced to watch while all his other sons were slaughtered in front of him. Then he suffered an agonisingly slow death, being shot to death with arrows. It was a bitter end but it would soon, in its own way, be avenged.

Quite what crime Chosroes had committed against Kavad is unclear but it must have been awful to merit such terrible retribution (though it is notable that Chosroes himself came to power by playing a part in the murder of his own father, King Hormizd IV). However, he was himself a vicious man – he had reputedly had the king of an enemy crushed to death beneath the feet of elephants – and perhaps his own excesses motivated others to be equally savage in return.

The peoples of the Arabian peninsula had not as yet made a dramatic long-term impact on history outside of their own region and its environs. It was true that they had earned a reputation as great traders and had played a part in developing mercantile activity between east and west. However, cut off to some extent by the vastness of the deserts, they had never yet been at the very heart of world affairs. There was some Arab involvement in these wars between Byzantium and Persia, but only peripherally. Little more than mercenaries, Ghassanids from Syria fought on the Byzantine side and the Lakhmids of Iraq with the Persians. Mecca remained the only independent Semitic city, guarded by the desert and the fierce protectionism of the Quryash tribe.

The tribes living in the Arabian Peninsula were epitomised by strong values of loyalty and honour as well as a pride in the uniqueness of their Arabic culture. It was in this relatively isolated society that a rich man by the name of Mohammed developed a new creed. Supported by his wife and protected by his father-in-law, he evolved a new set of doctrines based on the concept of the oneness of God and direct communication with the power of the Almighty, Allah.

This creed became known as Islam – 'submission'. It was a religious force with little initial focus on social revolution and even less on any forms of nationalism, although that would soon change. It was founded on a monotheistic purity of approach, in stark contrast to the convoluted and increasingly rhetorical nature of Christian theology. However, the Arabs had been affected by both Judaism and Christianity and this reflected itself in the evolution of the new faith.

When Mohammed's family were in danger of persecution in the early years of the new creed, they fled to Christian Ethiopia for safety. However, alongside its radicalism this apparently radical faith played on old links and traditions too, which had been paganised over time but were nevertheless very influential traditions as far as the evolution of Islam was concerned, and this helped to strengthen its position. This traditionalism is manifested, for example, in the reverence for the Kaaba, the sacred rock in Mecca with its associations with Abraham who, as a wanderer, was particularly attractive to a society where many were nomadic Bedouins.

If Islam's initial aims were not social revolution, it was not long before this position changed. Among early reforms introduced by Mohammed was a ban on the exposure of unwanted female babies, a feature of Arabian life previously. Islam was undoubtedly religious in its inspiration but, like all great faiths, would soon lead to political and social reform. Many of its original impetuses were egalitarian and revolutionary. Key to it was the *ummah*, the community of the loyal and faithful.

A seminal event in the evolution of the new faith was Mohammed's exile from Mecca. With the death of his father-in-law, he lost the protective influence that had previously shielded him from those who did not take kindly to his teachings. He managed to make his way to Medina, and while he was there he developed his philosophy still further and attracted new followers to his cause. This act of exile, the *Hegira*, was so important that it was used as the year from which the Islamic calendar started. So the date of the *Hegira* (24 September AD 622) became the first official day in the life of Islam and the point in time from which all future events in the new faith took their base date.

Islam became very militarised, with new concepts of total war that were in stark contrast with the rather gentlemanly arrangement of conflict in Arabia before that date. Decisive warfare had not in the past been an aim of military strategists in the Arabian world; now that position was turned on its head. As a result, it was not long before Mohammed was able to launch a successful attack on Mecca, which then became the focal point from which to launch further expansive activity.

Mohammed introduced the rituals of the *hajj*, pilgrimage, to Mecca, reclaiming the city from pagan overtones. Pagan idols in the city were suppressed in an act of symbolic purification. The rituals the Prophet introduced included seven circumambulations of the

Kaaba; seven trips between Safa and Mawat; prayer on the sacred mountain of Arafat; the stoning of Satan in the Valley of Mina; and, lastly, a sacrifice to complete this extended act of worship and submission.

However, if Mecca was the religious centre then Medina was Islam's first political capital. Here the first mosque was built. It would be the prototype for all others built afterwards. The mosque is a rather unique combination of enclosed building and surrounding enclosure, a place where the secular and the religious not so much exist side by side but merge imperceptibly, one into the other. In the great mosques of the world, such as the Umayyad mosque in Damascus, the Great Mosque in Cairo or the Blue Mosque in Istanbul, the glory of the experience is as much in the perambulations across the surrounding courtyards as it is in the rarefied atmosphere of the solemn and elegant but sometimes austere interior.

Here, the community came together as one, collectively acting out their forms of ritual worship. They sat together in lines, seated on the floor, the great and the meek, undifferentiated. Only the teacher, the *imam*, was separated, as befitted the leader of the flock. Symbolically, the Prophet himself was always present in his seat, the *minbar*. The architectural pattern that all mosques followed was one that was square, neat and, at its heart, fortified.

The oldest Muslim building now standing in the world is the Dome of the Rock, built between AD 688 and AD 691 at the heart of Jerusalem as Islam expanded dramatically. It is right in the middle of what one modern magazine called 'the most explosive piece of real estate in the world'. It was on the site of Solomon's Great Temple, in the same city in which the Christ of the Christians was killed.

It is not difficult to understand why this magnificent statement of faith has been a cause of division for so long. However conciliatory most faiths might claim to be, adherents of each of them will see their way as the only true path to enlightenment, salvation or whatever other term might be applied to it. For Muslims, this is a truly sacred place, built on the rock from which Mohammed ascended into heaven in a vision. It remains one of the most emotive pieces of architecture in the world.

So much of Islam's architecture, what of its core doctrines? Much was emulated from other religions at the higher level if not in the detail. There were (and are) at its heart five core beliefs, the Pillars. The first is that there is only one God and Mohammed is his Prophet; this put it rather closer to Judaism than Christianity, with its Trinitarian dogma, which was anathema to the Muslims.

Then there was the importance of ritual prayer, hardly unique in the annals of religious history. The concept of fasting was important too, hence the month of Ramadan, when strict rules of fasting apply. This took existing Jewish practices around the Feast of the Passover to much greater lengths and the underlying concepts of self-denial are also reflected in Christian beliefs, such as fasting during the period of Lent. The fourth Pillar was that of pilgrimage. This was also not of itself new; believers of many faiths have visited the holy places of their religion for millennia, hoping to gain some vicarious benefit as a result.

The last Pillar was that of the giving of charitable alms, at a rate that was prescribed as 10 per cent of earnings (reflecting the percentage normally applied to the Christian tithe). This emphasised the fact that the religion was concerned with the care of others and supporting the religious establishment as well as one that was undoubtedly in possession of militaristic tendencies.

There were other good practices outlined in the sayings of the Prophet, the *hadith*. Other important beliefs included that of *jihad*, one that symbolised the inner struggle of man for the triumph of his soul over his animal instincts but later came to be irrevocably associated with the struggle of Islam against other faiths. Circumcision and the prohibition of eating certain foods such as pork, both adopted from Judaism, also became part of the new faith.

In social terms, Islam allowed polygamy, with up to four wives permitted, each of whom would enjoy equal rights in all areas including that of the boudoir; sensual enjoyment was never an issue for Islam as it had been for some of the more extreme Christian sects. Paradise was stocked with perpetual virgins who attended to the every need of the righteous; anything further removed from the austerity of the Christian heaven would be difficult to imagine.

It was one thing to found Islam and create its power base, another to maintain its unity. As the French scholars Bresc and Guichard perceptively noted, the problem was 'how to define the legitimacy of power'. Put more simply, when Mohammed died, who was to succeed him? Another wider question should also be addressed; for how long was Islam a unifying influence?

The answer, in common with many other faiths (Christianity most definitely included), was 'not long'. The power of Islam, as in all religions, is in the force of a potentially unifying idea. Constantine recognised as much when he introduced Christianity as a state religion and so too did the Soga dynasty in Japan and the Sui in China. But there is a paradox, for these tendencies towards unity typically soon turn to disuniting pressures emphasising differences rather than similarities between sects within the faith.

Islam came along at a propitious moment when the two great powers to the north, Byzantium and Persia, were in the early stages of state senility, an inexorable and one-way journey of decline towards eventual extinction. As a result, Islam was not strangled at birth but instead fed on the weakness of its neighbours and voraciously consumed them. However, like all revolutionary movements (and not just religious ones; communism provides an equally apt example – both are ideologies) the early euphoria drives the emergent creed on to initial victory. But then it is only a matter of time before factions emerge, each unhappy with the philosophies of the other and soon becoming inimically opposed to them.

But this is to get ahead of ourselves. At the beginning of the seventh century there was no Islam. By its close, it dominated Arabia, the eastern coast of the Mediterranean and much of North Africa, Persia and large chunks of Central Asia. How did this happen?

It was through the unique coincidence of an amazing, dynamic energy emerging from the desert lands and the cataclysmic demise of those two old powers of Persia and Byzantium, though the latter managed to hang on to life by its fingertips. Yet, irony of ironies, the great man who gave life to this new force did not live to see this amazing destiny fulfilled. It was not until AD 630 that the Prophet entered Mecca. Two years later he was dead.

His place was taken by Abu Bekr as caliph or 'representative'. In the beginning, it seemed that he might not even hold on to Arabia and a rebellion needed to be put down. But then

Arabs in Syria asked for help against the Byzantines and an era of conquest began, with little thought as to a master plan. Abu Bekr also did something else which had an impact that still reverberates down the centuries; he had the teachings of Mohammed formulated into the Quran.

The military power behind the fledgling Arab army was a general named Khalid who made great use of wonderfully effective cavalry forces. He first of all raided Persian territory and then moved to Syria. It was here in AD 634 that one of the decisive battles in history was fought by the banks of the River Yarmuk. The army of the Byzantines were commanded by Vahan the Armenian, at the head of a force of up to 20,000 men.

What followed was such an extended battle that it was almost a small campaign in its own right. It lasted for six days. In the early stages of the fight, the Muslim forces were at some points on the verge of retreat and it was only, it was said, the haranguing of their womenfolk that drove them back into battle. Although the exact course of the battle is somewhat unclear, it seems as if it was on the fourth day that fortunes started to turn. By the next day, Vahan was trying unsuccessfully to negotiate a Muslim withdrawal.

There was a legend that a sandstorm on the sixth day led to final Byzantine defeat. Some of the army were killed either in battle or by plunging down the steep cliffs by the River Yarmuk but many just fled. Syria and the lands beyond were now wide open to Muslim conquest. After this amazing triumph Jerusalem soon fell, to be followed by much of the surrounding territory. By AD 640, the Muslim armies had moved in to Egypt. Islam simplistically divided the world into two: *Dar al-Islam*, the House of Islam, where the faith had been established, and *Dar al-Harb*, the Land of War, where it had not.

Persia by this stage was already virtually conquered. In AD 637, the Persian general Rustam was defeated by Islamic forces at a battle at Kadasiya. It was a shattering blow for the Sassanid regime that ruled Persia, and presaged their demise in very quick time. A final and decisive battle was fought just five years later and the age-old empire of the Persians was no more. Incredibly, the country was now in Arab hands.

The Arabs came from the desert but they were quick to make their impact in an urban setting. New towns emerged such as Basra, from which trading missions would soon be setting out for India. A great city re-emerged, one of the world's oldest; Damascus would soon become the supreme political capital of Islam, though Mecca would always remain the beating heart of its spiritual existence.

But Islam was cursed by the same problems that beset many new religions, that of internal division and debate. As it turned out, to conquer militarily was far easier than to triumph theologically. Or perhaps it all came down to a very human quest for power among the potential successors of Mohammed. At any event, the murder of the caliph Omar in AD 644 was an ominous sign of serious problems ahead for Islam and heralded bitter and brutal struggles for dominance.

It was only a few decades before Islam had divided into a number of divergent groups. At the highest level, three might be broadly discerned (though, again in common with most faiths, smaller and more radical extreme sects would also form, adding to this overall number). There were first of all the purists, those who believed that the initial pure beliefs of Islam had been quickly corrupted as power was gained and turned the heads of the victors. This group was known as the Kharijites. Then there was the party that supported the concept that the caliph (the ultimate leader of Islam and the heir to Mohammed) should be from the line of Ali, the Prophet's son-in-law. These were known as the party of Ali, more widely recognised as the Shia.

There was a third party, those of more moderate and consensual persuasion. During the latter part of the seventh century, as Islam sought for its true soul, they gathered around the standards of the ruler of Damascus, a man named Muawiya, from whom they took their name, the Umayyads. Hussein, the young son of Ali, marooned in Mecca, decided to move to Iraq to face up to the threat of Umayyads. In response, a much larger army moved out to meet him.

They met near the city of Karbala in AD 680 (the year 61 in the new Islamic calendar) in what would be, in terms of its long-term effects, one of the truly great battles of history. The numbers involved were small but the impact was ultimately so profound that it echoes down to this day. Hussein made no attempt to escape and was slaughtered along with his small band of adherents. The Umayyads were triumphant but their victory was far from complete, for they had completely underestimated the power of a martyr.

Martyrdom is one of the most powerful inspirers of emulation that there is. Christ himself was a martyr whose sacrifices continue to inspire Christians. The martyrdom of Hussein similarly moved his followers and made them determined to fight on. They dressed themselves in black and the movement as a whole moved towards more millenarian and radical tendencies. There on the dusty plains of Karbala the Shia–Sunni split was made permanent; over thirteen centuries on, the scars left by it are as vivid and important as ever.

Despite the lesson, all too often we still do not understand the power of a martyr. Basic human instincts are often driven by thoughts of revenge, and such motivators, understandable though they often are, can have very negative long-term results. Martyrs become symbols of resistance with the power to inspire men to die for a cause; think of the Scottish freedom fighter William Wallace, for example. Think too of Hussein, whose martyrdom is still keenly felt many centuries later.

Islam's triumphs had brought the faith into contact with other worlds. By the middle of the seventh century, Arab warriors had conquered lands as remote as Transoxiana in Central Asia, always a frontier zone, where, before the coming of Islam, Buddhism and Zoroastrianism had competed for religious supremacy. It also brought Islam flush against Chinese territory. It could only be a matter of time before a clash resulted.

In the other direction, Islam moved unstoppably along the southern Mediterranean coast, hungrily devouring the coastal regions of North Africa as it went. Raids against Carthage were launched in AD 648, though it was not until AD 692 that the full-scale invasion of North Africa began. When it did, the underpowered Byzantine regimes there were incapable of stopping the Muslim armies for long. The Arabs had also quickly developed seafaring skills and by the middle of the century they were attacking Cyprus. Thirty years later, they were launching their first raid on Spain at the other end of the Mediterranean.

By AD 653, they had captured Rhodes and taken away what remained of the great Colossus, one of the remaining ancient Wonders of the World that had survived from antiquity. Between AD 673 and AD 680 they laid a desultory and ultimately unsuccessful siege against Constantinople, which was always a hugely iconic target for Muslim forces, but the fact that they got there at all speaks volumes for the comprehensiveness of their initial triumphs. These were evidenced in other ways; for example, by the end of the century the official language of Damascus had changed from Greek to Arabic.

Constantinople, the city that the great Constantine had founded, the heir of all that had been great in Rome, appeared to be on its last legs. There were two things alone that saved the city from conquest by the forces of Islam. The first was the inexperience of the attackers in the arts of siege warfare, which meant that they were unable to breach the towering walls that protected the city. The legacy of Justinian continued to be a powerful one.

The second was one of the most fearsome weapons of medieval war. It was a chemical substance known as Greek fire, a weapon so powerful that once its flames took hold of something it was almost impossible to put them out. Given its chemical composition, even water was useless against it. No wonder it has been described as the nuclear weapon of the medieval age. It took five years for the besiegers to be fought to a standstill but at the end of it Byzantium emerged in the ascendant again – in its own backyard at least.

It was something of a miracle that Byzantium not only survived this early Islamic attempt to bring its life to an end but would also live on for more than half a millennium despite its own best efforts to destroy itself. To be an emperor of Byzantium was to take on one of the most dangerous roles imaginable. In AD 688 Justinian II took the throne, soon after defeating the Islamic armies (already called 'Saracens') and wresting back Armenia from them.

Despite this success, Justinian II was later deposed, having his nose cut off and being sent off into exile; he had been a harsh and unpopular ruler, leading one modern historian to describe him as 'a monster whose only attributes were a pathological suspicion of all around him and an insatiable thirst for blood'. Then his successor, Leontius, suffered a similar fate of deposition, also losing his nose in the process.

It was part of a trend for Byzantine emperors, who would over the centuries be deposed at a sometimes alarming rate, regularly suffering mutilation in the process. Such acts were deemed to be sufficient to deprive the emperor of the necessary accoutrements to be a ruler (blinding would become a particularly popular method) and death was often, though not always, avoided as a result. However, there were exceptions to the general rule that mutilation debarred an emperor from reclaiming his throne, as we shall see.

Byzantium was in increasing contact with further-flung corners of the world. The founding of the T'ang dynasty in AD 618 marked another change of direction in China, the first emperor of this new ruling class being known as T'ai-tsung. To some extent, this change in government saw an opening up to the outside world. Between AD 628 and AD 635, missionaries from Byzantium reached the kingdom, as well as Nestorian equivalents from Persia.

Nestorianism was an offshoot of Christianity with a particularly eastern emphasis that would later become popular with many Mongols when that empire was in its heyday, leading to quite ridiculous assumptions that they would be ready to participate in a joint crusade against a common Muslim enemy. It proved particularly resilient in the east, though Catholics and Orthodox Christians alike would regard supporters of the creed as little better than heretics.

The T'ang took over from the Sui a China that was theoretically united. No one could doubt the Sui's ambitions, but they were in fact requiring too high a price to be paid. An expedition against Korea in AD 612 reputedly required an army that was over 1 million strong, and the huge resources required resulted in rebellions from within an overstretched state. This would bring the dynasty crashing down, excessive ambition again proving a death warrant for a state that did not know when or where to stop.

Delegations from Islam also reached China within a very short time of the new religion's conception. Neither was the process of interchanging ideas all one-way. A Chinese traveller named Hsüan-tsang reached India in AD 629 and sent back positive reports on prosperity and good government from there. The world continued to shrink, with ideas flowing from west to east and east to west alongside a growing trade in exotic goods that the wealthier inhabitants of Central Asia, the Middle East and ultimately even parts of Europe longed for.

The century also saw what might be thought of as the Golden Age of Tibet. The warrior Srong-brtsan-sgam-po became ruler of the country and forged a powerful state. Buddhist monks were invited in from India and the great city of Lhasa was founded. The warrior turned scholar, and it was even said that he retired from active government for four years so that he could learn to read and write. In AD 648, the year of Hsüan-tsang's eventual return home, a delegation was sent from China to Tibet. It included a Chinese princess, an offering that spoke volumes of Tibet's raised status in the wider world.

But the year after, AD 649, T'ai-tsung died. His had been a significant reign in which the country's wealth and prosperity had increased. The T'ang Empire now stretched as far as Bukhara and Samarkand in Central Asia. However, the tactics by which this had been achieved had been innovative, relying more on diplomacy than military conquest. Such skills were needed as the borders of China were exposed to increased levels of external threat, particularly from Turkic groups from Central Asia.

The T'ang introduced several attributes which were to form an ongoing part of future Chinese evolution. One social innovation was the development of tea drinking almost as an art form. The T'ang also left the first known legal code from China, prescribing a light beating for minor offences and execution for those at the other end of the scale. Dating to AD 653, the code's principles, if not the exact detail, formed a crucial part of subsequent legal developments in China.

Confucianism continued to be exploited by the ruling elite, who hoped that the traditional values of loyalty and deference to the 'natural order' of things would ensure the longevity of the dynasty. Civil service examinations were used more widely and were more meritocratic than those previously in use and the ambitious, with talent but not necessarily with wealth, were at least given a chance to progress.

Despite these changes, this period of history is often seen as a 'Dark Age'. Certainly India, after a forty-year resurgence ushered in by the accession of Harsha of the old Gupta line, by the middle of the century seems to have been in one. And far to the west in Europe, a Dark Age is commonly held to have blacked out all vestige of civilisation.

Yet it is ironic that roots were taking hold in Europe that would provide the foundations for the great and dominant continent it would become. Take England, for example. The few manifestations of art might be pagan, barbaric almost, with *Beowulf*, which dates to around AD 650, being by far the best-known example. The story's main character walks in the land of legend, where 'down from the moorlands' misting fells came Grendel stalking'.

Further vestiges of this pagan tradition emerged from the bowels of the earth when the funeral ship of a king of the East Angles, probably named Raedwald, was unearthed by archaeologists in England in 1939. The finds were staggering, most remarkably a helmet with a face mask that gave the wearer the appearance of a warrior from the depths of the underworld, a worthy companion to the monster Grendel.

There was little in England to connect it to the future world power it would be; it was a hotchpotch of Germanic tribes – Angles, Saxons, Jutes – and survivors from an older Romano-British world that hung on ever more precariously in diminishing pockets. Nothing seems to link this was the later world. But a new power was already taking root, tentatively at first but soon to drill roots so deep they would be impossible to remove until threatened by the much, much later threat of apathy. The name of this power was Christianity.

Sometime in the seventh century a church was erected near London at a place called Westminster, a very modest precursor of what would later stand there. And on the other side of the Channel, another new kingdom was to increasingly subscribe to the faith. The Franks too had pagan origins but by the end of the seventh century they were sending Christian missionaries to the forests of Germany.

Even in Eastern Europe, movements were happening which would shape future history right up until the present day. The region was painfully open to great 'barbarian' sweeps from Central Asia and when the Slavs entered into Illyria and Pannonia in the middle of the century they appeared just to be another group of vandalising pagans. Yet they too would eventually be in thrall to Christianity, though one group, who would become known as Croats, subscribed to Roman Catholicism and the other, to be known as Serbs, to the Orthodox branch of the faith.

It is tempting to imagine this was a dark and largely localised world across the globe but it was not so. There is evidence that East Africa was trading with Persia, Arabia, India, Indonesia and China by this time. The Arabs who saw the African peoples living along the coast gave them the collective name *Sahili* ('sahil' means 'coast' in Arabic), from which the language now known as Swahili gets its name. By the end of the century, Madagascar was the recipient of a large number of migrants from Indonesia, thousands of miles to the east, showing how well developed ocean transport then was.

So this was in many ways an age of paradox. While the new faith of Islam (which owed much in fact to two old faiths, Christianity and Judaism) appeared to be all-conquering, the world of old Rome struggled to survive in the shape of Byzantium. Christianity in the west appeared to make as yet little difference. Vestiges of the faith had been most marked in the region by isolated monastic settlements but these had produced larger-than-life proselytizing missionaries like the great Columba. Here, Christianity was beginning to take root for a second time among the pagan tribes who inhabited the lands once ruled by the Western Roman Empire, and the foundation of a golden age for Europe, although many centuries away from full fruition, had already been laid.

21

HIGH-WATER MARK

Islam Fragments (AD 701–800)

No doubt to those overwhelmed by the all-conquering armies of Islam it seemed that the world that they had come to know was about to disappear forever, and in some ways it did, for nothing would ever be quite the same again. However, although few would have known it at the time, the initial wave of Islamic conquest was starting to run short of energy and there would be something of a realignment during the eighth century; nevertheless, the new faith was here to stay and would continue to have a huge impact across the globe.

It seemed that few could stand up to the armies of Mohammed. Byzantium was the main hope for Christendom and that appeared, to be frank, a feeble one. The so-called successor to Rome seemed more interested in her own internecine struggles than any external threat, however dangerous. She appeared to be incapable of learning the lesson that in unity was strength. Self-serving emperors put their own interests before those of the people they sought to rule for their own benefit.

In AD 704 (hereafter referred to without the AD designation), Justinian II returned to power in Byzantium with the help of barbarians from the Crimea and the Bulgars. It was a dangerous move to concert with foreign powers that possessed objectives conflicting with those of Byzantium, and it showed that little had been learned from the demise of Rome when 'friendly' barbarians had bitten the hand that fed them. Justinian did not live up to the great name he bore. A spiteful man who knew little about how to win the hearts of his subjects, his new reign was announced with reprisals against those who had ousted and mutilated him in the first place.

True to form, within a few years Justinian suffered a defeat against the Bulgars, who had predictably taken advantage of the situation for their own ends. By 711, the cruelty of Justinian had become too much. When an attempt was made to remove him for the second time, his army and navy simply stood aside. Justinian lost both his throne and also, this time, his life, lamented by few. He was lucky to have had a second chance, but did nothing to merit it.

That same year, the Muslim armies stormed into the west of Europe, across the narrow straits guarding the escape route from the Mediterranean into the mighty Atlantic. At their head was Jebel al-Tariq, who gave his name to a new fortress overlooking the narrow crossing point: Gibraltar. Spain was then a Visigothic kingdom, with little support among the indigenous population. The defence of Iberia quickly disintegrated. Count Roderick, last Visigoth king of Spain, was defeated and killed at the Battle of Rio Barbate.

Another great Islamic warrior, Musa, followed up this initial success. He soon took Seville, Merida, Toledo and Saragossa. Any semblance of resistance collapsed with awesome and frightening totality. It was as if a hammer was smashing its way through walls made of wafer-thin balsa wood. The Visigoths may have successfully conquered Spain, but they had done nothing to govern the people in a way that won their support, let alone their hearts. By 720, in historical terms in the blinking of an eye, the Muslims had crossed the Pyrenees and had reached Narbonne in what is now southern France. Spain was now behind them, in their wake. It seemed as if it was destined to forever remain part of Islam.

Part of the problem was the fragmented nature of Western Europe and its immediate environs. As Rome collapsed, independent tribal groupings that had never been assimilated into the empire had reasserted themselves in the vacuum that resulted; they included the Basques in the north of Spain and the Berbers in north-west Africa. In many places in the region, town life also went into reverse. Alongside the conquests, trade routes across the Mediterranean went into serious decline and in many parts of the new Islamic Empire coastal towns virtually disappeared.

But Islam was not at this time a movement of zealots, and this in some cases certainly helped their cause. There was a degree of religious tolerance for the 'Peoples of the Book' (Jews, Christians and Zoroastrians), who were allowed a degree of freedom. In some Christian regions like Iraq, Syria and Egypt there was actually a revival among certain minority groups that had previously been suppressed by Byzantine Christian orthodoxy.

Tolerance did have its limits, though. Church bells could not be rung, these other faiths were allowed no public worship and proselytizing (attempting to convert individuals to religious movements other than Islam) was out of the question. Non-Muslims could not own Muslim slaves and could not witness in court against a believer. However, there was no forcing of non-Muslims to convert to Islam.

Tax also acted as a differentiator. Non-Muslims were required to pay a poll tax, the *jizya*, which Muslims were exempted from. Instead, Muslims were required to pay a land tax, the *kharaj*, on any land they owned. In addition, the requirement to pay tithes was often as onerous as that to stump up for the *jizya*. On occasion, exemption might be made to the normal rates for tithes if its economic effects were particularly debilitating.

However, there seems little doubt that the *jizya* was an important part of the funding of the Islamic state. In the longer term, the voluntary conversion of former taxpayers to Islam would have a serious effect. Within the space of 150 years, the revenues of Egypt would decline from 17.5 million dirham per annum to 4 million dirham as a result of such matters of faith. There was a clash between theological concerns on the one hand and economic realities on the other.

The requirement to pay tax was rigorously enforced; travellers were required to wear a cord around their necks to prove that they had already paid the tax required of them. The land tax was so extreme for some that there was a marked movement from rural areas to the towns and in some areas there was significant decline as a result, a state of affairs made worse by Islam's adoption of partibility, that is the breaking up of inheritances into small chunks so that each son might have a portion of it. There were therefore huge social changes in some parts of the Islamic world as a result of the new religion.

Not that these were by any means all negative. Under Caliph Walid, many important reforms were introduced; schools, roads and hospitals for lepers were all constructed, for example. Irrigation, which had largely disappeared in many instances, was reintroduced to Mesopotamia. The great mosque of Damascus was built between 706 and 715 and remains one of the most beautiful edifices in the world to the present day. At its heart is a tantalising clue to Islam's links with Christianity, a shrine to the great saint of the latter, John the Baptist. Walid also beautified mosques in Jerusalem, Mecca and Medina and was a musician of some talent. To those misguided observers who see Islam as a fundamentalist religion intent on creating a cultural wasteland, all this beauty must come as something of a shock.

Nor did Islam solely move west. By 715, contingents of Arabised Iranians, *mawali*, had conquered Bukhara, Samarkand and Khwarezm, moving into the heart of Central Asia. This brought them directly to the borders of China. Here, just three years previously, Hsuan-tsung had come to the T'ang throne. It was the start of a notable reign, as the new Chinese emperor invigorated cultural life, encouraging poets, artists, scholars and establishing a music academy.

During his reign, the T'ang dynasty reached its zenith. A man who enjoyed the trappings of power, Hsuan-tsung codified state ceremonials until they became almost an art form. He had a fond taste for women too, siring thirty sons and twenty-nine daughters. However, he also took care to look after the more serious aspects of everyday life. The excessive power of both Buddhist institutions and greedy relatives of the imperial line was curbed.

While Hsuan-tsung struggled to maintain his borders against the Islamic threat, Byzantium was soon under threat again. Between 717 and 718, Constantinople was besieged by the forces of the new religion once more. The besiegers clearly expected to be there for some time, for they brought seeds with them to plant around the walls and grow into wheat. However, the Islamic armies could still not execute the siege sufficiently robustly to break down those massive walls and Greek fire once more forced them away. It would be the last attempt by the 'Saracens' for a while. The Byzantines, in the meantime, offered their fervent thanks to the Virgin, represented by her mystical icon, whom they deemed responsible for their salvation.

Far to the west, a block was also about to be made to Muslim progress. In 714 a count by the name of Charles Martel began the moves that would eventually lead to him becoming the undisputed ruler of the Franks a few years later. Charles would refuse to take the title of king, suggesting a certain humility on the one hand and wise political manoeuvring on the other. Nevertheless, it seemed that he had much on his hands with the Muslim threat from across the Pyrenees.

He had an able lieutenant to help him. In 721, the invading armies were checked near Toulouse by Duke Eudo. This was just as well, for it was not the only threat Charles faced. In 725 we find him holding back attacks from the Alemanni and Saxons, launched from the German forests at the other end of his territory. Duke Eudo was still manfully fighting his battles against the Muslim threat far to the south.

It was far from one-way traffic. Eudo was defeated in 731 near the city of Nimes, most famous for its great Roman aqueduct, and four years later he was dead. Throughout this period, the ebb and flow of conquest moved first one way and then the other, the Muslim tide crashing against the defences of the Christian opponent and then receding again. Charles added Aquitaine to his possessions and took the fight to the Muslim enemy. A climax was reached at Tours in 732, when the Muslim army was shattered and forced back towards the rock barrier of the Pyrenees.

It was the high-water mark of Islamic conquest in Western Europe. Historians now frequently suggest that the essential energy that drove the Muslim conquests forward was already spent, making the battle almost an irrelevance. This is part of a relatively modern historical interpretation, which commonly strives to underplay the role of battles and looks instead for greater, sweeping movements over an extended period that are responsible for changing the world. They may well be right to suggest that few battles in isolation change the course of history, but that should not underestimate the symbolic importance, particularly at the time, that was attached to the triumph of Charles Martel at Tours.

With the Islamic forces batted away from the gates of their capital and now seemingly distracted in the west, Byzantium, relieved of the burden of fighting the Muslims, now returned to fighting itself. When the emperor Leo III was enthroned in 717 the scene was set for a bitter and deeply felt dispute that threatened to tear his empire asunder. Some things never changed.

Theology was at the heart of the problem. Byzantine society was one that considered religious matters deeply and intensely. They were not alone, of course, even in Christendom. Yet when one looks at the wonderful artwork of the Lindisfarne Gospels, produced in around 715, particularly its intricate scrolling, with animal heads entwined as if in the coils of a serpent, there seem to be strong links to an older religion, one of paganistic nature.

Byzantine religious belief seems to have been much more introverted and inward-looking. It comes across as being a matter of intellect as much as of religious belief. A visitor to the city tartly remarked of Constantinople that 'the city is full of workmen and slaves who are all theologians. If you ask a man to change money, he will tell you how the Son differs from the Father. If you ask the price of a loaf he will argue that the Son is less than the Father. If you want to know if the bath is ready you are told that the Son is made out of nothing'. These debates were deeply felt and were about to manifest themselves in an extraordinary manner. The battle that was about to break out was crucial; it was for the soul of Byzantium.

At its heart was the role of icons. Emperor Leo was shocked at the veneration of such images, yet many of his people gave heartfelt thanks to the Virgin, represented in the form of her holy icon, for saving them against their enemies on several occasions. Theologically Leo might have been on sound ground; the worshipping of graven images was prohibited by the Old Testament, and for theological reasons Muslims prohibited the use of such images; so, going to the other extreme, did Protestants argue against their worship in later times.

Yet no doubt many of Leo's people turned on him for this swipe against one of their core beliefs, that of the efficacy of such icons. After all, many put Byzantium's triumph over the armies of Islam down to divine intervention, and the icons were seen as protecting angels. But the moves towards iconoclasm – literally the 'smashing of the icons' – began in 726 and created a groundswell of resentment. After an initial meeting held with the senators and bishops, complete removal of all idols was required. All representations of Christ and the Virgin were forbidden.

So shocked were some that a rival empire was declared in Greece and an abortive attempt was launched by dissentient elements on Constantinople itself. Pope Gregory II in Rome was also against the iconoclastic policy. In 730, the Patriarch of Constantinople, the most important churchman in Byzantium, rebelled against Leo and was deposed for his pains.

The luxury of such internal conflict was only possible because great tensions were also being played out in Islam, which had diverted its attention from efforts to conquer Constantinople. The Umayyad dynasty was becoming increasingly stretched and unpopular. As a result, a palpable sense of tension was building. Over time there were a number of revolts, especially in Iran and Egypt; the latter might well have been brought on by excessive taxes, but in the former a type of nationalism whereby Persians looked on the past as a golden age also played a part.

This concept of a lost golden age should be remarked upon, as it is a consistent feature found throughout history. The dangers of a distorted view of the past should never be underestimated. Revisionism can play a huge part in creating tensions in the present; history is littered with such examples. Even now, some are trying to reinvent Stalin, nostalgics attend the grave of Ceauşescu in Bucharest armed with flowers and Mao looks benignly on over Tiananmen Square. Perceived history is usually more powerful than real history, and the power of a legend to inspire, without facts getting in the way, continues to play a key role across the world.

The Umayyads had also been increasingly oppressive towards their Arab subjects, which further unnecessarily overstretched them. In response a revolt broke out, led by a group known as the Abbasids. This lasted for twenty years, a political and military campaign waged with vigour and hatred. The Shiites supported the uprising, having been wooed by its leaders. However, their hopes would be disappointed. Indeed, the attraction of the Abbasids was their very vagueness, by which many hoped to prosper if they triumphed, though few could be confident that they knew how. The Abbasids did not hesitate to make these vague policies clearer when they finally came to power and many, including the Shiites, were to be bitterly disappointed at their reward, or rather the lack thereof.

The rebellion was fought vigorously. Suffice to say that eventually it became clear that a climactic point was being approached. There were definite points of significance along the way, for example in 744 when Walid II, the Umayyad caliph, was assassinated after a short period in office. By 750, the crisis point had been reached.

Open rebellion was declared at Merv in 747. The weakness of the Umayyad dynasty was shown by the speed of its collapse after this point; by 749 all of Iran and Iraq was lost to them. The Abbasid leader, Abul Abbas al-Saffah, was declared Caliph at the great mosque of Kufa and the armies of the victor continued to move west. All but one of the Umayyad leaders was slaughtered in an ambush in Syria the following year. However, the escape of this one man was very significant for he fled west to Spain, where he managed to establish what would be a glorious Islamic flowering in its own right in the city of Cordoba.

In 750, Damascus, the political capital of Islam, was besieged by Abul Abbas. He called himself 'the Bloodthirsty', giving an insight into his philosophy. The epithet was fully merited by his acts when the city fell, involving the digging up of the corpses of recent Umayyad caliphs, and then their subsequent scourging, hanging and burning. It was the symbolic end of a great Muslim dynasty.

In reality, by now the Muslim powers were facing up to counter-attacks on several fronts. In 751 the Chinese tried to win back land from Islam in Central Asia but were thrown back. Islam was now involved in frequent frontier wars; with China here, with Byzantium in the Caucasus and with African groups in Nubia, that old frontier zone, at a junction between different worlds since the time of the pharaohs.

For the time being Islam managed to retain most of its gains but the long, slow fightback had started in several parts of the globe. In recognition of this, to the 'House of Islam' and the 'House of War', the latter being that part of the world that it was the duty of all Muslims to bring into the fold of the faith by conquest, was added another entity – the 'House of Truce' – consisting of those parts of the world where for the time being a non-Islamic status quo had to be accepted.

If there was any theme that emerged from the century, it was that of great internal conflict. Byzantium and Islam have both been referred to in this respect but China would also experience much self-induced trauma, a tragically frequent marker of Chinese history. In 755 there was the revolt of a military governor, An Lu-shan, against the T'ang. It was to usher in an era that was truly cataclysmic; in the next ten years it was said that 36 million people died as a result of the infighting and, although the figure must be treated with great suspicion, there is no doubt that it created immense upheavals. It ranks almost certainly as one of the deadliest conflicts ever fought – to put the numbers in perspective, 36 million amounts to approximately 14 per cent of the world population at the time.

At its heart is a very personal story, that of a great love affair. When nearly sixty, Hsuan-tsung fell in love with a much younger woman, Yang Kuei-fei. She was all he desired, both for her great beauty and the love she shared with him for music and dance. Unfortunately she did not have much in the way of political judgement. She was close to An Lu-shan and, besotted with her as he was, the emperor failed to notice the threat that his governor posed until it was too late.

In the course of his flight, his army mutinied against Hsuan-tsung and forced him to execute Yang Kuei-fei. With all that he cared about gone, Hsuan-tsung abdicated in favour of his son. The revolt was put down and Islamic troops were sent to the aid of the emperor. Saracen mercenaries stayed behind in China and became the core of a new Islamic society there. This was an act with long-term significance; to this day, some of the greatest tensions in modern China are found in regions with significant Islamic communities.

There were other important developments further afield in the Far East taking place. Buddhism continued to expand, much in the same way as Islam in other parts of the globe, though some advocates of Buddhism might say that it was more of a philosophy than a religion. In any event, by the mid-century Java had been taken over by a Buddhist dynasty from Sumatra and the island officially adopted the philosophy. By the end of the century (the exact date is not known) the great temple of Borobudur had begun to be built.

Buddhism was continuing to strengthen its hold elsewhere, too. In about 747, a great colossal Buddha was built in Japan with the intention of propitiating the gods who had visited the islands with smallpox; a terrible outbreak in the 730s had virtually wiped out the population in some localised areas. Social trends were at least working in favour of some of the population, with the private ownership of land opened up to peasants in Japan in 743 though, in negative compensation, the tax burden also increased on them.

As far as we are aware, out of sight of Eurasia the civilisations of Central America were most remarkable in this period for a flowering of Mayan civilisation. Although the Maya did not leave written records, from their pictorial legacy as well as archaeology/architecture we can see that there must have been great wealth around. More kings with splendid names such as Jaguar Shield the Great and Jaguar Bird IV built wondrous monuments as well as fighting many wars.

The great city of the Maya was Tikal, where a magnificent temple 65 metres tall was erected. There was still no such thing as a Mayan kingdom, rather a collection of city states that often seem to have been at each other's throats. Most of what we know of them and their beliefs comes from archaeology. The tomb of one chieftain, Ah Cacao (died in around 734), was found surrounded by shells, pearls, skins and assorted jewellery.

It was perhaps as well for the Maya that they were unaware of the way that Western Europe was starting to take shape for, many years into the future, inhabitants of that then unknown region spelt a death sentence for the Central American civilisation. If talk of 'Dark Ages' in Europe at the time is over-simplified, an insight into undeveloped views of the world is provided by the contemporary case of St Vergilius, who was castigated for saying that the earth was round and condemned as a heretic for insisting on the existence of the antipodes.

One of the most significant re-shaping exercises taking place was in the land of the Franks. The Merovingian dynasty had been in power for several hundred years but in 751 Pepin the Short deposed the last of the line, setting the scene for a dynasty that was to have a much more pan-European impact: the Carolingian. The focus became more internationalist, with Pepin quickly crossing the Alps to attack the Lombards in their territories and, hinting at a closer alliance that was to have significant ramifications, giving the captured province of Ravenna to the Pope.

His cause was helped significantly by a relative decline in Islam which, although still immensely powerful, was showing increasing signs of fragmentation. In 756, the

Muslims in Spain split away from the Abbasid dynasty far to the east. Three years later, Pepin was able to eject the last of the 'Saracens' from France. Important regional bridges were built; during succeeding decades a powerful new King of Mercia (one of the English kingdoms) named Offa assumed a degree of dominance on his own island and forged links with the Franks on the wider stage.

Islamic fragmentation was further emphasised in 765 when, following the deposition of the seventh imam, a breakaway group of Shia Muslims formed the Ismaili sect, a relatively small but nevertheless important faction from whom a shadowy and threatening group called the Assassins would develop several hundred years into the future.

The balance of power had tangibly shifted within Islam. In 762, Caliph Mansur built himself a new capital at Baghdad, close by ancient Ctesiphon. Here had been one of the great palaces of the mighty Persian Empire of old and, in tacit recognition that the Persian influence was increasingly strong, Mansur made great use of advisers from the region rather than relying on men of Arabic background. Men from the Persian, Greek and Jewish world flocked to Baghdad and books of classical Greek science were translated into Arabic. Baghdad would become the great seat of world learning for a while, a place of truly international significance.

In comparison, developments in Western Europe, in the first instance, had a more localised impact. In 765, Pepin tried to convert the Saxons in Germany to Christianity by use of the sword – very much a foretaste of things to come. When he died three years later, his kingdom was divided between two of his sons, Charles and Carloman. Perhaps predictably, they were soon at each other's throats but a bitter war was averted, first by the timely mediation of their mother and then by the even more timely death of Carloman in 771.

The field was now clear for Charles to reign alone. He continued to fight to convert the Saxons by fire and sword and also built closer links with the papacy, still struggling to build a meaningful position on the political as well as the spiritual stage. Charles moved to the aid of the Pope when he appealed for help against the Lombards, sensing a mutual advantage in so doing as his own legitimacy would be enhanced. The journey down the path along which Charles would become Charlemagne had already begun.

In fact, the second half of this century would see some important changes in the balance of power. It was also one in which, certainly in Europe, after several centuries of fragmentation and localisation, the world would begin to shrink again. Charlemagne was one of the great figures of history, laying the foundations not only for a Frankish kingdom but also an empire that would be a force in the European political landscape for years.

Here was the ultimate Christian warrior, with a bible in one hand and a sword in the other. One group who particularly felt the force of his powers were the German Saxons, defeated by him in 776 and given a rather unpalatable choice between conversion to Christianity and death. Confident that he had overcome this particular challenge, Charlemagne then turned his attention to another great enemy of Christendom, the 'Saracens' in Spain.

Unfortunately, once his back was turned his campaign in Spain was cut short when news of a revolt by the Saxons was received. He had no option but to turn back and put down this challenge to his authority. As he left, his rearguard, under the command of his nephew Roland, was attacked and cut to pieces by Basques. The legend of Roland, vainly blowing his horn in an appeal for help, became one of the great parables of medieval chivalric literature, the ultimate story of a heroic acceptance of a Christian death rather than the alternative possibility of cowardly flight and a ruined life thereafter. As such, it had huge significance on Western European medieval thinking.

In 773 we find our first historical reference to the 'Ghana Empire', though it is certain that it had existed for many years before that. King lists, admittedly from a later time, suggest that it may have already been a power for half a millennium. From Ghana (not totally synonymous with the country we now call Ghana, which is a much more recent creation), caravans regularly criss-crossed the scorched wastelands of the Sahara to Tripoli and Tunis. Ghana would soon be a source for much trade, particularly in the form of salt and gold.

Further east, the Byzantine Empire was to some extent resurgent. Constantine V died in 775 and under his successor, Leo IV, iconoclasm was moderated. However, it would appear that the real power behind the throne lay with his wife, the empress Irene, and she increasingly became the dominant figure in Byzantine politics.

Soon, the worlds of Eastern and Western Europe were to collide again. Charlemagne was an enthusiastic supporter of the papacy but Italy, where the papal lands were, was still in the Byzantine sphere of influence. A crucial agreement made in 781 between the papacy, Charlemagne and Irene saw Byzantium give up its claims to the Papal States. This left Charlemagne free to return to his Christian warfare back in the west. The year after, a book he had ordered to be prepared, the *Capitulatio de partibus Saxoniae*, lay down harsh punishments, including death for practising pagan beliefs among the Saxons.

Byzantium still had many problems of its own to concern it. Between 782 and 784, the caliph al-Mahdi sent troops into Asia Minor to fight the Byzantines. His son, in command of the army, was successful and became known as Harun al-Rashid ('the Upright'). Soon after, when in Europe Charlemagne had finally defeated the German Saxons, Irene had reversed the iconoclastic edicts in Constantinople and King Offa of Mercia had built a dyke to keep the troublesome Welsh out of England, Harun became caliph.

This ushered in one of the great caliphates. Within a few years, Harun had increased patronage of the sciences, especially medicine, astronomy and chemistry. He also fostered interest in astrology and alchemy. So began a major revival of Islamic learning that would last for several hundred years. Poets were also encouraged at his court, such as Merwan and Abu Nawas. Under his patronage, stories and legends from older times were recorded, giving rise to the amazing tales of the *Thousand and One Nights*.

This outburst of cultural energy was centred on Baghdad but on the westernmost edge of the Islamic world the tide was, for the time, ebbing slowly against the Muslims. After a successful campaign between 788 and 791 against the Slavs and Avars, Charlemagne again crossed the Pyrenees, this time establishing a small strip of land under his rule, known as 'the Spanish March'. It was the beginning of a war that would last for half a millennium in Spain in what would eventually become known as the *Reconquista*.

While this was not the start of an unblemished Christian reconquest in Iberia, and there were many more Islamic successes yet to come, it was a symbolic gesture that marked the beginning of a road, however indistinctly, that would end up with that ultimate episode of medieval warfare, the Crusades.

The flaw in this Christian fightback lay largely in the extraordinariness of the man behind it. Charlemagne would be irreplaceable. He had built a strong, centralised state in his own image. By the end of the century, he had introduced military service into his kingdom on a feudal model and had organised regular meetings of his bishops and nobles, at which new laws would be discussed; essentially an unelected form of parliament.

His power was still on the rise and was about to reach its zenith. When in 799 Pope Leo III was imprisoned and badly beaten by his opponents, he managed to escape, fled to Charlemagne and appealed for help. Sensing a magnificent opportunity to cement his power, the Frankish ruler came to his aid in a move that would make him into a European emperor. Charlemagne and his armies moved on Rome, reinstalling Leo and summoning his opponents to the city in the following year to construct a permanent peace.

Elsewhere in the globe, important but mostly regional events were taking place. By the century's close the city of Kyoto, the 'Capital of Peace', has been founded in Japan, while in Cambodia the Khmers had begun their rise to prosperity. In Central America, the Maya had started to decline and a new warrior power, the Toltecs, was threatening to take their place. Of wide global significance in the longer term, the colonisation of the Pacific had also begun, with bold and brave adventurers island-hopping into the unknown in their long but flimsy canoes. Australasia had developed well out of sight of the wider world since the beginnings of history, but the process by which they would be brought back into vision had already begun.

In Europe, at century's end it appeared that stability had been restored. Charlemagne was about to stake his claim to be the first effective Roman emperor in the west for hundreds of years. It seemed that the Islamic threat had been halted and, given its problems as it began to fragment, the risk from that quarter to Europe appeared to have diminished significantly. Yet all was not well.

The abbey of Lindisfarne in Northumbria was one of the great monastic institutions of Western Europe. In 793, as the monks were going about their business, sleek dragon-headed ships, greyhounds of the seas, hove into view. They bore down on the abbey like a pack of hunting dogs moving on an immobilised and horrified prey. They stormed ashore, stabbing, slaughtering, burning, looting. When they left again, a pall of smoke marked the remains of what had once been one of the great Christian monuments in England.

These raiders were ruthless, fierce and skilled in the arts of war. As pagans, they also had no qualms about killing Christian monks or pillaging Christian goods. The ravens from the north had announced their arrival on a global stage in spectacular fashion. The Vikings had appeared, and they brought chaos in their wake.

22

TERROR FROM THE NORTH

Charlemagne and the Age of the Vikings (AD 801–900)

The collection of records known as the *Anglo-Saxon Chronicles* is not just a unique and priceless insight into a world that might otherwise be lost. It also offers a glimpse into the souls of cultures and peoples that were about to be radically changed. As much as being historical records, the chronicles are full of auguries and evil omens. It is not therefore surprising that for the year of 793, when Lindisfarne went up in flames, we read that 'terrible portents come over the land of Northumbria, and miserably frightened the people: there were immense flashes of lightning and fiery dragons were seen flying in the air'.

In many ways the sacking of Lindisfarne was the '9/11' of its day. It came as a bolt from the blue and its impact was felt across the European stage, even in those days of relatively undeveloped communication. Most frightening of all was both its unexpectedness and the fact that the slaughtering of God's servants suggested that the Almighty was displeased with the world. What, people wondered, would be next? Or, more pertinently, where?

There had been little warning of the raid. Scandinavia was on the edge of the world and therefore mostly ignored. Yet ironically, from here would come a bold if violent people who would bring the world closer together. The people known as the Vikings were not, of course, a civilising influence. Although they certainly valued art, their creations were pagan, almost shamanistic, relics of a world that was already dying. They rather played the role of a conduit, travelling as far as the interior of Russia in the east as well as, for the first time that we know of, from Europe to America in the other direction.

This is not to underestimate their importance. The Vikings, for all their savage practices, were also great adventurers. The spirit of exploration that would before long see them reaching out across the Atlantic in one direction and towards Central Asia in the other made them forerunners of the great age of European adventurism that would have such a dramatic impact on the world.

But the Vikings would also transform into something different. The cultures that they came into contact with would shape them much more than they would shape those they attacked. They would eventually throw off the old gods and accept Christianity. They would legitimise themselves by knocking off some of the rough edges at least, eventually entering into alliances, even sometimes accepting vassalage as the price to be paid for holding onto their lands without constant warfare. Such would, most pertinently of all, be the direction taken by the Normans, who were themselves of Viking stock but eventually entered right into the heart of European affairs as a permanent power rather than a bunch of opportunistic raiders.

Yet at the beginning of the ninth century it might have seemed that the early raids were aberrations, albeit terrifying ones, that were a throwback to the old days of barbarian raids on the fringes of Europe, and did not in themselves threaten to overturn the existing order. 'Order' was indeed the right word as, under the brilliant leadership of Charlemagne, Western Europe achieved a continental profile that seemed to have been lost with the demise of the Western Roman Empire four centuries before. It also achieved a form of unity that had seemed lost forever.

Charlemagne was a star of his and later times. Over 6 feet in height with piercing blue eyes, his physical presence was striking. However, even that does not account for his political achievements. Charlemagne's rise to greatness was confirmed in Rome on Christmas Day 800, when he was crowned emperor by Pope Leo. It was a moment of massive symbolic significance, when a new Roman Empire was established. This 'Holy' Roman Empire was to play a critical role in Europe for over 500 years. Yet even amid the triumphalism of the moment, the emperor knew that his world was already under threat, for in that same year Charlemagne also arranged for the defence of the Channel coast against the Vikings.

That could not disguise the sense of triumph he felt. To be made an emperor was not an everyday occurrence. There were several important impacts from this development. The first concerned the papacy. Pope Leo's position was under threat and he needed allies and a strategy to improve his position. Leo had therefore previously sought sanctuary with Charlemagne. Now, in formalising Charlemagne's position by crowning him, Leo officially had a protector who helpfully also happened to be the strongest man in Western Europe. Additionally, by taking upon himself the duties of anointing the emperor he had done something that no Pope before him had ever done; by conferring power on the emperor he had symbolically emphasised the superiority of the spiritual power over the temporal.

On the other hand, the prize was obviously also huge for Charlemagne. But it was equally a slap in the face for Byzantium, which could no longer claim to be the sole successor of the glory of Rome. This was in many ways a snub that reflected tensions between Byzantium and the Pope. While the Byzantines might look down judgementally on Western barbarian princes who could normally barely write (if at all), the West was equally dismissive of an empire that could have a murderer on the throne; a murderer, to make it worse, in the shape of a woman.

The empress Irene was deeply unpopular. She had arranged for the deposition of her own son, Constantine, and for his eyes to be removed – a regular feature of so-called Byzantine civilisation – in such a cruel fashion that he died soon after. Sensing a number of enemies around her, and keenly feeling the risk to her own position that this threatened, Irene explored the possibility of a marriage alliance with Charlemagne. Before it could come to anything, she was deposed in 802 and conveniently died the year after.

But in some ways Charlemagne's rise to power papered over a number of cracks. Even as it appeared to be resurgent, Western Europe would face threats from several directions. Although Islam continued to fragment, some of the new regimes formed out of this collapse of unity proved to be aggressive and troublesome neighbours to the Western Europeans, especially those based around the Mediterranean such as the Aghlabid dynasty of Kairawan, which was established in north-west Africa in the same year as Charlemagne's coronation.

Charlemagne was an archetypal Christian warrior. He continued to push into Muslim territories in Spain, for example capturing Barcelona in 801. But wanting to be a man of letters as well as war, Charlemagne also encouraged learning in his court, his greatest scholar being Alcuin of York, who presented an improved translation of the Bible to him, of which many copies were made. Even as this was being done, in 801, on the far side of Asia the T'ung Tien was produced, the first Chinese historical encyclopaedia. At around the same time, the first treatise on tea was written by Lu Yu.

Following the destruction of Lindisfarne, the first decade of the century witnessed much of the same in Europe. The holy sanctuary of Iona was sacked by the Vikings in 802. But while Christianity was under threat in some areas, in others it continued to expand by means of sword and fire. Two years after the sack of Iona, Charlemagne depopulated much of northern Saxony. By the end of his campaign there, Germany as far as the River Elbe was firmly established as one of his territories. Then he turned his attentions further afield, conquering Venetia, Dalmatia and Corsica far to the south while his son campaigned in Bohemia. In 806, Charlemagne – thinking that his empire was already becoming too unwieldy for one man to govern – started to take steps for its eventual division among his sons, a neat reversion to old Roman ideas, when the empire was regularly split.

While Charlemagne was strengthening his grip on power in Europe, Harun al-Rashid was doing the same in his caliphate in the Middle East. In 803, he ruthlessly eliminated the Barmakids, the Persians responsible for his administration, seeing them as a threat to his power. Then three years later he turned on Byzantium, directing a successful campaign in Cappadocia against the Byzantine emperor Nicephorus I. The emperor in Constantinople was stretched on several fronts and sent a fleet to Venetia to try to recover the territories that he had lost there.

Byzantium was squeezed between two powers, a situation that soon threatened to become more permanently established when Harun al-Rashid and Charlemagne entered into a correspondence to strengthen diplomatic ties between them. This reflected the fact that they both led substantial power blocs that were not in direct competition with each other but had common enemies, particularly in the form of Byzantium. In 807, the caliph sent a water clock to the Holy Roman Emperor, a small enough gesture perhaps but symbolic of a wish to build closer ties towards a mutual common interest.

For the caliph, however, time was running out. He died in 809 after putting down a revolt in Samarkand. His reign had been extraordinary. Included in his achievements was the foundation of a state-of-the-art hospital in Baghdad, the establishment of a good postal service and the idea, if not put into practice, of a canal across the Suez Isthmus. But now his kingdom was divided among his sons and the caliphate was about to experience an alarming slide in its influence and status.

In other parts of the world, different philosophies were continuing to expand their impact. Links between China and Japan were becoming ever closer, fostered in particular by the spread of Buddhism. Quite predictably, there was no 'one size fits all' of its teachings and several different sects were established in Japan, notably the Tendai and Shingon variants of Buddhism. By the end of the first decade of the century, an important innovation could be seen in China in the shape of what was called 'flying cash', that is money drafts rather than coin. In effect paper money was now in circulation as well as copper coinage. Chinese attempts to introduce tea growing into Japan at this time, however, literally failed to take root.

By 810, important events had also taken place in Venetia. Venice would achieve a worldwide status out of all proportion to the size of the city in its lagoon in the north-east corner of Italy. Originally formed by refugees from the barbarian hordes that swept into the peninsula as the Roman Empire collapsed, Venice was still an inconsequential actor on the world stage. But in 810 the Venetians accepted the resumption of Byzantine overlordship and started to build a city around an area known as the Rialto.

Two years later, in a display of realpolitik, Michael I, the Emperor of Byzantium, sent a delegation to Charlemagne, recognising him as the emperor in the west. In return, Charlemagne dropped his claims to Venetia. Little good would this do Byzantium in the long run, as Venice would prove stubbornly independent; in fact, in a few centuries the inhabitants of Constantinople would have good cause to shudder at the very mention of the city on the Adriatic. The Venetians had introduced something remarkably innovative for the time: the election of their 'prince', the doge, in a semi-democratic process that was so complicated it is almost impossible to describe.

Despite the rising power and influence of the Franks, Europe was under increasing threat from external forces. The Vikings were spreading their wings, bringing their own unique brand of terror (as well as occasional trading) with them. By 807, they were raiding Ireland. Within the next fifteen years, they were starting to probe deeper into France.

Nor were they the only danger to Europe. In 813, the emperor Michael was defeated near Adrianople by the Bulgars, who then moved on Constantinople, though those mighty walls managed to keep them out as they had many a raider over the years. The Bulgars, under their great leader, the khan Krum, had been an ongoing threat to Byzantium for a number of years now. Just two years before, the emperor Nicephorus had been killed in battle against them; his skull had been turned into a drinking vessel for Krum.

Despite the threats, Charlemagne appeared unconquerable, but even he could not cheat death. When he died on 28 January 814, the imperial crown went to his only surviving son, Louis. The new emperor, who was given the flattering title of the Pious, did his best to deal with an almost impossible challenge, namely to even come close to emulating his father. He confirmed the existence of the Papal States in Italy but also interfered directly in church affairs, ordering all monasteries in his empire to conform to the Benedictine rule.

In the east as well as the west, the death of great men had brought with it uncertainty and decline. However by 819, years of incessant internecine warfare in Harun al-Rashid's old empire had been brought to an end by the suppression of a revolt in Baghdad. But Islam was continuing to disunite, and this was only a temporary respite in a journey that was leading rapidly and inevitably to the continuing relative decline of this young politico-religious institution.

Yet ironically, as the power of the caliph, the great figurehead of Islam, diminished alarmingly, elsewhere new Islamic powers were threatening the heart of Europe. They came from an unexpected direction: the sea. In a short space of time, the forces of Islam had transmuted from Arab warriors, whose mode of transport was often the ship of the desert, the camel, to fighters who felt comfortable with the intricacies of naval warfare.

A chain reaction had been started when Muslim fugitives from Cordoba had been expelled from Alexandria. With no obvious home to head for, they took the island of Crete, which they made a centre for piracy in the Mediterranean. In 827 Ziyadat Allah I of Kairawan made the short crossing north over the Mediterranean from North Africa and began the conquest of Sicily. The island, the heel to the long boot of Italy, was strategically vital. By 831, Palermo had fallen to the forces of Islam and a long process of conquest was well underway.

There was also another emergent force to consider. They had existed for a while, penumbral and influential yet invisible beyond their immediate world. These were the great roving bands of Turkish warriors – still largely shamanistic and pagan in their beliefs but in many cases soon to become devotees of Islam – who would subsequently have a critical effect on shaping the future direction and fortunes of that religion.

Their influence spread across Asia. At the same time, in some places their powers were waning. By the 830s, a confederation of Uighurs in Manchuria was beginning to unravel. The Turkish peoples (for there were many separate tribes, not one homogeneous whole) also started to lose their dominance in Central Asia, where for several centuries they had been a guarantor of a form of safety for those travelling along the Great Silk Road to China and back. Many of them therefore started to look westwards.

The fact that China was strengthening helped encourage this change of focus. The T'ang had recovered to some extent from the great rebellions of the previous century, though the dynasty would never again hold quite the same power. Nevertheless, by 821 they were strong enough to attack Tibet. Progress in civil engineering was also being made at about this time, with canal lock gates appearing in China. Yet China too was under threat, with a Thai state, Nanchao, attacking Szechuan in 829. By 832 the Nanchao had destroyed the Pyu people in Burma and were clearly a growing threat in the region.

There was in fact an ongoing internal struggle for power being fought in China over a long period in which these events were just phases. For one thing, the power of the eunuchs in China had been growing. In 835, a night of the long knives known as the 'Street Dew Incident' ended when the emperor Wen-tsung's attempts to regain power from his eunuchs was defeated, his ministers being massacred.

This was an appropriately chaotic time in China for the decade was indeed one of turmoil across the globe. There was a long catalogue of disturbing events to report. In 834 the Vikings raided Frisia and then began almost annual assaults on the coast of France. The year after, they attacked England and also set up camps in Ireland. Something significant was happening; the attacks were changing from raids into migrations, with Vikings increasingly looking to set up home.

In the Middle East, a weakened caliphate was now forced to rely on the services of Turkish mercenaries to protect it. In 836, the year that the Vikings sacked London, the caliph al-Mustasim moved his capital from Baghdad to Samarra, where he was virtually a prisoner of his Turkish bodyguard. The year after that, the 'Saracens' from Sicily intervened in the affairs of mainland Europe more closely, firstly helping to relieve the siege of Naples and then sacking Brindisi. Soon after, they pillaged Marseilles.

The fabric of Western Europe was starting to stretch alarmingly at the seams. In 839, Louis the Pious divided his threatened empire between his sons. He died the year after, but the threats to his kingdom continued to increase. The Vikings sailed up the Seine to Rouen while Muslims from Sicily took Taranto and Bari and plundered the Adriatic coast as far as Venice. Increasing strains on Charlemagne's old empire were apparent.

The Treaty of Verdun of 843 formally divided the Carolingian Empire in an attempt to make it more manageable in the eye of the approaching storm. One son of Louis, Lothar, stayed as emperor, ruling Italy, the lands between the Rhine and the Rhone-Saône and Frisia; another, Louis, received Germany; and a third, Charles, was given France and the Spanish March. Also in 843, a new kingdom was formed off the coast of Europe: Scotland, created by Kenneth McAlpin, King of Scots and King of the Picts (though historians suggest that there is evidence that Kenneth was not the first ruler of a unified state but he whose name has survived longest in the annals of history).

This year also saw the end of a bitter dispute, when the Byzantine emperor repealed the iconoclasm laws that had created so much controversy and division, effectively bringing an end to the controversy over the place of idols in the Orthodox Church. This was a vital step forward as the schism created had been so great that it threatened to tear Byzantium apart. A succession of emperors had done what they could to divorce their people from what they saw as a dangerous superstition but without success. Even as they banned such practices from their palaces, their own families were adhering to the old beliefs in secret. The year 843 saw a triumphant return of the images, celebrated in ritualistic pomp on a day still known as 'Orthodox Sunday'.

And so the marvellous yet mystical artistry that typified the religious iconography of Byzantium was restored, though interestingly religious sculpture as opposed to paintings was not, perhaps still being considered too close to the graven images prohibited by biblical commandment. There was a majesty in Byzantine art rarely, if ever, equalled and yet consistently underrated in the West in particular. Yet it is notable that the icons were officially restored by a regent, the regal widow Theodora, rather than an emperor, for the ninth century in particular was typified by a bewildering succession of emperors who in the main were deposed, mutilated or murdered.

Religious and philosophical debate was not the exclusive preserve of the West. In the Far East, those in power were becoming increasingly resentful of the influence of Buddhism. In 842, Langdarma, the King of Tibet, tried to suppress Buddhism and was killed by a lama as a result, hardly the pacific response one might have anticipated. The Manichean religion, of Persian origin, was suppressed in China, having previously been protected by the Uighurs whose power had now collapsed. Then in 845 all alien religions were forbidden in the country (something of a precursor of trends in modern China at the height of the Cultural Revolution). Buddhism was particularly targeted, with a widespread confiscation of property and the production of a book, the *Li-tai ming-hua chi*, describing how Buddhist monasteries were suppressed, almost a pre-echo of Henry VIII's draconian moves in England 700 years later.

Viking journeys in the meantime became ever bolder. In 844 they were driven off from Lisbon but sacked Cadiz, Seville and Cordoba in the south of Spain. The year after, it was the turn of Paris to receive a fearful visitation from these ravens from the north. By the close of the decade, they had started to colonise Iceland and reached as far east as Kiev. Here they would form a Varangian Empire. It was named the empire of the Rus', from the Swedish word for seaman, and it was from this that Russia got its name.

Kiev would become a great trading centre, at a crossroads of worlds, where goods could move from the east to the west with the Viking middleman taking a fair share (or more) of the profit. It would become a role model for other great trading cities and would be a linchpin for hinging the then loosely connected trading blocs of Eurasia together.

It is certainly true to say that the Vikings were very adept traders as well as warriors, but it is for the latter 'quality' that they remain best known. In 851, they wintered in England for the very first time, suggesting that the move towards settlement rather than raiding was gathering pace. Within the decade, they had established a kingdom in Ireland with a capital established by the blackwater (in Celtic *Dubhlin*). By 860, they had burned Paris, had ravaged the Balearic Islands and Provence and were at the very gates of Constantinople though the city's mighty walls again proved impervious to assault.

To make matters worse for Europe, there were also ongoing assaults from the south chipping away at the edges of Christendom. Muslim armies had established themselves in Bari, on the mainland of Italy itself, from where they launched attacks further north up the spine of the peninsula. However, this was no longer a consolidated Muslim attack, as the first great attacks on an unknowing world launched from Arabia had been but an onslaught from one part of a now increasingly fragmented power bloc.

In the meantime, the sad demise of the caliphate continued. It is true that there were increasing trading links far to the east to China, evidenced best by the appearance of a book in 851 called *Silsilat al-Tawarikh*, which included stories of the journeys of Suleiman the merchant – the source of the tales of Sinbad the Sailor. But ten years later, the caliph al-Mutawakkil was killed by his Turkish bodyguard, evidencing just how much the power of the prestigious institution had diminished. Days before, he had ridden on horseback between two lines of soldiers 4 miles long but these trappings of earthly power could not protect him from the assassin's blade.

In 866, his successor al-Mustai'in had been deposed by men from the same group who were there ostensibly to protect him. In 870, the caliph al-Mutadi was assassinated by his bodyguard. Whatever compensations there might have been in taking on the role of caliph, they must have been significant if they outweighed the dangers.

With the Viking menace gathering pace in Europe, new alliances needed to be forged to protect against their depredations. In 862, the emperor Michael III of Byzantium sent missionaries to convert Slovakia. Two years after, he forced Boris I, Khan of the Bulgars, to be baptised as a Christian. But the year after, the Vikings were again hammering unsuccessfully at the doors of Constantinople. This was a dangerous time to be a ruler of any kind. Michael III was murdered and succeeded by Basil I in 867, while three years later the Anglo-Saxon king Edmund of East Anglia was shot to death by Viking arrows, being ritually slaughtered in an act that would later lead to his canonisation.

The Byzantine missionary incursions into the Balkans and beyond were very important in several ways. One of the missionaries, Cyril, found that the Slavs did not have a written language, so he developed one that tried to capture it phonetically and so the first moves towards the 'Cyrillic' alphabet were made. But the papacy in Rome coveted these lands also. While the Orthodox hierarchy nominally recognised the Pope as first among equals, reality did not always match the stated case. In the Balkans in particular there were tensions. Areas like Serbia moved into the Orthodox sphere of influence, while others like Croatia were in the Catholic camp. The effect of these divisions continues into modern times.

With the Saracens of Kairawan growing in strength and taking Malta, the Holy Roman Emperor Louis II entered into an alliance with the Byzantines and together they ejected the Muslim armies from Bari in 871. A crucial event happened soon after when an Orthodox bishop was sent to Russia as a missionary after a treaty between the Byzantine Emperor and the Vikings in Kiev. So were laid the foundations of the Russian Church, later to be so powerful in state affairs in that country. In the twenty-first century, the Russian Church still exercises great influence in one of the world's great powers, a situation that can be traced back to these early steps twelve centuries ago.

In places, it appeared that the Viking threat could not be defeated. In England, the Viking advance appeared unstoppable. The invaders here were Danes, as opposed to the Norwegians who made up most of the force that had attacked Ireland (and for that matter the northern and western islands off Scotland) or the Swedes who had spearheaded the incursions into Russia. It seemed here that the English kingdoms would disappear forever, especially when, by 878, Alfred – the young King of Wessex in the south of the country – was hiding away on an island in the marshes around Athelney in the west of England.

The kingdoms of England had long been divided. In fact the whole idea of an 'England' was a concept before its time. What had always existed since the time of the first incursions into Roman Britain was a group of separate Anglo-Saxon kingdoms: Northumbria, Mercia, East Anglia, Sussex, Wessex and others. From time to time, a prominent king, known as the *bretwalda*, would emerge and claim titular supremacy over the others. Occasionally, one kingdom would become more prominent that others: Northumbria in the seventh century, Mercia in the eighth and Wessex in the ninth. Beneath the surface, there was always a tendency for the individual kingdoms to reassert themselves. But now it seemed as if no residue of the Anglo-Saxon kingdoms was to survive.

But Alfred fought back from a seemingly impossible position. The subsequent war of resistance that he led lasted for over a decade, with a vigorous ebb and flow of fortunes. In the end, a compromise of sorts was reached. Alfred developed a system of defence based on fortified towns known as *burhs* and put together a navy. Guthrum, the leader of the Danes, was baptised and in the end a partition was agreed. The south of England, broadly speaking, was left to Alfred while the north was left to the Danes, becoming known as the *Danelaw*.

On the far side of Asia, the T'ang dynasty was beginning to creak. From about 860 onwards, there had been an increasing loss of centralised control and bandit gangs roamed the land. There followed decades of violence, which peaked in ferocity in 879 when 120,000 foreigners were said to have been slaughtered in Canton; probably many of them were Persians and Arabs who dominated the export trade, especially with Korea and Japan. In any event, it was symptomatic of the xenophobia that can occur when the world becomes a smaller place, a problem we are still struggling to come to terms with over a millennium later.

At the head of the most successful band of raiders was Huang Ch'ao. He had attempted to pass the civil service exams then much beloved of the Chinese but had failed. He had graduated instead to the highest prize of all, for in 881 he set up a government in the now disintegrating country. The T'ang dynasty was overwhelmed and died a lingering death over the next twenty years.

Huang Ch'ao did not live long to enjoy his triumph. He was defeated and killed in 884 by the Turk Sha-t'o, whose leader, Li-K'o-yung, fought for control of northern China. China, whose real strength lay in unity and whose weakness was associated with fragmentation, started to decline.

The T'ang had been the driving force in holding China together but recent times had seen centralised control break down. This was not all bad news; the removal of the heavy hand of central bureaucracy meant that local initiative and entrepreneurship was encouraged in its stead, evidencing one of the age-old and, as yet, unsolved conundrums of where to strike the appropriate balance between state control and individual and local responsibility. In the absence of this all-invasive centralised influence and control, sparks of economic initiative took root on a local basis.

Yet to others it must have seemed as if the world was about to end. Reinforced by the rigid framework of Confucianism, which had encouraged men to think of status and roles as well as mere wealth and land, a strong bureaucracy and civil service had developed. Men measured their success by progress through the ranks. Now this outward measure of achievement was increasingly irrelevant and a vacuum was created which, for a while, men struggled to fill.

It was the end of a remarkable period of rule. The T'ang had introduced good government into China, a strong civil service and a fair tax system. The early period of their government was often later seen as a golden age that unfortunately could not be sustained. At least other civilisations in the region continued to develop; in 881, for example, Indravarman I built Bakong Temple in Cambodia, the first terraced stone pyramid at Angkor.

The T'ang had also built strong links with other parts of the world, lessening China's sense of isolation. Some of them had been to the east, to Japan and Korea. Others had been to the west, to Persia and the Middle East. To the south a greater knowledge of India had also been gained. But the Indian Subcontinent was still a divided region. The ninth century had been marked by yet more battles between different parts of the peninsula, each trying to gain supremacy over the other.

One man in particular had gained a reputation for himself, Govinda III of the Rashtrakutas, who was renowned as an Indian equivalent of Alexander and lived at the beginning of the ninth century. Yet despite his many successes, he or those who came after him showed little desire to build a great empire covering much of the Subcontinent and were instead far more content to dominate locally rather than regionally.

It is appropriate perhaps to move towards the end of this review of the ninth century as we began in Western Europe. There was in some ways a neat symmetry to events. Charlemagne had been crowned in 800 at one end of the epoch, while at the other Alfred – the only English king to be honoured with the accolade 'Great' – died in 899.

Yet there was a world of difference between Charles the Great and Alfred the Great. For the former, the Vikings had been an irritant, an annoyance, nothing more. For the latter, they had almost been the cause of his death and that of his kingdom. He had hung on and managed to turn the tide but it had been touch and go, a world away from the great empire that Charlemagne had governed.

The era of Viking expansion was not yet over. These remarkable voyagers had brought the world into closer contact. From the steppes of Russia to the shores of America, from the Arctic Circle to the gates of Constantinople (where Viking graffiti can still be seen in Hagia Sophia, though that was from tenth-century visitors), nothing remained untouched or, at least, untouchable. They might not have brought culture with them in their travels but they did help to make the world a smaller place. Their activities in Russia brought them adjacent to the great trade routes from China, which thus stayed in view of the West, albeit still far removed from the everyday knowledge and understanding of most Europeans.

Significant developments were also taking place far away. For Central America, this century was one of important changes. Several notable city states had emerged by this time, including Tikal and Calakmul. The history of these states is poorly understood and the details are sketchy. Occasional shards of light only illuminate the scene dimly. We know for example that in Tikal, the last important governor was a man known as Dark Sun, who ruled after 810. He erected the last great pyramid on the site, some 55 metres high. Despite the mention of several rulers later in the century, it is clear that by the time of its demise later in the century Tikal was much more sparsely populated than had previously been the case and a great deal of its riches had disappeared.

Similarly, there were no great monuments erected in Calakmul during the century. This is especially surprising as in the Mayan calendar the year 830 was the particularly significant baktun 10.0.0.0.0. What seems to have happened is that widespread outbreaks of war across the region diverted everybody's attention elsewhere. Recent research suggests a change in the nature of war, evolving from conflicts based around capturing the chiefs of rival cities for ritual sacrifice to campaigns of utter destruction.

One of the problems appears to have been demands handed down from the ruling classes for ever greater tributes, which led to a brutal exploitation of the peasants and extensive social discontent. Whatever the reason for this, there is solid evidence of widespread malnutrition among the population at the time and signs exist of this being a particularly nasty period to live through in Central America.

This was a world in upheaval, from the west of Europe to the far shores of China as well as in the Americas. Some long-lived dynasties were starting to run out of steam. The situation was well summed up in a chronicle written by Regino, Abbot of Prüm in Francia, which simply said under the year 888, 'Each kingdom decided to create its own king drawn from its own entrails.' Francia was indeed already starting to dissolve as a political entity. By the end of the century, the Languedoc, the southern lands of what is now France, had started to become a region without a king as the local aristocracy there became far more powerful.

There were in addition still a number of so-called barbarian incursions to contend with; the Turks were becoming increasingly troublesome, and within Europe particular elements such as the Bulgars or the Magyars, who were wandering destructively around central and eastern Europe in an attempt to find a permanent home, were also creating difficulties. Then there were the Saracen incursions from the south to distract the west as well. Although Christian armies had started to reclaim the Iberian Peninsula (as evidenced by the opening of a hospice for pilgrims to the shrine of St James de Compostela in 893), this was only the very beginning of the *Reconquista*. Saracen raids into the underbelly of Europe continued to create anxiety.

Further afield, Islamic fragmentation and internal dispute continued to eat away at the unity of the faith. In 899, a group known as the Qarmatians established an independent state in Bahrain. They proved to be a particularly aggressive breakaway faction and used their base in the gulf to launch terrorist raids.

These events in the Middle East were, when allied to the Viking raids which had now affected an area covering thousands of miles, symptomatic of an age in ferment. The decline of the T'ang dynasty merely reinforced the general picture. For a century that had started so brightly, the world seemed to have turned around 180 degrees. Great uncertainty seemed to mark the way ahead.

23

THE TWILIGHT OF THE DARK AGES

The Rebirth of Christianity (AD 901–1000)

The tenth century was one in which new powers emerged but also when some older ones, seemingly on the brink of extinction, managed to hang on for dear life against the odds. It was also one in which the waves of 'barbarian' incursions continued to lap across Eurasia. Rather than thinking of the phenomenon of such invasions as being solely connected to the decline and fall of Rome, in fact the second half of the first millennium AD in the Christian calendar saw ongoing probing from a number of different sources. Whereas centuries before it had been Saxons, Goths, Huns and Vandals, now it was Norsemen, Bulgars, Pechenegs and Magyars, not to mention various other Turkic tribes.

The impact of these huge migrations was felt across a wide area, from the borders of Europe to the edges of Central Asia. For those states in the front-line - and there were many of them, especially as some of these incursions were seaborne and ignored land boundaries – it was a matter of survival.

The Magyars were one group that was particularly active. What comes as a surprise to the uninitiated was just how widespread their incursions were. They were peoples of the Central Asian steppes originally and, given this, it is understandable that they were superb horsemen. This gave them great mobility and it explains why their raids took in huge sweeps of Europe such as Bavaria and Italy (in 900), Carinthia – now part of Austria – in 901 and Moravia (Central Europe) and Saxony in 906. Later on, in 924, they were raiding Italy again but were forced out into southern France. Thirteen years later they were raiding as far into France as Rheims.

The Magyars swept across Europe for a time without any clear sign that they would stop and settle anywhere. In the eastern part of the continent, Byzantium was one state potentially in the front line and the Magyars were indeed raiding in the region of Constantinople in 934. But the Byzantine Empire was to see something of a revival during the tenth century. It was not that those who held the exulted position of emperor were any more secure; there were ten emperors in the ninth century and eight in the tenth; not statistically hugely different. Neither did it mean that the plotting, the depositions and the murders of unpopular rulers did not happen. But some very good emperors did emerge during the course of the century and this, allied to weaknesses among Byzantium's neighbours, helped to create the conditions for a Byzantine revival of sorts.

However, the emperors in Constantinople had new challenges to contend with. The infusion of Viking blood into Russia seems to have sparked an expansionist spirit into the region. By 907, Russian raiders were at the very gates of Constantinople (they would return again in 941) though the massive walls – perhaps the most significant construction project ever undertaken in the millennium following the collapse of Rome – again prevented any serious threat emerging, though the suburbs of the city were sacked. Despite their failure, these raids launched from Russia had given a clear indication that another new power was emerging. Just four years later, a peace treaty was agreed between the Byzantines and the Russians at Kiev.

Byzantium also had renewed ambitions in the west. In 915, Byzantine forces, co-operating with local Christian allies, drove the Saracens out from their base on the Garigliano, bringing to an end the Muslim presence in central Italy. However, the ability of these Islamic forces to act as fast raiders was still a problem and as late as 934 they were launching lightning strikes on Genoa, Corsica and Sardinia, using their by now well-developed naval skills to do so. Six years later, they got as far into Europe as Switzerland.

In the Middle East, the decline of the Abbasid Caliphate continued. After the death of the caliph al-Mu'tadid in 902, his successors effectively continued as puppets with their strings pulled by their Turkish bodyguards. There were, admittedly, some signs suggesting a recovery of sorts; for half a century, a dynasty known as the Tulunid had broken away from the Abbasid Caliphate in Egypt and ruled in its own right. However, in 905 it was invaded and both Egypt and Syria were restored to Abbasid rule.

It was a false dawn. More symptomatic was the reign of the Abbasid caliph al-Mustada in 908, which lasted for one day. The year after, an event of great significance occurred when the Aghlabid dynasty in North Africa was overthrown. The dynasty nominally owed allegiance to the Abbasid Caliphate and this was yet another sign of the institution's seemingly permanent decline.

The leader of the victorious army, Sa'id ibn-Husayn, was proclaimed 'Ubaydullah al-Mahdi'. And so was founded the Fatimid dynasty, which would play a critical role in Islam for the greater part of the next three centuries. Significantly the Fatimids were adherents to the Shiite branch of Islam, in contrast to the Abbasids, who saw themselves as protectors of Sunni orthodoxy. The fault lines of Islam were becoming increasingly marked.

This weakening of Islam helped Byzantium, which was also assisted by events elsewhere. The Bulgars, frequently hostile to the Byzantines though they had been, were actually useful in providing a buffer state against the Magyars to the north of Constantinople. The power of the Bulgars declined as the century went on, though this only became apparent over time.

In 913, the Bulgarian khan Symeon led his army to the very suburbs of Constantinople, though those immense walls frightened even him off. But not for long. Four years later, Symeon demanded that he should be recognised as the Byzantine emperor. He defeated the imperial forces deployed to check his ambitions and effectively made himself master of the Balkans, though Constantinople was still far too tough a nut to crack.

In 923, Adrianople – after Constantinople one of Byzantium's foremost cities – fell to Symeon. However, when Symeon died on 27 May 927 Bulgar dominance died with him. He was replaced by his son Peter, who made peace with the Byzantine emperor, who then recovered his authority over Serbia. During the course of the century, imperial power in the Balkans steadily grew and a terrible reckoning awaited the Bulgars for their temerity in challenging the regional supremacy of Byzantium.

Byzantium was characterised by two paradoxical phenomena: an incredible artistic achievement and a seemingly endless ability to self-destruct. One of the key causes of the latter state of affairs was the frequent jostling for position between the emperor, the secular head of the empire, and the Patriarch of Constantinople, its spiritual leader. Over time, the secular increasingly came out on top but it was a foolish emperor who ignored the patriarch in his political calculations.

A similar situation pertained in Western Europe, where the Pope was still very much a junior partner to the secular powers even after the formation of the Holy Roman Empire. But the power of the Church was about to increase. In the eleventh century, several powerful Popes would emerge who would considerably strengthen the papacy's position. The tenth century, however, helped to lay the foundations for this situation through an amazing surge of spiritual energy emanating in particular from the abbey of Cluny in France.

The abbey at Cluny was founded in 910. A new church was opened there in 927. Success was not an overnight phenomenon. However, as the century progressed the influence of a revitalised monastic movement grew significantly. This was in some ways a quite necessary counterbalance to an aggressive nobility that was increasingly hard to control. A constant battle for dominance was being fought, leading to a delicate and often volatile state of equilibrium between the competing elements. This would come to a head during the eleventh century.

Both the situation of the papacy and that of the Byzantine patriarchs – and for that matter the role of the various Islamic caliphs – serves to emphasise that such positions in religious establishments also had a heavy say in secular politics too – something that we might not choose to recognise today, when increasingly there is a drive (certainly in Western Europe at least) to keep Church and State separate. Such a situation would have been unthinkable a thousand years ago.

That said, it was clear that a counterbalance to the brutal norms of secular society was needed. Western European society remained violent and divided, and the situation in Francia deteriorated alarmingly when measured against the relative stability of Charlemagne's reign where, though violence existed in abundance, there was still an element of control exercised by central authority. Those on the wrong end of this 'controlled violence' of course suffered terribly, but the situation became much worse as local warlords took full advantage of the lack of central restraint. The Holy Roman

Empire continued to exist but the dominant driving force behind it was now German rather than Frankish. In 911, Louis the Child, the last Carolingian ruler of Germany, died.

The Franks also had new neighbours to worry about. That same year, Charles the Simple received the homage of Rollo, a Norse leader who had established himself on the Seine. Rollo was baptised as a Christian and in return was granted Rouen and other towns in Normandy. So began the formal life of the Duchy of Normandy. This established a permanent base for a new power in the west, the Normans, as well as bringing about an end to the Viking raids on the north of France. To the Frankish king, it no doubt seemed a price well worth paying. To other regions, though, who would suffer from the opportunistic talents of the Normans, the cost must have seemed exorbitant.

However, the Normans were just one strand of the Viking threat. The name 'Viking' has been found on old rune stones in Scandinavia and means 'an overseas expedition'. It is in some ways a rather careless title because different groups of raiders emanated from Scandinavia owing little, if any, allegiance to each other (in other words, the 'Vikings' were nothing like a homogeneous group). In similar fashion to the Turks, different groups might co-operate on a specific venture but generally speaking these were autonomous war bands. Even if Rollo's Vikings were now relatively quiet, Danish raiders continued to cause trouble elsewhere in France. In 921, Count Robert of Neustria expelled the Danes from his land but allowed them to settle near Nantes. Two years later, they were also raiding Aquitaine and the Auvergne.

Across the Channel in England there had been something of a resurgence as the Saxon parts of the country accelerated their attempts to reverse the effects of the Viking invasions. In 914, King Edward the Elder began the reconquest of the area approximately covering the northern half of England, known as the Danelaw. Four years later, he took control of Mercia and conquered the Danish Midlands. Then when a Viking warlord, Ragnald, seized York and became King of Northumbria, he acknowledged the overlordship of Edward the Elder.

When Edward died in 924, he was replaced by his son Athelstan. On 12 July three years later, in a historic meeting on the borders, the kings of Scotland and Strathclyde recognised the overlordship of Athelstan. It was more a token gesture than anything else and any formal integration between England and Scotland was still nearly 700 years in the future; it was nevertheless a very strong signal of just how successful the fightback from southern England had been.

But in Francia, in contrast, the Frankish dynasty was an increasingly weakened power. In 917, the Magyars raided Alsace and Burgundy. King Charles asked for help from his nobles to rebuff them. He was completely ignored in response, further evidencing the loss of monarchical power in Francia. Then in 919 the Germans declared their own king, the duke Henry of Saxony, who became known as Henry the Fowler because of his great love of hunting. This was a direct act of defiance against the Carolingian dynasty.

The year after, Charles invaded in an attempt to reassert his authority in Germany but soon retreated again. By the time of Henry's death in 936, many of the German peoples were united under his rule and a new power had emerged in the region. Not only had the position with regards to Francia been changed heavily in Germany's favour, but Henry had also forced King Gorm of Denmark to make peace and a march had been established in Schleswig, while Magyar attacks on his lands had also been successfully repulsed.

To the south, the Islamic territories in the Iberian Peninsula were enjoying a renaissance, helped by the decline of Frankish power in the north, which had previously pushed itself into their territories. In 929, the ruler of Cordoba, Abd-ar-Rahman III, declared himself caliph. There were now three Caliphs claiming to be the figurehead of Islam: Abd-ar-Rahman in Cordoba, the Fatimid caliph in North Africa and the Abbasid in Baghdad. It was yet another sign of the fragmentation of the Muslim world.

Yet the Cordoba caliphate, though short-lived, was to lead a glorious life, typified by sumptuous architecture such as the Great Mosque of Cordoba. Later in the century, the caliph Al-Hakam enlarged Cordoba University, making it probably the foremost educational establishment in Europe and the Muslim world at the time. Al-Hakam's army would also destroy the Idrisid dynasty of Fez in North Africa, reinforcing their regional dominance as far as Islam was concerned.

Trade also thrived and Abd-ar-Rahman managed to reverse some of the gains made by Christian powers in the previous century (for example, in 937 he took Saragossa from the Christian kingdoms of Leon and Navarre in the north of Spain). The King of Navarre was forced to recognise his suzerainty. The conquest of Toledo soon after Abd-ar-Rahman had been declared caliph had effectively reunited the Muslim lands in Spain, which had previously become fragmented, returning it to a coherent whole.

Despite this resurgence, much of the Islamic world was shocked to the core by momentous events that took place in 930. The Qarmatians were a Shiite fundamentalist breakaway movement who believed that a great leader, the Mahdi, would be sent into the world to usher in an age of Islamic renaissance. In some ways, their regime seems surprisingly liberal, with their belief in equality and reason. But they also regarded the annual *hajj* to Mecca as nothing more than a superstition. When they raided the city in that year, they removed from it the fabled Black Stone which was said to date back to the time of Adam and Eve, the very founding of the world. It would only be returned several decades later, when a massive ransom payment was paid over.

A state of affairs that might once more fairly be described as chaos existed in China in the first half of the century. With the loss of the centralised control that had gradually been eroded as the T'ang lost their grip on the tiller of the ship of state, local powers had increasingly stepped into the gap created as a result – in many ways a replication of what was happening in Francia at the same time. Local warlords were quick to seize the opportunity to build up their status and wealth as a result. An especially significant year was 907, when the T'ang were finally extinguished, the last emperor being deposed by the warlord Chu Wen, who declared himself ruler. So began what was known as the 'Period of the Five Dynasties and the Ten Kingdoms'.

Yet it would be wrong to think of the same situation pertaining all across China. The characteristics of the land in the south, more suitable to agriculture and a settled population, were quite different than those in the tougher, drier north. Although the south fragmented, the situation was not one of permanent warfare but one in which smaller states that had been formed traded freely and openly with each other.

The north was different. Here there were many Turkish warriors prepared to move into the vacuum created by the decline of the T'ang. The five dynasties that existed in the latter T'ang period characterise just how volatile the situation was. In 937, one of the claimants to the throne turned to the Khitan tribes of Mongolia for help in securing his claim. They fulfilled their part of the bargain but the successful claimant soon found out, like many a claimant before and since, that inviting in such help was a double-edged sword. Once the Khitans had smelled power, they were reluctant to give it up again.

The Khitans were in many ways the pre-echo of the Mongols. They came from beyond Manchuria, in the far north of China, where they had existed partly by farming, partly by hunting. They sent tributes to the T'ang when they were in power but were not above raiding either. At one time divided, they now entered into a federation; the man responsible for this, Abaoji, also replaced the traditional leadership election process, where chiefs served for limited terms, with a system of hereditary succession.

In 947, the Khitans established a separate dynasty in the north of China, the Liao, which would survive until 1125. They imitated Chinese customs, formally adopting Confucianism but also patronising Buddhism. Next to them, to the west, another group, the Tanguts – related to the Tibetans – had also established a state, known as Hsi Hsia. These states would essentially act as a northern barrier to protect China when a strong state was restored further south.

In the wake of the decline of T'ang control, other regional powers took the opportunity to assert their independence. So in 939 Ngô Quyen defeated the Chinese and founded the kingdom of Dai Co Viet (north Vietnam). Half a century later, the then king of Dai Co Viet, Le Dai Hanh, defeated a Chinese invasion of his country. Then in 983 he destroyed Indrapura, capital of the Champa kingdom in south Vietnam. Conflicts between north and south Vietnam have a surprisingly modern ring about them.

Close by, in 936 Wang Kŏn reunited the Korean peninsula after half a century of war-torn chaos. Adopting the techniques of administration he admired from T'ang rule, he founded the Koryŏ dynasty. Despite being a general, he was a devout Buddhist who believed that the great Buddha's protection was vital for the well-being of his fledgling state, which he welded together with the judicious use of marriage alliances with some of the aggressive warlords in the region.

The Indian Subcontinent still remained divided at this time. For example, in the south by now there was the Tamil Chola kingdom. Under a long-lived king Parantaka I, who reigned from 907 to 955, the Chola state expanded steadily, picking off adjacent territories such as Pandya, the neighbouring Tamil state in the south. Although surviving records are sketchy, it seems that Parantaka was a mighty warrior and for much of his reign the extent of the territories he held increased.

However, there is always a danger that such ambition leads to overstretching, and from 940 onwards the Chola kingdom was increasingly on the defensive. Opposition in particular came from the Rashtrakuta dynasty to the north. Krishna III, also known as Kannara, led his armies against the Chola and later won a crushing victory. By the end of his reign the extent of Rashtrakuta territories covered much of the Indian Subcontinent. Even the King of Ceylon paid homage to Krishna. But, by the time Krishna died in 967, he had been far too generous in his granting of lands to his key commanders and in this lay the ultimate undoing of the great empire he had built.

In Germany, on the death of Henry the Fowler in 937, his son Otto succeeded him and pointedly was crowned in Aachen, Charlemagne's old capital. This was evidence that he was aiming to be proclaimed not just king but also emperor. Before Otto could make good on his ambitions, he first of all had to keep his own dukes under control, which was no easy task. Once he had done this, he launched a series of campaigns against both Francia and Italy, culminating in the capture of Pavia in 951.

Otto also cultivated good relations with the Church. These led to the Pope, John XII, seeking and gaining his protection and in return crowning him emperor in 962. Charlemagne's days of Frankish glory seemed an awful long way in the past, as the Franks were now very much the junior power in Western Europe. But Otto proved an unreliable ally to the papacy. The year after being crowned by John, Otto deposed him and installed Leo VIII as Pope instead. John recovered the papacy shortly after but died in the following year. His successor, Benedict, was then replaced by Leo once more. It was a portent of far greater struggles between Church and State in the following century.

As the century progressed, the Fatimid caliphate grew ever stronger. In 969 al'Mu'izz, the fourth Fatimid caliph, conquered Egypt and exterminated the ruling Ikhshidid dynasty, which had been in power for just a few decades and had been established by Turkic warriors. After the decisive battle, the capital at Fustat was reconstructed and given a new name, al-Qahira, 'the Victorious'. It would become better known in the west as 'Cairo'. For the next 200 years, the Fatimid dynasty in Egypt was to play a crucial role in the Islamic world.

Neither was this the last Fatimid victory. Within the next fifteen years, they had pushed on into Palestine and southern Syria (which the founder of the Ikhshidid dynasty, Muhammad al-Ikhshid, had seized in 937). It now seemed only a matter of time before the Abbasid Caliphate was at last extinguished. The decline of Abbasid power was epitomised by the emergence of an increasing number of small Muslim states in Syria; for example, in 944 Sayf ad-Dawla established himself in Aleppo, marking the start of the Hamdanid dynasty based there.

This was yet another sign of fragmentation in the Muslim world. During the tenth century the Fatimids made a partially successful attempt to step into the breach in Syria. From the north, the Byzantines also nibbled away at the borders and won back lost territory. Syria and the surrounding region became a fault line where three powers bordered each other: Byzantine, Abbasid and Fatimid. The inherent weakness created as a result laid the foundations for a threat from quite a different direction in the following century.

But future salvation for the Abbasid caliphs was to arrive from an as yet unsuspected source. The Turks were major if unpredictable players in the shaping of both Asia and Europe and their vigorous activities were evident over a wide area. For example, in 962 a Turkish warlord, Alptigin, founded the dynasty of the Ghaznavids with the seizure of Ghazni in what is now Afghanistan. Their influence on the future development of the Middle East and Eastern Europe would eventually be profound.

In 960, the Karakhanids of Central Asia became the first Turkish tribe to convert en masse to Islam. The Turks, fierce horsemen with a penchant for plunder, had traditionally been shamanists. However, they were to become fierce defenders of their newfound faith. Another group, the Seljuks, had originally lived to the north of the Caspian and Aral Seas. They too took up Islam as their faith. During the tenth century they moved into Khorosan, on the borders of Persia. From here they would, in the next century, burst forth spectacularly into the consciousness of the lands further west, with some rather surprising results for the Abbasid Caliphate. Superb horsemen, and equipped with the powerful composite bow, they were formidable warriors.

The decline of the Abbasid Caliphate allowed Byzantium to make significant strides down the road to recovery. So too did other factors. To the north, the Bulgars were starting to run out of steam, removing a significant and frequent threat from that direction. What also helped Byzantium no end was the emergence of several emperors of distinction. That is not to say that the insuperable problems of internal strife and usurpation came to an end, merely that the men who emerged victorious from them were often of a superior ilk to those who had done so previously.

The first of them, Romanus I, steered the helm of the ship of state very adroitly and managed as a result to take the momentum out of the Bulgar advance. Although never loved by the people whose throne he had seized – usurpation was a very common route to the role of emperor – his achievements were important in the light of the revival that he launched. When he himself was the victim of a coup in 945 – a coup, it must be said, in favour of the legitimate emperor, Constantine VII – he was at least allowed to live, albeit humiliated and forced to become a monk.

Constantine was a man of great learning, whose own writings provide an invaluable window into tenth-century Byzantium. Later on in his reign, two outstanding generals emerged, Nicephorus Phocas and John Tzimisces. They both scored significant successes against Muslim armies in Asia Minor and beyond. Then, in 960, in the reign of Constantine's successor Romanus II, Nicephorus won a stunning victory when he overwhelmed the Islamic base on Crete, from which so much troublesome piratical activity emanated. It was a hard-won victory, due more than anything to the ability of Nicephorus to motivate his men during a long-drawn-out siege of the main city, Candia.

However, successful generals were a threat to emperors and Nicephorus was snubbed and deprived of the triumphal return to Constantinople he was due. This was a dangerous step to take. On the death of Romanus II, Nicephorus showed the same skilfully executed strategic insight he had demonstrated on the battlefield to successfully manoeuvre himself to the throne. A reign typified more than anything by triumph after triumph against Muslim armies in the east followed; Tarsus, Cyprus and, most significantly, Antioch returned to the empire. Even the ruler of Aleppo recognised Nicephorus as his sovereign lord.

Yet even such victories could not secure his place on the throne. During a fierce blizzard on a December night in 969, a party of plotters burst into Nicephorus's room. There, watched by the man who would take his place, that other successful general John Tzimisces, Nicephorus was beaten mercilessly by his enemies and finally run through with a sword. Then, his body was thrown out of a window into the snow, to lie there untended until a passing monk took pity and buried the corpse. Such was the gratitude of Byzantium for the triumphs Nicephorus had won.

Despite starting his reign with blood on his hands, John Tzimisces proved a capable leader. He was faced with a great challenge at the outset, another invasion from that new and vigorous power, Russia. Prince Svyatoslav of Kiev led his men into Bulgaria but Tzimisces was ready for him and won a stunning victory. Svyatoslav was no quitter and continued the campaign but was completely outmanoeuvred. He was forced to retreat and the kingdom of the Bulgars was – ironically, given past events – given the formal protection of Byzantium. This was just a cynical ploy; shortly afterwards, Bulgaria was absorbed into the empire.

Tzimisces then turned his eyes east, where the decline of the Abbasids and the emergence of the Fatimids had created huge instability in the Levant. Using this destabilisation to full effect, Tzimisces advanced into the region, taking parts of Palestine, Lebanon and Syria. But his successes were brought to an end by his death in 976. There were, perhaps inevitably, persistent rumours that his lingering demise was brought on by poison. Such claims were never proven, but they were certainly believable.

His successor, Basil, was faced with a number of challenges. He was a young man, overshadowed by his chamberlain and faced with revolts from several directions. But he managed to hang on to power before launching himself vigorously into a series of campaigns in several directions. A major challenge came from the Bulgars, led by their able khan Samuel, who used the seemingly fragile state of the empire to fight back against Byzantium. There would be terrible consequences for the Bulgars.

Basil sought help from Russia, from where 6,000 men of Viking extraction set out. So was born the Varangian Guard, the most famous of all Viking warrior bands. But the Russians were unhappy that they did not receive the reward they were promised for their help and seized Byzantine-held territory on the northern coast of the Black Sea as a result. Seeing that he needed Russian support, Basil decided to mend his bridges and, as he had previously promised but not yet delivered, he sent his sister to marry the Russian prince, Vladimir.

Quite what the thought of this must have seemed like to the young princess, Anna, is hard to imagine, though politically expedient marriages of the kind were by no means unheard of as a way of building useful alliances. But the distance between the civilisation of Byzantium and the harshness of the world of 'barbarian' Russia must have seemed considerably greater than the 400 miles or so as the crow flies that separated the two. Yet this was one of the most significant acts of medieval history. For, though Russia was still largely pagan, it would not remain so. As part of the marriage terms, Vladimir was baptised.

This must have seemed to many just a cosmetic ceremony, yet it truly seems to have transformed Vladimir. Before his marriage to Anna he had enjoyed many wives and concubines. Now these were all sent away and a vigorous process of proselytising among the rest of his people followed. Russia was moving inexorably towards lasting integration into the Orthodox flock. It was as if the legitimacy gained from adopting Christianity would mark some transition in Russia's status, and indeed in many ways it did.

Russian delegations that had visited Constantinople were seemingly influenced by the majesty of Byzantine ceremony; one visitor from Kiev described how, when visiting Hagia Sophia, 'we knew not whether we were in Heaven or earth. For on earth there is no such splendour and beauty, and we are at a loss as to how to describe it.' This is a feeling that many modern visitors to this incredible building (this author included) can surely still empathise with.

Such conversions to Christianity were not unprecedented; in a number of places previously pagan cultures were becoming Christianised; in 950 Gyula, the Magyar leader – whose wanderings had stopped by the end of the century, the Magyars having found a permanent home in Hungary – was baptised in Constantinople and returned home with the first Hungarian bishop as a missionary, and in 959 the German king Otto sent a missionary to Russia at the request of Olga of Kiev.

Mieszka of Poland had also converted to Christianity in 966, the year after King Harold Bluetooth had made Christianity the official religion of Denmark. But the conversions did not always last; the Wends, a fierce people on the far fringes of Northern Europe, had been nominally Christianised by missions from the west but a great rising in 983 threw the missionaries out and saw the Wends reverting to paganism for several centuries.

With the support of Russia, it seemed Basil was free to destroy the Bulgar threat once and for all. However, just as he was preparing for a final and crushing campaign in 995, dramatic news came in of a massive attack from Fatimid forces in Syria. Basil in response launched one of the most incredible counter-attacks in history. Leading his army hundreds of miles across harsh terrain in just sixteen days, he arrived at Aleppo before the Fatimids could take it and drove off the threat. It was the mark of a man who was not possessed of flair or obvious innovatory military genius but who, instead, won his victories through ruthless persistence, indefatigable energy and quite brilliant organisational skills.

In China, an end of sorts to the disintegration of centralised power was signalled with the emergence of the Sung dynasty. Led by Zhao Kuangyin, better known as T'ai-tsu, who took power in 960, the new dynasty offered hope of the restoration of a more stable way of life for many of his subjects. T'ai-tsu managed to bring most of the autonomous regional armies in the south of China under his sway. He succeeded in removing the generals who had in the first place brought him to power and establishing a strong state administration in the place of what had amounted to military rule.

This was not a case of demilitarisation, though; by the time of T'ai-tsu's death in 976, there were reputedly 378,000 men in his army. The position of the ruling dynasty was simply not secure enough to dismantle the army. There were other improvements in a number of important areas though – judicial, fiscal and logistical – through the improvement of transport links.

Yet this was not a complete return to the strong power of the T'ang. The Khitans around Beijing were too tough to budge and were instead bought off. They continued to reign in the north, a minority in a Chinese-populated area (at their peak there were estimated to be 750,000 Khitans ruling several million Chinese) using Chinese administrators and methods of rule to ensure that their government was successful. But, although heavily outnumbered by the Sung-governed population in the south, their military superiority was enough to ensure that they survived for several hundred years.

Other events at around this time emphasised the changed nature of the Chinese world, such as when, in 968, Dinh Bo Linh, the ruler of Dai Co Viet, was recognised by the Sung emperors in China. What the Sung did do was expand China's trading opportunities. Guangzhou developed as a major trading port with links to a number of areas in the South China Sea. Trading grew with areas further afield such as Indonesia, and Guangzhou served as a conduit for traffic on to more local bases in Korea, Manchuria and Japan. By the end of the eleventh century, the city would have a population of 300,000, dwarfing anything in Europe.

It is often thought that Japan has, until recent times, lived in splendid isolation from the rest of the world. That is only true as far as Europe is concerned. In contrast, links with China and Korea were very significant. There was substantial trade with mainland China, initially focussed through the port of Fukuoka but later other entrepôts to Japan emerged such as Hakata and Nagasaki. Silk, porcelain and ceramics flowed in, to be followed from 1200 onwards by tea.

The world elsewhere was also continuing to become smaller, though the process was not rapid. Slowly but surely, without knowing it, Europe and America were starting to travel down a path that would lead, half a millennium later, to a head-on collision. A significant step forward in this respect was about to be made. As well as being raiders and traders of the first order, the Vikings were also wonderful seafarers and intrepid adventurers. One of them, known as Erik the Red, was banished from Iceland and sailed west. Here he found a new land, inhabited by only a few Inuit, which he thought offered the opportunity for permanent and successful settlement.

With his period of exile over, Erik later returned to Iceland and told those there of a new 'green land' he had found. He returned to Greenland and established several permanent settlements in 985. The island settlements never housed a large number of people, a few thousand at most, but provided a potential stepping stone to the as yet unknown lands further west. By the end of the century the Vikings had also reached Newfoundland. Although only here for a short time, perhaps a decade in total, they left behind them the only surviving evidence for pre-Columbian links between Europe and America at the archaeological site of L'Anse aux Meadows.

But the new Viking territory of Vinland in Newfoundland did not last long. The sagas suggest that this was because, as well as fighting each other, the Vikings also found themselves at war with the indigenous population, whom they called skraelings, a word of uncertain origin which might mean 'foreigner' or refer merely to the skins that they wore. The settlement did not ultimately take root but contact had been made.

Given Newfoundland's proximity to it, it is quite likely that the Norse adventurers made landfall on the mainland too; the name 'Vinland' may refer to grapes, and the mainland was a more likely home for these than the exposed island offshore (though the presence of grapes in Canada suggests that the climate was warmer then than now). Dependent on future discoveries, Columbus's claim to have discovered the Americas may one day be in need of significant re-evaluation.

By the close of the tenth century, the 'barbarians' surging into Europe were increasingly transforming themselves into settled peoples rather than raiders. The raids did not stop altogether; the Vikings were back raiding England, for example, by the century's close. But there was an increasing organisation evident in their attacks, which made them far more dangerous. New powers were emerging and with them new threats. As the best example, Viking raiders had gone through a metamorphosis into Normans, whose thirst for adventure and profit was about to make itself known right across Europe. It was debatable whether parts of Europe were any safer due to this transition.

That these were violent times in the west, where local warlords were becoming increasingly powerful, was evidenced by the emergence of a new style of architecture, demonstrated at the century's close when Fulk of Anjou built one of the earliest known castles at Langeais in France. It was an apt metaphor for what was to follow, for a century of blood was nigh when east and west would clash as they had not done for nearly a thousand years. The consequences of this clash are with us to the present day.

In the year 1000, a year of almost inevitable apocalyptic significance in the Christian world, there were those who believed that the world would indeed come to an end. Biblical scholars warned that, one thousand years on from the birth of Christ, the time for his return to earth had come and a terrible judgement was therefore close at hand.

Just how widespread such views really were in a Europe, where communications were poor and literacy limited to a select few, is a matter of debate. However, legends grew that the papacy was so concerned that it ordered Charlemagne's tomb to be opened and his imperial crown recovered just in case. The world did not end, but at many times during the coming century it appeared that Armageddon had not been cancelled, only postponed.

24

THE CENTURY OF BLOOD

The Dawning of the Crusades (AD 1001–1100)

Ninety-nine years after the Christian world thought that its end was nigh, Muslim and Jewish Jerusalem was filled with the screams of the dying and the victorious war cries of Western European invaders. The streets, it was said, in places ran knee-deep with blood. These two events bookend what was one of the most significant periods in history, the events of which resonate down to the current day. Some historians might dispute this, saying that the long-term impacts of the Crusades have been over-egged. They miss the point that perception is more powerful than reality in shaping the way in which human beings think and act.

One question that to the modern mind is hard to understand is why so many ordinary people, men and women, young and old, as well as men of war should abandon all they had in the west and set out on Crusade. One of the answers is that many of them had little to give up. The chroniclers of the time weave a harrowing tapestry, vividly creating an image of an era of violent lawlessness when robber barons helped themselves to what they wanted. The vast majority of society, now trapped in what was fast becoming an exploitative feudal system that treated them little better than cattle, was powerless to resist; the dictates of the law allowed them to be pillaged just as much as they were subject to banditry. Life was harsh; as well as war, there were frequent famines and outbreaks of disease.

Although lazy stereotypes should be avoided, the surviving chronicles of the period leave little doubt that this was indeed a tough time to be alive. The castles that were increasingly dotting the landscape represented something sinister; partly the result of powerful lords that increasingly cocked a snook at monarchical authority (as well as that of the Church) and partly a base from which to exert maximum pressure on the local populace to give up the pitifully few things they possessed, which, in most cases, were needed more to keep them alive rather than provide any tiny measure of comfort. It was not that previous centuries lacked violence; Muslim, Viking and Magyar raiders prove that. However, the violence was increasingly localised, one lord against his neighbour. And, worst of all, it was often legitimised by the law.

Yet this was the century when Western Europe started to play a role that would lead for a while, some centuries into the future, to a position when it was without a doubt the dominant world power. It would take some time to arrive at this point but the eleventh century was a crucial step in that direction. It would not only most obviously represent a clash between faiths when Christendom collided with Islam (as we have seen already, warfare between the two was very much a feature of earlier centuries, though there were distinguishing characteristics of the Crusades that we will consider) but also between the eastern and western halves of Christian Europe.

An insight into the social structure at this time is given by Bishop Adalberon of Laon, who described three classes: *oratores*, *bellatores* and *laboratores*, that is those who pray, those who fight and those who work. There were clear delineations between the three and the hierarchy was rigid. Those who prayed, the monks and clergy, sought constantly to assert their rights against those who fought, the knights, whose often violent exploits threatened to overturn the position of the clerics. Those who worked formed the very base of the pyramid, pitilessly crushed by supporting the weight of the structure on top of them, expected to do as they were told by the two other parties.

At the century's outset it seemed as if Byzantium and the West might become closer. In 1002 Zoë – the niece of the unmarried Byzantine emperor Basil II – set out for Italy, where she was due to be married to the Holy Roman Emperor, Otto III. By the time she completed her voyage, her groom-to-be was dead, taken by a fever at the age of twenty-two. Given the lack of a male heir to succeed Basil, it is tempting to speculate whether Eastern and Western Christendom might not, after all, have been reunited peaceably if things had been different. It is one of those great what-ifs of history that can never be answered, though the different world views espoused by the two halves of Christendom were so marked that such an outcome is inherently unlikely.

The first decades of the century were marked by events that were notable, even in those often violent times, for the letting of copious amounts of blood, events that seemingly assured the future of Byzantium. The most shocking of them perhaps occurred in Bulgaria, which would lead to Basil earning for himself one of the more sinister sobriquets of history – *Bulgaroctonus*, the Bulgar slayer.

Early in his reign Basil had been severely defeated by the Bulgars. Although he was a rational, even clinical man, his actions suggest that he bore a personal grudge in addition to wanting to embed Bulgaria as part of his empire for good strategic reasons. In 1014, after a decisive victory at Cimbalongus, he found himself in possession of 15,000 Bulgar captives. They were divided into batches of 100; of each century, ninety-nine were completely blinded while the hundredth was deprived of only one eye so that he could be tied to the rest and lead them back to the khan Samuel as an unmistakable message that Basil was not to be trifled with.

Terror has been a frequently used tactic to bring subjugation to an enemy; for Genghis Khan and many others throughout history (Alexander, Hitler, Cromwell in Ireland – the list is a long one) it has been a strategic tool to frighten an enemy into submission. In this case, it most certainly worked. Samuel promptly died, it was said of shock, leaving Bulgaria at the mercy of Basil. After these actions, it is something of a surprise to find that the emperor, now that his aims had been achieved, proved to be a surprisingly tolerant and benign ruler of his newfound subjects, who formed an invaluable buffer against further attacks from the north on Constantinople. Perhaps the terror had done its job.

The dead khan Samuel is largely a forgotten presence outside of his own region, but there are clues to his existence still there for those who care to look. His castle, heavily reconstructed, still stands on top of a hill overlooking a lake at Ohrid in Macedonia. It is a place of breathtaking beauty, a bowl in a ring of hills generously dusted with snow in the winter months, a poignant reminder of a once great ruler who is now, in many accounts of history, little more than a footnote.

By the lake not far below the castle stands the church of St Sophia, now much renovated after being neglected for some time. There are still some of the eleventh-century icons left, with a power and a spirituality that can still reduce a sensitive viewer to the verge of tears. These awe-inspiring windows into the soul of the past are residues of Byzantine attempts to assert a new identity that would subdue the old and they are artistically and spiritually wonderful. Here is one of those great paradoxes of history, that even from suppression beauty can form. Beauty is, of course, in the famous cliché, in the eyes of the beholder.

Basil died in 1025, unaware that the real threat to his empire came no longer from the north and only partly from the east. That there was some danger from the west was clear enough but he could not have known how great that threat would be. The Byzantines continued to hope for the recovery of their lost lands on the Italian Peninsula, which had been seized by both Western Europeans and Muslims in the south. When Basil expired, he was planning a raid on the Muslim island of Sicily, which was thus saved for a few decades longer.

Basil did not inspire affection among his people, and his passing, though perhaps regretted because of his achievements, was not widely mourned. He had failed in one thing and in this, in the absence of further relevant information, it appears he had been quite deliberate. He had died unmarried and without an heir, leaving an unclear line of succession. In the aftermath, a succession of weak emperors and empresses appeared, under whom the demise of Byzantium was so marked as to be alarming. Basil had papered over the cracks but the foundations of the Byzantine Empire were subsiding.

His immediate successor Constantine VIII was both weak and cruel. Basil had subdued the power of the aristocracy and introduced strong centralised control; this soon changed. The power of local nobles grew, with sometimes devastating results for their peasantry, especially in Asia Minor, which was both the granary of the empire and the source of large reserves of manpower for the Byzantine army. Constantine did not live long and was, again, without an heir when he died.

His sister Zoë, no longer the young princess who might, if fate had been kinder, have united east and west, assumed the throne and shared it with the husband, Romanus Argyrus, who had been found in amazing haste when Constantine died. The fact that he was already married proved no obstacle; Romanus was threatened with the choice of accepting the easily arranged divorce he was offered or losing his eyes. It proved an easy decision to make.

Little good did it do him. The reign of Romanus III was short. Almost inevitably, when he died in 1034 there were widely believed suggestions that he had been murdered. This time it would be half a century before a ruler of note would emerge to pick up the baton carried by Basil II and he would inherit a very different state of affairs to that pertaining when the Bulgar slayer died.

The decline was already apparent when an attack on Muslim Sicily was finally launched in 1038. In the Byzantine ranks was a Viking who would earn a fearsome reputation, Harald Hardrada; he was on his way back from a pilgrimage to Jerusalem, which suggests that these were changed times from when the Scandinavians had first launched their raids two centuries before. After initial success, the campaign quickly became one of abject failure for the Byzantine army. The invading army was sent back east with its tail between its legs. The defenders congratulated themselves on their victory but would have been better served turning their attention northwards.

Events in the west of Europe were generating forces that would be hard to control. By the end of the tenth century, a movement known as the Peace of God had started which aimed to stop or at least limit the excesses of the robber barons of Western Europe. It was a cause enthusiastically espoused by the increasingly influential monks from Cluny. By about 1040, it had been decreed that certain holy days were to be treated as times of 'non-violence' when it was a sin to fight.

Yet this led to strange effects. In 1038, the peasants of Limoges, who were understandably sick to the back teeth of being on the wrong end of exploitation, took up the cause of peace so enthusiastically that they formed into armed bands and started to attack castles. The peace movement was turning violent. The establishment, which included the Church, grew nervous at a movement that threatened to overturn the established order. A number of bishops were heartily frustrated at the ministrations of Cluny.

A movement later developed during the course of the eleventh century known as the Truce of God. The title may sound similar but it was essentially differently motivated than the Peace of God. Its purpose was not to protect the weak but to stop feuding between the nobles so the interests of the establishment could be properly respected. By this time, these interests were quite clearly enshrined in the law in a way that meant that the feudal system was almost impossible to resist for the vast majority of the population. At the apex of the inverted pyramid were the Church and the lords, each offering the underclass their 'protection' in return for payments of taxes, tithes and other dues. Where there was a king, he was in effect just a first among equals and often found it difficult to assert his full authority effectively.

Amid these difficult social trends, the western and eastern fringes of the Mediterranean were starting to see increased interaction, a situation that was not always blessed with positive results. In 1016, a group of Norman warriors were passing through Salerno when they were recruited as mercenaries. In their wake, others followed. A recurrent lesson, never seemingly learned, was that when mercenaries were hired by weak kingdoms, they preyed on that weakness and undermined those who sought to buy their protection. Norman mercenaries would become infamous for their innate ability to turn and bite the hand that fed them, as Byzantium would later find out. The Normans liked what they saw in Italy and decided to stay, starting to carve out a territory for themselves on the peninsula.

By the middle of the century, there was a growing menace making itself felt around the Mediterranean. The Normans had moved north up the Italian Peninsula and were soon at odds with the papacy. So alarmed was the institution that in 1053 Pope Leo IX personally led an army against them. At Civitate he was overwhelmed and captured. Forced to renounce his actions to obtain his release, he made his way disconsolately back to Rome, where he died soon afterwards.

The Byzantines were well aware that it might not be long before the Normans were threatening them too. Their cause was not to be helped by a major falling out with the papacy, who could have provided an ally against a common enemy. For some time, differences in Christian doctrine and practices had been emphasising tensions within Christendom. It was unfortunate that the Patriarch of Constantinople at the time, Michael Cerularius, was both tactless and arrogant. When a delegation was sent from Rome to try to resolve differences it had exactly the opposite effect.

Unfortunately the delegation was composed of men of a similar ilk to the obstinate patriarch. When Cerularius was rude to them, they responded soon afterwards in the most inflammatory way possible. At three o'clock on the afternoon of 16 July 1054, they strode down the aisle of Hagia Sophia during the Eucharist service and lay a Bill of Excommunication on the high altar. They then withdrew, symbolically wiping the dust from their feet as they left the building. Just when unity was most required, it was least in evidence.

The excommunication, which was directed against Cerularius personally, led to the patriarch excommunicating the members of the delegation in response. Nothing could better symbolise the growing gap between east and west as far as Christendom was concerned. It was attitudes like this that explained why Pope Gregory VII could say a few years later, on the very eve of the Crusading movement, that 'it is far better for a country to remain under the rule of Islam than be governed by Christians who refuse to acknowledge the rights of the Catholic Church'.

This clash between the two churches forced the Pope into the arms of the Normans, a dangerous place to be as far as Constantinople was concerned. In 1059, a new Pope, Nicholas II, was installed after Benedict X had been deposed. The same year he appointed Robert Guiscard Count of Sicily, as well as giving him several other titles. Robert was the finest warrior of his generation and his investiture suggested that Byzantium was under great threat.

So too were the Muslim rulers of Sicily. For his new title to mean anything, Guiscard would have to take possession of the island by force. He also still had a few Byzantine territories on the mainland to occupy his attentions. The last of them, Bari, fell in 1071. It was the end of Byzantine involvement in Italy, over 500 years after Justinian had intervened so spectacularly and established a flourishing capital at Ravenna.

It was a sad end to a glorious late blossoming of Byzantine culture on the peninsula. But it left the Normans free to complete their systematic conquest of Sicily. Intriguingly, rather than destroying Muslim culture on the island it created the conditions in which it could blend with western styles and forms, leading to a rich infusion of ideas that created wonderful and unique art and architecture all of its own.

The ejection of the Byzantines from Italy demonstrated just how much Byzantium was weakening. At the opposite edge of empire, the Seljuk Turks continued to push into the far corners of Asia Minor, strategically so vital to the empire. Romanus Diogenes was not the worst man ever to wear the imperial purple, but he was about to lead it into its greatest military catastrophe.

The Turks were spreading their wings far and wide, impacting on both Asia and the fringes of Europe. From Ghazni Sultan, Mahmud descended with monotonous frequency on the northern borders of India, inflicting terrible destruction on the Hindu states whose people he regarded as being no better than heathens. Yet despite the frequent and terrible violence, which understandably horrified those who were exposed to it, Mahmud did not take a significant amount of land in India on a permanent basis.

These conflicts were in some ways a surprise. Early relationships between Hindus and Muslims when they came into contact were remarkably tranquil. The different states in India were more concerned about the threat posed by each other, so they did not at first see a greater challenge from further afield. It was a fatal error. Mahmud saw the Hindus as little more than idolaters and was quick to burn some of their greatest temples in the north to the ground (after removing the precious gemstones he found in them, of course). On one raid he allegedly returned with over 50,000 slaves and 350 elephants.

At the other end of the Subcontinent, the Cholas continued to be predominant. Indeed, as the century advanced they grew more powerful and intervened further north than their traditional southern strongholds. One of their kings, Rajaraja I, ordered the construction of the wondrous temples of Tanjore (now called Thanjavur), among the greatest of India's treasures. It was a monument as much to the king as to the deity, Lord Shiva, that it professed to exult. Rajaraja contributed enormous sums to it, including 230 kg of gold.

The Cholas also pushed north into Odisha (formerly Orissa) and even into Bengal, though these were more in the nature of raids than conquests, with the prime target of one of them being jars of holy water carried back south from the sacred Ganges. Rajaraja's successor, Rajendra, also looked further afield and is believed to have directed expeditions to the Malay Peninsula and Sumatra, suggesting access to decent naval power, the existence of which is also hinted at by Chola trading missions to China.

But the Cholas were not completely untroubled. Ceylon (Sri Lanka), raided by Rajendra I, was lost in 1070 and, on the mainland Subcontinent, the neighbouring Pandya state continued to nibble away chunks of territories from them. There were ambassadorial exchanges, however, with regions as far away as China and also with the Khmers of Angkor.

Neither did Ghaznavid dominance in the north of the Indian Subcontinent last that long. As is often the case with empires that are founded by outstanding individuals, it did not long outlast its greatest ruler, Mahmud. Following his death a series of vicious succession disputes weakened it. Khorosan was lost to the empire in 1040, shifting its focus further east towards India, bypassing eventually even Ghazni and moving to Lahore. Ghazni eventually fell to an Afghan power, the Ghorids, who may have originally been Persian.

As well as the Ghaznavids, the Seljuk Turks were also an increasing factor in world affairs. Toghril Beg had ascended to the leadership of the Seljuks, then in Central Asia, around 1016. Defeated by the mighty Mahmud of Ghazni, he had led his people westwards, into Persia. He eventually got his own back on Mahmud by sacking Ghazni in 1037. However, his warriors then moved west rather than east and it was they who took Khorosan from the Ghaznavids. In 1055, the Seljuks took possession of Baghdad. There was a rebellion there soon after and for a short time a Fatimid ruler was installed. However, it was back in Seljuk possession by 1060; when it was retaken, Toghril personally strangled the usurper with a bowstring.

Once in Baghdad, there was the Abbasid caliph to consider. Both parties had something to offer each other. While the Seljuks could offer protection, the caliph gave them legitimacy. The Seljuks were in historical terms recent converts to Islam but, like many new religious affiliates, were enthusiastically devout. They were firm adherents to the Sunni cause, whose notional leader was the Abbasid caliph. As for the caliph, he might have wished for power as well as status but a man in his position should not expect too much. Therefore, the Seljuks became the guarantors of the Abbasid Caliphate.

Even before Baghdad was taken, the Seljuks had been raiding on the fringes of Anatolia, threatening the Byzantine Empire. The threat could no longer be ignored as the raids were becoming more frequent and dangerous. In 1071, the same year that Bari fell, Romanus Diogenes led a large army against the encroaching Turks led by Alp Arslan. He was walking straight into a trap, which he fell into at Manzikert, near Lake Van. He would be ensnared in two directions. In front of him, the highly manoeuvrable horse cavalry of the enemy tempted him to attack them, only to avoid the ponderous attempts of the Byzantine vanguard as easily as if a horde of flies were being chased by a platoon of lumbering tortoises.

The soldiers behind Romanus, supposedly on his side, were no better either. Worst of them was Andronicus Ducas, an ambitious man who had no time for the emperor. When the emperor's men became isolated from the rest of the army, Ducas was so quick to escape without going to the aid of Romanus that it is hard not to conclude that it was all part of a treasonous plot on his part. Nor was this the only sign of treachery in play. The Byzantine army was forced to rely on mercenaries, some of whom were Turkish and quickly showed where their true allegiances lay. There were also Normans present in the Byzantine army, whose involvement in the battle was unenthusiastic to say the least.

The battle ended with a Byzantine emperor a captive in the hands of an enemy for the first time in half a millennium. However, Romanus was treated with dignity and respect by Alp Arslan and sent back to Constantinople soon after. His treatment there was somewhat different. He had been replaced in his absence by Michael Ducas, the name giving a clue to the familial connection with the presumed traitor at Manzikert, whose motives were therefore fairly transparent. Romanus was blinded so savagely that he died in agony from his mutilation soon afterwards.

The disaster at Manzikert, one of the decisive battles of the Middle Ages, was truly catastrophic for Byzantium. It exposed Asia Minor to the encroachment of raiding Turkish war parties who quickly devoured large chunks of it. Yet, even though important, the significance of one battle should not be overplayed. It merely provided evidence of what was already clear; Byzantium was in decline, a state of affairs not helped one jot by the actions of self-serving men like Andronicus Ducas.

It was Byzantium's good fortune that in 1081 another usurper, Alexius Comnenus, inveigled his way to the throne. He was not Byzantium's greatest emperor but he was in every way a man for his time, astute, determined, focussed. He managed to survive the attacks led by Robert Guiscard on the Adriatic coast a few years later (Guiscard conveniently dying while the campaign was underway) before deciding that the threat posed to his empire by the Turks was so great that he needed to seek help from elsewhere.

Guiscard is one of the great forgotten figures of the medieval period. A superb military tactician as well as a wily political strategist, he came within an ace of greatness. He was routinely accompanied into battle by his formidable wife Sichelgaita, who was the archetypal Valkyrie; the chroniclers tell us she was immense in build and fiery in spirit and she seems to have loved nothing more than charging into battle, the loudness of her battle cry piercing the air and her long, blonde hair flowing from beneath her helmet. Guiscard himself was ruthless – when his armies sacked Rome the rapine and pillage that was unleashed destroyed some of the great treasures of antiquity that had survived the incursions of Alaric and his like half a millennium before. But this was a violent and tough age, and he had been one of its foremost figures.

Norman conquests were not, of course, limited to Sicily. In 1066, Duke William of Normandy sailed across the English Channel to make good his claim to the crown of England. Just twenty days after Harald Hardrada and his army had been decimated at Stamford Bridge – King Harold, the Saxon ruler of England, fulfilling his promise to provide his enemy with 'six feet of earth or as much more as he needs, for he is taller than most men' – the victor himself lay dead on Senlac Hill, just outside Hastings.

These were events of great significance. Saxon England was no more, exposed to the harsh depredations of an invading power who established a ruthless, grasping regime. The 'harrying of the north' between 1069 and 1070, a systematic scorched earth policy to crush any resistance to the new regime, left perhaps 150,000 dead and seared itself into the consciousness of those unfortunate enough to be on the wrong side of it. The great Domesday Book, commissioned at Christmas 1085, was nothing less than a tool by which to ensure that every last penny due from a subject people was extracted – hardly the most welcome to presents. It was said that 'there was no single hide nor a yard of land, nor indeed one ox nor one cow nor one pig which was left out'.

The death of Harald Hardrada, though less remarked upon than that of the Saxon king at Hastings, was also significant. He was the last great Viking King of Norway and his demise, if it did not mark the total end of Viking raiding, symbolised an essential loss of vitality from that direction, which was no doubt a great relief to those who had been their potential victims. Three hundred ships had arrived to carry the raiders to Stamford Bridge; only twenty-four were needed to take the survivors home, a crushing defeat that marked the symbolic if not literal end of an era.

This was indeed quite a change since the start of the eleventh century when England, 'led' by its infamously weak king Ethelred the Unready (which actually means 'no counsel' but 'unready' in its usual sense would do just as well), had resorted to buying the Vikings off at regular intervals. Eventually, a Danish dynasty had taken over the country in 1016, led by Cnut, but it did not last long. A Saxon had been restored to the throne by the time of Duke William's conquest.

The times were certainly changing for the Norsemen; in 1000 King Olaf had unified Sweden and established Christianity. The pagan scourge of the monasteries was increasingly becoming part of mainstream Christendom. Later, another King Olaf had done the same for Norway. Cnut in 1029 had succeeded in uniting England, Denmark and Norway, forcing Olaf to flee for sanctuary in far-distant Kiev with its ruling dynasty, once Viking, now increasingly a hybrid with a mixture of Norse and Slav bloodlines. By the century's close, the north was once more returning to the periphery of world affairs.

We also find in 1067 a rare reference to a prominent African figure from the time. His name was Tunka Manin, King of Ghana. His kingdom now had significant Muslim elements living within it. They were allowed to coexist with others as long as they obeyed the laws of the land. Tunka Manin's army was strong, their weaponry – iron-tipped spears in particular – being superior to anything else in the region. His empire, known as the Wagadu, was a significant regional power which would dominate its neighbours such as Senegal. It was said that 'Wagadu was a lion among the wildebeest'.

The evidence we have, from a Spanish Arab writer called al-Bakri, is of a highly organised empire with well-developed tax-collection systems and a series of local governors and sub-kings who sent Tunka Manin regular tribute. Gold finds in particular were subject to taxation and essentially the ruler had a monopoly on its production, which was of course the basis for his wealth. Western Europe got most of its gold from this region so Wagadu became very rich, though the empire was still far from the political mainstream of Europe.

The face of Western Europe had changed radically by the close of the century. The Normans in particular were proving mighty warriors and adventurers, and groups from other areas of France, the Low Countries and Germany were also growing in strength. In Constantinople, Emperor Alexius thought that mercenaries from the west might help him to drive back the Seljuks. But his plan to ask for aid from western knights ironically opened the way for another huge threat to his empire, one which would in the end lead to its long, lingering death. For it led directly to what would become known as the First Crusade.

Just why the Crusades happened when they did is one of the key questions to consider. They were far more than just a simple military expedition to the east and they were certainly not launched just because of a desire to help Byzantium. In part, they happened because the papacy wished to increase its power. It had already done so in spectacular fashion. Pope Gregory VII had been elected in 1073. He threw himself with vigour into increasing the power of the Pope.

One of the main issues to resolve at the time concerned the interference of secular rulers into the appointment of bishops and even popes, a process known as investiture. The papacy now sought to break free of such unwelcome intrusion. But the Holy Roman Emperor, Henry IV, saw that his powers would be diminished as a result and refused to accept the situation. A power struggle between Church and State ensued, with Gregory using the ultimate sanction available to him when he excommunicated the emperor.

The fortunes of Henry and Gregory ebbed and flowed. In 1077, Henry – weakened by revolts in Germany which ate away at his power base – was forced to do penance, kneeling in the snow dressed in a hair shirt at the feet of Gregory at Canossa in Italy. However, that was not the end of it. The emperor understandably burned with the humiliation meted out to him and sought to get his own back. It was not long before he had declared his own 'Anti-Pope', Clement III.

Henry then attacked Rome itself. Gregory was forced to call on the help of the Normans in Italy to come to his aid. They rescued him from the clutches of the emperor in 1085 but he died soon after. In the struggle for supremacy, chaos had been unleashed. Although the papacy was undoubtedly stronger than it had ever been, it was certainly not dominant.

One of the issues was the ongoing propensity of secular warlords to engage in acts of gratuitous violence. When Pope Urban II was elected in 1088, he sought to continue the quest for papal supremacy. When he received an appeal for help from Alexius Comnenus in 1095 at Piacenza in Italy he listened with the greatest of interest.

'Holy wars' were already being fought in Spain. In the process known as the *Reconquista* Christian armies were striving to recover territory in Spain. Prominent among the driving forces behind this was King Ferdinand I of Leon. On his death a bitter civil war broke out between his sons, from which emerged one of the most famous names of the era – El Cid Campeador.

The story of El Cid is steeped in legend. Rodrigo Diaz de Vivar, as he grew up, was born around 1040 and soon showed himself to be a formidable warrior, from which his nickname El Cid – 'the Lord' – emanated. As he grew more successful, others inevitably became jealous of his fame and he found himself in exile from the court of Alfonso, the son and successor of Ferdinand. But his success continued. In 1094, he took the important Muslim-held city of Valencia. It is perhaps sad to report that he died peacefully five years later and not, as Hollywood would have us believe, with his corpse propped up on his horse, leading his men one last time in a sally from Valencia to drive a Muslim army off.

During the course of these raids against Muslim Spain, the papacy had adopted the tactic of offering spiritual privileges to those who took part in the war, including those who came from beyond her borders, such as the French. The use of spiritual benefits was therefore already well established and would be an important part of the Crusading movement that was about to be born.

In an attempt to assert papal power, and as a fortunate by-product redirect military activity away from launching attacks on the Church and its property, Urban decided to introduce a new idea, that of the 'Crusade'. It was several things. It was first of all a pilgrimage, but one with an added dimension; the pilgrims would be encouraged to fight against the enemies of Christ. It was therefore, in effect, a papally sanctioned war.

Urban preached his Crusade in November 1095 at Clermont. The response was overwhelming. Men (and women) flocked to take the Cross. However, it quickly transpired that a genie had been released from the bottle that would be rather hard to control let alone return to where it had come from. For not only did warriors offer themselves as Crusaders but so did thousands of the masses, many of them with little or no military contribution to make whatsoever.

The 'armies', if so they may be called, that first set out included many humble folk, hence the slightly misleading name of the 'Peasant's Crusade'; misleading both because there was more than one such expedition setting out and also because there were others from the higher ranks of society as well as humble peasants involved.

These poorly disciplined hordes tramped across Europe and into Byzantine territory, to the utter horror of Alexius Comnenus, who had not expected or wanted this type of expedition at all. A number of them were cut down en route, often at the hands of Byzantine soldiers when they threatened to get out of control. The rest were shipped over to Asia Minor as quickly as possible. Here they were quickly massacred by the soldiers of Kilij Arslan, the Turkish warlord whose capital was at Nicaea.

However, the next wave of Crusaders was of an altogether different ilk. Again there were several expeditions, very poorly coordinated, although some coordination would emerge later in the campaign only to disappear again. These armies were led by prominent warlords such as Count Raymond of Toulouse, Geoffrey of Bouillon and, most worryingly of all for Alexius, Bohemund, son of the late Robert Guiscard. They posed a far greater degree of threat than did the earlier movements – both to Byzantium and to the Turks.

When constituent parts of this second wave reached Constantinople, Alexius showed great skill in isolating the individual commanders from each other and one by one forcing them to swear an oath to restore all future conquests of former Byzantine territory back to him. Unfortunately, getting them to comply with it proved more difficult. Not that his actions altogether inspired trust. When the Crusaders were on the verge of taking Nicaea in June 1097, he negotiated its surrender behind the backs of the Crusaders. It played to an image of an untrustworthy and devious view of Byzantium that had already been created in the minds of many in the Western European armies. Misunderstandings between the eastern and western parts of Christendom existed from the start; they would only get worse with time and closer contacts.

The Crusade moved on, fighting off a fierce Turkish counter-attack at Dorylaeum. Then on 3 June 1098 Antioch, one of the most prominent of former Byzantine cities, which had only been held by the Turks for a few years, was taken. An awful massacre ensued, followed by a stunning Crusader victory when a large relieving force was driven off, partly because of its own disunity.

The Crusaders moved inexorably on towards Jerusalem. Reaching its environs, a tight siege was laid. After many days of hard fighting, on 15 July the walls were breached. It was not long before the gates were opened to the baying mob outside, a Crusader army that had suffered terrible hardships and severe depredation now keen to salve its wounds with the blood of the enemy of Christ. A terrible bloodletting followed that seared itself into the soul of the Muslim world.

Once the carnage had stopped, a ruler needed to be found. It was Godfrey of Bouillon who was to emerge as Jerusalem's first Christian head since Heraclius nearly four centuries before. So sacred was Jerusalem in the Christian psyche that he refused to accept the title of 'King' in God's holy city and made do with 'Defender of the Holy Sepulchre' instead.

This was clearly an act of enormous significance, yet there were crucial things to note as well as the return of Jerusalem to Christian rule. Firstly, it was a victory that owed as much to fragmentation in the Muslim world as it did to the power of Western arms. The Muslim response to the invasion had been largely patchwork and uncoordinated. It would require a much more coherent response if the Crusaders were to be ejected.

But there was another consideration too. Jerusalem had once belonged to the Byzantine Emperor and therefore it might be argued that it should be returned to Alexius. If it was a debatable point given that the city had not been Byzantine for so long, it was far less so with Antioch, which had only recently been conquered by Muslims.

Yet the Crusaders showed no intention of returning their conquests to anyone. Instead the leaders of the Crusade sought to carve out their own lands; Godfrey in Jerusalem, Bohemund in Antioch, Count Raymond of Toulouse in Tripoli and Count Baldwin of Boulogne in Edessa. It was clear that the Crusaders were here to stay and had no intention whatsoever of meekly handing their conquests back to a Byzantine emperor who had done very little to help win them. What was not so clear was how the Muslim world would fight back or what the long-term consequences for international relations would be. The next century would shed a great deal of light on these issues, with dramatic long-term impact.

25

SWORD AND SCIMITAR

The Crusading Movement (AD 1101–1199)

This was a century that saw the emergence of some major figures on the world stage, affecting both west and east. It also gave birth to a literary flowering in several parts of the globe. In 1123 *The Rubáiyát of Omar Khayyám*, one of the outstanding works of medieval Islam, appeared. Twelve years later, Geoffrey of Monmouth wrote *The History of the Kings of Britain*, which described the story of King Arthur, including the life of the arch-wizard Merlin, as well as other important semi-mythical figures such as King Lear and Cymbeline. In 1155, the writer Wace of Jersey, in his *Brut*, included a reference to a Round Table. The Arthurian theme continued when, in 1191, the great king's alleged tomb was uncovered in Glastonbury (though the need of the monks to find funds to refurbish their abbey might, to cynical minds, provide some explanation for this fortuitous and timely event).

These events were symptomatic of a quite incredible flowering of civilisation, especially in Western Europe where it was much needed. The driving force behind this was the Church, not through its spiritual ministrations but as a power, *ecclesia* as it was known – rich, powerful, hugely influential and capable of underwriting an amazing development in art and architecture, a 'great eruption of ecclesiastical splendour' as the late art historian Kenneth Clark called it. He also recognised that this was a time of deeper philosophical thinking about man's place in the world, a period of both contemplation and action as he called it.

The great architectural movement in Europe led to the emergence of the first great cathedrals of the later medieval era, in particular the rebuilt church of Saint Denis near Paris in the 1140s and the magnificent edifice of Notre Dame, the building of which began in 1163. Such building projects spread across Western Europe, but France was undoubtedly the driving force. Alongside these achievements were some great men (and women), including such personalities as Abbot Suger, who gave impetus to the re-emergence of Saint Denis, and the German mystic Hildegard of Bingen.

Hildegard was born into a noble family in 1098, living until 1179. She entered a nunnery, as did many rich younger daughters in the period, becoming abbess of Bingen near Mainz in 1141. A remarkable woman, whose music is among the earliest to survive into the modern era, she was also an incredible visionary; her visions seemed to tap into the great mystic and poetical urges of the time, which was something of an early Renaissance. She described herself in an allegory which captures well the spirit of the age in the west:

> Listen: there was once a king sitting on his throne. Around him stood great and wonderfully beautiful columns ornamented with ivory, bearing the banners of the king with great honour. Then it pleased the king to raise a small feather from the ground and he commanded it to fly. The feather flew, not because of anything in itself but because the air bore it along. Thus am I.

She was no weak-willed woman, though, and refused to be meekly subservient in what was still a male-dominated era. When directed to exhume the body of an excommunicate that she had ordered buried, she refused to do so for months. She eventually tired of life in the nunnery where she had first become a nun and uprooted herself and her sisters to start up anew many miles away. Though subject to visions, she was no pure dreamer but also a woman of action, of strength, of courage and of perseverance.

But if in the west this was a time where a mystical woman could think of herself as a 'feather on the breath of God', it was also an era of hugely significant political realignments, especially in the Middle East. In Byzantium, Alexius Comnenus, continuing to rule in the first decades of the century, remained the perfect emperor for his times. Following his accession, he had managed to extricate his empire from a series of parlous situations. During his reign he reintroduced a stability that appeared to have disappeared from it for good. It is true that his reign was one more characterised by defensive rather than offensive action, but in the process he built a foundation that succeeding generations could build upon.

Yet in one respect his reign was disastrous. By inviting the West to involve itself in Byzantine affairs, he had unwittingly initiated his empire's long-term demise. His own handling of the situation once he saw it emerging was, it is true, masterful. He was also helped enormously by the Crusaders' own incompetence and petty squabbling as well as, irony of ironies, by the re-emergent power of the Turks that he had sought the help of Western warriors against. Yet once he was gone, it would be impossible for later emperors to protect themselves and their people against the joint pressures created by the exploitative intentions of the West and the resurgent powers of Islam.

The Muslim Levant had been caught badly off guard by the onslaught of Western warriors. But after the initial amazing success of the Crusaders in taking Jerusalem, the Turks in Asia Minor put their differences behind them and united for a short period against the threat now facing them. It was just in the nick of time. Euphoric after the triumph of the First Crusade, new armies of Crusaders made their way out to the Middle East.

The kingdom that they were on their way out to had already changed. Godfrey of Bouillon had died in 1100. His decision not to declare himself a monarch in Jerusalem did not set a precedent; his successor was duly crowned as King Baldwin I. The year after, Raymond of Toulouse's Crusader army, on its way with reinforcements from the west, was destroyed by Danishmend Turks in Anatolia. This heavy blow was followed by another Crusader force being crushed the month after. Clearly, Crusading success could not be taken for granted.

The Kingdom of Jerusalem nevertheless continued to consolidate. In 1104, Baldwin of Jerusalem took the vital port of Acre. It would become the main entry and exit point of Outremer, the 'Land Beyond the Sea' as the Crusader kingdoms were collectively known. But success did not smile on everyone. Bohemund of Taranto, disappointed in his ambitions after having been captured by the Turks, once released decided to turn his attentions towards what he regarded as a weak and feeble Greek empire. It was a grave miscalculation. Bohemund was outwitted and outfought by Alexius and ended up having to publicly and humiliatingly sign the Treaty of Devol, which ended his hopes to claim Byzantine lands and also forced him to do homage for Antioch.

Alexius Comnenus died in 1118 after a long and successful reign. He was a contradictory emperor in some ways. His achievements were immense. He had rebuilt an army that had seemingly lost belief in itself. He had restored pride to an empire that had lost most of it. He also reshaped the shattered economy that he had inherited.

Yet for all of this he was not widely loved by his people. In some respects this was an inevitable result of some of the harsh measures that needed to be taken to restore a degree of health to Byzantium, putting more gold into the treasury coffers and more fight into the battered army. But he could also be devious and he was perceived to be nepotistic in his appointments. This latter trait was by no means unique to Alexius and was partly inevitable given the fact that recent history showed a Byzantine emperor needed to be surrounded by people he could trust. But he took it to heights rarely reached in the past and he was not therefore held in universal high regard. While this is understandable it was not right, for without him the people of Byzantium would have been exposed to parlous danger.

Alexius nominated his son John as his successor and it quickly became apparent that beneath the surface little had changed in Byzantine politics. Even as his father's funeral took place there was an abortive coup against John, led by none other than his own sister, Anna. She had at one stage been heir presumptive before John's birth, and frustrated personal ambition was no doubt high on the list of motivations for her treacherous actions. John dealt with her leniently and she retired to a convent where she devoted the rest of her life to the writing of a Byzantine history that is the source of much of what we know about the period.

This was a time of significance further west in Europe too. Warfare with the 'Saracens' was not limited to the Levant. In 1113, Raymond-Berengar of Barcelona and the Pisans began to reconquer Balearic Islands from Muslim forces, beginning a process that would drive them from the western Mediterranean. War against the Islamic world continued on and off for centuries and would only intensify as both power blocs became more expansionist in their ambitions.

Also in 1113, one of the great ecclesiastical figures of medieval history entered the abbey of Citeaux. His name was Bernard (later Saint) of Clairvaux. His appearance coincided with the birth of a new monastic movement, the Cistercians, who would become hugely powerful and influential. From France, they would spread across many parts of Europe, the famous 'white monks' who were renowned for building their monasteries in out-of-the-way and beautiful places. Eschewing wealth, they were nevertheless contradictory, for the order would become very rich. By the middle of the century, the Cistercians would own more than 400 monasteries.

A few years later (1119), another religious order appeared in the Crusader kingdoms of Outremer. Formed with the intention of escorting pilgrims to Jerusalem and therefore equipped as warriors, this order, known as the Knights Templar, was nevertheless managed on quasi-monastic lines. The Knights Templar, too, would give up all wealth at a personal level but the order they were pledged to would become extremely rich. Other military orders followed suit, particularly the Knights Hospitaller and much later the Teutonic Knights, but the Templars would excite both the admiration and the envy of many like no other order.

The emergence of the orders, alongside the development of the Arthurian legends, show that this was an age when a new concept was developing fast, that of chivalry. This was a code which in theory regulated the behaviour of the knightly class, but in practice this was a contradiction. War was as brutal as ever, rapine and pillage common. The reality was that chivalry existed in two ways – firstly in some idealised imagination and secondly as a code that regulated behaviour only within narrowly delimited class lines. This was as much as anything pragmatic; sparing a captured knight in battle offered the opportunity of lucrative ransom, much more useful than a profitless death.

The military orders, which undoubtedly appealed to both religious and chivalric motives among their recruits, were a much-needed development. Military resources were sorely needed in the undermanned Kingdom of Jerusalem and the other elements of Outremer, and eventually the military orders would play a crucial role in this respect. Finding enough soldiers was a perennial problem. In 1119, the Frankish army of Antioch was destroyed on the graphically named 'Field of Blood' by Ghazi, ruler of the Danishmend Turks. Although this was a long way from a fully fledged Muslim resurgence, it did not augur well for the future as far as the Crusader kingdoms were concerned.

Europe was beset by religious controversy during these years. Bernard of Clairvaux was a hard-line conservative but other men were starting to show a tendency to adopt a more questioning approach to religion. One such was Peter Abelard, a remarkable free thinker and a radical genius. In his secular life Abelard had seduced a beautiful woman, Heloise, an act which cost him dearly, as he was castrated for his indiscretion.

This moved him to join the Church, where his brilliant mind and piercing wit soon showed him to be a dangerous enemy of religious conservatism. He stated that acts were good or evil depending on the intention behind them and he also took pleasure in identifying apparent contradictions in the Bible. This brought him much condemnation, most notably in 1121 and then later in 1140, but he was one of a new breed of theologians who were increasingly prepared to challenge the status quo and in the process make many in the Church extremely uncomfortable.

In Byzantium, John Comnenus took up the reins he had been handed by his father and turned imperial policy into one of expansion rather than defence. Resurgent Turkish tribesmen, the Danishmends, felt his wrath and he recovered territories in Asia Minor that had been long lost to his empire. In the process he found himself adjacent to Christian territories in Anatolia and further south held by the Crusaders and their allies. These were in theory still Byzantine territory and John sought to reassert his authority.

When he appeared before the walls of Antioch with his army in 1137, a state of shock descended on the Crusader ruling caste inside it. But they were instructed by King Fulk of Jerusalem to recognise the right of the emperor to rule there, which they grudgingly did. However, their obeisance was only theoretical and John was unable to enforce it. Distracted by problems elsewhere, John was forced to leave the problem of Antioch as unfinished business. However, he would die before he had a chance to make good his claims on the city.

Manual Comnenus, successor to John, was the last of a triumvirate of outstanding Byzantine emperors to rule in the twelfth century. The end of his reign would herald in an era of mediocrity which would have disastrous results. But it started well. There would soon be important developments affecting the relationship between Byzantium and the West. On Christmas Eve 1144, a Muslim warlord named Zengi of Mosul captured the Crusader city of Edessa, slaughtering the Crusader Christians he captured in the aftermath. Zengi had become Emir of Mosul in 1127 and since that time had worried away at the edges of the Crusader kingdoms, but the loss of Edessa was one of those events in history which, in retrospect, marked a turning point.

News of the city's loss sent shock waves across Western Europe and an armed response was planned. The so-called Second Crusade, summoned by Eugenius III in 1146, crossed Byzantine territory but was badly cut up traversing Asia Minor. The still sizeable remnant that remained arrived in the Crusader states of Outremer, where their subsequent actions were entirely negative. They decided to attack Damascus, the Crusaders' only Muslim ally of significance in the region, thus driving the city into the welcoming arms of a rising Islamic power in the region led by Nur al-Din, Zengi's successor.

For the spectacularly unsuccessful end result of all the effort and money that had been expended on the Crusade, the French king, Louis VII, one of the key participants, unfairly blamed Byzantium when he would have done better to look to his own inadequacies. He returned to France with a sense of injustice, partly brought on by his failed military exertions and partly by the antics of his strong-willed and flighty wife, Eleanor of Aquitaine, from whom he would soon be divorced (she would be married to Henry II, the then future King of England, within two months of the annulment). Damascus, the strange target of this failed venture, fell into the hands of Nur al-Din in 1154, a major and entirely avoidable change in fortune as far as the Western European settlers in Outremer were concerned.

To live in the land where Christ had walked was for many European settlers in Outremer an incredible experience. Their religious devotion was epitomised by the erection of many churches on the holy sites that meant so much to them. The most famous were the church of the Holy Sepulchre, marking both the site of the Crucifixion and Resurrection, and the church of the Nativity in Bethlehem. But everywhere one looked there was a sacred place. From the Mount of Olives, Christ supposedly ascended to Heaven; a church built on the spot had a hole in the roof so that if needed He could do so again. The impression of His footprint was also allegedly in the rock there, letting the curious know that, if genuine, Christ had size 6 feet.

But these were worrying times for those in the West who sought dominance over Islam. Not only was the situation in Outremer deteriorating, there was a change in fortune for the Islamic states in Spain too, evidenced when in 1164 Muslim armies in Spain recaptured Cordoba and Almeria. If the end of the eleventh century generated sensations of triumph for Christendom, the twelfth century created ones of doubt.

There were other significant events affecting the Crusading movement during the century too. In 1147, Bernard of Clairvaux preached against the heretic movements that had become increasingly noticeable in Languedoc in the south of what is now France. It did not immediately lead to a change of direction in the movement but did place a marker down the road that led to a massive diversion from the original idea of a Church-sanctioned war against Islam. In 1157, the Council of Reims condemned the heretical movement known as the Cathars. Within a century the Crusades would be used as both a way of destroying heretical movements that preached doctrines that were contrary to Catholic orthodoxy as well as a political tool by which the papacy sought to strengthen its political position. The Cathars would feel the effects of this more than any other group.

When he eventually became king, Henry II of England established himself as a major player on the European stage. An act of historical significance occurred in 1155 when the English Pope, Nicholas Breakspear, granted him Ireland, a significant step down the road that led to 800 years of bloodshed and mistrust between two unequal neighbours. Three years later Henry was eating away at the remaining independent territories in Wales and he also became the overlord of Sicily. Allied to the massive Angevin territories he ruled in France, he had become a very powerful man indeed.

But in 1162 Henry took a step which he subsequently came to regret bitterly when he appointed his long-time friend Thomas Becket to the position of Archbishop of Canterbury, no doubt thinking that here was a man and a prelate who would be easily manipulated. But the hitherto pliable Becket was transformed, stridently standing up for the rights of his Church against the secular power of the king. It famously ended up with the murder of Becket in his cathedral at Canterbury on 29 December 1170.

Henry was forced to undertake a very public and humiliating penance and Becket soon became a very unlikely saint. Yet the power of Henry appeared for a time to be unabated; Ireland might nominally have been his over a decade previously but it had not yet been conquered. That was about to change, as his lieutenants were now achieving by the sword that which the word of a Pope alone was not enough to bring about.

But the story of Henry II was a very human tragedy. He would finally be destroyed by those nearest and dearest to him, his family, who all showed in various degrees that they had inherited their father's ambitions and their mother's cunning. For one of them, Richard, the call of the Crusades would be irresistible. Yet before he was to appear on the scene, the lands of the Middle East were about to undergo great – and, as it turned out, permanent – change.

We must return once more to Byzantium, for its position was about to change fundamentally. Manuel Comnenus made massive strides during his reign. He established a dominance of sorts over the Crusaders in the Middle East and reclaimed large chunks of territory from the weakened Hungarian king with whom he was at war between 1151 and 1167. He skilfully forged diplomatic alliances with a range of players. But all this was a false dawn.

In 1176, Manuel's army was badly beaten by the Seljuk sultan Kilij Arslan at Myriocephalum. Although it was a decisive triumph, the sultan was magnanimous in victory and Manuel escaped with lenient terms. But it was a symbol that Byzantine resurgence had come to an end. Manuel died in 1180, perhaps one of the most brilliant of emperors but one whose promise was unfulfilled because he was unable to concentrate and focus his energies on a manageable portfolio of projects. As a result, the empire he left behind was weaker than the one which he inherited.

This was epitomised by the emergence of new independent powers in the Balkans. By 1180, Stephen Nemanja, perhaps the greatest name in Serbian history, was ruler of an independent state, able to hold its own against both the Byzantines in the south and the Hungarians in the north. Confident in his position, Nemanja was able to turn his attentions towards the construction of some wonderful Orthodox monasteries, adorned with lavishly coloured wall paintings that spoke eloquently of both the mysticism of eastern Orthodoxy and of the fears of hell and damnation that tortured the minds of contemporaries.

In an unusual (though not unique) act for the time, Nemanja voluntarily abdicated the throne and spent his final years as a monk. However, the Serbian state would struggle to survive into the longer term as an independent entity. Its emergence was due to a drastic decline in the Byzantine Empire but this was in the end only to lead to the exposure of the Balkans to another aggressor: the Ottoman Turks. Indeed, even in Nemanja's own time there were signs of changing fortunes when in 1189 he was defeated by the Byzantines and forced to surrender some of his conquests.

There was one event of Manuel Comnenus's reign in particular which would have catastrophic consequences for Byzantium, though not until over three decades after it happened. In 1171 Manuel had ordered the arrest of all Venetians in the empire. In response, Venice attacked Dalmatia, a Byzantine possession on the shores of the Adriatic. Venice had become a source of some envy, her obvious commercial success making her too powerful to be tolerated. But these acts, to be followed a few years later by atrocities against the Venetians in Constantinople, led to a huge amount of resentment from Venice towards Byzantium and there would be a heavy price to pay in return in 1204.

Following Manuel's death, the mediocrities arrived in Constantinople. His successor, Alexius II, was soon removed by the adventurer Andronicus Comnenus. In many ways a glamorous figure before his coup, Andronicus the emperor proved to be cruel and spiteful. Worse still, he was unsuccessful and Byzantium was invaded by Count William II of Sicily.

Deposed when it appeared that the count would win and stake a claim to the imperial purple, Andronicus suffered an agonising death at the hands of the mob in Constantinople. His successor, Isaac II Angelus, fought off the Sicilians, as if by a miracle, but proved equally inept at being an emperor in the long run – by 1187 he was forced to recognise Bulgarian independence in the north. This weakness was to have fatal consequences, for more Crusaders from the West would come and, in the end, sense easier pickings in the Byzantine Empire than in the Muslim states in the Levant.

Byzantium's deterioration was accompanied by an upsurge in the fortunes of Muslim forces in the Middle East. In 1171, the same year that Nur al-Din seized Mosul, he increased his powers greatly when his young lieutenant Saladin took Egypt for him from al-Adad, who therefore had the dubious distinction of being the last Fatimid caliph. Egypt was now a Sunni land and, equally importantly, there was now a Muslim superstate surrounding Outremer and wrapping it itself around the Crusader states in a vice-like grip.

Two years later, Saladin's brother Turan-an-Shah conquered the Sudan. In 1174, on the death of Nur al-Din, Saladin claimed power in Egypt for himself. Within a short period of time, Saladin had taken over a large proportion of the other territories once ruled by Nur al-Din too. In 1175, the Caliph of Baghdad recognised Saladin as ruler of Egypt and Syria. By 1176, Turan-shah had conquered southern Arabia. These were moves that carried enormous threat to Outremer.

But Saladin was overconfident. He was badly beaten in a battle at Montgisard in 1177 when he invaded the Crusader kingdoms, thinking that victory was a formality. Indeed for a time it appeared that the Crusaders were re-emerging as a threat. The strong-willed Crusader baron Reynald of Chatillon attacked Muslim shipping in the Red Sea in 1182 and raided as far as Mecca. Although he was beaten off, this caused great offence to Islam and left Reynald a marked man.

Saladin, though, was just biding his time. In 1183 he took Aleppo and made Damascus his capital. Then he decided it was time to destroy the Crusader territories once and for all. On 4 July 1187 around the parched hills known as the Horns of Hattin, near Lake Tiberias, the largest Crusader army ever assembled was wiped out by Saladin, having been lured into a carefully set trap. The boorish Reynald of Chatillon was executed, in some accounts by Saladin personally, after the battle (among more lurid tales was one that Reynald had ravished Saladin's captured sister, which would have meant that such personal retribution was understandable).

Within two months Jerusalem itself had fallen. The great mosques that had been converted to Christian buildings, holy edifices such as the Dome of the Rock and the al-Aqsa Mosque, were purified with rosewater and restored to their former status. The pride of Christendom was lost and for a while it seemed as if all of Outremer would follow suit. However, the terrible reverse of Hattin had a short-term positive effect in terms of uniting some at least of the powers of Western Europe in a common cause, although it was only for a very limited period of time.

By 1190, a great Crusade was on its way to the rescue under Frederick Barbarossa, the Emperor of Germany, Philip Augustus, King of France and Richard I, now King of England. Disaster threatened before the expedition had even arrived in Palestine. On 10 June Frederick Barbarossa died while crossing a river in Asia Minor, whether from drowning or a heart attack is unclear. In any event, it was a major blow to the Crusade.

Barbarossa had been one of the giants of the century. Coming to the throne in 1152, his early years were marked, as they had to be, by a struggle to achieve a form of unity in Germany. He also strove to restore to his imperial crown the rights it had once enjoyed in Italy. This brought him into opposition with some formidable figures such as Henry the Lion, Duke of Saxony, and most significantly the papacy, continuing a century-long tradition of conflict between emperor and pontiff. The situation became even worse when Barbarossa's son, Henry VI, married the heiress to Sicily, thereby threatening to leave the Pope surrounded by an empire that controlled Italy both to the north and to the south of Rome.

With Barbarossa dead the German involvement in the Crusade dissipated, but Philip and Richard, unlikely allies as they were fighting each other for supremacy in France, continued their separate journeys to the east. Richard seemingly wanted to practice his martial skills on the way out, seizing control first of all of Sicily and then of Cyprus. The two rulers then set to work conducting the siege of the crucial port of Acre, which fell to them in 1191. However, there was soon a falling out between Richard and Philip and the latter returned home, to threaten Richard's substantial lands in France when he reached there.

Despite a victory over Saladin at Arsuf, Richard was unable to take and hold Jerusalem. A truce was agreed with Saladin (whom Richard, sadly for romantics, never actually met) and Richard returned home in 1192 to England, where his brother John had been causing difficulties in his absence. Contrary to the general impression of the results of this so-called Third Crusade, as a consequence of which Richard is widely regarded as a hero and a warrior without equal, it was something of a disappointment. A thin sliver of land had been recovered for a substantial outlay of men and materials. Outremer was living on borrowed time.

In Spain too the Muslim revival continued. For several centuries Christian forces had been steadily pushing down the Iberian Peninsula in the process known as the *Reconquista*. Now, however, there was something of a fightback, epitomised when in 1195 Berber forces inflicted a heavy defeat on Alfonso VIII of Castile at Alarcos. It would be nearly 300 years before the last Islamic foothold in the region would be taken by Christian armies.

Islam was also making significant inroads into Africa. In the eleventh century, what was to become known as the Sayfawa dynasty was founded; it would last for about 800 years. This dynasty existed in a region known as Kanem, which would at its maximum extent cover Chad, the southern part of Libya and the eastern areas of modern Niger. From its capital, Njimi, caravans would set out for and arrive from Tripoli and Tunis. The dynasty would prove itself a strong supporter of the Muslim faith, and an earlier ruler of Kanem, Mai Hume – who lived in the eleventh century – was the first ruler of the kingdom to make the *hajj*. Later leaders would even build a hostel in Cairo for pilgrims from their lands who were on their way to Mecca.

In Asia, as the century progressed, a strong dynasty emerged in the north of Rajasthan and the east of the Punjab in India. The Chauhamanas (also known as the Chauhan dynasty) may well have initially been a desert tribe from further west. In the middle of the century, one of their kings named Vigraha-raja took Delhi, an event which is recorded by an addition to a much older column that referred to the victories of Ashoka. His kingdom stretched as far north as the Himalayas.

He was no doubt partly helped by internal divisions in the Islamic states to the north, best epitomised when in 1151 Alā-ad-Din Husayn, Sultan of Ghor in Afghanistan, was given the title of 'World Burner' when he destroyed Ghazni. Such disunity was to be the curse of Islam for centuries.

Following the death of Vigraha-raja, Mohammed of Ghor started to pick at the edges of the Subcontinent in an attempt to expand his territories. He first moved into Sind and then into Gujarat where he was initially unsuccessful in his attempts at conquest. So he then moved on to Lahore. Before long, he found himself opposite the borders of Punjab, not far away from the modern border of India and Pakistan. Rich pickings lay beyond and the stage was set for an early inter-religion struggle, for Mohammed was of course a Muslim and the new king of the Chauhamanas was a Hindu.

In 1191, Mohammed invaded. An early success led to an inevitable response from the Chauhamana king, Prithviraj. A battle at Tarain led to the apparent defeat of Mohammed, who was injured during the conflict. However, he merely retreated to Ghazni to lick his wounds and came back with another army, over 100,000 strong, a multi-ethnic force including Persians, Afghans, Arabs and Turks.

The two armies met again, coincidentally once more at Tarain, in 1192. Prithviraj, a young man with a huge force at his back, was full of confidence. There was desultory talk about a truce, which threw the Chauhamana king off his guard. When the battle started, Mohammed used classic Turkic tactics of launching wave after wave of cavalry assaults and then retreating to wear the enemy out. It worked and the Chauhamana forces broke; 'like a great building [the army] tottered to its fall and was lost in its ruins'.

It was said that 100,000 men died. Prithviraj was captured and soon joined the ranks of the slain. It was one of the most decisive moments in the history of the Subcontinent. A ruthless raping and pillaging of the Hindu glories of northern India followed. Delhi fell to Mohammed. From here, the Ghorid Empire pushed further east into Bengal and Assam.

There were other important events occurring in the Far East during the century, in distant lands far removed from the sight of Europe. For long a centralised state, new factions had emerged in Japan known as *bushi* (warriors) or *samurai* (retainers). These groups entered into alliances and started to eat away at the structure that held together the governing class. The rivalry that emanated from these alliances led eventually to violent struggles between two groups, the Taira and the Minamoto. The former party emerged victorious.

Their leader was a man named Taira no Kiyomori, and he had an eye for beautiful women, not least the concubine of his defeated enemy, Yoshimoto of the Minamoto faction. Her name was Tokiwa and she had six children by Yoshimoto. Unusually for the time, Kiyomori spared them, an action he would live to regret.

By 1180 Kiyomori seemed to be at the peak of his powers and, now an old man, he nominated a two-year-old grandson as his successor. This led to a revolt from disaffected nobles who felt they had better title to the throne. Prominent among the rebel leaders was one of the spared children, Minamoto no Yoritomo. Kiyomori died of a fever and by 1185 Yoritomo was the most powerful man in the land.

He claimed a new title in 1192, that of seii taishōgun ('barbarian subduing great general'), a nomenclature that is normally abbreviated to that of shōgun. He set up what was effectively a feudal system held together by a small group of nobles who owed allegiance to him. However, his was not a happy rule. He saw enemies everywhere around him and even ordered the assassination of his own brother. He died in 1199 after an unexplained fall from his horse; there were inevitably suggestions that this was not an accident.

But unknown to anyone, a new threat was growing in eastern Asia to the north-west of China. A nightmare was about to be unleashed on an unsuspecting world. China would be the first to feel its power before it turned 180 degrees and made itself known to the Middle East and the West, as well as the fringes of India. It was a force of apocalyptic intensity, unlike any ever known before.

China was divided and therein lay its weakness. To the north, a federation led by the Ju-chens from the mountains of eastern Manchuria had founded the Chin dynasty under the auspices of their leader Aguda. Allying with the Sung, they defeated the Liao in 1125, taking their capital Beijing in the process, and then predictably turned on their former allies. This was ironic, for the Liao, as the Khitans, had themselves been usurpers and were now suffering a nasty dose of their own medicine. The year after, Korea became a client state. China was now split in two, with the Chin holding the north and the Sung the south, with the Hsi Hsia to the north-west bordering on the lands of a number of steppe tribes, including the – at the time – relatively unimportant Mongols.

The Ju-chens were quick to incorporate captive siege engineers into their armies, a precedent that was soon to be followed by others with far greater impact. Capturing the important city of Kaifeng, they also captured some of the Sung royal family, who were released for a large ransom. The Sung retreated still further south. The Chin moved their capital from Manchuria, first to Beijing in 1153, then soon after to Kaifeng. They assimilated many of the practices of the Chinese civil service, but never treated those who held high offices of state with the respect that had been accorded them under previous dynasties.

It was quite a turnaround, from peripheral tribesmen to the ruling caste, but it was but a mild precursor of what was to follow. Sometime in the 1160s (the exact date has never been proven), a son was born to the chief of a small tribe in the steppes, the Mongols. His name was Temüjin and it was said that when he was born he came forth from his mother's womb clutching a clot of blood. It was a very apt portent of the life that was to follow.

His father was murdered when he was still a child and years of hardship followed, with his life under threat a good deal of the time. But eventually he returned to prominence in his own tribe and then slowly started to conquer and assimilate others. It was a long and drawn-out process, and it would take many years for it to reach fruition. But the inexorable rise to greatness of the man who would later be known as the Universal Ruler, Genghis Khan, had begun. By the end of this century, he was still largely unknown. By the end of the next, his name would be spoken of in tones of horrified awe and abject terror.

26

THE MONGOL CENTURY

Genghis Khan, the World Emperor (AD 1201–1300)

The thirteenth century was remarkable for seeing the last of what might be called 'the barbarian invasions', which had pockmarked the landscape of history for a millennium and more. The latest and greatest of these saw the creation of the largest empire in terms of contiguous landmass that the world had ever seen. The Mongol invasions came to the West like a bolt of lightning from a clear blue sky and even to the Chinese, more used to raids from the region in which the terrifying horsemen lived, the intensity of these attacks was overwhelming.

Yet although there is no doubting that these were for those who lived through them years of abject terror, they were also crucial in the process of shrinking the world. Regions which had up until now been close to unknown suddenly became linked to each other, even if this was an imperfect arrangement under the aegis of a ruling class that only survived as a coherent entity for a short time. The impact of the Mongols was truly global. The same army that attacked Poland and Hungary attempted to invade Japan, and the same whirlwind that descended on Java also struck Syria (though with very different results).

Yet at the century's start the Mongols were virtually unknown beyond the Mongolian steppes and the borderlands of China. Their very location hid them away from much of the outside world, cloaked as it was to the south by the harsh expanses of the Gobi Desert and on other sides by steep mountains and harsh rolling plains that made travel difficult. Mongolia had no riches to speak of and indeed it was a region of rugged terrain, unsuited for agriculture and only of use to the sturdy pastoralist nomads who eked out a difficult and uncertain living there. There was little sign of the reign of terror that was about to unleash itself across vast expanses of Eurasia.

Europe was certainly oblivious to the threat as the century began and had distractions closer to home to divert its attentions. The Crusading movement was still alive, if not thriving, and was about to cause one of the most controversial events in the medieval period, if not all of history. Plans for a Crusade to recover the lost lands of Outremer continued to evolve, and in 1202 another expedition attempting to achieve this objective set sail. This time large numbers of ships had been hired from Venice, but from the outset the Crusade started to lose sight of its objectives. When the Crusading army that had been assembled arrived by the city in the lagoon it was less than a third of the size that had been expected.

As the costings of the expedition had been based on the original, larger manpower figure and there was now a serious shortfall of funds, the financing of the Crusade was a disaster. Venice was owed significant sums of money and there was no means by which to pay it. So a deal was struck. To pay off its debts, the Crusade was asked help the Venetians recover their lost city of Zara on the Adriatic coast from the King of Hungary. This they did, which so angered Pope Innocent III that he excommunicated the entire army.

Despite Innocent's decisive action, worse was to follow. The Crusade next found itself involved in an attempt to restore the deposed Byzantine emperor Isaac Angelus and his son and heir Alexius, who had been deprived of their throne by a usurper. The effective leader of the Crusade, a wily octogenarian named Enrico Dandolo, sensed a vast opportunity and was quick to exploit it. With the Crusade's help, the blinded Isaac and his son were restored to power.

Unfortunately for the Angelus family, they could not pay the vast bill that they were left with as a result of their restoration. Unable to gain what they saw as their just desserts, the Crusade launched an attack on the city of Constantinople. On 9 April 1204, the unthinkable happened and the Crusaders broke through the unbreakable walls. The rank and file were then given three days to indulge their base desires in the fallen city in whatever way they wished.

There was no love lost between Eastern and Western Christendom. The former regarded the latter as the lands of barbarians, while the Westerners in return regarded the Byzantines as heretics. An orgy of destruction followed the capture of the city; churches were ransacked for their treasures, Orthodox nuns, vowed to chastity in the service of Christ, were raped in their convents by Christian warriors and the smell of death, fire and destruction hung heavy over the city.

It was a disgraceful act from which few benefited in the long term. Even those who did, primarily the Venetians, should have hung their heads in shame. Doge Dandolo, who had bowed before the altar of St Marks before setting out, vowing to lead his men against the Muslim enemy, would now send back ransacked treasures from a Christian city to decorate it. Accompanying these would be the famous four bronze horses that decorate the basilica of St Marks in Venice (though those there presently are copies, with the originals inside the glorious church for their protection); the basilica itself is decorated even now with the magnificent artefacts looted from Constantinople.

But the Catholic Church, despite its outrage at the diversion to Constantinople, must take its share of the blame because in sanctioning the use of violence for religious purposes it was unleashing a tempest that it could not control. That same year, 1204, Pope Innocent granted a charter to another military order, the Sword Brothers, who were to be used to forcibly convert the pagan Liv tribes in Lithuania. During the course of the century, many more shameful acts would be committed in the name of Christ.

The Crusade of 1204 went no further. No Muslim enemy was attacked during its course. Instead, a new empire was established around Byzantium by the victorious Crusader army. It was short-lived. Independent remnants of Byzantium hung on elsewhere, in Epirus in Greece, in Asia Minor around Nicaea (Iznik) and further east at Trebizond (Trabzon) on the Black Sea coast. Within half a century the Latins would be expelled from Constantinople with the aid of the Genoese, the arch-enemies of Venice, who relished the chance to get one up on their rivals.

There was something of a revival in art after the return of the Byzantines to Constantinople halfway through the century; the period is known as the Paleologus Renaissance after the emperor who led the fightback. Evidence of it can still be found in places like the church of the Holy Mother in Ohrid (now in the Former Yugoslav Republic of Macedonia), which remains a place of awesome beauty. But the last remnants of Byzantine energy would be exhausted in the process of restoring their fortunes, and the inheritor of Rome was now living on borrowed time. The key bastion of Christendom against the expansion of the Turks into Christian Europe had effectively been destroyed by the so-called Crusade that had been visited upon it, and many Christians in Eastern and Central Europe would feel the effects in the longer term.

But how much had changed in that half-century between the capture of Constantinople by the Crusaders and the Paleologian Restoration? Much of Eurasia had been affected by the Mongol onslaught. Europe was not alone in its troubles. Even India had not been immune. At the start of the century, the empire of Mohammed of Ghor to the north of the Subcontinent appeared supreme but it was not really so. It fell apart, starting in the western part of the empire, in Khorosan first of all, where Mohammed was ousted by Khwarezmians who themselves would soon feel the wrath of the Mongols. In 1206, Mohammed was assassinated. That same year Genghis Khan was elected as leader of the Mongol tribes in Mongolia.

When the Mongols struck Central Asia just over a decade later a huge number of Muslims were displaced, many of whom made their way to India. Here, a number of competing Muslim powers emerged in the north. They were as likely to fight each other as Hindu states across the Subcontinent, and what followed was a series of wars driven much more by personal ambition than any religious conviction. Genghis Khan himself crossed the Indus in 1222, although he did not push further south and India, for a short time, was reprieved from Mongol attentions.

Yet many an innocent victim died in these wars in the north of India. A Muslim warlord, Iltutmish, who ignored any claims to central power that rulers in Delhi attempted to impose, was confused when, on sacking a large settlement at Odantapuri near the Ganges, the shaven-headed citizens of the place made no resistance, even when slaughtered in vast numbers. He did not realise that he had come across a Buddhist seat of learning, ill-equipped to fight back. But it proved very difficult for the Muslims to agree on a common purpose and some areas such as Bengal managed, to all intents and purposes, to stay independent.

On Iltutmish's demise, there was a surprise when, after his son's short-lived and ineffectual reign, a daughter, Raziya, seized power in his lands. However, although she ruled well enough, the obstacles presented by her gender were too great; a contemporary Muslim chronicler noted that a woman's place was 'at her spinning wheel' (a later historian noted that this was the first reference to such an implement on the Subcontinent, where textile production would later become so important, leaving him to surmise that it was Muslims who first brought it into the region).

A revolt removed Raziya from power and soon after, in 1241, the Mongols sacked Lahore. But the actions of a stubborn leader, Ghiyas ud din Balban, a former slave who seized power in Delhi, kept the Mongols out of that city at least. The Mongol threat in fact helped Hindus elsewhere in the region; with the successors of Genghis threatening them, Muslims in the north could not be diverted elsewhere. Eventually, in 1260, Balban came to a compromise agreement with Hulagu, grandson of Genghis. It did not always hold, but Balban had a remarkably long reign of forty years, eventually expiring in 1287.

During these astonishing decades there was an amazing ebb and flow across Eurasia as the Mongol Empire grew with incredible speed, their rapacity for more conquest seemingly unquenchable. As the thirteenth century moved, on the pace of that change would slow, but it remained powerful. It was an incredible period of conquest for a people with little previous history of note beyond their frequent raids of China.

China was immensely rich by the standards of the rest of the world. She had developed significant trading links, and not just with regional entities like Japan and Korea; connections were established further afield too, for example with Indonesia and India, but also thousands of miles distant, with Sri Lanka, the Islamic world and Africa. In many ways China pre-empted the later maritime links of Britain, though focussed very much in the Pacific and Indian oceans and not reliant on conquest but on trade. But the wealth of China proved an irresistible lure for the Mongols.

The driving force behind the rise of the Mongols was one of the most famous names in history, Genghis Khan. He had grown up as an outcast and an outlaw following the murder of his father, a minor chieftain. He directed the bitterness generated within him into a driving ambition for power and conquest. Through perseverance as much as anything – for this was no overnight process but one which took decades – he gradually built up his armies, selectively assimilating those of conquered enemies into his own.

There were several reasons for the success he enjoyed. As always, the weakness of his enemies contributed – Han T'o-chou, the emperor of the southern Sung Empire in China, was killed attacking the north in 1207 as one example – but that alone cannot explain what followed. Genghis's men were meticulously drilled and disciplined, his tactics confused his foes and his success was in the main attributable, in the beginning at least, to his horsemen – some heavy cavalry, others lightly armed archers, every bit successors to the Huns of a millennium before.

The Mongols had raided China for as long as anyone could remember and had also been used by Chinese rulers as mercenaries. Genghis now coveted China for himself. China was divided into several kingdoms and it would take the best part of a century to complete the conquest. The capital of the Chin kingdom in the north, Zhongdu

– close to modern Beijing – was attacked in 1211 and finally taken in 1214. The south would remain out of reach for several decades longer. But in the process of conquest the Mongols also obtained new skills in siege warfare from among the Chin engineers they conscripted, and these were to prove invaluable in the future.

So the armies of Genghis were well armed, organised and led, but one further feature was added to this irresistible cocktail of conquest, an attribute for which the Mongols would become notorious, namely the use of terror as a tactic to subdue resistance. Certainly the use of such an approach was nothing new, but the Mongols would take it to previously unseen heights. The use of this tactic was about to be horrifically demonstrated in Persia and the surrounding region.

Genghis also sought to build links to the west, and in particular the independent and powerful kingdom of Khwarezm, on the borders of Persia. But when a group of traders was slaughtered by the governor of the frontier town of Otrar in 1218, a terrible price was to be paid. Genghis swept into the region, completely outmanoeuvring the Khwarezmian generals who sought to defend their lands against him.

A long and bitter campaign followed that ended in the virtual obliteration of many cities in the region, a roll-call of devastation that included the names of the great settlements of Nishapur, Merv and Balkh. Even allowing for the conventional exaggeration of the casualty lists by contemporary chroniclers, it is likely that millions died both from the attrition of war and the resulting destruction of agriculture in the region.

It has been estimated that 18 million people died because of Genghis Khan, an unenviable record that puts him on a par with any twentieth-century dictator. News of these dreadful events, horrifying even for the times, no doubt served a salutary propaganda purpose, discouraging other cities from resisting, but even surrender did not guarantee survival. The brutal and seemingly motiveless slaughter of the latter parts of this campaign were among the worst in recorded history, a not inconsiderable claim when there are so many benchmarks with which to compare.

Europe, too, soon became aware of the Mongols. In 1221, a Mongol reconnaissance was launched into Russia. Two years of raiding followed. The Mongols on this occasion initially avoided pitched battle, but were left with little option when they were caught up by the Russian army near the Kalka River in 1223. The Mongols won a decisive victory but they did not at this stage follow it up; this was only a scoping mission for a later full-scale onslaught. Genghis died in 1227 but the Mongols returned to Russia and beyond a decade or so later, in the process decisively beating European armies in both Poland and Hungary.

In those early decades of the century, Europe had other issues to concern it closer to home. In England, King John came into conflict with his barons, a confrontation that ended humiliatingly, with the monarch forced to agree to recognise the rights of his barons with the signing of Magna Carta in 1215 (an important development, but hardly the declaration of universal rights that later generations made it out to be).

Across the water in France, there were significant upheavals in train. The full force of the Crusader movement was directed towards the heretic regions of the south, where the Cathar faith had taken root. Its doctrines, emanating initially from the Balkans, preached a number of radical ideas, including a complete abstinence from acts likely to lead to procreation. More importantly, these doctrines ran directly contrary to the teachings of the Catholic Church.

In 1209, an army whose existence had been sanctioned by the Pope, Innocent III, marched into the south of France. Outside the city of Beziers there were a number of soldiers in the Crusader army who were anxious about attacking, for there were Catholics in the city as well as Cathars and they had no means of identifying members of one group from those of the other. In response to the uncertainties expressed by Crusaders who did not wish to murder innocent Catholics, a man of the cloth with the expedition advised, 'Kill them all; God will recognise His own.'

Devastation duly followed. The ensuing campaign was harsh in the extreme and at the end of it the Cathar 'aberration', as it was seen by the Catholic Church, was crushed. Their mountain citadels were all taken, most poignantly of all their headquarters at Montsegur, the final place to fall over thirty years later in 1244. At its base a huge funeral pyre was lit, on which over 200 human torches were consumed, those captured who had refused the offer of life if they renounced their faith and accepted Catholicism. Now the meadow where they died so horribly is a place of rare beauty, overlooking mountains decked with flowers, with little evidence of the terrible events that took place there. Then it was a place of death and sacrifice.

For all the awfulness of these events, they were important in uniting the north and south of France and building a more viable kingdom, a process fuelled by French successes in the north against the Angevins in Normandy (now the rulers of England), who lost most of their French lands as a result.

However, it would be easy to ignore the many positive changes that were happening in Western Europe in contrast to these harsh events. It was to be seen in art, evidenced for example by the construction of Rheims Cathedral, which began in 1210. There were many developments in learning, too. A number of students had left the base of their learning in Oxford, England, the year before to go to a newly founded establishment at Cambridge, though some would move back before too long. In Europe these were years of paradox, of beauty alongside death, of intellectual challenge often fighting against religious conservatism.

Spiritual motivations were still strong and led to some renewed outbreaks of Crusading enthusiasm. In 1212, a large body of young people from Germany marched down through France, seeking to launch a Crusade for the conquest of Jerusalem. They had no organisation and no idea of how they would find transport to get there. But somehow ships were provided and this so-called Children's Crusade set out. It ended in disaster, many of the participants being captured by pirates and taken into a life of slavery.

At the same time, the Arthurian legend continued to take root alongside a general development of the concept of chivalry, which had no doubt been fuelled by the evolution of military orders of knights who fought ostensibly for Christian purposes. It remained a hypocritical contradiction; the orders were rich and exploitative, the wars knights fought brutal and bloody, their ends characterised by rapine and pillaging that had little to do with chivalric ideals. But with the emergence in Germany of epics like Wolfram von Eschenbach's *Parzival* in 1212, the Grail legends developed and the mirage of chivalry continued to grow apace, supported by the emergence of Gothic architecture, perhaps more extravagant and fantastic than any building style before or since.

A rich young noble from the Italian Peninsula reacted against this concentration on worldly goods. While out riding, the young man came across a member of the community of the poor and gave him his cloak. He soon after rejected all material possessions and started off down the road that would end with his canonisation as St Francis of Assisi, perhaps the greatest of all medieval religious figures. The order that he founded, the Franciscan (whose monks became known as the 'Friars Minor'), would ironically achieve great material wealth, and the Church as a whole, while embracing his image, rejected his message. When a group called the Fraticelli emerged after his death, espousing the beauty of poverty and the rejection of worldly goods, they were denounced as heretics and treated as such.

In 1216, a Spanish canon named Dominic started his own movement, the 'Friars Preacher', which soon attracted its own following. But a more sinister side to this movement developed. They would play a very active part in the Inquisition tribunals that were established to strike down heresy. By 1233, Pope Gregory IX had formally organised the Inquisition but the challenges it was up against were demonstrated when, in that same year, Conrad of Marburg, who was leading a harsh persecution of heretics in Germany, was murdered.

The Church did not only have rebellious heretics to concern it; secular rulers could prove troublesome too. The German emperor Frederick II (reigned 1208–50) was one such man. He seemed determined to assert his rights at the expense of the papacy at every turn. Eventually he was cajoled into agreeing to launch another Crusade to the Holy Land, but when he prevaricated for too long before actually setting out he was excommunicated.

Counter-intuitively, he then set out on Crusade at last; whatever he was commanded to do or not to do, he would do exactly the opposite. In another supreme irony, by entering into an alliance with local Muslim powers for whom the sacred city of Al-Quts (the Muslim name for Jerusalem) was no more than a bargaining chip in return for which Frederick would help them against their rivals, in 1229 he regained the Holy City for the Crusaders without a blow being struck in anger.

In a final bizarre twist, his coronation in the Holy Sepulchre took place against the backdrop of a Christian cleric outside hurling insults at the excommunicate who dared take the throne in such a fashion. Frederick left Outremer soon after. Fifteen years later, a virtually defenceless Jerusalem was sacked and taken by Khwarezmian mercenaries who had been forced from their own lands by the Mongol hordes. Jerusalem would not be in Christian hands again for 673 years.

Following the death of Genghis, although there were tensions in the Mongol succession and serious internal confrontation threatened, his son Ögedei took his place.

The process of Mongol expansionism continued. In 1234, Kaifeng fell and the Chin dynasty in the north of China was at last assimilated into the Mongol Empire. Large chunks of Russia were added more securely as well, after more horrific sacks such as that of Kiev in 1240; this would become the base of the Mongols who later became known as 'The Golden Horde'. But eventually fragmentation would occur and different rulers would emerge to govern in Central Asia, China, Mongolia and Russia. Civil war would eventually start to grind the empire down from within, fuelled by excessive ambition.

This had some important effects. The Mongols were never strong enough to permanently assimilate the lands they temporarily conquered. Often they would appoint a puppet ruler on the throne of conquered lands and, provided they paid the tribute and honour that was due, they would be left more or less alone. In other areas, more on the outer limits of their expansion, their raids decimated lands and left vacuums for others to move into. So, following raids into Poland in 1241, German settlers moved in and the destroyed town of Wroclaw became Breslau, sowing seeds of interracial tension that would last for centuries.

In some crucial ways, the impact of the Mongols continues to impact on the modern world. It has been argued, for example, that the paradigms of Russia as regards the world and its place in it are shaped by the effects of the Mongol incursions and the Golden Horde. The BBC correspondent Martin Sixsmith, who spent several decades in Moscow, believes that the fall of Kiev was a seminal moment in history, arguing that 'from then on, there has been a fear of the outside, the dangerous lurking enemies all around Russia's borders. It has been deep-seated in the nation's psyche.' He further notes that the establishment of a strong ruling hierarchy introduced the Russians for the first time to 'that centralised iron fist' that so often epitomises Russian government.

But it is the fate of all empires to overreach themselves and perish. Sometimes that demise is not immediate but a protracted, drawn-out process. Yet with the gift of hindsight we can identify steps along the road to ultimate ruin that appear to be decisive. One such moment was to occur in Palestine. In the early decades of the century, the Mongol tide appeared to be irresistible. Everywhere they shattered all resistance. As the century passed its halfway point, more awful events were about to take place in Persia and Iraq.

In Persia, the Mongols came up against the shadowy group known as the Assassins. They were well known for their uncompromising elimination of opponents through assassination and the lack of concern on the part of the killers about whether they died in the attempt or not. An extreme Shia group from the Ismaili branch of the faith, they believed that their death in what they saw as a religious act would buy them their entry into Paradise. Their opponents claimed erroneously that they were drugged on hashish, hence the derogatory term *hassishiyya* – 'hashish takers'.

But they were foolish enough to be implicated in a plot against Mongol leaders, an act which the Mongols never forgot or forgave. And so when they moved into Persia they moved against the Assassin (more properly known as 'Nizari') fortresses. The Assassins were a small group with an impact out of all proportion to their size. They depended for their survival on several features: the ability to spread terror in their wake; an amazing adaptability that allowed them to superficially change their religious doctrines to survive while underneath remaining true to their core beliefs; and their choice of out-of-the way, inaccessible fortresses to which they could retreat.

The Mongols systematically turned their minds to overwhelming these fortresses one by one. They were helped by their control of the Assassin leader, Rukn al-Din, who foolishly believed that by co-operating with the apparently invincible Mongols he would save his people. When in 1256 they moved on the greatest fortress of all, the so-called 'Eagle's Nest' at Alamut in the north of Persia, he had to watch on while the fortress, including the great library there, went up in smoke.

Worse was to follow. Rukn al-Din's people were called to an assembly where, they were informed, a census of them all would be held. It was, however, a trap. Once they were all together, the real reason for the assembly became horribly apparent. These people, all of them, had been called together to be slaughtered. And so the killing began, an act of brutal genocide with the aim of nothing less than the removal from the face of the earth of every known Nizari, regardless of age, sex or guilt.

Although this was shocking, most Muslims would have had little sympathy for the Assassins, who were, in their eyes, no more than heretics. But what happened soon after shocked Islam to the core.

Baghdad had seen better days, as had the Abbasid Caliphate that was still based there. But both still had great symbolic resonance. In 1258, the Mongols resolved to destroy both. The city fell after vain resistance and an apocalyptic bloodbath followed. Some of the great sites of Islam went up in flames; only a few Christian churches survived, these due to a small number of the Mongols being Nestorians.

Syria now lay virtually defenceless before the Mongols, who were quick to move in and take advantage. Aleppo and Damascus both fell; the latter was entered by Crusader warriors walking triumphantly alongside the Mongols, with whom they had entered into a truce. Regardless of how rewarding it might have seemed to those involved in the celebratory procession and who soon after joined in the desecration of Muslim monuments in the city, it was a terrible miscalculation on the part of the Crusaders.

To understand why, we must look to Egypt, from where a remarkable Muslim revival was about to be launched. Following the infamous Fourth Crusade that sacked Constantinople and enriched Venice in particular, two substantial Crusader expeditions had followed in 1220 and 1249. Both of them targeted Egypt. Both ended in abject failure for the Crusaders.

The latter failure had been particularly notable. At the head of the Crusader army was a King of France, a saintly man with undoubtedly genuine piety but limited success in war. Louis IX, or Saint Louis as he would become, lived a life of unimpeachable Christian devotion. Yet he was not without his blemishes; he was a stern man and he was also a proud king. Therefore, when his Crusade fell apart and he found himself a captive of the Muslims in Egypt, he must have been a chastened man.

Louis would eventually be released but only after a huge ransom had been paid. He would return home with his mission to recover Jerusalem unfulfilled. His defeat was a huge shock. The mission had been meticulously planned and extravagantly funded but it had met its match because of the rise of a new power in Egypt. When the Crusades began, their initial success had been regarded as a sign of God's approval. This defeat suggested that exactly the opposite was now the case.

To understand where this power in Egypt came from, it is necessary to look back for a few decades. When Saladin died in 1193, his extended empire soon began to fragment. In part this was because of his deliberate policy of putting in place a quasi-feudal hierarchy where some of the captured territories were ruled by family members with a great deal of autonomy. Without his unifying influence (which had anyway never been absolute) the tensions pulling at it inevitably increased.

The fragmentation that followed has already been referred to through the alliance that briefly brought Jerusalem back into Crusader hands. It was tragic for Islam as, just in the period which immediately preceded the First Crusade, in the face of the approaching Mongol onslaught, it was divided. This meant that the attacks of the Mongols were faced with disunited and weak opposition, making the process of conquest that much easier.

There was only one ray of hope for Islam and it came from Egypt. The Crusaders had been bested there through the exertions of a powerful warrior caste known as the Mamluks. They had been a part of the Egyptian army for centuries. They were captives, taken from their homes – often far away in the Caucasus Mountains – in their childhood. But theirs was not a life of bondage and drudgery. They were treated well and looked after, for they were trained from their first days in captivity as elite warriors.

These were not, in the conventional understanding of the word, slaves. To be a Mamluk signified not shame but honour. The warriors trained together with boys and then men of their own age, forming elite regiments that bonded unbreakably together. But to the ruling caste of Egypt they also represented danger. As the central government of Egypt weakened, the Mamluks seized power for themselves.

As the Mongols greedily eyed Egypt, their next obvious prize, from their newly won possessions in Syria, they were about to be taken by surprise. First of all, the death of the Mongol Khan Möngke in 1259 meant that many of the army and its leaders returned east to ensure they were not disadvantaged in the forthcoming manoeuvres in the succession process. Then, rather than meekly wait to be attacked, the Egyptian army moved on the offensive against the Mongols.

The battle that followed at Ain Jalud in Palestine in 1260 was brutal and hard-fought, but it ended in something little-known before; a Mongol defeat. In the aftermath, Syria was abandoned and the Mamluks moved in. In the years that followed, those Crusaders who had been misguided enough to side with the Mongols paid heavily, most notably the people of Antioch, which was sacked and lost to the Crusaders forever.

The driving force behind the Mamluk advance was a formidable warrior by the name of Baibars. While Saladin may be to the West the epitome of Islamic chivalry, Baibars is as highly regarded by the Muslim world. Baibars was a ferocious warrior who systematically drove back the Mongols and destroyed the Crusaders until just a pitiful rump of their kingdom was left. He was not sultan at the beginning, but, ambitious and ruthless as he was, it was no surprise when he later seized power for himself. Few were rash enough to resist him. When he eventually died in 1277, the Middle East was unrecognisable from the region that had existed thirty years before.

Further south, in West Africa, a new power had emerged. Ghana – more accurately the Wagadu Empire – was no more. It had been assailed by powerful forces from North Africa and weakened, but a new regional force had emerged to take its place. A vacuum was left and into it stepped Sundiata, the King of Mali, who, in the best traditions of all great leaders, returned from exile to lead his people to freedom and regional dominance.

A great and rich empire would emerge to dominate the region into the fourteenth century, with kings who lived in large palaces and scribes who wrote fluently in Arabic script, for Mali would become almost completely Muslim, although local tribal beliefs would remain important. They would also become explorers, and there are accounts that suggest that Malian sailors voyaged across the Atlantic and found America some 180 years before Columbus did.

A twentieth-century explorer, Thor Heyerdahl, sailed across the Atlantic from Africa in a raft built of local materials that he named the *Ra*. He completed two successful crossings of the Atlantic on such rafts, using the Canary Current to good effect. In so doing he proved that the voyage of the Malian sailors was a distinct possibility. African historians might comment with some justice that it is strange that Heyerdahl's name is still well remembered while the legendary voyage of the Malian sailors is not.

Nearby, the Yoruba people were producing works of great craftsmanship in brass in particular, with works that have been claimed to be among the best examples of their type in the world, a salutary reminder that when we talk of art we should avoid a Eurocentric bias that is to the detriment of other cultures. The Yoruba lived in small towns and among their achievements was a massive earth embankment called the Great Eredo, which was enclosed by a circular trench nearly 100 miles around, with a bank that was 60 feet tall in places.

Much further south again, another African civilisation was approaching its peak. Zimbabwe means 'place of stone houses' in the Shona language and the great city that formed the main settlement in the kingdom fully lived up to its name. The city, Great Zimbabwe, was constructed of large dry-stone walled buildings. It was the centre of an important trading network; within its walls goods from Persia, India and even China were traded. In return, gold and ivory flowed east. The peak of this kingdom was witnessed between the eleventh and the fourteenth centuries, but afterwards decline would set in until the kingdom faded into oblivion by about 1450.

Recent research also suggests that this was an era of amazing exploration in another area – the Pacific. Radiocarbon dating suggests that in a very short space of time, perhaps not much more than a century, a huge expanse of the vast ocean came within the reach of colonisers. It is believed that the expansion began in the Samoa–Tonga region. Between 1200 and 1250 they had reached Rapa Nui (Easter Island, where the famous statues were erected), arriving in New Zealand between 1230 and 1280 and in Hawaii between 1220 and 1260.

A marked 'El Niño' peak increased the frequency of tropical westerly and subtropical easterly winds, which helped the process. However, the impact that these human interlopers made on previously uninhabited territories was, some argue, catastrophic; native wildlife was devastated within decades and the damage caused to flora was also profound. Easter Island provided a microcosm of the problem; all the trees were chopped down as part of the efforts to build those gargantuan statues and the land became waste as a result.

These were events that made no impact on the consciousness of mainstream Eurasia. After their defeat by Baibars, the Mongols had turned their attentions east once more. In 1263 the emperor Kublai Khan had decided to establish a new Mongol capital close to Zhongdu in China; his palace, later destroyed, was near the modern Tiananmen Square in Beijing.

Believing that destiny had decreed that the khanate should rule the world, the islands of Japan attracted his attention too. However the vast fleet he sent to conquer them was destroyed not by the enemy but by tempestuous seas and winds – though the Japanese did put up stubborn resistance when the Mongols managed to get troops ashore. The Japanese not unnaturally believed that greater powers were at work here, the gods of Japan protecting the sacred isles. So in honour they gave the storm the name 'divine wind' – *kamikaze.*

Not all historians agree that the *kamikaze* story is entirely true, though it must be said that if bad weather conditions were going to occur anywhere, it would be in Japan – this part of the Pacific coast is terribly exposed to typhoons. However, recent archaeology suggests that there were other contributory factors, including some very shoddy workmanship on the part of the shipbuilders and a lack of coordination in the attacks, hinting perhaps that this invasion was something of a 'rushed job'.

There were in fact two invasion attempts on Japan by the Mongols, and in the gap between the first and second a substantial wall was built by the defenders that also played a key part in keeping back the Mongols. But whether or not the *kamikaze*, the divine deliverance, provided the whole picture, what is undoubted is that eight centuries later the legend would inspire young Japanese pilots to crash aircraft into enemy craft attacking their homeland. Henry Ford once famously said that 'history is bunk'. This suggests that he knew much more about the production of motor cars than he did about human nature.

Japan in fact had, like Britain in the west, good reason to be thankful for that narrow strip of water, about 60 miles broad, that separated the islands from the mainland of Asia. It was a natural wall, very difficult for an enemy to breach given the vagaries of naval warfare. Not until 1945 would Japan be subject to foreign occupation – almost 1,000 years since the English were defeated by the Normans at Hastings and 2,000 since the Romans successfully invaded the southern half of Britain.

The invasion attempt on Japan would not have been possible at all without Chinese sea power. The conquest of the Sung had brought the opportunity to launch amphibious assaults within the capacity of the Mongols, though their very mixed success suggests that they may have been better off sticking to land-based warfare. The Sung, increasingly hemmed in by land over the previous century and cut off more and more from exploiting trade advantages offered by the great Silk Road, had sought to compensate with maritime adventures and recent archaeology has shown that they built craft with watertight compartments, way ahead of anything available in the West.

Kublai would become far more Chinese than he was a Mongol. He would enthusiastically adopt Confucian teachings on how to govern, though he introduced Mongol concepts of religious toleration to the Chinese, allowing the introduction of both Islam and Christianity and encouraging something of a rebirth in both Buddhism and Taoism. He encouraged other Mongols to build their palaces around him. Chinese civil servants provided the bureaucracy that ran the empire, though they were kept firmly in their place. Even if Kublai did not try to destroy China and its culture, he attempted to rule it for his own and Mongol interests.

Europe would find out much more about Kublai when a young Venetian, Marco Polo, set out for his court. Rather unfairly, two previous adventurers to visit the Mongols, Friar Giovanni Carpini and Friar William of Rubruck, both beat the Polos by several decades but their accounts are largely forgotten. Neither was Marco the first Polo there. Members of an elder Polo generation, Maffeo and Nicolo, had set out for China in 1260 and also accompanied Marco on this later expedition.

But if Marco Polo was not the first Westerner to make the journey, he did spend several decades in the East and left a lively and vivid account of his time with Kublai and his court, which made a huge impact. It was 1271 when the Polos set out and the tales they brought back with them when they at last returned created tantalising visions in Europe. It is said that when Christopher Columbus set out looking for the Indies, in his luggage he carried a copy of Marco Polo's writings with him.

Those who heard Marco Polo's tales were both amazed and, in many cases, frankly disbelieving when he told them of the wealth and scale of the scenes that he had witnessed. They called him 'Mr Millions' in deference to the descriptions of the excess of everything – gold, riches, invention, population – he related to them; a somewhat sarcastic allusion, it would appear. But at the time he was right. China was more advanced technologically and could even feed its people better; according to the eminent modern historian Niall Ferguson, one Chinese family could live on an acre of land producing rice for them – in Europe, 20 acres of land were needed to feed a family.

Marco Polo would return to Europe and its environs to find much had changed, especially in the Middle East. What remained of the Crusader kingdoms of Outremer had been living on borrowed time. Little now remained once Baibars had finished with it. At the end, only Acre and a few other isolated towns and castles was left. When an act of vandalism against Muslim traders in Acre was perpetrated by new arrivals from the west who were ignorant of local realpolitik, incurring the wrath of the sultan Qalawun in Egypt, the end was nigh.

Qalawun died of natural causes just as the campaign he launched in retribution started, but the banner of vengeance was at once picked up by his successor, al-Ashraf Khalil, who led an army against Acre. The kettledrums beat their incessant rhythms out and the rhythmic thud of the huge boulders fired from the trebuchets and mangonels against the city walls soon mixed with the screams of the wounded and dying. For centuries, the major military orders, Templars and Hospitallers, had fought each other almost as much as they fought Muslims. Now they fought and died side by side. The Muslims, hugely superior in number and armament, broke in and launched a vicious sack in retribution for that unleashed by the Crusaders in 1099.

The loss of Acre neatly bookended the history of the Crusades to the east. The final cataclysmic scenes resonated perfectly with those seen when the Crusaders had first taken Jerusalem. What was left of Outremer was soon abandoned by the Crusaders. After 191 years, a dream, often misguided, rarely glorious, ended after sowing seeds of hatred, mistrust and bitter legacy in its wake. If the Crusaders genuinely believed that their God was on their side when they took Jerusalem in 1099, then surely their sins must have been great now that the Holy Land had once again been lost?

The Crusading battlegrounds had by now moved to Europe. The Templars were soon to face an ignominious end, though the Hospitallers lived on for centuries longer. For a while the newest of them, the Teutonic Order, was in the ascendancy, founded in Jerusalem but now very much based in Prussia, where they would fight for decades in vigorous and bitter conflict with pagan enemies.

They would return to a Europe much changed in terms of social structure. Whereas earlier centuries could be addressed very simply in a binary sense, with society composed of two classes – namely *potens/pauper* (powerful and poor) – there was now a third, creating a hierarchy of *maiores*, *mediocres*, *minores* (great, middling and small), with the intermediate class composed of city burghers, merchants, who had become more prominent with the development of urban life.

During this period, a new power started to emerge in South America. Fairly recent archaeological finds suggest that the Inca civilisation began to strengthen between 1200 and 1300, earlier than previously thought. The reason for their emergence has a surprisingly topical ring about it – a warming climate. This enabled more land to be farmed than previously and, with this happy effect, agricultural surpluses were harvested. This enabled more roads to be constructed, as well as large armies to be formed; both of these developments aided in the conquest of neighbouring tribes. In the process, the Inca managed to lord it over the Huari warlords who had previously dominated the region before a severe drought badly affected them.

On the other side of the globe, India continued its erratic and tempestuous development. There were a number of rulers in Delhi throughout the thirteenth century. They were members of what was known as the 'Slave dynasty'. They were not, however, downtrodden serfs rising up and throwing off their shackles. They were much closer in spirit to the Mamluks who were emerging in Egypt, members of a warrior elite possessed of excellent fighting skills and fierce temperaments.

But, as so often happens, the death of a long-lived and strong leader, the redoubtable Balban, brought chaos in its wake. Three years of weak rule followed before a new ruler emerged, Jalul ul din (also known as Feroz Shah I), bringing an end to the Slave dynasty. He also brought an end to something else. The Hindu states further south had enjoyed virtually a century or relative peace. The new regime would end that situation with a vengeance.

The historical records of that period in southern India and the Deccan (mid-India) are, as is often the case, sketchy. However it is clear that there were a number of separate states still in existence (as was the norm in the Subcontinent until modern times). One dynasty, the Hoysalas, emerged as the dominant power for a time under their king Ballala II, until Sundara Pandyan of the Cholas fought back in the 1250s.

However, the ambitions of Muslim warlords in the north were growing. In 1293 there was a Muslim raid in Bhopal, still some way north but further south than most previous excursions. Then in 1296 a warlord named Ala-ud-din pushed further southwards into western India. The precipitous citadel of Devagin, ruled by the Yadavas (also known as the Seuna), appeared unconquerable. It was not, for in a week the defenders had run out of provisions. A peaceful agreement was reached whereby Ala-ud-din returned north with enormous wealth and the promise of future co-operation.

However, Ala-ud-din proved a dangerous man to have around. He had shown himself to be a powerful and successful individual, far stronger in fact than Feroz Shah, whom he nominally served. Feroz Shah was soon deposed and Ala-ud-din took his throne in Delhi. He then restarted raids further south, though more Mongol attacks from the north between 1297 and 1303 kept him distracted for some of the time. He managed to push the Mongols back, even pushing into Afghanistan as well as regaining Sind and the Punjab.

These attacks by Ala-ud-din into southern India were raids, not conquests. Resistance to them could be fierce. In Rajasthan Hindu warriors threw their wives onto funeral pyres before charging out to certain death against the attackers rather than surrender; it was a suitably brutal postscript to a harsh century. But it was an appropriate precursor to the century that was to follow, where a new terror was to emerge – one which would, ironically, act as a catalyst for significant social reform, an important step down the road towards the modern era. This new terror would not come from warfare, but would bring Europe and Asia to their knees far more effectively than any human enemy could.

27

THE CENTURY OF DEATH

The Black Death Attacks the World (AD 1301–1400)

At the outset of the fourteenth century, there occurred an event of great importance for Western Christendom that in itself gave warning of the turbulent waters into which the the world was about to sail. The origins of this event were in Italy, a region of competing city states usually in open (and often hostile) competition with each other. These were not only maritime competitors such as Venice, Genoa and Pisa but also land-based powers like Rome, Florence and Siena. Italy was a fragmented region, a kaleidoscope of small states where power politics was duplicitous, and armed confrontation frequent.

The constant manoeuvring for advantage in the peninsula inevitably embroiled the papacy, as much a political as a spiritual power. The Roman nobility, headed by the Orsini and Colonna families, were in a state of perpetual feud with each other, which eventually led to Pope Clement V (pope from 1305–14) seeking refuge in Avignon. Here Clement, a Frenchman, was inevitably subject to the influence of the French monarchy. It marked a serious weakening of the papacy.

The fourteenth century was one of fundamental political change. The age of Mongol domination was perceptibly coming to an end. Other great cultures were living out their last years, while in the East an outstanding Chinese dynasty would emerge from the rubble left behind by the demise of the Mongol ruling caste. The balance of power was shifting in Europe and new dangers were emerging there. But all of this paled into insignificance before the onset of the greatest natural disaster to visit the world since the beginning of recorded history.

Few parts of Eurasia were unaffected by the Black Death (a name that would be given to the pestilence many years later but is so synonymous with the epidemic that it is pointless to try and call it anything else) and the politics of virtually every power were in some way shaped by it. For some states, though, it was just the greatest of a series of problems to face them during the century. Byzantium, for one, was faced with challenges that were soon to prove insuperable. The decline of the empire was evidenced early on in the century when it was forced to resort once more to mercenaries for help.

This time they came from Catalonia, but they proved as dangerous as the forces that had theoretically come to the aid of Byzantium in the past. Andronicus II, who was responsible for enlisting them in the first place and reigned for nearly half a century, found that he could not get rid of them once they were no longer needed. His ham-fisted and ultimately futile strategy to deal with the issue resulted in a massacre of a number of them. Those that remained understandably proved to be completely unmanageable as a result and Andronicus's acts persuaded them to raid into and settle in Greece, marking yet another downturn in the empire's fortunes.

The decline of Byzantium was evidenced, as well as caused, by the rise of other powers in the region. To the north, the Bulgarians and Serbs in 1331 conspired to form a great Slav state which was a direct threat to Byzantium. Parts of Macedonia were lost to the empire forever.

But this was not the greatest threat, which came from quite another direction. In 1302 a Turkish army bested the Byzantines near Nicomedia in Asia Minor. The victory was not a decisive one but was ominous in terms of suggesting a change in the balance of power, with significant longer-term consequences. The leader of this Turkish army was named Othman, and it was from him that the Ottoman Turks got their name. Further Turkish victories against the Byzantines followed, most notably at Pelekanon in 1331. None of these triumphs were decisive in their own right but the big picture did not bode well for the empire.

Muslim armies were on the offensive elsewhere too. In 1307, Ala-ud-din attacked the Seuna in India; they had been insufficiently enthusiastic in their allegiance. Once more, a monetary gift did the job and bought him off. But then a captured Hindu-turned-general, Malik Kafur, pushed much further south against the Hoysalas. From there he pushed even further, to the southern tip of the Subcontinent. The far south-eastern cities of Madurai, Srirangam and Chidambaram were robbed of their wealth and Malik Kafur returned to Delhi with treasure that included 612 elephants, 20,000 horses and huge amounts of gold (some 241 tonnes of it), pearls and other jewels. It was quite possibly the biggest treasure trove in history.

Delhi and the north of India were attracting unwelcome attention from the Mongols. Inspired no doubt by the wealth of the region, they had unsuccessfully attacked Delhi in 1303 and had been driven out of the north of India in the following year. India would always prove a tough nut to crack for the Mongols, though there would be one man with Mongol connections who would, later in the century, prove rather successful in his raiding into the Subcontinent.

Elsewhere Mongol powers appeared to be in decline, though their ultimate demise would not have been foreseen by many at the start of the century. China was one fault line; for example, in 1307 a state of civil war existed in some areas, something that evidenced another decline of centralised Mongol power and was as such a symptom of the problem. Yet the portents were still mixed at this time, for in the same year Mongol forces succeeded in annexing Rūm (Asia Minor). The picture was not yet one of consistent decline but rather of fragmentation as far as the Mongols were concerned.

The Muslim incursions into India did not lead to out-and-out conquest there. There were no forced conversions and there was no religious bigotry. Ala-ud-din's reign was most highly regarded for the fact that he reduced the price of basic commodities.

But the end result of this well-intentioned experiment was deflation and a drop in production. On his death, the command and control economy he had introduced collapsed and the old laissez-faire attitudes returned.

A bitter succession dispute followed his demise, from which a cruel tyrant, Mubarak, emerged. Among his more bizarre indecencies, he assembled a group of prostitutes to walk along the terraces of his palace and had them urinate over those entering his court, which was an unusual gesture of welcome to say the least. The end of his line was not far off and a new dynasty, the Tughluqs, was about to emerge to take its place.

From this dynasty emerged one of the most controversial figures in Indian history. This was Muhammad bin Tughluq, sometimes known as 'Muhammad the Bloody'. It has been said of him that he was India's answer to Nero or Ivan the Terrible. While his ferocious temperament is indisputable, he was not without merits. He was intelligent, an attribute demonstrated by his ability to write poetry. He was also a great patron of the arts and an authority on medicine and mathematics.

But alongside this he had dreams of conquest. At one stage his eyes spread as far west as Afghanistan and Iran but, this proving too ambitious a scheme, he turned instead to the Himalayas. However, his greatest challenge came from within. Facing a succession of revolts, he put down the rebels with brutal efficiency. One of the first to fall into his hands was flayed alive, his skin stuffed and put on display while his flesh was fed to his family (a delicacy later allegedly copied by Vlad Tepes 'Dracul', the medieval Romanian prince).

Unfortunately Muhammad's dreams had huge costs. Taxes were high, which in turn just fed the revolts that broke out against his regime. Reprisals were so harsh that the land went uncultivated and famine stalked his realm. Economic experimentation included the issuing of new brass and copper coins, which were so easy to forge that they soon became worthless and had to be withdrawn. Neither were the citizens of Delhi impressed when he abandoned their city as his capital and instead established it at Devagiri. Although there may have been sound strategic reasons for doing this, it was also the case that he was widely despised by the ruling Islamic elite of Persians, Turks and Afghans in the city and he was safer moving elsewhere.

He reigned, despite his severity, from 1325 to 1351, no mean achievement given the turmoil that was spreading across India. His successor, Feroz Shah Tughluq, ruled for even longer, thirty-seven years. However, his kingdom was limited in size. Campaigns in Gujarat and Sind were not far off disasters, there was no attempt to take lands in the Deccan ('Middle India') and the south was left virtually untouched. Only in Odisha was any sizeable military action taken and even here, although this was successful enough, there was no permanent addition of lands to his kingdom. Despite this, there was little hint of the devastation that was imminent; a decade after the death of Feroz, Delhi was about to face its blackest day.

Within Islam at the time there were those who sought not to conquer but to explore, to set out on great adventures driven by an unquenchable thirst for knowledge and enlightenment. The greatest of them all was Ibn Battuta, a resident of Tangier initially, for whom his own city was simply too small. His journeys began when he set out to reach the holy places of Arabia, a mere 4,000 miles on foot. Passing through the fabled city of Cairo, he found that he could simply not stop wondering and wandering.

So an odyssey of epic proportions began, which took him to the sun-kissed island of Zanzibar and the frozen depths of Mongol-held Central Asia. He became an adviser in Delhi and an emissary from there to China, passing through Ceylon and Sumatra on his way. In all perhaps 75,000 miles were travelled by this extraordinary enthusiast for life whose quest for discovery knew no bounds. Whenever possible he made sure that he never travelled the same road twice.

One place that Ibn Battuta visited on his travels was Mali and it was from here that the king Mansa Musa set out on a *hajj* to Mecca in 1324. This was perhaps one of the great spectacles of the Middle Ages, for it was said that he had with him 60,000 people and 100 camels, each carrying 300 lbs of gold. So great was the volume of gold that when he reached Cairo so much was spent that the price of the precious metal plummeted, a situation that was later repeated in Mecca.

Ibn Battuta also travelled through the Middle East on his journeys, a region where there had been profound changes that also impacted on Europe. One very specific consequence was on the Christian military orders that had been given the responsibility of protecting pilgrims travelling to the Holy Land and also provided crucial inputs to the standing army of the Crusader kingdoms. Now that 'Outremer' was no more, their raison d'être had gone.

Some of the orders were more successful than others in finding a new one. In 1306, the Hospitallers began their conquest of the strategically important island of Rhodes, just off the coast of Asia Minor. They would live on for another 500 years, though towards the end of that time their power would be vastly diminished and more symbolic than real. Only with the final conquest by Napoleon Bonaparte of their last redoubt on Malta would their effective existence be ended.

The Teutonic Knights were about to increase their power because of their effective ejection from the Middle East. They found a new target for their crusading zeal in north-east Europe. In 1308 they were admitted to Danzig (Gdansk) where they seized the city and massacred the inhabitants. The year after, they took the region of East Pomerania. The Grand Master, who had taken up temporary residence in Venice, moved to a massive fortress at Marienburg. With many pagan tribes still extant in the region, there remained a useful role for the Teutonic Knights to carry out. By 1330 they had occupied Riga, and throughout the century their power continued to expand in Europe.

Such was not the case for the most famous order, the Knights Templar. They had no effective role with the loss of Crusader possessions in the Middle East, but they still had plenty of wealth. This was a terminally dangerous position for them to be in. Their vast stock of worldly possessions came to the notice of the French king, Philip the Fair, who was in great need of more resources for himself. With the Pope at the time effectively a French puppet, Philip engineered outrageous charges of heresy against them and, on the morning of Friday 13 October 1307 – the source, some say, of the later superstition that Friday the 13th is an unlucky time – he raided their properties across France.

During the next few years the Order was systematically plundered of its possessions and suppressed across Europe. In France, the persecution against them was brutal. The last Grand Master, Jacques de Molay, was burned alive on the Île de la Cité in Paris in 1313. In other countries the Templars were also suppressed, though not always with such viciousness as in France. But their final elimination was nevertheless completed everywhere within a few years.

In modern times, it has been suggested that some of the Templars found a refuge in Scotland and, lest this theory be dismissed completely out of hand, a visit to the remote ruined chapel of Kilmory in south-west Scotland does provide evidence in the form of an unusually high number of gravestones with what clearly appear to be Templar symbols. While this does not in itself mean that the order continued to thrive clandestinely, it is nevertheless an intriguing theory.

There is less conclusive evidence for the occasionally postulated claim that the Templars took part in the battle which won Scotland's independence. For several decades, Scotland had been a target for the kings of England, particularly Edward I, a formidable warrior but a stern and ruthless monarch. His execution of the Scottish warrior William Wallace in 1305 by the terrible method of hanging, drawing and quartering only succeeded in creating a martyred hero for Scots to rally around (though whether that effect was immediate or has perversely got stronger rather than weaker over time is perhaps a matter of debate).

His successor, Edward II, was of very different mettle to his father, weak and indecisive in comparison. After years of dilly-dallying, his belated attempts to defeat the rising power of his opponent Robert Bruce were decisively rebuffed on the field of Bannockburn near Stirling. Although it was not the end of English attempts to dominate Scotland or at least install a puppet king of their own choosing, it was an important step towards protecting Scottish independence and an even more crucial symbol of Scottish identity and separateness. Bannockburn became part of the legend of Scotland that continues in its own way to act as a rallying point for nationalist support to this day.

Other significant events took place in the very same year as Bannockburn, 1314. The ruling Muslim dynasty in Egypt placed an Islamic ruler on the throne of Dongola (northern Sudan) replacing a Monophysite Christian monarchy that dated back to the sixth century. Elsewhere Dante's *Divine Comedy* (perhaps the greatest poetic work of the Middle Ages) was begun. Dante was inspired by the Gothic, and his characters inhabit a terrible and terrifying world, amply artistically displayed by the contemporary painter Giovanni di Paolo.

Dante's famous visions of Hell were a suitable portent for times that were already liberally provided with reminders of the frailty of human existence. In 1316, there was a terrible famine affecting much of Europe, with widespread mortality as a result. There were other reasons to be fearful too. In 1323, Bernardo Gui, one of the most famous of all Inquisitors of the Middle Ages, produced a manual for officers of the Inquisition which included detailed guidance on the subject of witchcraft. The face of European warfare was changing too, with the first mention of cannon in Europe at Metz in 1324.

Another great semi-mythical figure also belongs to this time. The most famous story about the Swiss patriot William Tell concerns his skills with a crossbow and it was supposedly on 18 November 1307 that he broke an apple in two with a well-directed bolt when it was perched on his son's head. This was in response to a supposed slur against an Austrian governor, Albrecht Gessler, that Tell had delivered when he refused to bow before Gessler's hat, which had been put up on a pole in the village where he lived as a symbol of Austrian dominance. Tell was offered his life if he performed the feat with the apple, which he duly did.

Tell would later become renowned as a great freedom fighter for the Swiss against the Austrians. Yet his story also has shades of those other great patriots of the time, William Wallace and Robert Bruce, for each of them would develop legends that would grow in later times when their example was a spur to later movements seeking to reinforce national identity; in Wallace's case, his great monument near Stirling was erected in the nineteenth century, about a century after Tell had become a revolutionary symbol in the fight against tyranny (French revolutionaries were quick to claim inspiration from him). With both Tell and Wallace there was a core of truth, but legends accreted around them until it was hard to tell the man from the myth.

There was much violence and uncertainty around in the first decades of the fourteenth century. Yet this was also an age of contradictions, for it saw the first stirrings of what would become known as the Renaissance, and in particular the marvellous artwork of Giotto di Bondone, the Florentine genius of whom a writer in more recent times would say, 'He made a decisive break from the crude traditional Byzantine style, and brought to life the great art of painting as we know it today.'

There was a freshness about Giotto, a brilliance about his colours and a beauty about his portrayal of the human form that outmatched anything that had gone before. His masterpiece is often felt to be the so-called *Arena Chapel* in Padua, executed in around 1315 and depicting the life of the Virgin and Christ. Much of his work and life is surrounded in controversy and uncertainty, but few are in doubt as to his genius. He would die in 1337 and was buried in Florence.

The fourteenth century is often remembered as a period of death and great uncertainty, but it was also a time of artistic flowering. Not only did artists like Giotto emerge; so too among the pampered rich did art collectors, the most famous of which was the French Duc de Berry, who lived at the end of the century and who lived, it seems, solely for art, having the huge material wherewithal necessary to compile the greatest art collection of the medieval world. The wealth came from heavy taxation on his feudal subjects, little better than slaves; one assumes they did not necessarily appreciate art in the same way that their lord and master did. That said, the parts of his collection that survive are among the finest of all medieval art, particularly the famous *Very Rich Book of Hours*.

Such artistic stirrings could not disguise the great upheavals widely present in these often troubled times. In 1325 there was a popular rising in China against the Mongols, who were still hanging on to power there but with increasing signs of strain. In 1328, the Karamanids took Konya in Asia Minor from the Mongols, whose Ilkhanate in

Persia was beginning to disintegrate. On the opposite side of the world at around the same time, the Aztecs settled on an island in Lake Texcoco that would become the city of Tenochtitlan, the site of what would later be Mexico City.

The exact date of the establishment of this new city is still the subject of some debate, but there is consensus that it was sometime in the fourteenth century. There were a number of clans within the Aztec tribal hierarchy and the people that were responsible for this new settlement were known as the Mexica. The creation of Tenochtitlan brought to an end many years of migration. The site had birds, fish and other aquatic life which offered many alternative food sources. It was an island location, which meant that it offered easy transport communications with the use of canoes. This would become the centre of a great Mesoamerican civilisation.

These were years of upheaval in Japan where, in 1331, the co-emperor Go-Daigo refused to abdicate and was defeated and deposed by the Hōjō Regency. Yet this was only the beginning of a bewildering see-saw of changes. Two years later Go-Daigo was back, having defeated the Hōjō Regency. The year after, he was deposed once more. By 1338, Takauji had restored the shogunate, though its control of Japan was never complete and feudal anarchy prevailed for several centuries thereafter.

Nearby, more weakening of Mongol power was apparent. A series of famines in China in 1335 loosened their grip still further (the year after, food shortages were also experienced in India). Rivalry between various Mongol princes, allied to economic stresses (inflation was rampant) and the natural disasters, weakened the ruling Yüan dynasty dramatically. At the same time, in Western Europe one of history's more protracted conflicts was on the verge of starting, presaged in 1336 by King Edward III of England's prohibition of the export of wool from his realm to Flanders.

A year later, Philip of France announced the seizure of Gascony, a source of substantial volumes of wine even then and the jewel in Edward's crown. Edward responded in the only way he could – with force – and so the Hundred Years' War began. Those early decades were ones of great English success, with the sea battle of Sluys (more of a land battle fought on ships in terms of tactics) and the crushing victories of Crecy and Poitiers. Yet for all these triumphs, a conclusive and definitive victory would prove stubbornly elusive.

As the century progressed, Byzantium proved incapable of helping itself. Following the death of Andronicus III, several years of mismanagement followed before one of the empire's most prominent generals, John Cantacuzenus, took the throne. He had been shabbily treated and virtually forced to claim it in order to ensure his own survival. The state of the empire was given graphic symbolic emphasis by his coronation. This took place in a half-ruined Hagia Sophia, part of which had collapsed, and no crown jewels were available as they had been pawned to Venice in an attempt to fill an empty treasury; cheap glass replacements were used instead. In 1343, John conquered Thrace (Bulgaria) but even this victory was ominous, for he did so with the support of Turkish mercenaries who would prove very hard to shift from Europe in the longer term.

Elsewhere it appeared that traditional threats were weakening. In 1344, Casimir of Poland defeated the Mongols on the Vistula and Lewis of Hungary expelled them from Transylvania. Yet, as much as anything this marked a diminution of Mongol might rather than a strengthening of European power. New dangers were emerging to challenge Europe, sometimes from unexpected directions.

The world was about to change, facing perhaps its darkest moment in recorded history, certainly within Eurasia. The same year, 1346, that the English trounced the French at Crécy, there were outbreaks of a terrible pestilence noted in Georgia and the surrounding regions in Central Asia. The Black Death had arrived, though there are accounts suggesting that it had been present, for example in India, as long ago as two decades previously.

Plague and pestilence were of course not new, but it was the sheer scale of this outbreak that created such terror. Whereas previous plague outbreaks had had a disproportionate impact on the peasantry and the poor, no one was exempt from this virulent assault. Rich, poor, young, old, all were affected, although some groups were even more exposed than others – losses among priests, for example, were particularly high as a result of their close contact to the dying in the administration of the last rites.

The outbreak that was about to hit Europe seems to have originated in the lands of the Golden Horde and the Crimea. It spread west from there, perhaps as a result of some intermixing between Genoese traders and Mongol forces at Kaffa in the Crimea, for episodes of the terrible disease were certainly present among the latter. By 1347, it was in Constantinople, Naples, Genoa and southern France. The year after, it arrived on the shores of England as well as more widely in Italy, in Spain and across France. By 1349 it was in Ireland, Scandinavia and Germany, while, when it arrived in Switzerland, there were atrocities committed against the Jewish community there who were blamed for it.

A plausible theory for the spread of the disease has Genoese forces returning home from Kaffa (where the siege had disintegrated due to the large losses from pestilence among the Mongol forces) and stopping off in Constantinople, thereby planting the seeds of death and destruction there. However, other commentators suggest that the timings are not quite right and that plague had already made its way to Constantinople in other ways.

Whatever its source, from Constantinople the plague spread to Alexandria. Then it moved west across North Africa. It may also have arrived here by ship transport from Sicily, the Black Death having already established itself there too. A poet in Tunis wrote how 'there is fear and death, stirred up by tumult and pestilence'. It had certainly reached Morocco by 1348.

Its spread was facilitated by the close trading relationships between Europe the Middle East, Central Asia and Africa. Nothing seemed able to stop it. In some areas 60 per cent of the population probably died. Estimates suggest that up to 65 per cent of the general population in Spain died, 62.5 per cent in England and 60 per cent in France. These almost unbelievable losses were not due just to the plague, but also to what are called by experts 'secondary catastrophe effects', such as famine and malnutrition.

The impact of this pestilence was immense. The losses were catastrophic, with perhaps a third of the overall European population wiped out. In 1351 a Statute of Labourers was introduced to regulate wage rates in England, which were rising as a result of the Black Death and the consequent labour shortage. The feudal system, with its domination of the peasantry by unaccountable landlords, started to erode.

There would within decades be social unrest, evidenced in England by the revolt led by Wat Tyler, as well as the appearance of new religious groups challenging the status quo. Neither was this a specifically English phenomenon; there were also uprisings in France and Flanders, for example, usually crushed with brutal force. But they evidenced the fact that everything was now different. So enormous were the losses caused by the Black Death that it seemed as if the world had been turned on its head and nothing could be taken for granted anymore – there was no such thing as the 'natural order' of things.

The Black Death spread across Asia too; there was an outbreak in Russia in 1354. There would be another flare-up in 1361, almost like the aftershock of a great earthquake; there would be yet another in England and France in 1369. Economies were impacted on an ongoing basis too; wages, despite attempts at regulation, continued to rise rapidly as those fortunate enough to survive took advantage of the situation to improve their lot by hiring themselves out to the highest bidder.

Yet it has also been shown that the main impact of the pestilence was to slow down what had been centuries of population growth (population in Europe was assessed to be 80 million before the outbreak; to contextualise this, population registers show that there were 60 million Chinese in 10 million households in 1393, though these latter figures may have been reduced significantly by natural disasters in the period there too since the time of the Black Death). The world would recover even from these losses, but it would look a rather different place when it did. Ironically, long overdue social change was driven by the harsh economic effects of the pestilence.

Political changes continued apace. In 1354, John of Byzantium abdicated in order to become a monk. The Serbian Empire of Stephen Dushan to the north was now larger than his, but did not have long to survive itself and would in fact be outlived by Byzantium. The origin of the ultimate demise of both empires was not yet obvious. When on 3 March in that year a party of opportunistic Turks crossed over to Europe and settled at Gallipoli in the aftermath of a disastrous earthquake that had decimated the defences, no one thought much of it. But from the acorn of this first Turkish settlement on European soil a mighty oak tree would grow.

Within a few years the Turks had started to push their way into an Eastern Europe that was powerless to resist it. Local populations were forcibly removed to Anatolia and replaced by Turks. Embarrassingly, Emperor John V was forced to travel around Europe with his begging bowl in an attempt to prop up his dying empire. Several times he was effectively held hostage, an unmistakable sign of how far Byzantium had fallen.

By this time, the Mongol Empire was falling apart. After decades of revolt by the Chinese against their unwelcome overlords, the Yuan dynasty was about to be finally overturned. Natural disasters played their part, as they always have in China. A later visitor to China wrote tellingly of the great river that so often flooded and left chaos in its wake, saying that 'this Yellow River has no respect at all for Chinese law and order'.

When the end of the Mongol dynasty in China came, the catalyst was surprising, a Buddhist monk named Chu Yuan-chang, a peasant who joined a famous secret society known evocatively as 'the White Lotus'. He later denied that he ever did such a thing but few believed his protestations. By 1355 he was the leader of a rebel band but his real breakthrough came with the capture of Nanking the year after.

In 1368 he moved on Beijing, which fell to him soon after. The capture of the city from the Mongols marked the symbolic end of the Yüan dynasty. A new dynasty took its place, the 'Mandate of Heaven' now bestowed on the Ming, 'the Brilliant'. Although the Mongols hung on in other parts of China for a few more years, they were now increasingly an irrelevance. As far as the Ming were concerned, the cultural driving force of their civilisation was a rejection of all things foreign – especially Mongol.

Of course, the Ming years are best known for the extraordinary ceramics that would centuries later be exported in vast bulk to Europe. But the reality was that Chinese art had continued to develop even under Mongol rule. The Mongols in fact made virtually no permanent impression on future Chinese culture (with the rather sad exception of Kublai's claim to Tibet, the bitter legacy of which continues to be felt).

The Mongols would survive for over a century longer in Central Asia but it would not be easy to do so. As an example of the instability that reigned there, the khan of the 'Golden Horde', Jani Beg, was murdered in 1357 and succeeded by his son Berdi Beg. Two years later, Berdi Beg was murdered and was then succeeded by his brother Qulpa. Just a year after, Qulpa was also dead. All this was evidence that here, too, the Mongol were in terminal decline.

Other powers were emerging to take the place of the Mongols. Some were commercial. In Northern Europe, the Hanseatic League had established itself based on Visby. In 1361 the city was sacked by Danish forces following a murderous battle of which striking evidence was found centuries later when thousands of bodies, often still wearing their armour, were discovered in mass graves. In response, the Hanse entered into an alliance with Norway, Sweden and the Teutonic Knights against Denmark. It was a powerful organisation that had progressively increased its influence using a range of weapons in its armoury, from such quasi-military alliances to trade embargoes such as that against Bruges in 1356.

But in the east another new political power was about to take up the Mongol mantle. In Central Asia, a man named Timur had by 1367 effectively become the ruler of the Asiatic Mongols. With his rise to power, Islam took hold among the Mongols and Christian missions to Central Asia ceased. To the north Russia breathed a sigh of relief and turned to more lofty ideas than the Mongols. In Moscow, work continued on what would become the Kremlin. Meanwhile Timur continued to consolidate his power in Central Asia, though it would not be long before he turned his attention further afield. Further Mongol raids were defeated by Dmitri of Moscow and in 1380 they suffered a decisive defeat at the Battle of Kulikovo near the River Don.

By this time Western Europe was faced with another divisive threat, which came from within. In 1378, the exiled papacy returned to Rome from Avignon but this did not heal the wounds of division but rather aggravated them. Pope Gregory XI, the returning pontiff, did not have the support of all the cardinals and some of them elected a rival pope. The so-called Great Schism resulted in the existence of two rival popes, which hardly helped to strengthen Western Europe in the face of external challenges.

Europe was by now under increasing threat from Asia. In 1371, the Turks destroyed the Serbian army on the River Maritsa. The advance into Europe threatened to become an unstoppable deluge and in 1385 they took Sofia. They moved as far west as Albania and then in 1387 took Thessalonica, one of the foremost cities in an empire that was just a pale shadow of its once great self. Then, in 1389, one of those battles of history with a legacy exceeding its practical effects took place. On the 'field of blackbirds' in Kosovo, the Serbian army was decimated in a battle which still forms a key part of national consciousness in the twenty-first century and explains why Kosovo is regarded like no other territory by the Serb people.

Only the assassination of Sultan Murad during the battle gave any palliation to the cause of Christendom. He was replaced by Bayezid, 'the Lightning', who continued the drive for expansion. The tone for his reign was set by his first act. His brother, Yakub, had fought heroically in the battle; so heroically in fact that he appeared to be a likely rival for Bayezid, who consequently had him strangled with a bowstring. It set a nasty precedent for future Turkish successions, most notably when Mehmet III, who became sultan in 1595, had nineteen of his brothers slain on his succession. Manuel II, the new Byzantine emperor, somehow managed to keep Constantinople from the Turks, though his empire was increasingly beleaguered and isolated.

But the Turks were still victorious against most other opponents. There was still Crusading fever in parts of Europe, though the visible manifestations of this were patchy and the motivation more to do with delusions of chivalric grandeur inspired by the development of, among other writings, the Arthurian literary corpus, rather than spiritual motivations, especially among the French court.

However, such delusions did not often lead to major expeditions. There were some exceptions; in 1365 a Crusade led by Peter I of Cyprus took and sacked Alexandria, though this led only to a few days of pillaging and rapine rather than any permanent resettlement. But the Turkish threat did create some momentum towards a fightback and in 1396 a large Crusade was despatched from Western Europe. A fiasco followed, with the French-dominated Crusader army refusing to co-operate properly with local forces composed largely of Hungarian and Wallachian forces (the latter region now in modern Romania). In the battle that followed, the Crusader army was comprehensively beaten at Nicopolis in Bulgaria. Thousands were slaughtered in an action that augured dangerously for future conflicts between the West and the Ottomans.

But the Turks, or at least Bayezid, were about to meet their nemesis from another direction, though there would be a long and winding road to the decisive confrontation between the Turks and the forces led by Timur, better known as Tamerlane. Over the course of decades, he steadily and ruthlessly expanded his kingdom. Not himself of Mongol stock, Timur was wise enough to realise that, rather than claim to be khan himself, he would be better placed to govern through a puppet ruler from the bloodline of Genghis, which is exactly what he did.

His rise acted as the catalyst for a period of uncertainty and chaos in the lands around Central Asia. A rival leader emerged of Mongol stock, Tokhtamysh, who in 1382 sacked Moscow – this in the very same year that the last Mongol forces were ejected from China. Tokhtamysh also raided Lithuania and Poland. These actions, from a man whom Timur had previously sponsored, were an act of defiance to his authority. It merely served to inspire him to greater efforts.

Timur moved into Georgia, decimating the city of Tiflis in 1387. His enemies naturally vilified him, one contemporary chronicle describing him as 'merciless, cruel, treacherous, filled with all the evil, impurity and stratagems of the tempter Satan'. There was no doubting his brutality, evidenced for example by the massacre of the population of Isfahan in Persia.

In 1392, Timur took Baghdad. From his capital at Samarkand, his power still seemed to be in the ascendancy. But the act that would perhaps prove the most memorable and terrifying was to take place in India in 1398. Attracted like so many would-be emperors by its enormous wealth, he led a huge army towards Delhi.

By December of that year, the city was under a tight siege. The Indian defenders, equipped with mighty war elephants, rashly sought an open battle with Timur. They were heavily defeated and the gates of the city were now opened to the invader. At first all was quiet, but then a small incident quickly sparked an outbreak of violence. Emotions soon ran out of control and the situation deteriorated into one of the worst atrocities ever seen in the Subcontinent. By the end of it all, Delhi was in ruins and thousands of its people lay dead in the streets. The city was abandoned soon afterwards as it was no longer fit for human habitation.

Europe was largely oblivious to these goings-on, though not entirely so as Timur sent emissaries to Western Europe, including London and Paris, to seek alliances. Nothing came of these approaches, nor in the long term from those led by the Byzantine emperor Manuel to Venice, Paris and London to seek help against the Turks in 1399. The Turks seemed the far greater threat to Europe and indeed they were. Despite this, Europe would be slow to realise the danger and Manuel would return to his increasingly isolated capital in Constantinople a bitterly disappointed man.

There were also important events that would help to shape other parts of the world in this century, especially in the Far East. Although they did not have profound immediate effects globally, they still helped to shape the world in which we live. For example in 1350 Ramadhipati was crowned as the first King of Ayudhya (Thailand/Siam) and introduced a legal code. In 1389 the death of Rajasanagara, King of Java, saw the end of his empire, which covered most of Indonesia. In 1394 Yi Seong-gye established a Korean capital at Seoul. All of these events had important regional effects.

Unknown to Eurasia, an extraordinary ruler was now enthroned in Tenochtitlan. Tezozomoc governed what was known as the Tepanec Empire of the Aztecs, assuming the position in 1371. He would reign for fifty years. Although accounts of his reign were not written down until a century after his death, when Spanish colonisers had taken over the region, they offer an insight into a reign that was characterised by a number of personality traits that would have done a European Renaissance prince proud: flattery, bribery, assassination and treachery allied to ruthlessness and downright terror.

The Aztec world reflected the structure of other earlier civilisations in Central America; this was still not a composite empire but a region characterised by rival city states who, for all their shared cultural values, were often at each other's throats, and where the survival of rulers was linked to their success in both war and alliance building. In Tenochtitlan, succession was by election; there was no hereditary passing of rule from father to son.

The preceding events went unseen by those across the ocean, but soon the Americas would come to the attention of Europe. The West and the East had become increasingly aware of each other, but from a distance. All that was about to change; Europe was about to reach out for China, and in the process stumble across something completely unexpected.

28

BRAVE NEW WORLDS?

Columbus and the Beginning of the End of Native America (AD 1401–1500)

If any century deserves to be called 'the century of discovery', this was it. What may be the most famous year in history was 1492, when Columbus and his increasingly disillusioned crews saw a new world looming out of the mists. They thought that they had come across the Indies; they had not. But the fact that they were looking for the Indies at all speaks volumes for the spirit of the age.

Since the journeys of Marco Polo, Giovanni Carpini and William of Rubruck, the distant and mysterious East had continued to fascinate the West. There was, of course, a stream of exotic products flowing from the East through relays of middlemen that whetted the appetite too. Columbus was the most famous of all explorers, but the immense repercussions of his discoveries have obscured others unfairly. Some of the largely forgotten adventurers came from Portugal, and the most incredible voyages were perhaps made by a man from China.

But at the beginning of the century all this would have seemed unlikely. The trends of the late fourteenth century continued and war continued to blot the landscape in several parts of the globe. Asia was a major battleground. In 1400 the ferocious Timur had defeated the Egyptians at Aleppo and Damascus and then took other Syrian cities. The following year he returned to Damascus and ferociously sacked it. Baghdad followed soon after – it had barely recovered from the terrors inflicted on it by the Mongols 150 years before. Timur was a devout Muslim and his excesses earned these campaigns the bitter epithet of 'the Pilgrimage of Destruction'.

Of course, it is easy to concentrate on such major events; however, there were a number of other apparently minor ones also occurring that were going to have significant long-term repercussions. For example, the seemingly mundane discovery of the process of curing herring enabled Dutch merchants to take on traders from the Hanseatic League. The latter were also hampered because fish stocks, perhaps because of climate change, had moved away from the Baltic.

Byzantium was now virtually at the mercy of the Ottoman Empire, a small and beleaguered island in the midst of a stormy sea that threatened to submerge it at any moment. It lived by sufferance alone and it seemed likely that every year might be its last. The 'empire' was now just a rump centred around Constantinople, with a few small enclaves in Asia Minor and Greece. The situation was so desperate that Emperor Manuel visited Italy, Paris and London in person to drum up support. It was in vain.

Then, a miracle. There was, after all, a power greater than the Ottomans. On 28 July 1402, the mighty Timur, now in his sixties, destroyed the Ottoman army at Ankara. Bayezid was captured and, according to some accounts, lived out his days in a cage. If we believe the Elizabethan playwright Christopher Marlowe, he committed suicide by dashing his brains out against the bars of his prison. It was a cruel way to end his life, but perhaps merited in light of the cruelty that he had meted out as Sultan. It was said that his wife was forced to serve naked at Tamerlane's table. Everything had changed, it seemed. Although the Ottomans retained their European possessions, they were forced onto the back-foot for a while. Byzantium was reprieved.

Yet if the battle appeared decisive, it was not. The Ottoman Turks seemed to be finished but such was far from the case. Those in Europe, now settled there in their thousands, were left unmolested by Timur. Within a few decades they would experience their greatest triumph. On the other hand, by 1405 Timur would be dead, conquered by that irresistible adversary, old age. He was on the verge of leading a major attack on China, which had done nothing to deserve his jealousy other than exist as a major power. His empire, vast but fragmented, did not long survive him.

He was buried in Samarkand, a city to which he had added some marvellous architecture. In this respect he was very different from the early nomadic Mongols, whose legacy he had inherited (though he himself, as noted, was not of Mongol stock). A fine tomb was erected for him. It was said that if ever his grave was disturbed then woe betide those responsible. Over five centuries later, Russian archaeologists disinterred his skeleton. Days after they did so, the country was invaded by Hitler's armies.

In the same year that Timur died, China set out in search of the world. An admiral, a eunuch named Cheng Ho, led a naval expedition, first of all to South East Asia, then to Burma, India, Ceylon and East Africa and possibly even Australia. This was an amazing feat of navigation and exploration nearly a century before Vasco da Gama and Columbus set out on their journeys. Alongside exploration went conquest. In 1407 Yung-lo, the emperor of China, occupied Hanoi and annexed Dai Viet (now part of Vietnam), extinguishing the Hi dynasty in the process. But the Vietnamese were fierce and proud fighters even then and resistance continued despite savage reprisals. In 1409 the Chinese even took Ceylon, though they would not hold it for long.

The year after, Yung-lo campaigned in Mongolia and bought the neutrality of some of the tribes there. He tried everything he could to strengthen his grip on power, including having a number of editions of the Confucian classics republished and reintroducing traditional Confucianism and the civil service examination system. Confucianism, with its emphasis on respect for the established order, could be a useful tool for a wise emperor, and Yung-lo would reign until 1424.

Other apparently fading powers continued to hang on tenaciously to the vestiges of control that they still had. In 1408, Edigu, khan of the Golden Horde, unsuccessfully besieged the growing city of Moscow but still managed to restore the 'Tatar Yoke' in parts of Russia. Elsewhere, though, the bright light of the Renaissance continued to increasingly illuminate a dark world, best exemplified in this year by Donatello's famous statue of David commissioned for Florence Cathedral. The city would become the driving force behind both mercantile growth and artistic development, though it was an evolution accompanied by internal friction and domestic strife.

Early in the century, the rediscovery of texts from antiquity – by authors such as Tacitus, Plato and Cicero – reintroduced ideas long hidden from the world. For this, we have to thank monastic institutions that had shielded knowledge from the destructive influences of 'barbarian' invasions during the so-called Dark Ages as if they were protecting precious gems, which indeed they were. Some stirrings of a remarkable rebirth of lost knowledge had already been present during the fourteenth century, when great minds such as the poet Petrarch were active, as was another great literary figure, Giovanni Boccaccio. As a result of their collective efforts, a new force entered into Florentine life, what has been described as 'the heroic age of scholarship', which laid the foundations for that amazing flowering known as the Renaissance.

Europe was evolving quickly, and new powers were taking shape while older ones were diminishing in strength. In 1410, the armies of Jagiello of Poland and Vytautas of Lithuania defeated the Teutonic Knights at Tannenberg. It was a heavy defeat for the order, whose powers were waning. The year after, by the Treaty of Torun the Teutonic Knights made peace with Poland and Lithuania, ceding some of their lands in the process. The ambitions of Vytautas were fuelled by this and he soon after fortified the Dnieper in Russia to control its passage to the Black Sea; he used some Mongol troops called 'Cossacks' to do so. He would be the head of a sizeable empire, now generally forgotten in the West but at one stage a powerful player in Eastern Europe and Russia.

In 1413, an event of great future significance occurred. Mehmed I, a son of Bayezid, with Greek help defeated his brother Musa at Çamurlu in Serbia and reunited the Ottoman lands fragmented after Timur's victory at Ankara. This was an enormous tactical error on the part of the Greeks, a now largely emaciated power whose sole hope of survival rested with the disunity of their enemies. Their very existence hung by the frailest of threads, one which was now under increasing strain. Their support for Muhammad would have fatal repercussions.

In the meantime, the never-ending war between England and France appeared to have reached a decisive conclusion on the muddy fields near the small settlement of Agincourt in north-west France on 26 October 1415. Henry V's weakened army, heavily depleted through disease, was greatly outnumbered (though some historians postulate that the numerical disparity was less than normally suggested) but fought with far more intelligence than their French enemy who, seeing a small force before them, charged with little discipline on a narrow front where their very numbers were a handicap.

The French were fossilised by the constraints of chivalry, the English forced by circumstance to rely on pragmatism. Pragmatism won, in itself a sign of changing times. What followed was a slaughter and the terms that followed the battle appeared to seal the English victory. Henry married Catherine of Valois, daughter of the French king, and it appeared that the succession would pass to the English Crown in the future. But it was not to be. Henry died young, and with him the hopes of English triumph in the Hundred Years' War.

Reforming tensions were abroad in Europe that were to have dramatic and long-lasting repercussions. There were a number of men who had emerged to challenge Catholic orthodoxy in the West. One of them, a religious reformer from Prague named Jan Hus, attracted many supporters; so many, indeed, that he could not be allowed to live by those wishing to protect the status quo and he was burned at the stake in 1415.

The destruction of Hus was carried out with ruthless thoroughness. As an ordained member of the Church, his anticlericalism had to be wiped out in the most public way possible. So, before he was burned his hands were scrubbed as a symbolic cancellation of his ordination, he was dressed in clothes adorned with devils to emphasise the evil he espoused and, after his death, his ashes were scattered in a lake to stop his relics becoming a rallying point for opposition. It did not have the desired effect of dampening the drive for change at all; in fact, in succeeding years the draconian response to his threat would seem to reflect the very opposite.

By 1419 an extreme Hussite sect called the Taborites had formed. The base of the Hussite movement was in Bohemia, and the year after their establishment they won a battle against the Bohemian Catholics at Sudoměř. In July of that year they defeated a Crusading army led by Sigismund near Prague. The following year another Crusading army was bested in Austria. Bitter tensions had been unleashed; civil war broke out in Bohemia, but the challenge to Catholic orthodoxy was now firmly established.

Byzantium was now under real pressure. Murad II became sultan in 1422 and laid siege to Constantinople. The year after, Thessalonica – recovered from the Turks only a few years previously – was handed over to the Venetians as the Byzantines could not defend it anymore. Seven years later, it was taken and sacked by Murad.

The end was clearly nearing for the once great city of Constantinople. Not only had it outgrown its history, it had also outgrown its people. The walls were far more extensive than they needed to be to accommodate the number of citizens left, and farms and orchards were abundant inside them. As one of the last Byzantine emperors, Manuel II, remarked, Byzantium no longer needed a great emperor with big, inappropriate ideas; in its current emaciated form it required a good manager. Despite Murad's efforts, the city would survive this latest attempt to breach its formidable walls – but time was running out.

While these upheavals were scarring the landscape of Europe, on a more global basis European adventurers were seeking new horizons. The age of exploration that would soon lead to Europe dominating much of the globe either militarily or through trade (or indeed a combination of the two) had already started. The impetus came not from an established great power but from Portugal, whose expansion across land was barred by Spain, still divided and opposed by the Muslim powers that remained in the peninsula. The discovery of Madeira in 1418 was followed in 1425 by the start of the conquest of the Canary Islands. Far more ambitious voyages of exploration were to follow.

The Renaissance too was beginning to spread its light, a paradox in an age of violence and upheaval. It was illuminating regions outside of the Italian Peninsula, which was itself in a state of political uncertainty, with city states vying for power and bands of mercenary *condottiere* hiring their services out to the highest bidder. To the north the court of Burgundy was the centre of chivalry and art, a position that was consolidated in 1425 when the Flemish artist Jan van Eyck was appointed court painter to Philip of Burgundy. The Florentines in fact were great sculptors, and van Eyck was their counterpart in painting. His portraits for perhaps the first time expressed personality in those whose likenesses he captured, personalities, further, that were draped in light in a way that again offered something quite new.

But the violence in Europe continued alongside the artistic development. There was not far to search to find enemies both without and within. An unsuccessful third anti-Hussite crusade launched by the Church in 1426 was followed by another failure the year after. The exuberant Bohemians invaded parts of Germany in its aftermath. The Hanseatic League found itself at war with Denmark once more and the Muslim threat continued to create problems, with the Egyptians successfully invading Cyprus, and the Ottomans, now on the march again, taking Thessalonica.

The conflict in France was about to reach a decisive stage. A young dauphin, Charles, hung on tenaciously to the few portions of France that he had inherited. The English still appeared to have the upper hand, though, and when they laid siege to the significant city of Orleans in 1428 it seemed that a decisive victory loomed.

Far across the world in that same year, China found its expansionism to an extent checked when a man named Le Loi declared himself Emperor of Dai Viet; the Ming recognised him after he admitted Chinese suzerainty, so they still had notional power over him but not to the extent that they wished.

The year 1429 saw a turning point in France, one which came from the most unlikely of directions. A young peasant girl from Domrémy in Lorraine arrived on 23 February at the dauphin's court-in-exile at Chinon. She said that she had received divine instructions to help restore Charles to his rightful glory. Mystical intervention was no stranger to the spirit of these centuries, with figures such as Hildegard, Teresa of Ávila and others both male and female. The fact that the peasant girl was a virgin added to the power emanating from this young and inexperienced figure who became known, of course, as Joan of Arc.

The turnaround was spectacular. By the end of April Orleans was relieved; on 17 July Charles was crowned king at the traditional coronation site in Rheims Cathedral, which had long been in English hands. The story of Joan almost demanded that it ended with her martyrdom. This duly followed when Joan was captured by the vengeful English and burned at the stake in Rouen on 30 May 1431. Of course the power of martyrs by definition lies more in their death than in their life, and by killing her the English judges who found her guilty on trumped-up charges merely served to create an example of heroism for others to follow. In doing so, they had signed the death warrant of the cause for which they were fighting.

The Hussite wars continued apace and yet another Crusade against them, the fifth, this led by a cardinal, Cesarini, was beaten back by its stubborn opponents, who were proving astonishingly obdurate. In that same year, 1431, the Portuguese discovered the Azores, though an attempt by them on Tangier a few years later was beaten off.

The Hussite uprising (for such it was, at least as far as the established Church was concerned) did not last into the longer term. It was too marginal a movement to do so. However, the tensions that its supporters had fed on and the teachings that they espoused would survive and eventually thrive until another discontented cleric, a worthy successor to Hus by the name of Martin Luther, would pick up the mantle of religious dissent.

The old order continued to be threatened in other ways. In 1435, Sigismund of Lithuania defeated the Teutonic Knights at Wilkomierz, driving another nail into their coffin. The year after, the French took Paris from the English and in the process made their ultimate triumph more certain. At the same time, Chinese scribes (one in particular by the name of Fei Hsin) were penning an account of the epic voyages of Cheng Ho while, close by in relative terms, the kingdom of Cambodia was starting to settle into its newly established capital, Phnom Penh.

Time was now running out for Byzantium. Delegations to the West from the city achieved next to nothing, save to emphasise the ongoing religious differences between the two halves of Christendom. Even on the brink of destruction, the Greek theologian St Mark Eugenicus could say that his people should 'flee from the papists as you would from a snake and from the flames of the fire'. When help came in 1444, it was from Hungary, itself threatened by the advance of the Ottomans. It was given the status of a Crusade but it made little difference. It was shattered at Vàrna on the Black Sea coast and the death sentence of Byzantium was thereby decreed.

What made matters worse was that it had seemed for a time as if Europe had a military leader who might be successful in fighting back the Turks. In 1443 a Crusading army led by John Hunyadi from Hungary had taken Sofia, although he was later ejected by the Turks from Thrace. Other leaders emerged to take the fight to the Turks too, including George Kastrioti (better known as Skanderbeg), a renowned Albanian warrior whose statue still adorns many Albanian cities across the Balkans.

Albania can be employed as an example of the complex history that has shaped the Balkans and continues to do so to this day. Although it would later be assimilated by the Ottomans and would become predominantly Muslim, before it did it was also on a fault line between Orthodox and Roman Catholic Christianity. Catholicism tried to assert its authority over the Balkan regions, but the surviving art we find in its churches is evidence enough that the region still looked to the east rather than the west for its religious motivation.

Skanderbeg would also become a symbol of Albanian cultural identity. This is why he is still a rallying point for Albanians in the Balkans, and his statue can be found not only in what we now call Albania but also in Kosovo and Macedonia. The latter both still have strong Albanian elements – in Kosovo they form by far the greatest part of the population. Ethnic and cultural tensions, rooted in history, still simmer just below the surface in the Balkans. And as we know, cultural tensions in regions that are on fault lines of the world can still flare up into open hostility and conflict with alarming speed.

In the aftermath of Vàrna in 1448, Murād II defeated Hunyadi at Kossovo Polje and regained most of the Balkans except for Albania. Constantinople was now completely isolated and exposed, though it seemed that it might still earn a temporary reprieve when the sultan died and a young, inexperienced successor took his place.

Sultan Mehmet II was only a young man of twenty-one years of age when he decided that the drawn-out demise of Constantinople must be brought to an end. In the spring of 1453, his forces surrounded the city. Inside, the population had been much reduced by hunger, disease and desertion and was hugely outnumbered by the Turks. Nevertheless, the fight they put up against a massively superior enemy, armed with huge cannon, was nothing short of heroic.

It was the cannon that made the difference. Previously the mighty walls of the city, normally well maintained even in times of economy, had proved impervious to all assault. But this new form of weapon smashed the walls as if they were made of flimsy timber. One cannon was 27 feet long, one of the longest ever founded. Against this, a weakened and demoralised Byzantium had no answer. To those inside the walls, this first concerted cannon bombardment in European history was terrifying; one witness described it as being like 'the awful resurrection blast'.

On the evening of 28 May it was obvious that the Turks were preparing for a final assault. The population of the city crowded at dusk into the hallowed environs of Hagia Sophia to perform the last rites of an empire that was over a thousand years old and heir to one much older still. In that service, perhaps the most poignant ever held in the history of Christianity, those who had argued for and against the merits of closer union with Rome during the final attempts to summon help from the West were as one. They breathed out their prayers, hoping that the Virgin who had so often come to their aid would do so once more.

It was not to be. The next day the Turks smashed into the city. The Byzantines fought to the death. Emperor Constantine XI, eighty-eighth and last ruler of Byzantium, threw off his imperial regalia and died fighting alongside his soldiers. An orgy of death, rape and destruction took hold. After it ended, Sultan Mehmet converted the church of Hagia Sophia into a mosque. Byzantium was no more. Its death might have been long in coming but its life had spawned some wonderful art, much learning and a unique culture. The world was infinitely the poorer for its passing, though the Ottoman culture that replaced it also produced some sublime works of art and played its own part in the history of the region and the world.

Mehmet's troops sacked the city so thoroughly that the conventional three days of pillage were over in one as there was nothing left to loot. Some of the citizens were taken into slavery, especially the good-looking youths, male or female. But the ordinary population was allowed to live on, given a degree of rights inside the city. The sultan appointed a new patriarch, the leader of the Orthodox Church in the city. Christians would be allowed freedom of religion. Eight centuries on, the head of the Orthodox Church still resides in what is now Istanbul, a very Turkish city; his local flock is now tiny but his wider responsibilities for the Church worldwide still make him an influential figure.

The West was shocked at the death of Byzantine Constantinople, but it was the shock of the hypocritical. At the end, it did nothing to help protect Byzantium and its earlier actions had contributed much to its demise. Now Europe lay with its underbelly exposed to the Ottoman thrust. Not for two centuries would it be able to stop the spread of the Turks, at the very gates of Vienna. Thousands of Europeans would come to curse the day that the West had done its damnedest to destroy Byzantium. It was the end of an era in history, made sadder still both by the long, lingering death that it had suffered and by the final, glorious, defiant demise.

Robert Byron, a twentieth-century travel writer, called Byzantium a 'triple fusion' – a Roman body, a Greek mind and an oriental, mystical soul. It was a typically brilliant and clever comment, made more brilliant and clever by the fact that it was both completely accurate and captured totally the essence of a dead and lamented culture.

Only it is not dead. Despite the efforts of Western historians – particularly the famous but not always trustworthy Edward Gibbon – to paint Byzantium as some kind of immoral and tainted freak show that fully deserved to be obliterated, it lives on, most especially in the great frescoes of Hagia Sophia or the Chora in Istanbul, or indeed in other great Orthodox churches and monasteries and the Orthodox religion practised in them – the likes of those found in Ohrid, the great painted monasteries of northern Romania such as Sucevița or Moldovița or the monastic retreats of Mount Athos in Greece; all bear witness that the flame of Byzantium still flickers, albeit more tenuously than it once did.

After the fall of the great city, there were only occasional flashes of light to illuminate the darkness for those who wished to prevent the Ottomans from expanding further into Europe in the years that followed. One such was the successful defence of Belgrade against them in 1456, which seemed little short of a miracle at the time. In an undisciplined but successful sally from the city after many of the Janissaries (the Ottomans' elite troops) who had broken in were slaughtered, the Turks were so badly defeated that Mehmet barely escaped with his life. But it was a short-lived success; within a month Hunyadi, the great hope of Hungary and neighbouring Christian nations, had died of the plague.

Hunyadi was a magnificent warrior, though he experienced the bitter taste of defeat on several occasions. It is perhaps appropriate that in what is still, just beneath the surface, a divided part of Europe, both Romanians and Hungarians claim Hunyadi for themselves. But although the victory at Belgrade is sometimes held as a seminal moment in European history, it only slowed the Ottomans down and could not stop them altogether. With Constantinople now firmly in Ottoman hands, Europe was wide open to further incursions.

In 1456 the Turks took Athens, ending its relatively long-lived Latin duchy. Three years later Serbia fell and in 1460 Morea, with its beautiful capital of Mystras, was also taken. In 1461 the Turks conquered the Greek empire of Trebizond in Asia Minor, an isolated last outpost of Byzantium. In the aftermath St Jonas became the first metropolitan of Russia to be independent of Greece, which was now firmly under Ottoman rule.

These enormous and history defining events, which shattered the last remnants of the Byzantine Empire, the successor to Rome, overshadowed other important political developments elsewhere. In 1450 the French, now unstoppable in their fight against the English, defeated them in Normandy at Formigny. On 12 August the English surrendered Cherbourg, a crucial seaport. The year after, the wealthy region of Gascony, the jewel in the English crown in France, was conquered when Bayonne fell. Only Calais now remained to the English. Finally, in 1453 the French victory at Castillon ended the Hundred Years' War.

Other significant events included the formal union of Denmark and Norway in 1450 and Vasily II of Moscow's securing of Novgorod, a crucial city in Russia, an important signal that Russia was becoming a stronger power. So too was Poland, which, in 1454, under its leader Casimir, incorporated Prussia into its realm at the request of rebels fighting against the Teutonic Order, though they would fight back and defeat him at Chojnice. Then in 1455 England, shattered and exhausted after the Hundred Years War, went to war with itself in that bitter dynastic conflict that would later be known as the Wars of the Roses, giving it a romantic veneer that its violence did nothing to merit.

These were years of great uncertainty, with frequent internal disputes disfiguring the landscape of Europe and beyond. So in Italy, for example, civil rivalries continued to be bitter and savage; in one uprising Ferrante of Naples summoned the help of the renowned Skanderbeg, who alone seemed capable of keeping the Ottoman Turks out of his territories. In the same year that this happened, 1462, Vasili II of Moscow died and was succeeded by his son, Ivan III. This proved to be a particularly important point in the history of Russia for it marked the first time for many years that the khan of the Golden Horde was not asked to approve the Russian succession. Old powers appeared to be dying all over the world and new ones were rising to take their place.

Central and Eastern Europe was now in great danger from the Ottomans. There was resistance against the Turkish side, but the problem was that it was fragmentary and relied on a few great leaders whose successors did not come up to the mark of those they replaced. One such staunch fighter was Matthias Corvinus, who in 1458 was elected as King of Hungary, now virtually on the front line. In 1463, he defeated the Turks in Bosnia. He then turned his attentions west, where his position was under challenge from Frederick of Austria. He was able to force Frederick to give up his claims to Hungary.

That same year, Pope Pius II, better known as Piccolomini, became the last pontiff to call a Crusade against the Turks. There was a poor response to his summons and, despite suffering from a fever, he left Rome in an attempt to drum up support. All this did was make his illness a terminal one. From his deathbed he watched helplessly as the Crusade ground to a halt before it had even left Italy. The time of the Crusades was effectively over, although there would be the occasional flare-up in decades and centuries afterwards.

Meanwhile, the power of Poland was growing; the Poles could, and would on occasion, form a powerful barrier against Turkish incursions into Europe. The Peace of Toruń in 1466 effectively ended Poland's conflict with the Teutonic Knights, who gave up many of the order's lands as part of the agreement, although they hung onto Königsberg.

Skanderbeg in the meantime was still proving a formidable foe for the Turks and in 1466 defeated the army that was besieging his fortress of Croya. But two years later he was dead and there was no one of the same calibre to take his place, though the rocky fastnesses of Albania would still prove a difficult nut to crack.

One of the most well-known of the defenders of Eastern Europe at this time was Vlad Tepes, *voivode* (or prince) of Wallachia (now part of Romania), who fought a determined defensive campaign against the Ottomans. He also looked to increase his power to the west, in particular in the mountains and forests of Transylvania. As well as being a brave and tough leader he was also renowned for his ferocity, and his nickname of 'Vlad the Impaler' tells much about his harsh techniques for increasing his power.

He is best known for another reason, though. Over four centuries later, an Irish writer was searching for a name for his anti-hero in his Gothic tale. Looking through a rather dry history book on medieval Wallachia, he found a reference to a medieval ruler whose nickname was (some say inaccurately, though this is disputed) translated as 'son of the devil' – Dracula.

This association with vampirism is most unfortunate for Romanians, who see Vlad as a hero, but the legends have proved hard to destroy. Even his burial place is a site of mystery, on a small island in a lake where even now the only way to visit the monastery that hosts his grave is by means of a small rowing boat. Some years ago his tomb was searched in an attempt to establish some facts about the legends surrounding his burial. When it was opened it was found to be empty. This author once visited the monastery on an overcast day with leaden clouds overhead. On reaching the island, a black-cloaked, thick-bearded Orthodox priest was on hand as a welcome party. The journey back to the shoreline in a tiny boat, interrupted halfway across when a violent thunderstorm broke out, is one that will be hard to forget.

Other parts of the world were now also making an impression on the world stage. In West Africa, Sunni Ali, the ruler of Gao in the middle Niger, took the important trading settlement of Timbuktu, founding an empire – the Songhay – that would last until 1591 when it was finally defeated by a Moroccan army.

Two years after this, he began the siege of the important city of Jenne. It fell after a siege of seven years, seven months and seven days. A further seven days was added for the victors to celebrate alongside the vanquished as Sunni Ali – only a Muslim in name, as he supported many African religions – married the widow of the former ruler, who had died in the siege. There was no bloodletting of any kind to mar the euphoria of victory. In case we visualise this kingdom as an undeveloped territory, it was replete with a university and a hospital so advanced that surgeons could remove cataracts.

In 1467, a vicious conflict, the Ōnin War, began in Japan, a feudal confrontation on a large scale with the Shogunate now having little real power. Two years after, on the far side of the world, as yet still out of sight of Eurasia, Montezuma I, the fifth Aztec king, died. He had created a formidable empire that extended to the coast of the Gulf of Mexico. He cannot have known that it was now living on borrowed time.

The Americas were enjoying their last few decades of obscurity, at least as far as the West was concerned. However, the achievements of the Aztecs were great; wonderful architecture, with layered pyramids climbing up to the heavens like giant stone staircases to the gods, while their craftsmen created some amazing artefacts in gold and other metals. But theirs was a civilisation of contradiction, for alongside this beauty human sacrifice was still widely practised.

Contradictions of different kinds also existed in Europe. If we look at the year

1470 for example, we would find geniuses such as Botticelli and Bellini at work in renaissance Italy. In that year, an Englishman called Thomas Malory finished his *Le Morte d'Arthur*, the definitive summation of the Arthurian legends. Yet Malory wrote his *magnum opus* as a prisoner in the bitter civil war that still raged in England. Florence, too, was in many ways contradictory; a patron of arts and at the same time a lover of money and materialism. It was no coincidence that a consummate political dynasty, the de Medicis, was in power during this period.

Europe was still a place where violence walked cheek by jowl with breathtaking artistry but it was also on the verge of greatness, or at least dominance. The Iberian Peninsula was at first the place where the driving force of European expansionism was found: England was still too busy fighting itself and was not yet a strong international power, while France was still barely out of the recovery stage after the exhausting travails of the Hundred Years' War.

At first it was the smaller (territorially speaking) power in the peninsula, Portugal, who gave the impetus, finally conquering Tangier in North Africa in 1471. This was also the year when a king named Pachacutec died in South America. He had established a great Inca empire that covered Peru, Bolivia, Ecuador and parts of Chile and Argentina. It would provide rich pickings for aggressive Europeans less than half a century later.

Pachacutec had systematically conquered the lands to the south of his kingdom. The territory around Lake Titicaca especially caught his eye, as it was a region of great wealth. It was conquered with ruthless efficiency. The Incas were a remarkable civilisation; unlike the Maya in Mesoamerica, they did not have hieroglyphic writing but were possessed of remarkable organisational genius. They also mummified their dead and, on great state occasions, the mummies of former rulers were brought out and sat in chairs to share in the festivities.

They were also capable of spectacular building and engineering feats. In the difficult landscape in which they lived, water was particularly vital. They constructed a series of canals and terraces to bring the precious liquid to their mountain fields. At one site, Tipon near Cuzco, boulders and rocks were piled high to form a natural filter, creating irrigation canals that allowed the local farmers to grow two crops of maize a year, which was vital.

Spain, the future conqueror of the Inca Empire, was still far from a united entity and, until it was, external expansion was bound to be limited. However, steps were being taken to address this disunity. Following the capture of Barcelona in 1472 by John of Aragon, for example, Aragon and Castile were reunited. The next year John entered Roussillon and Cerdagne in what is now France and added them to his empire.

One seminal date in Spanish history was 1474, for it was then that Ferdinand of Aragon and Isabella of Castile were declared king and queen of Castile. They would prove a potent double act, the figureheads while Spain united itself internally and prepared itself to expand externally.

Yet despite the fact that Europe was about to launch itself across the globe, it still appeared that the Turkish threat was a source of great danger. In 1475, the Turks took the significant Genoese trading base of Kaffa in the Crimea. The Mongol khan of the Crimea became their vassal, showing just how much the state of power politics in the region had changed. The truth was that the Mongol power was now in terminal decline, as was evidenced in 1476, when Ivan of Moscow refused to do the khan of the Golden Horde homage and subsequently defeated him in battle.

On the global stage, some conflicts were starting while others were finishing. The Ōnin War in Japan ended in 1477, largely through exhaustion, though civil war in the country remained endemic. Two years later Buhlūl Shah of Delhi conquered Jaunpur while Le Thanh Tong of Dai Viet captured Luang Prabang, capital of Laos, having previously conquered parts of Champa and formed an empire in South East Asia.

But it was in Europe that the shape of the immediate future could be seen. Alongside the artistic outpouring of the Renaissance, another important development was the introduction of printing to the continent. Johannes Gutenberg developed a printing press in around 1439, while William Caxton established his in London in 1476.

The printing press was one of the most crucial inventions ever made, enabling the mass dissemination of information to a population that as a result became far better informed (or, more cynically, manipulated), especially as levels of literacy also began to rise. There were certainly some great minds around; in approximately 1485, Leonardo da Vinci designed a prototype parachute. Work also began on the amazing edifice of King's College, Cambridge, though some art was less aesthetically pleasing, with Hieronymus Bosch, the painter of hellish landscapes, active at the time.

In 1480 the Canary Islands were ceded to Spain by Afonso of Portugal. The Turks were still active, attacking Rhodes but being repulsed by the Hospitallers, who were based there. However, the Turks remained a threat, taking Otranto in Italy, although they were soon driven out again. The drive for expansion from Iberia continued, with the Castilians winning Alhama from the Moorish kingdom of Granada in 1482. Exploration continued further afield, with Diego Cão, a Portuguese explorer, reaching the Congo in the same year. The Portuguese also established a settlement on the Gold Coast (now Ghana).

Cão's landing in Congo deserves further consideration, if only as an exemplar of the development of a sin that would scar the world for the next half-millennium: slavery. He was astounded when he approached the coast to see that the ocean had turned brown; this was a result of the enormous outflow of the mighty Congo River. The local inhabitants were terrified when they saw the Europeans; the white skin of these strange creatures whose ship had appeared from the bowels of the earth were *vumbi*, ghosts. It was an appropriate explanation of what they might be and the sad story of the rape of Congo, resonant of what happened in many other parts of Africa, would reach unbelievable heights of savagery before it ended (and in some ways it still goes on).

There were other ominous sides to these developments, best evidenced when Tommaso de Torquemada became the inquisitor-general of Castile in 1483. Four years later, *Malleus Maleficarum*, the most famous handbook of witchcraft, was published. As if to emphasise that this was an age of both exploration and persecution, in 1488 the Portuguese Bartholomew Diaz rounded the Cape of Good Hope while Torquemada's rules for the Inquisition in Spain were adopted. Despite having some Jewish blood in the family line, he would be a harsh persecutor of non-Catholics in Spain. Terrible persecutions were to follow as the Spanish monarchs sought to unite their country by destroying perceived enemies – Jews, Muslims and Nonconformist Christians – within.

In 1491 Ferdinand and Isabella signed their famous contract with Christopher Columbus, under the terms of which he would search for the Indies and bring wealth and glory to Spain, important for a new power seeking to establish itself on the world stage. But they might even have been beaten to it; in the same year, sailors from Bristol possibly rediscovered Newfoundland.

The scene was now set for events that would reshape the world. The year 1492 was a decisive one, and not just because of Europe's discovery of the Americas. On 2 January the Spanish completed the conquest of Granada, signalling the end of Moorish power in Spain. It did not take long before the persecution of other faiths started in the aftermath of this great event. By 31 March the Jews in Spain were given three months to convert to Christianity or leave; many opted for the latter and crossed to North Africa. It was an apt precursor to the period of Spanish expansionism that was about to begin.

And so to that epic voyage. Columbus set out with the idea of finding a route to the Indies that was better than that being sought by the Portuguese around the Cape of Good Hope – this was ironic as he had already unsuccessfully appealed for financial support from the court of Portugal. He knew of the existence of lands in the Far East and of Japan from the writings of Marco Polo. He believed that there was a distance of 2,300 statute miles from the Canaries, from where he set out, to the islands; the distance was in fact 12,200 miles.

About half the funding came from private Italian investors, Columbus being Genoese. He was offered great rewards but no one really expected him to return. He departed from Palos on 3 August 1492 and sailed into the great unknown. He made his way to the Canaries, which he left on 6 September.

Rodrigo de Triana has been unfairly forgotten by the writers of history, for it was he who first spotted land looming through the mist on 12 October. Columbus had in fact found one of the Bahamas, a small island which he named San Salvador, known by the native population as Guanahani. He later sailed to Cuba before making his way back to Palos. Convinced (or perhaps hoping) that he had found a route to the East, Columbus called the residents of these lands *indios* (Indians).

The year after, Pope Alexander VI issued a papal Bull assigning all territories 100 leagues west and south of the Azores and the Cape Verde islands (a league being a measurement no longer routinely used but approximating to 3 miles) as areas ripe for colonisation by Spain – the fact that these lands were already occupied being no obstacle. The papal Bull *Inter caetera*, which gave the legal basis for this, did not succeed in keeping other European powers out of America but gave legitimacy to the enslaving of native peoples in the Americas. Attempts were even made by indigenous peoples to have the Bull repealed in the late twentieth century.

Columbus soon set out on another expedition and discovered Dominica, Puerto Rico, Antigua and Jamaica. All this was taking place at a time when the Turkish threat was growing from the east, invading Dalmatia and Croatia, so Europe itself was far from secure. The Treaty of Tordesillas in 1494 added further detail concerning the division of territories by Spain and Portugal in the so-called New World (it was in fact an old world, just one that had not been previously discovered by Europe, a temporary visit by Vikings centuries back excepted). Three years later John Cabot was commissioned by Henry VII to also find new lands, the treaty apparently having little significance in England. He came across 'Newfoundland', which he believed to be the home of the Great Khan.

Europe still had internal divisions to deal with, though. Charles VIII of France invaded and took Naples (which would remain under foreign rule until 1870), leading in 1495 to the so-called Holy League with the German Empire, Spain, Venice and Milan uniting, ostensibly to fight the Turks but really to eject Charles VIII from Italy.

Great art continued to thrive alongside religious persecution on the continent. Leonardo da Vinci started to paint his masterpiece *The Last Supper* in the same year that the Jews were expelled from Portugal. Three years later, in 1498, Girolamo Savonarola, a Dominican Friar, was executed in Florence. An outspoken critic of excessive luxury and moral laxity, he was burned to death on the same spot where, the year previously, he had incinerated piles of books that he did not like in what was known as 'The Bonfire of the Vanities'. While the friar played out his death agonies, a young man called Niccolò Machiavelli watched on. He would yet have his own moment of fame in the world.

Persecution went cheek by jowl with progress in this century of contradictions. In 1498, when Savonarola met his end, Vasco da Gama explored the coast of Mozambique and then made his way across the Indian Ocean to the Malabar coast. Another way to the Orient had been found. That same year Columbus made his third voyage west and discovered Trinidad and South America (though the Portuguese explorer Duarte Pereira may have discovered it at around the same time). And so the century drew to a close, with more adventurers, such as Alonso de Ojeda and Amerigo Vespucci, leaving Spain – they would discover the mouth of the Amazon. Another fortune seeker, Vicente Yáñez Pinzón, also explored the Brazilian coast.

But in 1499, when these final discoveries of a history-making century were made, back home in Spain Ferdinand and Isabella were adopting an increasingly aggressive policy against the remaining Moors in Granada. A great civilisation was being suppressed. The Age of Exploration was underway. So too, sadly, was an Age of Intolerance.

29

RENAISSANCE AND REFORMATION

Leonardo and Luther (AD 1501–1550)

The first fifty years of the sixteenth century are among the most important ever in terms of shaping the world in which we live. During this period ships ploughed their way across the stormy seas from Europe, across the Atlantic, into the Indian and even into the Pacific Ocean. In the process they set in train the events that would, for good or ill, shape the colonial movements that would see empires emerge in the Americas, in Asia and in Africa. One could argue long and hard about the merits of colonialism, but we cannot in a historical sense ignore its impact on the world in which we now live. It created prejudices and resentments that still reverberate deeply, as well as continuing to shape territorial boundaries across the globe.

All this on its own would be remarkable, but there was another series of events within Europe that would dramatically reshape the continent. This was an age of reformation and reform within the Church. New interpretations of the Christian faith would emerge to challenge the power and dominance of the Catholic Church, turning Christendom on its head and leaving a radically changed landscape in their wake.

All this was against a backdrop in Europe of a remarkable Renaissance in the arts and sciences. At the century's outset artists such as da Vinci, Bosch, Michelangelo, Cranach and Dürer were all active, a remarkable array of talent that was taking European art to places where it had never been before. Bellini and Raphael, too, were creating their masterpieces and in 1503 da Vinci began his enigmatic *Mona Lisa*, perhaps the most famous painting ever produced (another of his works, *The Last Supper*, finished in 1498, has a strong claim to be second), while five years later Michelangelo would begin working on his magnum opus in the Sistine Chapel. Most ages would be happy with one genius; this age undoubtedly had two, in the shape of da Vinci and Michelangelo, and Raphael could plausibly aspire to that august rank too.

Another great work was Michelangelo's monumental statue of David, gigantic, heroic, godlike; Man was the offshoot of God and, in Michelangelo's eyes, appeared to be capable of ultimately emulating him. Yet there was political meaning in this too. Michelangelo was a Florentine, and the citizens of that great city had recently ousted the dictatorial de Medicis and become a republic (although this would prove to be a temporary change in management arrangements). David, the giant-slayer, was an apt symbol for the Florentines, who had managed to throw off the suffocating grip of the de Medicis.

Michelangelo was regarded even during his lifetime as the supreme embodiment of the Renaissance; he was known as *Il Divino*, 'the divine one'. It was suggested in the past that he was asked to paint the Sistine Chapel because he would have to use a medium he was unused to and would therefore suffer in comparison with his rival Raphael (though modern historians tend to dispute this). The ceiling would take him four years to complete and is a vast work with over 300 figures. In the Counter-Reformation within the Catholic Church later in the century some of his works would be considered too risqué, and fig leaves were applied to some of his male figures to hide their genitalia, which were considered too explicit.

Da Vinci, on the other hand, built realism into his sketches and paintings. He made copious notes on a range of issues – what was man's place in the world, why did he age, how did a storm build – there seemed no limit to the interests of this remarkable man. But in the end his conclusion on the key issue was the antithesis of Michelangelo's; man was not godlike at all, but feeble and fated from the moment he was born.

Yet alongside the enlightenment that their work might have suggested there were darker elements to take into account; religious reform would soon be evidenced by acrid clouds ascending into the air from the funeral pyres of martyrs from rival sides of the Christian fence.

Nor was this all. Just as Europe was setting out to invade the world, it was itself invaded. The power of the Ottomans threatened to completely overrun parts of Eastern and Central Europe and spread its influence into Arabia and Africa as well. When we consider these events alongside the death of the Maya, Inca and Aztec civilisations in America and the emergence of the Mughals in India, we have a remarkable sequence of events to consider.

But when we talk of European colonialism it is important to note that it was at first largely driven by adventurers from the Iberian Peninsula. Almost every year new territories were being 'discovered' by the West (they had of course been discovered by indigenous populations centuries or even millennia before). The very first year of the century, 1500, was an apt portent for what was to follow. On 22 April, Pedro Álvares Cabral landed in Brazil, which he claimed for Portugal. In the Indian Ocean Diogo Dias discovered Madagascar, while in North America Gaspar Corte-Real explored the coasts of Greenland and Labrador. It seemed that nowhere was safe from colonising Iberians, a trend that would continue as the century progressed.

But while this expansion was going on, events in Iberia were troublesome. That same year, Dom Miguel, who was heir to the thrones of both Spain and Portugal, died, shattering hopes of Iberian unification. At the same time, Ferdinand of Aragon was forced to suppress a Moorish revolt in Granada, the intolerance of his regime leading to discontent among his newly annexed Muslim subjects. The year after, this intolerance was perfectly illustrated when Ferdinand declared Granada to be a Christian city and the repression continued.

In 1501, an Italian adventurer named Amerigo Vespucci left Portugal to explore South America; he was convinced that a new continent had been discovered, a conviction that was, of course, absolutely right. Six years later, a man named Martin Waldseemüller proposed that the New World should be named America after Vespucci, a proposal which, as we know, was accepted. The year after Vespucci set out, Columbus made his last voyage west across the Atlantic, visiting Honduras and Panama.

We should not assume that all this colonial energy was unopposed by the peoples that the Iberian adventurers stumbled across, but as well as having energy, they also were starting to enjoy advantages in technology, at least when compared to what was available to those with whom they came into contact.

So by the end of the first decade of the century, Francisco de Almeida, who had been declared viceroy of the Indies, defeated the Muslim princes of north-west India. He later took on the combined Indian and Egyptian fleet at the Battle of Diu, establishing Portuguese supremacy of the Indian Ocean. By 1510, the Portuguese had acquired Goa in India, and the year after they took Malacca. The tentacles of Europe were beginning to spread greedily across the world, though at this stage there were really just two limbs on this octopus – one Portuguese, the other Spanish.

It is also worthy of note that, while Italy may have acted as the catalyst for the Renaissance (though its effects and proponents spread far beyond there; Bosch, for example, worked in the Netherlands, and Lucas Cranach in Germany), the peninsula itself was in a state of great disturbance. This was the time of the Borgias. As well as becoming synonymous with manipulation, extortion and terror, they were at the centre of events during one of the most amazingly creative periods in European history. Incidentally, they were also indirectly responsible for one of the wittiest comments on history ever made, spoken by the actor Orson Welles in the classic movie *The Third Man*:

> In Italy for thirty years under the Borgias they had warfare, terror, murder and bloodshed, but they produced Michelangelo, Leonardo da Vinci and the Renaissance. In Switzerland they had brotherly love, they had 500 years of democracy and peace, and what did they produce? The cuckoo clock.

One of the most famous of the Borgias was Lucrezia, the illegitimate daughter of Rodrigo, who later became Pope Alexander VI. Married three times, she and her brothers were adept at the art of political manipulation, never missing a chance to further their ambitions. Cesare was perhaps the most famous exponent of the political arts from this rather skilled family. As an example of his approach, he captured the city of Faenza in 1501 and then promptly ordered the assassination of its leader, Astorre III Manfredi, despite having previously promised him his life.

Italy was something of a playground for foreign powers as well as the Italian city states. The Spanish (at the time more properly termed the Aragonese) were actively trying to increase their possessions there as well as in North Africa, where they attacked some of the Moorish possessions along the coast in 1503. Nor were they alone, for the French had interests in the peninsula too. By 1502, the French and the Spanish had come to blows in Italy. The year after, the Spanish were victorious in the Battle of Garigliano but their triumph was not decisive.

Not unreasonably, some of the city states started to look around for allies. Venice was one such. In 1504, the city sent an ambassador to Turkey, seeking an alliance. This was by no means a major departure from policy for a city that had freely traded with Islamic powers in the eastern Mediterranean before, after and even during the Crusades. In the process, they also suggested the construction of a Suez Canal. However, this was not enough to protect them from the French, who, a few years later, would win a victory over them that effectively gave them dominion over the north of Italy.

There were new powers emerging further afield that would have important regional significance. In 1501 Ismail the Sufi, Sheikh of Ardabil, defeated the Persians and founded the Safavid dynasty. This had an important effect on the development of Persia. The Safavid would rule the greatest Persian empire since the time of the Islamic conquest.

They would also firmly establish Shia Islam as the main religion in the country, a state of affairs that exists to this day – a survey in 2009 estimated that over 90 per cent of the Iranian population was Shia, which represented nearly 40 per cent of the global Shia population, with over 10 per cent in neighbouring Iraq. Although this introduced its own tensions, especially with members of the Sunni community, the Safavids very successfully expanded the power of Persia, for example driving the Uzbeks from the important city of Khorosan by 1510.

To the north, in the vast reaches of Russia, another force was emerging. Having thrown off the 'Tatar Yoke' of the Golden Horde – though the Crimean Tatars would continue to raid into the sixteenth and seventeenth centuries – Russia now sought to increase its power further. Ivan the Great had become Russian ruler in 1462. He would then reign for over forty years. In 1500 his armies fought those of Lithuania and won a crushing victory at the Battle of Vedrosha. As a result of the peace treaty that was finally signed in 1503, the size of the Russian kingdom increased by about one-third.

Polish forces, often allied with the Lithuanians, were in the firing line as well. In 1512 the Russians (or, more accurately for the time, the Muscovites, based at the centre of the emergent state) invaded the territories held by the Lithuanians and two years later took the important trading city of Smolensk. They did not have everything their own way and suffered a serious defeat at the Battle of Orsha at the hands of the Lithuanians and the Poles. They also suffered heavy raids from the Tatars in 1521, but the following year another peace treaty was signed. As a result of this, Lithuania ceded another large chunk of land, including Smolensk, and the River Dnieper was agreed as the new frontier between Russia and Lithuania.

In 1513, the same year that a Florentine writer by the name of Machiavelli began to pen his famous work *The Prince*, which would become the classic book on Renaissance politics (though it would not be published until 1532), two further breakthroughs in the opening up of the world occurred. Firstly, the Spanish explorer Vasco de Balboa crossed the Panama Isthmus and sighted the Pacific Ocean, further evidence that the world was bigger than Europeans thought.

Secondly, a Portuguese expedition sailed into the harbour of Canton (now Guangzhou), opening the way up for the trade of many goods from China to Europe. Late Ming porcelain, typically blue and white and finely crafted, would become particularly popular in the longer term. The European explorers typically paid no regard to the fact that this territory already belonged to someone else, for they promptly claimed it (or more specifically Lintin Island) for Portugal. Four years later King Manuel I of Portugal commissioned another trade mission to Canton, though the Ming authorities would soon become hostile. By 1519 the Portuguese would also be enjoying trading privileges in Burma.

The Ottomans were also flexing their not inconsiderable muscles. In 1516, Sultan Selim I conquered northern Mesopotamia and then annexed Syria after defeating the Mamluks of Egypt. The following year they took possession of Cairo, ending several hundred years of Mamluk rule and ushering in a similar period of Turkish supremacy. The Sheriff of Mecca also surrendered to him and Arabia, too, became an Ottoman possession as a result.

Exploration had its dangers. The Spanish explorer Juan Díaz de Solís, who was looking for a passage to the Pacific, was killed while exploring the coast of Argentina by a band of warriors from the local Charrúa people. For the indigenous populations, though, the long-term effects would be disastrous. Yucatan was discovered by Francisco Hernández de Cordoba in 1517 and then the coast was further explored by Juan de Grijalva the year after, with ultimately catastrophic results for the indigenous population. It was also disastrous for many further afield, and the granting of a licence to Lorens de Gominot from the Holy Roman Emperor Charles V to transport 4,000 slaves from Africa to the New World in 1518 has an especially ominous ring to it.

But Europe was approaching a period of internal crisis as well as external expansion. When a young man called Martin Luther entered an Augustinian monastery in 1505, it was unlikely that anyone took much notice. Such was not the case just over a decade later when he nailed a notice of complaint to the door of the Palace Church in Wittenberg, the so-called *Ninety-Five Theses*, complaining against the sale of indulgences. His statement that 'all men are priests forever' was, to the Catholic Church, radicalism of the most dangerous kind.

As it happened, the rejection of the constraining orthodoxy of organised religion also made the European drive for expansion and, to be frank, exploitation across the globe possible. Colonial expansion was already well underway by this time, but the mercantile domination of much of the world would be made possible by the freedom to think, act and trade without constraint, which the liberation from orthodoxy had made a reality.

This went to the heart of Catholic doctrine. Luther had developed the radical idea that the way to get into heaven was through good works and not by purchasing from the Church exemptions from punishment for sins committed. This, of course, was a source of great danger to the Catholic Church and it reacted vigorously. The Church tried to force Luther to recant at the Diet of Worms the following year (1521), but to no avail. The scene had been set for a decisive confrontation.

It was not long in coming. In 1520, Luther publicly burned a papal Bull, *Exsurge*, about as clear a symbolic defiance of the Pope as one could get. However, this was not all. He also urged that the Germans should effectively nationalise their Church. Underscoring his rejection of the Catholic Church in its current form, he attacked all sacraments except for baptism and the Lord's Supper in his thesis *On the Babylonish Captivity of the Church*.

The response was severe; Luther was excommunicated, which cannot have been a surprise as he had rejected so much of what the Pope and his Church stood for. While Luther had some supporters, others were forthright in their rejection of his preaching; for example, his works were burned at St Paul's Cross in London. But there was no turning back the tide. In 1521, Luther appeared before the Diet of Worms and was examined by a papal nuncio but refused to change his stance. Europe started to take sides. The Holy Roman Emperor Charles V (who as Carlos or Charles I had become the first King of Spain, succeeding to the thrones of Ferdinand of Aragon and Isabella of Castile) also ordered the burning of Luther's works, but there were other undercurrents in support of Luther and his attempts to oppose the Pope.

The support from England for the Pope was no surprise, for the current monarch of the English, Henry VIII, was at the time a firm supporter of the traditional teachings of the Church. Henry was a man who believed in the settled order of things, which may seem surprising given his later actions. His protestations on behalf of the Pope against the increasingly radical teachings of opponents had earned for him the title 'Defender of the Faith' from Rome. He also desired greatness and had frequently sought to involve himself, not always successfully, in the affairs of mainland Europe. He had just taken part in that unreal demonstration of chivalric ostentation, 'The Field of the Cloth of Gold'.

The year 1520 was notable for other reasons. King Christian II of Denmark and Norway had conquered Sweden, briefly uniting Scandinavia under one monarch. A new Sultan, Suleiman, had succeeded to the throne of the Ottoman Empire; he would be called 'the Magnificent', a sobriquet that would be deserved both in terms of the trappings of power and wealth that he held and the events of his reign. Portuguese merchants would start to settle in China while a Spanish navigator, Ferdinand Magellan, passed through what would become the Magellan Strait into the Pacific and then on to the Philippines. He would be killed in a fight with hostile locals but his expedition continued under Juan Sebastián Elcano; he and his crew would become the first to complete a circumnavigation of the globe. To cap it all, a little-remembered inventor named Gaspard Koller invented rifling on firearms, with significant long-term impact on the conduct of war.

The stage was set for a traumatic decade that would change the face of significant parts of the globe and fundamentally affect the religious landscape in Europe. Neither were these events unconnected; the Iberian colonisers who were setting up an empire over vast regions of the world sought not only to impose their rule on those whom they conquered, but also their religion.

Spain had had plans in place to conquer Mexico since 1518. At the head of the army that landed in Yucatan in 1519 was a minor noble by the name of Hernán Cortés. He set out for Tenochtitlan in October, accompanied by a number of native warriors who had allied with him. His arrival at Mexico's second-largest city, Cholula, was heralded by a brutal massacre of thousands of nobles.

Despite this, he journeyed on to Tenochtitlan, where he was well received by the Aztec ruler, Montezuma II, who perhaps hoped to learn his weaknesses before striking back. Cortés later claimed that some Aztecs had believed that he was the incarnation of the god Quetzalcoatl, though some modern historians dispute this. Cortés did not have everything his own way. He had enemies among his own Spanish compatriots, and inevitably some of the Aztecs fought back against his attempts to destroy their empire. But on 13 August 1521, Tenochtitlan fell to him and with it the Aztec Empire. The city was soon given a new name – Mexico City.

The events of the next few years were traumatic indeed. Aztec temples were destroyed and Cortés initiated a determined evangelisation programme. Slaves were introduced to tend to the sugar that had newly been planted by the colonisers. However, the new empire was difficult to control. Several neighbouring Spanish territories attempted to operate as virtually autonomous entities and there were some serious blows struck between fellow Spaniards as a result.

Elsewhere exploring continued at a breathtaking pace. In 1521, when Tenochtitlan fell, the Portuguese were establishing a trading post in Amboyna in Indonesia. That same year Francisco Gordillo explored the North American coast up as far as South Carolina. In the following year Pascual de Andagoya led an expedition by land from Panama to Peru, while Portuguese ships reached Brunei, in north-west Borneo.

Then, in 1524, Giovanni de Verrazano explored the coast of North America from Cape Fear to Newfoundland, while Estêvão Gomes did so from Florida to Nova Scotia. A few years after, while the Portuguese visited New Guinea and Sebastian Cabot sailed up the Paraguay River, Lucas Vázquez de Ayllón founded a settlement in the Carolinas that was later abandoned. It was a breathtaking whirl of activity. Certainly, colonisation was not an instant success everywhere. The Portuguese had been expelled from China in 1523, but they would be back.

While this incredible energy was being expended by powers from Western Europe, the east of the continent was increasingly under threat. Suleiman was flexing his military might as the ruler of the Ottoman Empire. In 1521 he took Belgrade and then moved on to Hungary. The year after, he took the island of Rhodes from the Knights of St John. By 1525 Suleiman had signed a seven-year truce with Sigismund of Hungary and was then urged by France to attack Germany; incredibly, this dangerous power was being invited into the heart of Europe. Hungary fought on determinedly but Suleiman defeated her army at the Battle of Mohács in 1526, where Louis II of Hungary was killed. By 1529 Suleiman was at the gates of Vienna, though he was unable to take it.

The religious debate in Europe continued to eat away at the fabric of society. In 1522, Luther translated the New Testament, an act of such great impact that it was said that the Devil was in the room with Luther, trying to distract him, as he wrote it; so convinced of this was Luther that he allegedly threw an inkpot at him. Legends apart, the German translation was an important move as it brought the Bible within the reach of ordinary people, who would no longer have to rely on educated priests to read and interpret it for them.

If knowledge is power, then the Catholic Church was in danger of losing an important part of it. Making the Bible more accessible and removing the need for the Church to explain it was considered such a radical move that the English reformer William Tyndale was burnt at the stake in part for translating it into English. Luther also reformed the church service and introduced a liturgy in German. Nor was he the only opponent of the papacy. In Zurich, Ulrich Zwingli, a confirmed reformer who was if anything even more radical than Luther, condemned fasting in Lent and celibacy, again striking at the heart of Catholic control.

It was hard for the papacy to fight back as firmly as it wished because there was a genuine appetite for reform. In 1523, the Diet of Nuremberg saw the papal nuncio promising reform of the Church, but German princes demanded the summoning of a general council in Germany to discuss the issues. In other places, more Catholic in their leanings, there was a reaction; within a few years Lutherans were being tried for their beliefs in France and translations of the New Testament were being burned there.

The pressure on the papacy grew. The Pope was no longer even sure of his main power base in Rome, which was the centre of fierce conflict between France and its allies and Spain. The papacy had allied itself with France; with the gift of hindsight, a decision of debatable merit. In 1527, Imperial troops entered Rome and sacked it. The Pope was now effectively a pawn of Charles V. This would prove most troublesome when, in the same year, an unhappy Henry VIII of England, distraught at the lack of a male heir, started divorce proceedings against his wife. The problem was that Katharine of Aragon, his wife, was the aunt of Charles V.

Protestantism became a great issue across Europe. In 1527, Gustavus Vasa, who had ejected the Danes from Sweden and taken the throne, claimed most Church property for the Crown; the Swedish Church Council would soon start to direct that Protestant rites be adopted in church services. In the same year, the dissolution of the monasteries in Berne began. The year after, Cardinal Wolsey, Henry VIII's streetwise chief adviser, began to do the same with some small monasteries, though at this stage only on a minor scale.

There were other important developments in Europe during the decade too. In 1523, a marine insurance policy was first issued in Florence, an important commercial development. The year after, hops were introduced to south-east England. Hopped beer had been exported to the country from Holland for over 100 years and just a few years before hops had been condemned as 'that pernicious weed'. But England had now given in to the inevitable.

In India, a spectacular new era had been launched. A direct descendant of Timur named Zahir-ud-din Muhammad Babur led his army south from Central Asia and into the north of the Subcontinent. He brought with him some strong Persian cultural influences (some philologists insist that his name comes from *babr*, Persian for tiger, though others disagree). His career had not been an unmitigated success and he had failed to hang on to the crucial city of Samarkand after he had briefly captured it.

Disappointed in Central Asia, he moved into India. His army was armed with muskets, a relatively new innovation that had been copied from the Ottomans, who had used it to good effect. His main opponent, Ibrahim Lodi, was killed in the First Battle of Panipat in 1526. Agra and Delhi fell to him shortly afterwards. Soon after, he beat off a Hindu confederacy at Khanwa (he himself was a Muslim). So was formed the Mughal dynasty, which was to become famed for its amazing literature, architecture and artistry.

Taking advantage of his newfound dominance over the papacy, Charles V was crowned the Holy Roman Emperor by Clement VII. This was significant as it would be the last such crowning by a Pope. Charles put further pressure on Pope Clement VII to refuse Henry VIII's request for a divorce. It was perhaps a dangerous time to alienate currently friendly monarchs as Martin Luther was by now advising German princes to prepare for war rather than accept the dictates of Charles and, by definition, the papacy.

By 1531, Henry VIII had been recognised in his own country as Supreme Head of the Church of England. Not that he was by any means opposed to the majority of the Catholic rites, merely Catholic leadership. As if to prove his orthodoxy, in the same year Thomas Bilney, a critic of pilgrimages and images, was executed for heresy. But the tensions in England merely mirrored those elsewhere in Europe. War was about to break out in Switzerland between Protestant Zurich and her allies against rival Catholic cantons. Zwingli, the reformer, was killed in the subsequent Battle of Kappel but the resulting Peace of Kappel gave each canton the right to worship as they chose. Switzerland therefore effectively divided on religious affiliation grounds; Zurich, Berne, Geneva and Basle, for example, were Protestant, while Lucerne and others were Catholic.

These internal divisions were seen as a green light by Suleiman in the east and in 1532 he relaunched his campaign against Vienna. The Turkish invasion forced Charles to make peace with the German Protestants for the time being, though this was kept a secret from other Catholic powers. But this defensive measure was only a limited success. Ferdinand of Austria signed a peace treaty with Suleiman but was forced to pay tribute to him. Hungary was effectively under the control of the Turks, though Charles V continued a campaign in the Mediterranean against them.

In 1533 Henry VIII at last got his wish when he married Anne Boleyn, though the hoped-for male heir would not arrive, at least not until the new queen had been replaced by yet another. Anne would die a traitor's death on a scaffold three years later, having failed to produce any heir other than one subsequently proclaimed a bastard (who, as Elizabeth I, would become one of England's greatest monarchs). This was also the year when the famous Dissolution of the Monasteries would begin for real. Just a few years later there was not one monastery left in England; all their wealth had been transferred to the Crown and more than one English abbot had suffered the ultimate penalty for their so-called treason towards the king.

Also in 1533, another great empire fell in South America, ironically just as it was reaching its peak in terms of territorial possessions. The first great Inca was a man known as Manco Cápac, whose tribe in the Cusco region had started their rise to prominence in about 1200. They would grow into the largest known empire in the Americas until the Europeans arrived. However, it was only in 1438 that much of Peru was conquered, so this was a short-lived empire. They revered in particular Inti, the sun god. Like the Aztecs and the Maya further north, human sacrifice played a part in their religious rituals. They possibly discovered the methods of freeze-dry storage, leaving items out to freeze overnight, stamping on them in the morning and then leaving them to sear in the sun. They had no iron or steel but were skilled workers in bronze.

But the sacred places, or *huacas*, of the Inca were about to be destroyed. A bitter civil war in the Inca Empire left it divided just when it could least afford to be. A Spanish *conquistador* (the Spanish word for conqueror) named Francisco Pizarro took full advantage. He had with him less than 200 men and facing him was the Inca army under their leader, Atahualpa, with an estimated 80,000. But the Battle of Cajamarca that followed ended in a stunning triumph for the invaders.

Atahualpa was taken and fulfilled his promise of providing one room filled with gold and two filled with silver, but this did not buy him his life, let alone his freedom. He was condemned to death and brutally executed by being garrotted. A year later, Cusco was occupied and with it the fate of the Incas was sealed. In 1535, Pizarro decided that a new capital was needed and so Lima was founded. He ruthlessly exploited the resources of the empire that he had conquered (as indeed colonisers typically do) but would himself be killed by assassination about a decade later.

The Incas did not die without a fight. When Atahualpa was butchered, a replacement was foisted on the Incas in the form of a young man named Manco Inca Yupanqui. Within three years, the puppet king was rebelling against his colonial masters. When he was defeated he carried on with guerilla attacks from the city of Vilcabamba in the jungle. The Spanish would not take it until 1572. They also took the mummies of the dead rulers of the past Inca empires and treated them with great disrespect. When the mummies started to rot away they were buried and then lost. Other local peoples suffered too in the lust for gold and the search for the fabled city of El Dorado – 'the golden one' – that inspired Europeans to pillage the cultural heritage of the region, an act accompanied by the brutal suppression of 'devilish' Pagan practices.

The colonisation further north also continued. Yucatan fell in 1533, the same year that Cortés attempted to set up a base in Lower California. However, the Iberians would no longer have everything to themselves in the Americas, for in 1534 a French explorer, Jacques Cartier, made his first voyage to North America, in which he sighted the coast of Labrador and explored the St Lawrence River.

A year later, Cartier visited the sites of what would become Quebec and Montreal. This was evidence of a more ambitious foreign policy by France, who had already fought a not always successful war in Italy and were now allied with the Turks. It seemed that there was plenty of land to go around in the Americas, but in fact parts of the continent would become a battleground for European powers. It is fair to report that none of this would do any good for the indigenous populations, who had lived there for thousands of years.

The rest of the decade saw yet more exploration; the Spanish probed into Arizona in 1536 and also founded a settlement called Buenos Aires far to the south in that year. They would soon be pushing into Florida. By 1539, the same year that Cuba was annexed, Bogotá had been established. The Portuguese in the meantime had set up a trading settlement at the island of Macau, perfectly based for the Chinese market. They would be there for 500 years.

Because of the sheer scale of events it is easy to concentrate solely on the horrific exploitation of the great American cultures by Western colonists. However, the move to exploit Africa was also gaining momentum. This period of history introduces a rarity for the times – an African voice that was heard in Europe.

That voice came from a remarkable man, King Afonso of Kongo. He became an enthusiastic Christian convert, though given his intelligence this might have been an attempt to improve his position vis-à-vis the white traders who were increasingly robbing his kingdom of its prize assets. These were not just natural resources such as copper but, most alarmingly of all, people.

Slavery was common in Africa and slaves were often poorly treated. However, what was happening now was on an altogether different scale than what had gone before. Afonso was alarmed enough to write to his fellow Christian monarch in Portugal. He told him that 'each day the traders are kidnapping our people … This corruption and depravity is so widespread that our land is entirely depopulated.'

King João III wrote back that his traders told him 'how vast the Congo is, and how thickly populated that it seems as if no slave has ever left it'. This sordid and discreditable tale ended in personal tragedy when Afonso sent ten of his young grandsons and nephews to Portugal for religious education. He never saw or heard of them again – they had in fact been transported to Brazil as slaves.

In India, Hamayun – the son of Babur – had succeeded to the throne in 1530. He had subsequently lost much of it but with Persian help had managed to win much of it back again. Having then been expelled from Delhi by the Pashtun leader Sher Shah, he made his way to Persia, where he was well received and lavishly treated. Having reluctantly converted from Sunni to Shia Islam, he was given a substantial army to lead in an attempt to rebuild his fortunes. By 1547, he would take the important cities of Kandahar and Kabul. He would eventually return to India, where he would boost the fortunes of the Mughals even more and would be buried in a magnificent tomb in the style of the famous Taj Mahal, whose magnificent architecture it would help to inspire.

There were also European influences at work in India by this time. A young Spanish monk, Francis Xavier, had arrived in Goa in 1542. From here, he would start evangelising in other parts of southern India and eventually Sri Lanka. He then journeyed to Indonesia, where, by the end of the century, there would be 60,000 Catholics. A series of missionary expeditions also took him to Canton and then on to Japan, where Portuguese seamen had landed on the island of Tanegashima in 1543. The organisation to which he belonged, the Society of Jesus, better known as the Jesuits, would be the only Christian missionaries in Asia for a time, although they would later be joined by the Franciscans.

These early missionaries were important in laying the foundations for religious as well as political colonialism in certain areas. Though Christianity was by no means universally accepted in a part of the world where other religions like Buddhism, Hinduism and Islam were already strongly in evidence, in some regions it did make an impression. This was not always a peaceful process. Xavier introduced the Inquisition to Goa and ruthlessly suppressed local belief systems when he could. Among the

Inquisition's victims would be local Hindus and, with tragic irony, Sephardic Jews whose ancestors had fled from Iberia to escape persecution.

It was a paradox that Catholicism was spreading its wings internationally while it was still under threat in Europe. Luther now had allies. John Calvin was a Frenchman who, in 1530, broke from the Catholic Church and started to develop his own brand of Protestant theology in Basel, the place to which he had fled. In particular he espoused the doctrine of predestination, which argued that God predetermines everything and that man has no free will to make his own decisions, particularly on matters that affect his soul. The future is shaped and nothing can be done to change it.

This was still more subtle a rejection of Catholic teachings than some others, but a rejection it was. It meant that the Church could do nothing to affect the future; God's predetermined plan was pre-eminent and omnipotent. It completely contradicted the authority of the Catholic Church. God alone arbitrated on who was destined for eternal damnation and who was not; the Church could do nothing to intervene. This argument went against all kinds of instruments that gave the Church its power, such as indulgences.

Having been active in cities like Bern and Geneva, Calvin was not always popular and at one stage left for Strasbourg. However, he was invited back to Geneva, where he took up residence again in 1541. Here he would be renowned as a preacher – it was said that he preached 2,000 sermons in Geneva alone. Luther was still active too, and the two men initially shared similar views. But the two men went their different ways over their respective interpretations of the rites of the Eucharist.

These differences of opinion show that the adherents of any new religion (or in this case a new interpretation of an old religion) soon start to argue among themselves. It is normally not long before the persecution starts. In 1553, an opponent of Calvin's named Michael Servetus was burned as a heretic. Servetus was an interesting character; as well as developing a theory about the pulmonary circulation of blood, he also denied that Christ was the eternal son of God. Calvin's pleas for mercy on his behalf had extended no further than asking that he should be beheaded rather than incinerated. This was just ten years after the first Protestant martyr had been burned alive in Spain. The flames of suppression were well and truly ablaze and not especially selective about whom they consumed.

But then these were harsh times pretty much everywhere. In 1547, an act of great significance was played out in Moscow when, at the Cathedral of the Dormition, a tsar was crowned. Just sixteen years old, Ivan IV – better known to history as 'the Terrible' – was crowned. In many ways here was the classic Renaissance prince, a veritable alter ego for that other great tyrannical ruler of the time, Henry VIII.

There was much that would be good about Ivan – the introduction of new laws, the creation of self-governing arrangements for remote rural areas, a love of learning that saw the printing press introduced to Russia for the first time – but also much that was, as his sobriquet would suggest, terrifying. Possessed of a violent temper, it was said that in a rage he killed his own son and heir. In fact, it was said that he ordered his first killing when just thirteen years of age and then had the slain man's body (the victim was a plotting courtier) thrown to the dogs.

He would also do much to increase the possessions of his own empire inside the boundaries of what we now know as Russia, and in this he was also very much in tune with the spirit of the age, as seen in the increasing exploitation of the Americas. Soon the profits of empire were swelling the coffers of some of the great powers of the world; silver from the mines of Potosi in Peru or precious metals from Zacatecas in Mexico. Reasonably enough, not everyone was happy with this arrangement. The Spanish were forced to put down rebellions from their discontented Maya subjects, for example.

But it was an inescapable fact was that the world had now changed forever, and the shape of the globe as we would now recognise it was being created. This was an extraordinary sequence of events, the bringing of America, Asia and some parts of Africa into the European sphere of influence. Science, too, was making progress – in 1546 the Flemish cartographer Gerardus Mercator was to proclaim that the world had magnetic poles – but it was more than anything for their imperialism that these years would craft world history, even more than the art of Michelangelo, da Vinci or Raphael would. For the greatest lesson of the age, for all its intense religious debate, was that age-old one: might equates to right.

30

EUROPE IGNITES

The Beginnings of the Modern World (AD 1551–1600)

Many of the trends of the first half of the sixteenth century were continued in the second. Colonisation continued, though perhaps it was not quite as dramatic as in the preceding half-century; the Aztecs, Maya and Incas were now firmly subdued and were being rapaciously exploited for their wealth and raw materials. On the other hand, the tensions apparent in Europe over the thorny issue of religion, if anything, became worse. Open war broke out, presaging the terrible conflict known as the Thirty Years' War, which would affect Europe in the next century.

The Ottoman threat to Europe was still very real, though it did appear that the vigour of the Turks had diminished. In 1551, for example, they expanded their lands in North Africa by the conquest of Tripoli but were unable to take Malta. Hungary also proved easier to defeat in battle than subdue permanently. In 1552 the Ottoman Turks invaded Hungary and won the Battle of Szegedin, but they were forced to return to reconquer the country on a number of occasions in the future. Their fleet continued to raid the Mediterranean, however, aided by their French allies. At one stage they provoked a rebellion on Corsica, which was put down by the Genoese with the help of the Spanish.

England, soon to become a more influential player on first the European and then the world stage, went through a period of upheaval when, in 1553, Lady Jane Grey was cajoled to usurp the throne in the interest of the Protestant succession on the death of Edward VI, who had so enthusiastically embraced the new creed. However, she was deposed after just nine days by Edward VI's legitimate successor, Mary, a confirmed Catholic. As a result there was soon a steady stream of Protestants leaving for Geneva and Zurich, as the old faith was quickly restored.

In 1553, an expedition left England under Hugh Willoughby and Richard Chancellor, searching for the Northeast Passage to China. The search for this shortcut to the Indies, matched by the quest to discover the Northwest Passage, which goes around the top of America, would become something of an obsession for many years. Willoughby reached the Russian coast but died while wintering on the Kola Peninsula. Chancellor reached the site of Archangel and travelled on to Moscow. It was a useful start to developing links between Russia and England. Just two years later, the Muscovy Company was founded in England for the purposes of trading with Russia.

The reception with Tsar Ivan IV must have been intimidating; it was said that one group of ambassadors who unadvisedly did not remove their hats in his presence subsequently had them nailed to their heads. Certainly Ivan was now showing himself to be a forceful ruler, even if still a young man, and he had recently begun the conquest of Kazan and Astrakhan from the Tatars in the south.

He was not the only rising power. A new emperor of the Mughals named Akbar soon after defeated the Afghans at the Second Battle of Panipat. He would continue to expand the Mughal territories throughout his long reign. The city of Gwalior followed in 1558, and then two years afterwards the Rajput kingdom fell as well as Lower Bengal. Akbar then established a new capital at Agra; it seemed appropriate to mark his triumphs by establishing a new base from which to proclaim his power and glory. Whereas twenty years before his dynasty seemed doomed to disappear, he had now taken it to renewed greatness, well beyond the imagining of Babur, who had started the process off.

Religious tension, meanwhile, continued to pockmark the landscape of Europe. In England the decision of Mary to marry the pre-eminent Catholic monarch Philip II of Spain proved deeply divisive. Her subsequent persecution of Protestants later earned her the dubious honour of being known as 'Bloody Mary'. But she only mirrored her times. Calvin was still busily defending the decision to eliminate Servetus, but others, like the writer Sebastian Castellio, were arguing that religious toleration should be the norm. By the so-called Peace of Augsburg in 1555, certain territories were free to practice Lutheranism and some Lutheran states were to enjoy equal status with those that were Catholic. But innovative and forward-thinking as these policies might seem, they were uncomfortable compromises brokered by expediency rather than conviction, and the illusion of harmony would not survive for long.

In the meantime the process of colonialism continued. In 1554, São Paolo had been founded in Brazil and in the following year the French established a settlement in the bay of Rio de Janeiro. However, this expansionism was not without its negative consequences even in Europe. Soon after came a spate of bankruptcies in France and Spain caused by an influx of American silver, which had flooded the market and forced prices down. The colonial rivalry between some of these European powers was also apparent occasionally in open conflict; France was at this time typically trying to hold her own against Spain, who was in turn often allied with England so that in 1558, for example, a Flemish army in the service of Philip of Spain, aided by an English fleet, destroyed the French at Gravelines.

Spain appeared to be very much in the ascendancy and on the verge of becoming the world's greatest superpower, if she were not so already. As if in recognition of this relatively recent status, a new capital was found for what was still a fairly new country. Less than a century before there had been no Spain; there had been Castile, Aragon, Navarre and others. Now, in recognition of the new united polity that existed, it was decided in 1560 that Madrid would be the new capital.

In the east of Europe, a new reality also existed. Livonia (modern Latvia and Estonia), in fear of a Russian attack, transferred its allegiance to Poland in an attempt to protect itself. The states of the Teutonic Knights were secularised, the old order increasingly an anachronism in this new world. It was a wise, though not completely successful, move. A few years later, Ivan IV conquered Polotski in eastern Livonia. Intermittent war then broke out between Russia and Poland; it would last until 1582.

But the move to religious confrontation continued apace. In 1561 the Edict of Orleans was issued, by which the persecution of the Protestant Huguenots in France was suspended. It was one thing to pass such an ordinance, quite another to make it work, and the very next year 1,200 French Huguenots were slaughtered at the Massacre of Vassy. This provoked the First War of Religion in France, the first of a bewildering sequence of such conflicts, which were in part civil wars and in part an excuse for outside powers to intervene in the affairs of the country.

It was at about this time too that the first Calvinist refugees from Flanders took up residence in England. The Low Countries formed part of the Spanish patrimony and, despite enjoying its own Renaissance – for example in 1560 Pieter Bruegel the Elder was painting his masterpiece *The Adoration of the Kings* – the whole region was about to enter a period of turmoil from which it emerged very much changed.

The reason for the Flemish emigrations was straightforward. There was a new monarch on the English throne, the so-called 'bastard' Elizabeth, the daughter that Henry VIII could not imagine ever becoming an effective or powerful monarch. She had undone the Catholic reforms that her half-sister Mary had introduced and would increasingly change her foreign policy too, an approach that would bring her and her nation into direct confrontation with Spain.

There were early signs that the English, too, were starting to increasingly think of some kind of international expansionism though the first moves were more mercantile than colonial. In 1562 John Hawkins left Plymouth for Sierra Leone to establish the slave trade between Africa and Hispaniola, adding to the terrible burden suffered by Africa, which would so often be the target for exploitation either of its people or its natural resources. Hawkins would return with exotic goods from the New World to trade, including tobacco in 1565, which was introduced to England for the first time.

There were others who were also increasingly interested in colonialism. In 1562 Jean Ribault, a French naval officer, claimed Florida, ignoring the fact that the territory already had occupants in the shape of native tribes such as the Timucua. Such colonial adventurism was perhaps a distraction from the increasing tension in Europe but the bitter undercurrents between European powers also started to affect the wider world. A Spanish force soon attacked the settlement that Ribault had established at what was called Fort Caroline. When it was taken, many of the defenders were executed as the Spanish considered them no better than pirates.

Europe itself was under great strain. It was as if, as punishment for ransacking so many other parts of the globe for its material wealth, Europe was doomed to struggle to find its own soul. France was fighting on two fronts, for example, against dissentient religious elements and against the foreign supporters of those whom the ruling elite regarded as 'rebels'. So in 1562, at the Battle of Dreux, the Duke of Guise barred the progress of a German army moving in support of the Huguenots.

The war ended the following year with the Edict of Amboise, but it was merely an interlude to allow the participants to catch their breath. Three years later the Second War of Religion would break out in France. Neither was it just on the battlefield that the Catholic Church attempted to protect its position. In 1563 the Counter-Reformation began in Bavaria, with the Jesuits taking control of Ingolstadt University. This was shrewd strategy; it is wise to capture a man's mind and then his body in order to gain his support. To control the soul through the mind and through this to possess the physical being became the aim of both the Catholic and Protestant movements.

The friction that was present was increasingly to undermine that great power, Spain. There were particular problems in the Low Countries, where the efforts of the religious reformers had borne much fruit. In 1566 there were iconoclastic riots in the Netherlands, an open expression of the rejection of the images and icons that formed the basis of much of the ritual of Catholic religion. The current ruler of the region, the regent Margaret, abolished the Inquisition in an attempt to subdue tensions, but it was a very limited success.

The Turks in the meantime sought to take advantage of Europe's inner turmoil to extend their own empire. The Ottomans had won a crushing victory over a fleet mainly composed of Spanish ships at the Battle of Djerba off the North African coast in 1560. Half the Christian fleet was destroyed. In 1565, the Turks moved on Malta. One of the most famous sieges in history followed. The Knights Hospitaller garrisoned the small but strategically crucial island and fought with great obduracy against the Ottomans.

It was as if, having ejected the order from Rhodes, the Turks had a personal vendetta against them. Despite an overwhelming numerical advantage of, according to some commentators, six to one, the Ottoman army was unable to decisively breach the defences. After having lost perhaps a third of their force to combat or disease, the Turks eventually withdrew. The victorious Grand Master of the Hospitallers, Jean de la Valette, then turned his attentions to building a new city, which would be named Valetta after him.

It is worth briefly moving away from the field of politics and war, for the period also saw a crucial point in the development of art, in this case of music. In the previous century, there had been a new style of music developed in Europe known as polyphony after its multi-part harmony. Two men in particular, Guillaume Dufay and Josquin des Prez, had given the movement its impetus and during the sixteenth century other men had taken it up. The greatest of them perhaps was Giovanni Pierluigi da Palestrina.

There were those who did not approve of this ornate and highly decorated music, which to them was too reminiscent of the profane rather than the divine. They sought for a return to the old days, to the simple unison lines of plainsong. The matter was due for discussion at the Council of Trent of 1562–63. There is a legend – and sadly it is no more than that – that Palestrina was so concerned at the threat that he wrote a Mass called *Missa Papae Marcelli* that was so exquisitely scored, with such heavenly harmonies, that the council decided it was inconceivable that such music should be banned. True or not, it is fitting to consider that if music is an ongoing process of evolution, where the great composers often take an existing style and develop it to new heights, without Palestrina we may have been deprived of the glorious choral music of Monteverdi, Vivaldi, Haydn or Mozart.

While Europe returned to war in 1566, when John Casimir led an army of German Protestants to fight for the French Huguenots, by this time an important change had taken place in Japan. Oda Nobunaga succeeded in taking power over a significant portion of the islands. Japan had previously split into a number of clan territories and, as a result, was scarred by the effects of civil war and a general breakdown in law and order. Nobunaga was ruthless but also strategically skilled and possessed of great patience in his military campaigning. He would not complete the conquest of all the islands, but he would lay the path for someone else to do so and usher in a period where the Shogunate would be restored and the country much strengthened as a result.

By 1571, the port of Nagasaki was open to European trade. Francis Xavier had already visited the islands some twenty years before and made some conversions there. Now Portuguese traders sought to introduce a virgin Japanese market to new goods as well as new ideas, tobacco and textiles in particular. They also acted as a conduit for goods from China.

European impact in China was very significant. In the 1580s an Italian Jesuit named Matteo Ricci set out on a mission to the region. At first unsuccessful, he began to appreciate that the way to change this was to adapt more to local circumstances. He took to dressing himself as a Confucian scholar and subtly adapted his message to appeal specifically to the Chinese mind. The fact that the Chinese thought differently to Europeans about the world might seem a statement of the blindingly obvious, but Ricci saw the need to change the thrust of his teachings to allow for these differences. As a result, the Jesuits would, over time, exercise a disproportionate impact over China.

Europe in the meantime continued to divide on religious and political grounds. Spanish ships were increasingly harassed by privateers, while in Spain itself Philip was forced to put down a revolt from the Moorish population of Granada, who were enraged at the ongoing suppressive treatment to which they were subjected. In the rising, they desecrated some of the Christian churches in Granada. In return Philip I ordered the slaughter of many of the Moors in a brutal stamping out of the revolt.

The pressures rising in Europe persuaded Pope Pius V to issue a document known as *Regnans in Excelsis* (literally 'ruling from on high', a reference to its supposed divine inspiration). This was highly significant as it excommunicated Elizabeth I of England and absolved her subjects from allegiance to her. From now on, the Queen of England was always a potential target for an assassin. The document merely reflected the divisions elsewhere in Europe; for example, in the same year that it was issued, 1570, Calvinists, Lutherans and the Moravian Brethren in Central Europe united in common cause against the Jesuits, who were threatening them.

The tension was also rising in the Mediterranean. When Venice refused to relinquish the island of Cyprus to the Ottomans, the Sultan declared war on the *Serenissima*, as the city state was known. The Venetians had a powerful fleet and an illustrious history but eagerly welcomed the support of Spain. Nevertheless, the Ottomans were able to attack Nicosia and later they took Famagusta after an eleven-month siege; many of the inhabitants were massacred in the aftermath.

The Turks also harried shipping in the Adriatic but on 7 October 1571 they were met by a combined Christian fleet off the coast of Greece at Lepanto. The coalition arrayed against the Turks included Venice, Spain, the Knights Hospitaller, Genoa and the papacy. The Christian fleet in fact had some decisive technological advantages; they had more guns and their footmen on board the ships were armed with arquebuses, while the Turks were mainly armed with bows.

The result was a crushing victory for the Christian fleet, marking the beginning of the end for the Turks as a naval power. The Peace of Constantinople in 1573 ended the war between the Turks and the Venetians. Venice ceded Cyprus and paid an indemnity of 300,000 crowns to the Turks so it appeared as if the original war aims of the Porte in Constantinople had been met. But Lepanto was a resounding success that boosted morale in the West, as one can still see in the magnificent painting by Vicentino that still hangs in the Doge's Palace in Venice.

Spain, however, would not be able to dwell on its success for very long. In 1572 the Dutch War of Independence began with the capture of the town of Brielle. What were known then as the 'Spanish Netherlands' had formed part of the patrimony of the Emperor Charles V. Charles had decided to split this up among his heirs, and Philip II had inherited the Netherlands as well as Spain. He had appointed a regent to rule in his northern territories on his behalf. There were certainly many religious tensions that had been brutally crushed by the Catholic Spanish, particularly when the Duke of Alba had been sent to restore order in 1567. However, it was the cost of financing Philip's wars against the Turks that proved the final straw. After seeing their taxes significantly increased, rebellion flared up.

The perfect storm that Spain feared was an attack over the border from France in the south. It seemed to have inspired them to acts of extraordinary ferocity including allegedly herding all 3,000 citizens of the town of Naarden into a church and setting fire to it – only sixty people survived the slaughter. But the Netherlands would prove very hard to subdue. Privateers known as the 'Beggars of the Sea' began to harry Spanish shipping and despite determined efforts the Spanish failed to capture Haarlem from the rebels. In 1573, the Dutch defeated the Spanish in a sea battle off Enckhuysen. This was clearly going to be a hard war for the Spanish to win.

Just a short distance across the North Sea (the name even came from Dutch, Noordzee, to contrast it with the Zuiderzee – southern sea – further south), England would become increasingly connected with the Netherlands as they both had a common enemy. It had not taken long for the Pope's excommunication to have an impact. In 1571, Robert Ridolfi had left England to arrange a plot to rescue Mary, Queen of Scots (who was a prisoner of the English queen having fled from Scotland), and depose Elizabeth I. Shortly thereafter, the English Parliament demanded the execution of Mary, Queen of Scots, but Elizabeth refused to contemplate it at this stage, realising that it would only serve to increase the likelihood of a huge Spanish reprisal attack in return.

In France there was a terrible escalation of violence in the so-called St Bartholomew's Day Massacre in Paris. This was in fact a number of targeted assassinations followed by mass mob violence directed against the Protestant Huguenots. The most prominent victim was the admiral Gaspard de Coligny, who had been involved in plots against the Spanish in the Netherlands. He had been seriously wounded in an assassination attempt a few days before and was now finished off and his body thrown into the streets. A terrible bloodletting followed, with the mob quickly out of any semblance of control. Across France it was estimated that between 5,000 and 30,000 were killed in the violence that followed. The violent reaction to this led to the Fourth War of Religion. The Huguenots withdrew to places of refuge, such as La Rochelle on the coast, and a number of refugees left for England and Germany.

Relations between England and Spain became increasingly complex. English privateers launched unrestrained attacks on Spanish ships, which of course led to tension. But Elizabeth did all she could to avoid all-out war, which would be a serious drain on her country's resources. In 1574 the Treaty of Bristol brought a temporary end to the fighting between Spanish and English, which had flared up following the seizure of Spanish treasure ships five years before. The Spanish were happy to sign this. They still had problems elsewhere and not just in the Netherlands. Despite their defeat at Lepanto the Ottomans were still a major danger. They had laid waste to Moldavia and had now taken Tunis from the Spanish, which became a Turkish regency with an elected bey. Despite the setbacks in the north of Africa, further south the European adventurers were still having success, with the Portuguese founding a settlement at São Paulo in Angola.

Elizabeth played a canny game. In 1575 she signed an agreement with Luis de Requesens, Governor of the Netherlands, by which she agreed to prevent Dutch rebels from using English ports and also to banish all refugees from the Low Countries from her kingdom. Two Dutch Anabaptists were later burnt at Smithfield on her orders. This was welcome for the Spanish, who were faced with a massive financial crisis and could not even pay their army in the Netherlands.

In India in the same year Akbar had further strengthened the position of the Mughals by annexing Bengal. Although a man who could on occasion by absolutely brutal against a defeated enemy, he was also a ruler who learned the benefits of tolerance in securing a conquest. After initially treating the Hindus harshly, he introduced greater freedoms for them. He also reached an accommodation with the Portuguese, who quickly worked out that the Mughal army was too formidable for them to conquer. In return for the good trading relationships with them that Akbar fostered, they in their turn issued passes for Muslims from his lands to make the *hajj* to Mecca.

Trading relationships between China and the West were also good by this stage. There was something of a threat in the open trading conditions for the Chinese; in 1575, the first European imitation of Chinese porcelain was made at Florence. But on the whole at this stage the Ming economy was stimulated by the trade with Europe.

China would also foster closer trading relations with Japan, and in return silver would flow freely into the country from both east and west, so much so that silver would become the basis of cash trading in place of banknotes.

By 1576 a mathematician named François Viète was active in France, making important developments in the study of algebra and decimal fractions. This was an oasis of learning achievement in a nation that was still in a state of turmoil; the following year, another War of Religion (the Sixth) broke out in the country. Across the Channel, Elizabeth of England was increasingly nervous. When, in 1577, Don John of Austria was appointed Governor of the Netherlands and issued an edict by which all Spanish troops must leave the country, Elizabeth insisted that they should do so by a land route, afraid that if they went by sea they would try to invade England rather than return to Spain. She also continued her support for John Casimir, who was returning to France with more troops to support the Huguenots.

But she was playing a dangerous double-game, for that year also saw Francis Drake leaving on his voyage around the world with the aim of attacking Spanish settlements and shipping along the way. While he was gone for several years, much would change in Europe. The Union of Utrecht in 1579 was signed by Holland, Zeeland, Utrecht, Gelderland, Friesland, Groningen and Overijssel. This effectively marked the creation of the Dutch Republic, though the Spanish fought back, capturing Maastricht shortly after.

The following year the Spanish successfully invaded Portugal. They were now a great superpower, holding huge territories in the Americas and with important outposts in Africa and Asia as well as the lands that they held in Europe. They were a dangerous enemy and England would do well to avoid antagonising them. Despite this, when Drake returned he was knighted, as clear a sign of approval that a monarch could give. The signing of a commercial treaty with Turkey, one of Spain's greatest foes, soon afterwards cannot have helped to improve relations.

The next few years saw some important changes and discoveries. Some were scientific, such as the discovery of the principle of the pendulum by Galileo. Another was the introduction of a radical change that would have a huge effect in Europe. In 1582, a papal Bull from Gregory XIII decreed that a revised calendar should be introduced. One of the main reasons for this was that there were some inaccuracies in the calculation of leap years. There was in fact an eleven-minute annual difference between the Gregorian calendar and the Julian calendar that had been widely used before it. While this might not appear much, the accumulated difference between the two was now at ten days. As the date of Easter was linked to the date of the spring equinox, this was a difference that the Church was no longer prepared to tolerate.

There had already been other changes to the calendar in recent decades. Many European states had not used 1 January as the start of their year, using, for example, Christmas Day, Easter (used in France) or in England 25 March, which was known as Lady Day (the celebration of the day of the Assumption, when the Virgin Mary was informed by the Archangel Gabriel that she was pregnant with Jesus). Many European countries had already changed to a 1 January start date a few years before the Gregorian calendar was introduced, though England (some might say predictably) was slow to give up its traditions and would not change to a 1 January start date for the legal year until 1751.

Not everyone instantly adopted the Gregorian calendar. In 1582 it was accepted by the Papal States, Spain and Portugal, closely followed by France, Denmark and Norway. But eventually it would be adopted by most states as a suitably consistent method of calendarisation; for example, in China and Japan. Russia and Greece only switched in the twentieth century, having to 'lose' thirteen days in the process. However, the Orthodox churches of most countries where the organisation is present still do not recognise the Gregorian calendar and continue to use the Julian, which has given the present writer the chance to experience two Easters in the same year, on opposite sides of Europe.

Eastern Europe and Russia were about to see a shift in the balance of power. On the one hand, in 1581 the Russians began the conquest of Siberia, which would be completed by 1598, adding a significant amount of territory to the country that would become the biggest in the world. But in the western part of Russian territory, the equilibrium was moving in the opposite direction; also in 1581, Stephen Báthory, King of Poland, invaded territories held by Russia and would soon become the Prince of Transylvania as well.

The year after, the Treaty of Jam Zapolski between Russia and Poland was signed. This abandoned Russian claims to Livonia and Estonia to Poland, and she therefore lost her immediate hope of access to the Baltic. Given the fact that her northern ports were often icebound in winter, this was a significant consideration. It was also clear that the irascible Ivan was becoming more temperamental – it was in 1581 that he killed his son (also Ivan) in a fit of rage. Just three years later he was dead. He was succeeded by Feodor, who was dominated by his brother-in-law, Boris Godunov. Fifteen years later, Boris seized the throne for himself.

Ivan would later be lionised by Russians, who saw him as a national hero. Among those who greatly admired him was no less a person than Joseph Stalin, which, given the authoritarian tactics he adopted, is perhaps no great surprise. In 1565, Ivan had introduced his own version of the secret police, the *Oprichnina*, who would terrorise the population, another apposite precursor of the twentieth-century Soviet regime. A contemporary Russian chronicler of Ivan's time, I. S. Peresvetov, excused him by saying that 'justice cannot be established in the land without such terrors'. If ever a stark contrast between these times and our own could be quoted, surely this is it – though in all too many parts of the world terror is still used as an excuse for the implementation of justice.

These were significant years in Japan too, with events that would provide some important precedents that still impact on our world today. In 1582 there was a crisis in the islands as the most powerful warlord, Nobunaga, was assassinated by Akechi Mitsuhide who was himself then defeated by Toyotomi Hideyoshi. Hideyoshi would prove himself a great unifier of the islands. He took a firm grip on power and among the restrictions he introduced was one that only the Samurai class could carry arms. He built himself a powerful castle in classic Japanese style at Osaka.

By 1585 he had been appointed dictator (it should be noted that Japan also had an emperor but the role was more symbolic than anything else). Seven years later he hatched an ambitious plan to attack China, a lucrative target now that so much wealth was flowing into the country. He was not the first Japanese adventurer to cast envious eyes across the Korea Strait. During the course of the century, there had been so much Japanese piracy that parts of the Chinese coastline had been evacuated. The most obvious route into China was through Korea, which gave the shortest sea crossing for a Japanese army. But when Korea refused to allow Japanese troops through, the peninsula was then invaded. Tensions between Japan, Korea and China have, as we can see, strong historical roots.

In Europe events were leading towards a decisive confrontation that would mark the beginnings of a slow but steady transfer of power from the south-west of the continent to the north. This did not just involve the English but also the Dutch and the French, who would become increasingly active on the wider international stage. The figurehead of the Dutch movement towards independence was William of Orange (also known as William the Silent). William was assassinated in 1584 at the orders of Philip II and was succeeded as stadtholder by his son Maurice of Nassau. The Spanish were far from defeated, though, and Ghent soon submitted to the Duke of Parma. But later that year the Dutch established a trading post at Archangel on the White Sea, the initial steps towards becoming what would be another significant international power.

The English too continued to cast their eyes across the wide oceans and sought out opportunities for further international expansion. In 1583 Sir Humphrey Gilbert unsuccessfully tried to found a colony in Newfoundland, while Ralph Fitch and John Eldred, two English merchants, made an expedition to the Persian Gulf, Mesopotamia and India. Nor were continential European powers the only ones intent on expansion; in 1584 a Turkish fleet failed in an attempt to capture Zanzibar from the Portuguese.

To some it seemed that the fates of England and the Netherlands, who shared a common potential enemy in the Spanish, lay together. A Dutch commission offered the Netherlands to Elizabeth I, which she declined, not wishing to further provoke the Spanish. But when Sir Francis Drake set out for the West Indies, he would attack the Spanish ports of Vigo and St Domingo. The Spanish in return confiscated English ships in Spanish ports, effectively a declaration of war. They also launched the Sack of Antwerp, which effectively ended the city's days as an internationally significant trading port; it had previously been a centre of the spice trade and the hub of the international money market.

In 1585, an expedition financed and organised by Sir Walter Raleigh but under the command of Richard Grenville and Ralph Lane landed at Roanoke in Virginia to plant what was effectively Raleigh's first colony there. There were, of course, residents in the region already: the people of the Croatan tribe. These were a tribe who were part of the Algonquian Indian peoples. Making a living out of hunting, fishing, corn, beans and squash, the Algonquians were spread over north-east America, with a number of different tribes, some with vaguely familiar names, such as the Massachusett, others less well known now, like the Passamaquoddy.

The colony did not establish itself, and a further attempt to colonise Roanoke in 1587 also failed in unknown circumstances. It is known that there was conflict between the settlers and the local tribes, and disease or starvation might have also played their part. In any event, Roanoke would later be termed 'the Lost Colony'. But the fact that there was a colony at all was a direct challenge to Spanish supremacy in the Americas. Other English explorers were also active too, such as John Davis, who visited Greenland and discovered what is now the Davis Strait while looking for the Northwest Passage.

Europe, though, was about to explode. The fuse to the powder keg was lit in 1586. Mary, Queen of Scots, nominated Philip II as her heir, in itself an incendiary act to the Queen of England. But when the Babington Plot in England was uncovered and Mary was implicated in it, there was no turning back. Mary was sentenced to death and, despite Elizabeth's grave reservations, was beheaded.

In response, on 9 June 1588 an armada under the command of the Duke of Medina Sidonia set sail from Lisbon with the intention of uniting with a Spanish army in the Low Countries and invading England. The following month, the armada was sighted off the coast of England, and it was soon attacked by fireships at Calais. Subsequently, the Battle of Gravelines saw the armada defeated, with many other ships lost on the return voyage to Spain. This was not the ultimate destruction of Spanish power; there would be several other attempts to launch armadas in the next fifteen years. But they came to nothing and the immediate threat to England was crushed.

And so England started to emerge from the shadows of a world that was becoming much more widely understood. A map by the famous cartographer Gerardus Mercator in 1587 showed – besides the relatively familiar continents of Europe, Africa and Asia – the Americas, New Guinea and other islands of South East Asia as well as a still-undefined *Terra Australis*. In this new world, England continued to develop and several great talents emerged to help cement her new-found position, most notably Shakespeare, of course, but also other great playwrights like Ben Jonson and Christopher Marlowe. There were not alone, and great artists continued to emerge elsewhere in Europe to further add to her artistic heritage; men like El Greco and Tintoretto, for example.

Shakespeare plays an important part in history, not just because of his status as a writer but also because he has played a key role in shaping our view of it. It is to him, for example, that we owe the image of King Richard III of England as a hunchbacked villain. Whether or not he murdered his nephews in the Tower of London (which we must accept as a strong possibility, though without definitive proof), Shakespeare's depiction of the king was exaggerated to say the least. It is to Shakespeare that we owe our stereotype of Richard, and we should be careful to consider a writer's motives when studying their views of history. Shakespeare, after all, was aiming to be entertaining, not historically accurate. And he was hardly likely to court controversy with his Tudor sponsors by attempting to protect one of the dynasty's arch-enemies.

The legacy of Shakespeare was and is profound. Not only is he highly regarded still in the English-speaking world, but elsewhere too he is held up to be one of the greatest literary figures in history. In 2012, for example, a BBC report announced that he had just been translated into Somali, while the same bulletin referred to the fact that the name 'Shakespeare' is a popular choice for children in twenty-first-century Armenia in the Caucasus region. These random examples give a clear demonstration on how 'the Bard's' unique ability to sum up and comment on the human condition in all its facets remains moving and powerful, 400 years after his death.

Literary impact was one thing, expansionism quite another. There were further examples of European colonialism throughout the rest of the century. In 1592 the Portuguese settled at Mombasa, while, six years after this, the Dutch took Mauritius and sent traders to Guiana. But these were not the only expansionist movements evident. In particular the Mughals continued to grow ever more powerful. In 1581, Akbar had conquered Afghanistan; by 1590 Odisha in India was also his, and then, two years afterwards, Sind in what is now Pakistan.

This was a significant empire and posed a threat even to Persia to the west, a state that was uncomfortably sandwiched now between Akbar on one side and the Ottomans in the other. It was perhaps no surprise, then, when Shah Abbas I of Persia made peace with the Ottomans, abandoning Tabriz and Georgia, so that he could deal with yet another threat, this time from the north; the Uzbeks had advanced into Khorosan (they would eventually defeat the Uzbeks in 1597).

So did Europe begin to make the transition from the Middle Ages to the modern world. It had been a century of some scientific achievement; as one example, towards its end (the exact date is disputed) Zacharias Janssen invented a microscope. It was an era of discovery, primarily of a world that Europe had no prior knowledge of, but also of the past (during the last years of the century Pompeii was rediscovered). But this was only the beginning. The north of America was barely explored, and in Africa and Asia only the fringes had been accessed. There were still many lands left to explore and exploit as Europe continued on its drive towards world domination.

31

EUROPE AT WAR

The Thirty Years' War and the Building of New Empires (AD 1601–1650)

The next fifty years would see the already serious religious tensions between the Catholic and Protestant strands of Christianity flare into widespread open violence that threatened to drag in much of the continent of Europe – it would also impact on immigration to the Americas. This would involve civilian populations in a brutal way that harked back to the darkest times of the Middle Ages. But internal strains would not stop the drive of European powers to spread their empires ever wider across the globe, being prepared to use force or commercial enterprise in equal measure as the occasion demanded.

At the century's outset, this drive was typified by the foundation in several countries of various 'companies' to look after colonial interests in many regions across the globe. This was, in modern parlance, a private sector approach to colonisation, even if it was backed by the state; private individuals, sponsored by the Crown to a greater or lesser extent, were to look after their designated spheres of interest and expand European interests there. So, for example, in 1600 one of the most famous, the English East India Company, was founded, to be followed two years later by an equivalent organisation from the United Provinces. A French version would follow in 1604.

There was a very significant development in the British Isles when Elizabeth I died in 1603. The 'Virgin Queen', as her nickname would intimate, had left no direct heir so on her death the crown was offered to James VI of Scotland, the son of the executed Mary. Unlike his late mother, James had been brought up as a Protestant and was therefore an acceptable monarch for England. So the crowns of England and Scotland were, to an extent, united, though James would be known as James VI of Scotland and James I of England.

A formal unification of England and Scotland would not arrive for another century. However, not everyone in England would be satisfied by the new monarch's actions. Catholics who had hoped for more freedom were bitterly disappointed, leading to the infamous actions of Guy Fawkes and his colleagues, who, in 1605, failed in an attempt to blow up both James and his Parliament in the Gunpowder Plot.

In Japan, Hideyoshi had died and left a five-year-old heir to take his place. Inevitably other, more experienced, men sensed weakness. One of them, Tokugawa Ieyasu, won a decisive victory at the Battle of Sekigahara in 1600, one of the most crucial in Japanese history. Ruthlessly executing his leading opponents in the aftermath of battle, he became ruler of Japan in practice if not in name. Hideyoshi's heir was left a token amount of territory, but any power he had had was effectively lost. In 1603, Ieyasu became shogun and instituted the Tokugawa Shogunate, which would last until 1867. Nominally, the shoguns – a title given to someone who was effectively a military dictator – owed their power to the emperor in Kyoto, but in practice this was not the case.

At this time Russia was faced with a period of crisis. A shadowy figure emerged claiming to be Dmitri, the youngest son of Ivan IV, and attempted to take the throne from Boris Godunov. He was defeated in 1604, but Boris died in the following year. These years were known in Russia as the 'Time of Troubles', not only because it was uncertain who was the rightful king but because the country suffered a terrible famine in which perhaps 2 million people died.

After Boris's death, the throne at first went to his son Theodore. Dmitri, however, advanced on Moscow and soon had the city in his possession. Predictably, Theodore was soon dead. More Godunov heads followed and the late tsar's daughter, Xenia, was raped and kept as Dmitri's concubine. He was married soon after, but not to Xenia. Instead he married Marina Mniszech, a Polish noblewoman. This reflected his foreign policy, which was to build alliances with Poland, Lithuania and the papacy (Marina was a Catholic).

However, he quickly lost the support of his subjects. Marina's refusal to convert to the Orthodox faith (which was expected in such circumstances) alienated the Russian Church, a dangerous enemy to make. This so-called 'False Dmitri' was killed soon afterwards. His body was cremated and the ashes symbolically fired from a cannon towards Poland.

This did not discourage Marina, who returned to Poland. Not long after, she claimed to have miraculously discovered that her husband was still alive and as a result a so-called 'False Dmitri II' appeared, a bizarre case of an impostor pretending to be an impostor. He died not long afterwards, but Marina returned to Russia to try to reclaim her inheritance; she had a young son named Ivan. It would end in awful failure. Ivan would be ruthlessly executed and Marina would die in prison shortly afterwards.

Russia was in a state of ferment during these years. A Muscovite prince named Basil Shuisky had been behind the removal of the first 'False Dmitri', but he had been in a weak position. In 1608 he had asked for help from Sweden, to whom he ceded Karelia in return, but this did not work. The Swedish army sent to protect him against the Poles was defeated. The Russian throne was offered to Władysław, son of Sigismund III of Poland, but the latter wanted it for himself and continued his advance on Moscow. He took it while law and order fell apart across parts of Russia.

But the Russians, as has been proved subsequently in history, do not like a foreign invader. They united and rose up against the Poles and drove them back. Mikhail Romanov, who had ordered that the three-year-old Ivan should be hanged and Marina killed in prison, was made tsar, founding a famous dynasty in the process. By 1618, treaties had been signed with Poland and Sweden, restoring Russia to independence.

During these years, the process of Western exploration of the globe continued. All across the world more annexations of territory were taking place. In 1605 the Dutch had seized Amboyna in Indonesia, while in the same year Barbados was claimed as an English colony, though settlement would not begin there until 1624. The Spanish navigator Luís Vaz de Torres (though some historians believe he was Portuguese) sailed between New Guinea and Australia in 1606, an important opening up of another unknown part of the world.

In that same year the London Virginian Company sent three ships with 120 colonists to Virginia. When it arrived, the settlement of Jamestown was founded under the captaincy of Captain John Smith. Smith, who appears to have been something of a disruptive influence on the journey out, was later captured by warriors of the Powhatan people and famously had his life saved by Pocahontas, a chief's daughter. She would later marry an English settler, John Rolfe, and travel to London, dying of disease just as she was about to return to America.

In 1607, a new musical form appeared in Europe. An Italian musician, Claudio Monteverdi, more famous for his church music, took what had previously been an experimental form and produced what was probably the first famous opera, *L'Orfeo* (though another Italian composer, Jacopi Peri, produced a work called *Dafne in Florence* in 1598 which preceded it, but this is now lost). It was perhaps appropriate that an Italian should be responsible for the first foray into this form. Opera developed from what had been known as the *intermedio*, played between the acts of a play, into a fusion of drama and music that would prove extremely durable. It would, of course, become a mainstay of the Italian musical scene.

By signing a nine-year truce with Spain in 1609, the United Provinces in the Netherlands virtually secured their independence. The provinces also signed a twelve-year truce with England and France. The Spanish still had a massive empire further afield to concentrate on, and in the same year the Jesuits were given complete control of the Catholic missions in South America, establishing their first at San Ignacio Guaza in Paraguay.

New fashions were being introduced from the colonies; in 1609 tea was first shipped from China by the Dutch East India Company. Coffee also became far more popular during the course of the century, being previously frowned upon by some Europeans as an 'Arab drink'. The first coffee shop in Europe is thought to have been opened in Vienna in 1645. Interestingly, in the previous century there had been debates about the acceptability of coffee within Islam as many conservative imams were unhappy at its stimulative effects.

Internationalisation had its problems, though, even for the colonisers. In 1610 there were skirmishes between Dutch and English settlers in India. France was also opening up routes into the heart of North America; Samuel de Champlain, who would become known as 'the Father of New France', was active at this time and had recently laid the foundations for what would become Quebec City. He would prove very adept at building relationships with native tribes such as some of the Algonquin peoples or the Huron, taking the side of the latter in wars against the rival Iroquois. But other European powers were active in the region too, and in 1610 Henry Hudson discovered Hudson's Bay. The scene was being set for a major confrontation between England and France in North America. Alongside these developments, scientific discoveries crops in what was known as a Little Ice Age, and before long they would be in serious difficulties.

In 1620, the group that would be known as 'the Pilgrim Fathers' set out from England in an attempt to find the freedom to practice their religious beliefs without outside interference to stop them. Attempting to escape persecution for their Puritan Protestant beliefs, on 21 December they landed at what would become Plymouth, Massachusetts (the anniversary is now celebrated on 22 December, as a result of an erroneous translation from the Julian to the Gregorian calendar). This would be the second permanent English settlement in the New World. By 1623 English settlements had also been founded in New Hampshire and Maine, while nearby the Dutch had established a province in what would be called the New Netherlands.

But in the meantime the war in Europe continued. The Protestant forces suffered another significant reverse at the Battle of Wimpfen in 1622. The next few years saw a number of determined sieges undertaken by the Catholic armies and by 1625 the two sides had more or less fought themselves to a standstill. For a time, the war ground to a halt and Europe breathed a premature sigh of relief.

It was short-lived. By the following year the war was underway once more. The Danes decided to protect their near neighbours in Protestant Lower Saxony against the Imperial forces and intervened on their behalf. But the armies of Christian IV of Denmark were defeated at Lutter in the Harz Mountains. This placed North Germany at the mercy of the Catholic League. The war moved to the borders of the Baltic, but the lack of naval forces inhibited a conclusive victory on the part of the League.

This violence did not put a stop to further international expansion. In 1626, the Dutch agreed a deal with the local tribes to take legal possession of the land on Manhattan Island. A settlement, New Amsterdam, was established; later, under British ownership, it would be renamed New York. The French, too, were keen on expanding their interests and founded their first settlement on the Senegal River in the same year.

By now, Richelieu had risen to prominence and was the dominant force in France. One of his early moves was to declare the publication of works against the state or religion as a capital offence. Then in 1627 he signed a peace treaty with Spain. This was likely more out of expediency than conviction, as France still had some major internal issues to resolve. The Huguenots had suffered a number of defeats but were still not beaten.

The Huguenot base at La Rochelle on the French coast was the target for what would be one of the iconic sieges of European history. Urged on by the support of England, the Protestant defenders of the port refused to submit to the armies of King Louis XIII, though the hand behind everything belonged to Richelieu. But despite several attempts, some half-hearted, by English fleets to relieve the city it was eventually forced to surrender. It effectively marched the end of the Huguenot cause in France and was also a powerful symbol of the increasing strength of centralised authority in France.

In 1628, Richelieu founded the French companies for Canada and Senegal, marking another important development in the growth of European imperialism as France was increasingly a key player in the process of colonisation. In the same year, European initial Swedish victory when war started again in 1636, France was less fortunate and was invaded by Spain, with Paris itself under threat at one stage. The Spanish were eventually forced back, but the war still had twelve years to run. By its end, Richelieu was dead and much of Europe was exhausted.

These events in Europe were important in shaping not only European but also world history. Although religion played a key part, it was more complex than just a religious war. France and Spain were both Catholic but they were on opposite sides; later in the war the Danes would switch sides and fight alongside the Holy Roman Empire against the Swedes. Increasingly, the motivation was power politics rather than religious conviction. This was reflected in the antagonism that existed between colonial powers, tensions that would become more marked in the next century until the whole globe was the stage for war between European powers.

However we should not lose sight of important events across the globe. In 1636 the Manchus proclaimed the Ch'ing (or Qing) dynasty at Mukden (Shenyang). Several important successes in battle followed and the Koreans, traditional allies of the Ming, renounced their allegiance after being defeated by the Ch'ing. International affairs exacerbated Ming problems. Anyone who believes that globalisation is a purely modern phenomenon may be surprised to know that it contributed significantly to their ultimate decline.

The Spanish king, Philip IV, had cracked down on illegal smuggling of silver from South America to China and instead insisted that it should all flow through Manila. This slowed down the flow of silver into China. An increasingly protectionist regime in Japan, particularly when a new regime came to power in 1639, slowed it still further. A major economic crisis followed, playing right into the hands of the Ch'ing.

Large numbers of Chinese peasants, unable to pay their taxes or feed their families, organised themselves into large bands of rebels. An unpaid and hungry army proved completely incapable of resisting either the peasants or the Manchu. On 26 May 1644, Beijing fell. The last Ming emperor hanged himself from a tree outside of the Forbidden City. China was still protected by the Great Wall, which ran for thousands of miles along its borders, but it may as be well have been made of sand, as the commander of the forces defending it simply opened the doors and let the enemy in. The Manchu streamed through and on to Beijing where in June Shun-chih was proclaimed the first ruler of the Ch'ing to actually reign in China. Once more, the losses suffered in China in these events were of almost incredible magnitude, with perhaps 25 million dead.

Other significant events during these years saw the establishment of a college in Cambridge, Massachusetts. Originally founded as a training establishment for Congregationalist and Unitarian clergy, it would eventually become a secular establishment, taking its name from its first benefactor, John Harvard. Harvard, founded in 1636 but given its famous name in 1639, is the oldest higher education institute in North America and is of course now renowned as a centre for academic excellence across the world.

In the same year, 1637, that English traders set up a factory at Canton, the shift in world power was illustrated further by the Dutch expulsion of the Portuguese from the

Gold Coast. The year after, Sultan Murad IV recovered Baghdad from Shah Abbas I of Persia. The Ottoman Empire had gone into serious decline in recent decades. Murad blamed decadence for this and banned tobacco, alcohol and coffee; it was said that if he saw any of his subjects breaking this ban he would personally execute them on the spot. A huge man physically, he was the last sultan to lead the Ottoman armies into battle.

His excursion into Mesopotamia succeeded in restoring not only Baghdad but also Tabriz and Yerevan to the Ottomans. These gains were confirmed by the Treaty of Qasr-e Shirin the year after. However, in 1640, he died at the tragically young age of twenty-seven. His brother and potential successor was believed to be mentally incompetent and on his deathbed Murad ordered that he should be killed, but this command was not carried out.

In 1640 English settlers founded a fort in India that would later become Madras City. The Mughal Empire in the north of the Subcontinent remained both powerful and rich but around the fringes of wider India the roots of further European expansion into the region had been firmly laid down and would lead to European dominance in subsequent periods.

But internal problems were about to distract the English. In 1642, the King of England, Charles I, and his Parliament came to blows. There had been a struggle ever since Charles had become king seventeen years before. Charles believed explicitly in the 'Divine Right of Kings' to rule as they wished, with the absolute authority of God behind him. In this he reflected the views of his father, James I, but whereas James could be reasonably skilled in building consensus and compromise, Charles was not.

His decision to marry a Catholic bride did not help either. England was, on the whole, firmly in the Protestant camp now, and although Charles was in fact quite committed to the Anglican and not the Catholic Church in his country, many of his subjects were distrusting of his religious policies. On the political side, he had tried to rule without Parliament and some of his key advisers were deeply unpopular. All this was a recipe for conflict, which now started, condemning the British Isles as a whole to war that would last on and off for another century.

The year 1642 was also significant for wider international reasons. In August, a Dutch seafarer named Abel Tasman was despatched from Batavia in the East Indies to explore the southern oceans. An epic voyage followed. Sailing first to Mauritius, he then made his way east into the unknown. In November he came across Tasmania, which he claimed for the Dutch and named Van Diemen's Land after the governor in Batavia.

On 13 December his men became the first Europeans to sight New Zealand. The Maori population, however, was not pleased to see these newcomers and in a skirmish four of Tasman's party were killed. Tasman was not very sure where he was and assumed that the lands he had found were attached to Argentina, a miscalculation of many thousand miles. Returning north, he sighted both Tonga and Fiji. Another voyage in 1644 further explored some of the coastline of Australia.

The way of life of the indigenous peoples here was under great threat from these explorations. The Maori, for example, are believed to have lived in the islands since about 1300, but they would suffer badly from later European colonisation. Linguistic similarities suggest links between the Maoris and the Cook Islands and Tahiti, hinting that epic voyages must have taken place for them to have reached these far-flung lands. Now their very existence, and that of others like the Aboriginal peoples of Australia, was under threat.

The Dutch were increasingly successful on the world stage. In 1642, now that the Japanese had ejected Portuguese traders from their islands, they were given a monopoly of foreign trade there. The Tokugawa shoguns, though, placed severe restrictions on activities. They generally strengthened the role of the samurai and introduced restrictions on aspects of everyday life such as dress and hairstyle, which had a deep symbolic significance. They increasingly established the role of the city of Edo (now Tokyo) as a centralised point of power for their regime.

In 1637, they had been forced to put down a strong rebellion from disaffected peasants and Christians in what was known as the Shimabara Rebellion. Foreigners were placed under much tighter control as a result. Only Dutch and Chinese traders were allowed, and they were limited to an island in Nagasaki Bay and a few other scattered trading outposts. This led to an extended period of relative seclusion, though it should not be assumed that no outside knowledge came into the country. Nevertheless, it was a significant change in direction.

Japan in effect turned its back on the rest of the world. Laws were passed saying that no Japanese ships could pass out of the sight of Japanese lands. This had a beneficial effect on her near-neighbours in China and Korea, who were spared the predations of the Japanese pirates who had raided their territories for hundreds of years. But the isolation would have a drastic impact when Japan was forced away from it in the nineteenth century; the transition to a modern state that arose as a result was both painful and far-reaching in its results.

In Europe, important scientific advances continued to be made. In 1643 an Italian physicist, Evangelista Torricelli, invented the mercury barometer. The year before, Blaise Pascal, a French mathematician, had started developing calculating machines, a very early ancestor of modern computers. Great artists continued to produce outstanding works of art. At this time, Rembrandt painted *The Night Watch*, perhaps his most famous legacy. With its concentration on everyday people as opposed to divinities and saints, it was a perfect symbolic affirmation of the different world views of Protestantism and Catholicism, the former far more secular in its outlook than the latter.

Internally, Europe was in need of a breathing space and it was soon to get it after a fashion. The defeat of Charles I at Naseby in 1645 effectively brought the civil war in England to a temporary close, though it would flare up again soon after. On the continent, the Thirty Years' War was finally reaching a conclusion. Reinvigorated, the Swedes took Prague in 1646. Two years later, the Peace of Westphalia ended conflict.

There were in fact a number of treaties signed [illegible] collectively ended the war. Sweden gained lands in Pomerania and access to the mouths of the Elbe, Weser and Oder as part of the terms. France obtained ownership of Alsace and key towns like

Metz and Verdun. Brandenburg in Germany took over towns such as Minden and Magdeburg. The independence of the Netherlands, the German states and Swiss cantons was guaranteed. Overall, this was a settlement very much in favour of the Protestant powers. The map of Europe had been permanently changed.

In some areas the conflict had had devastating results. Parts of Germany saw population decline that was as high as 30 per cent. There were casualties not just as a result of war but also of disease and malnutrition. Plague also shattered local communities. In one of them, Oberammergau in Bavaria, the inhabitants made a vow that if God would protect them from the pestilence they would perform a Passion Play in His honour, a vow that is fulfilled once a decade to this day.

Politically, the end of the war also marked the conclusion of the Eighty Years' War between the Netherlands and Spain, and the former's independence was now permanently achieved. Sweden was established as a significant force and Spain and France were deadly rivals for regional dominance. There had been a shift in the balance of power across much of the continent.

In Britain, though, the revolution would reach a dramatic climax. Tired of the duplicity of Charles I, Parliament – and in particular a successful cavalry commander named Oliver Cromwell – would order the execution of the English monarch. Other English kings had died violent deaths before, but never so publicly. On 30 January 1649 (though as the English were still using the old system of calendarisation at the time it was then regarded as still being 1648), Charles was executed in Whitehall. A republic was declared that would last to all intents and purposes for eleven years, though some Royalist supporters proclaimed a new king, Charles II. However, he was in no position to enforce this claim until 1660.

Instead, England (and the rest of Britain) would become within a short time a military dictatorship. Cromwell, for all his rejection of kingship, would have all the power and absolute authority of a monarch. Religious to the point of fanaticism – everything was inspired by God – Cromwell and his followers would take control of many aspects of everyday life, down to the banning of the celebration of Christmas. It was a strange and so far unique interlude in English history, but the successful establishment of other republics, such as that in the Netherlands, gave others an interesting precedent to follow in the future.

Shortly after the execution of Charles, Cromwell was sent to Ireland as commander-in-chief. Here, a combination of xenophobia and religious fanaticism on his part revealed itself. Several brutal massacres followed at the towns of Drogheda and Wexford, similar in their harshness to the excesses unleashed on civilians in the Thirty Years' War. It was a turn of events that would sear itself into Irish consciousness and help create the situation that would blight relations between Ireland and Britain until the present day.

32

TURNING POINT

The End of Ottoman Expansion (AD 1651–1700)

The second half of the seventeenth century formed an important bridge between the old and the new. Many developments that would take place during this period would help to shape the modern world. It would see the end of the republican experiment in Britain and the emergence of a great king in France. There were important political developments matched by equally significant ones in the arts, especially literature and music, as well as in the sciences – this was, after all, the age of men like Isaac Newton.

With the elimination of Charles I, England became a republic. However, the late king had a son, also Charles, who would not accept the loss of his throne. Throwing in his lot with the Scots, he marched into England with an army at his back. However, this was destroyed by Cromwell at the Battle of Worcester and the civil wars in Britain were over. Their repercussions were not.

However, the new-found ascendancy of Cromwell was challenged at several levels. Parliament did not operate in the way he thought it should; therefore Parliament was dissolved. The man who had more than any other removed the monarchy in Britain became as authoritarian as any absolute king. This was no experiment in democracy but in the end a military dictatorship that vested huge powers in the hands of one man, who was entitled Lord Protector.

But there were international challenges too. There were now two north-western European republics close to each other and seeking regional supremacy; the region was not big enough for both of them and the Netherlands and England were soon coming to blows with each other. In 1652 the Dutch, under Admiral van Tromp, defeated the English fleet off Dungeness. Confident in their relatively new-found freedom, the Dutch also continued to expand internationally. They had become particularly powerful in the East Indies, but it took an epic voyage to reach them from Europe. Victualling points were needed en route and one was founded near the Cape of Good Hope (named after the sense of optimism that was engendered there). It would remain a small and insignificant settlement for many years, but the place that would become known as Cape Town had now been established.

The First Anglo-Dutch War ended in 1654, with the English tactical victors for the time being. The Treaty of Westminster of 1654 brought to an end a conflict that had been fought entirely at sea, but this would prove to only be a temporary cessation of hostilities. And, as is always the case, an absence of war does not mean peace. The Dutch and the English remained bitter rivals on the high seas. It was not clear who would come out on top in this unneighbourly rivalry on the north-western shores of Europe, a contest that was being waged across the globe. The quest for pole position saw one side moving ahead of the other for a short time, only to be outpaced by the other soon afterwards.

The two emerging would-be superpowers from the margins of north-western Europe continued to suggest that at some stage they might grow to punch far above their weight. There were inevitably ups and downs along the way, such as in 1654 when the Dutch were ejected from Brazil by the Portuguese. The year after, the English took the small but strategically significant island of Jamaica in the West Indies, from where they could eventually dominate part of the Caribbean. The Dutch, under the command of Peter Stuyvesant, partially compensated for their losses by seizing New Sweden in the north (around Delaware) and adding it to their foothold around New Amsterdam.

There were pressures in Eastern Europe, too. It is the misfortune of some countries to be geographically placed in the wrong spot, hemmed in between great powers who seek to use their territory as a doormat. Romania is one such unfortunate, for centuries precariously perched between Russia, the Ottoman Empire and the Austro-Hungarian Empire.

Poland was another and indeed in the twentieth century this would lead to catastrophe, not just for the region but for the world. But there was nothing new in this situation at all. In the seventeenth century she found herself trapped between not only the German states to the west and Russia to the east, but also a powerful Sweden to the north. In 1654 Tsar Alexis took Smolensk from her and the following year Charles X of Sweden invaded. In response, the Elector of Brandenburg, one of the German states, intervened but could not stop Charles from entering Warsaw and later claiming Prussia, though he did not hold on to that for long.

The scene was set for one of the most famous rulers in French history to emerge from the shadows in which he had been hidden for some time. Louis XIV had officially become king in 1643, but as he was then only a child of four this was a fairly meaningless title as far as real power was concerned. He was not formally crowned king at the traditional coronation site at Rheims until 1654 and did not actually achieve real power until 1661, after the death of his powerful Italian prime minister, Cardinal Mazarin.

France was in a mess. She was split by civil war and had suffered from the overspill of the Thirty Years' War that had pockmarked the face of the continent for so long. It did not augur promisingly for the reign that lay ahead. But in the event Louis would rule for over seventy-two years, one of the longest recorded reigns of any European ruler (the longest incidentally being the lord of the German state of Lippe, Bernhard VII, who supposedly reigned for eighty-one years in the fifteenth and sixteenth centuries. The great days when Louis would be known as the 'Sun King' were yet to come but when they did they would resonate down through French history.

By this stage, the republican experiment in England was coming to an end. Cromwell had been more authoritarian than most absolute monarchs, though there were moments of leniency, such as when the Jews were readmitted to the country in 1655. In 1657, Cromwell was even offered the crown but laughed it off, mocking that a country squire would cope poorly with the extravagant lifestyle. In the event, though, his power was even more absolute than that of Charles I. Cromwell's years in power were largely joyless and the majority were pleased to welcome King Charles II back in 1660 after the dictator had died two years earlier.

Despite the ostensible end of the Thirty Years' War, peace in Europe was still more theoretical than real. By 1657, Charles X of Sweden found himself at war with Denmark, Russia, Poland and Austria at the same time. There were still external threats to be faced too. The Ottoman Turks started to re-emerge as a danger once more. The same year they made important gains from the Venetians in the Eastern Mediterranean and shortly afterwards they were beginning to probe into Transylvania, from where they would be able to nibble away at Central Europe.

But there was an irony in all this. While much of Europe was exhausted, the north-west corner of it exhibited signs of energy and expansion, often at the benefit of older European powers that were now clearly in the decline. So while France, England and the Dutch Republic carried on their empire building, the older powers, Spain and Portugal, found it difficult to retain all their influence.

As one example, in 1658 the Dutch captured Jaffnapatam from the Portuguese in India, which was significant as this was their last possession there. In fact, the pressures were already starting to build up on the Subcontinent, presaging a struggle for European pre-eminence in the region between France and England in the following century.

But it is important to be reminded that the India we talk of still had a sizeable independent element for many years to come. The Mughals still had a huge and very wealthy empire and in 1658 one of them, by the name of Aurangzeb, imprisoned his father after a battle at Shamgarh and declared himself emperor the following year.

This heralded in a reign of half a century. Aurangzeb was a conservative Muslim and Sharia law was introduced in his territories, in contrast to the relative liberalism that had existed there before. Christian missionaries were stopped from trying to get a foothold in his territories and there were strict prohibitions on the use of music, which would have created great tensions with Hindus in his kingdom.

His seizure of power ushered in a period of expansion and Muslim territories to the south were annexed to the Mughal Empire. He acquired a massive army and it was needed, considering that most of his reign was taken up with warfare. In the end he appears to have overstretched himself. He came into conflict with other Indian powers such as the Maratha and the Ahom in Assam. He was also assailed internally, having to put down several rebellions, particularly from the warrior Pashtuns in what is now Afghanistan.

By the end of his reign Aurangzeb enjoyed great wealth and power and had overseen consistent – though interrupted – conquest, but his empire was starting to show serious signs of wear and tear. Succeeding generations would be unable to live up to his legacy and his kingdom would start to decline, leaving a gap that first other Indians and later acquisitive Europeans would start to exploit.

The following decade was hugely significant for both events in Europe and also across the globe. There was something of a cultural flowering. In 1658, a Frenchman called Molière (christened with the much less memorable name of Jean-Baptiste Poquelin) formed a company of actors. During the next decade they would achieve prominence in Paris due to the generous patronage of senior members of the aristocracy and royal circle.

Plays that Molière wrote, such as *The School for Husbands* and *The School for Wives*, were biting satirical comedies that caused offence with conservatives and the Roman Catholic Church but were much loved by many others. In the end, Molière would work himself towards an early grave with his concerted efforts to keep producing the next masterpiece, but he would earn himself an exulted place in posterity along the way. Other great playwrights such as Jean Racine would also appear, making this a golden age of French theatre.

On the other side of the English Channel, the return of the king brought a release to artistic talents that had been too long suppressed. The poet John Dryden was active, and during the next few years some classics of religious austerity were penned, especially Bunyan's *The Pilgrim's Progress* and Milton's *Paradise Lost*. Music would take longer to recover from its repression by the joyless Puritans, but it was perhaps appropriate that just a few months before Charles II's return, Henry Purcell appeared in the world. Within two decades his star's rise would be meteoric, a situation that would owe much to the new king.

With the real accession of Louis XIV following the death of Mazarin, the young French king was soon to stamp his mark on affairs when, just a year on, in 1662, he started to build a palace at a place called Versailles just outside Paris. It was not just the arts that were progressing either. In 1660 the Royal Society was founded in England (it was officially given its royal charter two years later). Initial membership included Sir Christopher Wren and Robert Boyle, a founding father of modern chemistry. In 1672 a young man by the name of Isaac Newton would become a member, a stepping stone along the road to greatness.

Alongside this blossoming of arts and science, though, the rough and tumble of international politics continued apace as Europe sought to expand her empires beyond the treasure troves of South and Central America that she had so ruthlessly exploited during the previous century. Charles II found himself involved, partly because of his Portuguese wife. He was given Tangier (which would not be of long-term importance to the English) and Bombay (which would be) as part of the marriage terms.

All this came at a cost; Charles was expected to pull his weight on the international scene and this involved him negotiating a treaty between Portugal and the Dutch Republic that allowed the former to hang on to Brazil and the latter to Ceylon. Again, though, the Dutch were not having everything their own way and in 1662 the Chinese managed to seize the island of Formosa from them.

But even as some parts of Europe looked outward – the province of New France was established in North America, with Quebec as its capital, in 1663 – others were increasingly in danger, for in the same year Neuhäusel was surrendered to the Turks, who now threatened Germany itself. Suddenly the Ottoman Turks were poised like an arrow, threatening to strike at the very heart of Europe.

The year after, the Turks were defeated at the Battle of St Gotthard in western Hungary. The Treaty of Vasvár ended the war and both sides retired from Transylvania, with the Ottomans getting the better of the peace deal. This had very much the feel of unfinished business about it.

So too did the confrontation between England and the Dutch, and 1665 saw another outbreak of war between the two. Imperial tension was once more at the heart of the issue. This had been well demonstrated the year before when the English seized the North American trading base of New Amsterdam and renamed it New York, a name which has stuck rather well.

The Dutch continued to expand at every opportunity, and in 1664 they had purchased the Swedish colonies on the Gold Coast. England continued striving to expand her influence internationally too, such as when she supported the Portuguese in their struggle to remain independent from Spain. But she had internal problems to distract her, with the Great Plague to contend with in 1665 and a Great Fire in her capital the year after.

England was therefore happy to make peace with the Dutch in 1667. The game of musical chairs this time stopped with England retaining – via the Peace of Breda – Antigua, Montserrat and St Kitts in the West Indies, the New Netherlands on what is now the north-east coast of the USA and Cape Castle on the Gold Coast; the latter to play a shameful part in the ongoing slave trade out of Africa. France, who had also got herself involved, retained Acadia in North America, strengthening her grip on the Quebec region. The Dutch kept Guiana and Surinam but agreed to drop their claim to New Amsterdam.

In fact, England and France were ganging up on the Netherlands. In 1670 the secret Treaty of Dover gave the French a free hand in the Netherlands and Spain, in return for which England would receive substantial subsidies. France also confirmed a treaty with Sweden. France was keen on acquiring territory, while England was more concerned with finance. In the following century and beyond, she would seek to have both. The year after, the famous engineer Vauban was constructing seemingly impregnable fortifications on the borders of the Netherlands.

This was, of course, just a prelude to out-and-out war. The Dutch may have carved out an impressive overseas empire but it was hard for them to ignore the fact that they were a small nation surrounded by much larger and more powerful states. They had much in common with the English, but the latter had one particular advantage that their close neighbours did not; they lived on an island, and that short, 22-mile crossing from Calais sometimes appeared as wide as the Atlantic Ocean. The Dutch had done well to move from Spanish domination to illustrious independence in such a short space but now, faced by France and England and with the Swedes also joining in against them, the future suddenly did not look so rosy.

In fact, the seeds were actually being sown for increasing confrontation between England and France. In 1669 the French established their first trading station in India. Within three years, they occupied Pondicherry. Soon after that, they took Chandannagar, north of Calcutta, and were confident enough to send an expedition against Ceylon. England sought at the same time to protect her own position in the region, a policy evidenced a few years later when Sivaji, the founder of the Mahratta state, declared himself independent of the Mughals and concluded a treaty with the English, who were already beginning to play an important role in the politics of the area.

But French efforts were not limited to the Subcontinent. In 1673 the explorers Marquette and Joliet descended the Mississippi to Arkansas, while Frontenac arrived in Canada and placated the Iroquois Indians there. In the end, the French would gain more traction in the northern parts of North America and would establish a foothold that continues within Canada to this day.

By 1680 they had created an empire in North America from Quebec to the mouth of the Mississippi and, further afield, had also founded a factory in Siam (now Thailand). They were continuing to open up the hinterland of North America when La Salle explored the Great Lakes in Canada and, in 1682, when the same man claimed Louisiana for France. Not long after, they constructed Fort Niagara as a barrier to further English expansion. Over the course of the following decades the process would be put in chain that led to what some have described as 'the first world war'.

England also continued to strengthen her hand, sometimes in some quite unscrupulous ways, such as when the English Royal Africa Company obtained a monopoly on the slave trade; the company subsequently built forts in several places, including Sekondi and Accra in what is now Ghana, to protect their interests.

Unsurprisingly, the Dutch did not meekly accept the attacks launched against them. William of Orange entered into a defensive alliance with Denmark in 1673 and Dutch forces managed to retake New York in the same year. The following year, England withdrew from the war by signing up to the Treaty of Westminster and this saw the settlement on the Hudson returned to them. The Dutch and French would settle their differences by the Peace of Nijmegen in 1678.

Despite her success in building an empire, England was always on the lookout to increase her influence without the expensive distraction of war. Charles II, always short of money, needed funds for other things. For one, London needed to be rebuilt, and in 1675, soon after the war with the Dutch ended, work began on a glorious new cathedral of St Paul. There were also developments in the arts and sciences, evidenced by the establishment of Greenwich Observatory in 1675.

This was something of a glorious age for music, too. In 1680, the twenty-year-old Purcell was appointed organist of Westminster Abbey, a seminal moment in a prodigious career that blossomed over the following decade with an amazing stream of works notable both for their quantity and their quality. No wonder that it was said of him that 'sometimes a hero in an age appears; but scarce a Purcell in a thousand years'.

But if Purcell's music, heavily influenced by fashion from France and Italy but finished with a distinctly English touch, marked a resurgence in English music that seemed to have gone forever with the demise of Tallis and Byrd a century before, brilliance was not limited to England. Also in 1680, a man named Stradivarius made his first known musical instrument, while the following year, in Lully's ballet *The Triumph of Love*, professional female dancers appeared at the Paris Opera for the first time. With kings who were lovers of the arts in both France and England, it appeared that Europe was keen to be rid of the wars of religious fanaticism that had scarred the landscape of the continent for what must have seemed forever to those who had lived through the first part of the seventeenth century.

Several remarkable characters were to make an appearance on the Indian Subcontinent during this period. In 1675, a nine-year-old boy became the ninth guru of Sikhism. Gobind Singh would be both a warrior and a poet. He would also be considered an exemplar of chivalry. His establishment of the Khalsa in 1699 would lead to one of the longest-lasting influences on Sikh ideology.

He would also prove a resilient defender of the Sikhs against the expansionist tendencies of the Mughals. His prime opponent was Aurangzeb, the sixth emperor. Aurangzeb also sought to expand his empire southwards during his reign of half a century, but it would symbolise the high-water mark of the Mughals. Aurangzeb pushed into the Punjab and Afghanistan in the north and north-west and, when the East India Company stepped out of line, they were soon put firmly in their place. The time for English expansion in India had not yet arrived.

Elsewhere, old rivalries continued. Turkey sought to expand her territories once more and in 1671 declared war on Poland, then the owner of vast lands in Ukraine abutting Turkish territory. Poland had decidedly the worst of it and the following year was forced to cede Ukraine to Turkey by the terms of the Treaty of Buchach. However, the Polish king, John Sobieski, defeated the Turks at Khorzim and for the time being brought a halt to their advance.

But the Ottomans had not yet finished with Europe. They had long had their eyes on one particular target – Vienna, a crucial junction between the different parts of Europe, east and west, north and south. Already repulsed there in 1529, the Ottomans returned in 1683 with a massive army. It would be easy to see this as a classic battle between Islam and Christianity; easy, but wrong. The Ottomans had been working closely with Protestant forces and the counter-action was definitely Catholic rather than Christian in inspiration.

As the Ottomans moved through Hungary towards Vienna, the opposing forces were marshalled by the Habsburg emperor Leopold, who had entered into an alliance with John Sobieski of Poland. Vienna was besieged and the traditional demand for its surrender issued on 14 July. But it proved a tough nut to crack, and a relief force led by Sobieski moved to drive away the Turks. There followed what may have been the largest cavalry charge in history, 'like a flood of black pitch coming down the mountain, consuming everything it touched', which saw the Ottomans fleeing in chaos from the field.

This marked the peak of the Ottoman threat. There were grave consequences as a result, not least for the defeated Turkish commander, who was strangled with a silk bowstring in Belgrade, the traditional end for shamed generals. Whether the battle itself was decisive or merely confirmed the decline of the Ottomans is argued by historians, but if the latter were the case then how had the Turks managed to make it so far into Europe?

Within a few years they had also been badly beaten in battle at Mohács in Hungary and had lost Belgrade, so there was clearly something of a shift in the balance of power going on. Russia joined in the war against the Turks too, in the process also managing to seize Kiev from Poland. One sad side effect of the Ottoman decline was that the Venetians sought to increase their influence in Greece and, in a bombardment of Athens, caused considerable damage to the Parthenon.

Following the Ottoman loss of Belgrade (though they would recover it briefly in 1690), the Austrians moved into the vacuum that was appearing. They subsequently occupied lands in the Balkans and beyond (such as Bosnia, Serbia and Wallachia). In the process tensions were aggravated that would eventually lead to one of the greatest conflicts that mankind has ever suffered. Alongside this expansion and its attendant evils modern economic institutions also started to develop, such as when a group of London underwriters began to meet regularly in Lloyd's Coffee House in 1688 to establish a pooled insurance arrangement, or when, six years later, the Bank of England was formed.

Other events were also to have a long-term impact on the shape of the world, or, more accurately, on its colonisation. Louis XIV had expansionist ideas and took advantage of the siege of Vienna by grabbing land from his neighbours while their eyes were facing eastward. Even as John Sobieski won his reputation as the saviour of Catholic Europe, French forces bombarded and took Algiers, laying the foundations for a lengthy period of colonisation in north-west Africa. As the French moved in, the English moved out, soon after abandoning Tangiers. They would look in different regions for ripe targets for exploitation.

England had more internal problems to contend with. She was now effectively a Protestant country but her king, Charles, was Catholic. He at least kept this largely hidden but his brother and successor, James, was far more overt in his Catholicism. His reign lasted just three years before he was ejected in a virtually bloodless coup and replaced by his daughter, Mary, and her husband, William of Orange.

If the coup was bloodless, the aftermath was not. James invaded Ireland in an attempt to regain his throne, reckoning on Catholic support there. On 1 July 1690 (the date in the old calendar – it is now celebrated on 12 July), his army was defeated by the army of William and Mary at the Battle of the Boyne. The significance of this reverse still lives on; when Orangemen march the streets of Northern Ireland, emphasising their differences from Catholics, they still celebrate the victory on the Boyne. Nor were tensions limited to Ireland only, for in 1692 the infamous Glencoe Massacre occurred in the Highlands of Scotland.

Scotland indeed was about to experience yet more hardship. Still an independent nation, her government worried that she had missed the colonial boat. Therefore, an expedition was sent to Darien on the Panama Isthmus to set up a colony there. From the outset it was a disaster. It was poorly planned and led, and many of the colonists were attacked by disease. Then, in 1700, the Spanish sent a force to drive them out. Huge sums of Scottish money were invested, and lost, in the venture. Broke and hugely disappointed, Scotland would not remain independent for long.

These tensions merely reflected a continuation of the religious disputations that had characterised English life in the second half of the century. There were many still opposed to Catholic approaches to religion in the country, represented particularly well by the jailed recusant John Bunyan, who penned the *The Pilgrim's Progress* in 1678. It was an age where superstition still troubled the minds of men, as evidenced by the infamous Salem Witch Trials in North America in 1692.

As the British Isles were being reshaped, another great empire continued to evolve. In 1689, Peter the Great became Tsar of Russia. Seven years later he took Azov from the Turks and seven years after that Kamchatka was added to his territories, giving him a kingdom that stretched across from Europe to the far reaches of Asia. By 1692, the first trading relations between Russia and China were in place. This continued a process of opening up that characterised the later years of the century, such as when Dutch traders were admitted to Canton in 1683 or when K'ang-hsi opened Chinese ports to foreign trade two years later.

The reshaping of Europe was reaching its conclusion for the time being. In 1697 the Austrian hero Prince Eugene defeated the Turks at Zenta. That same year the Treaty of Ryswick ended the war between France, England, the Netherlands and Spain. France regained its lost territories in India while recognising William III as the rightful ruler of England. A treaty was signed soon after between France and Austria.

Colonialism was not just a Western feature, for the Chinese took possession of western Mongolia. Nor did it settle all internal problems for those expanding. Peter the Great, for example, was forced to deal with internal dissent by executing a number of rebels in 1698. In the same year he also imposed a tax on beards to raise more revenue; this was an age of innovative tax-raising measures, with the English government around this time imposing a charge based on the number of windows in a property.

Europe was being carved up in a new way to reflect the changed balance of power. In 1699 the Peace of Karlowitz was signed by Austria, Poland, Russia, Venice and Turkey. Hungary, Transylvania, Croatia and Slavonia were ceded to the Habsburgs in Austria, Poland gained Podolia and Ukraine, while Venice was given the beautiful Morea in Greece and Russia retained Azov. There was a Second Partition Treaty signed between France, England and the Netherlands. Archduke Charles was to receive Spain and her territories in South America, while the Dauphin was to receive the Two Sicilies. There were two branches of the House of Habsburg and they were effectively being divided.

Of course, this reallocation affected not just Europe but the entire planet. More and more regions were involved. The Dutch, for example, established a colony in Natal while French Huguenot refugees settled at the Cape of Good Hope. The battle lines were being drawn for future conflicts that would reach across the globe.

Other areas even further afield were being brought into the orbit of Europe. William Dampier had started his life as a sailor in the English navy and then adopted a rather less straightforward lifestyle as a buccaneer. After journeying to the Americas, he then sailed on into the Pacific. He spent some time exploring the coastline of New Guinea and then Australia and started to make notes on the wildlife of the region, still largely *terra incognita* to the outside world.

Dampier perhaps did not become as famous as he should have done, but he was certainly an inspiration in many different ways, not all of them expected. One of his crew, Alexander Selkirk, became a castaway and the real-life inspiration for Robinson Crusoe. His navigational records were studied by later, more famous seamen such as Captain Cook and Horatio Nelson. His studies of the breadfruit were enthusiastically reviewed and his methods emulated by William Bligh, master of the ill-fated *Bounty*. Another naturalist who would become an admirer was Charles Darwin.

A number of words that Dampier penned in his writings first entered the comprehension of the English-speaking world through him – these include 'avocado', 'chopsticks' and 'barbecue'. Dampier's intrepid journeys pointed towards a further opening up of the world into something much closer to the globe that we now know. Others would follow his example but it was pathfinders such as him that helped to make the modern world what it is, for good or ill.

33

MUSIC AND MONEY

The Age of the Baroque and the First Stock Market Crash (AD 1701–1750)

At the beginning of the eighteenth century, there was ongoing international rivalry between the rising powers of France and England. It was still unclear who would be the dominant power in North America, where, in 1701, the French founded Detroit. The world was not just a dangerous place because of evolving superpower tensions, though; ordinary trading had its own dangers and ships were subject to the predations of pirates on the high seas. One of the most famous of them, Captain William Kidd, a privateer who made most of his raids in the Caribbean and the Indian Ocean, was hanged for piracy in that same year.

Trade went hand in glove with war as a way of building imperial power. In 1703, England and Portugal signed the Methuen Treaty, by which the British would export wool to Portugal and in return wine would be sent north with a third less duty than French wines. Port became popular in Britain as a result. The wine from Portugal was fortified initially to preserve it on its journey to England, giving it its distinct taste and character.

At the time, Russia was led by one of her greatest tsars, Peter the Great, who was then at the zenith of his power. He had spent the early part of his reign modernising the country he ruled and the army in particular, turning it into a formidable fighting force. In 1697, he had toured Europe for eighteen months, building alliances against the still formidable Ottoman Empire. Juxtaposed with an enlightened and westward-facing foreign policy was the ruthless crushing of any kind of domestic opposition.

As a mark of his modernising policy, the Russian New Year would now run from 1 January instead of 1 September and in 1700 the Julian calendar was introduced to the country. In 1703, a new capital was established for his empire, to be named St Petersburg. Stonemasons were forbidden from working anywhere else so that all available labour could be deployed in the construction of this great new city.

The following year, Peter fortified Kronstadt to protect St Petersburg. It was a much-needed move. His main enemy, it turned out, was not the Ottoman Empire at all but the rather closer kingdom of Sweden, which was at war with Poland and Lithuania. If they should fall, Russia too would be threatened. Despite his great power Peter was still faced with a number of challenges, both external and internal, the latter evidenced when he was faced with revolution in Astrakhan in protest against his ongoing westernisation.

By this time, Western Europe was in the grip of a bitter war. The death of Charles II of Spain in 1700 led to a violent succession dispute. The great powers of Western Europe lined themselves up behind various parties and by 1702 England was dragged into the War of the Spanish Succession on the opposite side to France. Two years later the English Admiral Rooke captured Gibraltar, giving his country ownership of a crucial strategic port that remains a bone of international contention three centuries on.

The war would be fought for a decade and there would be a number of great set-piece battles, with much loss of life. Perhaps the greatest of all British commanders, John Churchill (who would become the Duke of Marlborough) would emerge as its outstanding military figure, though the French armies of Louis XIV would fight on resiliently despite a number of setbacks. In honour of his greatest victory, Churchill would have a magnificent palace erected at Blenheim. However, he would prove much less adept at fighting political as opposed to military battles; by the time the war ended in 1714, he was no longer in command of the British Army.

These were tough years, with economic warfare also being fought out on the high seas. There was though a good deal of ongoing scientific progress that continued to develop knowledge of the universe. The British scientist Edmond Halley, for example, predicted the return of a comet last seen in 1682 in 1758. It would indeed appear in that year and would be named after him.

The year 1707 proved particularly significant in several parts of the globe, for it was then that Aurangzeb died in India and his Mughal Empire soon began to fall apart. It was an immensely important year in the British Isles too, for, on 1 May, the Act of Union between England and Scotland became law. This provided for a Hanoverian succession – the current Stuart queen, Anne, had proved unable to produce a viable heir – as well as one Parliament for England and Scotland and the adoption of one flag, the Union Jack (though the flag had been in use for a century on ships at sea).

Russia continued to be faced by many challenges. The formation of a so-called 'perpetual alliance' between Prussia and Sweden provided Peter the Great with a further threat, though he continued to reform internally, with the division of his massive Russian Empire into eight administrative districts in 1708. The following year, he introduced a measure that continues to resonate into modern times when he sent the first Russian prisoners to the harsh wastelands of Siberia.

The world continued to open up and knowledge of the globe continued apace. In 1708, the first accurate Western map of China was made by Jesuit missionaries. Commerce in the area continued to flourish despite the conflict in Western Europe and novelties were traded that would embed themselves firmly in cultures on opposite sides of the globe, such as when magnolia trees were introduced to Britain from Japan in 1709.

The War of the Spanish Succession continued to scar the landscape of Western Europe. In 1709, Churchill and his fellow commander, Prince Eugene of Savoy, himself a hugely successful general for decades, defeated the French at the Battle of Malplaquet; Marlborough's political opponents in Britain (of whom there were many) named him 'the Butcher'. There had been over 20,000 Allied casualties and the French withdrew in good order with half as many. But a celebratory song, 'For He's a Jolly Good Fellow', was nevertheless improvised in Churchill's honour, though ironically as a satirical tribute by a French soldier mocking the size of the Allied losses.

Alongside this conflict, colonial adventurism continued. For example, in 1710 Mauritius, formerly a part of the Dutch East Indies, became French. The following year the French entered the Bay of Rio de Janeiro. But France needed peace to recover from the exhaustion of the War of the Spanish Succession and in 1712 an Anglo-French truce was signed (there were several treaties signed between 1713 and 1714).

The following year saw the agreement known as the Treaty of Utrecht signed. This had significant impact for the future shape of Europe. France agreed to recognise the proposed Protestant Hanoverian succession in Britain and also ceded Newfoundland and Hudson Bay to Britain but gained fortresses on the Canadian border in return. Spain ceded the Spanish Netherlands and it was agreed that no King of Spain could also be King of France. Prussia gained Neuchatel and Upper Gelderland. But this was not the end of war in Europe, for in 1714 the Battle of Storkyro led to the Russian domination of Finland. The two countries would remain uneasy neighbours for centuries.

The year 1715 saw the end of several eras in Western Europe. Louis XIV died on 1 September, the last rays of his golden reign finally fading into the twilight. Queen Anne of England had died the previous year, bringing an end to the tragic story of the Stuart dynasty, at least as far as effective monarchy was concerned. Not everyone was prepared to accept this, however, and there was a rebellion in 1715 against the new Hanoverian king, George I, led by the self-proclaimed James III, son of the late, deposed James II. The attempt to overturn the status quo, led by the so-called 'Old Pretender', would not succeed but he would leave a son to pick up the cause three decades later.

In 1717, the great Austrian commander Prince Eugene defeated the Turks at Belgrade. The great city that dominated the strategically crucial confluence of the Sava and the Danube had seen many crucial battles between East and West. In the aftermath of this latest version, the Austrians reconstructed much of the great Kalemegdan Fortress, still an evocative and memory-filled place centuries later.

This laid the ground for another realignment of European borders the year after. The Treaty of Passarowitz between the Austrian Empire and Turkey saw the former retain Belgrade and Hungary while the latter gained the Morea; Venice retained Corfu and the conquests she had recently made in Albania and Dalmatia.

This set off a quite spectacular outburst of diplomatic energy. On 2 August the Quadruple Alliance was signed between France, the Austrian Empire, Britain and the Netherlands against Spain, who had seized Sicily and was rumoured to be planning an invasion of England. Then, on 25 December, came the Alliance of Vienna between England, Hanover, Saxony, Poland and the Austrian Emperor with the aim of forcing the Russians from Poland and guaranteeing Polish borders (something that would again be an issue in the mid-twentieth century). Further afield New Orleans was founded, while the Spanish, still retaining a foothold in North America, established Pensacola in Florida. However, Chinese troops, trying to enter Lhasa in Tibet, were heavily beaten by Mongol forces.

These diplomatic and military upheavals should not distract from the fact that there was a great deal of scientific and economic energy being expended too. Daniel Fahrenheit, a scientist of Polish origin but who lived most of his life in the Dutch Republic, was experimenting by using mercury in a thermometer and was already well into the research that would lead to him publishing, in 1724, a treatise on a method of temperature measurement that would be named after him (this was followed in 1742 by the development of the Celsius scale – officially known as centigrade until the twentieth century – by the Swedish scientist Anders Celsius).

A few years earlier Abraham Darby had performed the first successful experiments smelting coke in a blast furnace to produce iron, laying some of the foundations for the Industrial Revolution. However, the new technology had also led to new economics and these were still largely experimental. Some unfortunate side effects would ensue.

In the aftermath of the War of the Spanish Succession, some of the national debt of Britain had been assumed by what was known as the South Sea Company. This had been granted in return for trading rights in the South Seas (which then meant South America rather than the South Pacific). The company had then traded shares in return for the debt. By 1719 nearly £12 million out of the £50 million of the total national debt of Britain was held by the South Sea Company.

Unfortunately, the shares of the company were not worth as much as they claimed to be. Some of the transactions had been underwritten by bribes. Further corruption had been evidenced by the inflated claims that had then been made concerning the value of the company. When it became obvious that the market was overheating and the shares were worth much less than people had paid for them, what would now be termed a 'Stock Market Crash' ensued and the fortunes of many were wiped out overnight. What was known as the 'South Sea Bubble' was well and truly burst. Heavy financial speculation in August led to mass panic and thousands of people were ruined by December 1720. These were dangerous and uncharted waters that economies were sailing into.

In 1722, a new emperor, Yung-cheng Ti, began his reign in China. It would be a significant period as he would attempt to consolidate the centralised power of those who held his position. He was not first in line for the throne, but when his brother became mentally unstable he took over. He secured his tenuous title by ruthlessly wiping out anyone who got in his way, including his own brothers. He changed the style of government in China so that he took personal control of many matters of state, holding daily conferences with his ministers to do this effectively. It was a significant tightening of centralised control in China, perhaps brought on by ongoing internal dissent, emphasised, for example, by rebellion on the troublesome offshore island of Formosa just before he ascended in 1721.

During this period the kingdom of Morocco also enjoyed one of its more remarkable rulers, Moulay Ismaïl. During the final decades of the seventeenth century and the early ones of the eighteenth, he led a determined fight against the Ottoman Empire, confirming the independence of his state as well as resisting the Spanish. His political achievements were notable but so too were rather more human activities, for it was said that he fathered nearly 900 offspring, suggesting that – if the law of averages is followed, which might not be the case with such a prolific individual – he would have had to have enjoyed sexual relations with nearly five women a day for forty years. Suffice to say that the number of children sired is widely held to be a record in recorded history.

Russian expansionism continued during this period, in particular when Peter the Great took Baku and Derbent on the Caspian Sea from the Persians. At his death, his empire covered a massive 3 billion acres. He was a great moderniser but also a harsh ruler; his own son, suspected of plotting against him, had effectively been tortured to death. Much of his later reign had been characterised by a bitter war against Sweden, the Great Northern War, in the course of which Peter had travelled indefatigably across Europe, drumming up diplomatic support for his empire. In the aftermath of the war, which ended formally in 1721, Finland was effectively divided up between Sweden and Russia.

Peter was not against interfering with the affairs of the powerful Orthodox Church in Russia either. He passed a law decreeing that men could not become monks until the age of fifty, believing that the manpower of Russia was being seriously weakened by the number of young men opting to join the ranks of the Church. The power of the Patriarch of Moscow was also reduced and a synod of ten clerics had instead been introduced to run Church affairs. The patriarch had enjoyed the potential to set himself up as a possible rival to the tsar and his power therefore needed to be broken.

In 1725, a magnificent palace, the Peterhof, in Saint Petersburg was completed. However, Peter had no time to enjoy it for early in the year a serious urinary tract infection would take his life after several years of suffering. His reign marked a massive expansion in Russian territory and power and laid the foundations for the great modern state that is still such an influential power in the world.

All of these great political events should not distract from the artistic achievements of the period. This was the age of the Baroque, magnificent church architecture, flamboyant, extravagant, flowing lines and rich gilt ornamentation. There was also music to match.

The greatest composer of the age was Johann Sebastian Bach. He did not invent the musical style of the period but he took it to new heights, particularly with the use of counterpoint and the adoption of influences from France and Italy into the musical heritage of Germany. He was in particular a master of the fugue, that flowing, seamless transference of a musical line from one part of the orchestra to another. It was ornate, majestic and spectacular, in keeping with the architecture of the period.

It was ironic that in his life he was renowned as a great organist but not necessarily a great composer. Recognition of his outstanding contribution to the development of music would long post-date his death. He would succeed in obtaining patronage from the highest levels though, in particular when he became Royal Court Composer to August III, King of Poland, Grand Duke of Lithuania and Elector of Saxony in the 1730s.

However, it was not always plain sailing. In 1721, he wrote perhaps his most famous work, *The Brandenburg Concertos*. It was effectively a job application for a position with the Margrave of Brandenburg. He was turned down, a decision that for its short-sightedness must rank alongside the rather more modern example of Decca Records, who, in 1962, told a young and ambitious group from Liverpool named The Beatles that 'guitar bands are on the way out'.

The crucial impact of J. S. Bach, though, was that he formed a bridge in the development of music that would eventually inspire others such as Mozart and Beethoven. He was not the only great composer active at this time, though, as his contemporary was 'the Red Priest' (so-called because of his hair colour), Antonio Vivaldi, who was prolifically producing music in Venice, in particular his most famous work (in modern times), *The Four Seasons*, as well as a range of opulent and spiritually uplifting church music. He would die in 1741, with little ceremony surrounding his burial. He expired in Vienna and his funeral took place in St Stephen's Cathedral; in the choir at the time was a young boy by the name of Josef Haydn.

There were achievements of note in other aspects of the arts, too. In 1726 one of the most famous books of all, Swift's *Gulliver's Travels*, appeared (though it had been in production for over a decade). The work had a transparently political message, being a satirical sideswipe at the state of politics in Europe and the pettiness of religious differences. It clearly touched a popular nerve as the first run sold out in a week.

Satire was clearly a popular medium, for at around the same time the famous engraver, William Hogarth, was starting to produce his works. He would carry on for several decades, leaving us some of the most impressive images of Georgian London. In the 1730s he produced two of his finest sets of engravings, first of all *A Harlot's Progress* and then his most renowned work, *A Rake's Progress*. The latter relates the progressive fall into madness of a 'rake' who wastes his money by gambling, whoring and other abuses of his position.

These were partly moralistic commentaries in pictorial form but also biting assessments of the world that Hogarth saw about him. It was in some ways another presentation of the world according to Jonathan Swift and his cast. It was a different form of dissent from that of the seventeenth century, without a lot of the religious baggage that underpinned it, altogether a more subtle approach than that of the century before (not to suggest that that particular earlier age was without its own intellectuals).

It was suggestive of a new and different approach by which men, more and more, thought for themselves, when the firm straitjacket of religious instruction was becoming less of a restriction and political freethinking was challenging the accepted norms of society in what would be known as an 'Age of Reason'. Increasingly men would put their thoughts to paper and a war of ideas would soon be waged. It would, however, lead in the end to the most violent of manifestations against the perceived natural order of things.

Yet it would be some time before these violent stirrings made themselves known. In the meantime it appeared that the world was going on much as before. There were, it was true, some new powers emerging – or rather, an old one was re-emerging. In 1733, conscription was introduced in Prussia, laying the foundations for a military power that would play a crucial part in the Europe of the eighteenth and nineteenth centuries and beyond.

Even as the Prussian state began to gain in power, another apparently failing one enjoyed something of a resurgence. In 1739, the Turks began a fight back in Eastern Europe against Austria. The crucial city of Belgrade was once again threatened and, in the peace that was negotiated later, the city returned to Turkish hands.

At the same time a great military leader had emerged in the Middle East in the shape of Nadir Shah of Persia. Sometimes described as 'the Napoleon of Persia', he was certainly an outstanding military leader. Inspired by men such as Genghis Khan and Timur, he was a ferocious warrior who emerged from a period of instability and uncertainty in Persia to briefly restore former glories. He was a man of great ambition who moved his armies on India even as the Turks moved back into their lost territories in Eastern Europe. One of his greatest moments was when he led his men into Delhi, which had fallen to him in February 1739. The year after, he would extend his influence into Central Asia and in particular Balkh and Bukhara.

Europe now seemed to be a continent in a virtually perpetual state of war. Another major conflict was about to start, again inspired by disputed succession rights. In 1740, Charles VI, the last Habsburg emperor, died (allegedly through eating poisonous mushrooms) and was succeeded by his daughter Maria Theresa, Queen of Bohemia and Hungary and Archduchess of Austria. He left a treasury virtually empty of funds and an empire that was dangerously overstretched and under-resourced.

Unfortunately for the empress, the power of Prussia was growing in the north and threatened to eat up big chunks of Austrian territory. Something of the size of the threat facing Maria Theresa can be realised from the fact that her Prussian fellow-sovereign and opponent, Frederick II, would be awarded the rare sobriquet of 'the Great'. One of the most significant figures in German history – Hitler himself would be inspired by his achievements – his reputation would resonate across the centuries.

Soon after Maria Theresa's accession, the War of the Austrian succession began. Frederick II won territory in Silesia (a Central European territory mainly in Poland) from her, leading to Britain attempting to assume a mediation role between Austria and Prussia. While all this was going on, Russia too had a new ruler, the empress Elizabeth, who seized power when she led a coup against those who sought to deprive her of her inheritance.

Unusually, this was a bloodless revolution; she gave her word that she would sign no death sentences as a result of her installation as empress and she kept to her word. Ruler of a vast and still growing empire, it looked as if expansion was due to continue into territories new when a Russian expedition led by Behring to Alaska opened up a fur trade and established the beginnings of a claim for Russia in what was still, to all intents and purposes, largely a new and unexplored continent.

This was a remarkable achievement as, despite the efforts of Peter the Great, Russia was significantly in the shadow of Prussia, and German advisers held significant sway in the country. Indeed German princes were now very powerful, with a German dynasty now ruling Britain. They brought with them not only their political advisers but also their own artists. One such was the great composer George Frederick Handel, who in 1741 wrote his great work, the *Messiah*, in an astonishingly short period between 22 August and 14 September.

The Peace of Berlin the year after ended the First Silesian War. Prussia retained Silesia and took over the Silesian debt to Britain and the Netherlands. However, it was only a temporary respite. In 1744, the Second Silesian War began with Frederick II's invasion of Saxony. The war for Silesia was the dominant feature of the War of the Austrian Succession but it was truly a pan-European conflict. Allied with Austria were Britain and the Netherlands as well as Sardinia and Saxony (Russia would also join the alliance in 1746). Allied against them were France, Prussia and Bavaria. The Prussians and French had rather the better of it. Marshal Saxe defeated the British at Fontenoy in 1745 and conquered parts of the Netherlands.

Clashes between the French and the British in India foreshadowed larger and more decisive clashes to come. The Treaty of Aix-la-Chapelle in 1748 brought the war to an end. Despite having much the worse of the conflict, the territories ruled by Maria Theresa survived largely intact, only Silesia being ceded. The French came away from the war with virtually nothing and her king, Louis XV, received a great deal of criticism for the fact.

An interesting by-product of the war was the invasion of Britain in 1745 by Charles Edward Stuart, popularly known as the 'Young Pretender'. He was supposedly supported by the French but landed with just a handful of men in the wilderness lands of north-west Scotland. Despite being hugely outnumbered he managed to gather together an army and catch the Hanoverian forces by surprise at Prestonpans. He then moved into England, but his command was divided and some of his military advisers were of dubious quality. The rebellion (as his opponents termed it) was crushed with ruthless efficiency at Culloden in 1746 and considerable hardship followed, especially for the people of the Scottish Highlands, whose way of life was forcibly suppressed in the aftermath of the battle.

On the wider front, 1746 also saw the persecution of Christians in China. The following year Nadir Shah was murdered – he had become increasingly cruel in later life and he was killed by men who believed that their own lives were in danger. Described by some as 'the last great Asian conqueror', his empire did not long outlive him. After his death, Afghanistan became a separate country under the rule of Ahmad Shah. He established what became known as the Durrani Empire and, in the view of some, established the modern kingdom of Afghanistan.

In many ways, the political events of the first half of the eighteenth century appeared to look back rather than forward. The pan-European wars harked back to the Thirty Years' War, though with the important difference that religion appeared to play a lesser part in the motivations of the key players. Rather it was about empire building, largely focussed in Europe but also impacting on the wider globe.

It cannot at the time have been clear how decisive the next half-century would be. Momentous events would reshape the world, new empires would accelerate their development and the true foundations of Europe's attempts to conquer the globe in the nineteenth century were laid. Yet at the same time there would be contrary movements, drives for greater political freedom that would shake the very foundations of the established order so much that for a while it threatened to crash to the ground. The world would never be the same again, even for those older powers that managed to survive the whirlwind.

34

THE WORLD AT WAR

The Seven Years' War and the Rise of Revolution (AD 1751–1800)

In 1762, a Genevan philosopher, Jean-Jacques Rousseau, wrote a seminal work, *On the Social Contract*. His basic argument could be summed up by the most famous phrase from the book: 'Man is born free, but everywhere he is in chains.' This was the most memorable sentence from his great opus, but others were perhaps even more radical, such as, 'The Sovereign, having no force other than the legislative power, acts only by means of the laws; and the laws being solely the authentic acts of the general will, the Sovereign cannot act save when the people is assembled.' For the time, these were revolutionary concepts indeed.

Such thoughts were not new – the Civil War in Britain over a century before had started off with not dissimilar overall motivations. Nor was it the first time that Rousseau had himself expressed such thoughts; he had written in similar vein in 1754 in his *Discourse on the Origin and Basis of Inequality among Men*. He was an outspoken critic of power and wealth and their abuse in civil society. Not unnaturally, a number of those who owned power and wealth in eighteenth-century Europe were not enamoured of his arguments.

Three years after *On the Social Contract* appeared, Rousseau's house was stoned and he fled into exile, ending up in Britain, where he was looked after by another philosopher, David Hume. It was not a happy life and serious doubts were expressed as to his mental state in later years. Yet, in 1789, crowds in the streets of Paris provided a physical manifestation of his ideas in action and no sovereign in Europe would feel safe as the 'people' took control of their own destiny.

Rousseau did not have far to look for opponents. Another famous philosopher, François-Marie Arouet, better known by his pen name of Voltaire, was a strong personal critic despite his own vigorous support for social reform. But collectively these great thinkers and others, which included the Irishman Edmund Burke, had a dramatic impact on the mindset of nations on both sides of the Atlantic.

Britain was the driver of other types of revolution, these more predicated on agriculture and industry, which, when allied to the political upheavals that were about to occur, in their own way laid the foundations of much of modern life, certainly in the Western world. Yet of course the effect was not universal and is still not so, with many parts of the modern world still resistant to many of the ideals of Western-style democracy. Yet even regimes in these countries are affected by it and cannot be oblivious to the impact made on the thoughts of their people by the idea of power being vested in society as a whole and not merely in the ruling class or political elite.

However, the effect would not be instantaneous – it rarely is. Ideas only change people and nations over time. One contemporary writer, the Scot David Hume, who produced his *Political Discourses* in 1752, would develop ideas not only on politics but also economics, ideas that would influence thinkers such as John Maynard Keynes several hundred years later.

In many ways, the world continued on as before despite the radical ideas that philosophers were developing. However, that this was a time of change was apparent in some quite obvious ways; Britain brought its calendar forward by eleven days in 1751 and also decided to start the year on 1 January, in common with a number of other countries who had already made the move many years previously. In the same year, China invaded Tibet.

The world was about to enter a truly momentous period of upheaval, quite appropriately presaged by the great Lisbon Earthquake of 1755, which may have measured as much as 9.0 on the Richter Scale and possibly killed up to 100,000 people in the Portuguese capital alone, making it one of the most destructive natural disasters in recorded history (though many commentators think this figure is overstated and earthquakes in China, Syria and Iran centuries before and in the twenty-first century in the Pacific and Haiti almost certainly exceed this number of fatalities). Cracks 15 feet wide appeared in the streets and the subsequent tsunami destroyed several coastal fortresses.

Then, in 1756, after having heard of an alliance between France and Austria, Frederick II invaded Saxony (Hitler later regarded Frederick's expansionist tendencies as early signs of the need to develop *lebensraum* for Germany). This marked the beginning of what would be called the Seven Years' War but has also been called by some the First World War as it saw action across the globe, encompassing North America, Europe, Asia and even regions further afield. Britain would soon come in on the side of the Prussians and other European nations would also be drawn into the conflict. Smaller German states and Portugal would at some stage be part of the Anglo-Prussian alliance, while at other times Spain, Sweden and Saxony would be joined with the Franco-Austrian alliance. In all, approximately 1 million people lost their lives as a result of the conflict.

There were particularly significant outcomes in North America and India. British public opinion was outraged by the event known as the Black Hole of Calcutta, where it was claimed that over 100 prisoners (though the figure is disputed and may be much lower) lost their lives overnight because of the appalling conditions that they were kept in.

Britain did not enjoy the best of starts to the war and in 1757 the loss of Minorca by Admiral John Byng led to his court martial and execution by firing squad, a harsh judgement in the eyes of many. The ultimate decision to execute Byng rested with George II, the British king, who refused petitions for mercy and the sentence went ahead, as the great satirist Voltaire put it in his famous work *Candide*, 'to encourage the others'.

But better news awaited in the form of the triumph of Robert Clive at Plassey in the same year that Byng met his end. Following the incident of the so-called Black Hole of Calcutta, the Nawab of Bengal and his French allies had allied themselves against the British East India Company. The two forces met at Plassey on 23 June and at the end of the day the French were effectively a spent force in Bengal, leaving the field literally and metaphorically clear for the British to establish their ascendancy in India, which would lay the foundations for their empire in the following century.

The year after, the British took the North American French fortress of Louisburg as well as French Senegal in Africa. Also in 1758, in an event unrelated to the war, the Chinese occupied what was known as East Turkestan in Central Asia. This continues to have resonance in the modern world, for East Turkestan would later become Xinjiang, a region of modern China that continues to have a strong separatist movement in the twenty-first century and as a result has seen a number of recent outbreaks of political violence.

An important step in the future shape of North America was the capture of Quebec by General James Wolfe in 1759 (the same year that the British Museum was opened). He famously managed to direct his troops up the steep Heights of Abraham unobserved by the French and deploy his army for battle without the enemy having time to stop him. Although he was mortally wounded in the fight that followed, his victory paved the way for Canada to become a definitive part of the British sphere of influence, though Quebec has strong separatist tendencies to this day.

The war continued for several years, but the momentum was diminishing. By 1762, the protagonists were ready for peace. The British were the undoubted territorial winners of the conflict; they had made a large number of conquests, including St Vincent, Martinique, Grenada, Havana and Manila. Peace preliminaries were held at Fontainebleau between France, Spain and Britain. Britain gained Canada, Nova Scotia, Tobago, Senegal, Minorca and Florida. France regained Martinique and Guadeloupe and was granted fishing rights off Newfoundland. French settlements in India were restored but no fortifications were to be built there. Spain acquired Louisiana from France and recovered Manila and the Philippines, and France retained New Orleans, so there were at least some territories retained by the losers. The year after, the Treaty of Paris was signed and brought the Seven Years' War to an end.

Yet even as British power was in the ascendancy, steps were being taken by the victors that were to jeopardise her dominance in North America, for in 1765 the British Parliament passed a Stamp Tax, imposing taxation on American colonies. Patrick Henry attacked the rights of Britain to do so. Delegates from nine colonies met in New York to draw up a declaration of rights and liberties and to respond to these unwelcome attempts from the supposed mother country to assert her dominance over the independently minded colonies.

Britain was still not the only country seeking to expand her power and influence. In Europe itself, Russia was actively trying to develop her influence, especially in the Balkans, then in the main in the Ottoman sphere of interest. In 1767, Russian agents were busy agitating in Bosnia and Montenegro against Turkish rule. Two years later,

Russian troops occupied Bucharest. Nor were they the only powerful neighbour in the world trying to impose themselves over weaker brethren, for in the same year Burma acknowledged the suzerainty of China.

While the world stood on the brink of political revolution, there were other massive changes taking place too. In 1769, Josiah Wedgwood opened the Etruria pottery works, epitomising the drive towards industrialisation that was taking place in Britain. The Industrial Revolution was of course not a one-off event, and many commentators hold that it did not reach its zenith until the nineteenth century. A number of key steps drove the process forward – in the same year that Wedgwood started his factory Richard Arkwright invented his spinning machine. This led to the possibility of the mass production of textiles. Great changes were taking place in Britain – they would eventually affect the entire world.

It was a combination of its industrialisation and its overseas conquests that led to Britain's global power in the following century. It was supported and made possible though by great advances in agricultural production and selective breeding of livestock, which also supported a burgeoning population with, eventually, more money to spend and a higher standard of living, even if conditions were harsh compared to modern life.

The following years saw more international expansion, and not just from Britain. There were increasing problems in Eastern Europe that would take centuries to resolve. In 1771, the year after Captain James Cook had landed at Botany Bay in Australia, Prince Henry of Prussia visited Russia and suggested the partition of Poland, a recipe that would be repeated in 1939. Russia was certainly interested in growing and she had recently added the Crimea (now part of Ukraine) to her empire. The following year, Frederick of Prussia put his plans to divide up Poland into action.

Despite ongoing successes in many parts of the world, British expansionism was facing a major challenge. In 1772, James Bruce explored Abyssinia and traced the source of the Blue Nile to its confluence with the White Nile, adding an important contribution to Europe's knowledge of Africa (a knowledge, incidentally, that would have very mixed results for those whose lands were subsequently to be colonised). The year after, Warren Hastings – the first British governor-general of India – made an alliance with the state of Awadh against the Marathas.

But the challenge for Britain came from North America. The colonists there were increasingly angry at what they saw as the interference of the British government in their way of life. Tensions erupted in 1770 in what became known as the Boston Massacre, where British redcoats fired on a crowd and left five dead. This was followed three years later by the renowned Boston Tea Party, inspired by an attempt to enforce a tax on tea which ended with disgruntled colonists throwing tea over the side of ships into Boston Harbour. It was one of those iconic events where the symbolism was greater than the practical impact and led to an outcome that would reshape the course of history.

The political situation in the thirteen colonies of North America had been deteriorating for several years. The British government, unable to impose its will on the colonists peacefully, had in some cases resorted to military rule to impose it. The Americans had responded by setting up a Continental Congress to protect the interests of the colonists.

It was only a matter of time before war broke out. An army was sent over to North America to impose British rule, but it suffered several early defeats at Lexington and Concord. In the year that the war began, 1775, an experienced Virginian, George Washington, was appointed Commander-in-Chief of the American army. It would take some time for his army to gain the upper hand. Yet an early British victory at Bunker Hill was a hollow success, as a large number of men were lost in the process.

One year into the war, on 4 July 1776, one of the most famous documents in history was signed. Drafted by Thomas Jefferson, with amendments by Benjamin Franklin and John Adams, the Declaration of Independence was a call to arms and an unmistakable declaration of intent from the Revolutionaries. One phrase in particular resonates across history: 'We hold these truths to be self-evident, that all men are created equal, that they are endowed by their Creator with certain unalienable Rights, that among these are Life, Liberty and the pursuit of Happiness.' It was a brave, bold statement, yet like many in the course of human history it would prove hugely difficult to live up to.

Over time, the British Army became increasingly stretched and its enemy ever more confident and competent. The Americans would find several important allies, drawn in more perhaps by the thought that 'my enemy's enemy is my friend' than altruism. France was one and Spain another – the latter certainly encouraged by the perceived opportunity (ultimately one that was unfulfilled) of recovering Gibraltar.

Even as the war progressed, British exploration of the globe continued. Captain James Cook ventured further into the South Seas and as an important by-product found a cure for scurvy, the eternal scourge of sailors deprived of fresh food for months on end. Cook was a combination of brilliant seaman, outstanding cartographer and intrepid risk-taker; among some of the dangerous regions to be first explored by him were the Great Barrier Reef and the edges of Antarctica.

Important changes took place in Russia too, such as those of 1776, when Admiral Potemkin reorganised the Russian Black Sea fleet and a few years later began construction of what would be the key port of Sevastopol in the Crimea. But the events to impact on the world were not just political, they were also profoundly ideological.

It would be wrong to think that they were all left-leaning in nature either. For even as America fought to free itself from what it perceived as tyrannical rule from thousands of miles away and the drive for social upheaval grew to fever pitch in France, one of the most influential economic treatises ever was about to appear.

Scotland had been blessed with so many thinkers of outstanding talent during this period that it was christened 'the Scottish Enlightenment'. From this small nation in the north of Britain, ideas spread out across the globe, not least those of Adam Smith, whose seminal work, *An Inquiry into the Nature and Causes of the Wealth of Nations*, appeared in 1776.

There is a neat symmetry in the fact that this was published in the same year that the Declaration of Independence was produced. It took Smith ten years to write *The Wealth of Nations*. It is widely considered to be the founding work of capitalism. But it would be misleading to consider him a man who wished to see widespread exploitation, for he was a passionate supporter of the concepts of liberty and free speech.

Smith held strong views on a number of things, for example believing – based on his own experience – that universities were far better in Scotland than they were in England; his experiences at Oxford were not happy years for him. A particularly close friend of another great Scot, David Hume, he would have regarded himself more as a moral philosopher than an economist. He himself may well have considered his first work, *The Theory of Moral Sentiments*, to be superior to *The Wealth of Nations*.

Yet it is for the latter that he is best remembered. He argued in it that individuals are driven by self-interest and in the end by so doing they also promote the interests of the society in which they live far more positively than if they actively set out to do so. So self-interest in a competitive market would keep prices low and benefit all as a result. But there have to be rules governing economic conduct – Smith was a strong critic of monopolies, which flew in the face of a free market. Instead, division of labour should be encouraged in the interests of efficiency, which would also in the end benefit consumers as much as producers, as costs would once again be minimised.

In modern society many doubts are frequently expressed against capitalism, yet Smith was in many ways a liberal man for his time, opposed to imperialism and slavery in equal measure. He was also a strong believer that everyone should pay their taxes, and the rich should pay proportionally more than the poor, saying that 'every tax, however, is, to the person who pays it, a badge, not of slavery, but of liberty'. Liberal philosophy was also a driving force behind the Revolution in America, where the home-grown (though English-born) Thomas Paine was a key driver of the moves to break away from British rule. Over time the war turned decisively against the redcoats, in particular in 1777 when Burgoyne and his army were captured at Saratoga. The year before, an American inventor, David Bushnell, developed the first ever prototype of a submarine, the *Turtle*, though it met with limited success.

The war's decisive moment came in 1781 when the British general Cornwallis was captured at Yorktown with 8,000 men, marking the effective end of land operations in the conflict. There were other important events in the same year unconnected to the conflict. Russia concluded a peace with Austria, with the two planning to drive the Turks out of Europe once and for all, and to create an independent kingdom of Dacia (now Romania) that would be ruled by an Orthodox prince.

Joseph II of Austria also brought an end to serfdom in his kingdom (something that had happened in the previous year in Hungary and Bohemia). A third of the monasteries in Austria were also dissolved as a blow against corruption. But globally it was a less felicitous year for Austria, as she lost Delagoa Bay (in what is now Mozambique) to the Portuguese, enabling the latter to strengthen their colonial claims in south-east Africa.

Despite the effective loss of the American colonies, Britain still found success in other spheres, capturing Trincomalee in Ceylon from the Dutch in 1782, while Admiral George Rodney defeated the French fleet under de Grasse at the Battle of the Saints, protecting British possessions in the West Indies as a result.

The year 1783 saw the Treaties of Paris and Versailles, which ended the War of Independence. The USA was henceforward recognised as an independent nation, something that the British king George III struggled desperately to come to terms with.

Britain at least recovered her West Indian possessions. France also benefited from her part in the war, gaining, among other territories, Senegal, Tobago and St Lucia.

While this was happening, Russia intervened in Georgia after an attempt by the Persians to gain control there and Heraclius of Georgia was forced to recognise Russian sovereignty as a result. Yet there were also important cultural events happening while these great political upheavals were taking place. A young composer called Ludwig van Beethoven published his first work in 1783, while a more established musician based in Vienna by the name of Wolfgang Amadeus Mozart also published his *Mass in C Minor* in the same year.

Mozart had actually been baptised with the rather less memorable name of Johannes Chrysostomus Wolfgangus Theophilus Mozart and from his childhood had demonstrated phenomenal musical ability. His first composition appeared when he was just five years old. The genius of Mozart is perhaps epitomised by the story that when he visited the Sistine Chapel in Rome he heard that haunting piece of music, Allegri's *Miserere*. The beauty of this composition was so renowned that the Pope kept the music a jealously guarded secret and no copies of it were allowed. Mozart heard it once, it is said, went home and wrote it from memory virtually without error.

Mozart moved from Salzburg to Vienna where he established himself in 1781. Here he would become great friends with another prolific composer, Joseph Haydn, and would study and be influenced by the works of J. S. Bach and Handel. Eventually writing forty-one symphonies (the official total, though a number of others of dubious provenance are sometimes attributed to him) and in total over 600 works, he was a key developer of the style of music known as Classical, taking the legacy of Baroque to an altogether different place and in the process leaving his own bequest of music that remains some of the most recognisable ever written, such as his evocative *Requiem* (started but not finished by him), great operas such as *The Marriage of Figaro* and *The Magic Flute*, and a powerful collection of piano concertos, as well as pieces for other solo instruments.

Developments of an entirely different nature took place in Paris in 1783, where, on 21 November, the Montgolfier brothers managed to launch a manned hot-air balloon, one of the earliest known flights of man in history. Joseph Montgolfier later suggested that he was inspired to develop the concept while contemplating how a successful assault on the apparently impregnable fortress of Gibraltar could be made and came up with the idea of troops carried in the air. The first public demonstration of the craft that the brothers developed took place on 4 June 1783 in Annonay, France, when they managed to fly for ten minutes, traverse a distance of 2 kilometres and reach a height of about 6,000 feet. It was the inspiration for manned flight that would lead ultimately to huge and unthinkable developments in the twentieth century.

This was a period of extraordinary change, some of it contradictory. For even as European nations increased their colonial possessions, they often experienced internal upheavals as a number of political philosophers sought to redefine the established social order. They would not meet all their aspirations, and it is debatable even now how egalitarian the Western world is, yet it cannot be denied that there were massive changes in train.

Evidence of the thirst for freedom and redefinition of the social order came from far afield. For example, in 1784 Andreas Bernstorff abolished serfdom and established a free press in Denmark. Two years later, a Parliamentary motion was introduced in Britain to abolish the slave trade. Yet there were contrary movements too. During the same period, the India Act was passed in Britain, bringing the East India Company under a government-appointed Board of Control and forbidding interference in native affairs. While on the one hand this could be seen as allowing a more enlightened method of government in the East India Company's territories, on the other it was an important building block towards the establishment of an Indian Empire for the British.

More everyday matters were affected by events during this period too. In 1791, the first recorded mention in the USA of a game called baseball was made, while three years before (the same year in which the first British penal colony was established at Botany Bay in Australia) the Marylebone Cricket Club codified the laws of their sport. Similar sports in a number of ways, both were great British social exports to the world, with baseball one of the prime sports of the modern US and cricket currently a national obsession in India.

And so to 1789, one of the truly significant years in world history. On 30 April, George Washington was inaugurated as the first President of the USA. On 4 July, the US congress established the States as an economic and customs union (New York had been made the federal capital the year before). Then, just ten days later, the Western world was shaken to its core.

France under King Louis XVI had been suffering serious economic problems. These had been partly caused by grandiose schemes of the ruling elite, including the French intervention in the American war with Britain. Economic hardships for the masses were exacerbated by their lack of involvement in government – France was under the effective control of the nobility, the so-called Second Estate, comprising just 2 per cent of the populace. Resentment festered beneath the surface until, on 14 July, it exploded spectacularly.

The explosion did not come out of a clear blue sky. The month before, the frustrated middle class – the Third Estate – had received begrudging agreement from the king to form a National Assembly, a theoretically more representative form of government. But it was not enough. The king foolishly attempted to reshape the government and in the process merely lit the fuse of a powder keg.

On 14 July, it exploded. Paris was in arms, with thousands of protesters on the streets and an army that was powerless, or unwilling, to stop them. They marched on the Bastille prison, a symbolic place that for many years had signified oppression and keeping the masses in their place. The few prisoners there were released (the protesters were far more interested in the building's stores of gunpowder – they had already liberated 30,000 weapons from Les Invalides but had nothing to fire them with).

The shaky edifice of the French ruling elite soon began to wobble. Some Royalists, seeing the writing on the wall, decided to emigrate while the unrest spread. On 2 November, all Church property was nationalised. The following month, with the repercussions already unfolding, the Austrian Netherlands declared their independence, naming their new country Belgium.

But the terror that followed did not arrive overnight. There was, soon after the storming of the Bastille (the key was sent to George Washington as a symbolic gift in 1790), the passing of *The Declaration of the Rights of Man and the Citizen*, which cemented the rights of many citizens in a very explicit way (though it specifically ignored the rights of women or slaves). The following year, two groups – the Jacobins under Maximilien de Robespierre and the Cordeliers under Georges Danton – increasingly dominated the political landscape.

But this was still a country with a king, not a republic. On 3 September a new constitution was passed by the National Assembly, confirming France as a constitutional monarchy. The attention of most of the Western world was on France to see what would happen next, which distracted attention from significant events elsewhere, such as Lord Cornwallis's defeat of Tipu of Mysore at the Battle of Seringapatam, which secured another large chunk of Indian land for Britain. On 22 August 1791 there was a slave revolt in the French part of San Domingo, the first known example of such an event. In the meantime, a new US capital, Washington DC, was being laid out.

If 1789 was the year that lit the spark of the French Revolution, 1792 was the one in which it reached its blood-soaked conclusion. On 13 August of that year, the French royal family was imprisoned. Louis XVI had tried to escape the year before and had, in a way that much emulated his monarchical predecessor Charles I of England, been negotiating behind the backs of the National Assembly with foreign heads of state to institute a counter-revolution.

Soon after, France (whose queen, Marie Antoinette, was Austrian) declared war on Austria, Prussia and Sardinia. The citizen armies marched into Brussels and conquered the Spanish Netherlands. By November 1792, the Girondins under Danton had seized power. There was an almost tangible shiver of fear across the monarchies of Europe. What did these 'rights of man' mean? In some countries it was quite clear, for in 1792 Denmark became the first Western European country to abolish slavery. But to many monarchs it meant a threat to their own privileged position and those of the nobilities that supported them. Thomas Paine's seminal work *The Rights of Man* led to him being prosecuted in Britain *in absentia*.

On 21 January 1793, Louis XVI was led to his death. France had been declared a republic a few months before. Despite almost unanimous agreement at his trial that he was guilty of high treason, there was a much smaller majority in favour of the death penalty. Despite these reservations, Louis met his appointment with the guillotine bravely (the emblematic machine of death was, by the way, not a French invention – very similar devices are known from England and Scotland centuries earlier).

As a new world formed, it appeared that the old wanted to continue unhindered. So even while Paris was in turmoil, Russia and Prussia were agreeing on the Second Partition of Poland. Britain, in the meantime, was also disturbed enough to enter an agreement with Russia to intercept all French traffic in the Baltic. The theoretical partition of Poland became a practical one on 7 May, with Russia taking Lithuania and western Ukraine while Prussia took Danzig and other centres.

Attention soon returned to France, though, where the death of the king rather marked a beginning than an end. On 6 April, a Committee of Public Safety was established in France with dictatorial power – it was dominated by Danton. The US cautiously proclaimed its neutrality in the conflict that clearly loomed with the rest of Europe, a wise move for a new state with many issues of its own to resolve if it wished to become a viable major power.

But Danton had released a genie from the bottle that he could not return once it was loose. The problem with revolutions is that they rarely result in the outcome that the revolutionaries require, certainly not as quickly as they would like. The lot of the masses was still dire and popular resentment grew so that on 2 June the Girondins, who had not delivered what they had promised, were overthrown and the Reign of Terror began.

On 13 July Jean Marat, a leading Jacobin, was murdered by the Girondin Charlotte Corday in his bath. Soon after, more leading Jacobins were appointed to the Committee of Public Safety including Maximilien de Robespierre; his view on the rights of the public has a ring about it that would be recognised by many who have lived under totalitarianism: 'Terror is nothing else than swift, severe, indomitable justice; it flows, then, from virtue.' Once more the argument of expediency and justice in support of terror was being espoused.

These sinister comments explain much about what happened next. On 5 October Queen Marie Antoinette was executed. She was followed by a number of prominent Girondins, among them Danton (who would die in April 1794). But it was not limited to politicians alone. Vigorous efforts were made to crush the church in France, in a way that eerily pre-echoes later communist-era attempts to suppress perceived superstition and its hold over the people. In a more positive development, the former palace of the Louvre was made a national art gallery.

A counter-revolution in the Vendée towards the end of 1793 led to some of the most shocking events of this time of turmoil. Hundreds, perhaps thousands, of people were executed at Nantes in a process known as the *noyades* – 'the drownings'. Catholic priests and nuns were particular targets but women and children also perished in the atrocities. The butcher who ordered these barbaric acts, Jean-Baptiste Carrier, would later be executed for his actions, falling a victim to the guillotine at the end of 1794.

The world did not stand idly by while these events were happening. After all, they threatened the established order across Europe. British forces occupied the island of Corsica. Soon after, a former Corsican resident by the name of Napoleon Bonaparte captured Toulon from British occupiers. However, the British had more success in India, where they seized a number of French territories.

Protected by these upheavals to some extent by the wide Atlantic, the USA continued its evolution. The cornerstone was laid of the Capitol building, which would be the seat of government in Washington, though it would take thirty years to complete. In 1793 Eli Whitney invented the cotton gin in the USA, which led to the establishment of the cotton industry in the Southern states. But therein was a bitter irony, for in the land of the free thousands of slaves were required to feed the beast that was the cotton trade, as well as many others.

This introduced, or perhaps more accurately reinforced, contradictions and tensions in the USA. A number of signatories to the Declaration of Independence, particularly Thomas Jefferson, argued that slavery was an undesirable institution. Yet he kept his own slaves to the end of his life and in later years kept remarkably silent about the need to abolish the trade. An example of the early US view on slavery was a 1793 law that required an escaped slave to be returned to his master. Such complexities would lead to the USA suffering its own civil war seven decades after, and ongoing racial problems far beyond that.

Events in France continued to impact on the wider world. In 1794 slavery was abolished in the French colonies (it was reintroduced by Napoleon a few years later – so much for *liberté, égalité, fraternité*). A year later, the Batavian Republic was declared in the Netherlands, which led to British forces occupying the Cape of Good Hope on behalf of the exiled Prince William V of Orange. On 1 October, Belgium was formally joined with France. The Treaty of San Lorenzo between Spain and the USA in the same year settled the boundaries of Florida and granted the US the right to navigate the Mississippi, an important step along the road towards American colonial expansion.

France sought to widen its own territories. In 1797, she occupied the Ionian Islands as well as establishing the client Cisalpine Republic, which brought together Milan, Bologna and other Italian territories. But the impact was not just military, it was also ideological. Unprecedented mutinies in the British Navy seemed to some to presage a revolution in Britain, too.

Certainly Ireland seemed ripe for rebellion, and indeed it broke out in January 1798. However, the rebel force was defeated at Vinegar Hill on 21 June and the rebellion was brought to an end. As this crucial century approached its end, there were some reassuring signs for those who wished to protect the status quo. Britain, Russia and Turkey established a Triple Alliance in 1799 and the French suffered several significant reverses. Russian forces occupied Turin and the Austrians defeated the French at Magnano. Tipu of Mysore was killed in another battle at Seringapatam and his kingdom was divided between the British and the Nizam of Hyderabad, while the all-conquering general of the French revolutionary forces, Napoleon Bonaparte, was forced to return to France from Egypt, his fleet shattered in Aboukir Bay largely due to the tactics of a Rear Admiral named Horatio Nelson.

Once back in France, Bonaparte quickly manoeuvred himself to grasp the reins of power. This manifested itself in some important ways, such as his adoption in 1799 of a new system of measurement, the metric, for France, which would eventually spread across large parts of Europe. Returning to Paris merely allowed Napoleon to put himself in the right place to advance his political ambitions. On 24 December he was established as First Consul for ten years. Far from being a revolutionary, he would show himself to be driven as much by personal motivations as any King of France had ever been. Europe would be at war for much of the next fifteen years as a result.

35

NAPOLEON

The Rise and Fall of the French European Empire (AD 1801–1825)

In 1804, Napoleon Bonaparte was crowned Emperor of France by Pope Pius VII, just over 1,000 years after the similar honouring of Charlemagne. Pointedly, although the Pope was there to give symbolic approval to the proceedings, Napoleon placed the crown on his head himself. Yet in some ways an analogy with Julius Caesar rather than Charlemagne would be better for Napoleon's rise to power, as his ambitions won him many enemies at home and abroad and he had to manoeuvre his way through plots and assassination attempts to win the imperial crown.

It had been a gradual process, a progressive accretion of power over time, having himself made First Consul for life and President of the Italian Republic in 1802. This followed a short period of peace the year before, under the terms of which Britain was to return all the conquests she had made in recent times save for Trinidad and Ceylon (Sri Lanka). This was irksome as British forces had been successful in Egypt, which was now to be returned to Turkey.

It at least allowed Britain breathing space for other matters, such as the formal Union of Britain and Ireland, which came into force in 1801, or the purchasing of the famous (one might say infamous) Elgin Marbles at around the same time. Europe took time to recover its breath but it was, in boxing parlance, only a breather between rounds.

Away from all this war and peace, the United States of America, still barely a quarter-century old, continued to consolidate. In 1800 the Library of Congress was established in Washington, while all the departments of state were transferred to the new city from Philadelphia. The new nation was also continuing to expand; states that had not been part of the original nation joined on a piecemeal basis, with Ohio, for example, becoming part of the Union in 1803. The US government also took advantage of the French embroilments in Europe, purchasing Louisiana and New Orleans from them.

The ceasefire between France and Britain proved very short-term. Napoleon solely sought time to lick his wounds after a number of years' hard fighting – it was merely a truce of convenience. His ambition was greater than ever and ongoing interference in Swiss and Italian affairs led to a renewal of hostilities soon afterwards. The British won a significant battle in India at the Battle of Assaye, adding more territories to their burgeoning lands in the Subcontinent. The victory was attributable to a rising young British commander named Arthur Wellesley. They also took Dutch Guiana in South America, their naval power proving an impossible obstacle for the French and their allies to overcome. Military innovations were emerging in support of the war; a new shell, designed by Henry Shrapnel in 1784, was adopted by the British Army in 1803.

There were also social changes occurring that in their own way would impact on the conflict. The reintroduction of slavery the year before had led to unforeseen difficulties for Napoleon. It resulted in an uprising in Haiti led by Toussaint Louverture and Jean-Jacques Dessalines. A combination of unexpectedly fierce resistance and yellow fever decimated the French troops and also led to Napoleon recognising that territories on the other side of the Atlantic were indefensible, particularly given British naval supremacy, resulting in the so-called Louisiana Purchase already discussed, at a nominal rate of 3 cents per acre.

It was not long before Europe returned to a continent-wide conflict, with France and Britain lining up supporters behind them. In 1804, France pressured a weakened Spain to declare war against Britain. The following year, on 11 April, the Treaty of St Petersburg saw Britain and Russia aligning with the aim of liberating the north German states (Austria would join them later in the year).

In the meantime, following his papal coronation Bonaparte appeared to have an insatiable appetite for power, for he was soon after seeking the kingdom of Italy (he was crowned in May 1805 in Milan Cathedral). To secure the ongoing allegiance of the army, he appointed a total of eighteen Marshals of the Empire, hand-picked generals who he relied on to help him drive forward the process of conquest across the globe.

These events – ongoing conquest and the reintroduction of slavery – were hardly in the spirit of the revolution, and a number of prominent European figures were bitterly disappointed at the course Napoleon had adopted. One of them was Ludwig van Beethoven. He had been born in Bonn, Germany, but was another of that remarkable group of musicians who blossomed in Vienna, where he studied with Haydn. In particular, he took the symphonic form to new, and perhaps unmatchable, heights with nine remarkable symphonies that perfected it.

It was his Third Symphony, *Eroica*, that marked a turning point towards something quite new and innovative. It was so different to what had gone before that when premièred it received a mixed reception (better, at least, than Stravinsky's *Rite of Spring* a century later, which almost started a riot). But, interestingly, his original dedication for this vast new work was to Napoleon, who initially inspired Beethoven with his vision. Now his clear imperial ambitions turned Beethoven against him and the title page was torn out, with the work now just dedicated to an unnamed 'great man'. Beethoven would have further cause to turn against the emperor when the latter's army bombarded Vienna in 1809. Beethoven hid in a cellar, afraid that he would lose what was left by that stage of his hearing.

But it is all too easy to assume, until one looks closer, that Napoleon's impact and legacy were military only. He was also an energetic and far-seeing organiser. In 1804 he introduced a new set of civil laws, the Napoleonic Code, which drastically reformed such matters. Napoleon would say much later, after Waterloo in fact, that no one would remember his forty victories, the lustre of which would be irrevocably tarnished by that one catastrophic defeat; what he would be remembered for was his Code. He was right, for it still underpins the civil legislation of perhaps a quarter of all nations across the globe.

Those who consider him an out-and-out tyrant may also wish to consider his abhorrence of anti-Semitism, which he objected to on both practical and moral grounds. He once stated that 'I will never accept any proposals that will obligate the Jewish people to leave France, because to me the Jews are the same as any other citizen in our country. It takes weakness to chase them out of the country, but it takes strength to assimilate them.' It is a remarkable statement that many other more recent and supposedly enlightened societies would do well to emulate.

The year 1805 would be seminal for the reputation and legacy of Napoleon. On the one hand, he won perhaps his greatest victory at Austerlitz, the so-called Battle of the Three Emperors, where Napoleon was up against the armies of Austria and Russia. Certainly Napoleon regarded it as his finest victory, and he commissioned the splendid Arc de Triomphe to commemorate it. A more practical result was that Austria was forced to concede large chunks of territory and as a result the Holy Roman Empire came to a formal end after a life of 1,000 years. A Confederation of German States was established to step into the vacuum – unsurprisingly, Napoleon was given the position of its Protector.

Yet Napoleon also realised that, in order to dominate Europe as he wished, he needed to knock Britain out of the war. The Royal Navy acted as a stranglehold around the trade routes across the Atlantic and was therefore able to exercise a considerable negative influence on trade. In particular, the key ports of Toulon and Brest were blockaded. However, when the French fleet managed to evade this and break out for the Caribbean, the British fleet gave chase. Napoleon hoped that this would distract the defences of Britain and allow an invasion force to make the short crossing from Boulogne, but it was not to be. His army instead marched to Germany and ended up on the field of Austerlitz.

At sea his navy now suffered a crippling defeat. This followed a chase across the Atlantic to the Caribbean and back after the French fleet escaped Nelson's attentions when he was blockading Brest as the British ships were blown off-station by the weather. The French managed to make their way back to Cadiz but soon after set out for Naples. En route they were spotted and engaged by the British off Cape Trafalgar.

The subsequent battle was fought on 21 October 1805, with the English inspired by Nelson's famous signal that 'England expects that every man will do his duty'. What followed was a crushing defeat for the combined French and Spanish fleet and indisputable confirmation of Britain's mastery of the seas, the spine of her burgeoning empire. It was won not just through Nelson's brilliance and his tactics, which had been honed to perfection through a succession of stunning victories, but also by a superb group of captains, his 'band of brothers' as he called them (no doubt inspired by the quote in *Henry V* from another great Englishman, William Shakespeare), and the vastly superior gunnery of his men over their opponents.

Nelson, of course, died at the moment of victory, perhaps the perfect heroic ending for a man who courted fame all his life. The victory did not, as is sometimes claimed, save England from invasion – Napoleon had already moved his army from Boulogne – but there would never be another serious attempt to face the British fleet in battle for the remainder of the war.

Despite the epic scale of the war, exploration of what was, to the West at least, an undiscovered world continued apace. One such was a Scot named Mungo Park who, for a decade, endeavoured to open up unknown regions in Africa. His finest moment came in 1805, when he was the first European to explore the Niger River. His spirit can be summed up in the following words:

> I shall set sail for the east with the fixed resolution to discover the termination of the Niger or perish in the attempt. Though all the Europeans who are with me should die, and though I were myself half dead, I would still persevere, and if I could not succeed in the object of my journey, I would at least die on the Niger.

These were fine and, for many Europeans at least, inspirational words and certainly many explorers from many European nations acted with great personal heroism in their efforts. But at the same time the opening up of Africa – or more to the point the largely successful attempt by European nations to own and exploit most of it for their own selfish reasons – proved to be in many (and in some regions virtually all) ways a disaster for the indigenous inhabitants. In the event, personal disaster would ensue too. Park disappeared, and it would later be discovered that he had drowned trying to escape hostile natives.

Art, too, continued to develop and was in many respects at a crossroads between the old and the new. A perfect example was the Spanish artist Francisco Goya. He had a long career and over it there was a marked change in the character of his paintings. His early works are pretty and conventional, and it was no surprise that the Spanish royal family were regular patrons; here was a man who could be relied upon to deliver exactly what was required with no newfangled experimentation to be concerned about.

But in later years his paintings would become, in conceptual terms, far darker and the art far more radical. Chilling representations of witches' sabats and harrowing visions of war haunt his later works. Serious physical and mental illness left its mark, as did the political unrest that was about to hit Spain. Although his most famous works, the prints known as *The Disasters of War*, would not be produced until the following decade, by this time Goya's style had fundamentally changed. Its surreal representations would provide an early step down the path that would lead eventually to Manet and Picasso.

Of a very different style but equally influential on future artists (particularly Claude Monet and the Impressionist School) was the English landscape artist Joseph Mallord William Turner. English painters had become well known for their landscapes (with John Constable the most famous of them), but Turner adopted a quite different approach. Rather than adopt a realistic approach to painting, Turner instead concentrated on colour, shade and atmosphere, earning him the nickname of the 'painter of light'. A controversial figure in his lifetime, Turner would nevertheless quickly become recognised for his greatness. Active over decades, he produced a typically atmospheric painting of the Battle of Trafalgar in 1806, just a year after it was fought.

The Napoleonic Wars impacted far beyond the shores of Europe. Napoleon would forge formal alliances with both Turkey and Persia, though his earlier ill-fated efforts in Egypt were not a promising precedent. Nevertheless, Europe was the main battleground and Napoleon sought to put Britain out of the war by hitting her trade. To do this, he pressured Prussia into shutting her ports to British ships, but this only helped to ensure that Prussia declared war once more on France on 9 October 1806.

By now, Napoleon's dynastic intentions were clear. On 5 June of that year, Louis Bonaparte, his brother, was made King of Holland. On land at least he appeared unconquerable. He crushed the Prussian army at Jena and also successfully egged on the Turks to declare war on Russia, another potential enemy. Late in the year, he entered Warsaw. By that time continental ports had been closed to British shipping – the so-called 'Continental System'; Napoleon was attempting to hit his arch-enemy in the pocket.

But all this succeeded in doing was encouraging the British to implement a blockade against the coasts of France and her allies. This war was assuming a strong economic as well as military aspect and was foreshadowing much more modern conflicts as a result. All ships sailing to ports where British vessels were not allowed were liable to capture. However, this created wider problems for the British, highlighted on 22 June 1807 when the US ship *Chesapeake* was stopped by the British vessel *Leopard*. There was outrage in the US, and war between the country and Britain again moved closer (it had already threatened to do so in 1805, again because of British interference with American shipping) but was averted for the time being by the pacific policies of Thomas Jefferson, then the President.

A feature of these years was the bewildering series of coalitions entered into by various nations to oppose Napoleon. As often as not, they would collapse because of the defeat or exhaustion of one or more of the members. On 26 April 1807, the Convention of Bartenstein between Russia and Prussia was entered into, allying the two nations against France. Predictably, just two months later the two were defeated by Napoleon at Friedland, though they were joined in the Convention soon after by Britain. While the British sought to fight a more global war, attacking Buenos Aires soon after with limited success, Napoleon pushed on to meet Tsar Alexander and Frederick William II of Prussia on the River Niemen.

This meeting of three great rulers was an enormous symbolic coup for Napoleon, who held the upper hand in the negotiations after his recent victory. It showed in the Treaty of Tilsit, established as a result of the meeting. Russia agreed to close all ports to British ships and to coerce Denmark, Sweden and Portugal to join the war against Britain. In return, the tsar got a free hand in Finland. Prussia lost all her possessions west of the Elbe as well as her Polish territories and also agreed to join the 'Continental System'.

While Napoleon's empire grew – the former Prussian territories west of the Elbe were given to Jerome Bonaparte, who became King of Westphalia as a result – Britain used her only currently available weapon to fight back. In September, Britain bombed Copenhagen from the sea, forcing the Danes to surrender. However, Denmark soon after joined France against Britain, and by the Treaty of Fontainebleau Spain and France agreed to conquer Portugal, a traditional British ally. On 7 November Russia broke off relations with Britain, effectively entering war against her. To cap what was a very negative year for the British, on 22 December the US Embargo Act was passed, by which the US withheld raw materials from both France and Britain.

Despite these turbulent times, there was still a great deal of artistic achievement going on. Two of the most famous poets of all, Byron and Wordsworth, were active during these momentous years. In other fields there were some memorable achievements too. In 1808, two of Beethoven's most famous works appeared, his Fifth and Sixth Symphonies, as did the first part of Goethe's *Faust*.

But militarily the French juggernaut still seemed unstoppable. On 2 February 1808 French forces occupied Rome after Pope Pius VII refused to join a proposed alliance against Britain. Later the same month, the French invaded Spain and soon after occupied Barcelona. Madrid was occupied in March and on 15 June Joseph Bonaparte became King of Spain. In response the British sent a force to protect Portugal. It was under the command of Arthur Wellesley, who soon after arrival defeated the French at Vimiero. The Convention of Cintra, signed soon after, saw the French withdraw from Portugal (carried out on British ships, which was the cause of great shame in some quarters) but there was little confidence that this would be anything other than a short-term respite.

And indeed the British forces suffered another crushing reverse, at Corunna in Spain as 1809 began, with their commander, Sir John Moore, dying and being buried in the field, though much of his force was able to evacuate. But even as Austria once more joined the war against France – only to be defeated soon after at Wagram – the course of the war on land began to turn, though at first only slowly.

On 28 July, Wellesley won a decisive victory against the French at Talavera and was later given a title, the Duke of Wellington, as a result of his triumphs. It was not obvious yet that this was a turning point, with Austria much diminished in terms of territories because of her defeat and forced to join the 'Continental System' against Britain. But Spain, given its geographical proximity to France, was something of a 'soft underbelly' for Napoleon (who had more personal problems to worry about, for he was about to divorce his wife, Josephine, for her failure to deliver an heir).

This was realpolitik kicking in. Napoleon had at first been smitten when he met Joséphine de Beauharnais, a well-known socialite and former mistress of several senior political figures (one of whom was allegedly happy to lose her as she had very extravagant and expensive tastes). Her previous husband had been guillotined in the Reign of Terror, and she had had several children previously (from whom the present monarchs of Norway, Sweden and Belgium, among others, are descended), but her relationship with Napoleon was unproductive in terms of children and Napoleon divorced her and married Marie Louise, daughter of Francis I of Austria, instead.

While the war had a very significant impact on the shape of Europe, it was about to have a decisive long-term effect globally. With Spain heavily preoccupied in Europe, her colonies in South America sensed an opportunity for freedom. On 19 April 1810, under the influence of Simón Bolívar, the Junta of Venezuela broke from Spain, using as their ostensible excuse that they refused to recognise Joseph Bonaparte as their king. Bolívar was descended from colonists who had come over from Europe in the sixteenth century and became very rich as a result of mineral extraction.

It was the start of a domino effect, led by Bolívar, who still has wide hero status in South America; in September the Junta of Chile followed suit. The next year Paraguay did the same. Spain was now forced to fight a losing battle to hang onto her colonial possessions, although for many of the indigenous peoples of South America, brutally exploited by their European conquerors, it was far too late to make a difference. Freedom in fact meant the transference of rule from the Spanish crown to a ruling caste of Spanish colonisers who had permanently established themselves in South America – a situation that still pertains to a large extent in some countries in the region.

The impact of the war was also manifesting itself in the field of Anglo-American relations. In 1811, the US renewed the Non-Intercourse Act against British commerce. The British situation was not improved when, soon after, King George III's perceived insanity meant that day-to-day affairs of the Crown passed to his foppish son, who became Prince Regent. On 4 April of the following year, the US implemented a ninety-day embargo in preparation for war with Britain (soon after, incidentally, Louisiana became the latest addition to the US). On 18 June, the US Congress declared war on Britain. It did not begin spectacularly well, as on 16 August General Hull surrendered Detroit to British forces, though matters would get much better for the Americans thereafter.

But the war in Europe was about to reach its defining moment. While Wellington continued to win victory after victory against Napoleon's generals in the Iberian Peninsula, this on its own was not enough to threaten France. Napoleon, however, was about to fatally overreach, the curse of many an ambitious leader over the centuries, be it Alexander and his ultimately unfulfilled plans in India in ancient times, or, after Napoleon, Hitler's grave miscalculation in the Second World War.

Russia was becoming increasingly confident and in February 1811 had captured the city of Belgrade and made a Turkish army there captive. The nineteenth century would see a consistent Russian policy of the country acting as a protector of Orthodoxy in Eastern Europe and a constant drive to try and take advantage of perceived Ottoman weakness in the region. At this point in time, the weakness of Austria, then a major player in Eastern Europe, also helped; the country had just declared itself effectively bankrupt.

The strength of Russia was something that Napoleon was not prepared to tolerate. In 1812 the French reoccupied Pomerania in order to put pressure on Sweden and prevent a Russo-Swedish alliance. Prussia was pressured to allow the free passage of French troops across the country if France attacked Russia, and Austria agreed to provide troops to supplement Napoleon's armies.

On 28 May of that year, the Treaty of Bucharest between Russia and Turkey gave Russia Bessarabia (in the region of the modern state of Moldova and still a bone of contention for some Romanians, who believe that it should be part of their country) but Turkey hung on to the regions of Moldavia and Wallachia (which, with Transylvania, broadly form the modern state of Romania).

This was welcome news for the Russians, who now had far more critical problems to contend with. On 24 June Napoleon crossed the River Niemen with his armies and entered Russian territory. Two days later, Poland declared herself an independent state, though Napoleon refused to acknowledge the fact. By 18 August the French had taken Smolensk. On 14 September Napoleon entered Moscow after winning a critical victory at nearby Borodino. Moscow went up in smoke and burned for five days.

However, taking the city was one thing and holding it quite another. As a later autocrat would find out, it is one thing to take vast amounts of Russian territory, quite another to crush the Russian spirit. And the Russians had something quite deadly on their side – their harsh winter. The French army, with its vast and overstretched lines of communication, had no alternative but to retreat and Moscow was abandoned in October.

On 19 October the disastrous retreat from Moscow began. The French were ill-equipped for the harshness of the conditions facing them and the march that followed had a brutal impact on the poorly equipped army. Napoleon rushed back ahead of the army to protect his position in Paris, arriving back there on 18 December, well ahead of his army, most of which indeed never made it back. It had been a disastrous miscalculation on Napoleon's part, and its long-term impact was disastrous for the French emperor.

There were major social changes in this period, too. In 1808 – the same year that Britain added another colony to her possessions in the shape of Sierra Leone – the USA prohibited the import of slaves from Africa. The year after, Pall Mall in London was lit by gas and the process of industrialisation and modernisation continued apace. Scientific and cultural developments continued despite the war. In 1812, the year in which a new dance, the waltz, was introduced to Britain, the steamship *Comet* sailed on the Clyde at a speed of 7 knots. In Germany, at the same time, two brothers named Grimm were putting together a collection of fairy tales that would become, and remain, bestsellers.

The war, though, continued to dominate. In the Iberian Peninsula, Wellington continued to beat general after general in the French army. With Napoleon's retreat from the wintry wastes of Russia, there was strong evidence that the tide of war was on the turn. The year after, on 17 March, Prussia declared war on France. There were popular uprisings in Hamburg soon after and the Russians moved in to occupy the city. A couple of months later, Britain agreed to pay subsidies to Prussia and Russia in a joint war effort. The coalition grew and on 12 August, Austria declared war on France.

On 19 October 1813, Napoleon was defeated at the Battle of the Nations (fought near Leipzig) and the Kingdom of Westphalia was dissolved. The month after, the French were expelled from Holland by a popular uprising. In December, the allies signed up to the Declaration of Frankfurt, by which they agreed to invade France as Napoleon's response to peace approaches had been very vague. It now appeared that the war was nearing a final, climactic stage.

In 1814, the allies signed the Treaty of Chaumont, by which they agreed not to negotiate a separate peace with Napoleon. By the close of March, allied forces had entered Paris and under the terms of the Treaty of Fontainebleau Napoleon unconditionally abdicated and was exiled to Elba. Louis XVIII became king in his place. By the Peace of Paris, signed on 30 May, the 1792 borders of France were re-established and she agreed to recognise the independence of the Netherlands and the Italian and German states. There was something of a colonial carve-up too, with the strategically important Cape of Good Hope becoming a British colony, having been previously Dutch.

Everything appeared to be returning to normal. Following the burning of Washington in August, the Treaty of Ghent would bring a notional end to the war between the USA and Britain by the close of the year. In the meantime a European realignment took place at the Congress of Vienna. Russia handed over Saxony to Prussia, hoping to obtain Poland in exchange (the tragic story of that country, trapped between two potential great powers, continued).

Europe now looked to resolve other issues. A secret treaty in 1815 between Austria, Britain and France formed a defensive alliance to resolve Saxon and Polish problems. But Napoleon, as is well known, refused to go quietly, escaped from his island prison and returned to France in March. A new alliance was hastily formed between Austria, Britain, Prussia and Russia.

Even as Napoleon rebuilt his power base in France, on 9 June the Congress of Vienna was concluded. Holland, Belgium and Luxembourg were to be united to form the Netherlands, Switzerland was to be neutral, East Poland was ceded to Russia and the western provinces of Poland given to Prussia, Krakow becoming an independent territory. Lombardy and Venetia were restored to Austria while Prussia regained the Rhineland and the northern region of Saxony. Britain retained most of her overseas conquests including Heligoland and Malta. Countries were moved around like chess pieces on the map of Europe and beyond. What their respective peoples thought about it all appeared to be of little relevance.

But on 18 June, Napoleon's dreams were finally shattered at the Battle of Waterloo in Belgium. An allied army led by Wellington but composed of troops from the Low Countries as well as Britain and supported by a large Prussian army, stood firm in its hilltop position against everything the French could throw at them. The French attacks lessened in intensity and then failed altogether.

Four days later, Napoleon abdicated for the second and last time and was shipped off to the remote rock of St Helena, from which escape would be virtually impossible. Europe breathed a sigh of relief. The revolutionary genie unleashed in France had been tamed, hopefully for good. Such was the hope among the ruling classes, but it was not to be.

In fact, everywhere social tensions were growing. Already 'Luddites', unhappy at the impact that 'progress' had had on their lot, had destroyed machinery in Nottingham and Yorkshire. Political upheaval too continued across the globe. In 1811, a centuries-old regime was eliminated when Muhammad Ali massacred the Mamluks in Cairo.

In the Americas in particular, the world map was being redrawn. In 1813, Venezuela became a republic for a second time under the control of Bolívar, to be followed a few years later by Chile. Bolívar soon after became the President of Republic of Colombia, formed of Venezuela and New Grenada (approximately synonymous with modern Colombia). Spain, the nominal owner of these lands, had been distracted by revolution, seriously interfering with attempts to fight off the uprisings in her empire.

The Spanish Empire in South and Central America collapsed like a house of cards. By 1821, there were rumblings of Mexican independence from Spain. On 24 June of that year, Bolívar secured Venezuelan independence by defeating Spanish forces at Carabobo. Peru then declared independence, followed by Guatemala, who aligned herself with Mexico. Panama also declared herself free of Spanish rule and joined the Republic of Colombia. Over 300 years of colonial domination were coming to an end, though the legacy of Spanish culture and language would of course live on.

In the north of America, too, there were significant events taking place. New states continued to be added to the 'USA' – Indiana in 1816, Mississippi in 1817, Illinois in 1818, Alabama in 1819 and Florida was bought from Spain in 1819, although it would not become a state until 1845. But underlying tensions simmered away, storing up significant explosive power for the future.

In 1820 the 'Missouri compromise' was agreed, by which Missouri was allowed to enter the Union as a slave state but slavery was to be abolished in the remainder of the Louisiana territories. It solved the problem for now, but in the future the tensions would emerge once more with dramatic impact. Elsewhere moves to abolish slavery had been in train for some time in Britain, driven on by William Wilberforce and others, and Spain had also abandoned the institution in 1817.

These great changes were only a beginning and the slave trade would remain in place across the globe long afterwards; indeed, in some forms it still exists today in parts of the world. But they were important beginnings, though they did not go well with the continuing drive for European colonisation.

Europe was still far from united and there were many upheavals in the political landscape looming. The Ottoman Empire for one thing was beginning to fracture and in 1817 the Sultan of Turkey conceded partial independence to Serbia. Revolts against Ottoman rule followed in Wallachia and Moldavia (part of modern Romania) in 1821. There was a bloody uprising in Greece, too, when many Turks were slain in the Morea, and the Turks retaliated with a reign of terror. The Patriarch of Constantinople lost his life as part of the retribution taken. The tensions between Greece and Turkey did not end with these events but festered on, erupting again spectacularly in the twentieth century, and they are still present even in the twenty-first.

In 1822, Greece declared its independence. The Turks, in response, captured the island of Chios and massacred many inhabitants in an act which is still seared into Greek memory. They then invaded mainland Greece but after initial successes were forced to retreat. The Turks, no longer strong enough to win their battles unaided, were forced to ask for help from Egypt, as a result of which Crete was retaken and then the Morea invaded by their joint forces.

In the wider world, those with imperial power continued to grow stronger, as much by trade and treaty at this stage as by conquest, though the results were still often far from positive for the indigenous inhabitants involved. In 1819, the East India Company through Stamford Raffles established a settlement at Singapore from which British mercantile influence could strengthen. Two years later, British West Africa was formed when the British government took over Sierra Leone, Gambia and the Gold Coast. In 1824, Russia and the US defined their respective rights in the Pacific and North America as they continued with their own colonial expansion.

Of course, colonists tried to recreate parts of their own familiar world while exploiting the benefits of the new one that they had moved into. Even today, dotted among the urban sprawl of African cities, relics of empire hint at a past now gone. The small and pretty cathedral in Freetown, Sierra Leone, would not – apart perhaps from its red-brick building materials – look out of place as an English parish church. Inside there are those memorials so familiar around Britain, commemorating family members who have died. There are clues of something different, however, when you look closely; the number of people who died young, the frequent references to fever and pestilence. Many colonists paid the ultimate price for their ambition. Occasionally one memorial stands out more than others, in particular (to this writer) that to ships' carpenter W. Bartlet, who died on board HMS *Rattlesnake* and was buried at sea.

While in many regions empires were growing, in South America affairs had gone the other way. In 1822, Brazil declared herself independent of Portugal. That same year, Liberia was founded as a colony for freed American slaves. Known as the Pepper Coast, the small West African country was the destination for a number of people whose move back across the Atlantic was inspired by several prominent politicians, such as Henry Clay and James Monroe. Monroe, the fifth President of the USA, would be well known for his Doctrine, which stated that no further European intervention would be tolerated in the affairs of his young nation.

The freedom of the South American nations did not bring an end to dissent in the region, though, as the newly freed nation states started to fight each other instead of the Spanish. In 1825 Bolivia became independent of Peru, and soon after Uruguay became independent of Brazil. Brazil then declared war on Argentina over Uruguay.

But it was also a time of both literary interest and scientific advancement. This was the period in which the Gothic came into its own, with Mary Shelley producing the epic *Frankenstein* in 1818, while in the previous year Sir Walter Scott published *Rob Roy*, somewhat less supernatural in spirit. In 1823, Charles Babbage began the construction of a calculating machine and Charles Macintosh invented waterproof fabric. William Webb Ellis created a new sport when he famously picked up a football at his school in Rugby and ran with it.

In 1825, the Stockton & Darlington Railway was opened, an example of a young and developing mode of transport that would, within a few decades, spread across the globe and make the world a much smaller place than it had ever been before. Scientific development and colonisation would go side by side as a small island off the coast of Europe continued its inexorable drive towards becoming an international force. The world was on the verge of radical and irreversible change.

36

THE CONCEPTION OF MODERN EUROPE

The Age of Evolving Nationalism (AD 1826–1850)

With the end of the Napoleonic Wars, it appeared that the great powers of Europe had restored the status quo. The French monarchy had been reinstalled and the might of other leading European states had been re-established. Austria and Russia, it seemed, were confirmed in their status, and Prussia was powerful in its own region.

Little appeared to have changed; Europe was still dominated by a few great powers. But it was a mirage. If the eighteenth century was one of industrial and technical development in Europe, the nineteenth was much more one of political change. It was true that these trends had started in the previous century, and they had come to fruition in the United States of America and, for a time at least, in France, although the French experiment with republicanism was over – or so it appeared. But Europe in 1850 would look very different than it would in 1825.

Russia, for one, was flexing its muscles and expanding further to become an international player. The Russian Empire had long sought access to reliable open-water ports and many of the policies adopted by her political opponents during the nineteenth century were based on stopping her achieving this aim. The northern ports of Russia were often icebound during the winter months and her only chance of accessing the high seas anywhere else during these periods was either through the Black Sea and the narrow straits dominated by Constantinople or, if the weather was more clement in the east, from Vladivostok, which was thousands of miles away from the centre of European action.

This made the position of Turkey, which was increasingly weakening, of paramount importance. Constantinople was pivotal to preventing Russian access to the Mediterranean. On the other hand, Russia had cultural connections with a number of the Balkan peoples and saw herself as the protector of their rights. There was an affinity of language and religion, a shared Orthodox faith and the chance of claiming that protecting the Balkans was also a means of protecting Christendom from Islamic exploitation. Such geopolitical considerations continue to impact on Russian international policy in the twenty-first century.

Russia adopted an increasingly aggressive stance on several fronts. In 1826, she issued an ultimatum to Turkey over the Serbian and Danubian provinces held by the

Ottomans. This was settled by the Akkerman Convention on 7 October, largely in favour of Russia. She was sensitive to threats in other areas, too, declaring war on Persia after the latter encroached into Transcaucasia. The narrow land bridge between Asia and Europe, the region where countries like Georgia, Armenia and Azerbaijan now sit, was always a source of tension and remains so. Russia and Georgia came to blows at the beginning of the twenty-first century, while just to the north the region of Chechnya remains a knife pointed towards the ribs of Russia.

The situation in South America was still continuing to evolve. The young independent states continued to push each other for room, to define what were still liquid boundaries and form alliances for mutual advantage as a new political reality developed. In 1826, a Pan-American Congress met in Panama and, under the influence of Simón Bolívar, made a vain attempt to unite the American republics.

The failure to agree was in fact a prelude to something much more serious. A year later, Peru broke away from Colombia in protest at the alleged dictatorship of Bolívar. On 20 February 1827, Brazilian forces were defeated at the Battle of Ituzaingó by the combined forces of Argentina and Uruguay. After centuries of colonial domination from Europe, the South American states now had a new enemy – each other. In 1828, Uruguay formally declared herself independent. Two years later, Simón Bolívar abdicated as the President of Colombia while a new republic, named Ecuador, was formed.

Developments during these years were not just military in nature though. An 1826 treaty of commerce between Prussia and Mecklenburg-Schwerin developed the idea of the Zollverein, a customs union, which would come to fruition within a few years. There were still a number of small German states in existence and these events were the precursor of ever closer relationships, leading towards unification in a larger German entity in which inevitably Prussia would be a major player.

The year 1827 saw another first, a small invention that still continues to play a regular if understated role in the twenty-first century: the introduction of a friction match, the 'lucifer'. It no doubt made a big difference to everyday life, but on the political stage much greater events were taking place. In south-east Europe, Greece was making a bid for freedom from Turkish domination. The Turks, of course, were not willing to accept this and on 25 June captured the Acropolis and entered Athens.

The great powers of Europe, however, decided that this situation was not acceptable. On 6 July the Treaty of London was agreed, by which Russia, Britain and France decided to recognise Greek autonomy and force a truce on the sultan. These moves were understandably rejected by the sultan but the combined Turkish and Egyptian fleets were destroyed at the Battle of Navarino on 20 October. However, this did not bring an immediate stop to the conflict, although it did have a significance of another kind – it was the last major sea battle fought entirely by sailing ships.

Ten years later, perhaps the greatest British artist, Joseph Mallord Turner, would paint his masterpiece, the *Fighting Téméraire*. It shows a sailing ship being towed to the breakers' yard by a steamship while behind it the sun sets. It was a poignant and evocative portrayal of the demise of the age of sail, foretold by the great battle in the Ionian Sea.

The war would continue for several years. Russia continued to chase after more territory. The year 1828 saw the Treaty of Turkmenchay, in which Persia ceded part of Armenia to Russia, further strengthening the latter's hold on the Caucasian land bridge. Later that year, Mehmet Ali formally agreed to British demands to leave Greece. But in the meantime the Russians continued their advance into Europe, on 11 October occupying the crucial Bulgarian seaport of Vàrna.

The 1829 Treaty of Adrianople (this was indeed an age of treaties) brought a formal end to the war between Russia and Turkey. Sultan Mahmud II guaranteed the territory of Greece and the independence of the Danubian territories and Serbia. Tsar Nicholas I also obtained land south of the Caucasus. The year after, a conference in London confirmed the independence of Greece under the protection of France, Russia and Britain.

But, again, other hugely important developments were taking place away from the political arena. In 1829, one of the most famous railway locomotives in history, George and Robert Stephenson's *Rocket* (co-designer Henry Booth's important inputs are, rather unfairly, usually forgotten) won the Liverpool & Manchester Railway competition.

The significance of this revolutionary transport development cannot be understated. It would open up huge areas that were previously only accessible with enormous difficulty, particularly in the United States, in the near future. The same year that the Stephensons won their competition, the first steam locomotive ran in the United States between Baltimore and Ohio. On the sporting front, a great British tradition started with the first Oxford and Cambridge boat race (though it would not become an annual event until 1856).

However, there were clear signs that nationalist tendencies were rising in Europe that threatened the status quo. In 1830, even as French troops began an invasion of Algeria, taking Algiers and establishing a colonial presence that would come to dominate this part of North Africa into the twentieth century, the political map was being redrawn.

France had her own problems. The July Revolution of 1830 led to the abdication of Charles X and his replacement by Louis Philippe. When Charles attempted to pass new legislation that was seen by liberals to be dictatorial, there was a three-day uprising in Paris, which led to the demise of Charles and the establishment of a more constitutional monarchy in his place. But it would not be the end of the matter; republican tendencies in the country were, as it turned out, far from crushed.

This led to another significant event to the north of France. There was soon after a rebellion in Belgium against enforced union with the Dutch. The Belgian congress voted for a monarchy and on 20 December another London conference, where representatives of Britain, France, Austria, Prussia and Russia met, agreed with Belgium on separation from Holland. Attempts by Dutch troops to resist these moves were quickly brought to a halt when French forces moved in to resist them. Nearly two centuries on, the position of Belgium, and its very future, still rests in the balance, with strong divisions evident between French and Flemish elements in the country.

In other places, too, the desire for more independence was evident. In 1831 the Polish Diet declared the country's independence and deposed the ruling Russian dynasty there. Austrian troops were forced to enter Italy to put down revolts. These moves were short-lived. On 26 May, Polish forces were defeated by the Russians at Ostrołęka. The year after, a new Polish Constitution was established and Tsar Nicholas I imposed a new government on Poland; there was provision within the Constitution for partial autonomy within this, but it meant little in practice.

These moves resonated across Europe. In 1832, a new country was born when the Greek National Assembly elected Prince Otto of Bavaria King Otto I – there would be several other instances during the nineteenth century (Romania was another example a few decades later) when a German princeling would be elected as the first king of a new country in Eastern Europe.

In 1831, Giuseppe Mazzini founded the 'Young Italy' movement, an important step towards the unification of what had been disunited interests on the peninsula. Even in conservative Britain, change was in the air. There were riots in Bristol in 1831 when a Reform Bill was thrown out in Parliament. It finally passed the Commons the following year and later became law. Outdated 'Rotten Boroughs', which had just a handful of voters, all in the pocket of the Member of Parliament, were thrown out and the franchise was extended, though it was still far from universal.

Everywhere, the world was on the cusp of change. This was not just in the field of politics. In 1831, a small sloop, the *Beagle*, set sail from England bound for South America on a voyage of scientific exploration. On board was a young naturalist by the name of Charles Darwin, who would be amazed by what he observed, although he would not unleash his revolutionary findings on the world for nearly thirty years. In the next year the railway reached mainland Europe, with the first line running between Budweis (now in the Czech Republic) and Linz (now in Austria). Further developments saw the first railway in Canada opened in 1836, the same year in which the first train ran in London.

But the world was still, in population terms, a much smaller place than it is now. In 1831, the population of Great Britain was 12.2 million (2013 figure approximately 63 million) and the United States 12.8 million (now over 300 million). Even though these figures are not in every detail directly comparable (for example, the United States did not then encompass the same land area that it does now), the figures are indicative of how in some areas population growth has been enormous while in others, such as Ireland, the impact of net emigration has been hugely significant.

The Ottoman Empire, in the meantime, continued on its road towards a lingering and painful demise. It was not just the European powers that sought to make the most of this situation. In Egypt, the khedive, Muhammad Ali, came to blows with the Turks after demanding Syria as his price for aid in the war against Greece. On 21 December 1832, at the Battle of Konya, Egyptian forces routed the Turkish army.

In the complicated realpolitik that epitomised the nineteenth century, on 20 February 1833, Russian ships entered the Bosporus as they moved to aid Turkey against Egypt. No one else could be allowed to benefit from the demise of the ageing power to the east, at least not in the European sphere. Nevertheless, Turkey was obliged to recognise the independence of Egypt and also ceded Syria and Aden to Muhammad Ali.

But on 8 July, the Treaty of Hünkâr İskelesi established a defensive alliance between Turkey and Russia and closed the Dardanelles to all except Russian warships – a major breakthrough for Russian foreign policy. Later, on 15 October in Berlin, Prussia, Russia and Austria agreed to support the integrity of the shrinking Ottoman Empire. Britain and France were noticeably absent from the agreement.

Social changes continued to mark the period. In 1834, the year that the Houses of Parliament in London were destroyed in a disastrous fire, leading to the construction of the iconic building that we see now, a group of labourers who had agreed to form a co-operative union, the so-called 'Tolpuddle Martyrs', were sentenced to deportation to Australia for making an illegal oath.

There was widespread outrage as a result – 800,000 signatures were appended to a petition for their release – and their sentences were cut short and they returned home, though most of them then moved on to Canada, where they lived out their lives. The over-reaction to their actions that led to their conviction was especially contradictory as, in the same year that they were sentenced, slavery was abolished in the British Empire. Events elsewhere in 1834 saw Michael Faraday discovering electrical self-induction.

While this was happening in Europe, in the United States an epochal event was about to occur. Texas was still a part of Mexico, but moves for independence were gaining momentum. On 2 March 1836, formal independence was declared. In response to the upheavals, Mexico had sent a large army into Texas to bring the rebels back into line. They were soon laying siege to a mission station at San Antonio named the Alamo.

The Battle of the Alamo ended with the Mexicans in control of the mission station and only two of the 'Texian' defenders left alive. But the cruelty of the Mexican commander, Santa Anna, only served to fuel resistance. Within weeks of the defeat at the Alamo, a Texan victory at San Jacinto helped ensure their independence.

The Alamo, of course, soon entered into Texas legend. Names of men like Davy Crockett, William Travis and Jim Bowie became part of a heroic pantheon. Alamo became a nineteenth-century Thermopylae, a sacrificial defeat against perceived overwhelming odds (about ten to one) that served as a symbol to inspire the resistance of others.

Africa was also starting to open up more to European expansion and in some areas this was to lead to clashes, the scars of which are still unhealed. Disenchanted with the abolition of slavery, the farmers of Dutch origin in South Africa, the Boers, attempted to escape from the constraints of British rule and set out on what became known as 'the Great Trek', a journey into the hinterland of the region. In 1837, they founded a new state in Natal, on the borders of the great regional power, the Zulus.

The Zulus had emerged from being a minor tribe to a major force in the space of just a few decades. One of Africa's great heroes, Shaka, was largely responsible for this transformation. A superb military organiser and a fierce and inspirational warrior, Shaka was also a cruel leader who killed thousands on a whim. But he transformed military tactics and built up a great regional empire. If there had been no Shaka, it is probable that none save the most expert anthropologist would know much about the Zulus today.

The reality was that the region was already becoming overcrowded even before Europeans arrived. In a dreadful event called the *mfecane* – 'the crushing' – a brutal land war between tribes left tens of thousands dead of wounds or starvation and millions on the move, effectively homeless. The Europeans and Zulus (Shaka had died a few years before) soon came to blows and the Boer leaders were massacred, followed by widespread killings among the isolated settler communities that had been established.

Some tenaciously held on, though, and were soon after reinforced by other settlers intent on revenge. In 1838, a small Boer army was attacked by a much larger Zulu force when it was encamped on the River Ncome. Despite overwhelming odds against them, what followed was little short of slaughter as the Boers, equipped with firearms and dug in inside their wagon 'laager', decimated the tightly packed Zulus, armed with spears, that tried in vain to break in.

What became known as the Battle of Blood River became an iconic part of Boer legend, from which it passed into the annals of the Afrikaners who for years formed a dominant part in the folklore of the South African ruling establishment. To them, 16 December, the anniversary of the battle, became the Day of the Vow, when they – as they saw it – were rewarded by God for the covenant they had made with him. Since 1994, when majority rule at last appeared in South Africa, it has remained a public holiday although now it is called the Day of Reconciliation.

The Zulu power was not yet broken – it would require a British army with a made-up excuse for war to do that some forty years later – but this marked a turning point. For the Boers too it formed part of a process by which they sought to expand their lands and move them further away from the controlling clutches of British overlords. But on another level it was a defining moment that marked the supremacy of modern weaponry over poorly armed 'savage' tribes, as they were perceived, and highlighted the fact that Africa was there for the taking for those unscrupulous enough to try.

While Africa would, over the course of the century, increasingly attract the interest of Europe – until, at its close, hardly a foot of it was not, nominally at least, in European hands – focus was about to switch for a time to Asia. The jewel in Britain's crown was India, and anything that threatened her security there was dealt with decisively.

The greatest threats to these interests were seen to come from the direction of Russia. Any attempts on her part to intervene in the affairs of Afghanistan in particular were seen as a move down the road towards India itself. When, in 1838, Persian troops (supported by their Russian allies) attacked Herat in the west of Afghanistan, the British decided to intervene.

What was effectively a British invasion force set out from Punjab in December of that year. The Afghans, not feeling the need for rescue or perhaps, more pertinently, nervous at the price they would have to pay in return, resisted. However, initial attempts to rebuff the British failed miserably and the key cities of Kandahar and Ghazni fell before Kabul itself was taken. The British moved in, confident that they had finished the business and that Afghanistan would meekly accept this turn of events as a *fait-accompli*. They were wrong.

An uprising in Kabul in November 1841 left a number of key British officials dead. Those that were left did nothing in response, which merely increased the momentum towards full-scale rebellion against British rule. More murders followed and the British commander, William Elphinstone, agreed to withdraw his men and their thousands of camp followers from Kabul.

A retreat followed that turned into perhaps the worst reverse ever suffered by the British Army. Afghanistan then – as now – was not a coherent country in the modern sense of the word but a patchwork of dozens of tribal areas, where central rule counted for little. Even if the nominal Afghan government in Kabul meant for the agreed truce to stick, they had no way of enforcing this across the country.

A nightmare then followed for the composite column that retreated from Kabul. There were 4,500 soldiers and perhaps 12,000 camp followers. They were attacked incessantly as they trudged slowly along, and to make matters worse this was now the heart of the Afghan winter and they were short of supplies. Their numbers were decimated and, in the end, of the British contingent among this large column, just one man made it back to safety. Apart from a handful of prisoners who were later released, the British with the party were virtually wiped out.

Of course, a defeat of this magnitude could not go unavenged and another force set out later in 1842, fighting its way through to Kabul. A hopefully compliant emir was established who would be faced with all the same problems of retaining some degree of centralised control in the country that every man before or since has had to deal with in Afghanistan. The British wisely withdrew, having learned a bloody lesson, though it was one they would forget over time. As for the original objective of keeping back the Russians, it failed miserably. Russia continued to push forward, over the next three decades taking Samarkand, Tashkent and Bukhara, though a warm-water sea port remained stubbornly elusive.

In 1839 (the year in which Charles Goodyear vulcanised rubber and a horse race called the Grand National was run for the first time at Aintree, Liverpool), Britain was involved in another overseas adventure. This involved war with China. The Canton System of 1756 restricted access to the country to one port. This did not, however, stop the British completely and the East India Company, faced with tight restrictions to trade, bypassed the barriers to entry by engaging in smuggling, with one item in particular in demand – opium (America traders were involved in the business too).

When the Ch'ing emperor Tao-kuang ordered that the trading be brought to a halt, the British Navy intervened. They ravaged the coastline with impunity and dictated the terms of the agreement, the Treaty of Nanking, which brought the conflict to an end in 1842. As part of the terms of this, Britain was given a territory known as Hong Kong. It was not the end of the matter, as another war would break out just over a decade later.

But it did eventually open up China to trade, as well as mark the start of what would be known as her 'Century of Humiliation'.

In the meantime, ongoing instability in the Ottoman Empire threatened to upset the delicate balance of power in Europe, a situation exacerbated by the death in 1839 of Sultan Mahmud II and his replacement by a young boy, Abdul Mejid. Near neighbours took advantage of the further weakening of the situation and a Turkish fleet surrendered voluntarily at Alexandria to Muhammad Ali.

Matters were coming to a head and the power brokers of Europe decided that the 'Sick Man', as Turkey was known, could not be allowed to die. So in 1840 – the same year that the Treaty of Waitangi, by which Maori chiefs surrendered their sovereignty to the British, was agreed, a man named Adolphe Sax was developing a musical instrument that would be named after him and when Queen Victoria married a minor German prince, Albert – Russia, Britain, Prussia and Austria formed a Quadruple Alliance in support of Turkey.

Muhammad Ali was offered Egypt as a hereditary possession and southern Syria for life in order to stop his pretensions regarding Turkish-held lands, though for the time being he dissimulated. In order to convince him, on 11 September a British fleet bombarded Beirut to force him to co-operate. Acre was also attacked and captured soon after, and by the Convention of Alexandria Muhammad Ali at last agreed to the terms of the Treaty of London.

The year after, France joined the Quadruple Alliance and it was agreed that the Dardanelles would be closed to warships of all nations during peace time – something that was much more of a problem to Russia than to anyone else. Russia remained unhappy at the situation. In 1844, Tsar Nicholas I visited London and proposed the partition of the Ottoman Empire. He got nowhere with the suggestion. Russian ambition in Turkey remained undiminished and Europe, though she did not yet know it, was well down the road towards her only major continental conflict between 1815 and 1914.

Although these conflicts and tensions undoubtedly created a climate of uncertainty, these were also times of exploration. In 1841, James Ross discovered the great Southern Continent. He found out that Antarctica was not merely a mass of ice but a land and he sailed along the coast, charting much of it.

Although he is less remembered than he should be, parts of the continent, such as Mounts Erebus and Terror, which were named after his ships, bear witness to his achievement. While he was exploring the Antarctic regions, thousands of miles to the north a missionary called David Livingstone was starting his work in Africa, which would also lead to significant long-term results in bringing this part of the world, largely unknown and unexplored among Europeans, to the attention of the public, with very mixed repercussions.

In the arts, too, significant things were happening. In 1843, the British writer Charles Dickens, who would become famous for his gritty social works, wrote what is perhaps his best-remembered book, *A Christmas Carol*. Some fine composers were active in the music world too: Verdi, Mendelssohn, Berlioz and Wagner, for example. In that same year, there was an important development in the business world when a magazine called *The Economist* was first published.

In North America, the United States continued to consolidate. The 1842 Webster–Ashburton Treaty between the USA and Britain agreed the borders of Canada, something that was important given the wild and in some parts still unconquered frontier lands that stretched along the artificial boundaries between the two.

The young country was already showing signs of the inventiveness and ingenuity that would mark it as it rose to prominence, typified by events in 1844, when Samuel Morse sent the first message on the US telegraph line from Washington to Baltimore. Although telegrams now seem anachronistic, the invention of the device was revolutionary. This early and rudimentary form of electronic communication was an incredible breakthrough, allowing long-distance and virtually instantaneous interaction between people miles apart. The world would never be the same again.

Nor would the United States. Increasingly confident, her territories continued to expand. Texas was appended in 1845, with Iowa coming in in the following year. In the south, the US again came into conflict with Mexico, and as a result of the war that followed – in which the Americans entered Mexico City – New Mexico was added. In the north, the border between Oregon and Canada was fixed at the 49th parallel. In other ways too the US was solidifying its identity, as when the Knickerbocker Club codified the rules of baseball in 1845. And she had ambitions further afield too, as demonstrated when in 1846 Commodore James Biddle of US visited Edo Bay in Japan, though he was refused facilities to trade there.

But the existing country was not big enough for everyone, as shown when the group known as the Mormons chose to trek west and into what were then lands that were not part of the United States. A trek inspired by altogether different motives took place in 1848 when gold was discovered in California, leading to the first gold rush. California was not then part of the Union but would become so in 1850 as a free state.

In the far north of America, most territory was still uncharted. The possibility that there might be an as yet undiscovered shipping route leading from the Atlantic to the Pacific had long tempted intrepid explorers. In 1845, the British naval officer John Franklin set out on an expedition to discover it. It ended in tragedy two years later with his ships ice bound and the crew slowly dying of hypothermia and starvation (and possibly lead poisoning).

Inuit hunters who came into contact with a party that a few years later journeyed to the region to discover what had happened told terrible tales of cannibalism. Forensic examination in 1997 of the bones of some of those who died showed cut marks on them, suggesting that these awful stories were most likely true.

But such was the price of adventurism, and elsewhere British efforts to explore and to conquer continued. In 1843, Natal was formally annexed to the British Empire and so was Sind (which is now part of Pakistan). Hostilities broke out between the Sikhs and the British in 1845, but were ended by the Treaty of Lahore the year after, which saw more territory added to the mushrooming empire.

Other European powers were also involved in imperialist adventures. The French were forced to put down revolts in Algeria in 1846, suffering heavy losses in the process, a precursor of events 100 years later. Within Europe itself, Austrian and Russian troops occupied Kraków after a Polish revolt there, poor Poland again suffering oppression due to her exposed position between several European great powers.

However, the ruling classes in Europe were about to experience an unnerving wake-up call. There had been signs of social upheaval for a while. Even supposedly stable Britain was not immune, with Chartist protests in Britain in 1842. The continent was then hit by natural disaster and economic hardship. The potato crop in Ireland failed in 1845 and for years thereafter. This was the staple diet for most of the masses, and as a result of the disaster perhaps 1 million people died and another 1 million emigrated. The British government did little to alleviate the suffering, and unscrupulous landlords added to the problems by evicting tenants from farms. It was perhaps the blackest chapter in Irish history, no small claim given the trauma that has often affected that beautiful but sadly treated island.

Exploitation and hardship were not limited to Britain and Ireland, though; in 1846, for example, there was a widespread agricultural and industrial depression in France. This set the scene for a truly momentous year – 1848. Not the least of the events that took place then was the publication by two men, Karl Marx and Friedrich Engels, of their *Communist Manifesto*.

The timing was perfect as there was a great deal of resentment against the ruling classes in many parts of Europe. On 15 May, a communist rising started in Paris. By the end of the year, there was a Republican Constitution promulgated in France, with a strong President, a single chamber and direct election with universal suffrage. It did not help the cause, however, that Louis Napoleon, a member of the Bonapartist dynasty, was elected President of France by a massive majority, for he would soon seek to restore the Napoleonic imperial dynasty.

But this was just one example of the upheavals that affected Europe in 1848. Italy, still a patchwork of small states, was in flames. In January, there was a revolt in Palermo, Sicily, against the corruption of the ruling Bourbon dynasty. A new constitution was declared in Piedmont and Sardinia. Revolution broke out in Venice, leading to the declaration of a republic. Much of the peninsula was under the control of Austria (though France had significant influence there too) and Sardinia declared war on her. There were uprisings in Milan and Parma, and a popular insurrection took place in Rome.

The uprisings spread. There was revolution in Vienna and then in Berlin. The emperor, Ferdinand I, fled from Vienna to Innsbruck (he later abdicated). A Czech revolt in Prague was put down by the Austrians. Everywhere Europe seemed to be falling apart, this time because of internal class struggles rather than religious divisions or motives of territorial expansion.

The most remarkable aspect of 1848 superficially is how little the revolutions achieved in the short term. Some states took advantage of the general chaos to take their own agendas forward. Prussia, a growing military power, invaded Denmark over the future of the borderlands of Schleswig-Holstein. The Russians invaded the Danubian Principalities at the request of the Turks; the other great powers of Europe had too many distractions to intervene.

If 1848 was a high-water mark for revolution, 1849 was a low point. Revolts in Dresden were suppressed by the Prussians and communist uprisings in Paris were easily put down. The French, wishing to protect their interests in Italy, entered Rome, despite heroic resistance led by a freedom fighter named Giuseppe Garibaldi. Louis Napoleon showed his true stamp when in 1850 universal suffrage in France was abolished and liberty of the press was restricted. The new president clearly wished to turn the clock back and for a time appeared to succeed in doing so. However, too much had changed and the great upheavals that had erupted in Europe had only temporarily died down.

But, for now, all appeared to return to normal. The British defeated the Sikhs at Chillianwala in 1849, although many British troops were lost in what was a gruelling battle. That same year, Britain annexed Punjab by means of a treaty with the Maharajah of Lahore. But there was also rebellion further afield. The year 1849 saw a rebellion in Montreal against British rule and the issuing of the *October Manifesto* by Canadians in support of union with the US. The year after, the Taiping Rebellion in China, led by Hung Hsiu-ch'üan, took Nanking and Shanghai; he proclaimed himself emperor and attacked Peking.

The world was indeed about to move into a new era – or at least parts of it were. The introduction in 1846 of a standard gauge in Britain had led to a rapid development of the railways. By 1850, there were 9,015 miles of rail in the United States and 6,635 miles in Britain, a remarkable achievement in the railway's short life. Improved transportation would continue to shrink the world and open up a whole range of new possibilities but, as this was happening, there was little sign that the world would become a more tranquil place to live in.

37

THE SICK MAN OF EUROPE

The Demise of the Ottoman Empire (AD 1851–1875)

As the second half of the nineteenth century began, in some ways it was like a return to the first. On 2 December 1851, Louis Napoleon launched a coup d'état in France. A plebiscite later in the month supported a new constitution to be drawn up by him. When it was presented in the following year, France became an empire once again. Unsurprisingly, fired by thoughts of emulating his illustrious Bonapartist ancestor, he dreamed of a revived and renewed France and for a time it seemed that some semblance of glory could be restored. However, he did not have the great Napoleon's talents and his reign would end up in disappointment for himself and rejection by his country.

Although the world was growing, it was still much smaller in terms of population than the one in which we now live. The Chinese population in 1851 measured approximately 430 million, that of Great Britain 21 million and that of the United States 23 million. It is noticeable that China was massive even in those days in terms of its population, but in proportional terms the United States has grown massively more in the succeeding 150 years.

The United States was still expanding in territorial terms, partly through its union with states that had previously been independent and partly through westward expansion and increasing annexation of Native American territories. The country's eyes would soon be directed far further west, way across the Pacific, towards the as yet unopened trading opportunities presented by Japan.

They were not alone in their expansionist ambitions either. It is all too easy to be lured by the increasing size of the British Empire, along with other European powers such as France, and forget that Russia was also a great imperialist power and that the modern state that we see is as much a result of colonisation and annexation as the situation in Africa was until the move towards widespread independence in the second half of the twentieth century. In 1852, Russian expansion on the Pacific Coast continued with the addition of territory at the mouth of the River Amur.

Russian expansionism looked west as well as east. In the following year, Prince Alexander Menshikov, the Russian emissary to Turkey, claimed that Russia was the protector of all Christian subjects in the Ottoman Empire. With millions of Christian subjects under Turkish rule, this was a significant assertion and many in Western Europe feared that this was just an excuse to strengthen Russian interests in the area. The Turks rejected a Russian ultimatum in support of these claims and Menshikov left Turkey in preparation for war. On 2 July 1853, the Russians crossed the River Pruth and invaded the Danubian Provinces, part of the Ottoman Empire. Negotiations followed, with the issue of the so-called Vienna Note, but these were not successful and in October Turkey declared war on Russia.

France and Britain were not prepared to see the Ottoman Empire devoured by the Russians, though this stance was based on self-interest and not altruism, and on 3 January 1854, the British ambassador in Constantinople, Stafford Canning, received an order that the British fleet was to sail into the Black Sea, an instruction that was duly carried out. As the sea was seen by the Russians as their own 'lake', this was a provocative act. In March, the French and British declared war on Russia.

A not unimportant issue in the events leading up to the war was that of who should protect the rights of Christians in the Holy Land. The Russians saw this as their role, but the French felt that this duty belonged to them. Extraordinary as it might have seemed 700 years after the end of the Crusades to 'Outremer', the great powers of the world were still arguing over who should have control of the holy places of Christendom in the region.

An expeditionary force of French and British troops, supported by soldiers from Sardinia, set out for the Crimean Peninsula. It would be a hard-fought campaign and in military terms it seems almost to be a crossover point from Napoleonic to modern fighting. The Russians had the advantage of short lines of supply and large numbers of men, 'cannon fodder' that could be thrown into the attack with little regard for loss of life. The assault of the French and British was supported by a large fleet.

But the tactics of the allies were inept. Both the French and British troops were poorly led, though the foot soldiers fought with remarkable fortitude at the Battles of the Alma, Balaclava and Inkermann. The war was remembered as much as anything for the disastrous 'Charge of the Light Brigade' and the appalling conditions in which the British, in particular, lived. Medical conditions were basic and led to the famous efforts of Florence Nightingale (though it should be said that those enjoyed by French soldiers were already far superior).

It also saw the real birth of the modern war correspondent, with reports sent back from the front by William Howard Russell of *The Times*, whose despatches made a great impact on the general public. The crux of the campaign (which in some respects need never have started as the majority of the occupied Danubian territories had been evacuated by the Russians before the outbreak of hostilities) was the port of Sevastopol, which could have been taken early on but due to blundering by those supposedly in charge was not, leading to an extended siege and a great deal of unnecessary loss of life.

Sevastopol would fall in 1855 and the war would end the year after. As well as fighting in the Crimea, there was also conflict in the Caucasus region and the Baltic. The British Army in particular did not come out of it well and the most significant long-term effect of the war was the introduction of a new award for gallantry, the Victoria Cross, by the queen. Tsar Nicholas I, who in his ambition had done much to start the war with his heavy-handed political tactics, died a broken man while the war was in progress.

The war ended with Russian ambitions defeated. The Black Sea was to be kept clear of the Russian fleet and the Western powers resolved to protect the integrity of the Ottoman Empire – a stance that would cause them significant moral difficulties within a few decades. The last survivor of the Crimean War would live on to the incredible age of 165 years old, only dying in 2004. Unfortunately, 'he' was not a human being but a tortoise named Timothy who had been a ship's mascot during the bombardment of Sevastopol and who was later discovered to be female.

The events of the Crimean War were significant but only delayed the eventual death of the Ottoman Empire. Perhaps more important in the longer term were other events in the Pacific. The United States was keen on expanding its trade opportunities and forced open the gates of Japan to international trade in 1854. In doing so, a Pandora's Box was opened, with awful long-term consequences.

A cult later developed around the emperor, Meiji. For centuries the emperor had been a largely insignificant figure, a mere totem while the real power was vested in nobles and samurai warriors. Now he became a figure of reverence, divine and incapable of making a wrong decision. A fierce Japanese national sentiment developed; the stories of the *kamikaze*, the divine intervention that destroyed the Mongols, were revived and the perception that Japan enjoyed the especial protection of the gods evolved.

A new religion, State Shinto, developed – a fusion of many other elements of Buddhism and Confucianism. It became irrevocably linked with the concept of nationhood and nationalism, of self-sacrifice in the service of the sacred islands and their emperor. While Western technologies were absorbed, Western ideals and perceptions were mocked and treated as objects of derision.

The navy was modernised, as was the army – not without resistance, as those who had been brought up on traditional values, especially the samurai, fought against the modernisation of Japan. They were doomed to fail, in the light not so much of the emperor, who still remained in practice a figurehead, but his advisers, who pulled the strings and exercised real power.

But Japan still faced problems, both of its past and its future. Resentment against those who had been traditional enemies of Japan, namely China and Korea, was stoked and a build-up towards aggressive action against them reached uncontrollable proportions long before the conflicts of the twentieth century.

Then there was the problem of the future: Japan's limited natural resources. It was not surprising that there was one Western ideal that the Japanese did aspire to emulate – colonialism. A representative said that 'we shall someday raise the power of Japan so that not only shall we control the natives of China and India as the English do today but we shall also possess in our hands the power to rebuke the English and rebuke Asia ourselves.'

The fact that this was said in 1882, six decades before Pearl Harbour (by when, admittedly, the Americans rather than the English posed the greatest challenge), shows how a long-burning fuse had been lit by the forced integration of Japan into the modern world.

But the United States had problems much closer to home to concern it. The states were divided, sometimes bitterly, over the vexed issue of the rights and wrongs of slavery. On 30 May 1854, the Missouri Compromise of 1820, which allowed Missouri to keep slavery while it was prohibited elsewhere in the former Louisiana territory, was repealed by the Kansas–Nebraska Act, which opened up new lands for expansion. A bloody civil war in the region followed that went on for four years. Conflict was not just limited to the battlefield; Congressman Preston Brooks of South Carolina beat Senator Charles Sumner with his cane in the Senate in a dispute over slavery.

This shows how deeply divisive the issue was, a festering sore which would not go away. On 3 March 1857 the largest slave auction in United States history, known as 'the Weeping Time', took place. Over a two-day period, 436 men, women, children, and infants were sold, all of whom were kept in stalls meant for horses at a racetrack in Savannah, Georgia, for weeks beforehand. And just three days later, in the case of *Dred Scott* vs *Sandford* the Supreme Court of the United States ruled that 'Blacks' were not citizens and that slaves could not sue for freedom, driving the country further towards the American Civil War (the ruling was not overturned until the passing of the Fourteenth Amendment in 1868).

Yet these were also times of exploration and discovery. In 1855, David Livingstone became the first European to see Victoria Falls. A year later, Christchurch in New Zealand was recognised as a city while prehuman remains were discovered in the Neanderthal Valley, Germany. In 1857, the first elevator was installed in Broadway, New York. Sheffield FC, the oldest association football team in the world, was formed.

Exploration could also take men up into the highest places, and in 1858 the first recorded ascent of the Eiger was made while, in a rather more tranquil field, the use of the 'Wedding March' by Felix Mendelssohn at the wedding of Queen Victoria's daughter (also Victoria) made it a popular piece of music that is still often played at weddings. This year also saw the invention of one of those items that still plays an understated part in modern life – the patenting by Hyman Lipman of a pencil with an eraser attached. And it witnessed the arrival of a new department store called Macy's in New York.

In 1856, the Second Opium War broke out when officials from the nominally ruling Ch'ing dynasty boarded a Hong Kong-registered ship, the *Arrow*. Already faced with the major stress of putting down the Taiping rebellion, the Ch'ing had little chance of winning any conflict with Western powers. Britain and France used force to resolve the issue and were supported by Russia and the United States. The final outcome of the war – which included the partial looting of Peking (Beijing) was the greater opening up of China to overseas trade, the legalisation of opium commerce and the paying of an indemnity to the victors. Further rebellions were to come, and again millions were to lose their lives in the upheavals that followed in China.

The British Empire was about to receive a nasty shock in 1857. For centuries the East India Company had acquired lands on a vast scale and had armies bigger than those of many countries. However the situation was looked at, they represented an occupying power against which Indian resentment grew. A dispute over the bullets issued to the

Indian soldiers ('sepoys'), over whether or not they were greased with the fat of cows and pigs, which would be offensive for different reasons to Hindu and Muslim alike, led to an outbreak of violence in Meerut.

The immediate reasons for the outbreak suggest just how insensitive colonial rule could be; more sensitive handling could easily have avoided the immediate problem, though it seems probable that other reasons for revolt may have taken the place of this particular issue. In any event, the British were caught completely off-balance at first. Delhi fell soon after, Lucknow was besieged and there was a massacre of civilians at Cawnpore. But by 20 September the British had recaptured Delhi, bringing to an end the Mughal Dynasty.

When the munity was finally put down in the following year, it was seen that it was no longer viable to retain all that territory in the hands of the East India Company, so they were transferred to the British Crown. The uprisings had been crushed with much brutality. Incensed by stories of atrocities, the vengeful British forces executed rebels by tying them up in front of cannon and blowing them apart and made the supposed perpetrators of the atrocities in Cawnpore lick up the blood of their victims before they were then put to death. Even Queen Victoria was shocked at the viciousness of British public opinion on the required response to the mutiny.

In the aftermath of the Crimean War, some reshaping was taking place in Europe. In 1859, Wallachia and Moldavia were united as Romania under Alexandru Ioan Cuza (Transylvania would not be added until after the First World War – although she had many citizens of Romanian descent, there were also a number with Hungarian blood in their veins, a situation that continues to create pressures in the twenty-first century). Italy too was being reshaped – in that same year the Battle of Palestro took place, the armies of Piedmont defeating Austria. This was followed soon after by the Battle of Magenta, with the armies of France and Piedmont getting the better of Austria.

This year also saw the publication of perhaps the most significant scientific work ever when Charles Darwin's *On the Origin of Species* was published. The controversy it caused with its suggestions on evolution are well known and still in some cases a source of debate. It was also a significant year for trade, with the first ground broken for the Suez Canal. A tightrope walker called Charles Blondin crossed the Niagara Falls; he performed this feat a number of times, including one time blindfolded and another pushing a wheelbarrow. In London, the chimes of Big Ben rang out for the first time.

Events were now gathering momentum in Italy. In 1860, Garibaldi led the 'Expedition of a Thousand', an army of volunteers, leading to the defeat of the Kingdom of the Two Sicilies and its incorporation into the Kingdom of Sardinia. This was an important part of the Italian unification process (the *Risorgimento*) along with the political efforts of Prime Minister Camillo of Cavour and King Victor Immanuel. Further successes in Sicily followed and the victorious armies crossed from the island to mainland Italy. Naples soon fell and was handed to Victor Immanuel. A new kingdom was in the process of being formed.

However, the focus of events was about to move across the Atlantic. In 1859 – the year that the state of Oregon was admitted to the United States, a gaunt-faced abolitionist named John Brown raided an armoury at Harpers Ferry. It was, in a military sense, a failure. Brown was captured and later hanged. But it added a further spark to the already slow-burning fuse.

Brown became a martyr for the cause. In the Civil War that was about to break out, the song immortalising his sacrifice was sung enthusiastically by troops from the abolitionist Northern states. By now, there were about 4 million slaves in the American South. On 6 November 1860, the United States had a new President, Abraham Lincoln, in the first ever Republican Party victory (the party had been formed in 1854 by a group of abolitionist politicians). A month after Lincoln's election, South Carolina became the first state to secede from the Union.

Early in 1861, the secessionist movement snowballed. By February, six states had effectively resigned from the Union. Jefferson Davies was elected the provisional president of what was known as the Confederacy. In March, Lincoln took up office in the North, after surviving an assassination attempt. Then, in April, Fort Sumter was fired on and taken by Southern forces. The American Civil War had begun.

Further states seceded from the Union and Lincoln called for 75,000 troops to meet the threat. The Southern army grew and a man called Robert E. Lee resigned his commission in the US army to take command of the army of Virginia. In response, in Britain the queen issued a statement of neutrality, which ensured that for the time being the rights of the Southern states to break away were recognised.

Richmond, Virginia, was made the capital of the Confederacy and in the first major battle of the war, Bull Run, the Southern states won a major victory. Later in the year a British ship, the *Trent*, was stopped by the Federal (Northern states) navy and two Confederate envoys en route to London were arrested by the North, leading to serious diplomatic tensions between the Union states and Britain.

The bitter struggle in the Civil War continued into 1862, with both sides enjoying some victories. However, in August the Confederacy won another crushing victory at the Second Battle of Bull Run, while this was also a notable year in naval history, with the first fight between two ironclads at the Battle of Hampton Roads. Other notable events in the USA in that year were the drawing up of plans for the first transcontinental railway and the introduction of a new body, the Internal Revenue Service, to collect tax.

In Europe, while these seismic events were taking place in the USA, an important development was the installation as Otto von Bismarck as the Prime Minister of Prussia. In a famous speech shortly after this event he declared that the union of the German states was an unavoidable necessity and that the time for speaking was over – the great questions of the time, he said, would be settled by 'iron and blood'.

On 1 January 1863 Lincoln issued his Emancipation Proclamation, which made the abolition of slavery in the Confederate states an official war aim (somewhat more mundanely, the famous American publication *Harper's Weekly* published the first drawing of the modern Santa Claus two days later). In the same month, the first section of the London Underground system was opened (the New York subway would start later the same year), while in February the famous dwarf General Tom Thumb was married and the first fire extinguisher was produced.

The American Civil War now increased in intensity. Terrible losses were occurring in the battles being fought as the full impact of modern weaponry started to make itself felt (it was no coincidence that during the war the famous Gatling Gun was invented by Richard Gatling, who thought, with tragic irony, that its massive firepower – 200 rounds per minute – would bring an end to the concept of war, which would now become too bloody to be considered).

At the Battle of Chancellorsville, for example, which saw a Confederate victory, there were 30,000 casualties, including the famous Confederate general 'Stonewall' Jackson, who was shot by his own side. Neither were civilians exempt from the carnage, as when Vicksburg was besieged by the Union army.

Each side enjoyed some advantage over the other. The Union had massively superior industrial resources and could also deploy more men. On the other hand, the Confederacy were fighting a defensive campaign and had great fighting spirit, so something of a deadlock ensued. In order to break it, the commanding general of the Confederate forces, Robert E. Lee, invaded the North and made a move which he hoped would end with his army marching into Washington.

The two sides met at Gettysburg, a massive battle fought between 1 and 3 July 1863. This was the biggest and bloodiest battle ever fought on American soil. At the end of it, there were over 50,000 casualties. The Southern invasion was rebuffed and the prospects of an imminent victory for either party dissipated. But with the superior resources of the North, the longer the war lasted, the greater the chances of a Union victory became.

Later that year, Lincoln attended the opening of the Gettysburg military cemetery and gave one of the most famous speeches in history: it was a short speech but one immortal phrase – 'Government of the people by the people for the people shall not perish from the earth' – is as good a rallying call for democracy as there is ever likely to be (though some have noted the resemblance to Pericles' Funeral Speech, as described by Thucydides over 2,000 years earlier).

However, these bold words did not convince everyone – there were riots against conscription in New York shortly afterwards, for example – and the divisions exposed by the war would continue long after the last shot was fired and to some extent remain to this day. In October, Lincoln instituted a great American institution with the celebration of the first Thanksgiving Day on the last Thursday in November (though some argue that such feasts date back several centuries before that).

This was an important year in other ways, too. A young French novelist called Jules Verne published his first work, *Five Weeks in a Balloon*, the Football Association was formed, the first ever *Prix de l'Arc de Triomphe* horse race was held in Paris and a young Dutchman by the name of Gerard Adriaan Heineken purchased a brewery in Amsterdam.

As well as the ongoing hostilities in North America, 1864 saw another outbreak of fighting between Denmark and Prussia over Schleswig-Holstein. In the American Civil War, the appointment of Ulysses S. Grant as commander of the Northern forces led to increasingly aggressive moves into the Southern states and by the end of the year the fighting had moved as far south as Atlanta, Georgia, and on into Alabama.

This year also saw bitter fighting between Russians and Circassians in the Northwest Caucasus region. Some commentators see the massacres that took place as the precursor of modern genocides. The war saw the mass deportation of ethnic groups who had pushed into the region in previous centuries. In those very different times, the Russian government did not try to hide the scale of the forced expulsions, proudly proclaiming that 90 per cent of the targeted peoples had been forced out.

The figures involved in these deportations are hard to ascertain, though estimates that as many as 1.5 million Circassians were killed or deported have been produced. Many of those exiled ended up in Turkey, though some were later allowed to resettle in their country of origin. Suffice to say that in 2011 the Parliament of Georgia issued a resolution declaring that these events should be declared a genocide. Even today, the Caucasus region remains a global flashpoint that could erupt at any moment.

The American Civil War ended in 1865, with the Southern forces fought to a standstill. Robert E. Lee surrendered to Ulysses S. Grant on 9 April at Appomattox Court House. Five days later, the recently re-elected President Lincoln was assassinated by John Wilkes Booth in Ford's Theatre in Washington DC. On 27 April, the steamboat *Sultana* blew up on the Mississippi killing 1,700 people, mainly recently released Union prisoners of war – a larger loss of life than that suffered on board the *Titanic*.

Other significant events of 1865 were the foundation of the Christian Mission in London (later to be renamed the Salvation Army), the publication of the famous children's story *Alice in Wonderland* and the introduction of the first speed limit in Britain (2 miles per hour in town, a spectacular 4 miles per hour in the country). But the end of the war in America did not bring an end to the tensions there. Only two Southerners were subsequently executed for war crimes (one of whom was the commandant of a prisoner of war camp named Henry Wirz) but resentment in the South was widespread and by the end of 1865 a new, sinister organisation called the Ku Klux Klan had been formed to organise resistance and secure the rights of white Southerners against the now freed black slaves.

The following year saw ongoing clashes in another war, this time in South America. With all of the countries there still in their infancy, the struggle to define national rights and territorial boundaries continued. The conflict, called the Paraguayan War, was hugely costly in terms of proportionate loss of life, with a large percentage of Paraguayan males of fighting age losing their lives as a result. The conflict was between Paraguay and a 'Triple Alliance' of Brazil, Argentina and Uruguay.

The Battle of Tuyuti, fought in a swampy area on 24 May 1866, ended with a decisive defeat for the Paraguayans and a total of 17,000 casualties, one of the bloodiest returns from any battle fought in South America. Europe, too, moved closer to conflict, with an increasingly ascendant Prussia declaring war against a now declining Austrian Empire and Italy making the most of Austrian distractions to declare war on them too. The Treaty of Vienna later in the year ceded Venetia to Italy.

The same year witnessed the laying of a transatlantic cable that allowed telegraph communication between Europe and North America for the first time. It also saw the discovery of dynamite by the Swedish chemist Alfred Nobel and the foundation of a cereal company, Nestlé, which even in the twenty-first century remains a global player.

In 1866, a remarkable monetary experiment was launched. The Latin Monetary Union was an attempt by several countries to fix their currencies against each other. Although they would retain their separate currencies, each would be acceptable legal tender in the other states involved in the scheme. The first members were France, Belgium, Italy and Germany and they were joined two years later by Spain and Greece, with five new members in 1889 – Romania, Bulgaria, Venezuela, San Marino and Serbia.

The scheme was based on the level of gold in the coinage of each member state (Greece would be expelled for a short time for reducing the amount present in its coinage) and would last till the outbreak of the First World War. Britain refused to join, partly because it refused to reduce the level of gold in its sovereigns and partly because it would not adopt a decimal system of currency. It was an interesting precursor of the modern introduction in Europe of a common currency. Such efforts to unitise the currency of different states are surprisingly old; in about 400 BC, seven different Greek city states did the same thing. The so-called Achaean League would last for over 100 years and would only end because of geopolitical shocks arising from the ascendancy of Rome and not through any economic difficulties.

The United States, in the meantime, continued to expand. New states continued to join and others who had seceded during the Civil War were reintegrated. Then, on 30 March 1867, another, more distant, future state joined when Alaska was purchased from Russia for $7.2 million. The agreement, signed by Secretary of State William H. Seward, was known as 'Seward's Folly' – it was not seen as a prize acquisition at the time, but the discovery of gold in the Klondike in 1896 and large oil reserves more recently have changed perspectives somewhat. Meanwhile, the discovery of diamonds in 1867 in South Africa led to an increased interest, especially from the British Empire, in that region.

In Central America, French attempts to impose a dynasty in Mexico ended in disaster for their cause, with the execution of the captured French-appointed emperor, Maximilian. Born in Vienna, Maximilian was in many ways a liberal reformer who showed genuine concern for the Mexican people, but that could not compensate for the fact that he was an imposed representative of an alien power and was essentially an extension of colonialism (though monarchists from inside Mexico had invited him over). Only maintained in power by French troops, he was eventually abandoned by them, and his opponents, supported in kind, if not in the form of actual troops, by the United States, captured him and put him in front of a firing squad in 1867. His body was later shipped back to Austria for burial.

Alongside these significant political events, other inventions that still have a place in the modern world appeared, such as the first traffic signal lights, installed in Westminster, London, in 1868. The following year, Mary Ward made her (now usually forgotten) mark on history when she fell under the wheels of an experimental steam car and was killed – probably the first person to die of such an accident in history (by means of comparison, estimates suggest that in 2002 about 669,000 people died as a result road traffic accidents).

Also in 1869, the first ever American Football match between two colleges took place in the United States, while a gangster by the name of Jesse James began his career. In December, the Wyoming legislature gave women the right to vote, the first known modern law to do so (Utah would follow in the following year).

The nineteenth century is often seen as an era of colonial wars and certainly there were many of them. But there were also conflicts between great powers that presaged events on a catastrophic scale in the twentieth century. Not only was there the American Civil War; tensions between Prussia and France came to a head in 1870. The power of Prussia had risen through the course of the century and now, with the Iron Chancellor Bismarck at the helm, she had already come to blows with Denmark and Austria.

Now it was the turn of France. A bitter succession dispute for the vacant throne of Spain saw Prussia and France on different sides. Insults were traded, national pride inflamed and an unstoppable momentum for war ensued. It was France under Napoleon III who declared it. What followed was not only portentous but also had long-term repercussions that would reverberate far beyond 1871, when the war ended.

Militarily the war saw a crushing Prussian triumph. Their efficient use of railways to mobilise presaged the mass movements of troops in the lead-up to the First World War and beyond, while their use of heavy artillery – especially those manufactured by the famous Krupp works – was an ominous foretaste of later wars, too (the use of hot-air balloons in the war could also be seen as a primitive first step in aerial warfare). Prussia went into the war in alliance with other German states, still not yet part of a united entity, but that would change soon after and Germany as we know it would be born.

Napoleon III was forced to flee France after the disastrous French military performance culminated in a massive Prussian victory at Sedan. The French soon afterwards decided that they no longer wanted a monarch or an emperor and declared themselves a republic, which they remain to this day. But they could not avoid humiliating terms at the war's end, seeing chunks of territory in Alsace-Lorraine surrendered, a source of shame that would help stoke the flames of the First World War.

The developed world could take something of a breather from major war for a while and instead pursue other more leisurely matters (or, alternatively, attempt to increase colonisation of other weaker nations). In the former category, in 1872 the Yellowstone National Park – the first ever in the world – was opened. In the meantime, Africa was being explored by white adventurers and missionaries. David Livingstone was more in the latter category, but he had disappeared somewhere in the heart of the continent. An Anglo-American, Henry Morton Stanley, had set out to find him and did so on 10 November 1871, allegedly uttering the immortal words, 'Dr Livingstone, I presume', though there is no definitive evidence to prove that he did so.

In 1873, a White Star liner built by the Harland & Wolff shipyard in Belfast sank off the coast of North America. She was not called *Titanic* but the RMS *Atlantic* and she sank with over 500 lives, the largest civilian loss of life in a shipping disaster at the time. She was the first White Star passenger ship to be lost at sea and sank in April, just as a more famous vessel from the shipping line did some thirty-nine years later just a few hundred miles away.

This was also a significant year economically. A global economic downturn created many problems. The reparations levied on France after her war with Prussia led to inflationary pressures in other parts of Europe. The stock market in Vienna collapsed and the contagion then spread to the United States, causing the New York Stock Exchange to close for over a week. Britain was particularly hard hit, and the low economic growth experienced in many parts of the developed world lasted for two decades. Once called the Great Depression, the slump of the 1930s took over that name and this period of economic hardship is now normally called the Long Depression.

Other modern institutions were starting to appear. In 1874 Levi Strauss was awarded a patent to make jeans, while in Bombay a year later the first Asian stock market made its debut. This year also saw the first performance of Bizet's *Carmen* and the first indoor ice hockey match, which was played in Montreal, Canada. This year also saw the first running of the Kentucky Derby.

As the world moved towards the final quarter of the nineteenth century, Western Europe appeared to be the dominant force but the power of the United States was growing. Within Europe itself, the emergence of Russia as a major power would have a dramatic impact in subsequent years, as would the ending of isolation for Japan.

But although it would be several decades before even the first glimpses were apparent, the power of Europe was approaching its zenith and less than a century later it would be well and truly over. In every measure this would be true; in terms of the colonies the Western European powers collectively held, in terms of military force, in terms of economic might and even in terms of influence. The world was changing again and events were afoot that would presage much of the modern world as we now know it.

38

THE RAPE OF AFRICA

Colonisation and Exploitation (AD 1876–1900)

'Mr Watson, come here, I want to see you.' Perhaps not the most memorable quotation, but this was supposedly the first ever phrase uttered using a telephone. But while 1876 might be remembered for being the year in which Alexander Graham Bell, a Scottish inventor, patented his first device (though there are many who insist he did not invent the telephone, with other claimants including Antonio Meucci, the Frenchman Charles Bourseul or the American Charles Grafton Page), or when Queen Victoria was proposed to be given the grand title of Empress of India, or even for the massacres committed by Turkish forces in the Balkans, it is instead best remembered for a battle fought in Montana in which just over 200 United States soldiers lost their lives.

The Battle of the Little Big Horn, which took place on 25 June, was by no means a decisive battle. In fact, if it decided anything it was that the victors would later be crushed by the much stronger American forces sent to avenge the 'massacre' (which was in fact nothing of the sort). But the death of 'General' (actually, a Lieutenant-Colonel at the time of the battle) George Armstrong Custer and the troops with him created shock waves in the United States at a time when the country was eagerly awaiting its centenary celebrations.

The battle was the last swansong of the free native American nations who for years, decades and centuries had been fighting a losing battle to preserve their way of life (or ways of life – there were many different tribes, cultures and ways of life in existence) against an overwhelming flood of colonisers of European origin. Within a year of the battle most of the victors were back in their reservations, their great leaders like Crazy Horse or Sitting Bull dead or fleeing north towards Canada for sanctuary.

The oft-quoted rationale for the conquest of these lands was the doctrine of 'Manifest Destiny' (a phrase coined by John O'Sullivan in 1845), which argued that the United States was destined to expand (this had already justified war against Mexico in 1840, as well as later territorial annexation that saw the United States spread to the Pacific by 1860). Purporting to be based on principle – in particular the association of territories who shared similar democratic principles – in fact it became a way of justifying aggressive expansionism and the denial of alternative ways of life that went against the grain of so-called 'civilised' principles. It was yet another example – and there would be many to choose from – of the injustices that would be committed in the name of civilisation. Perhaps more than any other era, the late nineteenth century was the Age of Hypocrisy, proving that in few instances, if any, does civilisation equate to humanity or morality.

It is one of history's truly tragic ironies that within fifty years of the abolition of slavery in most of Europe, and within just a decade of the American Civil War, resulting in the emancipation of the slaves in the Southern states, supposedly civilised states could not see a contradiction in the brutal exploitation of so many 'savages', as they were invariably called around the world. Some argue that there were benefits to colonisation – education and healthcare improvements, for example. This is nonsense. For a start, most of those colonised never had access to these, certainly not until well into the twentieth century. Secondly, millions died to meet the demands of the colonisers, without any rights at all to protect them. They would not live to enjoy any supposed benefits, even if they had been available.

Indeed, one of the conclusions drawn from Social Darwinism by many so-called 'civilised commentators' in the late nineteenth and early twentieth centuries was that it was the role of 'doomed nations' of savages to meekly lay down and die so that a white master race could take over. In case this is considered to be a liberal interpretation and an example of historical revisionism, consider the following statement, made in 1912:

> It is not right either among nations or among individuals that people who can create nothing should have a claim to preservation. No false philanthropy or race-theory can prove to reasonable people that the preservation of any tribe of nomadic South African Kaffirs … is more important for the future of mankind than the expansion of the great European nations, or the white race as a whole.

These were the comments of Dr Paul Rohrbach, ingloriously implicated in genocide in Namibia, and it is not difficult to see where Nazi theories about supposed 'master races' derived from. Yet such thoughts initially came from the previous century, when Europe in particular tried to parcel up Africa and parts of Asia, often, it must be said, with a Bible in one hand and a gun in the other.

Colonisation, like the poor, has always been with us. Stronger nations have often sought to overrun weaker states. This is not just a European phenomenon, even in modern times – witness China in Tibet, the Japanese in the Second World War or even the Bantu in southern Africa, who were not indigenous to the region but came for a short time to dominate it.

But European colonisation came accompanied with a Bible and claims to civilising influence, which all too often translated to exploitation and a complete lack of respect for different cultures, traditions and ways of life. These trends would be as easily perceived in the late nineteenth century in North America, Africa and elsewhere as they would have been in South and Central America when the Spanish, Portuguese and others were invading three centuries before.

It is indeed odd that in today's world most people are aware of the evils of slavery and the terrible suffering it caused. Yet at the same time, the Rape of Africa in the late nineteenth and early twentieth centuries has become one of the world's great forgotten sins. A terrible scourge was about to be unleashed on the unsuspecting peoples of Africa, one unleashed because of a misplaced sense of racial superiority, an unbridled hypocrisy from so-called Christian nations and a view of those already living there as somehow little better, if better at all, than animals. While not every coloniser thought that way, the examples of concentration camps in South Africa and South-West Africa (now Namibia) during the next few decades, or of the brutal exploitation of the Congo, stand as awful indictments of those who unleashed violence and brutality on an unsuspecting Africa – all in the name of 'civilisation'.

On 12 September 1876, King Leopold II of Belgium – a man whose excesses in the region would become a byword for evil – called a conference to discuss how Central Africa could best be colonised. It would be a few years before he launched his own personal adventure in the Congo, which would mark one of the most hideous examples of colonial excess, but he clearly was already thinking of some kind of involvement in the area.

The year 1876 was also a year of firsts. Two famous domestic products made their bow – Heinz Tomato Ketchup and Budweiser lager (of the American brand) first appeared. And a young German composer by the name of Johannes Brahms had his First Symphony premièred. Richard Wagner also ran performances of his operas at Bayreuth for the first time.

However, European minds were elsewhere. The massacres committed by Turkish troops in Bulgaria in this year caused outrage. There were widespread calls for the great European powers to intervene. A memorandum in Berlin called for an armistice but made little difference. The Ottoman Empire was expiring and the lid was coming off a pressure cooker. By the end of the year both Serbia and Montenegro (then two separate countries; they were stuck together at the end of the First World War and went their separate ways again in the twenty-first century) had declared war on Turkey.

Russia declared war on Turkey the year after, which led to a hard-won triumph against stubborn Turkish forces after a long siege at Plevna, Bulgaria. Although other powers such as Britain did not intervene directly, they were worried by Russian war aims, including the possibility of the Russians securing Constantinople. Russia would clearly win the war against weaker Turkish forces and this created concern among rival powers.

The terms extracted by the Russians at the subsequent Treaty of San Stefano were tough. Even though they were watered down when the Treaty of Berlin was signed in 1878, they still reshaped Eastern Europe significantly. Romania, Serbia and Montenegro were declared independent principalities. Russia took territory in Southern Bessarabia – a region which has shuffled backwards and forwards ever since and still remains a potential, if often overlooked, flashpoint in the twenty-first century.

Bosnia and Herzegovina was handed over to the Austrians. Bulgaria was given autonomy – though still nominally overseen by the Turks – as was Macedonia. The carve-up of the Balkans, as we well know, would solve nothing. It would provide the fuel that lit a spark at Sarajevo in 1914. It would do so again eighty years later, when a

Europe that thought Balkan massacres were a thing of the past was rudely reminded that it was not so. And, even now, the fault lines remain, only forgotten by most because the fighting has, for the moment, stopped. But wise men would remind us that an absence of war does not equate to peace.

The year 1877 was also notable for more mundane matters. Tchaikovsky's ballet *Swan Lake* was first performed and England and Australia played their first ever Test match in cricket. The All England Tennis and Croquet Club held its first tournament at Wimbledon. In the following year, the American inventor Thomas Edison patented a recording device known as a phonograph, the precursor to the record player.

These examples of technological progress went alongside ongoing international tension. By 1878, Britain was particularly concerned at Russian expansionism and had sent ships to the Bosporus to forestall a takeover in Constantinople. Now she was concerned about Russian intentions in Afghanistan and therefore decided to launch an expedition there to protect her interests. Not for the first time, nor the last, a war ensued that would threaten to prove disastrous for the invading army in Afghanistan.

Britain would unexpectedly find itself embroiled in another war early in 1879. Her colonial representative in South Africa, Sir Henry Bartle Frere, manufactured a war with the independent Zulu nation and an invasion force crossed the border in January. There soon followed the worst ever defeat of the British army against a native power when, at Isandlwana, the British camp was overrun and most of the defending soldiers annihilated. Over 1,000 British soldiers and native allies died.

The result was, in the longer term, a disaster for the Zulus. Such a defeat must be avenged and the British government, though angry with the colonial authorities that the war had started at all, sent massive reinforcements, overwhelming the Zulus. The war ended with Zululand conquered and divided up, a situation that led directly to a bitter civil war a few years later that further undermined the region.

The following year (which featured the first electric street lights installed in India and the first shipment of frozen mutton from Australia to the United Kingdom) saw an outbreak of war between Boer settlers in the Transvaal and the British Empire, whose forces had annexed the territory a few years previously. The British again suffered a bad reverse and the war ended with Transvaal independent once more. The British also suffered a bad defeat at Maiwand in Afghanistan (one of the fictional casualties being Dr John Watson, Sherlock Holmes's literary companion), though the war there did end with a British victory.

Some socially significant events took place in 1881, with Kansas becoming the first US state to prohibit alcohol. It also saw Andrew Watson (born in British Guiana) become the first known black soccer player to be capped internationally (he played for Scotland). On 26 October the famous gunfight at the O.K. Corral, fought out in Tombstone, Arizona took place, an event that has come to symbolise the rough and tumble of the Wild West, though largely because of cinema and not due to its actual historical significance; the shoot-out, which lasted for probably no more than thirty seconds, was little-known for half a century until a biography of one of the participants, Wyatt Earp, was released.

Another famous event in the history of the American West took place the following year on 3 April, when the outlaw Jesse James was shot in the head and killed while standing on a chair cleaning a picture on the wall. On the political front, 1882 also saw the British Empire making Egypt a protectorate, particularly important as the Suez Canal was now a key link on the route between Britain and India. Thomas Edison also opened the first commercial electric power plant in history (it was in Lower Manhattan), a crucial milestone down the road toward the modern world. In the world of music, it was also the year that Tchaikovsky's *1812 Overture* was first heard.

The dominant worldwide event of 1883 – which also saw the Orient Express running for the first time (it would finally close in 2009) – was the massive volcanic eruption on the island of Krakatoa, off the coast of Java. It took several months of build-up before the cataclysmic explosion occurred. Explosions on 27 August were so loud that they were heard over 2,000 miles away in Australia. The eruptions, earthquakes and associated tsunamis officially caused 36,000 deaths, though unofficial estimates quoting four times as many dead have been made. Tidal waves over 150 feet high were recorded and the average temperature worldwide fell by over 1 degree Celsius. One very noticeable side effect was the darkening of the sky due to ash clouds, creating spectacular sunsets for months after the event.

A war in Sudan in 1884 led by a religious figurehead named the 'Mahdi' saw an attempt to drive out Egyptian forces occupying the country. This led to the famous siege of Khartoum, which came to an end with the city being taken and the British General Charles Gordon's death in January the following year. At the other end of the continent, the Germans established a protectorate in South-West Africa (now Namibia). The Germans were certainly eager to catch up on their late start in the colonisation process, as Cameroon and Togoland also received similar treatment. The Berlin Conference, which started in November 1884 and went on into 1885, decided on the future colonisation of Africa.

This was a crucial part of the 'Scramble for Africa', where spheres of influence were allocated to European powers and an undignified, unprincipled carve-up of the continent began. By 1895, the only free countries in Africa were Liberia (founded by freed slaves) and Abyssinia (Ethiopia), which would also be fighting for her survival.

Colonisation was not limited to Africa. France and China went to war over the control of North Vietnam (though French attempts to colonise the region had been going on for nearly three decades); the French would achieve their war aims but in the process would suffer several defeats and the Chinese army performed considerably better than it had in previous conflicts with European powers.

The carve-up of Africa was to move towards one of its greatest tragedies when King Leopold II of Belgium established the Congo Free State as a personal fiefdom. There followed the most terrible exploitation, accompanied by brutality and inhumanity on an unimaginable scale. Vast numbers of African workers were conscripted into what amounted to slavery, paid a pittance in return and with no choice as to their participation. Rubber was the ultimate target for their labour (though ivory was also collected in the first days of Leopold's ownership) and the conditions in which they worked were horrific. Those who resisted often paid for their temerity with their lives; as a warning to others, they were not only killed but their hands were lopped off as a 'tally' of those who had had summary justice meted out to them (victims included young children – a photograph of a father staring blankly at the severed hand of his five-year-old daughter is one of the most harrowing I have ever come across).

The country was not owned by Belgium; it was Leopold's own personal possession. It took several decades for the true horror of his rule to emerge and, when news of it broke, he was forced to hand it over to the control of his country. By the time this had happened, millions of people were dead. It was perhaps the most awful example of European exploitation of the nineteenth century, though no colonising powers were free of such shameful incidents in their imperialist history.

Within the borders of Europe itself, other events presaged later horrors. Otto von Bismarck deported Poles and Jews from within the borders of Prussia. On a more positive note, 1885 also saw the introduction of items that remain a prominent part of the modern world. It was the year in which the Statue of Liberty arrived in New York, shipped over from France, in which the telecoms company AT&T was established and when the Congress Party was established in India.

By 1885, significant developments were also taking place in the field of transport. Karl Benz, a German designer, was working on a device called a Motorwagen, which was the prototype of the modern automobile, although steam-powered cars had been around for some time before. Gottlieb Daimler, another German, produced an internal-combustion motorcycle (he would later become the first man to produce a four-wheeled automobile; Benz's only had three). And John Kemp Stanley in the same year manufactured the first commercially successful safety bicycle, an alternative to the penny-farthing.

The reality of world politics at this stage was reinforced by the gift of the country of Burma as a present to Queen Victoria on 1 January 1886, shortly after it had been annexed to British India, as if it were a piece of expensive jewellery to be hawked around at European discretion to keep Her Majesty amused. It was followed later that year by the first moves in an opposite direction when the British Prime Minister, William Gladstone, placed the first Irish Home Rule before Parliament (though it was defeated).

Also in that year, a man named John Pemberton, who ran a pharmacy in Columbus, Georgia, formulated a new drink that he sold for 5 cents a glass. It was offered as a cure for all kinds of ailments, including impotence. It would carve out a niche in the market and the patent was bought up a couple of years later by an organisation called the Coca Cola Company. In 2013, the descendant of Pemberton's product was one of the most successful brands in the world – a long way from Columbus, Georgia.

The news of 1888 was dominated later on in the year – in Britain at least – by the sensational murders committed in the East End of London by the infamous and unknown killer simply called 'Jack the Ripper'. In the arts, the year was marked by an act of self-mutilation committed by the Dutch painter Vincent van Gogh while suffering a bout of mental illness, and the invention of a new Kodak camera that considerably widened the appeal of photography.

International tensions threatened to come to the fore in 1889, when German warships fired on an American settlement on Samoa. Three American warships entered the harbour to exact retribution. Before they could do so, a cyclone blew up and sank all of the vessels, American and German, that were there. An armistice was agreed, an inevitable result of there being no ships left to fight a war. It was all sadly ironic; presumably the native Samoans would have rather been left well alone by both parties rather than have an uninvited war on their doorstep.

On a rather more prosaic level, a Neapolitan tavern owner, Raffaele Esposito, is said to have produced a new dish, with a bread base, tomato, mozzarella cheese and basil (to emulate the three colours of the Italian flag). Named after the queen consort of the country, the Margherita pizza would become one of the most universally recognised dishes in the world. Esposito is believed in some quarters to be the founder of the modern pizza.

Among other firsts in that year of 1889 were the first jukebox and the opening of one of the world's most recognisable monuments, the Eiffel Tower in Paris (regarded by some critics at the time as inelegant). Almost unnoticed, in Japan a small company started making playing cards. As Nintendo, it lives on into modern times, albeit operating in a somewhat different market now.

The carve-up of Africa continued in 1890 (a year when the electric chair was used as a means of execution in the United States for the first time) with the establishment of an Italian colony in Eritrea in the Horn of Africa. Italy had wider ambitions in the region and was far from satiated with this initial chunk of territory that had been added to her domains. She too wanted to catch up in the race. It was as if Africa and Asia were part of a giant board game where Western players could take hold of a new territory at the throw of a dice.

The world was nevertheless changing in remarkable ways, with technological progress once again advancing awkwardly alongside brutality and exploitation. One such development was the opening up of the first long-distance telephone line in 1891 (it was between London and Paris). In the arts, Carnegie Hall in New York opened and a detective called Sherlock Holmes took his bow in the *Strand* magazine for the first time (though two novels had preceded this); he is still the most instantly recognisable literary detective well over a century later.

The United States remained the major target for emigrants from Europe and beyond, and early in 1892 the famous processing centre for such aspiring new citizens was opened on Ellis Island, off New York. In less than four decades leading up to this, 8 million new arrivals had been registered in the country. Annie Moore, a fifteen-year-old from Cork, Ireland, was the first arrival at Ellis Island and was presented with a $10 piece to mark the moment, the largest amount of money she had ever owned.

In the first year of opening, nearly half a million people would pass through Ellis Island. The building would burn down a few years later and a new building in red brick (the first one was in wood) would take its place. The new structure would be stretched to the limit during the years leading up to the First World War as the rate of immigration to the United States would carry on increasing.

Technology was continuing to develop, and in 1892 the first official fingerprinting agency in the world was opened in Buenos Aires. In the realm of sport, Lord Stanley of Preston, the Governor of Canada, presented a trophy for ice hockey – the Stanley Cup is still contested today. It has become one of the most iconic trophies in sport and has been played for more or less continuously ever since (though it was not in the 2004/05 season because of a strike). Among its more unusual moments was the occasion when it came under rocket-propelled grenade attack in Afghanistan, where it had been taken in 2007 as a morale-boosting measure for troops stationed there.

Afghanistan was in the news for another reason in 1893. Sir Mortimer Durand may not be a household name now but perhaps he should be, for his actions continue to resonate in the twenty-first century. Durand was given the responsibility of drawing up the border between Afghanistan and what was then British India (now Pakistan). In the process, he cut Pashtun tribal areas in half and expected the tribes to comply meekly with the notion that they were to stay on one side or the other of what was an artificial and meaningless boundary marker.

The fiercely independent Pashtuns, of course, had no intention of doing so, and even today the North-West Frontier province of Pakistan and the opposite side of the border in Afghan territory remains one of the most obstinately troublesome regions in the world. Durand appeared to have no idea of the practicalities of what he was suggesting; a child with a pencil in their hand could have done an equally useful job. We are still paying a heavy price for some of the follies of empire.

On the political front, 1893 saw the creation of a new group, the Independent Labour Party, in Britain, while United States troops intervened in Hawaii, causing the collapse of the government there. European expansionism continued with the addition of the Côte d'Ivoire to French possessions. Social changes were evidenced by the granting of the right to vote to women in New Zealand – the first country in the world to do so.

In the field of transportation progress continued, too, with Paris being the first city in the world in which car number plates were used. Rudolf Diesel received a patent for the engine that was named after him and the first gasoline-powered car was driven on the streets of the United States. However, transatlantic transportation could still be dangerous. In February, the White Star liner *Naronic* disappeared with no survivors while sailing from Liverpool to the United States. A message in a bottle subsequently recovered told of striking an iceberg in a storm (though some think that this and other bottle messages were a hoax).

A much bigger loss of life occurred when the Royal Navy ship HMS *Victoria* inexplicably collided with the *Camperdown* off the coast of Lebanon in perfect visibility due to confusion over signals sent as the ships were manoeuvring. The *Victoria*, which was rammed sideways-on by the *Camperdown*, sank in thirteen minutes and 358 lives were lost. Other ships in the line also narrowly avoided hitting each other. A court martial was held and found that Vice-Admiral George Tryon, who had issued the faulty orders and had gone down with his ship, was to blame. However, an important subsidiary finding concerning the responsibility of more junior officers to query orders if they were clearly faulty emerged and would in the future give more opportunity for them to do so.

The year 1894, which featured the opening of one of the world's most iconic bridges, Tower Bridge in London, saw important developments, both political and social. In Korea there was much social unrest, which spilled over into violence. Both China and Japan intervened in an attempt to keep the lid on the pressure-cooker situation but the opposite result occurred and the First Sino-Japanese War broke out. This foreshadowed further clashes between the two regional powers and would lead to cataclysmic repercussions four decades later.

The great powers of Europe continued to play their power-broking games on the continent as well as further afield. France and Russia entered into alliance. For a while, Britain was concerned that there would be negative repercussions for her, and tensions with France ensued. But in the medium term, the alliance between France and Russia would be one of those intermeshed arrangements that would drag the world into an unimaginably horrific confrontation in 1914.

This was a world of increasing social tension too. There were, for example, frequent strikes in the United States as workers sought to protect themselves from exploitation by those who ran the factories, mines and other industrial edifices that they worked in. In Europe there were a number of outbreaks of anarchist violence – there were several bomb attacks in Paris and London, for example.

Alongside this violence there were social improvements too, such as the introduction of the first minimum wage arrangement in New Zealand (Australia would follow a few years after). Prussia, perhaps not the most obvious source of social reform, had introduced an old age pension back in 1889 for all those retired workers who were over seventy years of age.

There was upheaval of a different kind in France when Captain Alfred Dreyfus, who was of Jewish descent, was found guilty of spying for the Germans and sentenced to a life of drudgery on the infamous Devils' Island. Two years later, in 1896, new evidence emerged that suggested his innocence and he was brought back to France for further examination. New charges were brought against him and France found itself split, with the writer Émile Zola launching into a scathing attack on the government in the famous pamphlet *J'accuse*.

Accusations of anti-Semitism (a form of racism, of course, just as colonialism was; the two go hand in glove) and cover-ups by the establishment followed and it was not until nearly a decade later that Dreyfus was fully exonerated and took up his place in the army once more. The treatment of Dreyfus and the case itself was important for its wider significance. It provided evidence of anti-Semitism in France, which re-emerged during the years of the Second World War when the Vichy government collaborated with Nazi Germany and sent vast numbers of people, including Dreyfus's granddaughter, to their deaths in Auschwitz and other production lines of mass murder. France still recognises the impact of the Dreyfus case and in 2006, the centenary of his exoneration, both President Jacques Chirac and the National Assembly of France formally honoured his memory.

The year 1896, which saw the first X-Ray photographs produced, also marked the production of the first vehicle by an American industrialist called Henry Ford, as well as witnessing the first publication of the Dow Jones Industrial Average. It also saw a disastrous reverse for the Italians in Abyssinia. Italy, still a young country, had arrived late on the colonial bandwagon and had been squeezed out of most of the scramble for Africa. However the north-east corner, the Horn of Africa, seemed to offer an opportunity.

Italy had tried to enforce a situation whereby Abyssinia would become a protectorate of Italy. Not unreasonably, the Abyssinians did not want this, presumably being well-informed of just how altruistic that protection might be in practice, so an Italian army was sent. However, the difficulties of living off the land soon emerged for both sides and before long the Italian force was faced with the choice of trying to force a decisive battle or retreating.

The Italians, with about 18,000 men and fifty-six guns, decided to force the issue and tried to do so at Adwa on 1 March. The Abyssinian forces of the Emperor Menelik perhaps outnumbered them by five to one (and also had Russian advisers with them). The Italians went on the offensive against a well-positioned enemy. The result was a disaster for the Italians, who were overwhelmed by their enemy.

There were over 10,000 Italians killed, wounded or captured in the battle and the retreat that followed. Italy was forced to agree to the Treaty of Addis Ababa, which confirmed Abyssinia's independence. There were demonstrations from outraged families and supporters in Italy and demands that the troops be brought home, which happened soon afterwards. Italian pride was deeply scarred, and in some quarters the defeat left a thirst for revenge (against a country that hadn't asked to be invaded in the first place, which hardly seems fair) that would re-emerge forty years later.

This year also saw the establishment of a modern institution – or rather the re-establishment of a very old one. Small-scale versions of the Olympics had been held before, with competitions in Greece in 1859, 1870 and 1875. However, the 1896 Games would be altogether a grander scheme. Two years before, the French Baron de Coubertin had assembled an Olympic Games Committee with the aim of restoring the old games (one of its first rulings was that only amateur athletes could compete).

Its first modern edition took place in Athens and appropriately the marathon race was won by a Greek, Louis Spyridon. The Games were a great success and the King of Greece appealed for them to be held on every occasion in Greece in the future. However, Paris had been already approached for the 1900 edition and the Games would not return to Greece until 2004. There were some surprisingly modern subplots to the 1896 Games, with Greece in financial difficulties and struggling to hold them and suggestions that the budget would be exceeded by 300 per cent. Despite all this, the Games went ahead and were very popular, and the concept has never looked back since.

An important breakthrough in the field of communication took place in 1897 when the Italian Guglielmo Marconi sent the first ever wireless message over open sea, across the Bristol Channel between England and Wales. The theoretical possibilities of radio waves had been identified a few years earlier and Marconi had taken up the challenge of developing this into a practical application. An extremely astute businessman, Marconi would found a substantial business empire on the back of his work but would, more importantly, open up whole new worlds of communication, with rapid contact between one point and another over distances of thousands of miles.

One of the most famous of all Gothic novels was about to appear too, with the Irish writer Bram Stoker producing his unforgettable work *Dracula*, a tale that brought together the priceless ingredients of an undead vampire, a haunting landscape and just about every other trick available to produce a work that gripped the imagination. Released in 1897, the work continues to do so to this day. Ironically, some of the book was plagiarised from travel guides; Stoker never went to Transylvania in person but his descriptions of the region are almost identical to those given by some contemporary travel writers. However, his work engrossed his readers as few other horror tales have.

Queen Victoria also celebrated her Diamond Jubilee in 1897. Events were held across her vast empire to mark the occasion. This included India, where, during the events, several British colonial officers were assassinated in an outbreak of violence that is considered by some to mark the first stirrings of an independence movement that would eventually lead to the emergence of an independent latent superpower half a century later.

Exploration must be considered too, with new spheres emerging all the time. The North and South Poles were some of the last parts of the world above water to be explored and in 1897 a Swedish expedition set out to fly across the North Pole in a hot-air balloon. The expedition was a shambles; the equipment was not properly tested before it was used and as a result the balloon came crashing down just a few days into the journey. All three men died as a result of starvation, exhaustion and hypothermia, a salutary reminder of the dangers of trying to discover areas of the world that were as yet unknown.

Across the globe it appeared that imperialist European powers still held sway across most of its surface. However, the balance of power was already shifting. Spain, for example, had lost most of its once great empire but was about to lose some of the last remaining territories it still governed overseas, namely the Philippines and Cuba. On 15 February 1898, an explosion on board the USS *Maine* in Havana Harbour killed 266 men. There was a revolt in train against the Spanish authorities in Cuba and, despite a lack of incriminating evidence, the United States declared war, holding the Spanish responsible. 'Remember the *Maine*, to Hell with Spain' was the war cry.

In the United States, a sharpshooter named Annie Oakley wrote to President McKinley offering the services of fifty female sharpshooters in any war that might break out. War was declared on 25 April and a fleet was sent to the Philippines, then also Spanish, and destroyed their Spanish adversaries in the Battle of Manila Bay. The United States was in the mood for imperialism. Guam was annexed, as was Hawaii (which was nothing to do with Spain). Puerto Rico was invaded. By August, the fighting in Cuba was over and the Treaty of Paris in December ended the war altogether, with the balance of world power definitively shifted (though further fighting would take place in the Philippines in 1899).

Confrontation was also taking place in Africa too. In belated revenge for the death of General Gordon over a decade before, a British army destroyed that of the dervishes in Sudan at the Battle of Omdurman on 2 September 1898. However, the British and French were about to come close to war in the Scramble for Africa. Unhappy at continuing British control of Egypt, a French expedition was sent to Fashoda on the White Nile, considered by the British to be in their sphere of interest. For a time, war seemed probable but the British won the diplomatic stand-off that followed. Nevertheless, relations between Britain and France were very strained as a result.

But Britain was already struggling to hold on to an extended empire. The Boers in South Africa had always resented British control and in 1899 open hostilities broke out. Britain was confident that the war would be short and sharp, the outcome a foregone conclusion. It was anything but. The Boers were tenacious opponents, skilled sharpshooters and long-term residents who knew their lands intimately. In contrast the British were conservative and unimaginative in their tactics and plodding and uncoordinated in their movements. They quickly found out that this was going to be a long and hard fight.

The events of 1900 were, in retrospect, foretastes of what was to come in the twentieth century. The British suffered several disastrous defeats in South Africa which, although the war was ultimately won, suggested that her empire was too big to be retained on a long-term basis. The situation in India was a case in point, where 3,500 British civil servants led a country of 300 million Indians. Factions in China, unhappy at ongoing foreign domination, broke out in open defiance in what became known as the Boxer Rebellion. China, too, would not take being bossed around for much longer.

In retrospect, the nineteenth century had been extraordinary. Few if any of the technological achievements of the twentieth century would have been possible without the work that had gone on in the nineteenth, be it in the field of communications, of engineering, of transportation or of industrialisation generally. There had been massive social changes too; the rights of workers, if still often exploited, had notably improved in a number of countries. New political parties had emerged to protect the interests of the workers. And voting rights were also being extended to include women.

However, the balance of power was also changing. Old empires like those of Spain and Portugal had already started to decline. But the new empires, such as those of Britain, France and Germany were also impossible to retain. Inside Europe, great dynasties such as those which ruled Russia, Germany and Austria were living on borrowed time, while in the distant East new superpowers were starting to emerge (though at different stages of development) in Japan, China and India.

All this presaged perhaps the most turbulent century of all, when remarkable progress was made in so many fields, living standards (in some parts of the world at least) would rise and life expectancy would expand almost universally. This was, of course, a massive improvement for so many people. But beside the progress in many areas, old prejudices would be reinforced and tensions that had, in many cases, always been there would reach unmanageable proportions. Technology would not only touch the positive aspects of human life, from medicine to energy provision to transportation; it would also give man – frail, flawed, self-willed man – the ability to destroy the world that he lived in, almost at the press of a button.

39

THE DEATH OF THE OLD WORLD

The First World War and the Rise of Communism (AD 1901–1925)

On 1 January 1901 the Commonwealth of Australia came into official being, with Edmund Barton becoming its first Prime Minister. It was an important development for the young country, although Queen Victoria remained the formal head of state. Not for much longer, though. Britain and her empire woke up on 22 January to the stunning news that, after nearly sixty-four years as queen, Victoria was dead. Although the queen's advancing years made such an event likely, it still came as a shock after so many eventful years on the throne.

It was the passing of an old world and somehow the timing was very appropriate, with a new century arriving. That these were days of progress and economic growth was evidenced soon after, in February, when the American financier J. Pierpoint Morgan entered into the first billion-dollar deal with the purchase of mines and steel mills in the United States. This also marked a realignment, with the economic power of America continuing to rise while that of Britain began to diminish.

Despite the fact that so much of the world was now known, the age of exploration was not yet over. On 6 August 1901, the British explorer Captain Robert Falcon Scott set sail in the *Discovery* with the aim of venturing into the Ross Sea in Antarctica. It marked a step forward in the ongoing race for the South Pole, with which, eleven years later, Scott would become so tragically connected.

A very significant breakthrough occurred on 12 December 1901 when Guglielmo Marconi made the first transatlantic wireless transmission. Although the 'message' was merely the letter 'S', the transmission from Poldhu in England to Newfoundland marked a further dramatic shrinking in the world and another opening up in communication. In the same year, wireless equipment was being fitted to ships, such as the Cunard liner *Lucania*, marking the application of the new technology to a very valuable use.

The rate of technological progress continued at an ever-increasing pace, in the case of automobiles literally, with the establishment of a new speed record, 74 mph, a mark set by the Frenchman Leon Serpollet at Nice in April 1902. However, any thoughts that man was now more powerful than nature were shaken from time to time, for example when the volcano Mount Pelée on Martinique erupted on 8 May 1902. The town of St Pierre was overwhelmed and 30,000 lives were lost – the most deadly volcanic eruption of the twentieth century.

In the meantime, the Boer War had turned into what was effectively a guerilla conflict fought by the Boers against the regular soldiers of the British Army. After several stunning victories for the South African farmers in open battle, the superior resources of the British Empire had carried on pouring into the country and the Boers were forced to resort to hit-and-run tactics. In response, the British opened up what were effectively concentration camps and, due to disease and malnutrition, thousands of internees, especially women and children, lost their lives. They were not the first examples of such, which had been set up in Cuba by the Spanish in 1896, and they would soon be emulated by the German colonial power in South-West Africa (now Namibia) in 1905, where Herero and Nama tribespeople were kept in horrific circumstances.

The Boer War became increasingly unpopular in Britain. At a cost of £200 million, the war was the most expensive fought by Britain between 1815 and 1914. Over 20,000 British troops died of wounds or disease – a higher rate of loss than the Crimean War – and nearly 10,000 Boer combatants. In addition, nearly 28,000 Boer civilians lost their lives (this does not include black internees – it is thought that perhaps 14,000 of these died but the final figure may have been much higher as few records were kept). Although the war ended in a British victory, marked by the Treaty of Vereeniging, it was at a high cost. Britain pumped £3 million into South Africa to assist reconstruction and the country would be given limited self-government a few years later.

On 15 February 1903, a remarkably resilient children's toy entered the market. Named after the American President Theodore Roosevelt and an incident on a hunting trip had took part in during the previous year, the 'teddy bear' became a quickly established favourite. In the same month, Cuba leased land at Guantanamo Bay to the Americans in perpetuity, a decision that would lead to much controversy a century later.

Later that year Prussia became the first country to require drivers of automobiles to carry a licence. More significantly, a major breakthrough in transportation was the short flight, just 120 feet in 12 seconds, made by Orville Wright on 17 December. Orville and his brother Wilbur had been experimenting with unmanned gliders for several years. Now this new invention opened up all kinds of possibilities, though it would have seemed incredible that within sixty-six years man would be flying a space rocket to the moon – an amazing pace of technological progress.

The flights of the Wright Brothers at Kittyhawk, USA, marked one of the major inventive breakthroughs in history. If anything made the world a smaller place, it was the ability, developed from the aircraft concept pioneered by the Wright Brothers, to fly thousands of miles in a few hours. Their claims to fame were ignored, especially in Europe, for several years before their invention was acknowledged. Another pioneer, the German Gustave Whitehead, was claimed by some to have actually flown in 1901 and 1902, though many were and are unconvinced by his claims (there is no photographic evidence to support them).

At the beginning of 1904, the Herero people of what is now Namibia rose up in revolt against their German colonial overlords. They were overwhelmed in battle and driven into the Namib Desert. They were then prevented from returning, with the result that thousands of them died of thirst. The aftermath represented a deliberate attempt to wipe out the survivors, effectively marking the first genocide of the twentieth century. There was no pretence about any of this; the object of the German strategy was extermination of the Herero people. Even now, for objective historians it is difficult to read about the brutality perpetrated by troops of a so-called civilised nation without the blood starting to boil. The neighbouring Nama people were similarly repressed.

Shark Island is not a name that resonates very much now with the wider world. But on this small piece of rock off the coast of Namibia, hundreds of malnourished and hopeless Herero and Nama men, women and children were in effect starved and worked to death. Any sign of slacking from the workforce was instantly punished by brutal whippings regardless of the age or state of exhaustion of the supposed offender. They lived in buildings where the walls were cloth rags supported by sticks. This might have been Africa, but the night-time temperatures were freezing as the island was right on the South Atlantic.

This appalling institution did not have gas chambers, but to most other intents and purposes it was a death camp. At the start of the war, it was estimated that there were 80,000 Hereros. At its end, 16,363 were left in South-West Africa, though a small number had managed to escape the country. Of the Nama imprisoned on Shark Island, 2,400 were incarcerated and only 500 came out alive. Half of the survivors would die within three years of being released, a number undoubtedly as a result of the appalling treatment they had suffered.

Soon after, a British consul named Roger Casement published a report into the horrific atrocities committed against the people of the Congo by the regime imposed by King Leopold II of Belgium. This started an unstoppable wave of outrage against the excesses of the king that would lead, four years later, to Belgium taking over responsibility for the shattered country.

Expansionism was still on the increase. The United States purchased the Panama Canal zone in Central America and soon after work on construction began. In Asia, the British sent a force to Tibet, whose poorly equipped army was quickly overwhelmed. Lhasa fell in August, although permanent occupation of the country did not follow.

An event of great significance in 1904 was the signing of the Entente Cordiale between Britain and France. A series of agreements helped to bring an end to tensions between the two nations and, along with the Anglo–Russian Convention and the agreements already made between Russia and France, led to the so-called Triple Alliance. The creation of this network of alliances (though some politicians refused to admit that any relationship as strong as an alliance had been created) would have dramatic repercussions ten years later in the lead-up to the First World War. In addition to the repercussions on European affairs, there were a number of supporting agreements concerning colonial matters and British and French spheres of interest that were sorted out by the Entente.

However, international relationships were about to become more complicated. Russia and Japan both had imperial ambitions in Korea and Manchuria. China and Japan had already come to blows a decade earlier over Korea, a conflict that the Japanese had enjoyed much the better of. Russia, however, was unhappy at the increasing involvement of Japan in what she saw as her sphere of influence and had rented Port Arthur in China as a warm-water port with access to the Pacific all year round.

Negotiations to ease tensions between the two powers had gone on without success in 1903. On 8 February 1904, the Japanese launched a surprise attack on Port Arthur – a declaration of war followed three hours later, an eerie precedent for the events of 1941. After a siege, Port Arthur fell. The Russians sent a fleet thousands of miles east from the Baltic in response. On the way, tensions with Britain were caused when the fleet attacked some British fishing boats in what became known as the Dogger Bank Incident. In the meantime, the Japanese won a major land victory at the Battle of Mukden. Then, in May 1905, the Japanese fleet delivered a crushing triumph over the Russian fleet at the Battle of Tsushima, virtually destroying the fleet that had been sent from the Baltic. A new world power was emerging.

Japanese territorial gains in the aftermath of the war, which ended in a complete victory in a tactical sense, were modest. The long-term repercussions were not. Russia was in a state of virtual revolution and the end of the Tsarist dynasty in the country was fast approaching. On the other hand, Japan was clearly a rising power in the East. She was still, as later events would prove, very much in the ascendancy.

Several significant events away from politics also took place in 1904. In London, a play called *Peter Pan*, which was to become an established favourite, was put on for the first time. On 31 December, Times Square in New York saw its first New Year celebration. The first working caterpillar track was produced, which would have significant long-term benefits. Two big stories to hit the news stands in the year involved major shipping disasters. Off New York, the steamship *General Slocum* caught fire, killing over 1,000 people. Then, on 28 June, the Danish liner *Norge* sank off Rockall. In all, 635 people lost their lives, and the 160 who managed to get off in the boats spent up to eight harrowing days before being picked up.

The year 1905 also saw some interesting developments. A new town called Las Vegas was founded in Nevada, while a young scientist called Albert Einstein was working on his theory of relativity. The British Navy began construction of a new battleship class, the Dreadnought, which revolutionised the design of such ships and effectively made all other warships obsolete overnight, leading to a major naval arms race. Wilbur Wright also flew a plane for thirty-nine minutes, the first flight of over half an hour in history.

In Ireland, a new political party called Sinn Féin was formed with the intention of obtaining Irish independence from Britain. Elsewhere, the upheaval in Russia led to Tsar Nicholas II calling into being an elected *duma*. If he hoped that it would stop the call for reform in his country, he was sadly mistaken. These struggles for independence and freedom marked part of an ongoing process of such movements. During the course of the twentieth century they would spread worldwide – one of the most striking features of the period.

Tensions still existed within Europe, where various regions were still in the process of being redefined. In 1908, Bulgaria declared its independence from the Ottoman Empire and Austria-Hungary annexed Bosnia and Herzegovina. Alongside ongoing achievements, such as the expedition led by the American Robert Peary that set off for the North Pole and the production of Henry Ford's first Ford Model T (by 1910 Ford were selling 40,000 vehicles a year), political tensions were also rising. If the twentieth century was anything, it was also an era of contradictions.

Polar exploration, for example, continued apace. An expedition led by Ernest Shackleton claimed to have been the first to reach the Magnetic South Pole in 1909 (though they may, it is now believed, have got the location wrong) and in the same year the French aviator Louis Blériot became the first man to fly over the English Channel. In 1911, the Norwegian Roald Amundsen led the first party to reach the South Pole (his competitor, Captain Scott, famously died on the way back after also completing the feat).

From time to time there would be natural disasters that would shake the confidence of humankind in their domination of the world. One such was the San Francisco earthquake of 1906, which cost thousands of lives and millions of dollars. The sinking of the White Star liner *Titanic* on 15 April 1912 would also provide a major shock; over 1,500 people died in the disaster, which demonstrated that nature could still be a powerful adversary.

In the east of Europe, the rapidly changing situation due to the Ottoman Empire's loss of power would lead to a turbulent realignment in the region. This would have horrific consequences, both in the lead-up to the First World War and even, eighty years later, at the end of the twentieth century. One of the recurrent lessons of history is that the death of mighty empires often leaves chaos in its wake (for example, the demise of Rome or the end of the Spanish Empire in South and Central America). It is not simply a question of handing independence to those who are no longer under imperial role. New structures and systems need to be put in place to govern and national boundaries have to be defined, which can sometimes lead to enormous difficulties.

The demise of the Ottoman Empire in Eastern Europe led to a number of confrontations. However, ironically it was in North Africa that a chain reaction started that was to have dramatic consequences. Sensing the essential weakness of the Ottoman Empire, the Italians attacked Libya in a quest to gain territory. The conflict (which saw the first ever aerial bombing in history) lasted longer than the Italians expected it to, and the Turkish army proved much more resilient than expected. Among the Turkish soldiers fighting vainly to stem the tide was a young officer, Mustafa Kemal, who, as Kemal Atatürk, would later play the pivotal role in leading Turkey towards its current position as a significant and economically growing modern society.

However, the tension was also building in Europe. In October 1912, the small mountain kingdom of Montenegro declared war on Turkey. She joined Serbia, Bulgaria and Greece in the so-called Balkan League, which attacked Turkey. Serbian forces moved quickly into Albania and south into Kosovo while the Turkish navy was defeated by the Greek fleet. A number of Ionian Islands also fell to the Greeks. The war was ended by the Treaty of London, signed in May 1913, which saw the Ottomans ejected from most of Europe.

This First Balkan War, fought against the Ottomans, was soon followed by a second that saw the Balkan nations fighting each other. Bulgaria declared war against Serbia and Greece in a dispute over territorial boundaries. Romania, Montenegro and the Ottoman Empire also got involved in the fight against the Bulgarians (the Turks managed to regain Adrianople, which they had recently lost – it remains part of modern Turkey as Edirne).

The war ended with a Bulgarian defeat and a number of boundaries were redefined. But it would have much greater international significance than just this. Germany had been a tacit supporter of Bulgaria, an ally in the region, and wished to see a 'Greater Bulgaria' formed. Those ambitions were now frustrated. Equally, Russia had hoped that the Balkan League would stay united and form a counterbalance against the Austro-Hungarian Empire. Those ambitions were also null and void. Both Germany and Austria-Hungary were alarmed at the increasing power and territorial possessions of Serbia in the region. This would prove to have consequences that were absolutely devastating for Europe and the world.

However, although hindsight shows us just how critical these events in Europe were, we should not let this distract us from other major changes elsewhere. These were most marked in China where, in 1911, the Hsin-hai Revolution began, which would eventually topple the Ch'ing dynasty and with it wipe away thousands of years of history. The Ch'ing had failed to cope with the challenge of moving into the modern world and had also been shown to be weak in the face of greater foreign powers. Ethnic tensions within the country added further fuel to the fire.

In the distraction caused by the infighting in China itself, both Mongolia and Tibet were able to declare their freedom from China (though in the latter case this did not prove to be, in historical terms, a particularly long-lived release). Early in 1912, Emperor Hsuan-tung Puyi abdicated and the Ch'ing dynasty had breathed its last. The Republic of China was born, though it would take several decades and a huge shedding of blood before it would assume the shape that we now recognise.

Though less immediately significant in the short term, upheavals in Mexico too would play a part in looming events. Revolution had started there in 1910 – it too would be long, hard and bloody – but its most famous participant, Francisco 'Pancho' Villa, became involved a year later. Initially enjoying widespread American support, Villa would eventually turn on the country to the north, crossing over the border to gain revenge against an arms dealer who had sold him and his army ineffective ammunition. Anti-American sentiment in the country would rise, and in the end German attempts to woo Mexico would lead to American involvement in the war that was about to begin in Europe.

And so the scene was set for what was known – at least until 1939 – as the Great War, or (rather optimistically, as it transpired) 'the war to end all wars'. It is a mistake to think that, even within Europe, the period since 1815 had been one of peace, for it had not. Not only did the destructive Crimean War take place in the interim but Prussia had risen, as much through force of arms as anything, and had badly bloodied France's nose. Italy had been forced to rely on her armies to win her freedom and in the east territories in Ottoman hands had seen much effusion of blood.

That said, no one was prepared for the full horror of the First World War, which brought new weapons of mass destruction up against immobile armies typically led by unimaginative generals. Machine guns, barbed wire and trenches would hold the upper hand for most of the conflict in what would become the ultimate war of attrition.

None of this was predictable when a young, disaffected Bosnian Serb nationalist, Gavrilo Princip, decided to eliminate the heir to the Austro-Hungarian Empire, Archduke Franz Ferdinand, when he visited Sarajevo on 28 June 1914. The archduke had already survived a grenade attack earlier that day and was on his way to the local hospital to see some of the victims. In a fateful error of judgement, their driver took a wrong turn and was backing up slowly in the very street in which Princip was waiting with a gun. He calmly walked up to the car and shot both the archduke and his wife. Both died soon after.

Princip was captured after trying to shoot himself and, because of liberal Austrian laws, was too young to face execution for his acts. But what followed next was a monstrous sequence of events with, at any moment, the opportunity to avert catastrophe if anyone had foreseen the consequences and acted differently.

Austria-Hungary blamed Serbia for being behind the assassination and sent a strongly worded and quite impossible ultimatum, which was rejected. Russia was Serbia's ally, and so came to her aid. Once Russia was involved, then Germany must come in with Austria-Hungary. Once this happened, France must come in with Russia. And, when the Germans then invaded neutral Belgium when the conflict started, her long-term protector, Britain, also found herself ensnared. Thus, a series of alliances intended to preserve the balance of power in Europe were, when it came to the crunch, singularly useless in doing so and indeed conspired together to make war inevitable.

Surprisingly in the light of later events, the war in the West was at first one of movement. The Germans had a scheme, named the Schlieffen Plan after its founder, tucked nicely away in case of a war and they pulled it out now. It worked to perfection for a time. It required the Germans simply to ignore the main French defences and sweep round to the right of them (as they advanced from the north) through Belgium. The architect of the plan had died in 1913 – his deathbed words were reputedly, 'Remember – keep the right wing strong.'

Though the plan worked spectacularly at first, eventually the French, supported by the British, regrouped and fought off the Germans to the east of Paris at the First Battle of the Marne. This led to a period where each side did their utmost to entrench in strong positions. The lines thus created stretched ever westward in what became known as 'the race to the sea' with trenches stretching from the English Channel to the borders of Switzerland. Within weeks, the war swung from one of mobility to one of stagnation. Soon, the war that according to some should be over by Christmas was set to last for considerably longer.

The situation on the Eastern Front was very different. Partly because the German army was (in terms of equipment and morale) far superior man for man to its Russian counterpart and partly because of the vast spaces involved, this war stayed much more fluid. A crushing defeat for the Russians at Tannenberg put them on the back foot for some time. The Germans made the most of their excellent railway networks to move their men around effectively and, ultimately, decisively. Curiously, the battle was not fought at Tannenberg at all but nearly 20 miles away. However, in the Middle Ages the Teutonic Knights (who of course had a strong German connection) had lost heavily there, and it seemed to be a good way of evening up the historical balance to pretend this later battle had been fought at Tannenburg.

The British Navy appeared to be supreme at the start of the war but received a nasty shock within a couple of months of its start when three old cruisers, *La Hogue*, *Crecy* and *Aboukir* were sunk by a U-boat within an hour of each other. Although at first merchant and passenger vessels were exempt from attack, this did not last long and in May 1915 the world was shocked when the large Cunard liner *Lusitania* was torpedoed off the coast of Ireland, with the loss of 1,500 lives, including a number from the neutral USA.

Unrestricted submarine warfare was a shocking departure from previous conflicts. The concept of naval blockade was far from new but the unseen menace from submarines had a terrifying effect, as well as making a huge dent in shipping resources, especially those of Britain. But neither was it a risk-free strategy; there was no guarantee that the only victims would be from combatant states, and indeed it was sometimes likely that they would not be. The effect on neutral opinion, especially within the United States, should not be underestimated. The U-boat war would reach its peak in 1917, when over 6 million tons of shipping was sunk (as against 1.4 million in 1915).

Another new, and again ultimately terrifying, development was the evolution of aerial warfare. At the outset of the war this was an undeveloped tactic. However, throughout the conflict some significant changes would take place. The Germans launched their first raids on British civilians from airships in 1915. As British air defences developed, heavier-than-air aircraft were used instead. Although the scale of civilian losses was not at the same level as that in the Second World War, they had a dramatic effect on civilian morale.

Aircraft also had battlefield uses, especially for reconnaissance purposes. As this use for airplanes developed, so too did the concept of fighter aircraft. Early attempts to provide such machines were primitive; the first air-to-air loss in the conflict (and indeed in history) occurred when an Austrian plane was rammed by a Russian aircraft on 8 September 1914. When guns were added, it proved problematic to synchronise their firing with the propellers on the planes. When this problem was resolved later in the war, though, aviation had made a significant step down the road to effective fighter aircraft.

Such innovation contrasted for a time with the war on the ground. Attempts were made to break the logjam on the Western Front. These involved mass attacks against entrenched positions, ending up with little ground gain and huge loss of life. The Second Battle of Ypres in April 1915 introduced another horrific innovation – gas. But it did not lead to a breakthrough for the German forces that used it.

Attempts in 1915 to widen the conflict ended in dismal failure and humiliating defeat for the British and their Allies at Gallipoli, Turkey. The high level of losses, especially for 'ANZAC' troops from Australia and New Zealand, seared itself into the consciousness of those young (in their current form) countries and remains a powerful force within their respective national psyches. The bravery of the Turkish forces in defending their land is, on the other hand, often overlooked (though not, it should be said, in Turkey). One of those inspiring the defence was Lieutenant-Colonel Mustafa Kemal, who said, 'I do not order you to fight, I order you to die.' His 57th Regiment suffered 100 per cent casualties, killed and wounded. As a sign of respect there is no 57th Regiment in the modern Turkish army. The attack on Gallipoli, the brainchild of the First Lord of the Admiralty in Britain, Winston Churchill, ended in an ignominious retreat for the invading forces.

The year 1916 marked another terrible period of attrition. The French and German armies fought themselves to a standstill at Verdun, and the latter's attempts to bleed the former dry ended, leaving them even more exhausted. It became perhaps the iconic battle of the First World War, where victory appeared to be based on which side had the last man left alive. The British Army, too, suffered one of its blackest days on the Somme, 1 July 1916, with 60,000 casualties in a single morning.

However, on 15 September 1916, in the same battle, a new invention offered an opportunity to change the course of the war. The tank, when it made its first appearance, was no doubt a shock to the Germans facing it, but did not immediately make a breakthrough, due to a shortage of numbers, a lack of understanding of how to use it to best advantage and basic unreliability. But in the long run it would turn land warfare on its head. It had come a long way from the ideas of earlier visionaries as varied as Leonardo da Vinci and H. G. Wells.

As the armies trundled on into the third full year of what seemed a war without end, signs of collapse were particularly apparent in the French army, with a number of units mutinying. The British were to suffer terribly at the Third Battle of Ypres, better known as 'Passchendaele', a battle marked by unusually wet weather that turned the fight into one as much against nature as against man.

Two significant events were to swing the course of the war, first one way, then the other. The U-boat war reached new intensity in 1917 and there were many attacks against neutral shipping, especially from the United States. The Germans foresaw that this would probably lead to American involvement in the war and made overtures towards the Mexican government, with whom US relations were strained. Unfortunately for the Germans, the so-called Zimmermann Telegram, which carried the details, fell into American hands and was made public.

After keeping a strained neutrality up to this point, the United States now declared war on Germany. Although the standing army was small, reserves of manpower and industrial collateral were substantial. American troops were soon making their way over to Europe, the so-called 'Doughboys'. Their baptism of fire was harsh. There were more American casualties in the first four hours of their war in the Argonne Forest than were suffered during D-Day.

But as one ally joined the war (though no formal alliance was ever entered into by the Americans), another dropped out. Tensions in Russia had, in truth, been rising for decades; they could no longer be contained. There had been a great Russian victory in 1916 in the Brusilov Offensive, which forced the Germans to transfer large numbers of men from Verdun. The losses incurred, though, were enormous, even by the inflated standards of the First World War – over 1 million Russian casualties and 1.5 million from the combined enemy forces from Germany, Austria-Hungary and the Ottoman Empire.

In Russia, the political situation deteriorated and a new power, the communist Bolsheviks, rose. The tsar had lost his dictatorial grip on power and the army was increasingly a spent force. In March of 1917, the unthinkable happened when Tsar Nicholas II abdicated. The Bolsheviks led a successful armed power grab in November and in the next month were negotiating with Germany for an armistice. This led ultimately to the signing of the Treaty of Brest-Litovsk in March 1918, which saw the Russians dropping out of the war.

The treaty was a massive fillip to German morale. The Germans gained vast areas of land, 90 per cent of Russia's coal reserves and a third of her agricultural land. The treaty said everything there was to be said about the state of Russian morale at this stage and convinced some in the German High Command that this was the turning point in the war – an impression that was reinforced when they were able to transfer fifty divisions to the Western Front.

Buoyed by this success, the Germans launched a stunning offensive in March 1918, hoping to strike a decisive blow before American resources were fully deployed in Europe. After a five-hour artillery bombardment, in which a million shells were fired, the initial advance seemed to be a triumph and 24 March was declared a day of celebration in Germany. It proved to be premature. The Frenchman General Foch was appointed overall commander of the Allied Forces and a crushing counter-attack was launched.

After years of stalemate, the war was all at once transformed into one of rapid movement. This was brought about as much as anything by exhaustion on the part of the so-called Central Powers. Rising discontent in Germany sapped away at the will to fight as much as the losses in battle did. By November 1918, it was time to call a halt. An armistice was signed, leading to the Treaty of Versailles in 1919, which imposed harsh reparations, particularly on Germany – conditions that some would say led directly to the causes of the Second World War.

The end of the war saw a world map that was unrecognisable from the one that had existed at the start. The Austro-Hungarian Empire disappeared, as did the Ottoman Empire. Germany lost its colonies in Africa and elsewhere. The Balkans were split up into new kingdoms, with an arbitrariness that played a not insignificant part in the conflicts in that region at the end of the twentieth century. The same could be said of the carve-up of the Middle East. And a great new force had appeared, though it was not yet obvious. The revamped Russia still appeared to be a weak, divided nation but its communist ideology, allied to not a little ruthlessness, would forge a mighty power where for so long had only existed delusions of grandeur.

The losses in the war were immense. It is estimated that there were 35 million casualties, 15 million of them killed, both military and civilian. Over 3 million of the dead were from Russia and nearly 3 million from the Ottoman Empire. These numbers include losses from a terrible outbreak of influenza that took the lives of millions in 1918. They also include losses in the so-called Armenian Genocide ('so-called' as the attribution of the term genocide to the horrifying events in eastern Turkey is still a source of bitter dispute between the Turks and others), which claimed the lives of up to 1.5 million Armenians in what many argue was a deliberate policy of extermination.

These horrific events of course dominated the headlines between 1914 and 1919, but there were other things happening during these troubled years. In 1914, for example, a film star by the name of Charlie Chaplin made his debut in the comedy *Making a Living*. Even as war was about to break out, an expedition led by Ernest Shackleton set out to try and cross the Antarctic via the South Pole. It failed to even begin its overland journey, but the incredible story of survival, in which all of Shackleton's men were saved after their ship was crushed in the vice-like grip of pack ice, remains one of the greatest survival epics of all time.

Also in 1914, an Indian lawyer by the name of Mohandas Gandhi returned to his home country after years in South Africa, where he had been involved in a campaign of protest against the imposition of racially discriminatory laws. In July 1916, a series of shark attacks occurred off the coast of New Jersey, USA, events which would, sixty years later, lead to the film and novel phenomenon that was *Jaws*.

In November 1917, Britain declared her support through the Balfour Declaration for the establishment of a Jewish state in Palestine. Britain also had problems nearer to home to worry about; a rising at Easter 1916 against what was seen as the occupying British power by a group of Irish nationalists was ruthlessly put down – so ruthlessly, in fact, that it only served to fan the flames of Irish nationalism.

On 6 December 1917, a huge explosion in Halifax, Nova Scotia, when two freighters collided resulted in what was until then the greatest man-made explosion in history. One of the ships was carrying munitions, and the resulting blast when she caught fire killed nearly 2,000 people and injured 9,000. One of the ship's guns was found over 3 miles away after the explosion.

But if 1919 saw an end to the First World War, formally brought to a close by what would prove to be the very controversial Treaty of Versailles, it did not bring an end to fighting. Russia effectively entered a period of prolonged and bloody civil war, running from 1917 to 1923, between the Bolshevik 'Red Army' and the opposition 'White Party'. Supporting the latter were some of the Allied forces from the First World War, explaining why some war memorials in Britain state that the conflict lasted from 1914 to 1919, although British interventions in the Russian struggle were in reality half-hearted and completely unsuccessful.

The years 1919 and 1920 saw the height of the fighting in Russia, with the Red Army ultimately victorious. It was a violent, unforgiving conflict which suggested that, after the losses of 1914–1918, life was cheap; a perception strengthened by the subsequent actions of the victors. Another half a million lives were added to the roll call of the lost. And the Soviet shadow (the Soviet Union came into existence in 1922) continued to loom ominously further afield.

To the south, for example, countries such as Georgia took the opportunity in 1917 to declare themselves independent states. But by 1921, Georgia had been returned forcibly to the Russian fold. Thousands of miles to the east, Mongolia was also overcome and, although the nation would remain nominally independent, the Russian alphabet was imposed on its people. In other parts of the world, communist parties were being established, in the USA in 1919 and in China in 1921 for example. It was not just through force of arms that communism appeared to be such a major threat but also through force of ideas.

There was no doubting the brutality of the new regime in Russia. The most public manifestation of it was to be found in their treatment of the ousted royal family. At about 1.30 in the morning of 16 July 1918, Tsar Nicholas, his wife, their children and several servants were taken to the cellar of their prison in Yekaterinburg and shot in cold blood. Although the evidence on who gave the orders is not conclusive, several of those connected to the executions suggested that it came from the top, from Lenin himself.

The Soviet revolution appeared unstoppable. Many in Western Europe saw it as a huge threat to the established order, which is, of course, exactly what it was. Even the death of the orchestrator of the Russian Revolution, Vladimir Lenin, in 1924 did not stop the momentum – his place was taken by a Georgian named Joseph Stalin. The stage was set for a confrontation between East and West that would last formally for sixty years – and often seems to continue to the modern day.

The spirit of revolution had spread to Germany. Disputes between factions about the ending of the First World War contributed to the problem. A revolt had broken out in German ports when sailors heard of plans to send the navy out into one suicidal last battle in October 1918. From the ports, the rebellion spread to other cities inland. Realising that his time was over, the kaiser, Wilhelm II, abdicated. A misguided, excessively proud, overambitious and frankly untalented ruler, his abdication was perhaps the best thing he ever did for his country.

The emerging Communist Party in Germany tried to take advantage of the situation. However, it did not have enough support to seize power and by the end of 1920 the so-called Weimar Coalition had been formed, with the SPD (the Social Democrat Party), the largest political force in the country, one of its major players.

Yet this did not end the problem. Neither left (communist) or right (nationalist) parties were happy with the outcome. The left felt let down by the fact that the communist dream was not being lived in the country, while the right considered that the ending of the First World War effectively amounted to a betrayal of the German people. The myth that somehow an exhausted Germany had been stabbed in the back, by communists and Jews particularly, would not go away and led to increasing support for nationalists in the country. On 9 November 1923, a frustrated war veteran by the name of Adolf Hitler tried to grab power in Munich. Unsuccessful in the attempt, he was sent to prison, where he had the time to write out his political thesis in a work known as *Mein Kampf* (*My Struggle*).

Military defeat in Germany was attended by economic collapse. Strangled by huge reparations, the economy was characterised by hyperinflation, with money being printed so quickly that it was worthless and famously, in some cases, pushed around in wheelbarrows. At the end of 1918, one German mark was worth 4.20 US dollars. By 1923, the exchange rate was 1 million to one. The reparations levied on Germany were heavy, in marked contrast to the Marshall Plan, which helped finance the recovery of the country in 1945; it seems as if some lessons, at least, were learned from the events following this earlier conflict.

Germany managed to resist the attempts of the nationalists, at least for the time being, but Italy did not. Fascism is a word of Italian derivation and the man who gave life to the concept in 1919 was a professor by the name of Benito Mussolini (ironically a man given his start in the First World War with the aid of a large weekly wage from the British security service, MI5).

Mussolini seized power in 1922. He quickly set about rebuilding the economy with large public projects (an initiative which was, in the main, a failure) and instituting a police state in Italy. Some of his targets appeared laudable ones, such as the Mafia in Sicily, but the measures he took to suppress them were brutal. This brutality and disregard of the law also found expression in foreign policy; Corfu was grabbed from Greece in 1923 and a puppet regime was set up in Albania. It was the preface to a particularly brutal intervention in Ethiopia ten years later that was without justification and without common decency.

How were these excesses possible? After all, after the First World War an organisation had been set up precisely to stop such disregard for international law occurring. The League of Nations had been established by the Paris Peace Conference at the end of that conflict and had among its goals collective security and disarmament. These two goals would sadly prove to be mutually exclusive in practice. It was soon shown that, when nation states who had no time for pacifism – aggressors such as Germany, Japan and Italy – seized the territory of others through force, no one was in a position or had the desire to enforce international law with a military response. The League, no doubt launched with good intentions, would prove to be a frustratingly weak international force for good, much, it must be said, as its post-war successor the United Nations has been in recent times.

But from the chaotic upheavals attending the end of the First World War, new states were emerging. Ireland at last got the independence that many of its people had been striving for for so long, though 'Northern Ireland' remained formally a part of the United Kingdom. Ireland was divided, but in reality it had been so for centuries. The remarks of a nineteenth-century French visitor have a surprisingly modern ring about them: 'The Irish themselves, from different parts of the kingdom, are very different. It is difficult to account for this surprising localisation. One would think, on so small an island, an Irishman would be an Irishman: yet it is not so.'

In the aftermath of freedom, as has happened so often elsewhere, the newly freed Irish started fighting each other. The divisions in this civil war arose over whether the self-government awarded by Britain went far enough or whether, on the other hand, an Irish republic, without the British monarch as head of state, should be established. In the end it was supporters of the latter who triumphed. The civil war was short but ruthlessly fought by both parties, and several of the leading figures who had led the push for freedom from British rule, most notably Michael Collins, lost their lives in this struggle between Irishmen.

The lives lost in the Irish struggle were painfully felt by all those affected, but the scale of them paled against those suffered in another conflict in the other side of Europe. With the decline of the Ottoman Empire, a new Turkey was emerging. The vision for it came from a man called Mustafa Kemal, who would later be given the name 'Atatürk' – 'Father of the Turks'.

Key to achievement of this vision was the establishment of a secular government, even though the majority of the population was Muslim. Old-style fashions were frowned upon – the fez, for example, was effectively barred – and new ones took their place. Conservatism was discouraged and everyone must be involved if Turkey was to take its place in the modern world. This included women; as Atatürk said, 'Our task is to modernise the Turkish nation, we will not modernise the Turkish nation if we only modernise half of them.'

Yet this was a painful transition. In particular, there were many Greeks in Anatolia who sought to become part of Greece. Between 1919 and 1922, Greece and Turkey went to war over the issue. Greece, despite being on the winning side in the First World War, failed to achieve most of her war aims (being on the winning side was no guarantee of success; little Montenegro was forced to amalgamate with Serbia and did not have very much say in the process). Greece was unhappy at the extent of the territories still held by the Turks that had sizeable Greek populations, especially in Thrace and the western coast of Anatolia, particularly around Smyrna.

The Greeks lacked the force needed to win the war and the Treaty of Lausanne, which brought it to a close, transferred some territory in Europe to the Greeks but kept most of it within Turkey. A major effect was the transfer of Greek populations from what was now definitively Turkey back to Greece and vice versa. But these events were overshadowed by atrocities committed by both sides that evidenced a deeply felt hatred within each community. The most awful atrocity was when perhaps 100,000 Greeks died when the Turks entered the city of Smyrna (since renamed Izmir) in 1922, but there were atrocities committed by both sides that were causes of shame for everyone involved.

Life was, after all, cheap and not just in the east of Europe. In India, a momentum for independence was growing though it had not yet reached its full force. It was helped no end by the appalling massacre at Amritsar in 1919, when Brigadier General Reginald Dyer ordered his men to open fire on a large crowd of unarmed protesters. The minimum estimate was that 379 people died as a result, though there are much higher estimates from some sources. The most chilling aspect of the massacre – not a shot was fired back, as the crowd had no guns – was its cold-blooded deliberateness.

This was no massacre fuelled by panic but a deliberate attempt by Dyer to teach the protesters a lesson. He had armoured cars with him with machine guns; fortunately the streets were too narrow for him to unleash them on the crowds. Dyer confirmed that he would have done so given the chance. No attempt was made to help the wounded, either; Dyer explained that hospitals in the areas were open, so the injured could have been taken there easily enough, but he did not see it as his job to help – a consistent if not a moral attitude, at least.

This was an era characterised by extreme violence, upheaval and uncertainty, as much as, if not more than, any era of antiquity had been. Yet it is important to keep some balance too, for it was also an era of remarkable achievement and progress, all too easily overshadowed by the millions of wasted lives – and in some cases even caused by them.

For example, women had often played a key part in the war effort, though mostly on the civilian front (with the exception of Russia, where a small unit of women soldiers was actually formed and fought in the war). After it, as a result, women were in some places awarded the vote, including in Britain (though there was still some degree of discrimination as the age at which they were allowed to vote was thirty, and was not amended to twenty-one– the same age as for men – until 1928).

There were some remarkable achievements in avionics too. In 1919, an American aviator, Lieutenant Commander Albert Read, became the first man to make a transatlantic flight, flying from Long Island to Plymouth, England. It took twenty-three days and included several stopovers. Only a couple of weeks after this epic journey, two British airmen, John Alcock and Arthur Brown, became the first men to fly non-stop across the Atlantic, taking off from Newfoundland and landing in a peat bog in Ireland less than seventy-two hours later – the time it took was important, as a British newspaper had offered a cash prize for the first flyers to make the flight across the Atlantic and do it within this time.

These men were brave pioneers; as one example of their sheer guts, Brown had to constantly climb out on the wings to clear them as they started to ice up. Nor were they the only pioneers to make a mark. Also in 1919, the British airship *R34* made the first return crossing of the Atlantic, taking 108 hours from east to west and 75 hours on the return leg. But this bravery often came at a cost; Alcock, for example, was killed in an air crash later in the year and the airship phenomenon would finally come to a halt in the 1930s after several dramatic accidents, most famously that of the German Zeppelin, *Hindenburg*, the British *R101* and the less remembered but, in terms of loss of life, most costly disaster, which involved the USS *Akron*.

There were other developments taking place, too, that were to change the social face of both individual countries and, in some cases, the entire world. The United States in 1919 introduced 'prohibition' (formally the National Prohibiton, or 'Volstead' Act), a ban on the sale, production and consumption of alcohol. While no doubt there were good health reasons motivating the ban, it was the best news that the criminal fraternity in the country had heard for a long time. In fact, in many places the ban was effectively ignored. An America increasingly frustrated at the ban in times of great economic hardship and high crime rates abandoned the experiment in 1933.

This was also a time of growth in the film industry; classics such as the horror movie *Nosferatu* (released in 1922) appeared. This new entertainment medium was a form of escapism that took people away from humdrum lives, a trend that was also assisted later by the evolution of television, the potential for which was first demonstrated by John Logie Baird in 1925.

The world was now full of paradox. On the one hand, there was still much disturbance in various regions of the world and the unmistakable strengthening of movements in some places such as India to break away from colonial rule. But on the other hand, technology was opening up whole new possibilities – to some of the world, at least – though the impact of this was often regionalised and not as yet global. These two trends would continue in the next quarter-century; more violence, more disturbance, death on an industrial scale on the one hand, and new technologies offering hope of better lives on the other. But sometimes the two trends would merge and new technologies that might in some circumstances be a possible source of benefit would instead become instruments of death rather than hope or escape. This phenomenon would find its symbolism in the shape of a mushroom cloud.

40

THE WORLD IN CRISIS

Economic Disaster and Another World War (AD 1926–1950)

The world continued to lurch uncertainly into the modern age. It was a journey that would be marked by more violence, unparalleled economic turbulence and major global realignments, with the power of Europe visibly on the wane. The next twenty-five years also saw the emergence of a new world superpower in Russia and the signs of another one evolving in China. The United States was already well on her way to becoming one, but her position would be firmly cemented by the end of the Second World War.

Some countries had still not switched to the Gregorian calendar, but Turkey did so in 1926 (they were not the last; Ethiopia still uses one based on the Coptic calendar, which is seven to eight years behind the Gregorian – a somewhat strange situation when the arrival of a new millennium was celebrated years after most other parts of the world in the twenty-first century).

In other parts of the world, new technology was taking off but it did not come without difficulties; a radio play in London about a worker's revolution created a panic when an unsuspecting public tuned in (much as, more famously, an Orson Welles-directed version of H. G. Wells' *War of the Worlds* would do in the USA in 1938 – a distant observer of the panic from this broadcast was Adolf Hitler, who noted that it was 'evidence of the decadence and corrupt condition of democracy').

Another sign of social change was the increasing power of cinema. This helped to make the world smaller than it had ever been: Hollywood movies could be seen across the globe, making stars of actors who in the past could only be seen live on a stage. It significantly boosted the cult of celebrity too. When the screen heartthrob Rudolph Valentino suddenly died at the age of thirty-one on 23 August 1926, there was widespread grief across the globe. Another celebrity to die that year was the famous escapologist Harry Houdini. The following year, in 1927, another major step forward was made with the release of the first full-length 'talkie' movie, *The Jazz Singer*, although silent films would be around for a while yet.

Alongside these signs of progress there were hints of social unrest, too. The year 1926 saw the famous General Strike in Britain. The problem started when mine owners attempted to cut the wages of miners. The government claimed that the strikers were revolutionaries.

The king, George V, apparently suggested that those calling them such should try living on their wages before doing so. At its height nearly 2 million workers were involved in the strike. However, it ended in defeat for the strikers.

The year that saw the first transatlantic telephone call (via radio) from New York to London, 1927, also saw British troops landing in China. The country was once more on the verge of disintegration, with increased tensions between communist forces on the one hand and the nationalist Kuomintang on the other. A civil war was about to begin that would last until 1949. China, which has perhaps suffered more than any other country in the world from the effects of conflict and natural disaster over the millennia, was about to see another tragic chapter written. As if to set the tone, a huge earthquake on 22 May in Xining killed an estimated 200,000 people.

Political tensions were starting to rise across the globe. Britain and Russia, for one, were at odds with each other, with accusations and counter-accusations of espionage. In May 1927 Britain severed diplomatic links because of the tensions; the following month several Britons were executed in Russia on charges of espionage. It seems that tensions were as bad as during the Cold War thirty years later, if not worse.

Man's sense of adventure was still strong, and in 1928 an expedition took off in an airship in an attempt to complete the first flight to the North Pole. Led by the Italian general Umberto Nobile, it completed the journey but disaster struck on the way back. The ship crashed in the remote wastelands of Svalbard and a rescue attempt was launched. One of those taking part was the famous Antarctic explorer Roald Amundsen, but his plane was lost and he was never found. In a sign that air transport was really here to stay, though, Amelia Earhart became the first woman to cross the Atlantic in 1928 (Charles Lindbergh had recorded the first solo flight the year before) and the Flying Doctor service in Australia was also launched.

This was also the year in which Alexander Fleming discovered penicillin. It was an accidental discovery, made when Fleming returned from holiday to find cultures growing around some samples that he had left. This was a crucial breakthrough as it marked the beginning of the evolution of antibiotics, which of course had a very significant effect on healthcare in the twentieth century and beyond. Fleming was quick to point out that it was important that penicillin was not used needlessly, as this could lead to resistance building up in the patient.

However, events with much more negative significance were also taking place in China. Already threatened by internal division, the situation in the country became markedly worse when nationalist troops clashed with Japanese soldiers in the Jinan Incident. Several foreign consulates had already been attacked in the previous year; the nationalist leader, Chiang Kai-Shek, had tried to build his power base around resistance to foreign intervention in China. In the Jinan Incident, twelve Japanese were killed. In return, Japanese soldiers killed thousands.

For the Japanese, who had strong imperialist ambitions in China and particularly in the region of Manchuria, the incident was a golden opportunity to increase their intervention in the region. They would take full advantage of it, culminating in hostilities of extreme brutality within a few years.

However, the world's attention was diverted in 1929 by the most famous financial meltdown of all time. The Wall Street Crash came after a decade of rising stock values had led to an air of overconfidence and financial speculation. On 'Black Thursday' (24 October), the US stock market lost 11 per cent of its value in a day – the following Monday it lost a further 13 per cent and the day after a further 12 per cent. These were unprecedented losses. Three years later, a review of the crash led to the Glass-Steagall Act, which directed that the actions of commercial and investment banks should be separated – a measure that continues to be debated into the twenty-first century.

The crash heralded the start of the Great Depression, which affected all Western economies and did not end in the United States until after the Second World War. Construction, heavy industry and agriculture were all badly affected by the economic downturn. Unemployment shot up massively in the United States, Britain and France, as well as in Germany, where it had especially devastating effects.

Various economic theories developed in response to the crisis, including the work of John Maynard Keynes, who argued that in times of recession governments should boost spending to keep employment up – in 1930, US President Herbert Hoover went before Congress and asked for large sums of money to boost the economy following this theory. Others opined that the cause of the depression was over-indebtedness (this was the view of the American economist Irving Fisher). This debate also continues into the twenty-first century.

Outside of the West, hard-line attitudes were growing. In Russia, for example, in 1929 Joseph Stalin launched his programme of collectivisation, which sought to increase the industrial might of the country but would in the process lead to starvation, suffering and death for millions of the Russian people. No opposition would be tolerated – among those exiled from Russia were Leon Trotsky, once at the heart of revolution in Russia. The wealthy farmers, the *kulaks*, were particularly targeted. Seen as enemies of the poor, they were deprived of their farms and sent to gulags. Hundreds of thousands (the lowest estimate) or tens of millions (the highest) died.

Amid these geopolitical changes there were other more everyday events making their mark on the world. In 1931, the United States formally adopted 'The Star-Spangled Banner' as its anthem, a song that had been around for some time and had been used for various official purposes but had not before been formally adopted. As if to mark the event, the same year saw the completion of an iconic new building, the Empire State Building, in New York (two years later it would take a starring role in the Hollywood epic *King Kong*).

Of huge long-term significance, a Chinese Soviet Republic was declared on 7 November, being announced in the small region of Jiangxi by a young communist named Mao Zedong. He became renowned both for his revolutionary fervour and his severe tactics; he himself said that 'a revolution is an insurrection, an act of violence by which one class overthrows another'. Not for the first time, nor sadly the last, a revolution ostensibly to improve society would claim millions of innocent victims.

China was in fact about to go through yet another dark age, and those who seek to understand the Chinese in the twenty-first century ought to study their history very closely, for the terrible events that have often overwhelmed the people explain much. The

Japanese, fuelled by imperialist tendencies, had moved into Manchuria in force late in 1931. At the beginning of 1932, the US Secretary of State, Henry Stimson, published the so-called Stimson Doctrine, which refused to recognise any territorial gains made by any party by force. However well-intentioned the doctrine may have been, it made little practical difference to the terrible events that were already beginning to unfold.

The League of Nations, formed to stop international conflicts, proved impotent in the dispute between China and Japan. In Germany, meanwhile, on 25 February 1932 an Austrian by the name of Adolf Hitler became a naturalised citizen, allowing him to run in the elections for president that were due to be held later that year. He would not beat the First World War veteran Paul von Hindenburg, but that would do little to interfere with his rise to power.

By the end of the year, Hindenburg would be negotiating directly with Hitler, who had won a sizeable vote in second place during the elections, with the aim of asking him to form a government. However, in the end the position of German chancellor was awarded by Hindenburg not to Hitler but to Kurt von Schleicher. It proved to be a very temporary situation.

There is a sense, looking back, that 1933 would prove one of the seminal years of the twentieth century, the latest year in which the free nations of the world might have been able to do something to stop the approaching apocalypse. Most notably, it saw Hitler's rise to power and the start of the persecutions that he would launch against his opponents and those he saw as threats.

This year also saw increasing political violence in Spain, which would lead to open hostilities soon after, and turmoil further afield – there were even rumours of a planned coup to remove Franklin D. Roosevelt in the USA. These came to nothing, and Roosevelt turned his mind to other things, especially his famed 'New Deal', which aimed for 'Relief, Recovery and Reform' in an attempt to deal with the country's economic woes.

Roosevelt marked the start of his presidency by addresses to the American people over the radio in what were known as his 'fireside chats'. A different kind of oratory would be practised by Hitler, who at last became Chancellor of Germany on 30 January 1933. The country's descent into totalitarianism was remarkably quick. This process was helped along no end by the burning of the Reichstag building in Berlin on 27 February.

An unemployed communist, Marinus van der Lubbe, was found near the scene. His political affiliations gave Hitler's Nazi Party an ideal opportunity to stifle dissent. Civil liberties were removed and the Communist Party suspended in Germany, creating a vacuum that Hitler was quick to fill. The trials held afterwards found Lubbe guilty – he was subsequently guillotined – but the court declared his alleged co-conspirators innocent. Hitler was so furious at this that he promptly radically altered the court system to ensure that judges would be more subservient in the future.

In the aftermath of the Reichstag fire political opponents were seized and sent to what would become the first Nazi concentration camp at Dachau. Not long after, boycotts of Jewish goods and shops in Germany were being organised. In May, trade unions were banned, followed soon after by the banning of all non-Nazi parties in the country and the public burning of books that were deemed unsuitable. Later in the year, Germany declared its intention to leave the increasingly irrelevant League of Nations (Japan had already done so not long before).

By the end of the year, Hitler had introduced eugenic sterilisation in order to, as he saw it, improve the ethnic and genetic quality of the German population. Those who understandably felt threatened by the racist policies of the Nazi Party left Germany, if they were able to do so. One such émigré was a Nobel Prize winner by the name of Albert Einstein, who took up a post at Princeton University. He would later play a key role in the development of the atomic bomb which, if it had been in Nazi hands, might well have led to a very different outcome to the Second World War, a strangely ironic and poignant repercussion of the impact of blind racism.

Regardless, the Nazi Party continued its usurpation of power in Germany. Their main rivals were the brown-shirted paramilitaries known as the SA. Between 30 June and 2 July 1934, a number of Hitler's main opponents were systematically eliminated, in particular by the recently formed secret police, the Gestapo, in what became known as 'the Night of the Long Knives'. With all obstacles to power removed, Hitler became the Führer, the absolute ruler of Germany, by August. These ruthless moves inspired others elsewhere; there was also a failed coup attempt by Austrian Nazis, but their failure proved to be only temporary.

It seemed that an attempt to assume power in China by the Chinese Communist Party was failing. Badly beaten in battle by the nationalists, the survivors began what was famously called the Long March. It became a defining moment in Communist Party history and as such the true details of what took place are hard to discover due to the layers of myth that have accreted around the historical reality. But it established the reputation of Mao Zedong and succeeded in giving the communist armies time to recoup. The nationalists would soon have distractions elsewhere to occupy them.

Several further deteriorations in the international situation in 1934 accelerated the move towards all-out global conflict. Italian troops exchanged shots with Ethiopian soldiers; Italian pride had never recovered from the humiliating reverse at Adwa four decades earlier. This would prove regionally disastrous, but even more widespread in its repercussions was the decision by Japan to repudiate the limitations on naval power imposed by the Washington and London Treaties of 1922 and 1930 respectively.

Of course, there were many great social changes taking place that would have long-term repercussions in the world too. At the beginning of 1935, Iceland became the first country in the world to legalise abortion on medical grounds. Later that year, the world's first parking meters were installed in Oklahoma, USA. The famous board game *Monopoly* was first released and the first television programme was produced in Germany. But in that same country higher-level events were to make their mark, with the decision by Hitler to tear up the constraints on armaments imposed by the Versailles Treaty and turn Germany into a great military power. Few would be prepared to stand in his way.

The tumble towards all-out conflict continued in 1936, when the Germans seized the territory known as the Rhineland and the Italians annexed Ethiopia. There had been hostilities here since 1934 but the League of Nations again proved unable, or unwilling, to interfere, despite the fact that both Italy and Ethiopia were full members. The League was proving to be completely ineffectual and did nothing while the invading forces, clearly superior in capacity, delivered a brutal knock-out blow against Ethiopia (though both sides committed atrocities in the war and its aftermath). With the invasion successfully accomplished, Benito Mussolini's power was at its zenith.

Almost unnoticed, in 1936 the first helicopter appeared, the German Focke-Wulf Fw 61. It was overshadowed by international developments, as Rome and Berlin entered into an alliance. Germany suddenly appeared to be the centre of the world; the Olympic Games of that year were held in Berlin. They were significant for several reasons; they were the first Games to be awarded by means of a vote among International Olympic Committee members and provided the first live televised sporting events. They also witnessed the first relay of the Olympic torch, from Olympia in Greece to Germany.

Famously, the black American athlete Jesse Owens, who won four gold medals in the Games, caused consternation among the hosts, whose belief in white Aryan supremacy was well known and who had sought to make the event a visible demonstration of this supposed phenomenon. As a result there had been pressure in the USA to boycott the Games and the left-wing government in Spain actually did so. Owens was approached just before the Games by a famous sports manufacturer to wear their running shoes and so became the first black American athlete to receive funding of this nature.

Elsewhere, it was a year of chaos. In Britain, the new king, Edward VIII, abdicated so that he could marry an American divorcee, which was against the British constitution, while in Spain tensions between right-wing nationalists and left-wing communists erupted into open civil war – a conflict that would act as something of a proving ground for the weapons of overseas states that would soon be using them across Europe.

The civil war in Spain increased in intensity in 1937. The League of Nations issued an edict that no foreign combatants should take part in the conflict, a constraint that was, predictably, almost completely ignored in practice. The most notorious events of the war took place in the northern Spanish mountain town of Guernica, where German and Italian bomber planes caused hundreds of civilian deaths. Artists were inspired by the atrocity to produce memorable works as a reminder of what had happened; most famously (though there were a number of others too) Pablo Picasso who, emulating the work of Goya nearly two centuries before, captured the brutality and slaughter of war more eloquently than mere words could. His work would become a cause célèbre.

Awful though these events were, they paled into insignificance against those that took place in Nanking in December 1937. The ferocity of the war between China and Japan had been increasing since the Japanese annexation of what they called Manchukuo (Manchuria) some years before. In the so-called Rape of Nanking, 300,000 Chinese were slaughtered in a campaign of horrific brutality, characterised by the mass rape of the female population and the cold-blooded public butchering of anyone who happened to antagonise the occupying Japanese army.

The sheer extent of the massacre epitomised the sense of racial superiority felt by the Japanese, the same myopic reasoning that also saw Hitler attempt to implement in 1937 the concept of *Lebensraum*, living space (first expounded by Friedrich Ratzel in 1897), which argued that the German nation needed to expand and this made it permissible to seize neighbouring territories not currently in German hands. The Rape of Nanking was also extremely inept politically, as it quickly exposed Japanese claims that they were liberators intent on setting occupied colonies free from European control.

Cultural developments elsewhere could not hide the fact that 1937 was a generally black year for the world. There were chinks of light; *Snow White and the Seven Dwarfs* became the first full-length animated feature film to be made, and one of the most well-known pieces of classical music, *Carmina Burana*, made its debut. The Irish Free State, as it had until then been known, became the Republic of Ireland. But the most memorable news story of the year was the dramatic destruction of the German airship *Hindenburg*, which crashed in flames. Its burning shell seemed a metaphor for the whole world.

For those who believed in omens, 1938 (a year that saw the first intimations that there were large oil fields in Saudi Arabia) began inauspiciously, with a brilliant *aurora borealis* seen unusually far south. Described in some quarters as 'a curtain of fire', in medieval times it would probably have been seen as the precursor of unusually bloody times; in this case, the interpretation would have been supremely appropriate.

In Germany, Hitler made himself Supreme Commander of the Armed Forces, something for which, in the long term, the world should be truly grateful given his strategic limitations, although in the short term it appeared to be a spectacularly successful move. It was followed soon afterwards by demands that there should be Nazi participation in the Austrian government. This was shortly after followed by full German annexation of the country in what was known as the *Anschluss*. It was a move heavy with significance, for it gave the world a warning that any country with a significant German population was a potential target: Czechoslovakia and Poland were particularly endangered.

The warning was badly needed. In the previous decade, the world had been focussed on disarmament and pacifism – well-intentioned moves no doubt, especially for a planet facing economic meltdown, but disastrous in the face of rising militarism on the part of states such as Germany, Italy and Japan. Yet even as the world was belatedly waking up to the threat, pacifism continued. Britain, for example, agreed to recognise the Italian annexation of Ethiopia in return for a pledge that Mussolini would withdraw all his troops from Spain at the end of the civil war there. The world then stood idly by when Hitler added Czechoslovakia to his growing empire.

The future of Czechoslovakia was discussed at an infamous peace conference in Munich; Mussolini and representatives of the British and French governments were present, but one from the Czech government was not. The British Prime Minister Neville Chamberlain returned with an agreement which decreed that this was a basis for 'peace for our time'. There were dissenters from this view; the British politician Winston Churchill believed that the Munich Agreement was a disaster, but his was very much a minority view at the time – in fact, he only narrowly avoided an attempt by his local constituency political party to remove him. There was little stomach for war in Western Europe.

Buoyed by his successes, Hitler announced an ambitious naval expansion programme in 1939. Hungary joined what was known as the Anti-Comintern Pact (originally an arrangement between Germany and Japan signed in 1936), an agreement formed to defeat the perceived evils of communism, while in Spain the civil war ended, with the right-wing nationalist party led by General Francisco Franco the victors. Franco would effectively become the dictator of Spain for the next four decades and help to isolate his country from the rest of Europe, especially after the Second World War. Inspired by the spirit of the times, Italy invaded Albania and soon after entered into a 'Pact of Steel' with Germany. Alarmed, Britain began to adopt a more belligerent stance. She offered guarantees of protection to both Romania and Greece, as well as to Poland.

Concerned by the deteriorating situation, the American government gave permission to start the Manhattan Project, which would ultimately result in the atomic bomb, when Albert Einstein wrote to President Roosevelt suggesting such a scheme. Then at 4.45 a.m. on 1 September 1939, a German warship began bombarding a Polish fortress near Danzig. These were widely regarded as the opening shots of the Second World War. Two days later, Britain, France, New Zealand and Australia declared war on Germany, soon to be followed by countries as diverse as South Africa, Canada and Nepal. Other countries, most notably the United States (where a man-made fibre called nylon had just made its appearance) but also Ireland, Spain, Switzerland and Sweden, declared their neutrality.

The Soviet Union, though, who had recently entered into a non-aggression pact with Hitler to the surprise and consternation of the world, took advantage of the situation to invade Poland from the east (the Soviets soon after attacked Finland too). Polish defence was brief and futile. By the end of the month, the country had effectively fallen. The German occupying forces quickly declared that all Jews in the country should be moved henceforth to ghettos.

Yet this was known as the time of 'phoney war' – it may have been in the west, but the Poles presumably took a somewhat different view. The Soviet Union found that the conquest of Finland was harder than expected, but when the inevitable triumphant outcome was achieved, extremely harsh terms were imposed. The British Prime Minister Neville Chamberlain proclaimed that Hitler had 'missed the bus'. He was, of course, wrong. In May 1940, Hitler launched what became known as the Battle of France. By the end of the month, the British Expeditionary Force was being evacuated from Dunkirk and France was effectively overrun. Winston Churchill took over as Prime Minister with the position critical.

The German army soon after moved into Norway and Britain seemed doomed to fall too. However, the German *Luftwaffe* failed to defeat the British Royal Air Force in the Battle of Britain and the country fought defiantly on. In reality, the Germans had already turned their attention elsewhere and soon afterwards they launched their fateful assault on the Soviet Union. Such an act was always likely, given the fact that the two countries were both driven by strong ideologies that were inimically opposed to each other, but it was a move that would prove to be decisive in the overall defeat of Germany, for she had badly overreached herself.

But for a time her Japanese ally seemed to be the rising force in Asia. Desperate for resources to drive her industrial expansion, Japan began her own expansionist thrust into the Pacific, announcing her intention to do so at the American naval base at Pearl Harbour, Hawaii, on 7 December 1941. Months of apparently unstoppable Japanese conquest followed, but their triumphant advance was eventually brought to halt.

An important step along the way was the Battle of the Coral Sea, fought at the beginning of May 1942. Although the Japanese and American fleets lost a carrier each, it brought the advance of the former to a halt. It was also important in the sense that it was the first ever sea battle fought where neither protagonist could see the other. But the Japanese received a far more serious reverse at the Battle of Midway in June 1942, when four of her carriers were sunk by American planes. From that point on, she was on the back foot.

The war by now stretched across the globe. Australia, for example, had already been attacked by Japanese air power. Then, in 1942, what became known as the Holocaust moved into full swing. This was the year in which a young Dutch girl, Anne Frank, went into hiding in Amsterdam and began writing her diary. The racial stereotyping that underlay this persecution was a brutal but logical extension of colonialism as practised in many parts of Africa and Asia during the nineteenth and early twentieth centuries, and even of the destruction of native cultures in South America centuries earlier. Those earlier events had been characterised by perceptions that these other races were subhuman or even non-human, and their lives could therefore be destroyed on a whim.

Indeed, in the attempts of Nazi Germany to find *Lebensraum* in Eastern Europe and beyond, no attempt was made to hide their belief in the subhuman nature of the brutal Slav races, as indicated in Nazi propaganda. They were there to work until they dropped, given the most basic of living conditions and were on no account to mix with the 'master race' in anything except closely defined circumstances. Their lands were to be exploited for all they were worth. Colonialism had moved to the mainland of Europe.

Civilians were dragged into the conflict in a way that they had not been before. Air raids continued, exposing non-combatants directly to violent assault. The U-boat war caused huge losses among shipping, in turn creating serious deprivation among civilian populations, though in reality starvation and disease had often been the vicarious lot of civilians in wartime since the beginning of time.

The Germans initially made great advances into the Soviet Union, where Stalingrad and Leningrad in particular became symbols of resistance to their invasion. However, the tide of war began to turn decisively in 1943. In February of that year, the German army suffered a heavy defeat when it surrendered at Stalingrad. The Japanese, too, began a long but inexorable retreat when driven off the island of Guadalcanal.

Allied forces then began an invasion of Sicily, following the conquest of North Africa, which would eventually lead to a move across to the European mainland and up the Italian Peninsula, and German citizens continued to suffer bombing raids on a huge scale. But even in wartime cultural changes made their mark, with the appearance of a new musical format in *Oklahoma!* on Broadway on 31 March, which would mark a new genre that remains popular to this day.

The German army were on the defensive now that Russian forces were fighting back. The Battle of Kursk, fought in July and August 1943, saw the largest tank battle in history. It ended in a decisive Soviet victory. It also destroyed much of the trust between Hitler and his commanders, which had great significance for the rest of the war.

The Soviet leader, Stalin, put much pressure on the allied leaders, F. D. Roosevelt and Winston Churchill, to open a second front. Although pressure on Germany from the air was increasing, the U-boat war in the Atlantic was at last being won and the Allies were advancing north up the Italian Peninsula, only an invasion of France would create the pressure that was necessary.

This duly came on 6 June 1944 when the Allies successfully landed in Normandy following the largest amphibious assault in history. The Germans were caught off guard and, despite fierce initial resistance, the Allies moved on Paris, which was duly liberated. It was a high-risk operation; the weather was unpredictable, the precedent for an amphibious assault of this size (Gallipoli) had been an unmitigated disaster and the Germans had invested significantly in building defences. But despite especially strong resistance against the Americans on Omaha Beach, it opened the gates to Paris and then Germany.

By 1945 the war in Western Europe was coming to an end. While Allied forces moved on Germany from France, from the east the Soviet army moved ever closer to Berlin. Squeezed between two massive invasion forces, resistance in Germany started to collapse, though it was most vigorous in the east where Soviet forces were determined to avenge the huge losses they had suffered at German hands in their own country, and they took a terrible retribution on the populations that they now overran.

By May, it was all over. Berlin was seized by the Soviet army along with the east of Germany, while the west was taken by armies primarily from the United States and Britain. However, the war in the Pacific went on. For some time, the Americans had been undertaking a top-secret experiment, the 'Manhattan Project'. Its object was to make an atomic weapon, a tool of power and terror unparalleled in all of history. They of course succeeded, under the scientific leadership of J. Robert Oppenheimer. He famously recalled words from the Hindu epic, the Bhagavad Gita, when the first successful detonation of the bomb was made: 'I am become Death, the destroyer of worlds.'

The truth of those words was, of course, demonstrated graphically in the twin strikes on Hiroshima and Nagasaki, within a few days of each other in August 1945. The Japanese now realised that the war was no longer sustainable, let alone winnable, and surrendered for the first time in the country's history (though not before a brief rebellion from some of the military and a firm stance by Emperor Hirohito that he would not sanction surrender if his imperial title would be abolished as a result).

The atomic bombs, the innocuously named 'Little Boy' carrying uranium and, at Nagasaki, 'Fat Man' carrying plutonium, caused enormous loss of life, nearly all among civilians, including over 20,000 Koreans conscripted into hard labour by the Japanese. One Japanese citizen, Tsutomu Yamaguchi, was unfortunately injured in both explosions, though he managed to survive both of them.

The bombs undoubtedly saved hundreds of thousands of Allied lives that would have been lost if Japan had been subject to invasion, and may even have saved civilian lives, which were already being lost in huge numbers through conventional bombing raids. Whether they were morally right is an argument that belongs more in a book on ethics than one on history. But they undoubtedly brought the war to a quick end, though at the same time instigating a deterrent terror that would define the state of world politics ever after.

So, at the end of it all, what was the impact of the Second World War? It certainly changed the political face of the world. Europe was effectively divided into two camps, with the eastern part of the continent within the Soviet sphere of influence. Locked in a firm grip behind what Churchill famously called an 'iron curtain' for the next four decades, this half of Europe would be under the dominant influence of communism, or at least Sovietism, while the western part initially struggled to rebuild its shattered economies, at the same time trying to cope with the loss of colonies that began barely after the war ended.

In Asia, India quickly moved towards independence from British rule, led by the charismatic Mahatma Gandhi, who was assassinated in 1948, soon after the country had exited the British Empire. Gandhi had espoused non-violent resistance to British rule, adopting the view that, to paraphrase a quote attributed to him, 'an eye for an eye makes the whole world blind' (an expression that reflects beliefs attributed to Christ and later successfully used by Martin Luther King).

But it was not a transition free from violence, as Muslim and Hindu in parts of the huge Subcontinent found the thought of living together impossible and, as a result, two new nations, India itself and Pakistan, emerged from the post-colonial shake-up. In Africa, too, movements for independence gained momentum. The Atlantic Charter of 1941 appeared to confirm that colonies would have more autonomy after the war was over, though there was a good deal of ambiguity about what was meant in practice. It would be another decade before the independence movements in Africa met with widespread success, but the conditions for such a result were already taking shape.

The shattered economies of the defeated German and Japanese states slowly began rebuilding, with the aid of financial assistance from the victors, a state of affairs that could not have been more different than the massive reparations imposed at the end of the First World War, suggesting that at least some things had been learned. Over time, both Germany and Japan would grow into major economic powers.

The Marshall Plan, the implementation of which started in 1948, helped rebuild Europe and in the result also assisted the development of a bulwark against the further expansion of communism across the continent. Japan would be occupied by Allied forces until 1952 (and indeed the island of Okinawa remained so into the twenty-first century) and as part of this process steps were also taken there to reconstruct the economy of the country.

But perhaps the most crucial changes took place in China. For a while, the vicious occupation of Japanese forces had helped limit the civil war between nationalist and communist forces. Now that the Japanese invaders had been thrown out, the two factions were soon at each other's throats again. By 1949, the communist forces would be successful, in spite of American backing for their opponents, who established themselves on Formosa (now Taiwan).

The losses of the Second World War had been horrific. Although exact figures are of course impossible to arrive at, the range of estimated fatalities are from 50 to 70 million – making it the deadliest conflict in history in absolute terms. Of these, the Soviet Union suffered staggering fatalities of over 20 million. China also suffered more than 10 million deaths. In both cases, civilian losses far exceeded those incurred by the military.

As well as the atomic bombs, conventional bombing had killed hundreds of thousands. Losses at sea were large, too; in one incident, the 1945 sinking of the *Wilhelm Gustloff*, carrying mainly German civilians trying to escape advancing Soviet forces, nearly 10,000 perished, by far the biggest loss of life of any shipping disaster in history.

Perhaps the most awful part of this slaughter, though, was that millions of civilians were deliberately massacred, whether through industrial-style genocide in Germany or ruthless, uncoordinated barbarity against Chinese citizens. In order to help prevent a recurrence of these terrible losses, the United Nations Charter was signed in June 1945, with fifty countries signing up to it. Eventually, most countries in the world would become signatories (Vatican City being a notable exception). As a replacement for the discredited League of Nations it was a notable move, though preventing worldwide conflict or genocide (and sometimes even recognising it) would remain a problematic aspiration.

Europe had been decimated by the war, and the balance of power was changed irrevocably. The world needed to be rebuilt economically, and austerity was the byword of the day. The first post-war Olympic Games, held in London in 1948, were notable for the spartan accommodation provided for the athletes, military barracks as opposed to the purpose-built villages of more recent times.

It was the first Games for twelve years, but conflict still continued elsewhere. The state of Israel declared its independence on 14 May 1948; the next day troops from her neighbours, such as Egypt, Syria and Iraq, invaded. The conflict followed a UN plan for partition in Israel that the surrounding states refused to recognise. There were several truces – followed by further outbreaks of fighting – over the next few months, but by 1949 Israel had secured her borders for the time being. In their conduct of the war, both sides had committed atrocities against non-combatants, a sad precedent which has of course been emulated on a number of occasions.

By this time, much had changed elsewhere since the war. In 1946, a new federal state had been established in the Balkans – Yugoslavia – and the kingdom of Transjordan had been given independence by the British (it would soon be renamed Jordan). By the end of the year, the Dutch had recognised an independent Republic of Indonesia and in 1948 Britain granted the same to Burma. Tensions were also rising in Vietnam, which remained a French colony; within the country, increasing resistance against this state of affairs was apparent.

Europe, too, was still on a knife-edge. Communist governments had been voted in in several countries, including Czechoslovakia and Bulgaria. The two remaining international superpowers, the United States and the Soviet Union, squared up to each other. Berlin proved a crunch point, a divided city and an island in the middle of Soviet-run East Germany; the non-Soviet areas could only be provisioned by an air corridor, a task that was successfully undertaken via the famous Berlin Airlift. It was not a happy augury for future international politics.

Eastern Europe would find itself in a vice-like grip for decades. Attempts to assert more democratic principles in nominally independent countries such as Hungary or Czechoslovakia were ruthlessly crushed, often with direct or indirect Soviet assistance. Citizens of East Germany would, by the 1960s, find themselves trapped behind a wall, not to keep the enemies of communism out but to keep disenchanted citizens in. Religion would be discouraged and suppressed, though as soon as the edifice of communist power started to crumble it would quickly re-emerge again. And of course the 'bomb' would not remain exclusive US property for long; in a short space of time the Soviets would have their own version and the world would find itself peering into a precipice of terrifying depth.

But alongside these politically significant events, social changes were taking place too. In Britain, the welfare state took a large step forward with the foundation of the publicly funded National Health Service, while in post-war Japan women were granted the vote for the first time. Change was also happening economically; the International Monetary Fund was founded in 1947. Internationalism was a key word in the new order after the Second World War, and the following year the Organisation of American States came into being. In 1949, the North Atlantic Treaty Organisation (NATO) was formed.

In their own way, these new organisations marked the end of empires; where in the past a few imperial powers would get together and formulate their own collective policies on issues, now consensus and collaboration were the drivers in these pan-national fora. It was a much more equitable and democratic way of developing policy, and as such eminently preferable to what had gone before. But it was not without its problems, as the search for consensus slowed down the decision-making process and, when quick and decisive action was needed, such institutions struggled to cope, and continue to do so.

There were other pointers to the future emerging too. One was in the field of aeronautics. In 1948, Albert – a Rhesus monkey – became the first monkey astronaut, part of a race into space between the USA and the Soviet Union. A number of experiments with monkeys were carried out in subsequent years – in which the animals, including Albert, almost invariably failed to survive – but collectively these events played an important role in paving the way for men to travel into space – less than half a century after the Wright Brothers' flight. In the process, more questions were asked about the origins of the universe and in 1949 the English astronomer Fred Hoyle made the first reference to the 'Big Bang' theory, though the theory itself was not new and the phrase that he used was an ironic jibe against it.

Another more worrying development was the first ever hijacking, a Catalina seaplane called *Miss Macau* that was taken by force over Macau on 16 July 1948, though the motive for this act was financial rather than political. It was the first in a number of terrifying incidents in succeeding years and decades that would scar the world in days to come.

The scene was set for the second half of the twentieth century, a time of extraordinary technological process and – in some places at least – increased living standards. However, it was again an age of contradictions, with violence a continuing part of the world picture, sometimes exercised by nations against each other but also by pan-national organisations, this time terrorist groups, who introduced a new element of fear into the global environment.

However, these unwelcome developments did not mean an end to conventional war, as evidenced by the Chinese invasion of Tibet in 1950 or the outbreak of the Korean War in the same year. One of the founders of the atomic age, Albert Einstein, had recently prophesied that the world stood on the verge of destruction; as if to prove the point, General MacArthur now threatened to deploy nuclear weapons in Korea. The world stood on the edge of great progress and hugely increased opportunity; it also peered uncertainly towards a future over which a large, mushroom-shaped cloud hung more ominously than ever.

41

A NEW EQUILIBRIUM

The End of Empires (AD 1951–1975)

In 1951, the conflict in Korea was marked by a number of violent battles. The roots of the dispute lay in the resolution of the Second World War in 1945, which saw the Korean Peninsula divided in two, with the northern part under Russian control and the southern under the US. Before long North Korea was under a communist regime while the south was capitalist. It was the Chinese who provided the troops in support of the northern forces in the war for ideological domination that then broke out, and the United States who provided most of the troops to support the south in what was as much as anything a battle of ideologies.

In the end, the war was fought to a stalemate but not before an initial burst of toing and froing that saw Seoul change hands on four occasions. Starting as a modern conflict of aerial attack and mobile infantry assaults, the conflict soon changed into one based on trench warfare more reminiscent of the First World War.

Neither was the battle between opposing ideologies confined to Korea. In 1951, communist insurgents were involved in a guerilla conflict in Malaya. Discontent for different reasons was also important in Egypt, where riots broke out and a state of emergency was declared. Nationalist emotions were running high and would soon lead to far bigger international tensions, with Egypt declared a republic two years later. What became known as the Mau Mau Uprising in Kenya was also about to begin and would be a long and brutal affair.

The world continued to become more dangerous. In 1952, the year that King George VI died and was succeeded by Queen Elizabeth II, Britain announced that it had joined that select group of nations that possessed an atomic bomb (the following year, the USA would announce that it had just developed a hydrogen bomb). United Nations National Security Council Resolution 162/2 of October 1953 stated that the United States must keep its nuclear deterrent and a policy was developed that it would be used against Russia or China if they invaded any countries of the so-called 'free world'.

Even as this was happening the repercussions of the Second World War continued to impact, for example when West Germany (Germany was now divided in two) agreed to pay damages of 3 billion Deutsche Marks to Israel, in recognition of the millions of Jews who had been murdered as a result of the Holocaust.

At a more mundane level, a play called the *Mousetrap*, a thriller by the British writer Agatha Christie, appeared for the first time in London on 25 November 1952 – at the time of writing it is still going, making it the longest-running play in history as far as is known. There were also some interesting social developments in train, too. The name of Christine Jorgensen may no longer be a household one but she was born as George William Jorgensen and in 1952 became the first person to have a sex change operation, which took place in Denmark.

The death of the Soviet dictator Joseph Stalin in 1953 heralded a new era in the politics of the ruling regime, though it was not one that noticeably made the world a safer place in which to live. His eventual replacement, after a power struggle that lasted several years, was Nikita Khrushchev. He would begin a process that to some degree would reduce the impact of Stalin's legacy and also started some liberal reforms in the vast country.

In 1953, the Korean War came to a notional end, with a border agreed between North and South Korea. However, although the fighting stopped, the tensions did not and, sixty years on, the frontier remains one of the greatest political fault lines in the world. On a more peaceful note, this was also the year that Mount Everest was conquered for the first time, with the news of the successful ascent by Sherpa Tenzing and the New Zealander Sir Edmund Hillary arriving in London to coincide with the coronation of the new British queen. Man's quest for exploration was not over, but new frontiers now beckoned, both above the earth and in the ocean depths. Another link with the modern world was also forged when the first ever colour television went on sale in the United States.

International tensions were still prominent. By 1954, the year that the first nuclear-powered submarine was put into service (the first nuclear-fuelled power station was also opened near Moscow), Senator Joe McCarthy was well into his famous investigations into the alleged prevalence of communism in the United States. Clearly the freedom of speech guaranteed by the American Constitution did not extend to communism and McCarthy was ably assisted by a young lawyer named Robert Kennedy. But the year was also a tipping point against McCarthy. At the start of the year, polls showed that the majority of the public supported him. By its end, critics, who were beginning to tire of what they saw as paranoia, comfortably outnumbered supporters.

In the Far East, the political landscape was also shifting fundamentally. A French army was crushed by Viet Minh communist fighters from North Vietnam at Dien Bien Phu. It was a total defeat for the French and a reverse from which they never recovered in the region. The division of Vietnam into north and south would soon follow, and by the end of the year Laos would also be free from French rule.

Tastes in music were changing. A single by the singer Bill Haley and his band, The Comets, created a sensation in much of the West with a song called 'Rock Around the Clock', just as another superstar named Elvis Presley made his first appearance. Such distractions were needed as international tensions were still strong, epitomised in 1955 by a number of communist states in Eastern Europe uniting with the Soviet Union in what became known as the Warsaw Pact.

International politics were also prominent in 1956 (when a game called Scrabble was launched), as during the year Tunisia became independent of France. There were clear signs that once-great imperial powers were in permanent retreat; the British Empire would also soon start to unravel. The end of the year would confirm the trend, when Britain and France were forced to withdraw, humiliated, having made attempts to intervene when Egyptian president Gama Nasser nationalised the Suez Canal. Not that tensions were limited to Western European powers; an uprising against communist rule was brutally put down in Hungary by the intervention of Soviet forces. Hungary's attempts to leave the Warsaw Pact were crushed at the source.

We can see looking back that these were times of great drives for freedom. Countries such as Ghana were granted independence (in 1957, in this particular case). Now that we live in a world where there are so many errors to put right, and when so many expectations have been disappointed, it is easy to forget that a free country makes its own decisions, and that includes making its own mistakes, with which it has to live. With freedom comes responsibility.

The 1950s were a decade of increasing independence, in Africa in particular. In the north, for example, Libya gained independence in 1951 and Morocco became a self-ruling state in 1956, as did Sudan and Tunisia. This was only a prelude, as a steady stream of states becoming independent in the 1950s became a flood in the 1960s. Fourteen African states became independent in 1960 alone, and over ten others in the next five years. Some stayed as colonial states until the 1970s and a few even beyond, but the 1950s established the trend.

This also happened in Asia. Singapore would be granted self-rule in 1958, the opening steps towards full independence and something of a modern economic miracle. Malaya too would be granted independence, later emerging as Malaysia. Not everywhere was this process painless, though.

In Kenya, Mau Mau uprisings were vigorously put down by the British colonial rulers and in Indonesia all 326,000 Dutch nationals were expelled after a number of businesses were nationalised. In Europe, a significant reaction to the diminishing international influence of individual states was the signing on 25 March 1957 of the Treaty of Rome, which established the European Economic Community (EEC) – it officially came into existence on 1 January 1958.

Humanity was also looking upwards. The launch of *Sputnik 1* saw the first artificial satellite launched into space (an event that took place in October 1957). When the Soviet Union successfully completed the task, it created a panicked reaction in the United States. *Sputnik I* finished over 1,400 orbits of the earth before crashing back to the ground in early January 1958. At the end of the month, the United States responded with the successful launch of *Explorer 1*. The struggle for dominance had now spread to the stratosphere. By 1961, the Soviet Union appeared to be in the lead, when Yuri

Gagarin became the first man to enter space, though their advantage would prove short-lived.

However, there were plenty of problems back on earth to worry about. In April 1958, a revolutionary army led by Fidel Castro (at his side, a young fighter called Che Guevara would play his part) advanced on Havana, Cuba, presaging the emergence of a state that despite its small size would prove itself a troublesome neighbour to the United States and within a few years would bring the whole world to the edge of a nuclear cataclysm. Nature, too, seemed to be alarmed.

A landslide on 9 July in Alaska (which a year later would become the forty-ninth state of the USA, to be joined soon after by Hawaii as the fiftieth) produced a tidal wave that was an amazing 520 metres high. Perhaps nature was disturbed by the nuclear-powered submarine USS *Nautilus* becoming the first submarine to pass underneath the North Pole. Or the crashing of *Luna 2* on the moon on 14 September 1959, the first man-made object to reach the earth's satellite.

On 1 December 1959, Antarctica was declared as a scientific preserve with all military activity banned. Twelve signatories to the treaty marked an important breakthrough in more than one way, as it was the first arms agreement in the Cold War. But it was not just superpowers that were involved in difficulties. In 1960 there was a violent uprising in Algeria against the colonial power, France, this year also seeing the first deployment of American troops to Vietnam.

But colonies continued to gain their freedom in 1960 – Togo, the Ivory Coast, the Central African Republic, Mauritania and Upper Volta from France, the Belgian Congo from Belgium, and Cyprus from Britain for example. Across Africa in particular, the political map was being redrawn. It promised a hopeful new future; a reality that would prove somewhat hard to achieve in practice.

Some ideas, though, just do not catch on. In June 1959 an experiment was tried; a number of letters were sent up in a guided missile from the submarine USS *Barbero*, aiming for Florida. The missile landed minutes later and the letters were recovered; the experiment had proved a complete success. The postmaster general, Arthur Summerfield, predicted that this was the future; letters could be delivered in short order right across America and indeed across the world. However ingenious the idea was, and however successfully it was executed, the experiment has never been repeated since.

The world was still expanding rapidly. By now, there were over 3 billion human beings on the planet, a figure that would double in the next fifty years. There were many tensions and the Cold War was still in full swing. Amid all this, an event that promised great hope was the election of a young US President in November 1960: John F. Kennedy. He would experience a short, memorable and turbulent career.

Even before he had taken up residence in the White House, the incumbent but soon-to-be ex-President Dwight D. Eisenhower severed diplomatic relationships with Cuba. Within months of his move to the White House in January 1961, Kennedy supported what became known as the Bay of Pigs invasion, when a group of Cuban exiles landed on the island in an attempt to take it. They failed in this objective, leaving the American presidency severely embarrassed. Kennedy was particularly scathing about the role of the Central Intelligence Agency (CIA) in the invasion. The problem of Cuba had not gone away, though, and would soon assume much greater significance.

Not that it was the only point of threat; the erection in short order of a wall dividing Berlin in 1961 between the western and eastern (Soviet-held) parts of the city created a symbol of division that summed up the great danger that faced the world as well as anything else did. And when American helicopters arrived in Saigon in South Vietnam at the end of the year, the fuse was lit for a conflict that would assume massive significance in the next decade.

But Cuba would become the focal point for international politics in the short term. Kennedy was bitterly opposed to the views and ambitions of the current Soviet premier, Nikita Khrushchev. In 1962, when Soviet missiles were, it was proposed, to be based in Cuba, less than 100 miles from the US coast, a crisis point was reached (though the presence of American missiles already in Turkey went largely unremarked at the time). A game of bluff and counter-bluff followed, with Soviet ships boarded en route to Cuba. In the end it was Khrushchev who blinked first. For a while it had seemed as if the world was on the edge of oblivion, perhaps the moment of greatest peril ever. Humanity had peered over the edge of a precipice and the view had been alarming.

There were other points of confrontation too. In the Congo in Africa, US and Soviet interests were diametrically opposed. The country had been given its independence in 1960 but soon started to splinter in a violent secessionist struggle. The new prime minister, Patrice Lumumba, was assassinated shortly afterwards, allegedly with CIA involvement. Peacekeeping efforts were made but were unsuccessful in keeping the lid on the underlying tensions. The Congo turned into a morass of violence, instability and terrible living conditions for many of its people. Half a century on it remains largely the same, the suffering there still representing one of the greatest extant disasters of humanity, although it is only remembered intermittently by the wider world.

Further north in Africa, in 1962 Algeria achieved its independence from France after much violence in the country and a great deak of internal bitterness among different factions in France. In the same year, South Africa found itself condemned for its racist apartheid policies by the UN General Assembly. But racial tension was not limited to this part of the world. On 28 August 1963, the American civil rights activist Martin Luther King gave his famous 'I have a dream' speech on the steps of the Lincoln Memorial in Washington DC.

American society was faced by great challenges. In fact, the divisions were graphically exposed by the very public assassination of John F. Kennedy in Dallas, Texas, on 22 November 1963, in what was probably the iconic moment of the second half of the twentieth century. The still relatively young medium of television came into its own, pictures of the events and the state funeral soon afterwards making a dramatic impact around the world. It also probably spawned more conspiracy theories than any other event in recent history. Although one man, Lee Harvey Oswald, was identified as the assassin, there are many who still insist that he was not acting alone; just who might have masterminded the murder remains a matter of fierce disagreement.

Despite all these grave international tensions and the threats of a very serious global confrontation resulting, the sixties was also famous for something quite different. The emergence of new musical 'pop' groups such as The Beatles unleashed all kinds of changes, including increased levels of sexual freedom, experimentation with drugs and – in its own way an extension of these two characteristics – a rejection of traditional authority constructs in the parts of the world affected. Opposition to the Vietnam War in particular became a focal point for such rejections of traditional authority. In their own way these opened up fault lines in democracy, for Western governments, however much they talked up its merits, still believed that they knew what was best for their people and did not react warmly to those who disagreed with them.

This only impacted on some parts of the globe, though. In much of the world, authoritarianism was still the order of the day. The prevalence of communist rule in the Soviet Union, China and much of Eastern Europe meant that people's lives there were dictated by others 'who knew best'. Dissension was dangerous and experimentation with Western culture was a rejection of sounder 'Party' values and therefore had to be crushed.

Fortunately, the human spirit will, in some cases, not be crushed so easily. But Jean-Jacques Rousseau's famous comment in the eighteenth century that 'man is born free but everywhere he is in chains' remained true for much of the world 200 years later. Ironically, in many such places the ruling government had replaced old autocracies in the name of the people. For those who value freedom it is always a bad omen to see the word 'people's' or 'democratic' in the name of a country, for too often these are anything but.

Yet there were signs that times were changing. In 1964, President Johnson signed a decree outlawing racial segregation in the United States. Of course, there is a difference between passing new laws and abolishing such practices in everyday life and thought (as race riots in Harlem soon afterwards amply demonstrated, and 1965 would see a number of similar incidents), but it was nevertheless a crucial step forward. Elsewhere the struggle for freedom went on, with an uprising taking place in Mozambique in the same year.

That year, 1965, saw a substantial build-up of American forces in South Vietnam. There had also been naval confrontations with American forces in the region and the North Vietnamese were deploying more sophisticated anti-aircraft devices. What had been a fierce but essentially limited conflict was now changing in character. With increased American commitment came greater military losses and more resistance from the American public to involvement in the conflict. There would also be an upsurge in the ferocity of the fighting, which would soon lead to serious atrocities, especially against unarmed civilians.

The escalation would continue into 1967. Pitched battles were fought alongside fierce raiding from both sides. There was a robust counter-reaction to the war in the United States, which saw tens of thousands of protesters on the streets. Worried at the strength and frequency of such protests, President Johnson sought advice as to how to make the war more popular, or at least less unpopular. The response – that he should use his public speeches to present an optimistic picture of the war – was hardly innovative.

Conflict in the Middle East loomed, too. The state of Israel had been threatened ever since it was formed. In response to a military build-up by Egyptian forces in Sinai, the Israelis launched a pre-emptive strike on 5 June 1967. An initial assault by the Israeli Air Force found the Egyptian defences totally unprepared. The Egyptian media reported that a great victory had been won over the Israelis. Nothing could be further from the truth. The Egyptian Air Force was effectively knocked out of the war on the very first day.

Several other Arab nations entered the war, including Jordan and Syria. However, the initial air successes enjoyed by the Israelis merely presaged further victories on the ground. At the end of the Six-Day War, Israel held East Jerusalem, the Golan Heights bordering Syria, the Gaza Strip and the Sinai Peninsula. Decades later, with the exception of the Sinai Peninsula, which was eventually returned to Egypt, all these territories remain areas of contention and strife.

Events in the Far East were also to have a dramatic impact. On 16 May 1966, a major development took place in China with the formal beginning of what would become known as the Cultural Revolution. Set in train by Chairman Mao, its declared aims were to completely establish socialism and abolish capitalism and traditionalism. The Revolution was typified by purges at the highest level and the persecution of millions of others at lower levels.

Although it helped cement Mao's personality cult, it was an abject failure and caused widespread suffering and resentment, being abandoned just over a decade later. Ironically, some good came out of it; medical conditions in rural areas, for example, did improve. But for millions these were terrible years and the country as a whole breathed a huge sigh of relief when these flawed policies were abandoned.

But while these political events were taking place, the pace of technological advance continued to accelerate. When the great ocean liner *Queen Mary* made her last transatlantic crossing in 1967, it seemed symbolic of the ending of one age and the beginning of another.

The symbolism seemed complete when, in the same year, the first supersonic passenger airliner, Concorde, took the stage, though it would be some time before it saw commercial use. Somewhat more unusually, on 12 January that year, Dr James Bedford (a professor from California) died and a few hours later became the first human being deliberately frozen in the hope that, one day in the future, medical research will have advanced so much that he can be brought back to life.

The battle in Vietnam intensified in 1968. During the celebration of the Lunar New Year ('Tet'), there was supposed to be a cessation in hostilities. However, the North Vietnamese Vietcong caught their South Vietnamese, American and allied opponents off guard by attacking during this period. The aim was to attack selected targets in Saigon but, after initial successes, the Vietcong were driven back, losing thousands of men in the process.

Yet in its way the offensive marked a turning point. When forced out of the city of Hué, several thousand South Vietnamese were slaughtered in cold blood by the Vietcong, fuelling a strong desire for vengeance. In February, a photograph was taken of a South Vietnamese officer shooting a handcuffed Vietcong soldier in the head. It soon achieved worldwide coverage and the opposition to the war accelerated in the West. The fact that the man executed may himself have been responsible for ruthlessly killing several dozen South Vietnamese, including his killer's godchildren, shortly before did not lessen the impact. The power of the media in an age of ever more rapid communication was clearly on the rise.

The infamous My Lai Massacre, when unarmed civilians were killed by American troops a few months later, merely added to the rising anger in the United States against the war. The country was indeed bitterly divided on several fronts and was clearly not at peace with itself, as evidenced by the assassinations of Martin Luther King in Memphis, Tennessee, on 4 April 1968 and of Robert Kennedy, a presidential candidate hoping to emulate the success of his late brother on 5 June in Los Angeles. America was distracted, with a presidential election looming, when in August democratic movements in Prague, Czechoslovakia (now the Czech Republic), were ruthlessly crushed by 200,000 Warsaw Pact troops and 5,000 tanks in August 1968.

Yet amid this war and violence, mankind was about to demonstrate its extraordinary creativity. On Christmas Eve that year, the American spacecraft *Apollo 8* entered orbit around the moon. Astronauts Frank Borman, Jim Lovell and William Anders became the first human beings to see the far side of the moon. Appropriately, they read from the Book of Genesis in the Bible as they did so.

This set the scene for an even more remarkable event. On 20 July 1969, Neil Armstrong became the first man from this planet ever to set foot on an extraterrestrial body, in this case the moon (less well known is the fact that Eugene Cernan was the last person to do so – to date – having stepped on the moon on 14 December 1972, travelling there in *Apollo 17*). The *Apollo 11* expedition marked a remarkable rate of progression, coming just sixty-six years after man had flown in an aircraft other than a hot-air balloon for the first time. Half a billion people watched on television, at that time the highest audience for any event. On their successful return to earth, all the astronauts were quarantined for several days in case they had brought back any lunar germs with them, though subsequent tests showed that the moon's lack of atmosphere made this an impossibility.

Another moon landing followed later in the year. The Soviet Union, having lost this particular race, did not stay idle and the year after the *Venera 7* spacecraft became the first man-made object to land on Venus and send data back to earth. Nor was this the only aeronautical achievement, for at around this time a large new passenger airliner, the Boeing 747 (more colloquially known as 'the Jumbo Jet'), also made its bow.

Such distractions were much needed. The American war effort in Vietnam continued to increase just at the time that public demonstrations against such moves also grew. The new President, Richard Nixon, asked the 'silent majority' to join him in supporting the war and a draft lottery was held for the first time since the Second World War. In Britain, John Lennon, one of the Beatles, returned his MBE in protest at the British government's support of the United States in the war. Britain had troubles of her own to occupy her attentions in 1969 as outbreaks of street fighting in Northern Ireland led to the British government deploying troops there in an unsuccessful attempt to prevent an upsurge in violence, which culminated in a loss of control and life in what became known as 'Bloody Sunday', an event that continues to haunt British politics.

In Africa, a bitter civil war in the Biafra region of Nigeria came to an end in 1970. The conflict had become iconic because of the photographs spread across the globe of the terrible famine suffered by many inhabitants of the state. It was perhaps the first African famine to register so sharply in the minds of the rest of the world, but it would not be the last. Civil war was not just limited to this region. On the far side of Asia another internecine conflict broke out in Cambodia, with a fanatical party known as the Khmer Rouge rising to prominence as a result. In response, President Nixon asked for substantial funds to assist the Cambodian government.

Africa was showing worrying signs indeed after so many countries had received their independence in the previous two decades. One potentially more prosperous country on the continent was Uganda, 'the Pearl of Africa'. A Ugandan Army officer, Idi Amin, seized power there in a coup in January 1971. It was the start of eight years of tyrannical rule, characterised by torture, murder and disregard for human rights. He ejected all those of Asian stock from his country and seized all their business assets; the end result of this inspired move was to destroy one of the few profitable parts of the Ugandan economy. In many ways, Amin was just a symbol for so many other African leaders at the time, who saw their countries as sources of personal wealth where democracy was just a pretty name without any meaning.

In 1971, a new country was born. When India gained its independence from Britain the Bengal region was split between Hindu and Muslim areas. The former were attached to India and the latter to Pakistan. However East Pakistan, as it was known, was separated from the rest of the country by a wide tract of territory, and resentment against Pakistani rule grew so intense that in 1971 a breakaway government was declared in India. A war of liberation followed, at the end of which the state of East Pakistan, with significant Indian support, became the new nation state of Bangladesh. It is a nation not without problems, with a number of low-lying areas, not insignificant shifting of tectonic plates and common extreme weather conditions. Of all the nations in the world threatened by climate change, Bangladesh is near the top of the list.

The start to 1972 was marked by an iconic diplomatic mission by US President Richard Nixon to China. There had been some signs that Chinese isolation was ending; the country had recently taken its place at the United Nations, for example, at the expense of Taiwan. The visit itself did not turn the world on its head overnight, but it opened the world up to the possibility that at some point in the future China might become a major global player, a prospect that has now come to fruition spectacularly.

In May of that year, acts of genocide were committed in Burundi. It is estimated that 120,000 Hutus died in them. The later genocide in neighbouring Rwanda, largely against the minority Tutsis and perpetrated by the majority Hutus, is very well remembered, but this earlier crime against humanity much less so. The reality is that this particular region is on a political fault line and one that has largely escaped the notice of the wider world in the past. As a result of this, millions have died and millions of others have suffered lives of unspeakable hardship and hopelessness.

Yet there was at least a wider sign of optimism for the world when Presidents Nixon of the USA and Brezhnev of the USSR signed an anti-ballistic missile treaty in Moscow, the SALT 1 agreement, on 26 May 1972. The build-up of nuclear weapons was now so great that the world could be blown apart many times over and the cost of maintaining and developing them was huge. Economic reality may have been the driver as much as a desire for world peace, but it was at least a step in the right direction.

It was ironic that, on the very day that this treaty was being signed, in President Nixon's capital on the other side of the world an apparently minor burglary attempt took place that would lead to international repercussions. The break-in at the Watergate building was a failure, as was one on the following night. A break-in the following month, however, succeeded. The offices were the headquarters of the Democratic Party National Committee and politics were suspected of being behind the actions. The failed attempts left a metaphorical smoking gun that would lead back to the very highest places.

It is often said that politics and sport should not mix. But on 5 September 1972, they came into contact with terrifying results. The Munich Olympics of that year would be remembered not for the sporting achievements but for the massacre that took place when a number of Israeli athletes were seized by Palestinian terrorists and eleven of them killed. Ironically, in an attempt to expunge the memory of Hitler's utilisation of the 1936 Berlin Games as a propaganda tool, security in the Olympic village had been deliberately low-key. In a bitter comment on how divided the Middle East was, only one Arab leader – King Hussein of Jordan – condemned the attack. The Olympic Committee refused to institute a memorial to the murdered victims, fearing it would alienate other states. The issue of terrorism was not new to the world, even in modern times. But the Munich incident was a massive escalation that shook the world to its core.

Early in 1973, President Nixon decided that he had had enough of so little progress for so much cost in Vietnam and a peace accord was signed by which American troops were withdrawn from the country and American prisoners were returned. By the end of March, the last American soldier had gone. Nixon had problems closer to home to worry about, anyway. The Watergate hearings were in full swing and the onus of responsibility appeared to be rising ever closer to the top (by 16 July, Nixon's name was firmly in the frame). Yet despite all this there were some signs of a thawing in relationships with the Soviet Union, demonstrated when President Brezhnev became the first Soviet premier to address the American public on television.

On 6 October, a major confrontation once more erupted between Israel and her neighbours. It started with an Egyptian army crossing of the Suez Canal and a coordinated attack on the Golan Heights from Syria. The Israeli Army was initially caught off guard but turned the tide and pushed both armies back, at one stage reaching points just 40 miles from Damascus and just over 60 miles from Cairo. Both the United States and the Soviet Union, supporting different sides in the war, were pulled ever closer and in the end a ceasefire was called. As a result, a chain reaction was started that led to the Camp David Accords and a normalising of relations of sorts between Israel and Egypt.

However, in a way the whole world was dragged into the conflict. In response to the US decision to resupply Israel during the war, Arab oil-producing states announced an embargo. The actions of the Organisation of Arab Petroleum Exporting Countries (a subset of OPEC) had a massive economic impact. Oil prices skyrocketed and inflation soared. The embargo lasted for six months and only ended when the Israelis negotiated a ceasefire with Syria. But the power of OPEC had been amply demonstrated and the reliance of the world on 'black gold' fully shown. The use of oil as a weapon of economic warfare showed just how addicted the world was to it – a situation which is still largely the case, even when moves towards 'cleaner, greener energy' are being made.

In the United States, the Watergate crisis came to a head in 1974. President Nixon was now deeply implicated in the course of events and there was a very real danger that he would be impeached for his part in them, which would have been a unique and humiliating experience for an American President. Instead he tendered his resignation and his Vice President, Gerald Ford, took over from him. One of his first actions was to grant a full pardon to his predecessor, though the infamy Nixon had earned would live with him for the rest of his days.

Elsewhere, a Turkish invasion of Cyprus helped cement a division in the small but strategically important island. From Antiquity, Cyprus has been a much coveted territory due to its situation just off the coast of Turkey and the Levant. In more recent times, it had been home to both Turkish and Greek populations. With the demise of the Ottoman Empire at the beginning of the century, there was something of a struggle for dominance by one party or the other. While the island had been under British rule, the lid was kept on the situation. However, with the island's independence the situation deteriorated significantly. The de facto division of the island continues to create problems inside the European Union to this day and is an important obstacle to be overcome regarding the possible accession of Turkey to that body.

Other events, though less politically notable, would have long-term repercussions, such as the introduction of the Universal Product Code (UPC) barcode system in 1974, which is now widely used in North America, the United Kingdom, Australia, New Zealand and other countries for tracking the sale and movement of items in stores. It may appear a humble invention but it opened up the world to the potential of computerised stock management, which forms a key part of retail activities in some parts of the world until this day. It has come a long way from when the first item sold in this way, a packet of chewing gum, was processed on 26 June 1974 in Ohio. A year of interesting innovations was topped off by the invention of the Rubik's Cube puzzle by a Hungarian professor of that name. It is currently the world's best-selling puzzle game.

The release of a micro-computer, the Altair 8800, in 1975 was a crucial step forward in computerisation across the globe. Computers had been around for some time but almost exclusively inside laboratories of sorts. The Altair 8800 brought it into the reach of ordinary people. Two young 'techies' approached the company owner, Ed Roberts, offering to provide a computer language to run on the micro-computer. One was called Paul Allen, the other Bill Gates. The offer was accepted and the two men soon formed a company, which they called Micro-soft. The hyphen in the name was dropped and the rest, as they say, is history.

April 1975 was an iconic month in other ways. On 17 April, the Khmer Rouge entered the Cambodian capital, Phnom Penh. The city was forcibly evacuated and the mass murders for which the communist victors would become infamous now moved into full swing, with devastating results for millions of people. Buoyed by their triumph, in the following month the Khmer Rouge seized an American ship, the SS *Mayaguez*, in international waters. The Americans launched a recovery operation and the ship was recaptured but a number of their soldiers were killed in the fierce fighting that followed.

Despite involving Cambodia, this incident became regarded as the last conflict of the Vietnam War. The last names on the famous monument in Washington DC commemorating it are of those killed in the fight to recover the ship, including three marines captured alive and subsequently executed. What made the incident more poignant was that, just a few weeks before, one of the most famous incidents in modern times occurred when the North Vietnamese captured Saigon. The scenes of American advisers and other non-South Vietnamese citizens being evacuated, while leaving so many of their local comrades behind, seared themselves into the consciousness of the wider world. With the disgrace of President Nixon, an ongoing energy crisis and the effective loss of the Vietnam War, these were troubling times for the United States.

With a neat symmetry perhaps, the year was also characterised by the last knockings of European colonial rule. Britain and France had already given up most of their overseas territories and now Portugal joined in, with Mozambique, Angola and the Cape Verde Islands all achieving independence, though the first two soon entered an extended period of bloody civil war. Spain gave up Western Sahara, its last colonial possession, and the Netherlands did the same with Surinam. Even Papua New Guinea received independence from Australia. It marked the effective end of European colonialism, though a few isolated examples remain even now, albeit on a minuscule scale compared to what previously existed.

Yet superpower politics still appeared to be largely unchanged. It is true that Nixon and Brezhnev had earlier got together and an arms limitation process had begun. But it was at its very formative stages and the communist world still faced the West as a potential enemy, while poor Africa became a battleground in which both sides manipulated the situation in order to obtain an ideological advantage. But all this was about to change, and in just over a decade the world would be turned on its head.

42

THE GREAT ROLLER COASTER

The Collapse of Communism and the Birth of New Democracies (1976–2000 AD)

The year 1976 saw the formation of another new computing company, called Apple, which would have a great impact on the modern world. It also saw the legal consolidation of North and South Vietnam, a symbolic confirmation that the war there had been definitively won and lost. Space exploration also continued apace with the Viking missions to Mars. *Viking 1* went into orbit around the planet in June and would stay there for four years, feeding useful information back to earth. The landing craft ('lander') itself would remain in useful contact with earth for six years after landing before an expensive mistake back at ground-control cut off contact, which has never been regained since.

Space exploration was in fact high up the agenda again. On 17 September that year a new spacecraft, the space shuttle (this particular one named *Enterprise*), made an appearance in California. It lifted eyes again from the earth, which was still in turmoil in places. The death of Chairman Mao in 1976 brought an end to the 'Cultural Revolution' in China, though even before his demise there had been public protests in Tiananmen Square against what now people regarded as a failed experiment. China had other problems, too. In Tangshan on 28 July a massive earthquake killed an estimated 240,000 people.

Health issues were also on the agenda. Recent years had brought great improvements in this area, but from time to time new diseases still appeared. While meeting at a convention in Philadelphia, twenty-nine members of the American Legion were inexplicably taken ill and died. Legionnaires' disease had made its first recognised appearance. So too did a horrific new virus. With up to 90 per cent death rates of those affected, the Ebola virus, which was identified for the first time in Zaire and Sudan, was potentially a major killer. There was something of a double-edged sword in its rapid onset and high death incidence, however; it meant that the potential for a major epidemic was limited, as potential carriers died too quickly to spread the virus. However, it has had a major impact on local chimpanzee populations and there have also been suggestions that gorillas may be impacted by the virus.

Air transport was now well established and had helped to make the world a much smaller place. Although statistically a relatively safe mode of transportation, when accidents happen they can create a huge loss of life. The collision of two 747 'Jumbo Jets' in Tenerife on 27 March 1977 left 583 people dead, currently the heaviest loss of life in any air disaster. On a happier note, that year Spain held its first democratic elections for many years. The era of the Franco dictatorship was at last at an end and the country stood ready to take its place within the mainstream of Europe once more. Pakistan was going the other way, though, with General Mohammed Zia-ul-Haq overthrowing Zulfikar Ali Bhutto, the first elected prime minister of the country.

Popular music was changing. This was the era of 'punk rock', an anti-establishment form of music where the musicians seemed to go out of their way to shock – in the West young people continued to express their opposition to the status quo through music and also through lifestyle choices that defied convention. The year 1977 saw the death of an older anti-establishment figure by the name of Elvis Presley at the age of only forty-two.

On 25 July 1978, Louise Brown was born in the United Kingdom. What made the small, sub-6 lb baby special was the method of fertilisation that led to her birth, for she was the world's first child born through in vitro fertilisation (IVF), more popularly known as a 'test tube baby' (though this is factually misleading as the initial development was via the medium of a Petri dish). Man was increasingly capable of interfering with the course of nature, something that continues to develop with the ongoing debate over cloning.

International affairs were to the forefront as 1979 dawned. The Vietnamese Army forced the regime of the notorious Pol Pot to flee from Phnom Penh, the capital of Cambodia, while in Iran, the ruler – Shah Mohammed Reza Pahlavi – was forced out of the country, marking the beginning of the end for monarchical rule in the country after thousands of years. Soon after, an Iranian cleric by the name of Ayatollah Ruhollah Khomeini returned after fifteen years in exile.

He would soon after become a religious head of state, heralding the onset of a new regime that would become a regional power and a source of challenge for some of the leading countries of the Western world. The events in Cambodia had a significant impact, too. China, Cambodia's ally, briefly invaded North Vietnam in a war that was short but bloody, and the pictures of Pol Pot's 'Killing Fields', which contained the remains of millions of dead human beings, created a sensation across a horrified world.

In the field of technology, 1979 saw the appearance of the first compact disc – the Sony Walkman would go on sale for the first time soon after, and an artist by the name of Michael Jackson released his first solo album. Major changes were also taking place in Africa, where the first black government took up office in Rhodesia, soon to be renamed Zimbabwe (the first prime minister of the new country, Robert Mugabe, was elected in the following year), and Flight Lieutenant Jerry Rawlings seized power in the West African state of Ghana.

In China, struggling to cope with a vastly increasing population, a 'one-child policy' was implemented, a social experiment that – however economically justified it might have been – was deeply controversial, and led to allegations of infanticide among female children. However, the event that shook the world the most in this year occurred towards its end when the Soviet Union invaded Afghanistan, an event that would have dramatic consequences. Britain in the meantime had its first female Prime Minister, Margaret Thatcher, though there had been a number of female prime ministers in other countries previously, such as Sirimavo Bandaranaike in Sri Lanka (first in post 1960),

Indira Gandhi in India (1966), Golda Meir in Israel (1969) and Elisabeth Domitien in the Central African Republic (1975).

The Soviet invasion quickly led to repercussions and early in 1980 the United States, supported by the European community, introduced a grain embargo. There were signs of other developments that would have an international impact too, when in January 1980 over sixty Muslim fundamentalists were publicly beheaded in Saudi Arabia. They had seized control of the Grand Mosque in Mecca in November of the previous year and in the firefight that followed over 200 people died. The world was headed towards an uncertain and troubling period that continues to reverberate.

The United States soon after decided to boycott the Moscow Olympic Games in protest at the invasion of Afghanistan, but also had other issues to occupy it when the American embassy in Tehran, Iran, was taken over and a number of hostages held; the Iranian embassy in London was also taken over in April, leading to a famous rescue raid that was beamed around the world. In Poland in the meantime, a new trade union known as Solidarity (*Solidarnosc*) was recognised; it would have a dramatic long-term impact, though it would take the best part of a decade for it to do so.

The hostage situation in the American embassy in Tehran eventually ended peacefully, after a rescue mission launched to free them had ended in an embarrassing failure. America also had a new President when the Democrat Jimmy Carter was replaced by a former actor, Ronald Reagan. Although Reagan had many critics, he would play an unexpectedly positive role in world events during the rest of the decade, though his period in office started off with difficulty when he narrowly survived an assassination attempt in 1981.

Challenges still existed in the Middle East, as shown when an Israeli bombing raid destroyed a nuclear reactor in Iraq. The region was as dangerous as ever and on 6 October 1981 President Anwar Sadat of Egypt was assassinated by jihadists who objected to the closer relations he had fostered with Israel; Hosni Mubarak took his place. Tensions were also present in Syria when a Sunni uprising in the town of Hama in 1982 was crushed with great severity by government forces supporting President Assad. The country had a Sunni majority, but the ruling minority Ba'ath Party fought ruthlessly against any attempt to diminish its power.

Tensions between the USA and the USSR were raised in 1983 when President Reagan introduced a missile defence plan, designed, he said, to secure the defence of his nation against foreign aggression, which popularly became known as the 'Star Wars' initiative after a well-known Hollywood movie series of the same name (though its more proper name was 'the Strategic Defence Initiative'). By potentially making obsolete the principle of mutual deterrent, the Soviet Union saw this as a hostile act and relations deteriorated between the two nations. Few could have foreseen at the time that there would be a 180-degree turnabout by the end of the decade.

The United States was in difficulties in some parts of the world and a problematic relationship with the Middle East was to continue to haunt foreign policy. A suicide-bombing attack on the US embassy in Beirut, Lebanon, on 18 April 1983 seemed to mark the beginning of a new tactic by fundamentalist Islamic groups, which, at the time of writing, shows little sign of diminishing on a permanent basis. The attack followed the despatch of a multinational force to ostensibly keep the peace in the Lebanese Civil War, which in its own way presaged another new tactic: large-scale intervention in the Middle East by the United States and her international allies.

Perhaps now little remembered by the wider world, this intervention in Lebanon in retrospect was a turning point in international strategy and relationships that has led to one of the most challenging issues currently facing our world. As if to prove the case, the even more deadly truck bombing in Beirut that occurred later in the year, which killed over 300 US and French troops and Lebanese civilians, appeared to signify an upturn in such deadly acts.

Now not widely remembered, but hugely significant in its own way, was the voyage of *Pioneer 10*, which launched from Florida on 3 March 1972 and then made its way across the solar system on an incredible journey. Passing by Jupiter and then Pluto and Neptune, on 13 June 1983 the unmanned spacecraft became the first man-made object to leave the inner solar system.

Pioneer's voyage continued on and contact was not finally lost until 2003. It was a remarkable achievement on the part of mankind to offset against his more dubious efforts in other areas, such as the development of weapons of mass destruction (a terrifyingly bland description for something so awful in its potential if there ever was one) and the impact of mass industrialisation on the health of our planet.

The appearance of a new computer device, the Apple Macintosh, in January 1984, was part of a trend that saw such technology move away from being the preserve solely of big business and more and more towards the home. It also saw the first appearance of a new device now taken for granted – the 'mouse'. Although the 'Mac' would have to reinvent itself in the 1990s it would do so successfully and remains one of the great successes of modern times – though past history suggests that its time at the top will be limited and something, probably as yet undiscovered or at least little known, will eventually take its place.

A turning point in international relations was about to be reached with the appointment of Mikhail Gorbachev as leader of the Soviet Communist Party and effectively the leader of the Soviet Union. Gorbachev was to develop a chemistry with President Reagan that would have far-reaching consequences. Ordinary citizens were also becoming involved in mass movements, stirred by reports of famine in Africa to launch several widely supported charity events known as Live Aid.

Technology continued to advance, though there were still challenges to be overcome, as evidenced when Japanese Airlines Flight 123 crashed, killing 520 people, the worst single-airplane disaster in history. Alongside that, the discovery of the wreck of the most famous ship in history, the *Titanic*, on 1 September 1985 marked incredible technological progress but also served to remind of the dangers of hubris. It was a sentiment tragically and very publicly reinforced when, on January 1986, the space shuttle *Challenger* exploded shortly after take-off, an event watched by billions across the world. The power of mass media to bring such images to the watching world is one of the most significant of all forces in terms of shaping modern global attitudes.

It was also forcibly brought home when, on 26 April 1986, a nuclear power station at Chernobyl, then in the Soviet Union, now located in Ukraine, failed spectacularly, killing over 4,000 people and causing billions of dollars' worth of damage. Widespread nuclear fallout led to the mass evacuation of hundreds of thousands of people and contamination to a greater or lesser extent across much of Northern Europe.

Later in the year, in an attempt to stop a nuclear disaster of a different sort, Presidents Reagan and Gorbachev met in Reykjavik, Iceland, to discuss the possibility of a reduction in the stocks of atomic weapons held by each country. Although these talks did not ostensibly succeed in their objective, they laid a foundation for positive developments in the near future.

The Middle East continued to remain a problem zone, though. Palestinian territories that had been occupied by Israel were areas of festering discontent and in December 1987 the suppressed pressures burst to the surface in what became known as the First Intifada. There were outbreaks of violent rioting and mass protests followed by many arrests. As relations continued to deteriorate over the next few years, violence between Palestinians and Israelis also worsened, symptomatic of ongoing difficulties that still continue to present what appears to be one of the world's insoluble problems.

The region was also destabilised by a bitter war between Iran and Iraq, in many ways a war of attrition that bore reminders of the First World War. Trench warfare, liberally scattered barbed wire and large-scale frontal assaults appeared to belong to another age and also led to terrible casualty rates in the hundreds of thousands. Disturbingly, the conflict saw the deployment of chemical weapons by the Iraqis both against their Iranian foe and also dissentient Kurdish elements in their own country.

December 1987 was notable for another tragic reason. Earlier in the year, the sinking of a roll-on, roll-off car ferry named *The Herald of Free Enterprise* in Zeebrugge Harbour had cost several hundred lives. Then, on 20 December, a passenger ferry named the *Dona Paz* sank off the Philippines. The loss of life was catastrophic, officially 1,749 in total. However, this was not all. It quickly transpired that there were huge numbers of passengers who were not listed. It was subsequently estimated that the death toll was around 4,000, making it by far the worst peacetime shipping disaster of all time – only six survivors were rescued.

During 1988, the Soviet Union began a process of economic reconstruction known as *perestroika*. This saw the introduction of some market-type changes and marked an important move down the road towards a major political realignment both within the country and in Eastern and Central Europe. These changes came home to roost in spectacular fashion in 1989, a remarkable year that had a profound impact on Europe and the world.

It became obvious that the experiment with communism had only led in many cases to serious economic pressures and an irresistible drive for change. As if to emphasise the impact of the winds of change, the Soviet Union announced in February 1989 that its last troops had left Afghanistan, marking yet another failed attempt by a foreign power to subdue the country. By the following year, a number of Central Asian regions within the Soviet Union were announcing their independence.

Across Eastern Europe, communism did not so much collapse as die of old age. The most iconic of images was the spontaneous destruction of parts of the wall that had for three decades divided Berlin in two. The bloodiest of ends came in Romania, where the dictator Nicolae Ceauşescu and his much-despised wife Elena were shot after a brief parody of a trial on Christmas Day.

Across Eastern Europe the first shoots of freedom at last blossomed into an ability for nation states to decide their own destiny without outside interference, though in some countries it was not too long before elements of the population were reminiscing nostalgically about what had been lost from the 'good old days'. Exposed suddenly to the icy blasts of market forces, some disadvantaged social groups, such as the elderly, were left to fend for themselves when the ability to plan long-term for such an eventuality had been denied them. But there was no going back. By February 1990, the two states of Germany, divided at the end of the Second World War, were making firm plans to reunify.

This was not everywhere a smooth transition. Particularly in the Caucasus, bitter disputes would emerge over territorial boundaries, and sharp cultural and ethnic divisions would in some cases lead to war – between Azerbaijan and Armenia, for instance, though there would also be significant tensions in Georgia. There would be problems in the Balkans, too. In 1990, the people of Slovenia overwhelmingly voted to extract themselves from the federation that was Yugoslavia and in Croatia a change in the constitution was also voted through, presaging massive regional problems not long after.

China continued to resist moves to dispense with communism. Widespread public disaffection was met with a thinly veiled threat of violence. One iconic image was that of an unarmed protester standing in front of a tank in Tiananmen Square, his only weapon his force of will. The ruling elite hung on to power, though even in Beijing later economic reforms seemed to suggest that there was a dawning realisation that things could not merely go on as before.

These reforms were the launch pad for a remarkable change in economic fortunes, the impact of which is still developing. The emergence of Deng Xiaoping as the leader of the nation gave impetus to the process and helped drive China to the position it currently holds, one which is only likely to get stronger in the near future.

The West, too, was under pressure. The threat of terrorism continued to grow and on 21 December 1988 the destruction of Pan-Am Flight 103 from London to New York over Lockerbie in Scotland killed 250 people. Suspicions were raised that this particular terrorist act was state-sponsored, with suspicion centred on the Gaddafi regime in Libya. Gaddafi would eventually admit Libyan involvement in 2003, though he would deny any personal knowledge of the crime.

There were also signs of change in Africa, where in the aftermath of independence many countries struggled to find their way and dictatorship was the norm rather than the exception. But in South Africa, a state run by a minority white population, the evil of apartheid, which discriminated against the black majority, was showing signs of coming to an end. In February 1990, the African National Congress, which had led the fight against white domination, was legalised. On 11 February, the leader of the ANC, Nelson Mandela, was released after twenty-seven years of imprisonment. Soon after, following seventy-five years of South African rule, the neighbouring state of Namibia was granted its independence.

In August 1990, Iraq invaded the neighbouring state of Kuwait. For reasons that some suggested were as much to do with the threat to oil supplies as anything else, a large multinational force was assembled to restore the status quo. The war that followed the year after was brief and one-sided. The Iraqi forces were soon ejected from Kuwait but the dictator, Saddam Hussein, hung on to power and Israel was hit by a missile strike launched by his forces. As far as Hussein and President Bush of the USA were concerned, it proved to be a case of unfinished business.

By the end of the year, there were signs of an imminent massive breakthrough in the field of communications. Tim Berners-Lee, a British inventor, was developing a new medium of electronic information interchange called the World Wide Web. In 1991, the internet address 'info.cern.ch' became the first to be created. It is safe to say that few, if any, can have anticipated just how dramatic the repercussions of this breakthrough would be.

The break-up of the Soviet Union would not happen without some dangerous consequences. In 1991, Georgia went to war with South Ossetia, the start of hostilities which in some way are still ongoing, with the latter currently watched over by Russian forces. Latvia, Lithuania and Estonia voted to become independent nation states. Others, such as Ukraine, Uzbekistan and Moldova followed suit.

Yugoslavia had long been a stubbornly independent part of the communist world, but that too was starting to show signs of disintegration, with large protests on the streets of Belgrade against President Milošević. There would even be an attempted coup against President Gorbachev in the Soviet Union. It failed, but by the end of the year he would voluntarily resign his position. The Soviet Union would effectively dissolve and be reformed, with the Russian Federation, Ukraine and Belarus forming the Commonwealth of Independent States.

However, by this time the Balkans was in flames. Wishing to hold on to the power it had, Serbia went to war with its neighbours to protect the structure of the former Yugoslavia. A bitter siege against the Croatian town of Vukovar was followed by a terrible massacre that set an unwelcome precedent for the succeeding years. Old enmities, which had been suppressed under the strict but stabilising leader Tito, now bubbled to the surface with terrible consequences. The situation would deteriorate still further with the declaration of an independent Serb state in Bosnia and Herzegovina early in 1992. Within a few months, the beautiful city of Sarajevo, home not too long before to a Winter Olympic Games, was under siege.

Neither would this be the only region with violent upheavals to contend with. The passing of United Nations Resolution 794 in December 1992 gave permission for external intervention in the massively troubled country of Somalia on the Horn of Africa. Later that month, troops were sent in to stabilise what was a lawless and violent state and help ensure the effective distribution of much-needed humanitarian aid. However, the involvement would end in failure and humiliation, which would have serious repercussions for future suggested expeditions to Africa and beyond.

With the agreement of the Maastricht Treaty on 7 February 1992, the European Union formally came into being, though of course it evolved from an already existing institution. It was in many ways a recognition that the once powerful colonial powers from the continent no longer held the international clout that they once had and that closer unity was needed if the region was to remain a powerful player on the world stage. The economic threat from the United States was obvious, but that from the East at the time less so, though within two decades it would become abundantly clear just how strong that challenge was.

The establishment of the North American Free Trade Agreement (NAFTA) in 1994 was a similar initiative to build trading relationships in North America.

It was perhaps ironic that as some institutions were getting bigger, some countries were choosing to become smaller. On 1 January 1993, Czechoslovakia divided into two – the Czech Republic and Slovakia – in a largely amicable move that became known as 'the velvet divorce'. But such amicability was far from evident everywhere, and the detonation of a bomb in the World Trade Centre, New York, on 26 February 1993 demonstrated that there were still issues to be resolved regarding terrorism. The death toll was six people, but it could, as the world would later find out, have been far, far worse.

If the United Nations was born in a burst of optimism in 1945, 1994 must mark its nadir. In that year UN forces, largely as the result of total political failure on the part of the higher authorities of the body, stood by while thousands were slaughtered in Bosnia and hundreds of thousands in Rwanda. Both sets of atrocities were entirely predictable and predicted but the inaction in response was recognised even by the UN as a source of shame. Yet, ten years on, the inactivity also marked the UN's response to events in Darfur, Sudan.

The late twentieth century was a time for big global institutions such as the UN, the World Bank, the Organisation of African Unity and the European Union. Yet what most threatens these institutions is the danger that they become self-serving, bureaucratic and lacking in leadership. It is true that at some levels much good has been done – for example, there are many committed UN humanitarian staff around – but the good intentions of those at this level do not sometimes seem to be matched by the political leadership of those they report to, daunting though their task is.

Perhaps the most graphic example surrounded the reaction to the truly incredible slaughter in Rwanda, where 800,000 civilians were murdered in 100 days. While this terrible bloodletting was going on virtually unchecked, various administrations studiously sought for new ways of describing 'genocide' without using the word, as under legal conventions the UN would consequently be virtually forced to take strong action. By carefully avoiding the term, the need for action was avoided. The world watched on while nearly a million innocent civilians were murdered, a rate of extermination that compared with the horrors of the Holocaust fifty years earlier and, in terms of the short timescale in which these events happened, even exceeded it.

At the end of the century, the UN was still dominated by the 'P5', the Security Council of the US, UK, France, Russia and China. All worked on occasion with self-interest at heart. The US, UK and France would sanction tough action if their interests were threatened but would otherwise remain aloof. As for Russia and China, their own interests and human rights records almost inevitably mean that any reaction against human rights abuses is almost doomed to be either vetoed or watered down so much that the suggested action is meaningless. Bureaucracy, the language of the words carefully picked to suggest much but mean little, have become the norm; a careful use of tone and appearing to say a lot without actually committing to anything has created governing institutions that Confucius would recognise and approve of.

At least elsewhere in Africa there were much-needed signs that things might change for the better. On 10 May 1994, Nelson Mandela was inaugurated as the first black President of

South Africa, ending a remarkable personal journey but also unleashing huge expectations among a population that looked forward to the future with unprecedented optimism.

The year 1995 – which saw the announcement of a new invention known as the Digital Versatile (or Video) Disc (DVD) – began with the official formation of the World Trade Organisation (the WTO) through the Marrakech Agreement, a body tasked with the agreement and implementation of efficient, effective and equitable trading conditions internationally, a challenging remit that has proved predictably difficult to achieve in practice. But the event that shocked much of the world that year was the brutal killing of 7,000 men and boys in the town of Srebrenica in Bosnia. It was the worst atrocity in Europe since the Second World War. There were several factors that dramatically increased the impact of this awful event.

The first was that it took place in Europe, where such atrocities were supposed to be a thing of the past. But worst of all was the fact that the town was supposedly under the protection of UN troops. The fact that brutality had characterised the war was well known, as some participants had already been formally accused of war crimes.

That, however, had not led to a proportionate response in terms of the troops sent to protect innocent civilians. The Dutch peacekeepers in Srebrenica were inadequately supplied and were not present in enough numbers to stop the killing, and in the event they did little to intervene. When mass graves were later found, it created a sense of shock and guilt that many found hard to come to terms with, especially as it came so soon after the abject failure to intervene in Rwanda a year before. But it perhaps also marked a turning point; by August NATO warplanes were attacking Bosnian Serb positions around Sarajevo.

The intervention of NATO helped force the participants around the conference table, and at the Dayton Agreements, negotiated in Ohio in November and signed in Paris in December, a complex partition of Bosnia and Herzegovina was agreed. It was not quite the end of the conflicts and there would be a further flare-up in Kosovo, then part of Serbia, before the decade was out, again marked by extreme brutality and ended in significant part because of NATO intervention.

The local repercussions of NATO involvement continue to divide the region, with Kosovar Albanians seeing the actions as heroic and some Serbs seeing them as an unwarranted intrusion by the West in Serbian affairs. The establishment of the International Criminal Tribunal for the former Yugoslavia (ICTY), tasked with bringing alleged war criminals in the region to justice, further fuelled these contrary perceptions.

With the war in the Balkans coming to an end, attention turned to serious fighting in the largely Muslim region of Chechnya in Russia, a bitter dispute taking place on a geopolitical fault line. There was at least hope in 1996 of some progress in the insoluble problem of the Middle East when Palestine dropped references to the non-recognition of Israel, who in return moved towards acceptance of a separate Palestinian state.

But the wider region remained problematic, with inspectors still looking for weapons of mass destruction in Iraq, leading to the destruction of a biological weapons factory in May. Not everyone though was convinced that the problem of 'WMDs', as they were known, had been finally solved in the country. In June, US attempts to sanction military action to resolve the problem failed to gain agreement in the UN. It is interesting, though, to note that these discussions predate the Bush (that is George W.) presidency in the United States by several years, something that appears to have been largely forgotten subsequently.

There were also other signs that the United States had cause to be nervous of events in the Middle East. On 23 August 1996, a radical Islamic cleric named Osama Bin Laden issued a proclamation entitled *The Declaration of Jihad on the Americans Occupying the Country of the Two Sacred Places*, which called for the evacuation of all American troops from Saudi Arabia. Although the significance of the event to the wider world was not fully apparent at the time, in Afghanistan – struggling to find any kind of stability following the departure of Soviet troops at the end of the previous decade and tearing itself apart – Taliban forces moved on the capital Kabul. Before long the country would be under Taliban rule, with dramatic medium-term consequences.

The shooting dead of sixty-two Western tourists outside of the Temple of Hatshepsut in Egypt during the following year also confirmed that there were a number of Islamic terrorist sympathisers prepared to undertake previously unimaginable acts in pursuit of their cause. However, this was not just a battle between Islam and the West, it was also a battle for the soul of Islam itself, a battle which spread across much of Central Asia and North Africa. This had terrible repercussions for the unfortunate people of countries such as Afghanistan, Algeria (where in one outrage in 1998, thirty-two infants under two years of age and twenty others were hacked to death) and Somalia, countries caught in the crossfire of a brutal fight for power, a situation that would be repeated fifteen years later in other countries with Islamic majorities such as Egypt, Syria and Libya.

The war without a nation-state enemy, that involving terrorist activity, continued to grow in intensity over the next few years. On 7 August 1998, US embassies in Tanzania and Kenya were bombed and over 200 killed as a result in a further escalation of violence that also widened the region of terrorist activity.

The shifting political landscape in Europe was confirmed in July 1997 when Poland, the Czech Republic and Hungary were all invited to join NATO, something that would have been unthinkable for these former Warsaw Pact members just a decade before. They and other states that had been communist until 1989 would soon also be working towards full membership of the European Union. Moves were meanwhile in train to introduce a single European currency for a number of nations and by the end of 1998 the exchange rates of these currencies were frozen in a move towards full and, it was hoped, permanent integration.

On the other hand, a different political realignment was marked in 1997 with the handing over of Hong Kong from Britain to China. It was in many ways symbolic of handing over an imperialist torch. Seeking to drive forward its own industrial revolution, China would soon be searching around Asia and Africa ever more aggressively to obtain control of, or at least influence over, the raw materials that were needed to fuel its vigorous economic expansion, just as Britain and other European powers had done in much of the nineteenth and twentieth centuries.

At least the signing of an agreement on Good Friday 1998 in Northern Ireland offered hope that the seemingly insoluble conundrum there might be resolved without resort to the further effusion of blood – a situation that has largely held since. It was a sign that the unthinkable might after all be thought, though it would require a great deal of compromise, an acceptance that the unforgivable must be forgiven and the necessity of accepting a form of coexistence if such an outcome were to be achieved, say, between Israel and Palestine, or India and Pakistan or in a number of other ongoing stand-offs around the world.

Such a problem area was to be found in the Congo, where a bitter civil war that started in 1998 would end five years later with nearly four million lives lost, a staggering loss of life unsurpassed since the Second World War, though it failed to register on the consciousness of the Western world as much as other conflicts closer to home had. At the time of writing, the Democratic Republic of Congo remains a mess, with accusation and counter-accusation flying between the parties embroiled in the festering conflict almost daily and the very real danger that pointed words may be replaced by bullets at any moment.

The year 2000 began with relatively few of the predictions of imminent cosmic disaster that had been witnessed 1,000 years before, but there were fears of a meltdown of another kind. This was perhaps strangely ironic; man himself had now become the potential destroyer of his planet in the place of God. This was not just because of the possibility of nuclear disaster. For years preceding the arrival of the millennium (which actually officially started in 2001, the calendar of years having no Year 0), it had been stated that there could be widespread computer malfunctions due to the move to the new millennium and huge efforts were made to prevent the chaos that seemed possible. In the event, no such technological meltdown ensued.

In fact, few events of huge dramatic significance characterised the year. Where there were incidents, they tended to be part of ongoing situations, such as the ongoing terrorist incidents around the world or the seemingly intractable debate with Iraq as UN inspectors sought access to confirm the existence or otherwise of WMDs.

Of much long-term significance was the fact that during the year India became the second country in the world to have more than 1 billion inhabitants. Population growth has almost become overlooked as a challenge to the future of humanity, though we see symptoms of its impact everywhere if we care to look: poverty, famine and malnutrition where there are not enough resources to go around, warfare and masses of refugees. It will not get any easier as the population continues to spiral, seemingly out of control.

However, there would be drama aplenty to mark the next few years. Events were about to shake the world of the West in particular to their very foundations. If the new millennium had begun peacefully enough, it was not a situation that was going to last for very long.

43

WHAT OF THE FUTURE?

New Threats Emerge (AD 2001 and Beyond)

On 11 September 2001, the world watched on, stunned, as an unbelievable scene was relayed through television sets across the globe. What the disbelieving audience watched was like a scene from a Hollywood disaster movie, burning skyscrapers lighting up the New York skyline while on the upper floors thousands of people were trapped. Except this was no simulated drama, this was all too real.

Few will forget where they were as this awful tragedy was played out, truly the 'JFK Moment' of the twenty-first century. The deliberate destruction of the World Trade Centre, the famous 'twin towers', became the iconic moment of the current century so far. Along with an attack on the Pentagon building and the hijacking of a fourth plane that was destroyed before it reached its target, it ushered in a turbulent and as yet unresolved conflict of a new kind, and continues to have great consequences for the world.

Within a month, US forces and their allies had invaded Afghanistan, where it was alleged the terrorist perpetrators of '9/11' had been trained. It was thought and hoped that the superior armament of the allied forces would be triumphant and that a new Afghanistan, one more stable and palatable, might emerge. However, the conquest of the country still appears to be the impossible challenge it has always shown itself to be. The war still goes on and there is no sign whatsoever that a stable and maturing political fabric will be in place once Afghanistan is left to itself again. If military and political planners were closer students of history, they would have known that such an outcome was always likely.

In response to the terrorist attacks, President George W. Bush soon after authorised the introduction of military tribunals in the United States for the first time since the Second World War, threatening to erode any claim to moral supremacy. There was much resentment among liberals in many countries, with long-term damage to the American reputation as a result.

Away from the potential for deliberate man-made Armageddon, there were increasing concerns that humanity might help destroy the lives of millions accidentally. Early in 2002, a large ice sheet in Antarctica, Larsen B, to all intents and purposes fell into the sea. The ice sheet had been stable according to scientists for the past 12,000 years. This was a huge block of ice, the size of the state of Rhode Island, and its demise had almost certainly been triggered by significant and constant warming of Antarctic waters since 1940.

Similar large collapses from the Petermann Glacier in the Arctic seem to confirm the trend, alongside much-reduced ice levels in the region. Although not all scientists agree that global warming is a man-made phenomenon, climate change is certainly happening at what appears to be a much faster pace than it has for millennia.

The start of a trial in 2002 in The Hague to judge the alleged war crimes of President Slobodan Milošević for atrocities committed by Serb forces in Bosnia marked an attempt to encourage heads of state to act more moderately. The attempts remain ongoing and the length of time required to secure a conviction is frustrating (Milošević died before the trial was completed) but it is at least an effort to seek some form of justice for the victims of war.

Outside human conflict, other challenges faced mankind. Alongside a burgeoning population, a new epidemic was creating great anxiety. HIV/AIDS had been present for several decades. By 2002, it was estimated that 40 million people were infected with the virus worldwide. It was claimed that immoral behaviour was the prime cause of its spread, for example through promiscuity or infected needles being used during the taking of prohibited drugs. This was a sweeping generalisation that ignored, for example, the fact that unborn babies in the womb are affected. South Africa for a time refused to accept that it had an HIV/AIDS problem at all, which maybe helps to explain why it is currently believed to have one of the highest incidences of HIV/AIDS in the world, though the age of 'denialism' there is now over as the evidence, sadly, is too strong to dismiss.

Even now, HIV/AIDS remains a major threat in parts of Africa, where life expectancy has in some countries diminished alarmingly as a result of the virus (as one example, according to World Bank data, life expectancy in the small country of Lesotho has dropped from sixty in 1992 to forty-eight in 2010, largely, it is believed, as a result of a combination of HIV/AIDS and increased tuberculosis incidence – there is a medical correlation between the two).

In 2003, the tension between Iraq and the United States and others came to a head. Tired of ongoing refusals to co-operate with UN inspectors on the vexed question of WMDs, a large force was put together with the aim of invading Iraq and destroying any such weapons as well as bringing the belligerent Iraqi leader, Saddam Hussein, to book. The war was by no means universally popular and an estimated 10 million people took to the streets to protest across the globe. This did no good, and on 19 March the allied forces invaded Iraq.

Within a month, the war appeared to be over. The allies entered Baghdad and Hussein was overthrown and went on the run. When President George W. Bush landed on the aircraft carrier USS *Abraham Lincoln* on 1 May, a banner behind him proudly exclaimed 'Mission Accomplished'. Nothing could be further from the truth, as in the next few years, following the capture and subsequent execution of Hussein,

Iraq unravelled and tens of thousands died in suicide bombings and related violence. Suicide bombings also took place in Chechnya, Russia, Saudi Arabia, Afghanistan and other countries, a relatively new technique no doubt inspired, if that is the right word, by the '9/11' attacks.

The aftermath of the war in Iraq was a mess. No WMDs were discovered and widespread criticism of the war increased in intensity, particularly impacting on President Bush and Prime Minister Tony Blair in Britain. The actions of some allied troops in some of the prisons holding captured Iraqis fell hugely below what was expected of democratic nations and there were widespread allegations of faulty information being used by the British government to justify the war. The suspicious death of Dr David Kelly, a leading weapons expert who played an important part in the lead-up to the war, did not reduce tensions either; not everyone accepted the subsequent verdict of suicide.

The suicide bombings spread into Western Europe, too. In March 2004, 191 people died in Madrid in a series of coordinated attacks, while there was ongoing terrorist activity in Israel and the Philippines. At the end of a troubled year, it seemed tragically appropriate that the world was shocked when, in the midst of Christmas celebrations in many places, a massive earthquake, measuring 9.3 on the Richter scale, produced enormous tsunamis in South East Asia and beyond.

The devastation was unbelievable, and what made it more disturbing was that video footage of the tsunamis was beamed across the world. The official death toll approached 187,000 and another 40,000 are still missing. Towns and cities were demolished as if they were made of matchwood, millions were made homeless and huge numbers of lives were destroyed. It was a salutary reminder of the essential weakness of man against the forces of nature.

A multiplicity of problems still faced the world. North Korea announced in 2005 that it had joined the club of those nations with nuclear weapons; despite frequent attempts to cajole the country into more 'acceptable' behaviour, North Korea remains a 'problem child' and a 'rogue state'. On the other hand, the United States and others were considered by some to be 'rogue states', with the refusal of their governments to sign up to the Kyoto Protocols of the same year, which attempted to get to grips with environmental issues. On 7 July, four terrorist attacks in London killed fifty-two people and injured many others.

Coming the day after the news that London had been awarded the 2012 Olympic Games, the country was shaken and many questions were asked about the origins of the suicide bombers, who were all British citizens. The attacks contrasted with the announcement of a cessation of hostilities from the Provisional IRA later that month, bringing an end to thirty-six years of militant action. However, elsewhere terrorist activity continued, and in December there was another attack, this time on the popular tourist destination of Bali, which had suffered even worse attacks in 2002.

Alongside this, there were positive developments too. The first ever face transplant took place in France in 2005, following on from kidney transplants (first performed in 1950), liver transplants (1963) and heart transplants (1967). Women were awarded the vote in Kuwait, a welcome increase in their participation in Middle Eastern affairs, and the second Chinese space mission was launched in this year, marking both the arrival of another serious player in the space race and the ongoing strengthening of China's economic power and worldwide importance.

The year 2006 began with a demonstration of the insecurity of energy supplies and the relative weakness of those who were consumers rather than suppliers when Russia cut its gas supplies to Ukraine. The point was emphasised in the following year when supplies to Poland and Germany were also cut for a short time. Later, in 2007, there were the first signs of a looming economic crisis of global proportions when problems in the US sub-prime mortgage market emerged.

These economic weaknesses led in 2008 to a sharp drop in stock exchange values. There was a classic contrary pressure when, at the same time, oil prices were rising to a historical high of $100 per barrel and would carry on increasing. There were signs soon after of a number of banks facing potential collapse. The demise of the American bank Lehman Brothers in September led to an extraordinary response, with President George W. Bush announcing that the US government was creating a $700 billion fund to purchase the assets of stricken banks. Even countries were at risk, with Iceland soon after at risk of financial meltdown.

The election in the US of its first African-American President, Barack Obama, seemed to mark a new chapter in history. However, consummate orator though he is, the problems facing his country and the wider world were and are immense. The economic crisis continued, the rates of American and European unemployment rose and even cash-rich Dubai was forced to ask for debt deferment on its massive building portfolio. It did not stop the world's tallest building, the Burj Khalifa, being opened there early in 2010, though it is unlikely to hold the record for long given the ambitions of other rising economic superpowers.

The essential weakness of humanity against nature was emphasised in 2010 when a large ash cloud from a volcano in Iceland closed much of European airspace for a time and created chaos and massive losses in the airline industry. Disaster of a different kind loomed when it became apparent that the finances of Greece were badly overstretched, leading to a bail-out from the European Union and the IMF. There appeared to be a real risk of 'contagion', that is the Greek crisis affecting other indebted countries, leading to the possibility of defaults and huge increases in borrowing costs for the countries involved when they could least afford it – a similar 'bail-out' scheme was required for Ireland by the end of 2010.

The most noteworthy developments of 2011 concerned the eruption of protests across the Arab world against governments that were seen in many quarters as undemocratic and unrepresentative. Starting in Tunisia, protests would spread across North Africa and the Middle East, with Egypt and Yemen particularly affected. The authoritarian regime of Colonel Gaddafi was also overthrown. Quite where these protests will end up is still hard to gauge. While there is no doubting the desire for change in these countries, history teaches us that out of turmoil change may not come as quickly as expected or desired, and indeed matters may get worse before they get better. Current experience in Egypt, for example, is not encouraging in this respect.

Nothing stays unchanged; even time changes. Samoa and Tokelau skipped a day at the end of December 2010 so that they could change their time and date zone to better coordinate with business partners. But some things stay constant, not least man's ability to both innovate and destroy. At the time of writing, Syria is at war with itself and the outside world seems unwilling or unable to help – though it is easy to criticise from the safety of a writer's study and the end result of intervention is far from clear, as can be witnessed by military involvements in Iraq and Afghanistan in recent times.

All these recent events are, in historical terms, 'work in progress'. We have no real idea of where they might end, though we can perhaps reflect on history and work out what might happen. At the moment, Iraq, for example, still stands perched perilously close to the edge of a precipice. For a time the bombing stops and the ruptured country disappears from the view of a world only too happy to forget. Then, with stark and shocking clarity, another atrocity stirs the world temporarily from its apathy. The miscalculation of those who gave the go-ahead for the invasion of the country has created widespread resentment across parts of the world only too keen to blame the 'West' for everything, while in many cases conveniently ignoring their own, all too obvious deficiencies. The same could be said of Afghanistan, where Western forces are due to leave in 2014.

The economic crisis of today also threatens to be much more than a blip. While Europe in particular is in decline, the East shows slowing growth but growth that is still much greater than zero. The United States is struggling to grow economically on the same scale that it did in the past. Africa remains in a somewhat ambivalent position, possessed of great natural wealth in the form of minerals but at great risk of getting insufficient value from them. In many countries in Africa now, one does not have to travel far to see a Chinese presence, and it is to be hoped that the African continent as a whole avoids replacing European colonialism with a different variety.

Europe meanwhile is ageing, its nation states spending beyond their means and, with the odd Teutonic exception, becoming less and less competitive. Its leaders struggle to find a solution that keeps everyone happy – which is, of course, impossible – and the streets of major European capitals resound with protests against austerity. It is a time of both fear and risk.

As I write these words, I am reminded how much we need to learn the lessons of history. Consider this scenario. A world of major economic readjustment, threats to living standards and significant stresses on major economies. A rising economy in the East, opened up to new technologies after being cut off from the mainstream for so long. Increasingly, international bodies seem powerless to intervene, with a lack of will and vision among member states. The new Eastern superpower desperately needs resources to fuel growth and searches far and wide to find them. However, existing superpowers feel uncomfortable with this growth and indeed have good reason to do so. Tensions rise until they become unbearable.

The scenario I have just described reached its unavoidable conclusion at Pearl Harbor in 1941. Yet there are some marked similarities with the situation in the early twenty-first century. Replace 'Japan' with 'China' and 'the League of Nations' with 'the

United Nations' and where this particular road might lead is obvious. At the time of writing, in the Pacific China is increasingly becoming more assertive in her actions. American naval policy is now to relocate forces from the Atlantic to the Pacific. This is said not to be in answer to a perceived greater threat from China, yet it is eerily reminiscent of the struggle for power in the Pacific between Japan and the United States in the 1930s. Let us hope it does not lead to the same end result.

Yet I have to wonder, as we look at today's world, how much has really changed? For example, we think of this as a secular world but that is certainly not true for much of it. We are perhaps all too conscious of the power of some regimes that still have strong religious principles allegedly underlying their policies (for example, Iran). Yet even in so-called secular societies like the United States of America, fundamentalist religious figures can still have an impact on policy formulation.

And what about those societies who have avowed secularist societies, for example China? Is not the figure of Mao virtually deified? Is not that huge photograph still dominating Tiananmen Square, godlike in its omniscience? Or take Turkey, where three-quarters of a century after his death the picture of Mustafa Kemal Atatürk still looms large over the urban landscape and over much of public policy (though in Turkey there are currently tensions about the extent of his legacy). Go to his mausoleum, itself not unlike a modernist version of the great Egyptian temples used to celebrate the pharaoh-gods, and it does seem that little has changed in our need to acknowledge the godlike qualities of certain outstanding individuals. A caption in the museum by Atatürk's mausoleum describes how his 'holy body' was buried there. It might, I accept, just be a loose translation – yet if it is, it appears to be a very apposite Freudian slip.

But in the West the suggestion that secularism is increasingly the dominant force is hard to avoid. It is true that in some areas Christian fundamentalists can still play a part in national policy. But the power of the Catholic Church in many countries, once undeniable, is now visibly diminishing (often, it must be said, a self-inflicted result of failing to tackle various emerging issues). And in Protestant-majority countries, church attendance is declining.

Without wishing to in any way argue against the rights of atheists and agnostics to encourage an approach that removes religion from the mainstream of the decision-making process, as yet it seems to me that the result has in part, in the West at least, been an ideological vacuum. The challenge for secularists is not to remove religion from the political system but to create an ideological framework in its place; something that communism, for all its vast centralised power, was unable to do. Without it, the West seems to be left merely with grubby, self-centred materialism, hardly conducive to strengthening society and bringing it closer together.

We can look ahead to times yet to come and speculate what might happen. Scientists predict, for example, that 50–200 million years into the future the landmasses of America and Asia will unite. They even have a name for the new supercontinent: Amasia. Our love of 'labelling' knows no bounds; we use it for entities that do not even exist yet. But it is quite probable that at some time in the hopefully very distant future our world will be destroyed by some cataclysmic universal event. Secularists may argue that this will be the result of nature and not God, but the end result will be equally terminal.

Civilisations, like people, are always looking forward with apprehension to their death. That is why, just as there are creation myths for the birth of our world, there are equally a number of predictions outlining how it will all end. We of course have the biblical Armageddon, and there is another account that states how Jesus Christ will return to the earth and lead a mighty battle against the powers of evil. It might surprise those who are unaware that this is the account according to the Quran.

The vision of Armageddon is surprisingly similar to the end of the world as predicted by the Vikings. Here too there will be a great battle – Ragnarök – in which all the gods will die; the Twilight of the Gods, as spectacularly employed by Wagner. The lead-up to the end will be chaotic and terrifying; 'brothers will fight and kill each other, sisters' children will defile kinship. It is harsh in the world, whoredom rife – an axe age, a sword age – shields are riven – a wind age, a wolf age, before the world goes headlong. No man will have mercy on another.' Despite the carnage, two humans will survive and through them the world of man will be reborn.

The world, according to some, was supposed to end in 2012, this apparently according to the Mayans. Fortunately they were wrong, as apart from anything else sales of this book would have been zero. But it would do us all good to look for a different future, when violence is a last resort, when the world's resources are shared between rich and poor and when we start to take the stewardship of our planet and its rare gifts seriously. This might be a naive, even Utopian, aspiration but it should not stop us from hoping that it might happen before a man-made Armageddon comes along to bring our vibrant and vivid world history to an abrupt, chaotic end.

Martin Waldseemüller's '*Universalis cosmographia*' from around 1507, the first document known to name America. (Courtesy of the Library of Congress)

Oronce Fine's '*Noua, et integra universi orbis descriptio*', dated to 1531. (Courtesy of the Library of Congress)

Ortelius Abraham's '*Theatrum orbis terrarum*', from 1570. (Courtesy of the Library of Congress)

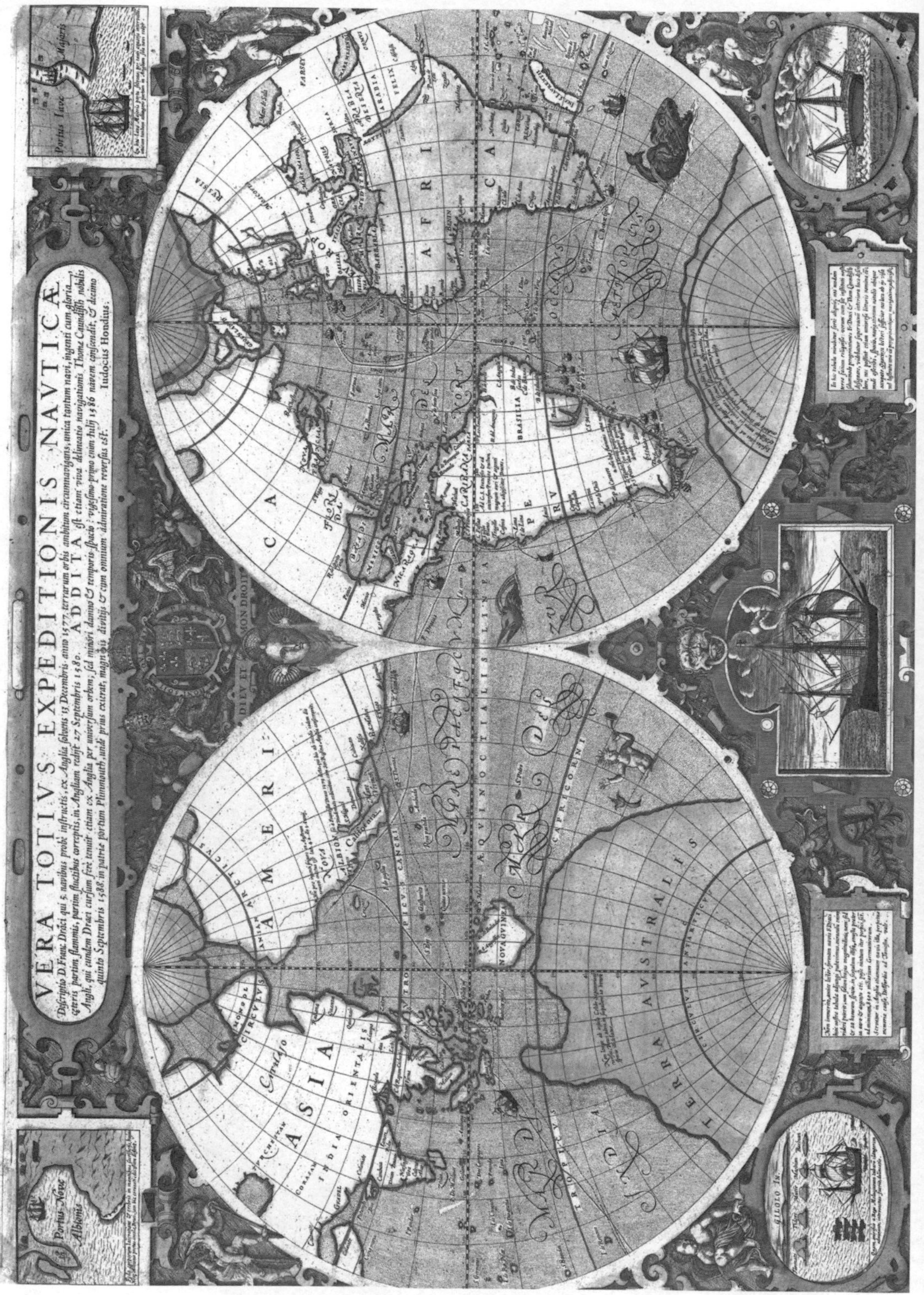

The 1595 '*Vera totius expeditionis nauticae*', created by Jodocus Hondius and dated to around 1595. This shows routes around the world used by Sir Francis Drake in 1577–1580 and Thomas Cavendish in 1586–1588. (Courtesy of the Library of Congress)

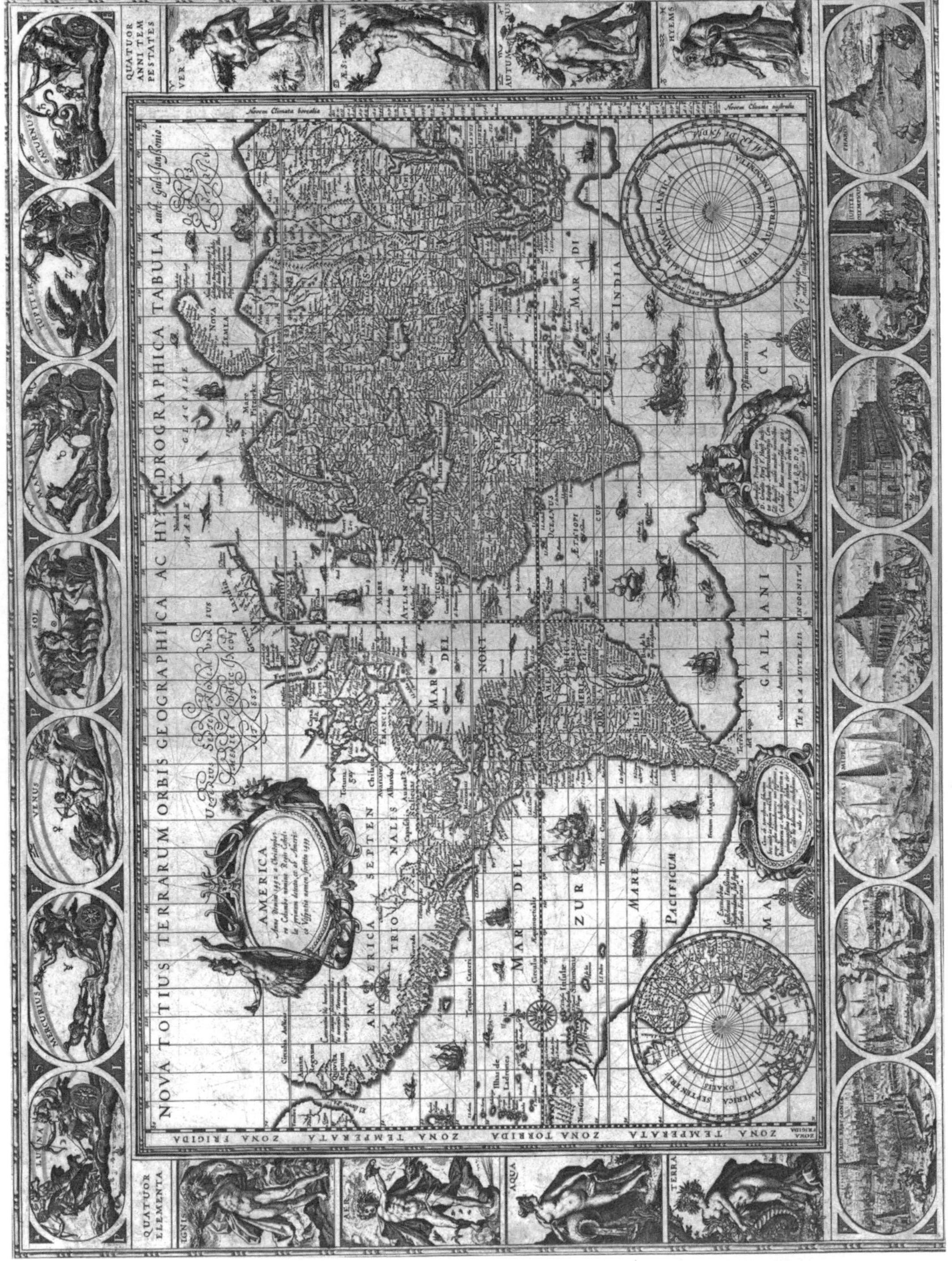

Willem Janszoon Blaeu's 1606 '*Nova totius terrarum orbis geographica ac hydrographica tabula*'. (Courtesy of the Library of Congress)

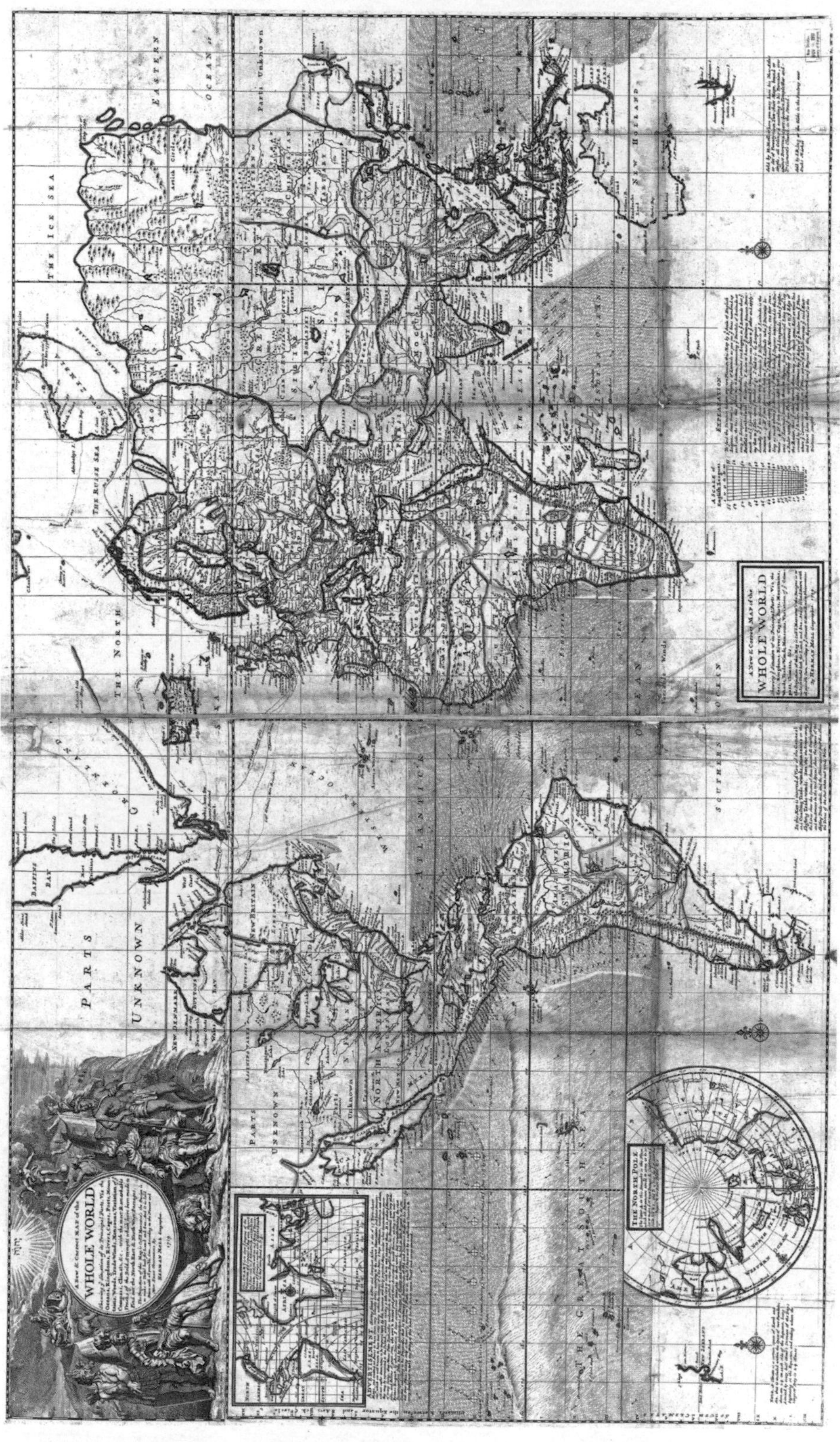

Herman Moll's 1719 '*New & correct map of the whole world*'. (Courtesy of the Library of Congress)

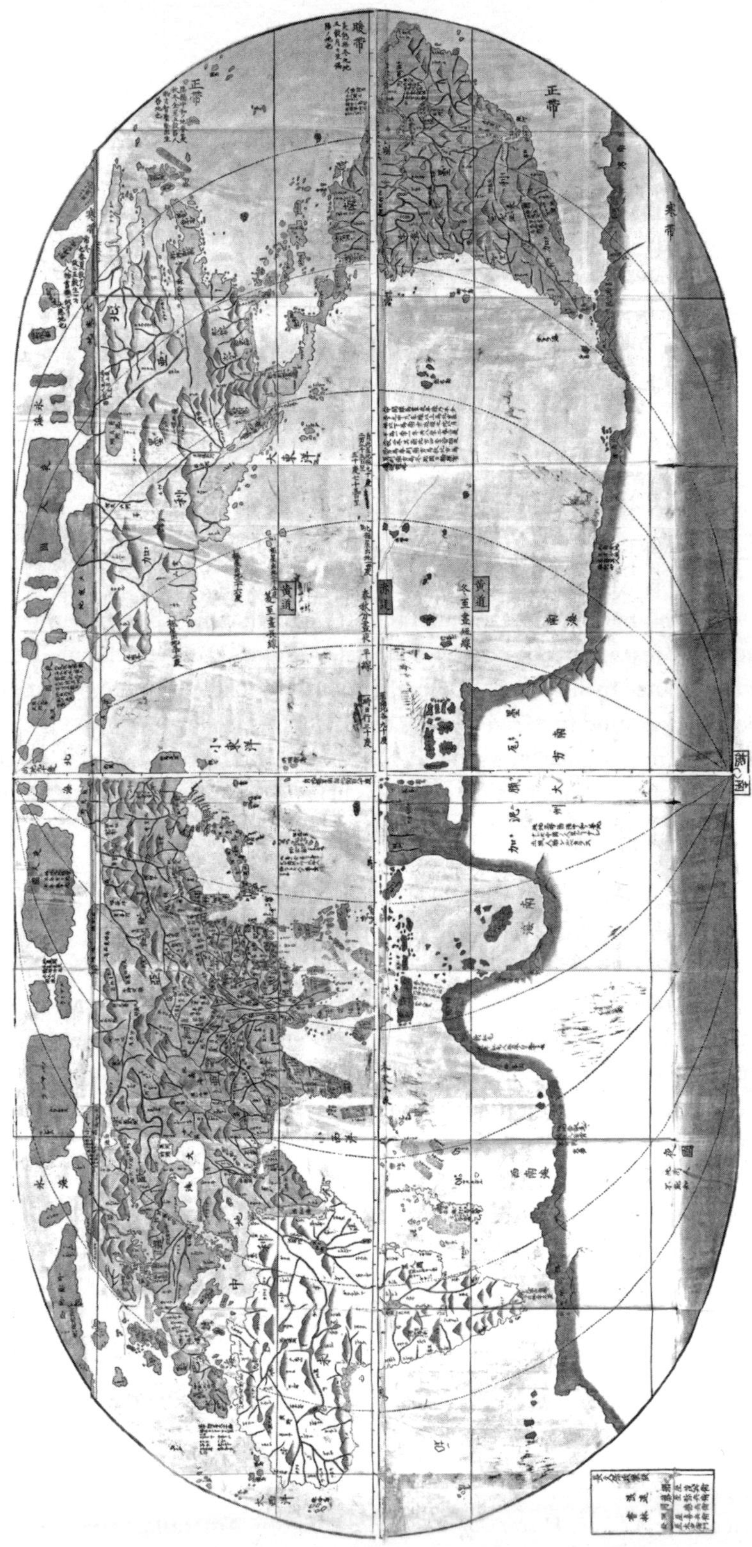

'*Sankai yochi zenzu*', a Japanese map from 1785 based on the 1602 map created by Matteo Ricci, a Jesuit missionary in China. (Courtesy of the Library of Congress)

SELECT BIBLIOGRAPHY

With a book of this nature, there are many other works that have been examined as part of the necessary research. What follows is a selection of those which have been most useful. It is of course by no means comprehensive but represents a cross-section of the most salient background material that has been accessed.

In terms of chronological background, the following reference books have been the primary initial source, though every effort has been made to cross-refer to more recent research that may have updated the information contained in them:

Mellersh, H. E. L.; *Chronology of World History – The Ancient World; 10,000 BC-AD799*, Helicon, Oxford, 1976 (1995 reprint)

Storey, R. L.; *Chronology of World History – The Medieval World; 800-1491*, Helicon, Oxford, 1973 (1994 reissue)

Williams, Neville; *Chronology of World History – The Expanding World; 1492-1762*, Helicon, Oxford, 1969 (1994 reissue)

Williams, Neville and Waller, Philip; *Chronology of World History – The Modern World; 1763-1992*, Helicon, Oxford, 1966 (1994 reissue)

In terms of wider background materials, the following have been especially significant:

Ackroyd, Peter; *Venice – Pure City*, Chatto & Windus, London, 2009

Ashley, Michael; *The Seven Wonders of the World*, Fontana, 1980

Bartlett, W. B.; *The Mongols – From Genghis Khan to Tamerlane*, Amberley, Gloucestershire, 2009

Bartlett, W. B.; *The Crusades – An Illustrated History*, Sutton, Gloucestershire, 2005

Bauer, Susan Wise; *The History of the Ancient World – From the Earliest Accounts to the Fall of Rome*, Norton, New York and London, 2007

Blainey, Geoffrey; *A Short History of the World*, Penguin, Australia, 2002

Chadwick, Nora; *The Celts*, Pelican, Harmondsworth, 1979

Cimok, Fatih; *The Hittites*, A Turizm Yayinlari, Istanbul, 2011

Clayton, Peter A.; *Chronicles of the Pharaohs*, Thames and Hudson, London, 1994
Daniel, Glyn; *The First Civilisations – The Archaeology of Their Origins*, Camelot, London and Southampton, 1968
Dawson, Doyne; *The First Armies*, Cassell & Co., London, 2001
Ebrey, Patricia Buckley; *Cambridge Illustrated History – China*, Cambridge University Press, 2007
Finley, M. I.; *The Ancient Greeks*, Penguin, Harmondsworth, 1963
Fossier, Robert (ed.); *The Cambridge Illustrated History of the Middle Ages* (3 volumes); Cambridge, 1997 reprint
Foster, R. F.; *The Oxford History of Ireland*, Oxford, 1992
Fox, Robin Lane; *Alexander the Great*, Futura, London, 1973
Gascoigne, Bamber; *The Dynasties of China*, Robinson, London, 2005 reprint
Gibbon, Edward; *The Decline and Fall of the Roman Empire*, Wordsworth, Ware, 1998 reprint
Gombrich. E. H.; *A Little History of the World*, Yale, New Haven and London, 2005
Goodwin, Jason; *Lords of the Horizons – A History of the Ottoman Empire*, Vintage, London, 1999
Grimal, Nicolas; *A History of Ancient Egypt*, Blackwell Publishers, London, 1995
Hale, John; *The Civilization of Europe in the Renaissance*, Harper & Collins, London, 1993
Hart, B. H. Liddell; *History of the First World War*, Book Club Associates, London, 1970
Hart, B. H. Liddell; *History of the Second World War*, Book Club Associates, London, 1970
Henshall, Kenneth; *A History of Japan – From Stone Age to Superpower*, Palgrave Macmillan, Basingstoke, 2004
Hillenbrand, Carole; *The Crusades – Islamic Perspectives*, Edinburgh University Press, 2006
Hochschild, Adam; *King Leopold's Ghost*, Pan Books, London, 2006
Holland, Tom; *Persian Fire – The First World Empire and the Battle for the West*, Little, Brown, London, 2005
James, T .G. H.; *An Introduction to Ancient Egypt*, Book Club Associates, 1979
Jones, Gwyn; *A History of the Vikings*, Oxford University Press, 1973
Joudallh, Fatima; *Syria – Source of Civilisations*, Dar al-Hassad, Damascus, 2004
Karabell, Zachary; *People of the Book – The Forgotten History of Islam and the West*, John Murray, London, 2007
Leakey, Richard E.; *The Making of Mankind*, Book Club Associates, 1981
Lee, Christopher; *This Sceptred Isle 55 BC – 1901*, Penguin, London, 1998
Lewis, Bernard; *From Babel to Dragomans – Interpreting the Middle East*, Oxford University Press, Oxford, 2004
Lichteim, George; *Europe in the Twentieth Century*, Cardinal, London, 1974
Lovell, Julia; *The Great Wall – China Against the World*, Atlantic Books, London, 2006
Maxwell Stuart, P. G.; *Chronicles of the Popes*, Thames and Hudson, London, 1997
Meredith, Martin; *The State of Africa*, Free Press, Great Britain, 2006

Moseley, Michael E.; *The Incas and their Ancestors – The Archaeology of Peru*, Thames & Hudson, London, 2004

Norwich, John Julius; *A Short History of Byzantium*, Viking, Harmondsworth, 1997

Norwich, John Julius; *The Middle Sea – A History of the Mediterranean*, Vintage, London, 2006

Phillips, Patricia; *The Prehistory of Europe*, Book Club Associates, 1980

Porch, Douglas; *Wars of Empire*, Cassell & Co., London, 2000

Roberts, Andrew; *A History of the English-Speaking Peoples Since 1900*, Weidenfeld & Nicolson, London, 2006

Roberts, J. M.; *The New Penguin History of the World*, Penguin, London, 2007

Service, Alastair & Bradbery, Jean; *Megaliths and their Mysteries – The Standing Stones of Old Europe*, Weidenfeld & Nicolson, London, 1979

Strachan, Hew; *The First World War – A New Illustrated History*, Simon & Schuster, London, 2003

Swanton, Michael (ed. & trans.); *The Anglo-Saxon Chronicles*, Phoenix Press, London, 2000

Townsend, Richard F.: *The Aztecs*, Thames and Hudson, London, 1992

Wood, Michael; *The Story of India*, BBC Books, London, 2008

Ziegler, Philip; *The Black Death*, Penguin, Harmondsworth, 1976

INDEX